International Capital Markets
Volume I

The International Library of Critical Writings in Financial Economics

Series Editor: Richard Roll

Allstate Professor of Economics
The Anderson School at UCLA, USA

This major series presents by field outstanding selections of the most important articles across the entire spectrum of financial economics – one of the fastest growing areas in business schools and economics departments. Each collection has been prepared by a leading specialist who has written an authoritative introduction to the literature. A full list of published and future titles in this series is printed at the end of this volume.

Wherever possible, the articles in these volumes have been reproduced as originally published using facsimile reproduction, inclusive of footnotes and pagination to facilitate ease of reference.

For a list of all Edward Elgar published titles visit our site on the World Wide Web at
http://www.e-elgar.co.uk

International Capital Markets
Volume I

Edited by

G. Andrew Karolyi

Dean's Distinguished Research Professor of Finance
Ohio State University, USA

and

René M. Stulz

Everett D. Reese Chair of Banking and Monetary Economics and Professor
of Finance
Ohio State University, USA

THE INTERNATIONAL LIBRARY OF CRITICAL WRITINGS IN FINANCIAL ECONOMICS

An Elgar Reference Collection
Cheltenham, UK • Northampton, MA, USA

Published by
Edward Elgar Publishing Limited
Glensanda House
Montpellier Parade
Cheltenham
Glos GL50 1UA
UK

Edward Elgar Publishing, Inc.
136 West Street
Suite 202
Northampton
Massachusetts 01060
USA

A catalogue record for this book is available from the British Library.

Library of Congress Cataloguing in Publication Data

International capital markets / edited by G. Andrew Karolyi and René M. Stulz.
    p. cm. — (The international library of critical writings in financial economics ; 12)
   Includes index.
   1. Capital market. 2. International finance. 3. Foreign exchange rates. I. Karolyi, G. Andrew. II. Stulz, René M. III. Series.

   HG4523.I574 2003
   332'.042—dc21
                                                                                    2002041386

ISBN   1 84064 723 X (3 volume set)

Printed and bound in Great Britain by MPG Books Ltd, Bodmin, Cornwall

Contents

Acknowledgements

The editors and publishers wish to thank the authors and the following publishers who have kindly given permission for the use of copyright material.

Blackwell Publishing for articles: Richard Stehle (1977), 'An Empirical Test of the Alternative Hypotheses of National and International Pricing of Risky Assets', *Journal of Finance*, **XXXII** (2), May, 493–502; Bruno Solnik (1983), 'International Arbitrage Pricing Theory', *Journal of Finance*, **XXXVIII** (2), May, 449–57; Michael Adler and Bernard Dumas (1983), 'International Portfolio Choice and Corporation Finance: A Synthesis', *Journal of Finance*, **XXXVIII** (3), June, 925–84; D. Chinhyung Cho, Cheol S. Eun and Lemma W. Senbet (1986), 'International Arbitrage Pricing Theory: An Empirical Investigation', *Journal of Finance*, **XLI** (2), June, 313–29; Campbell R. Harvey (1991), 'The World Price of Covariance Risk', *Journal of Finance*, **XLVI** (1), March, 111–57; Geert Bekaert and Robert J. Hodrick (1992), 'Characterizing Predictable Components in Excess Returns on Equity and Foreign Exchange Markets', *Journal of Finance*, **XLVII** (2), June, 467–509; Giorgio De Santis and Bruno Gérard (1997), 'International Asset Pricing and Portfolio Diversification with Time-Varying Risk', *Journal of Finance*, **LII** (5), December, 1881–912.

Elsevier Science for articles: Frederick L.A. Grauer, Robert H. Litzenberger and Richard E. Stehle (1976), 'Sharing Rules and Equilibrium in an International Capital Market Under Uncertainty', *Journal of Financial Economics*, **3** (3), June, 233–56; René M. Stulz (1981), 'A Model of International Asset Pricing', *Journal of Financial Economics*, **9** (4), December, 383–406; Simon Wheatley (1988), 'Some Tests of International Equity Integration', *Journal of Financial Economics*, **21** (2), September, 177–212; K.C. Chan, G. Andrew Karolyi and René M. Stulz (1992), 'Global Financial Markets and the Risk Premium on U.S. Equity', *Journal of Financial Economics*, **32** (2), October, 137–67.

Elsevier Science (USA) for article: Bruno H. Solnik (1974), 'An Equilibrium Model of the International Capital Market', *Journal of Economic Theory*, **8**, August, 500–24.

Oxford University Press for articles: Robert A. Korajczyk and Claude J. Viallet (1989), 'An Empirical Investigation of International Asset Pricing', *Review of Financial Studies*, **2** (4), 553–85; Wayne E. Ferson and Campbell R. Harvey (1993), 'The Risk and Predictability of International Equity Returns', *Review of Financial Studies*, **6** (3), 527–66.

Presses Universitaires de France for article: Piet Sercu (1980), 'A Generalization of the International Asset Pricing Model', *Revue de l'Association Française de Finance*, **1** (1), 91–135 [edited and reset, including Index to Notation].

Every effort has been made to trace all the copyright holders but if any have been inadvertently overlooked the publishers will be pleased to make the necessary arrangement at the first opportunity.

In addition the publishers wish to thank the Marshall Library of Economics, Cambridge University and the Library of Indiana University at Bloomington, USA for their assistance in obtaining these articles.

Foreword

Richard Roll

Globalization, integration and sustainable development are much in the news these days, but few journalists and investors are aware that financial economists have been modeling and measuring these phenomena for decades. The resulting research is sophisticated and highly pertinent to the passionate debates often conducted without much supporting foundation in the public arena.

Professors Karolyi and Stulz, both widely published and cited scholars of international finance, have provided in these pages an impressive collection of the most important research findings over the past 25 years. It would be altogether too much to hope that environmentalists, industrialists, government officials and others participating at the next international forum would each have the Karolyi/Stulz volumes with them in order to check on facts being alleged, yet the ensuing debate would rise to a higher level and be more likely to result in agreement if such an unlikely event actually were to occur.

Karolyi and Stulz divide the field of international financial economics into four sub-areas dealing with (1) asset pricing, that is, risk and reward; (2) portfolio diversification; (3) exchange rates and interest rates; and (4) barriers to international investments. In each sub-area, they offer a cogent review of the literature and a collection of the most influential papers.

Risk and reward is probably the single most important subject in finance. It is a difficult problem even domestically and all the more of a conundrum within the reality of an international setting. As noted by Karolyi and Stulz, if all international markets were frictionless, asset pricing would be the same everywhere. The same return/reward tradeoff would be available in all markets. The only technical problem is to account for differences in exchange rates

Unfortunately, this 'technical' problem is not all that easy, either. It depends upon whether exchange rates represent an independent source of risk beyond the risks of domestic markets. Karolyi and Stulz provide a fascinating survey of the theoretical development of this area, followed by an assessment of the empirical research. This alone makes these volumes worth possessing.

In reality, markets are not always frictionless. There are sometimes direct impediments to capital mobility, not to mention differential taxes, restrictions on foreign ownership, and other barriers, perhaps erected with good intentions but actually bringing unintended consequences. There are also material differences across nations in property rights, the rule of law, and the expropriation of capital, both historical and probable. The literature on barriers is surveyed in the fifth section of Karolyi and Stulz's introduction.

With respect to barriers, both the available theory and the empirical evidence are mixed and often surprising. Barriers have generally fallen over time, but they have been resurrected in some instances (Malaysia). Their influence depends on how easily they are evaded. Also, there is some evidence that investors naturally segment themselves, even in the absence of legal barriers. Finnish investors who speak Swedish, for instance, concentrate their holdings more in (Finnish) firms that issue annual reports in Swedish. Similar psychological proclivities might be responsible for some puzzling empirical anomalies, such as the dramatic home market bias (overweighting domestic securities), yet such an explanation is merely surmise at this point.

In the third part of their introduction, Professors Karolyi and Stulz survey the literature on international portfolio diversification, a subject about which scholars are somewhat more, though not universally, in agreement. There is an empirical surprise associated even with this subject, 'It is somewhat puzzling that international correlations across markets have not trended upward more rapidly. The existence of strong country effects in stock returns seems to have persisted more than one would have expected' (p. xv).

Low correlations are responsible for the benefits from international diversification, but whether such benefits could equally be achieved by appropriate domestic investments, via industry diversification or country funds, remains a controversial issue. Also, there is some evidence that the correlations are higher in down markets, precisely when diversification would have the most value. Needless to say, this subject and its ongoing research are not only of deep intrinsic interest but are also of great practical relevance for investors.

Section 4 of the introduction is devoted to exchange rates and interest rates. Within this general research area, there is literature concerning the determinants of exchange rates, the risk premiums (if any) in forward exchange rates as forecasts of future spot exchange rates, the rationale and extent of currency hedging, and the implicit risk premiums (if any) embedded in default-free short-term bonds because they are held by other than domestic investors. Resolution of such questions will ultimately lead to improved theories of international asset pricing.

These three volumes on international capital markets constitute an essential part of the Elgar series of critical writings in financial economics (which is itself an international venture). The research surveyed and included here integrates much of the domestically oriented literature printed in the other volumes of the series. Professors Karolyi and Stulz have provided a real service to scholars and the broader community of international investors by collecting and summarizing these critical papers.

Introduction[*]

G. Andrew Karolyi and René M. Stulz

Since the 1970s, the degree of international capital market integration has grown tremendously. Cross-border net and gross capital flows have increased dramatically. The value of daily foreign exchange transactions exceeds the value of annual international trade in goods and services. Almost as rapidly growing is the mass of scientific literature on international capital markets. This three volume set, *International Capital Markets*, serves to organize in one compilation the most important theoretical and empirical research in the field to date.

Our brief introduction surveys, describes and synthesizes this literature. To this end, we divide the field into four major areas of study: (a) international portfolio choice and international asset pricing models; (b) the structure of international returns and international portfolio diversification; (c) equilibrium models of exchange rates and interest rates; and (d) the impact of barriers to international investments.

1. International Portfolio Choice and Asset Pricing

When local investors can invest abroad freely and foreign investors can invest in the local market freely, asset prices in the local market are determined globally. The early contributions to the field of international finance in the 1970s established the conditions under which portfolios are chosen and under which asset prices are determined in internationally perfect capital markets. In such settings, assets have the same price regardless of where they are traded and no finance is local; there are no transportation costs, no tariffs, no taxes, no transactions costs, no convertibility restrictions, and no restrictions on short sales. Markets in which cash flows have the same price regardless of where claims to these cash flows trade are said to be integrated. Markets in which the price of cash flows depends on where the claim to these cash flows trade because of obstacles to trading these claims internationally are said to be segmented. If a market is segmented, that segmentation can be partial or complete. A market is completely segmented if local investors cannot invest abroad and foreign investors cannot invest in that market.

One can think of world capital markets as a collection of islands with different currencies. An island that is inaccessible is a segmented market. Islands that are easily accessible are perfectly integrated markets. A whole host of impediments can make it difficult to go from one island to another. When trying to explain how assets are priced internationally, one has to take a stand on how the markets are connected. This means that one has to assess the risks an investor bears and the obstacles he or she faces when investing in a foreign market. The literature has almost exclusively focused on foreign exchange risk as the main risk affecting foreign investors differently to local investors and on barriers to international investment as the obstacle affecting foreign investors. From this perspective, one has to make important decisions when pricing claims to cash flows in relation to: (1) how exchange rates are determined and (2) what barriers to international investment exist. In this section of the Introduction and in Volume I of this collection, we focus on models that assume that markets are internationally perfect. In section 4 of the Introduction and Volume III, we examine models that examine the implications of barriers to international investment.

Asset pricing models that assume that markets are internationally perfect differ in their assumptions about exchange rate dynamics. Exchange rate risk is important in asset pricing models because a domestic investor that owns a foreign security has to convert the cash flows from that security into the domestic currency to benefit from these cash flows. This conversion imposes on investors a risk that they do not face when investing at home. It is therefore important to understand whether that exchange rate risk is priced and how it affects portfolio choice.

The seminal work of Solnik (Vol. I, Chapter 1) assumes that all exchange rate fluctuations are real exchange rate fluctuations. Price levels are constant within countries, so that the exchange rate reflects changes in the price of the domestic consumption basket relative to the price of the foreign consumption basket. The assumptions of Solnik's model imply that a risk-free asset in foreign currency is a risky asset in domestic currency. Solnik assumes further that the return of a stock is uncorrelated with the exchange rate. This implies that a domestic investor holding an unhedged position in a foreign stock faces more risk than a foreign investor holding the same stock. However, investors can hedge foreign exchange rate risk by selling short the foreign currency which is equivalent to borrowing in the foreign currency risk-free asset. The ability of investors to hedge foreign exchange rate risk implies that this risk does not affect the proportions in which investors hold individual stocks because it is not optimal for investors to hold foreign exchange rate risk in the form of stocks. If investors want to bear such risk in their portfolios, they do so by holding foreign currency risk-free assets.

In Solnik's model, the domestic investor can hedge his or her holdings of the foreign risky assets against exchange rate risk by borrowing an amount in foreign currency equal to his or her holdings of foreign currency risky assets. Similarly, foreign investors hedge their currency risk by borrowing in domestic currency an amount equal to their holdings of domestic currency risky assets. If there is no reward for taking foreign currency risk, domestic investors short the foreign currency risk-free asset for an amount exactly equal to their investment in foreign currency risky assets and bear no foreign exchange rate risk. As the reward for taking foreign exchange rate risk increases, domestic investors decrease the extent to which they hedge the foreign exchange risk associated with their holdings of risky assets in foreign currency. Equilibrium in the market for the assets that are locally risk free makes possible the existence of a risk premium for bearing foreign exchange risk. Consequently, the Sharpe–Lintner capital asset pricing model (CAPM) does not hold in Solnik's model.

The model of Grauer, Litzenberger and Stehle (Vol. I, Chapter 3) is an alternative to Solnik's model, and assumes that purchasing power parity holds exactly.[1] When all investors have the same consumption opportunity set and the same constant expenditure proportions on consumption goods, the CAPM holds in real terms if there is a real risk-free asset. In such a model, there is no separate risk premium for foreign exchange. A currency for which the real rate of change is positively correlated with the real return on the world market portfolio has a risk premium as with any other asset for which the real return is positively correlated with the real return of the world market portfolio.

Solnik's model is significantly extended by Sercu (Vol. I, Chapter 2). Solnik's analysis was based on an important simplifying assumption, namely that nominal stock returns are uncorrelated with exchange rate changes. Sercu relaxes this assumption. With Solnik's model, the optimal currency hedge for a foreign stock is to sell short the foreign currency for an amount equal to the investment in the foreign stock. As the value of the foreign stock changes, the hedge has to be adjusted. This result no longer holds with Sercu. In Sercu's model, the optimal hedge depends on the currency exposures of the foreign stock. Nevertheless, in Sercu's model, investors hold any two stocks in equal proportions regardless of the country in which they live.

Adler and Dumas (Vol. I, Chapter 4) extend the Solnik/Sercu model to allow for inflation. In their model, investors consume different baskets of goods, and the price of their consumption basket evolves randomly over time because of inflation and relative price changes. Investors who are concerned about purchasing power risk can find it useful to hold foreign nominal bonds since the domestic currency purchasing power of such bonds can be less volatile than the domestic currency purchasing power of domestic bonds. This leads Adler and Dumas to demonstrate a two-fund theorem. An investor invests in the portfolio of risky assets if s/he has logarithmic utility and a portfolio that has the lowest real return variance given the consumption basket s/he consumes. The portfolio of risky assets an investor with logarithmic utility would hold is the same irrespective of the basket of goods s/he consumes and hence of his/her country of residence.

Purchasing power parity is more relevant for some countries than others. In particular, if a country experiences high inflation, purchasing power parity provides a reasonable forecast of exchange rate changes. However, purchasing power parity does not work well for countries that experience limited inflation. A model of international asset pricing should therefore accommodate not only countries where purchasing power parity offers a good approximation of exchange rate determination but also countries where it does not. Further, the exchange rate process is not an exogenous process. Exchange rates are functions of state variables on which other prices depend. General equilibrium considerations therefore preclude an exogenous process for the exchange rate. If the expected rate of change in the exchange rate depends on the state of the world, it is no longer correct to assume a constant investment opportunity set. Stulz (Vol. I, Chapter 5) derives a model that resolves these two issues. In his model, the exchange rate dynamics depend on state variables as do the dynamics of other asset prices. The assumed dynamics are therefore consistent with general equilibrium requirements. Further, the real expected return on an asset increases with the covariance of the real return of the asset with the rate of growth of world consumption.

The empirical evidence in support of international asset pricing models has come in two main waves. The first wave of research focused on unconditional tests of the international capital asset pricing model (ICAPM), the international asset pricing model of Solnik and his successors (IAPM), the international arbitrage pricing model (first developed in Solnik (Vol. I, Chapter 6)), and the consumption-based international capital asset pricing model. Early tests by Stehle (Vol. I, Chapter 7) of the international capital asset pricing model, by Cho, Eun and Senbet (Vol. I, Chapter 9) and Korajczyk and Viallet (Vol. I, Chapter 10) of the international arbitrage pricing model, and by Wheatley (Vol. I, Chapter 8) of the consumption-based capital asset pricing model find evidence that global factors are statistically important although more often than not the restriction that these factors are priced is rejected. The second wave of empirical tests focuses on a conditional setting with time-varying expected returns, variances and covariances. The first effort in this regard by Mark (Vol. II, Chapter 19) investigates the risk premium in currency forward contracts, but later studies by Harvey (Vol. I, Chapter 11), Bekaert and Hodrick (Vol. I, Chapter 12), Chan, Karolyi, and Stulz (Vol. I, Chapter 13), Ferson and Harvey (Vol. I, Chapter 14) and DeSantis and Gérard (Vol. I, Chapter 15) focus on national stock indexes as well as foreign exchange markets. These studies consistently find evidence that conditional covariances implied by the ICAPM or IAPM indeed have success in forecasting the national risk premia over time. Unfortunately, the risk premia tend to be quite large at times, leading to the rejection of the overidentifying restrictions implied by these models. In surveying these studies, the consistency of the results is remarkable in spite of the variety of statistical techniques applied, such as latent variables models, generalized method of moments (GMM), and generalized autoregressive conditionally heteroscedastic models (GARCH).

2. Structure of International Returns and International Portfolio Diversification

There has been a strong trend toward international diversification in all countries in the past decade, but especially among US institutional investors such as corporate and public pension funds. Indeed, the mere size of foreign markets justifies international diversification, even for US investors. By 2000, the world stock market capitalization hovered around $20 trillion, of which approximately half was accounted for by the US. In a fully efficient, integrated international capital market, mean-variance asset pricing models imply that it is optimal for investors to hold the world market portfolio of common stocks, but the case has not been fully built for the real world and numerous constraints may give a competitive advantage to domestic investors. These constraints may explain the existence of a home bias, namely that investors overweight their home market in their portfolio of common stocks (see, for instance, French and Poterba (Vol. III, Chapter 19)).

The first cases in favor of international investment programs by Grubel (Vol. II, Chapter 1), Levy and Sarnat (Vol. II, Chapter 2), and Solnik (Vol. II, Chapter 3) focus on the risk-reduction benefit of diversifying a portfolio by investing abroad. Of course, the prerequisite for this argument is that returns on the various capital markets of the world are not too highly correlated. However, the correlation of the returns of the various capital markets seems to have increased somewhat over time. Several papers have further pointed out that the correlation of the returns across markets seems to be higher in bear markets than in bull markets (see, for instance, Longin and Solnik (Vol. II, Chapter 6) and De Santis and Gérard (Vol. I, Chapter 15)). These results have led some to argue that diversification has become less valuable. Though early papers ignore issues of statistical significance, more recent papers have developed tools that make it possible to evaluate statistically the significance of the risk reduction brought about by international diversification. Some authors provide results showing that diversifying abroad does not lead to a significant decrease in volatility.[2] At the same time, however, international diversification has become easier to implement as it can often be achieved without buying securities that trade abroad directly. Bekaert and Urias (Vol. II, Chapter 7) show the diversification benefits that can be achieved by US investors in investing in closed-end country funds. Errunza, Hogan, and Hung (Vol. II, Chapter 11) show that US investors can obtain almost all available benefits from international diversification by investing in securities that trade in the US.

It is somewhat puzzling that international correlations across markets have not trended upward more rapidly. The existence of strong country effects in stock returns seems to have persisted more than one would have expected. Some studies have hypothesized that this can be explained by the growing competition among national economies and the resultant increased national specialization by industry that has resulted. Roll (Vol. II, Chapter 9) and Heston and Rouwenhorst (Vol. II, Chapter 10) have spurred a debate about the extent to which the industrial structure of markets can explain the benefits of international diversification.

Some investigators have attempted to find lead or lag patterns among market returns to better understand co-movements across markets. Some of this extension stems from nonsynchronous trading periods, some stems from attempting to understand how information in returns and the volatility of returns 'spill over' from one market to another. Eun and Shim (Vol. II, Chapter 4) and Hamao, Masulis and Ng (Vol. II, Chapter 5) employ vector autoregression analysis (VAR) and multivariate GARCH techniques to show how large lead and lag spillovers can be.

A related issue is whether the correlation across markets remains constant over time. It is often stated that the progressive removal of barriers to international investment as well as growing political, economic, and capital market integration affects international market linkages. Longin and Solnik (Vol. II, Chapter 6) was one of the first studies to confirm the instability of international correlations over time. Though they are unable to find strong systematic patterns in correlations with economic fundamentals, they find that the correlations tend to increase in turbulent periods (high global market volatility). A large literature on 'contagion' for Asian and Latin American markets during the 1990s showed that correlations are higher around emerging market crises.

All this effort at better understanding changing correlations has had limited success. Even when there appear to be significant changes in correlations using traditional estimation techniques, such as during crisis periods, recent papers raise questions as to whether such increases are spurious and the results of inappropriate techniques.[3] Despite the existence of dozens of papers on contagion, no consensus has been achieved among economists on whether it actually exists. Journalists and politicians by contrast, are assured about the economic importance of contagion.

3.   Exchange Rates and Interest Rates

The relation between asset returns and exchange rate movements is central to international asset pricing. Most economists reject the view that the short-term behavior of exchange rates is determined by balance of payments flows, preferring to view exchange rates as prices determined in asset markets that reflect future expectations about economic growth, inflation, and interest rates. Lucas (Vol. II, Chapter 13) develops a two-country money-demand model in which real growth in the domestic economy leads to increased demand for the domestic currency. This increase in currency demand induces a rise in the relative value of the currency. Because domestic stock prices are strongly influenced by real growth, this model justifies a positive association between real stock returns and domestic currency appreciation.

There is a considerable literature that uses the relation between forward exchange rates and expected spot exchange rates to understand better how foreign exchange risks are priced. In a risk-neutral world, the forward exchange rate should be equal to the expected spot exchange rates. There are several important studies that show that forward rates are biased predictors of future spot rates, including Hansen and Hodrick (Vol. II, Chapter 17), Fama (Vol. II, Chapter 18), and Bekaert and Hodrick (Vol. II, Chapter 25). The asset pricing models discussed in section 1 of this introduction have implications for the pricing of foreign exchange forward contracts. In particular, if the ICAPM holds, investors have to be compensated more for a long position in a foreign currency if that currency has a higher covariance with the world market portfolio. Mark (Vol. II, Chapter 19) finds support for this hypothesis. Dumas and Solnik (Vol. II, Chapter 23) test an asset pricing equation where foreign exchange rate risk is priced separately as in Solnik (Vol. II, Chapter 16) and find support for such an equation.

An important debate revolves around the rationale for currency hedging by investors. In a perfect markets model with no inflation (as in section 1 above), every investor would take positions in the domestic risk-free asset, in risk-free bills in foreign currencies, and in the world market portfolio of common stocks. Investors would take positions in foreign currency risk-free bills partly to hedge their holdings of foreign common stocks. However, they may still have a net exposure to various currency risks depending on how they are compensated for bearing these risks.

Although the weights of each national bill are complex functions, it is not unreasonable to assume that they are negative (except for the domestic bill), as this corresponds to selling foreign currency contracts which investors have to do to hedge holdings of common stocks. Perhaps the more important issue is how much investors sell of risk-free bills in a currency compared to how much they hold of stocks in that currency. The risk-free bills an investor sells in a currency expressed as a fraction of his or her holdings of common stocks in that currency is the investor's currency hedge ratio in that currency. Black (Vol. II, Chapter 14) draws heavily from Solnik (Vol. I, Chapter I), Sercu (Vol. I, Chapter 2) and Adler and Dumas (Vol. I, Chapter 4) to suggest that a 'universal hedging formula' exists, which every investor should use. In his model, every investor hedges the world market portfolio by selling risk-free bills in foreign currencies in the same way, since everyone holds the same portfolio of risky assets. The aggregate hedge ratio need not be unity. Black provides a historical estimate of roughly 0.70. Solnik (Vol. II, Chapter 16) shows that the simple fact that inflation differs across countries and varies over time destroys the argument that there exists a 'universal hedging formula'. An important element of the debate revolves around the application of Siegel's (Vol. II, Chapter 15) paradox to validate the arguments. The essence of this paradox is that because of Jensen's inequality, investors in two countries have different expectations for the exchange rate since if S is the spot exchange rate at home and $1/S$ the spot exchange rate abroad, the expected value of S differs from the inverse of the expected value of $1/S$.

Glen and Jorion (Vol. II, Chapter 22) conduct an empirical study of optimal asset allocations for a US investor with currency forward contracts and conclude that the importance of currency hedging depends on the proportion of the foreign assets held in the portfolio, but the extent of hedging may not matter so much in terms of risk-adjusted returns if the amounts invested in foreign assets are small.

Empirical evidence generally supports the finding that currency risk exposure is important and is priced in asset returns, but mostly for conditional tests. In unconditional tests, researchers assume that expected returns and risk are constant over time and most of these studies have had limited success in finding evidence that currency risk is priced. Conditional tests that allow expected returns and risk to vary over time have been more successful. Jorion (Vol. II,

Chapter 20), Dumas and Solnik (Vol. II, Chapter 23) and DeSantis and Gérard (Vol. II, Chapter 24) capture the pricing of exchange rate risk for equities, and Ilmanen (Vol. II, Chapter 21) for bonds.

4.   The Impact of Barriers to International Investments

The international asset pricing relations described in section 1 above apply to all securities only in an integrated world capital market. There are a host of direct and indirect barriers that can segment markets. In many countries, various types of institutional investors face severe legal constraints on their international investments. Official foreign investment restrictions, fear of expropriation, discriminatory taxes and higher investment costs push domestic investors to underinvest in foreign assets compared to the world market portfolio. Psychological, cultural and behavioral aspects of investing can be important factors, also. After all, investors are more familiar with their local market than with foreign markets, so they may feel uneasy about investing in a remote country or exotic currency. Models that explore the impact of these barriers on portfolio choice and asset pricing generally ignore exchange rate risk.

Black (Vol. III, Chapter 1) derives a model of international portfolio choice and asset pricing where barriers to international investment take the form of a proportional tax that is rebated for short sales. Barriers of this type might correspond to some types of taxes, but generally obstacles to investment are such that they reduce the return both for short and long positions. Stulz (Vol. III, Chapter 2) models such barriers as the equivalent of a tax paid on the absolute value of holdings of foreign stocks and shows that they imply that some foreign stocks are not held by domestic residents. This tax can represent explicit direct costs of holding foreign stocks as well as proxy for other indirect costs, such as information costs. Other barriers to international investment take the form of outright ownership restrictions. Eun and Janakiramanan (Vol. III, Chapter 4) and Errunza and Losq (Vol. III, Chapter 3) provide models that examine the portfolio and asset pricing implications of such barriers.

A number of contributions to the debate investigate empirically the implications of partial segmentation, where partial segmentation is defined to mean some equity flows take place either in or out of a country but these flows are limited because of explicit constraints or because of barriers to international investment. Many of the contributions discussed in section 1 use the hypothesis of segmented markets as their alternative hypothesis. In particular, it is common in the literature to contrast global pricing of assets to local pricing of country portfolios. Using data for developed markets for the 1980s and 1990s, authors generally find that their tests cannot reject global pricing of assets.

When barriers to international investment are known explicitly, a model that reflects these barriers can be tested. Errunza and Losq (Vol. III, Chapter 3) derive explicit predictions for the expected returns of securities that cannot be held freely by foreign investors and test these predictions on a short sample period, obtaining results that are not inconsistent with their predictions. Hietala (Vol. III, Chapter 5) tests a model where he incorporates the ownership restrictions that applied to Finnish companies over his sample period and finds supportive evidence that the magnitude of the premium of unrestricted shares relative to restricted shares can be explained by his model. Bailey and Jagtiani (Vol. III, Chapter 6) investigate the determinants of the premium of shares available to foreign investors in Thailand and show

how that premium varies over time. With explicit or implicit barriers to international investment, securities available to foreign investors may not be equally attractive to all foreign investors since the barriers may differ across investors, depending, for instance, on their tax status. In this case, the demand curves for domestic securities from foreign investors may be downward-sloping, creating incentives for firms to restrict their supply of shares available to foreign investors to increase the price of these shares. Stulz and Wasserfallen (Vol. III, Chapter 7) expand models with barriers to international investment to take into account the downward-sloping demand curves for domestic securities from foreign investors and find supportive evidence for Switzerland.

Over the last thirty years, however, barriers to international investment have fallen dramatically. Emerging markets took longer to remove explicit barriers to international investment. Even for emerging markets that have few such explicit barriers, sovereign risk often remains a significant barrier to international investment. Further, in these markets there have been instances where barriers have been restored – the most visible case being Malaysia in 1998. Bekaert and Harvey (Vol. III, Chapter 10) estimate a model where the degree of segmentation of an emerging market changes over time and then extract the extent to which the market is segmented from the data. With their approach, the risk premium on a market depends on its volatility if the market is completely segmented and depends on its covariance with the world market portfolio, or its world beta, if it is completely integrated. They allow a market's expected return to depend on both its volatility and its world beta. The degree of segmentation of a market decreases when the market's world beta becomes a more important determinant of the market's expected return. They find that the degree of segmentation varies over time – sometimes decreasing and sometimes increasing. Foerster and Karolyi (Vol. III, Chapter 9) examine firm-specific evidence of time-variation in market segmentation by studying the changes in expected returns, volatilities and market risks around the firm's decision to cross-list shares in US markets. They find large and significant declines in local market betas and only modest increases in world betas.

Bekaert and Harvey (Vol. III, Chapter 10) and Henry (Vol. III, Chapter 12) provide evidence on the impact of removing barriers to international investment for emerging markets. When a country's risk premium is determined locally, the mean-variance model implies that the risk premium increases with the volatility of that country's market. In contrast, when a country's risk premium is determined globally, the risk premium depends on the covariance of the return of that country's market portfolio with the return of the world market portfolio. Because emerging markets typically have high volatility but low betas, one would expect their equity to appreciate substantially when they move from local to global pricing. Henry (Vol. III, Chapter 12) shows that it is so.

A brief look at investors' portfolio holdings suggests that a major conclusion of the international CAPM and the IAPM is contradicted by the evidence. These models predict that investors hold common stocks in identical proportions regardless of their country of residence, but the portfolios of common stocks of investors are strongly biased toward domestic investments. US investors devote almost all of their equity portfolios to US securities, although these models would have them hold the world market portfolio. This is the home bias we referred to earlier. French and Poterba (Vol. III, Chapter 19), Gehrig (Vol. III, Chapter 20), Cooper and Kaplanis (Vol. III, Chapter 16), Tesar and Werner (Vol. III, Chapter 17) and Kang and Stulz (Vol. III, Chapter 18) present evidence of a home preference in portfolio investment and fail to find satisfactory explanations for such a large bias. This, of course, does not mean that financial markets are necessarily segmented. The model of Stulz (Vol. I, Chapter 5) is consistent with investors exhibiting a home bias in internationally perfect markets because investors hedge against unexpected changes in state variables, and state variables against which investors hedge can depend on the country of residence of investors. Nevertheless, it is difficult to ignore the fact that, though explicit barriers have fallen over time, the home bias phenomenon has persisted.

Foreign investors could be disadvantaged because of indirect barriers that stem from distance, differences in language and culture or information advantages for domestic investors. Gehrig (Vol. III, Chapter 20) derives optimal portfolios when foreign investors know less and shows how this leads to an overweighting of domestic assets. Kang and Stulz (Vol. III, Chapter 18) show that in Japan foreign investors have a bias towards large-cap stocks, which they hypothesize is related to their information disadvantage. Grinblatt and Keloharju (Vol. III, Chapter 24) show that in Finland language matters in an investor's portfolio allocation, in that Finnish investors whose native language is Swedish are more likely to own stocks of companies in Finland that have annual reports in Swedish.

Most studies that investigate whether markets are integrated do so by testing models that make predictions about expected returns. However, some papers investigate whether the law of one price applies to assets that have identical cash flows. Froot and Dabora (Vol. III, Chapter 23) show that three major cross-listed stocks that trade in multiple time zones around the world can trade at substantially different prices in different time zones.

Cross-border capital flows, especially to developing economies, have grown dramatically in the past three decades of market liberalization. A number of studies have asked whether changes in equity valuations can be traced to flows. Does the impact of capital flows on valuations reflect information known to foreign investors that is not yet incorporated into prices? Or is the impact of flows on asset prices the destabilizing by-product of excessively volatile flows as foreigners come and go on a whim? This is the focus of important contributions by Bohn and Tesar (Vol. III, Chapter 13), Brennan and Cao (Vol. III, Chapter 14), and Froot, O'Connell and Seasholes (Vol. III, Chapter 15). These studies, using different data and methods, show that foreign investors are positive-feedback traders, that is, they buy stocks which have experienced positive returns and sell stocks which have negative returns. Brennan and Cao provide a theoretical foundation for interpretations that suggest a cumulative informational disadvantage for foreign investors: foreign investors update their forecasts of future returns with greater frequency than local investors in response to public information about local markets, because their prior expectations are more diffuse.

5. Concluding Remarks

This three-volume compilation *International Capital Markets* brings together the major theoretical, empirical and institutional contributions to the field of international finance from the past 25 years. The scope of inquiry spans theories of international portfolio choice and empirical evidence on international asset pricing models, international portfolio diversification, exchange rates and interest rates, and theories and empirical evidence on international barriers to international investments. An important theme of this survey is that the dynamic nature of international capital markets is paralleled by the dynamic pace of research on those markets and how securities are priced within these. However, much research remains to be done.

Notes

*   In preparing this three-volume set, we solicited advice and input from a number of our colleagues who specialize in the field of international finance. We are grateful for advice and comments from Yiorgos Allayannis, Warren Bailey, Vihang Errunza, Cheol Eun, Campbell Harvey, Peter Henry, Ludger Hentschel, Robert Hodrick, Ross Levine, Rich Lyons, Sergio Rebelo, Carmen Reinhart, Dick Roll, Linda Tesar, and Simon Wheatley. We also thank Ben Booth, Nicola Mills and Edward Elgar for their support during the publication process.

1.   Grauer, Litzenberger, and Stehle also have results where purchasing power parity does not hold, but then they assume that all investors have the same risk aversion.

2.   See, for instance, M. Britten-Jones (1999), 'The sampling error in estimates of mean-variance efficient portfolio weights', *Journal of Finance*, **54**, 655–71.

3.   See, for instance, K. Forbes and R. Rigobon (2002), 'No contagion, only interdependence: measuring stock market comovements', *Journal of Finance*, **62**, 2223–2261.

Part I
Theories of International Portfolio Choice and Asset Pricing

[1]

JOURNAL OF ECONOMIC THEORY **8**, 500–524 (1974)

An Equilibrium Model of the International Capital Market*

BRUNO H. SOLNIK

Graduate School of Business, Stanford University, Stanford, California 94305

INTRODUCTION AND SUMMARY

Many of the existing studies in international finance are based on a segmented market approach which considers the different national capital markets as independent entities. Different currency areas, separated political organizations and trade barriers are usually taken as *a priori* justification for a segmented approach to analysis of international capital markets. However, the development of international investment is evidenced by the rapidly growing share of foreign investors on Wall Street and various non-American markets. Similarly, a large number of foreign stocks are being listed on the official exchanges of many countries, providing the investors with an easy way to obtain international diversification. Also, in many countries institutional investors have offered international mutual funds to the public (e.g., the French SICAV).

The purpose of this paper is to present an equilibrium model of the international capital market with the hypothesis that security price behavior is consistent with a single world market concept. An intertemporal model of the international capital market is developed in the framework of the Sharpe-Lintner-Mossin Capital Asset Pricing Model. A fundamental dimension of this international market is the existence of exchange risk and mechanisms providing protection to investors unwilling to carry that kind of risk. A mutual fund theorem is derived which states that all investors will be indifferent between choosing portfolios from the original assets or from three funds:

—a portfolio of stocks hedged against exchange risk (the market portfolio)
—a portfolio of bonds, speculative in the exchange risk dimension
—the risk free asset of their own country

* This article is derived from my doctoral dissertation at M.I.T. I am most greatful to Franco Modigliani, Jerry Pogue, and Myron Scholes for their help and advice. Thanks are due to Robert Litzenberger, Jack McDonald and William Sharpe for their comments and suggestions on an earlier draft of this paper. A large part of this work has been inspired by the pathbreaking approach of R. Merton. His benefic influence will be recognized throughout this paper. All errors remain mine.

500

The composition of these funds is independent of the investor's preference or nationality (except for the risk free asset).

The risk premium of a security over its national risk free rate is shown to be proportional to its international systematic risk. The coefficient of proportionality is the risk premium of the work market over a world bond rate. Similarly, the difference between interest rates of two countries is shown to be equal to the expected change of parities between these two countries plus a term depending on exchange risk covariances. This result has strong implications for the much debated interest rate parity theory; it implies that the forward exchange rate is a *biased* estimate of the future exchange rate.[1]

THE INTERNATIONAL ASSET PRICING MODEL

The Capital Asset Pricing Model developed by Sharpe, Lintner, and Mossin is the basis for a new theory of the capital markets.[2]

This model applied to a single national market suggests that all investors could make their investment decisions by choosing their portfolios from two funds: the market portfolio and the risk free asset. Besides, the model predicts that the expected extra return from holding an asset is proportional to the covariance of its return with the market portfolio (its "beta"). With a less restrictive set of assumptions, R. Merton [8], [9] has developed an intertemporal equilibrium model of the capital market. The *intertemporal* nature of this model allows it to capture effects which would never appear in a static model. This framework will be used to develop a theory of an international capital market, therefore the developments already presented in Merton [9] will be described more briefly here.

Even the intertemporal Capital Asset Pricing Model has important limitations because it only considers national investment. Therefore this theory can only hold in a completely segmented world capital market. It is not true that it could easily be extended by simply including foreign investment opportunities in the market portfolio; this model would not represent a general equilibrium and lose all economic substance and appeal. As a matter of fact very few attempts have been made to use this kind of approach to develop an international equilibrium model of the capital markets.[3]

---

[1] For an empirical test of the model presented here see Solnik [14] and [15].

[2] See Sharpe [2] and [13], Lintner [7], and Mossin [11].

[3] See for example Lee [6], Grubel [2]. Most of the work published is concerned with the investment behavior of citizens of *one* given country facing an enlarged investment opportunity set.

502   BRUNO H. SOLNIK

Among the various complexities of such a task are the nonexistence of a universal risk free asset (and different interest rates) and the presence of exchange risk which alters the characteristics of the same investment from different countries. Possible change in parities imply that a same asset might yield different returns (and therefore different expectations on returns) for citizens of different countries. In a mean-variance framework the investment opportunity set facing investors from various countries will vary, even in a perfect and integrated international capital market. The model developed below will attempt to deal with these problems in designing an equilibrium model of the international demand for capital assets.

1. *International Capital Market Structure*

A certain number of general assumptions have to be made about the capital market structure; they are mostly the standard assumptions of market perfection.[4]

Assumptions

A-1. The capital markets are always in equilibrium (i.e., there is no trading at nonequilibrium prices).

A-2. Capital markets are perfect, with no transaction costs, taxes, or capital controls. Investors are price takers.

A-3. Assets can be sold short.

A-4. In each country there exists a market (bond) for borrowing and lending at the same rate (however this rate does not have to be the same in all countries).

A-5. Trading in assets and currencies take place continuously in time. This implies a world of flexible exchange rates.

A-6. Investors hold homogeneous expectations about exchange rate variations and the distribution of returns in terms of the asset currency.

A-7. There are no constraints on international capital flows.

A-8. Investors' consumption is limited to their home country.

---

[4] I have given in sections 1, 2, and 3 a somewhat detailed description of the intertemporal formulation since the reader might not be familiar with it. However, since this formulation is not central to this paper, I have taken the liberty to make extensive use in this description of the original presentation of Merton [9], up to using some of his well-chosen words.

EQUILIBRIUM OF THE INTERNATIONAL MARKET   503

Assumptions A-1 to A-4 are the standard perfect market assumptions and their merits have been discussed extensively in the literature. Such a model of international market cannot be constructed without costs, and the doubtful assumptions of homogeneous expectations (A-6) has to be made here as well. As explained by Merton, A-5 follows directly from A-2. If there are no costs to transacting and assets can be exchanged on any scale, then investors would prefer to be able to revise their portfolios at any time (whether they actually do so or not).

The last two points summarize all the assumptions on international behavior and market structure. A-7 is central to this model. As far as the consumption pattern of investors is concerned A-8 implies a strict national separation, but does not forbid buying foreign goods with the local currency. This assumption will be discussed in more detail on page 505.

2. *Rates of Return Dynamics and Exchange Rate Structure*

It is assumed that expectations in real terms are homogeneous across all investors and that the price dynamics are described[5] by

$$\frac{dI_i}{I_i} = \alpha_i \, dt + \sigma_i \, dz_i, \qquad i = 1, 2, ..., n,$$

where

dI_i/I_i is the instantaneous rate of return on the market portfolio of country i,[6]

α_i is the instantaneous expected rate of return,

σ_i is the instantaneous standard deviation,

dz_i is the standard Gauss Wiener process with zero mean.

We also assume the existence of risk free asset B_i in each country:

$$\frac{dB_i}{B_i} = R_i \, dt,$$

where R_i is the risk free rate of country i.

---

[5] For a discussion of and further references to stochastic differential equations of this type see Merton [8] and [9], Itô [5].

[6] *Notation*: When the index k appears as a *subscript* it refers to a country k or its assets; when the index κ appears as a *superscript* it refers to a typical investor of country k (investor kappa of country k).

For simplicity of notation, only one asset per country (the market portfolio) will be considered. However it will be seen that investment decisions reduce the choice to market portfolios and not individual assets and identical results would be found if one started with all individual assets; unfortunately the notational crisis would be unsolvable.

504   BRUNO H. SOLNIK

For the time being we will further make the assumption that the investment opportunity set is constant through time (i.e., α_i, σ_i, R_i constant). This implies that the distributions of asset prices will be log-normal. Let us call f_{ik} the exchange rate between country i and country k. Then with the same assumptions[7]

$$\frac{df_{ik}}{f_{ik}} = \mu_{ik}\, dt + \varphi_{ik}\, dq_{ik}\,,$$

where μ_{ik} is the expected change of parity, φ_{ik} is its standard deviation. Then for an investor κ from country k, the instantaneous return on an investment in country i will be (by Itô lemma):

$$\frac{dI_i^{\kappa}}{I_i^{\kappa}} = \frac{d(f_{ik}I_i)}{f_{ik}I_i} = \frac{df_{ik}}{f_{ik}} + \frac{dI_i}{I_i} + \frac{df_{ik}}{f_{ik}} \times \frac{dI_i}{I_i}$$

$$\frac{dI_i^{\kappa}}{I_i^{\kappa}} = (\mu_{ik} + \alpha_i + \rho_{ik}\sigma_i\varphi_{ik})\, dt + \sigma_i\, dz_i + \varphi_{ik}\, dq_{ik} \qquad (1)$$

where

> ρ_{ik} represents the correlation coefficient between changes in the exchange rate f_{ik} and the returns on the asset i,
>
> $\Sigma = \| \sigma_{ij} \|_{n \times n}$ will denote the covariance matrix of assets returns (on real terms),
>
> $\Phi^k = \| \Phi_{ij}^k \|_{n-1 \times n-1}$ will denote the covariance matrix of exchange rates, for country k;

i.e.,

> Φ_i^{kj} will denote the covariance of change of parity of currency i (relative to k) with change of parity of currency j (relative to k).

If, for example, a devaluation is expected on currency i relative to currency k then μ_{ik} should be negative.

3. *Preference Structure and Budget Equation Dynamic*

Consider a world economy with n countries. Each consumer κ (of country k) is supposed to maximize his expected utility, given his current

---

[7] A characteristic of foreign exchange is the existence of a forward market which allows the investor to cover his foreign investment. In the Appendix it is shown how such a forward contract can be described in a mean variance framework and that it is equivalent to going short in the risk free asset of the foreign country (a well known result). Therefore the present model does consider the existence of a forward market and the possibility of covering exchange risk.

wealth, the states variables of the investment opportunity set and the distribution of his age of death.

In a continuous time model, this expected-utility maximization can be written as:

$$\text{Max } E_0 \left[\int_0^{T^\kappa} U^\kappa(C^\kappa(s), s) \, ds + B^\kappa[W^\kappa(T^\kappa), T^\kappa] \right], \qquad (2)$$

where $U^\kappa(\ )$ is the instantaneous utility function of investor κ; it is a function of time and the instantaneous consumption flow. Both U^κ and B^κ, the bequest or utility-of-terminal-wealth function are supposed to be strictly concave Von Neumann-Morgenstern utility functions.

$W^\kappa(t)$ is the wealth of investor κ at time t, T^κ is the distribution for his age of death. $C^\kappa(t)$ is the instantaneous consumption flow.[8]

We can write the accumulation function for the κth investor of country k as

$$dW^\kappa = W^\kappa \sum_{i=1}^{n} w_i^\kappa \frac{dI_i^k}{I_i^k} + W^\kappa \sum_{i=1}^{n} v_i^\kappa \frac{dB_i^k}{B_i^k} + (Y^\kappa - C^\kappa) \, dt, \qquad (3)$$

where

  Y^κ is the wage income of investor κ (of country k),

  w_i^κ is the proportion of wealth invested in country i stocks,

  v_i^κ is the proportion of wealth invested in bonds of country i,

therefore,

  $d_i^\kappa = w_i^\kappa W^\kappa$ is the demand for stocks of country i by investor κ.

In an intertemporal equilibrium model it is not generally possible to assume, at the same time, randomness in investment returns, consumption prices and income. We will make the simplifying assumption that wage

---

[8] Because the paper is primarily interested in finding equilibrium conditions, the model assumes a single consumption good in *each* country. As it was suggested to me by Merton, the model could be generalized by making c^k a vector and introducing as state variables the relative prices. While the analysis would be similar to the one-good case, there would be systematic effects on the portfolio demands reflecting hedging behavior against unfavorable shifts in relative, consumption goods prices (i.e. in the consumption opportunity set). We also assume that firms only issue securities denominated in their domestic currencies; although the existence of perfect capital and exchange markets implies that such an assumption is not important.

BRUNO H. SOLNIK

incomes are known for certain.[9] Substituting dI_i^k/I_i and dB_i^k/B_i in (3) we obtain:

$$\frac{dW^\kappa}{W^\kappa} = \sum_{i=1}^{n} [w_i^\kappa(\mu_{ik} + \alpha_i + \rho_{ik}\sigma_i\varphi_{ik})\, dt + v_i^\kappa(R_i + \mu_{ik})\, dt]$$

$$+ \sum_{i=1}^{n} [w_i^\kappa(\sigma_i\, dz_i + \varphi_{ik}\, dq_{ik}) + v_i^\kappa\varphi_{ik}\, dq_{ik}] + \frac{1}{W^\kappa}(Y^\kappa - C^\kappa)\, dt,$$

$$(4)$$

with $\sum_i (w_i^\kappa + v_i^\kappa) = 1$.

Let us transform the variables

$$x_i^\kappa = w_i^\kappa$$
$$y_i^\kappa = v_i^\kappa + w_i^\kappa.$$

This linear transformation will greatly simplify the algebra and is intuitively appealing

$$w_i^\kappa I_i + v_i^\kappa B_i = x_i^\kappa(I_i - B_i) + y_i^\kappa B_i.$$

This transformation corresponds exactly to the exchange risk hedging or coverage described in the appendix; $x_i^\kappa(I_i - B_i)$ indicates an investment in country i protected against exchange risk by borrowing in that same country. The quantity $y_i^\kappa B_i$ indicates a speculative position in currency of country i. Finally, by replacing $y_k^\kappa = 1 - y_i^\kappa$, we get

$$\frac{dW^\kappa}{W^\kappa} = \left[\sum_{i=1}^{n} x_i^\kappa(\alpha_i - R_i + \rho_{ik}\sigma_i\varphi_{ik}) + R_k + \sum_{i\neq k} y_i^\kappa(R_i + \mu_{ik} - R_k) \right] dt$$

$$+ \sum_{i\neq k} y_i^\kappa\varphi_{ik}\, dq_{ik} + \sum_{i=1}^{n} x_i^\kappa\sigma_i\, dz_i + \frac{1}{W^\kappa}(Y^\kappa - C^\kappa)\, dt. \quad (5)$$

4. The Equation of Optimality: The Demand for Assets

Let us consider the case of independence between exchange and market risks ($\rho_{ik} = 0$). This greatly simplifies the exposition while retaining the basic structure of the phenomena. The results derived in the general case can be found in Solnik [15].

---

[9] If we assume that there is no inflation (or as a matter of fact nonstochastic inflation), exchange rates can be defined as relative prices of national consumption goods. If stochastic inflation rates are taken into account, only real prices will enter in the individual utility functions; therefore, only real returns, dI_i/I_i, matter. The change of parity to be considered, $dfik/fik$ would result of both the difference of inflation rates between two countries and changes in relative prices. Therefore this formulation is quite general in dealing with inflation.

EQUILIBRIUM OF THE INTERNATIONAL MARKET   507

To simplify the exposition, it will temporarily be assumed that the *expected* change in parities is zero ($\mu_{ik} = 0$). This constant term does not affect in any way the derivations and it will appear in the final results when appropriate.

Let's define $J^\kappa(\cdot)$:

$$J^\kappa(W^\kappa, t) = \max E_t \left[\int_t^{T^\kappa} U^\kappa(C^\kappa, s)\, ds + B^\kappa(W^\kappa, T^\kappa) \right].$$

It can be shown[10] that the necessary optimality conditions for an investor who acts according to (2) in choosing his consumption-investment program are that, at each point of time

$$0 = \underset{(C^\kappa, x_i^\kappa, y_i^\kappa)}{\text{Max}} \left\{ U^\kappa(c^\kappa, t) + J_{W^\kappa} \left[W^\kappa \sum_{i \neq k} y_i^\kappa (R_i - R_k) \right. \right.$$

$$\left. + W^\kappa \sum_{i=1}^n x_i^\kappa(\alpha_i - R_i) + R_k \right] + \frac{1}{2} \left[J_{WW}^\kappa \left[\sum_i \sum_j y_i^\kappa y_j^\kappa \Phi_{ij}^\kappa (W^\kappa)^2 \right. \right.$$

$$\left. \left. \left. + \sum_i \sum_j x_i^\kappa x_j^\kappa \sigma_{ij}(W^\kappa)^2 \right] \right] \right\}. \tag{6}$$

Necessary conditions[11] for (6) are

$$(7a) \qquad 0 = \frac{\partial U^\kappa}{\partial C^\kappa} - J_{W^\kappa};$$

$$(7b) \qquad 0 = J_W^\kappa(R_i - R_k) + J_{WW}^\kappa W^\kappa \sum_{j \neq k} y_j^\kappa \Phi_{ij}^\kappa, \qquad \begin{array}{l} i = 1,\dots, n; \\ i \neq k \end{array} \tag{7}$$

$$(7c) \qquad 0 = J_W^\kappa(\alpha_i - R_i) + J_{WW}^\kappa W^\kappa \sum_{j=1}^n x_j^\kappa \sigma_{ij} \qquad i = 1,\dots, n.$$

Relation (7a) is the usual intertemporal envelope condition to equate the marginal utility of current consumption to the marginal utility of wealth (future consumption). The reader familiar with the single period capital-asset pricing-model will have recognized the similarity of relations (7c) with the standard CAPM results.

---

[10] Merton [9].

[11] For a proof of this derivation see Merton [9]; this assumes that the income is constant or deterministic. J_{W^κ} and J_{WW}^κ are the first and second derivative of $J^\kappa(\ )$.

508   BRUNO H. SOLNIK

From (7) we get

$$R_i - R_k = A^\kappa \sum_{j \neq k} y_j{}^\kappa \Phi_{ij}^\kappa ,$$

$$\tag{8}$$

$$\alpha_i - R_i = A^\kappa \sum_j x_j{}^\kappa \sigma_{ij} ,$$

where

$$A^\kappa = - \frac{W^\kappa((\partial^2 J^\kappa)/(\partial W^2))}{(\partial J^\kappa)/(\partial W)}$$

or

$$\| R_i - R_k \| = A^\kappa \Phi^\kappa y, \qquad n - 1;$$

$$\| \alpha_i - R_i \| = A^\kappa \Sigma x, \qquad n;$$

where y and x are column vectors.

The manifest characteristic of (8) is its linearity in the portfolio demands, and hence, we can solve directly for these demand functions by matrix inversion:

* demand for *stock* of country i

$$d_i{}^\kappa = \frac{W^\kappa}{A^\kappa} \sum_{j=1}^n s_{ij}(\alpha_j - R_j), \tag{8a}$$

where s_{ij} are elements of Σ^{-1}.

These functions are identical to the single period CAPM demand equations except that the risk-free rate R_j will vary according to the national origin of asset j.

* demand for the risk free bond of country i

$$e_i{}^\kappa = \frac{W^\kappa}{A^\kappa} \sum_{j \neq k} \eta_{ij}^\kappa (R_j - R_k) - d_i{}^\kappa, \qquad \text{for} \quad i \neq k, \tag{8b}$$

where η_{ij}^κ are elements of $(\Phi^\kappa)^{-1}$. While the terms under the summation sign do not depend on the country "k" for the stocks, they do depend on k for the bonds.

Since the demand functions for stocks and bonds are separable, it is easy to see directly that the ratio of demand for risky assets (stocks) will be independent of preferences and nationality. If one had considered all countries' stocks, formula 8a would have been similar with one term for each individual stock. Clearly the previous results hold.

These results suggest the following separation theorem.

SEPARATION THEOREM 1. *All investors will be indifferent between choosing portfolios from the original assets or from $n + 1$ funds, where a possible choice for those funds is*:

     —*the world stock market portfolio (hedged against exchange risk)*

     —*the n bonds of each country.*

The proportion of the risky fund invested in asset i is:

$$\sum_{j=1}^{n} s_{ij}(\alpha_j - R_j) \Big/ \sum_{j=1}^{n} \sum_{j=1}^{n} s_{ij}(\alpha_j - R_j).$$

N.B.: As expected the standard two funds theorem holds for all investors from one country; they can make their selection from two funds:

     —their domestic risk free asset

     —a portfolio of all risky assets (including foreign bonds) whose composition depends on the investor's *nationality* (not on his preferences). This fund will vary for each country.

5. *More About the Exchange Risk*

Up to now, we have not really postulated any structure for the exchange rates. However exchange parities and their fluctuations are not completely independent since they are only price relatives. These exchange rates need to be expressed in some arbitrarily chosen units.[12] Arbitrarily pick one country as the reference country (e.g., the USA and its key currency, the dollar); let it be the nth country.

Call Φ the $(n - 1) \times (n - 1)$ matrix of exchange rate covariance relative to that reference country,

$$\Phi = \Phi^n = \begin{pmatrix} \Phi^n_{11} & \cdots & \Phi^n_{n-1} \\ \vdots & \Phi^n_{ij} & \vdots \\ \Phi^n_{n-1,1} & \cdots & \Phi^n_{n-1,n-1} \end{pmatrix}.$$

Again, Φ^k_{ij} represents the covariance of changes in the exchange rate of currency i (relative to currency k) with changes in the exchange rate of currency j (relative to currency k).

---

[12] This implies that the dimension of the exchange risk, i.e. of the exchange risk variance-covariance matrix, is of rank $n - 1$ and not n.

How can we transform Φ^k into Φ? By definition

$$\Phi^k_{ij} = \frac{df_{ik}}{f_{ik}} \cdot \frac{df_{jk}}{f_{jk}},$$

$$\Phi^k_{ij} = \left(\frac{df_{in}}{f_{in}} - \frac{df_{kn}}{f_{kn}}\right)\left(\frac{df_{jn}}{f_{jn}} - \frac{df_{kn}}{f_{kn}}\right),$$

$$\Phi^k_{ij} = \Phi^n_{ij} - \Phi^n_{kj} - \Phi^n_{ik} + \Phi^n_{kk}.$$

Thus

$$\Phi^k = H^k \Phi H^{k^T},$$

where

$$H^k = \begin{pmatrix} 1 & 0 & \cdots & -1 & 0 & \cdots & 0 \\ 0 & \cdot & & & & 0 & \\ & \cdot & \cdot & \vdots & \vdots & & \cdot \\ & & \cdot & 0 & & & \\ & & \cdot & 1 & -1 & 0 & \cdot \\ \cdot & & & 0 & -1 & 1 & \\ \cdot & & & -1 & 0 & 1 & \cdot \cdot \\ & & & & & & \cdot \cdot & 0 \\ & 0 & & \vdots & \vdots & \vdots & & \cdot & 1 \\ 0 & \cdots & & 0 & -1 & 0 & \cdots & 0 \end{pmatrix}$$

column k

H^k is $(n - 1) \times (n - 1)$,

and H^{k^T} is its transpose.

Similarly we can observe that:

$$\| R_i - R_k \| = H^k \| R_i - R_n \| = H^k \mathbb{R}. \tag{9}$$

In the first set of optimality conditions we had $\| R_i - R_k \| = A^\kappa \Phi^k y$. It can be rewritten as:

$$H^k R = A^\kappa H^k \Phi H^{k^T} y \tag{10}$$

where $\mathbb{R}$ and Φ are *independent of the investor's preferences or citizenship* (purely technological) and y is a $(n - 1)$ column vector of y_i^κ.

Since H^k is invertible, we can left multiply by $(H^k)^{-1}$ on both sides of (10) to get (11):

$$\mathbb{R} = A^\kappa \Phi H^{k^T} y. \tag{11}$$

Then

$$\mathbb{R} = A^\kappa \Phi z^\kappa,$$

EQUILIBRIUM OF THE INTERNATIONAL MARKET 511

where

$$z^\kappa = H^{kT} y^\kappa,$$

$$z^\kappa = \begin{pmatrix} y_1^\kappa \\ y_2^\kappa \\ \vdots \\ y_{k-1}^\kappa \\ y_k^\kappa - 1 \\ \vdots \\ y_{n-1}^\kappa \end{pmatrix}.$$

z^κ is equal to the excess demand (over the demand for stocks) for bonds of each country, except for bonds of the investor's country. Like x_i^κ and y_i^κ, z_i^κ is expressed in *percentage* of the total investor's wealth, keeping in mind that $1 - y_k^\kappa = \sum_{j \neq k} y_j^\kappa$. This result is extremely interesting since it implies that

$$z^\kappa = \frac{1}{A^\kappa} \Phi^{-1} \mathbb{R},$$

or

$$z_i^\kappa = \frac{1}{A^\kappa} \sum_{j=1}^{n-1} \eta_{ij}(R_j - R_n), \qquad \text{for all} \quad k = 1,\ldots, n-1, \qquad (12)$$

where η_{ij} are the elements of Φ^{-1} and do not depend on k. Clearly, the ratio z_k^κ / z_j^κ is independent of preferences and nationality. The problem however is that z_i^κ does not really represent the demand for bonds of country i (minus demand for stock):

$$z_i^\kappa = y_i^\kappa \qquad \text{for all } i \text{ except } i = k \quad \text{where} \quad z_k^\kappa = y_k^\kappa - 1.$$

Similarly z_n^κ can be defined as equal to the demand for assets of country n by investor κ. Thus

$$z_n^\kappa = y_n^\kappa = 1 - \sum_{i=1}^{n-1} y_i^\kappa$$

but

$$\sum_{i=1}^{n-1} z_i^\kappa = \sum_{i=1}^{n-1} y_i^\kappa - 1;$$

therefore,

$$z_n^\kappa = y_n^\kappa = -\frac{1}{A^\kappa} \sum_{i=1}^{n-1} \sum_{j=1}^{n-1} \eta_{ij}(R_j - R_n).$$

BRUNO H. SOLNIK

SEPARATION THEOREM 2. *All investors will be indifferent between choosing portfolios from the original set of assets or from 3 funds, where a possible choice for those funds is:*

  — *a portfolio of all stocks hedged against exchange risk (the world market portfolio)*
  — *a portfolio of bonds, speculative in the exchange risk dimension*[13]
  — *the risk free asset of their country.*

The proportions of the funds invested in each asset are determined by market characteristics.

Proof. Let us build a fund which will hold a proportion δ_i in asset $I_i - B_i$ (hedged stock) with

$$\delta_i = \frac{\sum_{j=1}^{n} s_{ij}(\alpha_j - R_j)}{\sum_i \sum_j s_{ij}(\alpha_j - R_j)}$$

and another fund made of bonds B_i ($i = 1,..., n$) in proportions $\delta_i{}'$ with

$$\delta_i{}' = \sum_{j=1}^{n-1} \eta_{ij}(R_j - R_n), \qquad \text{for} \quad i = 1,..., n - 1,$$

$$\delta_n{}' = -\sum_{i=1}^{n-1} \sum_{j=1}^{n-1} \eta_{ij}(R_j - R_n).$$

Let $\lambda_i{}^\kappa$ be the fraction of the κth investor's wealth invested in fund i ($i = 1, 2, 3$). To prove the theorem we want to show that there exists an allocation $(\lambda_1{}^\kappa, \lambda_2{}^\kappa)$ which will replicate the demand functions (8a) and (12),[14] i.e.,

$$\lambda_1{}^\kappa \delta_i = \frac{1}{A^\kappa} \sum_{j=1}^{n} s_{ij}(\alpha_j - R_j), \qquad i = 1, 2,..., n,$$

$$\lambda_2{}^\kappa \delta_i{}' = \frac{1}{A^\kappa} \sum_{j=1}^{n-1} \eta_{ij}(R_j - R_n), \qquad i = 1,..., k - 1, k + 1,..., n - 1,$$

$$\lambda_2{}^\kappa \delta_k{}' + \lambda_3{}^\kappa = 1 + \frac{1}{A^\kappa} \sum_{j=1}^{n-1} \eta_{kj}(R_k - R_n), \tag{13}$$

$$\lambda_2{}^\kappa \delta_n{}' = -\frac{1}{A^\kappa} \sum_{i=1}^{n-1} \sum_{j=1}^{n-1} \eta_{ij}(R_j - R_n).$$

[13] Speculative in the exchange risk dimension means that this fund does not carry any "market" risk, but purely exchange risk due to the presence of foreign bonds.
[14] Since the net worth of the first two funds is zero, it will be required that $\lambda_3{}^\kappa = 1$.

EQUILIBRIUM OF THE INTERNATIONAL MARKET   513

It can easily be seen that the allocation

$$\lambda_1^\kappa = \frac{1}{A^\kappa} \sum_{i=1}^{n} \sum_{j=1}^{n} s_{ij}(\alpha_j - R_j),$$

$$\lambda_2^\kappa = \frac{1}{A^\kappa},$$

$$\lambda_3^\kappa = 1,$$

will satisfy (13). This demonstrates the theorem.

Intuitively, since the ratio x_i^κ/x_j^κ and z_i^κ/z_j^κ are independent of k, it appears that the following funds would be adequate,

$$
\begin{matrix}
I_i - R_i & B_i & & B_k \\
\begin{pmatrix} x_1 \\ \vdots \\ \vdots \\ x_n \end{pmatrix} &
\begin{pmatrix} z_1 \\ \vdots \\ z_k \\ \vdots \\ z_n \end{pmatrix} &
\begin{aligned} &= y_1 \\ &\;\;\vdots \\ &= y_k - 1 \\ &\;\;\vdots \\ &= 1 - \sum_{i=1}^{n-1} y_i \end{aligned} & \quad (1).
\end{matrix}
$$

Although a reference country n was arbitrarily used as a base to establish equations (11), the composition of the exchange risk speculation fund (and of the market portfolio) is *independent* of the country selected.

This three-funds theorem is in fact still a $n + 1$ funds theorem since the third fund (the risk free asset of the investor's country) will change according to the investor's nationality. However, it is a much richer theorem than Separation Theorem 1. The new "speculation" fund is made up of risk free bonds of all countries. Because of the symmetry of the exchange risk structure and of the mean-variance framework, this fund is the *same* for everyone. Thus any investor might invest his total wealth W^κ in the risk free portfolio and pick the desired level of risk by investing in the two risky funds; these are pure market risk or exchange risk funds since their net worth is zero in both cases.[15]

No one should ever be a pure speculator or a pure investor. In this model both types of risks are considered as independent. This is the reason why only three portfolios are necessary in the separation theorem. But

---

[15] One could make the analogy with the CAPM separation theorem by considering two funds:

— the risk-free asset B_F,
— the market portfolio "short" $M - B_F$ (with an expected return of $\alpha_M - R_F$ and a net worth of zero).

BRUNO H. SOLNIK

when he picks his desired level of risk, an investor's decision is only affected by expected returns and variances and not qualitative differences between exchange and market risk (at least in this theory).

6. *The Equilibrium Yield Relationship Among Assets*

Given the demand function (8a), we now derive the equilibrium market clearing conditions for the model. Since the demand function for stocks and bonds are separable the clearing conditions can be worked out independently. The equilibrium relationship between the expected returns on an individual national asset and the expected return on the international market can be derived from these conditions.

(a) *Stocks*

From (8a) the aggregate demand function, $D_i = \sum_k d_i^k$ can be written as:

$$D_i = \sum_k d_i^k = \frac{1}{A} \sum_{j=1}^{n} s_{ij}(\alpha_j - R_j) \tag{14}$$

where $1/A = \sum_k (W^k/A^k)$. If $D_i = \omega_i M$ where M is the total world market value, (14) can be transformed into:

$$\alpha_i - R_i = MA \sum_{j=1}^{n} \omega_j \sigma_{ij} .$$

Define

$$\alpha_m = \sum_i \omega_i \alpha_i$$

$$R_m = \sum_i \omega_i R_i$$

$$\sigma_{im} = \sum_{j=1}^{n} \omega_i \sigma_{ij} ,$$

then (15) is equivalent to:

$$\alpha_i - R_i = MA\sigma_{im} .$$

Multiplying (15) by ω_i and adding

$$\alpha_m - R_m = MA \sum_{i=1}^{n} \omega_i \sigma_{im} = MA\sigma_m^2.$$

Thus

$$\alpha_i - R_i = \frac{\sigma_{im}}{\sigma_m^2}(\alpha_m - R_m).\qquad(16)$$

THEOREM 3. *Equation* (16) *states that the risk premium of a security over its national risk free rate is proportional to the risk premium of the world market over an average international bond rate:* $\alpha_i - R_i = (\sigma_{im}/\sigma_m^2)(\alpha_m - R_m)$.

Since one can always get protected against fluctuations in exchange rates by going short in the risk free asset of the corresponding country (borrowing), it could be expected that only the expected return over that interest rate is relevant in the pricing of market risk. Because of the hedging process, this risk premium will be independent of expectations on change of parities or inflation.

In this model, the risk free bond of each country plays different roles. It is the risk free asset of the country but it is also a pure exchange risk asset for foreign investors, therefore allowing to hedge equity investment against exchange risk by going short in the foreign bond.

If the interest rates are considered to be exogenous to the system then the above pricing relations has important economic implications. Let us assume for example that a country arbitrarily decides to lower its interest rate due to internal economic considerations. Then relation (16) would tend to imply that expected returns on the stocks of that country would decline accordingly.

The most obvious differences between relation (16) and the Capital Asset Pricing Model relation are:

(1)   the systematic risk is the *international* systematic risk, involving the covariance of the stock return with the world market portfolio.

(2) R_i and R_m are in general going to be different.

The assumption that a country can arbitrarily control its interest rate will now be dropped.

(b) *Bonds*

In the previous derivation, it has been implicitly considered that the interest rates were exogenous to the model. This could be explained by the action of national governments setting rates determined by domestic economic policy and willing to borrow (or lend) an unlimited amount of funds at this rate. However this assumption might be very questionable in

BRUNO H. SOLNIK

an equilibrium model. We will rather make the assumption that the total demand for each national bond is zero (there is a lender for each borrower).

Let us derive the demand functions for risk free assets. The demand for bonds of country i is equal to the demand for all assets of that country minus the demand for stocks. The total demand for all assets of country i is

$$F_i = \sum_{\substack{\text{all countries} \\ k}} \sum_{\kappa \in k} W^\kappa y_i{}^\kappa = \sum_{k=1}^{n} f_i{}^k, \qquad (17)$$

where $f_i{}^k$ is the demand for assets of country i by investors of country k

$$f_i{}^k = \sum_\kappa W^\kappa y_i{}^\kappa.$$

By equation (12), it is known that:

$$f_i{}^k = \sum_\kappa W^\kappa y_i{}^\kappa = \sum_\kappa W^\kappa z_i{}^\kappa = \sum_\kappa \frac{W^\kappa}{A^\kappa} \sum_{j=1}^{n-1} \eta_{ij}(R_j - R_n),$$

$$f_i{}^k = \frac{1}{A^k} \sum_{j=1}^{n-1} \eta_{ij}(R_j - R_n), \qquad \text{for} \quad k \neq i,$$

with

$$\frac{1}{A^k} = \sum_\kappa \frac{W^\kappa}{A^\kappa},$$

and

$$f_k{}^k = \sum_{\kappa \in k} W^\kappa y_k{}^\kappa = \sum_\kappa W^\kappa (z_k{}^\kappa - 1),$$

$$f_k{}^k = \frac{1}{A^k} \sum_{j=1}^{n-1} \eta_{kj}(R_j - R_n) + W_k,$$

where W_i is the portfolio wealth of investors of country i.

By replacing in (17), we get

$$F_i = W_i + \frac{1}{A} \sum_{j=1}^{n-1} \eta_{ij}(R_j - R_n) \qquad (18)$$

where

$$1/A = \sum_{i=1}^{n} (1/A^i).$$

EQUILIBRIUM OF THE INTERNATIONAL MARKET   517

From the assumption of zero net demand for bonds, F_i should be equal to the demand for stocks D_i. From (14) and (18) we get

$$D_i = W_i + \frac{1}{A} \sum_{j=1}^{n-1} \eta_{ij}(R_j - R_n), \qquad i = 1,\ldots, n. \qquad (19)$$

Equation (19) gives a set of relations between the interest rates across the world as a function of the national wealth, its investment opportunities and the exchange rate relations. It is possible to estimate each risk free rate:[16]

$$R_i - R_n = A \sum_{j=1}^{n-1} \Phi_{ij}(D_j - W_j), \qquad i = 1,\ldots, n-1. \qquad (20)$$

$D_i - W_i$ is the net wealth invested in country i. If D_i is greater than W_i it implies a net foreign investment in that country; on the opposite, when W_i is larger than D_i, it means that investors from country i lack attractive investment opportunities in their home country and are net foreign investors. Besides,

$$\sum_i (D_i - W_i) = M - M = 0,$$

where M is the total market value. Let us define ω_i' as

$$\omega_i' = (D_i - W_i)/M,$$

$$\sum_{i=1}^{n} \omega_i' = 0.$$

Then replacing in (20):

$$R_i - R_n = MA \sum_{j=1}^{n-1} \omega_i' \Phi_{ij}, \qquad j = 1,\ldots, n-1.$$

Define:

$$R_W = \sum_{i=1}^{n-1} \omega_i'(R_i - R_n) = \sum_{i=1}^{n} \omega_i'(R_i - R_n) = \sum_{i=1}^{n} \omega_i' R_i,$$

$$\Phi_{iW} = \sum_{j=1}^{n-1} \omega_j' \Phi_{ij},$$

$$\Phi_{W^2} = \sum_{i=1}^{n-1} \omega_i' \Phi_{iW}.$$

[16] If one is known.

BRUNO H. SOLNIK

Then

$$R_i - R_n = MA\Phi_{iW}. \tag{21}$$

Multiplying by ω_i and summing:

$$R_w = MA\Phi_W{}^2.$$

Therefore the following relation can be derived, i.e.

$$R_i - R_n = \frac{\Phi_{iW}}{\Phi_W{}^2} R_W. \tag{23}$$

For simplicity of exposition, no expected change of parities have been considered so far. However non zero expected changes of parity can be easily introduced. Looking at the budget equation (5), it can be seen that μ_{ik} only appears in $R_i + \mu_{ik} - R_k$. This would transform the above relation into

$$R_i + \mu_{in} - R_n = \frac{\Phi_{iW}}{\Phi_W{}^2} R_W, \tag{24}$$

with still

$$\Phi_{iW} = \sum_{i=1}^{n-1} \omega_j{}'\Phi_{ij}$$

and[17]

$$R_W = \sum_{i=1}^{n-1} \omega_i{}'(R_i + \mu_{in} - R_n) = \sum_{i=1}^{n} \omega_i{}'(R_i + \mu_{in}).$$

We can rewrite this as

$$R_i - R_n = \mu_{ni} + \frac{\Phi_{iW}}{\Phi_W{}^2} R_W. \tag{25}$$

THEOREM 4. *The difference between interest rates of two countries is equal to the expected change of parities between these two countries plus a term depending on exchange risk covariances*:

$$R_i - R_n = \mu_{ni} + \frac{\Phi_{iW}}{\Phi_W{}^2} R_W.$$

---

[17] R_W is independent of n since

$$\sum_{i=1}^{n} \omega_i{}'(R_i + \mu_{in}) = \sum_{i=1}^{n} \omega_i{}'R_i + \sum_{i=1}^{n} \omega_i{}'(\mu_{ik} - \mu_{nk}) = \sum_{i=1}^{n} \omega_i{}'R_i + \sum_{i=1}^{n} \omega_i{}'\mu_{ik}.$$

Therefore

$$R_W = \sum_{i=1}^{n} \omega_i{}'(R_i + \mu_{ik}) \text{ for any } k.$$

EQUILIBRIUM OF THE INTERNATIONAL MARKET   519

Comments

It is shown in the Appendix that the forward rate of currency n in terms of currency i was such that the forward discount d_{ni} was equal to interest rate differential between two countries:

$$R_i - R_n = d_{ni} \tag{2}$$

The above relations imply that the forward exchange rate is a *biased* estimate of the future exchange rate. This is widely believed but generally for different and conflicting reasons. Here we demonstrate that the spread in interest rate should be equal to the expected change of parity plus a "hedging pressure" term. The premium charged is not a liquidity premium. These results are somewhat reminiscent of the "Habitat" theory (see [11]) if one interprets habitat as a stronger preference to hedge against changes in investment opportunities due to changes in parities.

The direction of the bias depends on the net foreign investment of each country. If a country has more tangibles than wealth (i.e. net importer of capital), then there is a hedging pressure of foreign investors who want to get protected against exchange risk on their equity investment in that country. To hedge their investment against exchange risk these investors will go short in the risk free bond of the country[18] (borrow) pushing the interest rate upwards. This conclusion can be derived from equation (25). At a first approximation Φ_{iW} is equivalent to its variance term,

$$\Phi_{iW} = \sum_j \omega_j' \Phi_{ij} \sim \omega_i' \Phi_i^2.$$

If country i is a net importer of capital ($\omega_i' > 0$), the hedging term would imply that, *ceteris paribus*, the interest rate in country i would be larger.

The term $(\Phi_{iW}/\Phi_W^2)\, R_W$ is the premium foreign investors have to pay to get their equity investment protected against exchange rate fluctuations. Hence it can be considered as a risk premium to speculators who provide that service. This relation (25) is very important because it outlines the determinants of the difference between any pair of interest rates. Only if all countries have a zero net foreign investment, would the spread between interest rates be an unbiased estimate of the change in parity. In this case no one would want to speculate on foreign exchanges since the expected gain on change in parities will be *exactly* offset by the difference in interest rate and no risk premium would be provided for carrying the exchange risk; investors would only invest (short) in foreign bonds to

---

[18] Or buy a forward contract, which is shown to be identical in the Appendix.

hedge their equity investment. The only *contrepartie* would be local lenders.

From equation (19) it appears that the proportions of the speculative fund (Theorem 2) invested in each country bond are equal (or at least proportional) to the net capital position of the country:

$$\delta_i' = \sum_j \eta_{ij}(R_j - R_n) = A(D_i - W_i) = MA\omega_i',$$

with

$$\sum_i \delta_i' = \sum_i \omega_i' = 0.$$

This speculative fund (with proportions, $\omega_i' = \delta_i'/MA$) will have an expected return of R_W .

While the market fund only depends on market value variables, this speculative fund composition only depends on international comparison variables. It is independent of investors preferences.

This result shows that a zero-beta portfolio (no market risk) does not necessarily have an expected return equal to the risk-free rate of the investor's country. This would be true for any portfolio of foreign bonds.

7. *Conclusions*

An intertemporal equilibrium model of the international-capital market has been developed. It takes into account exchange risk and the existence of different interest rates across the world. Some "mutual funds theorems" can be derived with important implications for investment policies. The most important of these theorems states that all investors will be indifferent between choosing portfolios from the original assets or from three funds, namely:

—a portfolio of stocks hedged against exchange risk (the market portfolio)

—a portfolio of bonds, speculative in the exchange risk dimension

—the risk free asset of their own country.

The first two portfolios are independent of investors' preferences or citizenship.

A risk pricing relation for stocks has been derived which states that the risk premium of any security over its national risk free rate is proportional to its international systematic risk. The coefficient of proportionality is the risk premium of the world market over a world bond rate.

EQUILIBRIUM OF THE INTERNATIONAL MARKET   521

Another set of risk pricing relations states that the difference between interest rates of two countries is equal to the expected change of parities between these two countries plus a term depending on exchange risk covariances. This implies that the forward exchange rate is a *biased* estimate of the future exchange rate.

These findings have important practical implications. They provide investors with a simple but powerful investment strategy. They also indicate the need for internationally diversified mutual funds. As a matter of fact, a single fund invested in all common stocks (with market value weights) would satisfy the needs of investors from any country.[19]

However one should keep in mind that these results depend on restrictive assumptions about homogenous expectations, consumption patterns and perfection of capital markets.[20]

APPENDIX

Exchange Risk: A Formulation

A fundamental dimension of international investment is the existence of exchange risk and mechanisms providing protection to investor unwilling to carry that risk. It will now be shown how exchange risk can be treated and described in a mean-variance framework.

There are two ways a foreigner investing on the American security market can be "covered":

— he can go to the forward exchange market and enter a contact to deliver an amount of dollars equivalent to its investment at a given date, or

— he can borrow dollars on the American market (or Eurodollar market) and sell them immediately (i.e., exchange them for his own currency at the spot rate). In turn he can invest them in his own country bond.

While the forward market is typically used for short term investment protection or speculation (90 days or less), the second method is more

---

[19] As of now it is much easier for any national to speculate on foreign exchanges (or hedge) through his domestic forward exchange market than to invest in foreign common stocks.

[20] If market and exchange risks are not independent a four-funds theorem can be derived instead of Theorem 2 (see Solnik (15)). However the derivation is very cumbersome and the composition of the funds is not intuitively appealing. Similarly a set of risk-pricing relations can be obtained wich mixes exchange and market risks.

522   BRUNO H. SOLNIK

adapted to portfolio investment. In the case of equity investment where the final return is uncertain, the protection only holds at the first approximation.

Let's now introduce some notation:

Let $\tilde{m}_{ik}$ be the change in parity of currency i relative to currency k.

μ_{ik} is its expected value.

d_{ik} is the discount or rate of coverage (in % of investment).

$$d_{ik} = \frac{\left[\begin{array}{c}\text{forward price of currency } i \\ \text{in terms of } k\end{array}\right] - [\text{today's spot price}]}{[\text{today's spot price}]} .$$

R_i is the interest rate of country i,
R_k is the interest rate of country k.

How can a forward contract be described analytically?

(a)   Let us assume that an investor from country k decides to buy his own currency k forward, i.e. he buys a contract to purchase currency k with currency i at a fixed date. The cost of coverage is d_{ik} (i.e. the change in exchange rate expressed in percent). d_{ik} can be positive or negative. Then the expected gain on this transaction is $d_{ik} - \mu_{ik}$.

The speculator can invest, in the meantime, in the risk free asset of country k up to the date of the forward contract. The total risk of such an operation will be the exchange risk φ_{ik} :

$$\tilde{R} = R_k + d_{ik} - \tilde{m}_{ik} ,$$
$$E(\tilde{R}) = R_k + d_{ik} - \mu_{ik} ,$$
$$\sigma^2 = \text{variance of } \tilde{m}_{ik} = \varphi_{ik}^2 .$$

For example, assume an American investor (country k) selling forward French francs for U.S. dollars:

—Today's spot rate is $100 for FF500;

—the 3 month forward rate is $(100)(1 + d_{ik})$ for FF500 (if $d_{ik} > 0$ the dollar sells at a discount).

In three months he will buy FF500 at the spot rate of $100 $(1 + \tilde{m}_{ik})$ and deliver them to get $100 $(1 + d_{ik})$ as agreed in his forward contract.

He will profit if:

$$100 (1 + \tilde{m}_{ik}) < 100 (1 + d_{ik}).$$

His profit per dollar is $d_{ik} - \tilde{m}_{ik}$.

EQUILIBRIUM OF THE INTERNATIONAL MARKET   523

(b)   If the speculator was instead selling his own currency forward, this contract could similarly be described as

$$\tilde{R} = R_k + \tilde{m}_{ik} - d_{ik},$$

$$E(\tilde{R}) = R_k + \mu_{ik} - d_{ik},$$

$$\sigma^2(R) = \varphi_{ik}.$$

Identically, the same investor from country k could have exchanged his currency for currency i at the spot rate (time 0), invested it in the risk free assets of country i (yielding R_i) and converted it into his currency k at the end of period. This operations could be described as

$$\tilde{R} = R_i + \tilde{m}_{ik},$$

$$E(\tilde{R}) = R_i + \mu_{ik},$$

$$\sigma^2(\tilde{R}) = \varphi_{ik}^2,$$

$$R_i + \mu_{ik} = R_k + \mu_{ik} - d_{ik};$$

therefore

$$d_{ik} = R_k - R_i.$$

This is a well known relation in international economics. This relation should hold since any investor looking for a *riskless* investment has the opportunity of either investing in the bond of his own country getting R_k, or exchanging currency to invest in the bond of another country (R_i) while buying a forward contract (d_{ik}) to repatriate his investment and profit at a fixed rate.

This relation also implies that both types of coverage should be identical. The left hand side represents the "cost" in the forward market while the right hand side represents the coverage "cost" of hedging. Since the two contracts are identical we will only use the second type of contract: going short in the risk free asset of the foreign country and long in the investor's risk free asset.

REFERENCES

1. F. BLACK, Capital market equilibrium with restricted borrowing, *Journal of Business*, July 1972.
2. K. BORCH, A note on uncertainty and indifference curves, *Review of Economic Studies*, **36**, January 1969.
3. H. G. GRUBEL, Internationally diversified portfolios: Welfare gains and capital flows, *American Economic Review*, December 1968, pp. 1299–1314.

524   BRUNO H. SOLNIK

4. N. H. HAKANSSON, Capital Growth and the Mean-Variance Approach to Portfolio Selection, *Journal of Financial and Quantitative Analysis*, VI, January 1971.

5. K. ITÔ AND H. MCKEAN, "Diffusion Processes and Their Sample Paths," Academic Press, New York, 1964.

6. C. H. LEE, A stock-adjustment analysis of the capital movements: The United States-Canadian case, *Journal of Political Economy*, **77**, July 1969.

7. J. LINTNER, Security prices, risk and maximal gains from diversification, *Journal of Finance*, December 1965, pp. 587–615.

8. R. C. MERTON, Optimum consumption and portfolio rules in continuous-time model, *Journal of Economic Theory*, **3** December 1971.

9. R. C. MERTON, An intertemporal capital asset pricing model, MIT Working Paper #588-72, February 1972, forthcoming in *Econometrica*.

10. F. MODIGLIANI AND C. R. SUTCH, Innovations in interest rates policy, *American Economic Review*, May 1966.

11. J. MOSSIN, Equilibrium in a capital asset market, *Econometrica*, October 1966, pp. 768–783.

12. W. F. SHARPE, Capital asset prices: A theory of market equilibrium under conditions of risk, *Journal of Finance*, September 1964, pp. 425–442.

13. W. F. SHARPE, "Portfolio Theory and Capital Markets," McGraw-Hill, 1970.

14. B. SOLNIK, An international market model of security price behavior, GSB Working Paper, Stanford University, October 1972.

15. B. SOLNIK, European capital markets; Towards a theory of an international capital market, Ph.D. thesis, Massachusetts Institute of Technology, August 1972.

[2]

This reprint is re-set and edited from P. Sercu (1980): A Generalization of the International Asset Pricing Model, *Revue de l'Association Française de Finance* 1(1), 91-135. Page numbers correspond to the original pagination. A table of symbols is added at the back. 91

A GENERALIZATION OF

THE INTERNATIONAL ASSET PRICING MODEL

Piet Sercu

Introduction and Summary

In the fifties and sixties, mean-variance optimal portfolio decisions and their implications for asset pricing were studied extensively. The basic model, developed by Markowitz (59), Sharpe (64), Lintner (65) and others, assumes that investors have homogenous expectation and opportunities, a unique riskless lending-borrowing rate exists, and purchasing power risk does not affect asset pricing—all investors consume the same good or commodity bundle at the same price, and this price is deterministic. In what Fama (76) calls "the basic Fisher Black model", the assumption of a riskless lending-borrowing rate is relaxed. Common to both models is the finding that, although portfolios differ among individuals, still any efficient portfolio can be decomposed into two "funds" that are the same for every investor. In other words, differences in portfolio compositions merely reflect differences in the relative weights in which the two funds are held, and these relative weights are uniquely related to the degree of risk aversion. Or in still other words: because in the basic model investors only differ with respect to risk-aversion, two funds suffice to form optimal portfolios for all individuals in the world.

In Solnik's (73) International Asset Pricing Model (IAPM), investors are assumed to differ not only with respect to risk aversion, but also as far as the composition of their consumption bundle is concerned. Thus, although investors are still assumed to have homogenous expectations with respect to nominal returns, they now have heterogeneous expectations about real returns: because of differences in consumption bundles, the real return on, say, a dollar Treasury Bill is not the same for all individuals. Solnik in addition assumes that commodity preferences are the same for all residents of one country, and that the central banks succeed in stabilizing the domestic-currency price of their country's domestic consumption bundle (no inflation in any country). Because of this characterisation of the world, exchange rates are equivalent to the reference-currency prices of the foreign consumption bundles; and there being no inflation in the reference country either, all exchange rate changes represent pure deviations from Purchasing Power Parity (PPP). That is, all exchange risk is "real". (Purely "nominal" exchange risk exists when all investors consume the same commodity bundle at the same relative prices, and when several numéraires exist with differently fluctuating purchasing powers. With PPP, real returns are the same everywhere, and therefore the currency or nationality of the investor will obviously not influence portfolio decisions). Finally, Solnik assumes a riskless lending-borrowing rate in every country, and "independence of stock returns and exchange rate changes". This last assumption, which was formulated somewhat imprecisely, does not mean that the covariance matrix of the returns on stocks and bonds, all measured in the same reference currency, is block-diagonal. Rather, it means that every firm has a single, clear-cut nationality, and that the price of that firm's shares, expressed in its home currency, does not tend to move into one particular direction when exchange rates change.

Solnik then decomposes any investor's portfolio into three funds:

(a) The investor's home country bond,

(b) A portfolio of stocks "hedged against exchange risk", that is, where investment in foreign (or domestic) stock is financed by a short sale of the corresponding foreign (or domestic) riskless bond. This fund is a zero-investment fund.

(c) A (zero-investment) portfolio of bonds of all denominations (including some domestic bonds), representing a demand for pure foreign exchange, or a demand for bonds in excess of the hedging demand.

A crucial result is that the compositions of the hedged stock fund and of the international bond fund are independent of nationality. Solnik then derives simple risk-return relations for hedged stocks and for foreign bonds.

Solnik's model has been criticized for its mean-variance foundations, for some unfortunate ambiguities (most of them cleared up in Solnik (77)), and for its independence assumption of stocks and bonds. Dumas (77), for instance, objects that "this assumption disturbingly changes meaning" depending on the currency one uses. This is a red herring, which may have been based on a block-diagonality interpretation of Solnik's independence assumption. Indeed, when the French Franc (FF) price of a French stock does not tend to move in a particular direction when exchange rates change, then each percentage rise of the FF in Brussels must tend to be associated with a one- percent rise of the French stock's Belgian Franc (BF) price. So the covariance matrix of BF returns on all assets is not at all block-diagonal; and there is nothing disturbing in the fact that, from the BF's point of view, a French stock's return is correlated with the change in the FF spot rate. A more fundamental criticism by Dumas is that in a world where exchange rates are based on relative commodity prices, it is unreasonable to assume that asset prices will be independent of exchange rates—except when the national economies are perfectly isolated. And perfectly isolated economies are not very compatible with perfectly integrated capital markets.[1]

The main purpose of the present paper is to relax Solnik's assumptions about the covariance structure of asset returns. The results obtained in the more general case may be summarized as follows:

1) *Demand for assets and separation theorems*: Solnik's three-fund theorem is basically a two-fund theorem, as he himself recognizes in his 1977 article. However, a more general two-fund theorem holds without having to impose any restriction on the covariance matrix. Solnik's independence assumption merely serves to provide a simple decomposition of the one nationality-independent stock-bond fund into, first, a hedged-stock part and, second, a pure bond part; but a more general decomposition into hedged stock and pure bond parts can be made without having to impose any restrictions on the structure of the covariance matrix. In addition, the nationality-independent fund is not a zero-investment portfolio. While Solnik's hedged stock fund can easily be re-interpreted as a standard portfolio, his characterisation of the bond fund as a zero-investment portfolio is based on an omission of cross terms, and this error invalidates his results on interest rates differentials.

2) *Risk and return for hedged stock*: the expected return on a stock is found to consist of three components:
- The risk-free rate of the numéraire;
- The expected cost of hedging the asset against exchange risk, which is defined as the expected (positive or negative) return on a basket of forward exchange contracts constructed so as to eliminate all covariances with exchange rate changes; and finally,
- A CAPM-like risk premium for all non-diversifiable risks not associated with exchange rate changes. It contains a risk measure (the sensitivity of the asset's return to the hedged market portfolio return) and a premium per unit of market sensitivity (the excess expected return on the hedged stock market portfolio).

3) *Interest rate differentials*. We obtain the familiar result that the forward premium is a biased predictor of the future rate of appreciation of the currency, because of a risk premium. The risk premium has two components:
- Covariance with the market return: this kind of risk, which disappears in Solnik's paper, always gets a positive premium. It implies that large, closed economies like the US will tend to have higher interest rates, although size may have an opposite effect via the second risk premium.
- Covariance with the return on a fund consisting of all bonds held as the nationality-dependent component in every investor's portfolio. The weights of each currency-bond in this portfolio depend on the national wealths and the national mean relative risk aversions. The price of this type of covariance risk is likely to be negative. The effect of national wealth on the interest rate differential is uncertain. More risk averse countries would tend to have lower interest rates.

4) *The representative consumption bundle, and a World Currency Unit CAPM*. Bringing together the equilibrium risk-return relationships for hedged stock and for bonds shows that a representative consumption bundle exists, in the sense that one can reason as if all investors consumed the same mean bundle. Constructing a world currency unit as a basket of currencies with the same weights as in the representative consumption bundle, one finds that a simple CAPM holds, where the market portfolio is defined as the capital

market portfolio of all stocks and bonds, and the risk-free rate is replaced by a weighted mean of the national interest rates.

I - MEAN-VARIANCE ASSET DEMAND: A GENERALIZED
TWO-FUND INTERPRETATION

The basic assumptions in this paper are the same as in Solnik (73), (77). In a nutshell, all investors hold portfolios that are mean-variance efficient in terms of their real units of account; but because of the assumptions of identical commodity preferences, identical relative commodity prices and no inflation within each country, this simply means that all investors hold portfolios that are mean-variance efficient in the currency of their home country. For an investor from an arbitrarily chosen reference country L+1, this implies the following demand equations for assets:

for the N risky assets: $\qquad W^i \, w_N^i \; = \; W^i \, \alpha^i \, \Omega^{-1} \, [\mu - r]$

$$(1)$$

for the investor's riskless bond: $\qquad W^i \, w_{N+1}^i \; = \; W^i \left\{ 1 - \alpha^i \, \underline{e}' \, \Omega^{-1} \, [\mu - r] \right\}.$

where W^i = investor i's wealth, measured in his own currency (currency L+1).

w_N^i = the N weights of the risky assets in investor i's total portfolio. The risky assets are the L foreign-currency bonds and n "other" risky assets, called "stocks".

α^i = the investor's relative risk tolerance (the inverse of relative risk aversion).

Ω = the N×N covariance matrix of the returns on these risky assets, all measured in the same reference currency.

$[\mu - r]$ = the N×1 vector of expected returns, μ_j, on the risky assets, measured in reference currency and in excess of the reference-currency bond rate r.

w_{N+1}^i = the weight of the reference-country risk-free bond in the investor's portfolio.

$\underline{e}$ = the N×1 vector with elements equal to unity (the summation operator).

Equation (1) is usually interpreted as meaning that every investor holds 1) a portfolio of risky assets with composition independent of risk aversion, and 2) a portfolio which contains only the riskless bond. For International Asset Pricing purposes this is not a convenient decomposition because each of these funds obviously depends on the nationality of the investor. Instead, it turns out to be useful to rewrite the last line of (1) as

$$W^i \, w_{N+1}^i \; = \; W^i \, \alpha^i \, \left\{ 1 - \underline{e}' \, \Omega^{-1} \, [\mu - r] \right\} \; + \; W^i \, (1 - \alpha^i) \, ,$$

and rearrange (1) as

$$
\begin{bmatrix} w_N^i \\ , \\ w_{N+1}^i \end{bmatrix} = \alpha^i \begin{bmatrix} \Omega^{-1}\,[\mu - r] \\ , \\ 1 - \underline{e}'\,\Omega^{-1}\,[\mu - r] \end{bmatrix} + (1 - \alpha^i) \begin{bmatrix} \underline{0}_N \\ , \\ 1 \end{bmatrix}.
\tag{2}
$$

Thus, expression (2) decomposes investor i's portfolio into two funds:

(a) A portfolio which in general contains positions in all stocks and bonds—including a nonzero weight for the investor's riskless bond. This will be the portfolio held by an investor with unit relative risk aversion (or unit relative risk tolerance, α^i).

(b) The investor's riskless bond (the portfolio held by an investor with infinite risk aversion or zero risk tolerance).

For another investor from a foreign country f, a similar equation (2) would hold, where the means and covariances would be measured in country f's currency and where the riskless rate would be the currency-f bond rate. The crucial property of the decomposition as in (2) is that the first fund, the internationally diversified stock-bond portfolio, has the same composition regardless of what the numéraire is in which the parameters are expressed. This is proven in Appendix A on the basis of the relations that exist between reference-currency and foreign-currency means and covariances.

The proof in the appendix however relies on a quadratic ("Ito") approximation between returns in different currencies. Solnik (73) uses a similar technique with the help of a linear approximation.[2] Since the result may be due to an inadequate approximation, it is prudent to look for an independent justification of the outcome. In the present case, such an independent justification is readily found by noting that this nationality-independent stock-bond fund will be the portfolio held by an investor with a utility function that is logarithmic in end-of-period wealth (up to the usual linear transformation). Such an investor, when living in the reference country, has an objective function of the type

$$
\text{Max } E_t\{\ U(C_t) + b_t \log \tilde{W}_{t+1}\ \},
$$

with end-of-period wealth W_{t+1} expressed in the reference currency. However, W_{t+1} can equally well be written as the product of the exchange rate and the foreign-currency value of that same wealth: $W_{t+1} = S_{f,t+1} W_{t+1}^f$ (the spot rate $S_{f,t+1}$ being the price, in reference currency, of one unit of currency f; and superscript f to W denoting that the investor's wealth is now measured in currency f). And in a log function these terms nicely separate. That is, we can also write this investor's objective function as

$$
\text{Max } E_t\{\ U(C_t) + b_t \log \tilde{W}_{t+1}^f + b_t \log \tilde{S}_{f,t+1}\ \}.
$$

With the standard assumption that all investors are price takers, no individual portfolio decision can affect the distribution of the future exchange rate. Thus, no derivative of $E[\log S_{f,t+1}]$ will show up in the first order conditions. In other words, the first-order conditions derived from $\text{Max } E_t\{\log W_{t+1}\}$ must be the same as the first-order conditions from $\text{Max } E_t\{\log W_{t+1}^f\}$; or investors with log utility functions hold the same portfolio whatever their nationality. This result was already used by Hakansson (69), and, more recently, by Stehle (77) .

Equation (2) therefore means that any investor's portfolio can be decomposed into:
(a) A portfolio containing all stocks of the world, and some bonds of all countries. This portfolio is the same for all investors (independent of nationality).
(b) The investor's domestic riskless bond, which depends on nationality.
Relative risk aversion determines the relative weights of these funds in the investor's total portfolio.

One implication of the fact that the nationality-dependent component of each investor's portfolio only contains the national bond is that nationality does not affect the relative weights of stocks among themselves. The ratio of the weights for two stocks j and k, w_j^i/ w_k^i, is independent of risk aversion and of nationality; or conversely the stock sub-portfolio in any investor's total portfolio always has the same proportions as the world stock market portfolio. This is due to the existence of a real riskless asset for each investor; without such an asset, the nationality-dependent fund would in general contain positions in all stocks and all bonds, as shown elsewhere (Sercu (80)). In the present context, one implication is that, since net outstanding amounts of each of the stocks are strictly positive, the asset demands by each individual are strictly positive for each stock. Thus, there is no need to assume that it is possible to short-sell stocks with full use of the proceeds.

II - DEMAND FOR HEDGED STOCK
AND FOR PURE EXCHANGE RISK

The previous section showed how any efficient portfolio can always be decomposed into a part which depends on nationality and which only consists of the investor's (real) bond, and a second part containing the stock market portfolio and some bonds from everywhere, in proportions that are independent of the investor's nationality. We now demonstrate that this internationally diversified fund can always be decomposed into a demand for hedged stock and a demand for pure exchange risk.

By convention, the stocks are the first n assets and the foreign bonds are the last L assets in Ω and $[\underline{\mu} - \underline{r}]$. There are L+1 countries, and the (L+1)-th bond is the reference-currency bond (the (N+1)-th asset). Accordingly, Ω is partitioned into:

$$
\Omega = \begin{bmatrix} \Omega_S & \Omega_{SB} \\ \\ \Omega'_{SB} & \Omega_B \end{bmatrix}. \qquad \begin{matrix} \text{(n stocks)} \\ \\ \text{(L foreign bonds)} \end{matrix}
$$

The (random) payoff of a foreign bond over a short period dt is just $r_f\, dt + \dfrac{d\, S_f}{S_f}$ where S_f is the spot rate of currency f (in units of the reference currency per unit of foreign currency); $\dfrac{d\, S_f}{S_f}$ is the (random) rate of appreciation of currency f; and r_f is the country-f risk-free rate per unit of time.[3] Thus, Ω_B is also the covariance matrix of exchange rate changes, and Ω_{SB} likewise is the matrix of covariances of stock returns with exchange rate changes. From multivariate regression theory, the inverse of the partitioned matrix can be interpreted as

$$
\Omega^{-1} = \begin{bmatrix} \Omega^{-1}_{S|B} & -\Omega^{-1}_{S|B}\,[\gamma]' \\ \\ -[\gamma]\,\Omega^{-1}_{S|B} & \Omega^{-1}_B + [\gamma]\,\Omega^{-1}_{S|B}\,[\gamma]' \end{bmatrix}, \qquad (3)
$$

where $[\gamma]' = \Omega_{SB}\,\Omega^{-1}_B$ is an n×L matrix, each row containing the L multivariate slope coefficients in the regression of the stock's return on all L exchange rate changes.

$\Omega_{S|B} = \Omega_S - [\gamma]'\,\Omega_B\,[\gamma]$ is the n×n matrix of disturbances ("residuals") of these n regressions, or, in the parlance of Gaussian regression theory, the covariance matrix of stock returns conditional on the exchange rates.

The vector $[\mu - r]$ is partitioned in the same way. The vector of the n common stock terms is denoted by $[\mu - r]_n$, and the vector of excess returns on the L foreign bonds is written explicitly as $[r_f + \phi_f - r]$, where r_f is the foreign interest rate and ϕ_f the expected rate of appreciation of the spot rate (per unit of time). Since, in our setting, stocks have no clear-cut single nationality, the exchange components in expected stock returns are left implicit at this stage.

The first n elements of $\Omega^{-1}\,[\mu - r]$, the weights of the common stocks in the stock-bond fund, are then given by

$$
y_n = \Omega^{-1}_{S|B}\left[\,[\mu - r]_n - [\gamma]'\,[\,r_f + \phi_f - r\,]\,\right]. \qquad (4)
$$

By analogy with Solnik (73), this expression can be interpreted as a demand for hedged stock. Following Dumas (78) and Adler and Dumas (78), a stock is said to be hedged if it is combined with forward exchange contracts (or zero-investment positions in foreign and domestic bonds) so as to make the total return on the combination uncorrelated with exchange rate changes. To implement such a hedge, we need the L slope coefficients, $\gamma_{j,f}$, f=1,...,L, of a multivariate regression of stock j's return on all exchange rates. It will probably be clear that, in order to hedge a stock j, it suffices to borrow, for every franc invested, $\gamma_{j,f}$ francs in each currency f. To see this, consider a portfolio with
- weight 1 for asset j,
- weights $-\gamma_{j,f}$ (that is, short sales or loans in foreign currency if $\gamma_{j,f}$ is positive) for each of the foreign bonds f = 1,... , L; and
- a weight $\sum_{f=1}^{L} \gamma_{j,f}$ for the domestic bond.

The return on this portfolio is

$$
\begin{aligned}
\frac{dP}{P} &= \frac{dV_j}{V_j} - \sum_{f=1}^{L} \gamma_{j,f}(r_f \, dt + \frac{dS_f}{S_f} - r\,dt) \\
&= \frac{dV_j}{V_j} - \sum_{f=1}^{L} \gamma_{j,f} \frac{dS_f}{S_f} - \sum_{f=1}^{L} \gamma_{j,f}(r_f - r)\,dt \ .
\end{aligned}
$$

Now consider the regression of dV_j/V_j on all dS_f/S_f. Clearly, the disturbance term from that regression is the only random component in the above portfolio return. It follows that this portfolio return is uncorrelated with all exchange rates, or the portfolio is hedged against exchange risk. That is, the bracketed vector in (4) is the expected excess return on hedged stocks. By the same argument, $\Omega_{S|B}^{-1}$ is the covariance matrix of hedged stock returns.

The next L elements in the internationally diversified stock-bond fund, the weights corresponding to the L foreign bonds, are:

$$
\begin{aligned}
y_L &= -[\gamma]\,\Omega_{S|B}^{-1}[\underline{\mu - r}]_n + \{\Omega_B^{-1} + [\gamma]\,\Omega_{S|B}^{-1}[\gamma]'\}\,[\,r_f + \phi_f - r\,] \\
&= \Omega_B^{-1}[\,r_f + \phi_f - r\,] - [\gamma]\,\Omega_{S|B}^{-1}\{[\underline{\mu - r}]_n - [\gamma]'\,[\,r_f + \phi_f - r\,]\} \\
&= \Omega_B^{-1}[\,r_f + \phi_f - r\,] - [\gamma]\,y_n \ , \quad\quad\quad (5)
\end{aligned}
$$

where y_n are the weights of the stocks in the stock-bond fund (see (4)).

To facilitate the interpretation of (4) and (5), just imagine that stock brokers or some other intermediaries actually attached the required amounts of hedges to each unit of each share, so that any stock purchased would be automatically hedged. In that case, the partitioned covariance matrix of hedged stock returns and bond returns would be block-diagonal, and the composition vector z_N of the new stock-bond fund would look like:

$$
\begin{bmatrix} \underline{z_n} \\ \\ \underline{z_L} \end{bmatrix} = \begin{bmatrix} \Omega_{S|B} & [0] \\ \\ [0]' & \Omega_B \end{bmatrix}^{-1} \begin{bmatrix} [\underline{\mu - r}]_n - [\gamma]' \, [\, r_f + \phi_f - r \,] \\ \\ [\, r_f + \phi_f - r \,] \end{bmatrix}
$$

$$
= \begin{bmatrix} \Omega_{S|B}^{-1} \Big[[\underline{\mu - r}]_n - [\gamma]' \, [\, r_f + \phi_f - r \,] \Big] \\ \\ \Omega_B^{-1} \, [\, r_f + \phi_f - r \,] \end{bmatrix}, \tag{6a}
$$

while the domestic bond would have a weight equal to

$$
z_{N+1} = 1 - \sum_{j=1}^{N} z_j . \tag{6b}
$$

Comparing (6a) with (4), one sees that

$$
\underline{y_n} = \underline{z_n} . \tag{7a}
$$

That is, the actual demand for stocks equals the demand for hedged stock that would be observed if brokers added the required amounts of forward contracts to each stock. Similarly, from (5) we have that for the foreign bonds:

$$
\underline{y_L} = \underline{z_L} + \{ - [\gamma] \, \underline{y_n} \} . \tag{7b}
$$

The last term in this expression is the amount of bonds necessary to hedge the stock in the optimal portfolio:

$$
- [\gamma] \, \underline{y_n} = \text{the L} \times 1 \text{ vector of } \sum_{j=1}^{n} (-\gamma_{j,f} \, y_j) \ , f = 1, \dots L .
$$

So the weights of domestic bonds in the log utility portfolio can always be decomposed into a part $(-[\gamma] \, \underline{y_n})$ which serves to hedge the stock positions, and a demand $\underline{z_L}$ which would be the solution if brokers had already hedged the stocks (if Ω were block-diagonal). Finally, the weight of the domestic bond in the diversified stock-bond portfolio, y_{N+1}, relates to its hedged-stock counterpart z_{N+1} as follows:

$$y_{N+1} \equiv 1 - \sum_{j=1}^{n} y_j - \sum_{f=n+1}^{n+L} y_f$$

$$= 1 - \sum_{j=1}^{n} z_j - \sum_{f=n+1}^{n+L} z_f + \sum_{j=1}^{n} y_j \sum_{f=1}^{L} \gamma_{j,f}$$

$$= z_{N+1} + \sum_{j=1}^{n} y_j \sum_{f=1}^{L} \gamma_{j,f} . \tag{7c}$$

That is, the weights of domestic bonds in the log utility portfolio can always be decomposed into the demand z_{N+1} that would be observed if stocks were already hedged (if Ω were block-diagonal), and a part which represents the investment of the proceeds of the foreign currency loans that hedge the stocks.

This leads to a generalised "three" fund theorem: all investors hold (a) their country's riskless bond; (b) a portfolio of hedged stocks, z_n ; and (c) a pure exchange-risk portfolio of bonds of all denominations, z_L . Funds (b) and (c) are the same for all nationalities, and are held in fixed proportions.

III - HEDGED STOCK: A CLOSER LOOK

In this section we discuss some interesting properties of the portfolio of foreign and domestic bonds that hedges a given stock. We will also make a comparison with Solnik's results.

Appendix B goes through the mathematics of the hedging portfolio. It focuses on the question whether the decomposition of the nationality-independent stock-bond fund depends on the numéraire in which the parameters are measured. Indeed, although the composition of this fund, as a whole, is independent of the numéraire, still Ω and $[\mu - r]$, taken separately, do depend on the numéraire. Thus, the decomposition of the bond component into a hedging part, $- [\gamma] \; y_n$, and a pure exchange risk part, z_L , may still depend on the numéraire. The issue is interesting in light of Dumas's (78) analysis of whether firms should hedge their exposure to foreign exchange risk: if hedging is meaningful at all (the answer to this question obviously depends on the assumptions one makes about the investor's opportunities) then the question is whether a universal hedge exists which eliminates exposure for all investors of all nationalities. If not, the firm first has to solve the problem of what set of investors it will serve—an extremely hard problem if there is an internationally integrated market.

The answer is that if a set of hedges is constructed which eliminates all covariance with exchange rate changes in an arbitrarily chosen numéraire d, then it suffices to add a single forward contract (a forward sale of currency d) to transform it into a hedging instrument for a foreign investor. Specifically, the hedging portfolios held by an

investor of country d (short for "domestic") and by an investor of country f ("foreign") are related as follows: per franc invested in stock j.
- both investors hold exactly the same amounts of third-currency bonds;
- d's holdings of his domestic bond equal f's holdings of that asset, plus one.
- d's holdings of the foreign bond equal f's holdings of that asset, minus one.

The same relation can be expressed in the following way: interpret the hedged stock as containing an investment in the stock financed by a loan in the investor's own currency (currency d for the reference country individual, currency f for the foreigner). This would transform the hedged stock fund into the investor's own bond plus a zero-investment position in hedged stock. And this zero-investment position in hedged stock would contain exactly the same assets for all investors of all nationalities.[4]

This property is related to the fact that the excess returns on hedged stock, or alternatively the (total) return on the zero-investment position in hedged stock, is independent of the numéraire in which the problem was initially stated. This property was in fact used by Solnik (73) to prove the independence of nationality in the special case of independence between stock returns and exchange rates. The differences with his results are, first, that the irrelevance of the currency is no longer detectable at first sight, and second, that this return no longer equals the excess return on (unhedged) stock measured in the firm's home currency.

This brings us to the question of how far the above results differ from Solnik's. The first difference is that Solnik assumes that each firm has a single clear-cut nationality, in the sense that one forward contract (or one loan in the firm's home currency) is sufficient to eliminate all covariances with exchange rate changes. In the case of one representative firm per country, Solnik's matrix of regression coefficients $[\gamma]'$ is of the form:

$$[\gamma]' = \begin{bmatrix} 1 & 0 & \cdots & 0 \\ 0 & 1 & \cdots & 0 \\ \vdots & \vdots & \vdots & \vdots \\ 0 & 0 & \cdots & 1 \\ 0 & 0 & \cdots & 0 \end{bmatrix}.$$

(stock of country 1, exposed to S_1 only)

(stock of country 2, exposed to S_2 only)

:

(stock of country L, exposed to S_L only)

(reference-country stock, not exposed)

Since $[\gamma]' = \Omega_{SB}\, \Omega_B^{-1}$, this implies that the $(L+1) \times L$ matrix of covariances of the $L+1$ stocks' returns with the returns on the L foreign bonds must be equal to:

$$\Omega_{SB} = \begin{bmatrix} \Omega_B \\ 0\,0\,0\,0\,\dots\,0 \end{bmatrix} . \qquad \begin{array}{l} \text{(L foreign stocks)} \\ \\ \text{(reference country stock, not exposed)} \end{array}$$

That is, a foreign stock is assumed to behave exactly as the corresponding foreign bond as far as its covariances with exchange rate changes are concerned. This assumption has its implications not only for the pricing of stocks, but also for the pricing of bonds, as we shall see.

The second difference between our results and those of Solnik is that his funds are zero-investment funds, rather than standard portfolios with weights summing to unity. As to Solnik's stock fund, there is no need to interpret it as a zero-investment portfolio. Using equation (A2) in Appendix A, one easily interprets Solnik's stock fund as a fund of shares to which forward exchange contracts are added. The pure foreign exchange fund, however, has to be defined as a zero-investment fund to obtain nationality-independence—at least with Solnik's math. Comparing his mathematics with Appendix A, it becomes obvious that Solnik's zero-investment property follows from the omission of the vector denoted $K_f = [0, 0,\dots,1, 0, 0]$, which picks up the cross terms that arise with a quadratic approximation. The omission of the cross-terms can be interpreted as an implicit assumption that, for all foreign currencies f and g, $cov_{f,g} = \sigma_f^2$. But if the variances of the exchange rate changes are non-zero, this implies that Ω_B has equal elements everywhere, so that it cannot be inverted. Moreover, it would mean that all pairwise regression coefficients of rates of changes of currencies, and all correlation coefficients, are exactly equal to unity. This means that all foreign currencies f and g move in perfect unison except, possibly, for their expectations. And if this has to hold for all possible reference currencies, there cannot be any exchange risk at all. Since this can hardly have been Solnik's intention, the omission of the cross terms may be interpreted as a linear approximation rather than a quadratic (Ito) one. This would not only be at variance with the Ito-process formulation in the beginning of Solnik's paper, but it also is inadequate for mean-variance purposes (a theory which basically relies on quadratic approximations). The inadequacy of the linear approximation shows up in the fact that, for unit relative risk aversion, the investor's portfolio in Solnik's world is not entirely independent of nationality: if the nationality-independent component of all portfolios were a zero-investment fund, any portfolio would contain a non-zero weight in the investor's own national riskfree asset.

IV - A GENERALIZED INTERNATIONAL ASSET PRICING MODEL

From equation (1), the vector of demands for stocks by investor i of any country is:

$$W^i \, \underline{w}_n^i = W^i \, \alpha^i \, \underline{y}_n \quad ,$$

where y_n is the vector of weights of the n stocks in the internationally diversified stock-bond fund. Summing over all investors and bringing in the market clearing conditions yields:

$$\sum_{\forall i} W^i \alpha^i \ y_n \ = \underline{V}_n$$

$$= M \frac{\underline{V}_n}{M} \equiv M \ \underline{x}_n \ . \tag{8}$$

In (8), the vector $\underline{V}_n$ denotes the vector of all outstanding aggregate values of all shares of each asset; M is the aggregate capitalisation of all stocks (the value of the world stock market portfolio); and $\underline{x}_n \equiv \underline{V}_n / M$ denotes the vector of weights of each of the stocks in the world stock market portfolio.

Define $W = \sum_{\forall i} W^i$, the world's aggregate invested wealth. This total wealth, W, will be equal to M, the value of the stock market portfolio, if there are no net outstanding amounts of bonds, viz., when all borrowing and lending is among investors and when there is no money stock outstanding. (See Fama and Farber's (78) analysis of the dual role of money as least cost medium of exchange and as a capital asset.)

Dividing both sides of (8) by M and bringing in aggregate wealth W yields

$$\underline{x}_n \ = \left\{ \sum_{\forall i} \frac{W^i \alpha^i}{M} \right\} \ \underline{y}_n \ = \frac{W}{M} \left\{ \sum_{\forall i} \frac{W^i \alpha^i}{W} \right\} \ \underline{y}_n$$

$$= \frac{W}{M} \ \overline{\overline{\alpha}} \ \underline{y}_n \ . \tag{9}$$

The term $\overline{\overline{\alpha}}$ is the wealth-weighted mean of all investors' relative risk tolerances α^i, henceforth called the world's mean relative risk tolerance. Since relative risk tolerance is the inverse of relative risk aversion η^i, the inverse of $\overline{\overline{\alpha}}$ is the wealth-weighted harmonic mean of all investors' relative risk aversions, henceforth called the world mean risk aversion:

$$\overline{\overline{\eta}} = \left\{ \sum_{\forall i} \frac{W^i \alpha^i}{W} \right\}^{-1} = \left\{ \sum_{\forall i} \frac{W^i}{W} \ (\eta^i)^{-1} \right\}^{-1} \ .$$

We can transform (9) into an expression of the familiar CAPM form by replacing $\underline{y}_n$ (the weights of the n stocks in the nationality-independent stock-bond fund) by its solution (4), premultiplying the result by $\Omega_{S|B}$ (the covariance matrix of hedged stock), and dividing by (W/M) $\overline{\overline{\alpha}}$. The resulting equation is

$$[\underline{\mu} - \underline{r}]_n - [\gamma]' \ [\ r_f + \phi_f - r \ ] \ = \frac{M}{W} \ \overline{\overline{\eta}} \ \Omega_{S|B} \ \underline{x}_n$$

$$= \frac{M}{W} \; \overline{\overline{\eta}} \; \underline{cov}_{j,M|B} \; . \tag{10}$$

where $\underline{cov}_{j,M|B}$ is the vector of covariances of the returns on the stocks $j = 1, 2, ... n$ with the return on the stock market portfolio, conditional on the exchange rate changes—that is, the vector of covariances of the returns on stocks $j = 1,...n$ with the return on the hedged stock market portfolio.[5] Equation (10) thus states that there is a linear relationship between the excess expected return on hedged stock on the one hand, and the risk of the stock (measured as its marginal contribution to the stock market portfolio's variance of hedged returns) on the other hand. The market price per unit of this covariance risk equals, or is proportional to, the world mean relative risk aversion. To operationalise this market price of risk, write (10) for the hedged stock market portfolio itself, as usual. Since the exposure of the stock market to currency-f exchange risk, $\gamma_{M,f}$, equals $\sum_{f=1}^{L} \gamma_{j,f} x_j$—the value-weighted mean of the individual stocks' exposures—, the price of risk equals

$$\frac{W}{M} \overline{\overline{\eta}} = \frac{(\mu_M - r) - \sum_{f=1}^{L} \gamma_{M,f} (r_f + \phi_f - r)}{\sigma^2_{M|B}} \; .$$

Therefore, for any stock j:

$$\mu_j - r = \sum_{f=1}^{L} \gamma_{j,f} (r_f + \phi_f - r) + \frac{cov_{j,M|B}}{\sigma^2_{M|B}} \left\{ (\mu_M - r) - \sum_{f=1}^{L} \gamma_{M,f} (r_f + \phi_f - r) \right\} . \tag{11a}$$

Equation (11a) says that the total risk premium on an individual stock consists of two parts:
- The expected cost of hedging the stock against exchange risk; and
- A CAPM-like risk premium for uncertainty not associated with exchange rate changes. One possible measure of this risk is the hedged stock's beta, that is, the stock's sensitivity to deviations of the hedged stock market return from its mean, or the regression slope coefficient of the stock's return on the hedged market return. The corresponding premium per unit of this market sensitivity is the expected excess return on the hedged stock market portfolio. As stated before, the excess returns are the same whatever the numéraire in which the analysis was started. So both the hedged beta and the reward for this risk are the same for all investors.

Equation (11a) can be criticized for at least two reasons. Firstly, it is arbitrary to remove from the market return everything that is correlated with exchange rate changes. To this objection one might reply that no causality is postulated. The statistical decomposition of the market return (into an exposed part and a component which is independent of exchange rate changes) arose naturally from the mathematics, rather than being an *a priori* assumption about a return generating process. Still, to accommodate whoever prefers to avoid this decomposition, Appendix D derives the following equivalent to (11a):

$$\mu_j - r = \zeta_{j,1} (r_1 + \phi_1 - r) + \dots + \zeta_{j,L} (r_L + \phi_L - r) + \beta_{j,M} (\mu_M - r), \qquad (11b)$$

where $[\zeta_{j,1}, \dots, \zeta_{j,L}, \beta_{j,M}]$ are the $L+1$ coefficients of the regression of the j-th stock's return on not only the L exchange rates but also on the market return. Equation (11b) avoids the decomposition of the market return, and may be preferable for empirical purposes (if the market return is observable, or if one sees a point in using proxies—see Roll(77)).

A second, more basic objection to (11a, b) and to the whole procedure followed to derive it is that any partitioning of Ω would yield mathematically similar results. One could, for instance, construct risk-return relationships for assets other than, say, steel companies. The expected return on a stock would then equal the expected cost of hedging the stock against fluctuations in the steel companies' share prices, plus a premium for risks not associated with "steel risk". This example is of course contrived, but it stresses the fact that the procedure would leave unexplained how the expected returns on steel companies themselves are determined in equilibrium. In the present case, there is some justification for treating the bonds as special assets. For one thing, they represent risk-free investments to at least some of the investors (if not to all investors, as in the basic CAPM). And secondly the results derived thus far allow one to determine risk-return equilibrium relations without knowledge of the composition of the bond market portfolio or of the national mean risk aversion per country. These parameters do enter into specifications that will be derived in sections 6 and 7.

V – EQUILIBRIUM INTEREST RATES

A problem with (11a, b) is that this model uses as explanatory variables the various interest rates that are themselves determined inside the model. This can be brought out by the following simple rearrangement of the premium for exchange exposure:

$$r_f + \phi_f - r = \phi_f - (r - r_f)$$

$$= [\text{expected appreciation}] - [\text{premium on forward exchange}],$$

because, as shown by Solnik, the term $(r - r_f)\, dt$ is the continuous-time equivalent of the forward premium in a short-term contract. So the premium per unit of exposure is the expected "return" from an open forward purchase of f. In a discrete-time notation, with $F_{t,t+1}$ denoting the forward rate set at t for delivery at t+1, this premium would have been written as

$$E_t \left\{ \frac{S_{t+1} - S_t}{S_t} - \frac{F_{t,t+1} - S_t}{S_t} \right\} = E_t \left\{ \frac{S_{t+1} - F_{t,t+1}}{S_t} \right\}.$$

Now in the present characterisation of the world, the expected appreciation of currency f is exogenous: the future spot rate is just the future price of country f's consumption bundle, measured in units of the reference country's consumption bundle; so the spot rate depends on relative prices of commodities and differences in consumption tastes, which are exogenous from the point of view of the capital market.[6] However, the forward rate set at t is a certainty equivalent, and as such it is obviously determined inside the model. It turns out that the crucial determinants are, first, the stock market covariance risk of the foreign bond (or of the foreign currency), and secondly the covariances among exchange rates, the national wealths, and the national mean risk aversions.

To demonstrate this, we assume in this and the next section that there is no net amount of bonds outstanding. We first discuss the case where all individuals' risk tolerances α^i are equal to unity—the case discussed by Stehle (77)—and next the more general case. Outside bonds are easily re-introduced later on, in Section 7.

From the demand equation (1), if $\alpha^i = 1$ for all investors i, then all asset demand originates from the demand for the internationally diversified stock-bond fund. The bond component in this fund is described in (6). If the net outstanding amount of bonds is zero and $\alpha^i = 1$, the market clearing condition therefore is

$$[\textstyle\sum_{\forall i} W^i]\left\{ \Omega_B^{-1} [r_f + \phi_f - r] - [\gamma]\ \underline{y_n} \right\} = \underline{0}, \text{ the zero vector },$$

or simply, because $\sum_{\forall i} W^i$ cannot be zero:

$$[r_f + \phi_f - r] = \Omega_B [\gamma]\ \underline{y_n}$$

$$= \Omega_B [\Omega_B^{-1}\ \Omega_{SB}']\ \underline{y_n} = \Omega_{SB}'\ \underline{y_n} .$$

But from (9), if M = W (that is, if there are no net outstanding amounts of bonds), and if all $\alpha^i = 1 = \bar{\bar{\alpha}}$, then $y_n = \underline{x_n}$ (with, it may be recalled, $\underline{x_n}$ being the weights of the n stocks in the world stock market portfolio). Hence, for every bond f,

$$r_f + \phi_f - r = cov_{f,M} .$$

In words, the expected excess return on a foreign bond equals the covariance of the bond's return (or of the exchange rate) with the return on the stock market portfolio, times a unit market price of risk. With log utility everywhere, bonds are priced exactly as in a Purchasing Power Parity (PPP) international CAPM with market price of covariance risk equal to unity. This is a very different result from Solnik's (77) equilibrium condition, where the premium was determined by covariances among bonds only. Recall from Section 4 that Solnik's independence assumption implied that covariances of stocks with exchange rates were the same as the covariances of the foreign bond of the same nationality with exchange rates. This is why covariances with the stock market disappeared—not because they were zero or irrelevant, but because they were indistinguishable from covariances between bonds themselves. The fact that covariances among exchange rates do not show up at all in our equation is due to the assumptions of unit relative risk aversion for all individuals and of zero outstanding net amounts of bonds.

A less attractive feature of this special case $\alpha^i = 1$ is that, since everybody holds the same portfolio and since bonds have zero weights in the market portfolio of stocks and bonds, nobody will hold any of the bonds. The interest rates in such a world are to be interpreted as shadow prices set to ensure that nobody is interested in these assets—a case also mentioned in Solnik (77) and in Fisher (75).[7] To ensure the existence of at least one of the bonds, one has to drop either the standard assumption of no net outstanding amounts, or the assumption of unit relative risk aversion.

In the more general case where the individual risk tolerances α^i are different from each other and from unity, aggregate demand for bonds will have two sources. First there is the demand induced by the demand for the international stock-bond fund, which is independent of nationality. The second source is the demand for bonds by the residents of the country (the country-specific fund). For the reference currency bond L+1, for instance, this second source induces a total demand equal to (see equation (2)):

$$\sum_{i \in L+1} W^i (1 - \alpha^i) = W_{L+1} (1 - \bar{\alpha}_{L+1}),$$

where $W_{L+1} = \sum_{i \in L+1} W^i$ is country (L+1)'s aggregate wealth, and

$$\bar{\alpha}_{L+1} = \sum_{i \in L+1} \frac{W^i \alpha^i}{W_{L+1}}$$ is country (L+1)'s mean risk tolerance.

So the market clearing condition for the foreign bonds is

$$\sum_{\forall i} W^i \alpha^i \left\{ \Omega_B^{-1} [r_f + \phi_f - r] - [\gamma] \ \underline{y}_n \right\} + W_f (1 - \bar{\alpha}_f) = \underline{0}. \tag{12}$$

From $\sum_{\forall i} \frac{W^i \alpha^i}{W} = \bar{\bar{\alpha}} = (\bar{\bar{\eta}})^{-1}$ and $[\gamma] = \Omega_B^{-1} \Omega_{SB}^{'}$, the expected returns must be equal to

$$[r_f + \phi_f - r] = \Omega_{SB}^{'} \ \underline{y}_n - \bar{\bar{\eta}} \Omega_B \left\{ \frac{W_f (1 - \bar{\alpha}_f)}{W} \right\}. \tag{13a}$$

Each term on the right hand side of (13a) can be interpreted as a covariance term with some portfolio return times a risk premium. For the first term, one can again use equation (9): when there are no outside bonds (W=M), the weights of the stocks in the international stock-bond fund $\underline{y}_n$ will equal the weights of these stocks in the world stock market portfolio $\underline{x}_n$, times the world mean risk aversion, $\bar{\bar{\eta}}$. That is,

$$\Omega_{SB}^{'} \ \underline{y}_n = \bar{\bar{\eta}} \ \Omega_{SB}^{'} \ \underline{x}_n = \bar{\bar{\eta}} \ \underline{cov}_{f,M} \tag{13b}$$

To be able to interpret also the second term in (13a) as a covariance with some portfolio, the weights have to be rescaled so as to sum to unity. If one sums the weights over all countries (including the reference country), then

$$\sum_{j=1}^{L+1} \frac{W_f (1 - \bar{\alpha}_f)}{W} = 1 - \bar{\bar{\alpha}} = 1 - \bar{\bar{\eta}}^{-1}.$$

So the last term on the right hand side of (13a) can be rearranged as

$$- \bar{\bar{\eta}} \, \Omega_B \left\{ \frac{W_f (1 - \bar{\alpha}_f)}{W} \right\} = (1 - \bar{\bar{\eta}}) \, \Omega_B \left\{ \frac{W_f (1 - \bar{\alpha}_f)}{W (1 - \bar{\bar{\alpha}})} \right\}. \tag{13c}$$

This is a risk premium of $(1 - \bar{\bar{\eta}})$, times the bond's covariance of return with the return on a portfolio of bonds with weights that depend on the country's national wealths and the national mean risk aversions. From the market clearing condition (12), one can see that this fund has a composition proportional to the aggregate holdings of the bonds as country-specific funds. The fund includes the reference-currency component (which, in this numéraire, is associated with a zero covariance term). Inclusion of the home country bond into the portfolio ensures that the composition of this portfolio is again independent of the numéraire, although the expected returns and covariances themselves obviously do depend on the numéraire. Furthermore, leaving out the reference country would not have allowed us to bring out the world mean risk aversion in the second term in (13a), a term which comes in handy in the next sections.

Substituting (13b) and (13c) into (13a), and denoting the bond fund with weights proportional to $W_f (1 - \bar{\alpha}_f)$ by a subscript F, equation (13a) simplifies to:

$$[\, r_f + \phi_f - r \,] = \bar{\bar{\eta}} \, \underline{cov_{f,M}} + (1 - \bar{\bar{\eta}}) \, \underline{cov_{f,F}}. \tag{14}$$

The first term in (14) looks quite standard. Indeed, if one ignores the second term on the right hand side of this equation, then one obtains the prediction of the expected return on foreign bonds when all investors consume the same bundle at the same (reference-currency) price (a PPP model) and when there is no inflation in that reference currency.[8] In such a PPP international CAPM, the covariance measures the marginal contribution of asset f to portfolio M, where M is the risky component of every investor's portfolio. If bond f is potentially held by all investors, it must be priced on the basis of its "similarity" to the market portfolio. From another angle, the term $cov_{f,M}$ can be seen to derive from the term $[\gamma] \, y_n$ in equation (12). So a high market covariance tends to be associated with high $\gamma_{j,f}$'s and/or high y_j's and hence with a strong demand for bonds as hedging devices. For instance, US stocks have large weights in the market portfolio of all shares; and as the US is, by European standards, a relatively closed economy, dollar loans would represent the bulk of the required hedging contracts. The strong demand for dollar loans, *ceteris paribus*, then tends to push up the US interest rates. This means that a high dollar interest rate needs not solely be explained by a weakness ($\phi_\$ < 0$) of that currency.

Note however the *ceteris paribus* clause: the second term on the right hand side of (14) may offset such an effect.

The second term in (14) has no analog in the basic CAPM. Firstly, the covariance with fund F is not a covariance with a market portfolio of bonds; rather, the weights in F are based on national wealths and national risk aversions, not outstanding values. And second, the premium for covariance with F is $1 - \bar{\bar{\eta}}$, not the usual $\bar{\bar{\eta}}$. In other words, the higher the world's mean relative risk aversion, the lower the premium; and for $\bar{\bar{\eta}} > 1$ this premium is even negative. This case is, in fact, the more likely one: if one accepts Friend, Landskroner, and Losq's (76) claim that the U.S. mean relative risk aversion probably exceeds two, then it is very unlikely that the world mean would be below unity. Otherwise, however, the premium for covariance with the bond portfolio would be positive.

Note, from the right hand side of (13c), that the sign of $(1 - \bar{\bar{\eta}})$ does not at all affect the comparative statics effectss of $\bar{\alpha}_f$ or W_f: assuming that the effect of the variance terms is not dominated by the covariances, a higher value of $\bar{\alpha}_f$ tends to increase the foreign interest rate, and so does a higher (lower) value of W_f if $\bar{\alpha}_f > 1$ ($\bar{\alpha}_f < 1$). The reason is that a higher risk tolerance decreases the demand for the country-f bond as the country-specific asset, while a higher national wealth has the same effect if $(1 - \bar{\alpha}_f)$ is negative. (In fact, when $\bar{\alpha}_f > 1$, the country is actually holding a negative position in its country-specific fund.) A lower net demand for this bond as the country-specific asset then increases the country's interest rate, *ceteris paribus*. The effect of national wealth here is the opposite of its effect via the first term in (14).[9]

Note also that the weight of a country's bond in portfolio F will be zero if its mean risk tolerance $\bar{\alpha}_f$ equals unity—if the country behaves as if its residents had log utility functions. In that case, the demand for the country's bond as nationality-specific fund from more risk-averse residents ($\alpha_f^i < 1$) is exactly satisfied by the supply of that same asset by more risk-tolerant investors ($\alpha_f^i > 1$) of the same country. Then all net demand for that bond would be induced by demand for the stock-bond fund; and by virtue of the market clearing conditions, the bond's weight in that fund must be zero. An important difference with the previously discussed case (where all individuals' relative risk aversions were equal to unity), is that now the bond will exist: it will be held short or long by investors in the corresponding country, although not outside the country. So a prerequisite for the emergence of an international bond market is that the countries' mean risk tolerances differ from unity. With $\bar{\alpha}_f < 1$ there is a net demand which must be satisfied by a supply of bond f through the international stock-bond fund. And this bond f must have a negative weight in that fund: foreigners will issue bonds denominated in currency f. A less risk-averse country with $\bar{\alpha}_f > 1$ would export bonds denominated in its currency, and invest the proceeds in the stock-bond fund. Finally, note that when $\bar{\alpha}_f = 1$—that is, when all lending and borrowing in currency f happens within that country—, still a premium for covariance with portfolio F will be included in the interest rate, unless the country's exchange rate is uncorrelated with all other exchange rates. Indeed, the interest rate must be set such that no foreigner is interested in the asset, and this of course has to take into account the covariances with and the expected returns on the other assets.

This section provided some insights into the workings of international bond markets, but the interpretation of equilibrium condition (14) was rather mechanical. In particular, we have not provided any economic interpretation of the new risk premium, $(1 - \bar{\bar{\eta}})\, \text{cov}_{f,F}$. This is the topic for section 7. First we will investigate the implications of (14) for the equilibrium conditions on hedged stock returns.

VI - RISK AND RETURN FOR STOCKS REVISITED

If one plugs back equation (14) (for the bonds) into its counterpart for stocks, (10), then it turns out that (10) becomes identical to (14). This should not come as a surprise, since both were derived from the same aggregate demand system. To see this, note that if $W = M$ (no outside bonds, as was assumed in (14)), we can rewrite (10) as

$$[\mu - r]_n = [\gamma]' \, [\, r_f + \phi_f - r\,] + \bar{\bar{\eta}}\,\Omega_{S|B}\,\underline{x_n}\, .$$

where $\underline{x_n}$ = the vector of the stocks' value weights in the market portfolio.

$[\gamma]' = \Omega_{SB}\,\Omega_B^{-1}$, the n×L matrix of the stocks' exposures to exchange risk.

$\Omega_{S|B} = \Omega_S - [\gamma]'\,\Omega_B\,[\gamma]$, the covariance matrix of stock returns conditional on the exchange rates.

Upon using the definitions of $[\gamma]$ and $\Omega_{S|B}$, substitution of (14) yields

$$[\mu - r]_n = \bar{\bar{\eta}}\,\left[\Omega_{SB}\,\Omega_B^{-1}\right]\Omega_{SB}^{\iota}\,\underline{x_n} + (1 - \bar{\bar{\eta}})\,\left[\Omega_{SB}\,\Omega_B^{-1}\right]\Omega_B\,\frac{W_f\,(1 - \bar{\alpha}_f)}{W\,(1 - \bar{\alpha})}$$

$$+ \bar{\bar{\eta}}\,\Omega_S\,\underline{x_n} - \bar{\bar{\eta}}\,\Omega_{SB}\,\Omega_B^{-1}\,\Omega_{SB}^{\iota}\,\underline{x_n}$$

$$= \bar{\bar{\eta}}\,\Omega_S\,\underline{x_n} + (1 - \bar{\bar{\eta}})\,\Omega_{SB}\,\frac{W_f\,(1 - \bar{\alpha}_f)}{W\,(1 - \bar{\bar{\alpha}})}$$

$$= \bar{\bar{\eta}}\,\underline{\text{cov}_{j,M}} + (1 - \bar{\bar{\eta}})\,\underline{\text{cov}_{j,F}}\, , \qquad (15)$$

where portfolio F again refers to the bond fund with weights proportional to $W_f\,(1 - \bar{\alpha}_f)$. Thus, the excess return on a stock j consists of the market price of risk, $\bar{\bar{\eta}}$, times the asset's covariance with the stock market portfolio (as in the CAPM), plus a premium $(1 - \bar{\bar{\eta}})$ per unit of covariance with the bond fund F. Comparing (15) with the risk-return relation for hedged stock (equation (11)), one notices that the stock market risk is now a standard covariance, not a conditional covariance or a covariance with the hedged market return.

And the exchange risk factor, $\mathrm{cov}_{j,F}$, is now the covariance with one basket F, the same for all stocks, while in (10) and (11) the hedging basket was different from asset to asset.

Equation (15) can be interpreted in the same way as (14). But a different interpretation is obtained if (14) or (15) are rearranged as

$$\mu_j - r - \mathrm{cov}_{j,F} = \bar{\bar{\eta}}\,[\mathrm{cov}_{j,M} - \mathrm{cov}_{j,F}]\,. \tag{16}$$

This is similar to the equilibrium condition obtained by Friend, Landskroner, and Losq (76), who studied not international asset pricing but the relationship, in a one-country (or PPP) framework, between nominal expected returns μ_j, the nominal bond rate r, the nominal covariance with the capital market portfolio, $\mathrm{cov}_{j,M}$, and the covariance with the uncertain inflation rate, $\mathrm{cov}_{j,I}$. Their nominal version of the equilibrium condition when all investors hold real efficient portfolios is:[10]

$$\mu_j - r - \mathrm{cov}_{j,I} = \bar{\bar{\eta}}\,[\mathrm{cov}_{j,M} - \mathrm{cov}_{j,I}]\,.$$

Thus, the only difference with (16) is that Friend *et al.* have a covariance with inflation (which they implicitly assume to be the same for all investors) where we have a covariance with the bond fund F. But the covariance with the return on the bond fund equals the covariance with the rate of change of a similarly weighted currency basket. Moreover, in the present characterisation of the world (no inflation in any country), each exchange rate just represents the price, in units of reference currency, of the corresponding foreign consumption bundle. This means that the covariance with the return on bond fund F can be interpreted as the covariance with a world representative inflation rate, constructed as some average of the national "inflation rates" (all measured in reference currency). The weights of each national inflation rate in the world average depend on national wealths and national risk aversions. In the special case where risk tolerances are equal across countries, then the world representative inflation rate would be a simple wealth-weighted mean of the national inflation rates measured in terms of the reference currency. (As Dumas has pointed out in a discussion, the same conclusion holds when risk tolerances are uncorrelated, across countries, with national wealths and with exchange rate covariances.) As before, if $\bar{\bar{\eta}} > 1$, then countries with higher risk aversions would have larger weights than expected solely on the basis of their national wealths.

The way of looking at the world is therefore as follows: assume that there is only one currency, but consumption bundles differ across people. Groups with homogenous tastes are called countries. The central bank agrees to keep the price of one (arbitrarily chosen) bundle constant; but to compensate the other countries for the loss of risk-free investments, the central bank creates a market for index bonds, one for each consumption bundle, paying out a known (real) interest rate plus the corresponding *ex post* inflation rate. If the world as a whole prefers positive covariance with inflation $(\bar{\bar{\eta}} > 1)$, and one group of investors is even more risk-averse than the average, then these individuals would be willing to pay a premium to obtain this perfect hedge against their own country's inflation.

In other words, that country would accept a lower real interest rate, and low interest rates would again reflect higher risk aversions. In equations (14) to (16), high national risk aversion (as compared to the world mean) leads to higher weights in the bond fund F, which via the negative premium $1-\bar{\bar{\eta}}$, indeed results in a lower interest rate.[11]

From this point of view, equation (16) says that there exists a representative inflation rate, in the sense that one can reason as if all investors consumed the same average consumption bundle. This representative rate has one crucial property of a true index, in that its composition is based entirely on beginning-of-period variables (national wealths and national mean risk aversions), that is, it is independent of the outcome of the investment decision, end-of-period wealth. Obviously, its composition is not constant through time: national wealths do change over time and so do national mean risk aversions. This poses empirical problems, not theoretical ones.

VII - RISK AND RETURN IN REPRESENTATIVE REAL TERMS

Since a representative world inflation rate exists, the obvious next question is what relationships exist among expectations and risks of deflated returns. Before doing so, we first present a quick re-derivation of (15) and (16), without worrying about the distinction between stocks and bonds, and now also allowing for positive outstanding amounts of bonds. Such positive net market values could be caused by the existence of money in each country (see Fama and Farber (78)).

If one aggregates (1) or (2) across investors, then the market clearing conditions for, respectively, the n stocks, the L foreign bonds, and the domestic bond can be written as follows:

$$
W \begin{bmatrix} x_n \\ , \\ x_L \\ , \\ x_{N+1} \end{bmatrix} = \sum_{\forall i} W^i \alpha^i \begin{bmatrix} \Omega^{-1}[\mu - r] \\ , \\ 1 - \underline{e}' \Omega^{-1}[\mu - r] \end{bmatrix} + \begin{bmatrix} 0 \\ \vdots \\ 0 \\ , \\ W_1(1 - \bar{\alpha}_1) \\ \vdots \\ W_L(1 - \bar{\alpha}_L) \\ , \\ W_{L+1}(1 - \bar{\alpha}_{L+1}) \end{bmatrix},
$$

with W the world aggregate wealth, W_f the f-th country's aggregate wealth, $\bar{\alpha}_f$ the f-th country's mean risk tolerance, and $\underline{x}_n$, $\underline{x}_L$, and x_{N+1} the weights of the n stocks, the L foreign bonds, and the reference currency bond in the world capital market portfolio of stocks and bonds. Premultiplying by Ω and dividing by W yields, for all risky assets,

$$
\Omega \begin{bmatrix} x_n \\ , \\ x_L \end{bmatrix} = \bar{\bar{\alpha}} \, [\mu - r] + \Omega \begin{bmatrix} 0 \\ \vdots \\ 0 \\ , \\ [W_1/W]\,(1 - \bar{\alpha}_1) \\ \vdots \\ [W_L/W]\,(1 - \bar{\alpha}_L) \end{bmatrix}
$$

or, after dividing and multiplying the last term by $(1 - \bar{\bar{\alpha}})$,

$$
\underline{cov}_{j,W} = \bar{\bar{\alpha}} \, [\underline{\mu - r}] + (1 - \bar{\bar{\alpha}}) \, \underline{cov}_{j,\bar{I}} \, .
$$

As before, $\bar{\bar{\alpha}}$ is the world mean risk tolerance; and subscript $\bar{I}$ refers to a currency basket with weights $[W_f\,(1 - \bar{\alpha}_f)]/[W\,(1 - \bar{\bar{\alpha}})]$. In the presence of outside bonds, we now have $cov_{j,W}$, the j-th asset's covariance of return with the return in the world capital market portfolio of stocks and bonds, instead of $cov_{j,M}$, the stock market covariance risk. As $\bar{\bar{\eta}}$, the world mean risk aversion, equals $(\bar{\bar{\alpha}})^{-1}$, it follows that for any j:

$$
(\mu_j - r - cov_{j,\bar{I}}) = \bar{\bar{\eta}} \, (cov_{j,W} - cov_{j,\bar{I}}) \, . \tag{17a}
$$

Equation (17a) also holds for linear combinations of assets. For the bond portfolio F with the same weights as in $\bar{I}$, equation (17a) takes the special form

$$
(\mu_F - r - \sigma_{\bar{I}}^2) = \bar{\bar{\eta}} \, (cov_{F,W} - \sigma_{\bar{I}}^2) \, , \tag{17b}
$$

where $\sigma_{\bar{I}}^2$ denotes the variance of the representative inflation rate or of the currency basket. Subtract (17b) from (17a), and add and subtract the terms $\sigma_{\bar{I}}^2$ and π (the expected inflation rate) on the left hand side. The result is

$$
(\mu_j - \pi - cov_{j,\bar{I}} + \sigma_{\bar{I}}^2) - (\mu_F - \pi - \sigma_{\bar{I}}^2 + \sigma_{\bar{I}}^2) = \bar{\bar{\eta}} \, [cov_{j,W} - cov_{j,\bar{I}} - cov_{W,\bar{I}} + \sigma_{\bar{I}}^2] \, . \tag{18}
$$

The expressions in parentheses on the left hand side are the expected deflated returns on assets j and F, respectively, where the covariances and variances represent the components of the second-order terms that are of first order of magnitude (Ito's Lemma; see e.g. Friend, Landskroner, and Losq (76) or Fisher (75) for the application of Ito's Lemma to the relation between real returns and nominal returns). For the bond fund F, these cross terms cancel because, by construction, F's covariance-with-inflation equals the variance of the inflation rate. The right hand side of (18) likewise is the covariance of the deflated return on asset j with the deflated return on the world capital market portfolio, W. Denoting parameters of deflated returns by an asteriks, (18) can be written more compactly as

$$(\mu_j^* - \mu_F^*) = \bar{\bar{\eta}} \ \mathrm{cov}_{j,W}^* . \tag{19}$$

Finally, note that the deflated return on the bond fund, μ_F^*, has zero variance. To prove this, recall that for portfolio F the second order terms cancel out, so that the deflated return simply is $dV_F/V_F - d\bar{I}/\bar{I}$. Using $x_{f,F}$ as shorthand for the country weights in the bond fund F and in the representative inflation rate $\bar{I}$, this deflated return therefore equals

$$\frac{d V_F}{V_F} - \frac{d \bar{I}}{\bar{I}} = \left[\sum_{f=1}^{L} (r_f \, dt + \frac{d S_f}{S_f}) \, x_{f,F} + (r \, dt) \, x_{L+1,F} \right] - \left[\sum_{f=1}^{L} \frac{d S_f}{S_f} x_{f,F} \right]$$

$$= \sum_{f=1}^{L+1} x_{f,F} \, r_f \, dt .$$

It follows that the ex post deflated return on F is indeed non-random, and equal to a weighted average of all countries' riskless rates. Adopting a more conventional mean-variance notation, this deflated return is denoted as r_F^*, the world riskless rate. Finally, eliminating $\bar{\bar{\eta}}$ in the standard fashion, one obtains

$$\mu_j^* - r_F^* = \beta_{j,W}^* (\mu_W^* - r_F^*) , \tag{20}$$

where

$$\beta_{j,W}^* = \frac{\mathrm{cov}_{j,W}^*}{\sigma_W^{*2}}$$

is the asset's real beta or real market sensitivity.

In short, there exists a kind of world currency unit (a basket of currencies) in which the standard CAPM holds even in the absence of PPP. The riskless rate is replaced by an average of the national risk-free rates, with weights equal to those of the individual currencies in the world currency unit. And the world capital market portfolio of stocks and bonds replaces the stock market portfolio when there is a net outstanding amount of bonds. This last difference is not important, since in the simple PPP CAPM one can also replace the stock market portfolio by the capital market portfolio without affecting the form of the relationship. As is easily checked, such a transformation would result in a market price of risk which is k = M/W times lower, and in market sensitivities that are k times higher.

As mentioned before, the problem with all expressions that involve a term in F or in $\bar{I}$ (equations (14) to (20)) is that the weights of the bonds or currencies are not directly observable. This problem also arises in F. Black's variant of the CAPM. However, as shown elsewhere, in the case of stochastic inflation the expected real return on the zero-beta portfolio is identifiable if the joint distribution of the nominal market return and the inflation rate is known: there is no need to invert the full covariance matrix of real returns, nor are Ω^* and $\underline{x}$ necessarily known.[12] In the same vein, the weights in F and $\bar{I}$ can be identified if the joint distribution of the market return and exchange rates changes is known in at least one of the currencies. The procedure is presented in Appendix D, and requires no additional information relative to equations (11a) and (11b).

VIII - CONCLUSION

It was shown that when real riskless assets are available in all countries, then optimal portfolios can always be decomposed into 1) a country-specific fund that contains the investor's domestic real bond only, and 2) an internationally diversified stock-bond fund that is efficient in all real units of account. This stock-bond fund can always be decomposed into a fund of hedged stocks and a pure bond fund. The excess returns on hedged stocks are independent of the numéraire in which the problem was originally stated, and simple relations exist between the hedge portfolios that are held by investors of different countries. A linear relation was found between the expected excess returns on hedged stock and the asset's covariance with the return on the market portfolio of hedged stocks. All this generalises the corresponding results that were obtained by Solnik (73) in the special case of independence between exchange rates and stock returns.

Interest rate differentials were found to be biased predictors of future rates of appreciation of foreign currency, because of a risk premium. This premium is related to the currency's stock market sensitivity (reflecting the hedging services provided by the bond), and to the covariances among exchange rate changes, the national wealths, and the mean national relative risk aversions. If the net outstanding amount of each bond is zero, then a necessary condition for the existence of these assets is that not all investors have unit risk aversion. (In a PPP mean-variance world, this condition is slightly more general: then not all investors should have the same relative risk aversion—whatever that value is.) Similarly, a necessary condition for the emergence of an international bond market is that countries' mean relative risk-aversions differ from unity.

Incorporating the results for interest rates into the equilibrium conditions for stocks, we showed that pricing of bonds and of stocks is basically identical. A world currency unit (a basket of currencies) was identified in which a CAPM-like risk-return relationship holds, with a basket of bonds taking the place of the riskfree asset. In other words, there exists a representative consumption bundle, in the sense that one may reason as if all investors consumed that same bundle.

Finally, it may be useful to point out some limitations of the model. First, it uses a mean-variance criterion. Secondly, it assumes homogenous expectations w.r.t. nominal asset returns, and it entirely assumes away the problem of partial segmentation of the international capital market. Also, it assumes constant opportunity sets (or alternatively, a one-period world). And finally, there is assumed to be no inflation. For this last reason, the model holds in an inflationary world only when all returns are deflated by the reference currency price level, when exchange rates are replaced by the product of the exchange rate and the foreign price level and when interest rates are index bond rates.

FOOTNOTES

[1] As Grauer, Litzenberger and Stehle (76) stress, there cannot be an international capital market if there is but one commodity per country which is moreover consumed only inside that country (no international trade): such a characterisation of the world, as in Solnik's 1973 paper, precludes international transfers of wealth, and exchange rates would not exist. Roll and Solnik's (77) reinterpretation of the model as set in a world where each country's commodity can be produced anywhere in the world is but a small improvement: the country's real wealth would still be determined exclusively by the total world production of its commodity, and international portfolio investment would only affect the internal distribution of wealth among the residents. Solnik's (77) formulation avoids this problem by assuming that investors consume many commodities, and that tastes are homothetic (there are no luxury goods nor inferior goods). The homotheticity of the utility function implies the existence of a single price level: the notion of "inflation" can be captured by one figure and "real" returns exist—see Samuelson and Swamy (74); see J. Long (74) for a mean-variance problem with many commodities and no homotheticity restriction. The overlap of the national consumption bundles makes international transfers of wealth possible. However, firms will no longer have an economically meaningful nationality. They will produce for various countries; and as each country's exchange rate is a homothetic function of the reference-currency prices of the commodities, firms' share prices can hardly be expected to be independent of exchange rates. Dumas (77) also warns against viewing the independence assumption as an empirical approximation: a mean-variance theory cannot drop covariances without losing internal consistency.

[2] With expected exchange rate changes equal to zero in the reference currency, the expressions $r_g - r$ and $r_f - r$ are the expected excess returns on the bonds of countries f and g. However, $r - r_f$ will not be the expected excess return, in currency f, on the reference currency's bond, because of Jensen's Inequality: unless the exchange rate is nonrandom, the expected appreciation of the inverse rate S is non-zero. With an Ito approximation, the difference between $E(dS/S)$ and $E(dS^{-1}/S^{-1})$ is captured by a variance term. With linear approximations, these Jensen Inequality terms are overlooked, as in Solnik (73).

[3] In general, the translation of returns gives rise to a covariance term which reflects the first-order component of the cross-product of the exchange rate change, dS/S, and the foreign-currency return on the asset, dV_j^f/V_j^f. This covariance disappears if the terms in the

product are non-random or otherwise independent. The interest rate being non-random, there is no cross term in the translated return on a foreign bond.

[4] These results only hold in the very short run, "dt". For longer periods, the cross terms become increasingly more important.

[5] The covariance of the hedged stock return with the hedged market return is obviously equal to the covariance of the "raw" stock return with the hedged market return.

[6] Grauer, Litzenberger and Stehle's (76) claim to the contrary is based on careless reading of Solnik's paper. He assumes no PPP and no inflation (only "real" exchange risk), while they impose PPP and stochastic inflation in different numéraires (only "nominal" exchange risk).

[7] Fisher shows that in a one-country (or PPP) model with uncertain inflation and index bonds, nobody will hold nominal bonds if their net outstanding value is zero. Obviously, when in addition all investors have equal risk aversion (whatever that level is) and equal commodity preferences, then even the commodity-indexed bonds will not exist if they are in zero net supply. In the present case where real units of account differ among investors, one has to impose that this value be unity in order to rule out the existence of real riskless assets.

[8] With PPP, one clearly has to assume inflation in the other numéraires if the foreign bonds are to be distinguishable from reference currency bonds. Note that in a setting with PPP and zero inflation in the home country, the reference-currency returns are the real returns, and the reference-currency bond becomes the index bond for foreign investors.

[9] This result assumes, reasonably, that rich countries are also large (relatively closed) and issue larger amounts of shares, and that $\bar{\alpha}_f > 1$.

[10] When no net amount of bonds is outstanding, the correction factor for wealth invested in bonds disappears. If outside bonds do exist, the market portfolio is better defined as containing these assets, especially in an inflationary model: this specification is in agreement with a "real" interpretation of the F. Black model, where the market portfolio contains all assets with purchasing power risk.

[11] If $\bar{\bar{\eta}} < 1$ however, the average investor prefers "speculative" portfolios with negative covariance with inflation, and requires an extra return $(1 - \bar{\bar{\eta}} > 0)$ for bearing positive

covariance with inflation. Countries with higher risk aversion would have smaller weights in fund F than expected solely on the basis of their national wealths; this weight would even be negative if $\bar{\eta}_f > 1$. Therefore such a country would tend to have smaller and possibly even negative covariance with F. Since $(1 - \bar{\eta})$ is positive, higher risk aversion would still result in lower real interest rates in that country.

[12] When the joint distribution of nominal market returns and the inflation rate is known, then the expected real return on the market portfolio and on the nominal bond, as well as the real risk of these assets, are known. With these data, it is easy to compute the expected real return on the zero-beta portfolio. See Sercu (80).

APPENDIX A:
PROOF THAT THE COMPOSITION OF THE STOCK-BOND FUND IS
INDEPENDENT OF NATIONALITY

The foreign-currency price (superscript f) of asset j, V_j^f, satisfies $V_j^f = V_j/S_f$, where S_f is the (domestic currency) price of one unit of foreign currency. From Ito's Lemma, then,

$$\frac{d\,V_j^f}{V_j^f} = \frac{d\,V_j}{V_j} - \frac{d\,S_f}{S_f} - cov_{j,f}\,dt + \sigma_f^2\;dt. \tag{A1}$$

I - FOREIGN CURRENCY RISK PREMIA

From (A1) it follows that, for any asset j, the excess expected returns in the home and foreign currency are related as follows:

$$\mu_j^f - r_f = \mu_j - \phi_f - cov_{j,f} + \sigma_f^2 - r_f$$

$$= (\mu_j - r) - (r_f + \phi_f - r) + cov_{j,f} + \sigma_f^2. \tag{A2}$$

That is, the foreign-currency risk premium is the difference between the (domestic) risk premia on asset j and bond f, respectively, plus some cross terms. Solnik (73) assumes that, for all assets j, $cov_{j,f} = \sigma_f^2$ (see Appendix C). For the domestic bond, which has $\mu_j = r$ and $cov_{j,f} = 0$, (A1) simplifies to

$$\mu_d^f - r_f = -(r_f + \phi_f - r) + \sigma_f^2. \tag{A3}$$

Let $K_f = [0, 0, ..., 0, 1, 0, ...0]'$, an N×1 vector with unity for bond f, zero elsewhere;

$$G_f = \begin{bmatrix} 1 & 0 & & 0 & 0 & 0 & & 0 & 0 \\ 0 & 1 & & 0 & 0 & 0 & & 0 & 0 \\ \vdots & \vdots & & \vdots & \vdots & \vdots & & \vdots & \vdots \\ 0 & 0 & & 1 & 0 & 0 & & 0 & 0 \\ -1 & -1 & & -1 & -1 & -1 & & -1 & -1 \\ 0 & 0 & & 0 & 1 & 0 & & 0 & 0 \\ 0 & 0 & & 0 & 0 & 1 & & 0 & 0 \\ \vdots & \vdots & & \vdots & \vdots & \vdots & & \vdots & \vdots \\ 0 & 0 & & 0 & 0 & 0 & & 1 & 0 \end{bmatrix},$$

which is an N×N matrix, with the −1 elements in the row that corresponds to bond f. With these definitions, one can relate the home-currency and foreign-currency expected excess returns as

$$[\ \mu^f - r_f\ ] \ = \ G_f^{\cdot} \{ [\underline{\mu} - \underline{r}] - \Omega\ K_f \} \ . \tag{A4}$$

This establishes the link between $[\ \mu^f - r_f\ ]$ and $[\underline{\mu} - \underline{r}]$, in the following way:

- all assets preceding bond f in the domestic opportunity set are translated according to (A2);
- all assets following bond f in the domestic opportunity set are translated according to (A2), but are stored one position higher. That is, asset j, which has the j-th position in $[\underline{\mu} - \underline{r}]$, obtains the (j–1)-th position in $[\ \mu^f - r_f\ ]$;
- the domestic bond is translated according to (A3) and the result is stored in position N.

2 - FOREIGN CURRENCY COVARIANCES

From (A1):

$$cov_{j,k}^f = cov_{j,k} - cov_{j,f} - cov_{k,f} + \sigma_f^2 \ . \tag{A5}$$

Hence, with the same change of positions,

$$\Omega^f \ = \ G_f^{\cdot}\ \Omega\ G_f \ . \tag{A6}$$

3 - INDEPENDENCE OF NATIONALITY

The composition of the stock-bond portfolio held by a resident of country f is

$$y_N^f \ \equiv \ (\Omega^f)^{-1}\ [\ \mu^f - r_f\ ] \ , \qquad\qquad \text{for the risky assets}$$

$$y_{N+1}^f \ \equiv \ 1 - \underline{c}'\ (\Omega^f)^{-1}\ [\ \mu^f - r_f\ ] \ . \qquad\qquad \text{for bond f}$$

From (A4) and A6, then,

$$y_N^f \ \equiv \ (\Omega^f)^{-1}\ [\ \mu^f - r_f\ ] \ = \ \{ (G_f)^{-1}\ \Omega^{-1}\ (G_f^{\cdot})^{-1} \}\ \left[G_f^{\cdot} \{ [\underline{\mu} - \underline{r}] - \Omega\ K_f \} \right]$$

$$= \ (G_f)^{-1}\ \Omega^{-1}\ [\underline{\mu} - \underline{r}] - (G_f)^{-1}\ K_f \ \ .$$

Multiplying both sides by G_f, we conclude that

$$G_f\ y_N^f \ + K_f \ = \ y_N \ \ ,$$

or

$$
\begin{bmatrix}
1 & 0 & & 0 & 0 & 0 & & 0 & 0 \\
0 & 1 & & 0 & 0 & 0 & & 0 & 0 \\
\vdots & \vdots & & \vdots & \vdots & \vdots & & \vdots & \vdots \\
0 & 0 & & 1 & 0 & 0 & & 0 & 0 \\
-1 & -1 & & -1 & -1 & -1 & & -1 & -1 \\
0 & 0 & & 0 & 1 & 0 & & 0 & 0 \\
0 & 0 & & 0 & 0 & 1 & & 0 & 0 \\
\vdots & \vdots & & \vdots & \vdots & \vdots & & \vdots & \vdots \\
0 & 0 & & 0 & 0 & 0 & & 1 & 0
\end{bmatrix}
y_N^f +
\begin{bmatrix}
0 \\ 0 \\ \vdots \\ 0 \\ 1 \\ 0 \\ 0 \\ \vdots \\ 0
\end{bmatrix}
= y_n \quad ,
$$

or

$$
\begin{bmatrix}
y_1^f \\
y_2^f \\
\vdots \\
y_{f-1}^f \\
1 - \sum_{j=1}^N y_1^f \\
y_f^f \\
\vdots \\
y_{N-1}^f
\end{bmatrix}
=
\begin{bmatrix}
y_1 \\
y_2 \\
\vdots \\
y_{f-1} \\
y_f \\
y_{f+1} \\
\vdots \\
y_N
\end{bmatrix}
. \tag{A7}
$$

Since an asset j following f in the domestic opportunity set is assigned the $(j-1)$-th position in the foreign opportunity set, (A7) establishes that both investors will hold exactly the same proportions of assets (other than the reference currency bond and bond f) in their internationally diversified stock-bond portfolio. Moreover, $y_{N+1}^f \equiv 1 - \sum_{j=1}^N y_j^f = y_f$: also the weights of country f's bond are identical. Finally, since the weights of both vectors must sum to unity, the investors must also obtain the same weights for the reference currency bond. Q.E.D.

APPENDIX B

PROOF THAT HEDGED EXCESS RETURNS ARE INDEPENDENT OF NATIONALITY AND THAT THE ZERO INVESTMENT HEDGED STOCK FUND HAS THE SAME COMPOSITION FOR ALL INVESTORS

From (A6), we know that

$$\Omega^f = G_f' \; \Omega \; G_f .$$

Partitioning G_f into parts corresponding to stocks and bonds, yields

$$G_f = \begin{bmatrix} I_{n \times n} & 0_{n \times L} \\ G_3 & G_4 \end{bmatrix} ,$$

where

$I_{n \times n}$, is an n×n identity matrix

$0_{n \times L}$ is an n×L matrix of zeros

$$G_3 = \begin{bmatrix} 0 & 0 & \cdots & 0 \\ 0 & 0 & \cdots & 0 \\ \vdots & \vdots & \vdots & \vdots \\ -1 & -1 & \cdots & -1 \\ 0 & 0 & \cdots & 0 \\ \vdots & \vdots & \vdots & \vdots \\ 0 & 0 & \cdots & 0 \end{bmatrix} , \text{ an L×n Matrix with elements } -1 \text{ for bond f; and}$$

$$G_4 = \begin{bmatrix} 1 & 0 & 0 & 0 & 0 & 0 \\ 0 & 1 & 0 & 0 & 0 & 0 \\ \vdots & \vdots & \vdots & \vdots & \vdots & \vdots \\ 0 & 0 & 1 & 0 & 0 & 1 \\ -1 & -1 & -1 & -1 & -1 & -1 \\ 0 & 0 & 0 & 1 & 0 & 0 \\ \vdots & \vdots & \vdots & \vdots & \vdots & \vdots \\ 0 & 0 & 0 & 0 & 1 & 0 \end{bmatrix} , \text{ an L×L matrix.}$$

With this partitioning of G_f, we can expand $\Omega^f = G_f'\ \Omega\ G_f$ as

$$\Omega^f = \begin{bmatrix} \Omega_S + G_3'\ \Omega_{SB} + \Omega_{SB}\ G_3 + G_3'\ \Omega_B\ G_3 & , & \Omega_{SB}\ G_4 + G_3'\ \Omega_B\ G_4 \\[2mm] G_4'\ \Omega_{SB} + G_4'\ \Omega_B\ G_3 & , & G_4'\ \Omega_B\ G_4 \end{bmatrix}. \qquad (B1)$$

Denoting the regression coefficients of foreign-currency stock returns on a foreign-currency exchange rate changes by $[\delta]'$, $n{\times}L$, we see that

$$[\delta]' \equiv \Omega_{SB}^f\ (\Omega_S^f)^{-1}$$

$$= [\Omega_{SB}\ G_4 + G_3'\ \Omega_B\ G_4]\ [(G_4)^{-1}\ \Omega_B^{-1}\ (G_4')^{-1}]$$

$$= \{[\gamma]' + G_3'\}\ (G_4')^{-1}. \qquad (B2)$$

Corollary 1: This implies that excess returns on hedged stock are the same for all investors.

Proof: We start by proving that the covariance matrix of hedged stock returns is the same whatever the currency was in which the problem was first expressed. This covariance matrix, in currency f, equals

$$\Omega_{S|B}^f \equiv \Omega_S^f - [\delta]'\ \Omega_B^f\ [\delta]$$

$$= \{\Omega_S + G_3'\ \Omega_{SB}' + \Omega_{SB}\ G_3 + G_3'\ \Omega_B\ G_3\}$$

$$\quad - \{[\gamma]'+ G_3'\}(G_4')^{-1}\ (G_4'\ \Omega_B\ G_4)(G_4)^{-1}\{[\gamma] + G_3\}$$

$$= \{\Omega_S + G_3'\ \Omega_{SB}' + \Omega_{SB}\ G_3 + G_3'\ \Omega_B\ G_3\}$$

$$\quad - \{[\gamma]\ \Omega_B\ [\gamma] + G_3'\ \Omega_B\ [\gamma] + [\gamma]'\ \Omega_B\ G_3 + G_3'\ \Omega_B\ G_3\}$$

$$= \Omega_S - [\gamma]'\ \Omega_B\ [\gamma] \equiv \Omega_{S|B}. \qquad (B3)$$

The fact that the covariance matrices of hedged stocks are identical, whatever the currency, suggests that the random components in the hedged stock returns must be the same in all currencies. An example in a two-country world will be worked out below. Moreover, also the expected excess returns on hedged stock must be the same, because $\underline{y_n}$ $= \underline{y_n^f}$ (Appendix A) and because of the definition of $\underline{y_n}$ (equation (4) in the text).

Corollary 2: The composition of a zero-investment version of the hedged stock fund is the same for all investors of all nationalities.

Proof: A zero-investment version of the hedged stock fund is obtained by financing the investments in stock j by a short sale of the investor's domestic bond. In other words, for each stock one constructs the following zero-investment portfolio:
- a weight equal to + 1 for stock j;
- weights equal to $-\gamma_{j,g}$ for each of the foreign bonds g=1,..., L
- a weight for the investor's domestic bond equal to

$$-1 + \sum_{g=1}^{L} \gamma_{j,g} , \tag{B4}$$

with the minus one representing the loan needed to finance the investment in stock j, and the sum representing the re-investment of the proceeds of the foreign currency loans.

Note that the holdings of the foreign bonds g = 1,...,L are equal to *minus* $\gamma_{j,g}$. Therefore the holdings of the investor's domestic bond will likewise be denoted by *minus* $\gamma_{j,N+1}$. The same notation applies for the investor of country f, except that a δ is used instead of a γ.

From (B2), then,

$$[\delta]' G_4^1 - G_3^1 = [\gamma]' , \tag{B5}$$

or

$$\begin{bmatrix} \delta_{1,1} , \delta_{1,2} , \; \dots \, , \delta_{1,f-1} , 1 - \sum_{g=1}^{L} \delta_{1,g} , \delta_{1,f} , \; \dots, \delta_{1,L-1} \\ \vdots \qquad \vdots \qquad \vdots \\ \delta_{n,1} , \delta_{n,2} , \; \dots \, , \delta_{n,f-1} , 1 - \sum_{g=1}^{L} \delta_{n,g} , \delta_{n,f} , \dots \, , \delta_{n,L-1} \end{bmatrix} = \begin{bmatrix} \gamma_{1,1} , \gamma_{1,2} , \dots, \gamma_{1,L} \\ \vdots \qquad \vdots \qquad \vdots \\ \gamma_{n,1} , \gamma_{n,} , \dots, \gamma_{n,L} \end{bmatrix} . \tag{B6}$$

This implies that for the currencies g that precede currency f in the domestic (reference currency) opportunity set,

$$\delta_{j,g} = \gamma_{j,g} , \tag{B7}$$

and for the currencies g that were placed after f in the reference currency opportunity set,

$$\delta_{j,g} = \gamma_{j,g+1}. \tag{B8}$$

But the g-th asset in the foreign opportunity set is the (g+1)-th asset in the reference currency opportunity set, because of the rearrangement of the rows described in Appendix A. Therefore the reference currency investor and the investor of country f will hold exactly the same amounts of third currency bonds per unit of share j.

The country-f investor's holdings of his own currency bond, $-\delta_{j,N+1}$ per unit of share j, relate to the reference country investor's holdings of that bond as follows:

$$-\delta_{j,N+1} = -1 + \sum_{g=1}^{L} \delta_{j,g} \quad , \text{by definition}$$

$$= -\gamma_{j,f} \quad , \text{from (B6)}. \tag{B9}$$

Finally, since the sum of total bond holdings per unit of share must be equal to minus unity (zero-investment), and since for all assets other than the reference currency bonds both portfolios are equal, the weights of the reference currency bonds must be equal in both portfolios. Indeed,

$$-\gamma_{j,N+1} = -1 + \sum_{g=1}^{L} \gamma_{j,g} \quad , \text{by definition}$$

$$= -1 + \sum_{g=1}^{f-1} \gamma_{j,g} + \gamma_{j,f} + \sum_{g=f+1}^{L} \gamma_{j,g}$$

$$= -1 + \sum_{g=1}^{f-1} \delta_{j,g} + (1 - \sum_{g=1}^{L} \delta_{j,g}) + \sum_{g=f+1}^{L} \delta_{j,g}, \text{from (B6)}$$

$$= -\delta_{j,L}, \tag{B10}$$

where the L-th bond in the foreign opportunity set indeed is the reference-currency bond. So both investors will also hold the same amounts of this last asset, per unit of stock.

Corollary 3. If hedged stock is defined as a full-investment position, then it suffices to add a unit forward contract to a stock which is hedged in terms of the reference currency in order to hedge it also in terms of a foreign currency.

Proof: To obtain the results for a non-zero-investment portfolio, it suffices to remove, from the proof of Corollary 2, the −1 term in the investor's holdings of his own country bond. It immediately follows that, if i(d) denotes an individual from the reference country and j(f) one from the foreign country, then

$$
\begin{aligned}
i(d)\text{'s holdings of bond d} &= j(f)\text{'s holdings} + 1 \\
i(d)\text{'s holdings of bond f} &= j(f)\text{'s holdings} - 1 \\
i(d)\text{'s holdings of other bonds} &= j(f)\text{'s holdings}.
\end{aligned}
$$

So if investor i of country d buys stock which is hedged from country f's point of view, he only has to add a loan in currency f and invest the proceeds in his own money market in order to obtain a stock which is hedged from his own point of view. This is equivalent to selling forward currency f.

A Two-country example. Assume two countries d and f. Denote the numéraire by superscript d or f to the market price V_j of stock j. By definition, the excess return on hedged stock from the point of view of a country-f investor is

$$\begin{bmatrix} \text{country f} \\ \text{hedged return} \end{bmatrix} = \left[\frac{d\, V_j^f}{V_j^f} - r_f\, dt \right] - \frac{cov_{j,d}^f}{(\sigma_d^f)^2} \left[r_d\, dt + \frac{d\, S_d^f}{S_d^f} - r_f\, dt \right], \tag{B11}$$

where $\dfrac{cov_{j,d}^f}{(\sigma_d^f)^2} = \delta_{j,d}$, stock j's exposure to currency d exchange risk (in numéraire f).

Below, we first expand the foreign-currency stock return using (A1); we then use (C2) and the definition $\gamma_{j,f} = \dfrac{cov_{j,f}^d}{(\sigma_f^d)^2}$. Thus, the first term on the right hand side of (B11) is

$$\frac{d\, V_j^f}{V_j^f} = \frac{d\, V_j^d}{V_j^d} - \left[\frac{d\, S_f^d}{S_f^d} + (\sigma_f^d)^2\, dt \right] - cov_{j,f}^d\, dt$$

$$= \frac{d\, V_j^d}{V_j^d} - \frac{d\, S_d^f}{S_d^f} - \gamma_{j,f}\, (\sigma_f^d)^2 . \tag{B12}$$

Likewise, one implication of (A1), (C2), and the definition of $\gamma_{j,f}$ is that

$$\delta_{j,d} \equiv \frac{cov_{j,d}^f}{(\sigma_d^f)^2} = - \frac{cov_{j,f}^d - (\sigma_f^d)^2}{(\sigma_f^d)^2} = 1 - \gamma_{j,f} . \tag{B13}$$

This last result confirms Corollary 3. Using (B12) and (B13), (B11) becomes

$$\begin{bmatrix} \text{country f hedged} \\ \text{excess return} \end{bmatrix} = \left\{ \frac{d\, V_j^d}{V_j^d} - \frac{d\, S_d^f}{S_d^f} - \gamma_{j,f}\, (\sigma_f^d)^2 - r_f\, dt \right\} + (1 - \gamma_{j,f}) \left\{ r_f\, dt + \frac{d\, S_d^f}{S_d^f} - r_d\, dt \right\}$$

$$= \frac{d\, V_j^d}{V_j^d} - r_d\, dt - \gamma_{j,f} \left[r_f\, dt + [- \frac{d\, S_d^f}{S_d^f} + (\sigma_f^d)^2] - r_d\, dt \right]$$

$$= \frac{d\,V_j^d}{V_j^d} - r_d\,dt - \gamma_{j,f}\left[r_f\,dt + \frac{d\,S_f^d}{S_f^d} - r_d\,dt\right], \text{ from (C2)}.$$

This last expression is the excess hedged return from currency d's point of view. So corollary 1 is also confirmed.

APPENDIX C

SOLNIK'S OPPORTUNITY SET

In this section, we add an expectations operator, E(), to products of returns, although in an Ito world the realisation and the expectation of such a product are indistinguishable from each other and from the covariance between the two returns. In this notation, Solnik's assumption is that, for a stock jf from country f,

$$E\left[\frac{d\,V_{jf}^f}{V_{jf}^f}\cdot\frac{d\,S_f^d}{S_f^d}\right] = 0\,. \tag{C1}$$

Assumption (C1) says that the stock's return, when expressed in its home currency, is independent of the rate of appreciation of currency f relative to any reference country (superscript d). But in a frictionless capital market,

$$S_d^f = (S_f^d)^{-1}\,,$$

so that, from Ito's Lemma,

$$\frac{d\,S_d^f}{S_d^f} = -\frac{d\,S_f^d}{S_f^d} + (\sigma_f^d)^2\,dt \tag{C2}$$

$$= [-\phi_f^d + (\sigma_f^d)^2]\,dt + \sigma_f^d\,dz_d^f\,,$$

where ϕ_f^d is the expected rate of appreciation of currency f in money d per unit of time, and the last term is the random component in the rate of appreciation. Equation (C2) shows that when currency f is not expected to appreciate in money d (i.e., $\phi_f^d = 0$) then the expected rate of appreciation of currency d in terms of f will be nonzero if there is uncertainty about the future exchange rate. We immediately infer that Solnik's assumption of zero expected rates of appreciation in terms of the reference currency is not sufficient to obtain zero expected rates of appreciation in terms of other currencies—unless all $(\sigma_f^d)^2$ are zero. Since this last condition rules out exchange risk, this can hardly have been Solnik's intention.

With the help of (C2), assumption (C1) can be reinterpreted as

$$0 = E\left[\frac{d\,V_{jf}^f}{V_{jf}^f}\frac{d\,S_f^d}{S_f^d}\right] = -E\left[\frac{d\,V_{jf}^f}{V_{jf}^f}\cdot\frac{d\,S_d^f}{S_d^f}\right] \quad \text{(from (C2))}$$

$$= -\text{cov}_{jf,d}^f\,dt\,. \tag{C3}$$

Equation (C3) is similar to (C1) except that both rates are now expressed in the same currency, namely f. In other words, the stock's rate of return, expressed in its home currency, is assumed to be independent of the rate of appreciation of currency d in terms of money f. Since the reference currency is arbitrary, similar conditions must hold for all third currencies g:

$$\mathrm{cov}^f_{jf,g} = 0. \tag{C4}$$

With these results, it follows that stock jf's return, measured in reference currency d, behaves exactly as a currency f bond as far as its covariances with exchange rates are concerned. First consider the covariance between the return on stock jf and the f-th exchange rate. From (A1), we have

$$\mathrm{E}\left[\frac{d\,V^f_{jf}}{V^f_{jf}} \cdot \frac{d\,S^d_f}{S^d_f}\right] = \mathrm{E}\left[\frac{d\,V^d_{jf}}{V^d_{jf}} \cdot \frac{d\,S^d_f}{S^d_f}\right] - \mathrm{E}\left[\frac{d\,S^d_f}{S^d_f}\right]^2$$

$$= [\mathrm{cov}^d_{jf,f} - (\sigma^d_f)^2]dt\ .$$

But (C1) assumes that the left hand side of this expression is zero. Therefore, (C1) implies that

$$\mathrm{cov}^d_{jf,f} = (\sigma^d_f)^2. \tag{C5}$$

Equation (C5) can be interpreted as follows. If the FF price of a French stock on average remains the same when exchange rates change, then a 1% appreciation of the FF in Brussels must on average be associated with a 1% rise of the stock's price in BF. Equation (C5) indeed says that, in a regression of the BF return from the French asset on the rate of change of the FF spot rate, the slope coefficient is equal to unity—under the independence assumption. An alternative way of summarizing (C5) is to say that stock jf behaves as bond f as far as its covariance with exchange rate f is concerned. To demonstrate that this last proposition also holds w.r.t. third currencies g, start from the arbitrage condition

$$V^d_{jf} = V^f_{jf}\,S^d_f\ .$$

This implies that

$$\frac{d\,V^d_{jf}}{V^d_{jf}} = \frac{d\,V^f_{jf}}{V^f_{jf}} + \frac{d\,S^d_f}{S^d_f} + \mathrm{E}\left[\frac{d\,V^f_{jf}}{V^f_{jf}}\frac{d\,S^d_f}{S^d_f}\right]. \tag{C6}$$

Consider the implications for the covariance of the return on asset jf with the country-g exchange rate. From (C6),

$$E\left[\frac{d\,V_{jf}^d\; d\,S_g^d}{V_{jf}^d\quad S_g^d}\right] \;=\; E\left[\frac{d\,V_{jf}^f\; d\,S_g^d}{V_{jf}^f\quad S_g^d}\right] + E\left[\frac{d\,S_f^d\; d\,S_g^d}{S_f^d\quad S_g^d}\right] \tag{C7}$$

On the other hand, the arbitrage condition $S_g^d = S_f^d\, S_g^f$ means that

$$\frac{d\,S_g^d}{S_g^d} = \frac{d\,S_f^d}{S_f^d} + \frac{d\,S_g^f}{S_g^f} + E\left[\frac{d\,S_f^d\; d\,S_g^f}{S_f^d\quad S_g^f}\right].$$

With the help of this result, we can expand the first covariance on the right hand side of (C7) into the sum of two covariances. (C7) then becomes

$$E\left[\frac{d\,V_{jf}^d\; d\,S_g^d}{V_{jf}^d\quad S_g^d}\right] = E\left[\frac{d\,V_{jf}^f\; d\,S_f^d}{V_{jf}^f\quad S_f^d}\right] + E\left[\frac{d\,V_{jf}^f\; d\,S_g^f}{V_{jf}^f\quad S_g^f}\right] + E\left[\frac{d\,S_f^d\; d\,S_g^d}{S_f^d\quad S_g^d}\right]$$

But from (C1) and (C4), each of the first two terms on the right hand side is zero. We conclude that, in terms of the reference currency, all covariance between stock jf's return and the rate of change of exchange rate g is due to covariance between currencies f and g:

$$cov_{jf.g}^d\; dt \;=\; cov_{f.g}^d\; dt\,. \tag{C8}$$

Finally, the independence assumption means that also for a stock jd of the reference country,

$$cov_{jd.g}^d \;=\; 0\;,\; g=1,\dots f,\dots L\,. \tag{C9}$$

Assuming, for national convenience, one representative stock per country and assigning row and column L to the reference-country stock, we conclude that the covariance matrix in any reference currency must look like:

$$\Omega \;=\; \begin{bmatrix} \Omega_S\;(L+1\times L+1) & \Omega_B\;(L\times L) \\ & \begin{matrix} 0\,0\,0\,0\dots0 \\ 0 \\ 0 \\ 0 \end{matrix} \\ \Omega_B\;(L\times L) & \begin{matrix} 0 \\ 0 \end{matrix}\;\Omega_B\;(L\times L) \end{bmatrix}
\begin{matrix} \text{(L foreign stocks)} \\ \\ \text{(domestic stock)} \\ \\ \\ \\ \text{(L foreign bonds)} \end{matrix} \tag{C10}$$

Corollary 1 : it immediately follows that the exposure matrix $[\gamma] \equiv \Omega_{SB}\,\Omega_B^{-1}$ has the form:

$$[\gamma]' = \begin{bmatrix} 1 & 0 & 0 & \ldots & 0 \\ 0 & 1 & 0 & \ldots & 0 \\ 0 & 0 & 1 & \ldots & 0 \\ \vdots & \vdots & \vdots & \vdots & \vdots \\ 0 & 0 & 0 & \ldots & 1 \\ \hline 0 & 0 & 0 & \ldots & 0 \end{bmatrix}, \qquad \begin{array}{l} \text{(L foreign stocks)} \\[3.5em] \text{(domestic stock)} \end{array}$$

that is, the domestic asset is not exposed, and an asset from any country g has unit exposure to currency g and zero exposure to any other currency. For foreign stocks, one forward exchange contract suffices to hedge the stock.

Corollary 2: the excess returns on hedged stocks are equal to the excess returns on the same stocks expressed in their respective home country currencies:

Proof: from Corollary 1 and the general definition of a hedged stock excess return, we obtain:

$$\frac{d\,V_{jf}^d}{V_{jf}^d} - r_d\,dt - \left[r_f\,dt + \frac{d\,S_f^d}{S_f^d} - r_d\,dt \right] = \frac{d\,V_{jf}^d}{V_{jf}^d} - \frac{d\,S_f^d}{S_f^d} - r_f\,dt$$

$$= \frac{d\,V_{jf}^f}{V_{jf}^f} - r_f\,dt, \text{ from (A1) and (C5).}$$

Q.E.D. Obviously then the covariance matrix of hedged returns and the expected excess return on hedged stocks are independent of the reference currency. This last property holds also in the general case, as shown in Appendix B.

Corollary 3:   Since covariances of foreign bond returns with stock returns are indistinguishable from covariances among foreign bonds, equilibrium conditions on expected returns for foreign bonds will seem not to contain covariance terms with the stock market portfolio.

APPENDIX D

DERIVATION OF THE COUNTRY WEIGHTS IN F AND Ī

In vector notation, (14), (16) or (17) can be written as

$$
\mu_j - r = (\text{cov}_{j,M}, \text{cov}_{j,1}, \ldots, \text{cov}_{j,f}, \ldots, \text{cov}_{j,L})
\begin{bmatrix}
\bar{\bar{\eta}} \\
\dfrac{W_1}{W}(1-\bar{\alpha}_1) \\
\vdots \\
\dfrac{W_f}{W}(1-\bar{\alpha}_f) \\
\vdots \\
\dfrac{W_L}{W}(1-\bar{\alpha}_L)
\end{bmatrix}.
\tag{D1}
$$

This must hold for the market portfolio M and for each of the L foreign bonds:

$$
\begin{bmatrix}
\mu_M - r \\
r_1 + \phi_1 - r \\
\vdots \\
r_L + \phi_L - r
\end{bmatrix}
=
\begin{bmatrix}
\sigma_M^2 & \underline{\text{cov}}'_{M,B} \\
& \\
\underline{\text{cov}}_{M,B} & \Omega_B
\end{bmatrix}
\begin{bmatrix}
\bar{\bar{\eta}} \\
\dfrac{W_1}{W}(1-\bar{\alpha}_1) \\
\vdots \\
\dfrac{W_L}{W}(1-\bar{\alpha}_L)
\end{bmatrix},
\tag{D2}
$$

so that

$$
\begin{bmatrix}
\bar{\bar{\eta}} \\
\dfrac{W_1}{W}(1-\bar{\alpha}_1) \\
\vdots \\
\dfrac{W_L}{W}(1-\bar{\alpha}_L)
\end{bmatrix}
=
\begin{bmatrix}
\sigma_M^2 & \underline{\text{cov}}'_{M,B} \\
& \\
\underline{\text{cov}}_{M,B} & \Omega_B
\end{bmatrix}^{-1}
\begin{bmatrix}
\mu_M - r \\
r_1 + \phi_1 - r \\
\vdots \\
r_L + \phi_L - r
\end{bmatrix}.
\tag{D3}
$$

Since the interest rates are observable, it suffices to know the joint distribution of market returns and the various exchange rates to obtain the country weights in bond fund F and the world representative inflation rate Ī, $[W_L(1-\bar{\alpha}_L)]/[W(1-\bar{\bar{\alpha}}_L)]$. Note that exactly the same information is also necessary in the hedged-stock IAPM (11a) and the multi-factor IAPM (11b).

From (D3) we also immediately obtain (11b). This follows upon using (D3) to eliminate the vector of premia in (D1), and because

$$[\text{cov}_{j,M}, \text{cov}_{j,1} \ldots \text{cov}_{j,L}] \begin{bmatrix} \sigma_M^2 & \underline{\text{cov}}'_{M,B} \\ \underline{\text{cov}}_{M,B} & \Omega_B \end{bmatrix}^{-1} = [\beta_{j,M}, \delta_{j,1}, \ldots \delta_{j,L}] , \quad (D4)$$

which is the vector of slope coefficients of the regression of j' s return on the market return and on all exchange rate changes.

REFERENCES

ADLER, M., and DUMAS, B.: Exchange Risk, Exposure, and the Relevance of Hedging; Working paper, revised November 1978, ESSEC, Cergy-Pontoise, France

BLACK, F.: Capital Market Equilibrium with Restricted Borrowing; *The Journal of Business* 45,July 1972, 444-454.

DUMAS, B.: Discussion (of Solnik (77)); *The Journal of Finance*, May 1977, 512-515.

DUMAS, B.: The Theory of the Trading Firm Revisited; *The Journal of Finance*, June 1978, 1019–1030.

FAMA, E.: *The Foundations of Finance*; Basic Books, New York, 1976.

FAMA, E. and FARBER, A.: Money, Bonds and Foreign Exchange; Working Paper, U.L.B. Brussels, Belgium, 1978

FISHER, S.: The Demand for Index Bonds; *The Journal of Political Economy*, 1975 (3), 509-535.

FRIEND, I., LANDSKRONER, Y., and LOSQ, E.: The Demand for Risky Assets under Uncertain Inflation; *The Journal of Finance*, December 1976, 1287–1297

GRAUER,. F.. LITZENBERGER,. R. and STEHLE, R.: Sharing Rules and Equilibrium an International Capital Market; *Journal of Financial Economics*, June 1976 3(3), 233-257

HAKANSSON, N.: On the Relevance of Inflation Accounting, *Journal of Accounting Research* 7, 1969.

LINTNER, J.: The Valuation of Risky Assets and the Selection of Risky Investments in Stock Portfolios and Capital Budgets; *Review of Economics and Statistics*, february 1965, 97–113.

MARKOWITZ, H.: Portfolio Selection; *The Journal of Finance*, March 1952, 77-91

MERTON, R.: An Intertemporal Capital Asset Pricing Model; *Econometrica*, September 1973, 867-887

ROLL. R.: A Critique of the Asset Pricing Theory's Tests, part 1; *The Journal of Financial Economics*, March 1977

SAMUELSON. P. and SWAMY, S.: Invariant Economic Index Numbers and Canonical Duality; *The American Economic Review* 64, 1975, 566-593

SERCU, P.: Mean-Variance Capital Asset Pricing with Uncertain Inflation and Deviations from Purchasing Power Parity; Working paper, K.U. Leuven, Belgium, 1980

SHARPE, W.: Capital Asset Prices: a Theory of Market Equilibrium under Conditions of Risk; *The Journal of Finance*, September 1964, 425-442

SOLNIK, B.: European Capital Markets, *Lexington Books*, 1973.

SOLNIK. B.: Testing International Pricing: Some Pessimistic Views; *The Journal of Finance*, May 1977, 503-512

STEHLE, R.: An Empirical Test of the Alternative Hypotheses of National and International Pricing of Risky Assets; *The Journal of Finance*, May 1977, 493-502

P. Sercu: A Generalization of the International Asset Pricing Model

Index to Notation

This table was not included in the original. Greek symbols are grouped at the back.

B (subscript)	denotes that the matrix refers to bond returns or exchange rates
$cov_{j,f}$, $cov^d_{j,f}$	covariance of the return on stock j with exchange rate f, all returns measured in currency d
$cov^f_{j,d}$	covariance of the return on stock j with exchange rate d, all returns measured in currency d
$cov_{j,\bar{I}}$	covariance of the return on stock j with the world currency basket (with price $\bar{I}$ in home currency)
$cov_{j,M\vert B}$	covariance of the return on stock j with the world market portfolio, conditional on the exchange rates (or on the bond returns)
$cov_{j,W}$	covariance of the return on stock j with the world market porfolio of all assets
$cov^*_{j,W}$	covariance between the real returns on stock j and on the world market portfolio of all assets, measured in terms of the world currency basket
$cov^f_{jf,g}$	covariance between the return on stock jf (from country f) and exchange rate (or bond) g, measured in currency f
$cov_{W,\bar{I}}$	covariance of the return on the world market porfolio of all assets with the world currency basket
$cov^d_{jf,g}$	covariance between the returns on stock j from country f and currency g, measured in the reference currency
$cov^d_{f,g}$	covariance between the returns on currencies f and g, measured in the reference currency
d	the domestic (reference) country
d (subscript)	refers to the reference country bond or exchange rate
d (superscript)	denotes that the variable is expressed in units of the reference currency
dz^f_d	random part in the rate of change of S^f_d
e	the N×1 vector with elements equal to unity (the summing operator)
f	a foreign country
f (superscript)	denotes that the variable is expressed in foreign currency
f (subscript)	refers to a foreign currency of bond
F	a bond portfolio with weights $[W_f(1-\bar{\alpha}_f)]/[W(1-\bar{\bar{\alpha}})]$
g(superscript)	denotes that the variable is expressed in units of foreign currency g
g (subscript)	refers to a foreign country other than f, its bond, or its exchange rate
G_f	N×N matrix defined on page 119
G_3	a partitioning of G_f, defined on page 122
G_4	a partitioning of G_f, defined on page 122
i (superscript)	denotes an individual investor
$\bar{I}$	price, in currency d, of a currency basket with $[W_f(1-\bar{\alpha}_f)]/[W(1-\bar{\bar{\alpha}})]$ as the weights
j, j subscript	denotes a particular stock of unstated origin
jf, jf subscript	denotes a particular stock from country f (in Solnik's model)

P. Sercu: A Generalization of the International Asset Pricing Model

K_f	1×L vector defined on page 119
L	the number of foreign bonds
L (subscript)	denotes the dimension of the matrix, or signals that the matrix includes foreign bonds (or exchange rates) only
M	the value of the world market portfolio (n stocks, but not including L+1 bonds if there are outside bonds)
M (subscript)	denotes the world market portfolio (n stocks, but not including L+1 bonds if there are outside bonds)
n	the number of stocks
n (subscript)	denotes the dimension of the matrix, or signals that the matrix includes stocks only
N	the number of risky assets (n stocks and L foreign bonds)
N (subscript)	denotes the dimension of the matrix, or signals that the matrix includes all risky assets (n stocks and L foreign bonds)
N+1	the total number of assets (N risky, and one riskfree)
N+1 (subscript)	denotes the reference-currency risk-free bond
r, r_d	the risk-free rate in the reference currency (d)
r^*	the risk-free rate in terms of the currency basket
r_f	the risk-free rate in currency f
$[\ r_f + \phi_f - r\ ]$	L×1 vector of excess expected returns on the L foreign bonds
S	a spot rate
S_d^f	value, in terms of currency f, of one unit of the reference currency (d)
S_f^g	value, in units of currency g, of one unit of currency f
S_g^d	value, in units of the reference currency (d), of one unit of currency g
S (subscript)	denotes that the matrix refers to stock returns
S_f^d, S_f	value, in terms of the reference currency, of one unit of currency f
V_j^d, V_j	value of stock j, measured in reference currency
V_{jf}^d	value, in units of the reference currency (d), of stock j from country f
V_j^f	value of stock j, measured in currency f
V_{jf}^f	value of stock j from country j, measured in currency f
w_n^i	n×1 vector of portfolio weights of the n stocks in investor i's portfolio
W^i	wealth of investor i (in reference currency)
W	the value of the world market portfolio (n stocks, plus L+1 bonds if there are outside bonds)
W (subscript)	refers to the world market portfolio (n stocks, plus L+1 bonds if there are outside bonds)
x_n	n×1 vector of weights of the n stocks in the world market portfolio
x_L	L×1 vector of weights of the L foreign bonds in the world market portfolio
y_n	n×1 vector of weights of the n stocks in the log utility portfolio
y_L	L×1 vector of weights of the L foreign bonds in the log utility portfolio

P. Sercu: A Generalization of the International Asset Pricing Model

$\underline{y}_N$	$N\times1$ vector of weights of the N risky assets in the log utility portfolio
y_{N+1}	weight of the N risk-free bond in the log utility portfolio
$\underline{y}_N^f$	$N\times1$ vector of weights of the in the log utility portfolio, computed from currency-f parameters
y_{N+1}^f	weights of the risk-free bond in the log utility portfolio, computed from currency-f parameters
$\underline{z}_n$	$n\times1$ vector of weights of the n stocks in the orthogonalized log utility portfolio
$\underline{z}_N$	$N\times1$ vector of weights of the N risky assets in the orthogonalized log utility portfolio
$\underline{z}_L$	$L\times1$ vector of weights of the L foreign bonds in the orthogonalized log utility portfolio
z_{N+1}	weight of the N risk-free bond in the orthogonalized log utility portfolio

$\bar{\alpha}$	the wealth-weighted mean risk tolerance of all investors from all countries
$\bar{\alpha}_f$	the wealth-weighted mean risk tolerance of all investors from country f
α^i	relative risk tolerance of investor i
$\beta_{j,w}$	regression coefficient of the return on stock j on the return on the world market portfolio of all assets
$[\gamma]$	$L\times n$ matrix of regression coefficients (n stocks on L exchange rates)
$[\delta]$	$L\times n$ matrix of regression coefficients (n stocks on L exchange rates), all returns measured in currency f
$\bar{\bar{\eta}}$	the inverse of $\bar{\bar{\alpha}}$, that is, the harmonic mean relative risk aversion
η^i	investor i's relative risk aversion
$[\underline{\mu}-r]$	$N\times1$ vector of excess expected returns on the n stocks, measured in home currency
$[\underline{\mu}-r]_n$	$n\times1$ vector of excess expected returns on the n stocks
$[\underline{\mu}^f-r_f]$	$N\times1$ vector of excess expected returns on the n stocks, measured in currency f
μ_F^*	expected real return on bond fund F, measured in terms of the world currency basket
μ_j	expected return on stock j
μ_j^f	expected return on stock j, expressed in units of currency f
μ_j^*	expected real return on stock j, measured in terms of the world currency basket
μ_M-r	the expected ecxcess return on the world stock market portfolio
μ_W^*	expected real return on the world market portfolio of all assets, measured in terms of the world currency basket

P. Sercu: A Generalization of the International Asset Pricing Model

σ_f^2, $(\sigma_f^d)^2$	variance of the rate of change of exchange rate f
σ_I^2	variance of the rate of change of the value of the world currency basket
$\sigma_{M\|B}^2$	variance of the return on the world market portfolio, conditional on the exchange rates (or on the bond returns)
σ_W^{*2}	variance of the real returns on stock j and on the world market portfolio of all assets, measured in terms of the world currency basket
ϕ_f^d, ϕ_f	expected rate of appreciation of currency f relative to the reference currency
Ω	N×N covariance matrix of returns on all risky assets (n stocks and L foreign bonds)
Ω^f	N×N covariance matrix of returns on all risky assets (n stocks and L foreign bonds), measured in currency f
Ω_B	L×L covariance matrix of L bond returns or exchange rates
Ω_S	n×n covariance matrix of L stock returns
Ω_{SB}	n×L covariance matrix of n stock returns with the L bonds or exchange rates
$\Omega_{S\|B}$	n×n covariance matrix of n stock returns conditional on exchange rates

[3]

Journal of Financial Economics 3 (1976) 233–256. © North-Holland Publishing Company

SHARING RULES AND EQUILIBRIUM IN AN INTERNATIONAL CAPITAL MARKET UNDER UNCERTAINTY*

Frederick L.A. GRAUER

Massachusetts Institute of Technology, Cambridge, Mass. 02139, U.S.A.

Robert H. LITZENBERGER

Stanford University, Stanford, Calif. 94305, U.S.A.

Richard E. STEHLE

University of Mannheim, Mannheim, West Germany

Received May 1975, revised version received December 1975

International capital market equilibrium is characterized for a world economy in which consumption preferences are defined multiplicatively over many commodities. It is shown that the set of relative asset prices under pure exchange in international capital markets depends on the real purchasing power of nominal payoffs under uncertainty and does not depend on the currency in which the nominal payoffs are denominated. A Sharpe–Lintner type international capital asset pricing model is derived as a special case. Proportional *ad valorem* commodity taxes and transportation costs are incorporated in the valuation model, interest rate parity and purchasing power parity are reinterpreted under uncertainty, and international differences in borrowing and lending are shown to reflect, in part, differences in risk aversion across countries.

1. Introduction

The international exchange of financial claims in a world economy composed of countries limited to consumption of a single but different commodity, such as in Solnik (1974), precludes the international transfer of financial claims on real wealth between residents of different countries. In the present paper, international capital market equilibrium is characterized for a world economy in which consumption preferences are defined over many commodities and are not strictly separated nationally. The international exchange of financial claims thus permits the transfer of real wealth between residents of different countries. Assuming individuals have multiplicative utility functions for consumption of many commodities, closed-form valuation equations for forward foreign exchange contracts and other risky assets are derived. Interest rate

*Comments of Fischer Black are acknowledged. Responsibility for any errors rests, as usual, with the authors.

parity, purchasing power parity, foreign exchange risk, commodity trade barriers and international capital flows are interpreted in this framework.

2. Asset choice and allocational efficiency in an international capital market

Assume individuals have concave Von Neumann–Morgenstern utility functions for lifetime consumption. Consider then the choice problem of an individual resident in the nth country in a two-period time–state preference model.

$$\text{Max} \sum_s \pi_s U_s(c_{10}, \ldots, c_{z0}; c_{1s}, \ldots, c_{zs}), \tag{1}$$

subject to

$$\sum_i c_{i0} P_{i0n} + \sum_j \alpha_j V_{jn} \leqq w_{0n}, \tag{2}$$

$$\sum_i c_{is} P_{isn} \leqq \sum_j \alpha_j X_{jsn}, \qquad \forall s, \tag{3}$$

$w_{0n} =$ the individual's nominal wealth in period 0 denominated in the unit of account of the nth $(n \in N)$ country;

$X_{jsn} =$ the nominal payoff in state $s(s \in S)$ of the jth $(j \in J)$ asset denominated in the unit of account of the nth country;

$V_{jn} =$ the market value of the jth asset denominated in the unit of account of the nth country;

$\alpha_j =$ the fraction of the jth asset owned by the individual;

$c_{i0}, c_{is} =$ the number of units of commodity i $(i \in I)$ the individual consumes in period 0 and state s, (period 1) respectively;

$P_{i0n}, P_{isn} =$ the price of commodity i denominated in the unit of account of the nth country in period 0 and state s, (period 1) respectively;

$U_s(\cdot) =$ the individual's strictly concave Von Neumann–Morgenstern utility function for lifetime consumption contingent on the occurrence of state s;

$\pi_s =$ the individual's assessment of the probability of occurrence of state s.

In Arrow's (1964) framework, the individual solves the choice problem recursively in an instantaneous sequence of markets. Under the assumption of time–state independent utility functions, the recursion may be viewed as having three stages. In the first stage and subsequent to the revelation of the state of the world, the individual allocates under certainty his nominal wealth in state s, $w_{sn} = \sum_j \alpha_j X_{jsn}$, among consumption commodities to achieve a consumptive optimum in period 1. In the second stage, the individual allocates under certainty his consumption budget in period 0, $c_{0n} = w_{0n} - \sum_j \alpha_j V_{jn}$, to achieve his consumptive optimum in period 0. The optimal solutions to the first two stages induce an indirect utility function defined over nominal consumption expenditures in period 0 and state-contingent claims on nominal wealth, $U_s(c_{0n}, w_{sn})$. In the third stage, the individual allocates his endowed nominal wealth in period 0 among consumption expenditure in period 0, c_{0n}, and investment in assets, α_j for all j. The individual's induced choice problem under uncertainty can be characterized by the following Lagrangean,

$$\max_{c_{0n}, \alpha_j \in J} \quad L = E[U_s(c_{0n}, w_{sn})] - \lambda \left(c_{0n} + \sum_j \alpha_j V_{jn} - w_{0n} \right). \tag{4}$$

From the first-order conditions, the individual's marginal rate of substitution between consumption expenditure in period 0 and investment in the jth asset equals the price of the jth asset where the currency of the nth country in period 0 is the numéraire (the price of one unit of c_{0n} is unity),

$$-\left. \frac{\partial c_{0n}}{\partial \alpha_j} \right|_U = -\sum_s \left[\left. \frac{\partial c_{0n}}{\partial w_{sn}} \right|_U \right] X_{jsn} = V_{jn}. \quad \forall j, \tag{5}$$

where

$(\partial c_{0n}/\partial \alpha_j)|_U$ is the individual's marginal rate of substitution between consumption expenditure in period 0 and investment in the jth asset;

$(\partial c_{0n}/\partial w_{sn})|_U$ is the individual's marginal rate of substitution between consumption expenditure in period 0 and claims on nominal wealth contingent on state s where $U = E[U_s(C_{0n}, w_{sn})]$.

Given unrestricted and costless movement of capital across national boundaries, the price of the jth asset in the nth and mth countries differs by a scalar, the spot exchange rate in period 0 between the respective currencies. That is, $V_{jn} = \Omega_{0nm} V_{jm}$, where Ω_{0nm} is the spot exchange rate in period 0 between the nth and mth currencies, or the number of units of the nth country's currency required to purchase one unit of the mth country's currency. The marginal rates of substitution between consumption expenditure in period 0 and investment in the jth asset for the hth and kth individuals resident in the mth and nth countries respectively differ, therefore, only by the multiplication of the spot exchange rate in period 0,

$$\left. \frac{\partial c_{0nk}}{\partial \alpha_{jk}} \right|_{U_k} = \left. \frac{\partial c_{0mh}}{\partial \alpha_{jh}} \right|_{U_h} \Omega_{0nm}, \quad \forall k, j, m. \tag{6}$$

Note that the multiplication of the hth individual's marginal rate of substitution by the spot exchange rate merely changes the numéraire for consumption expenditure in period 0 to the currency of the nth country. It follows from relation (6), that the international allocation of *existing* assets is Pareto efficient.

The international allocation of *existing* assets is Pareto efficient if no individual can be made better off by a redistribution of existing securities and present consumption without making one or more individuals worse off. A Pareto optimal international allocation of existing assets is obtained by distributing securities and present consumption to maximize a convex combination of the expected utility functions of individuals subject to conservation equations. From the first-order conditions for maximization, relation (6) follows.

The degree to which payoffs from existing securities span the state–space constrains the set of feasible allocations of state-contingent claims on nominal wealth. However, the currency in which a payoff is denominated does not affect its linear independence from (or linear dependence on) the real payoffs of other assets. That is, since the state of the world resolves all uncertainty with respect to spot exchange rates in period 1, the currency in which an asset payoff is denominated does not affect the spanning of the state space. Therefore,

$$\frac{\partial c_{0mh}}{\partial w_{smh}}\bigg|_{U_h} \frac{\Omega_{0nm}}{\Omega_{snm}} = \frac{\partial c_{0nh}}{\partial w_{snh}}\bigg|_{\bar{U}_h}, \tag{7}$$

the international allocation of *state-contingent* claims on nominal wealth is Pareto efficient if and only if the marginal rates of substitution between present consumption and state-contingent claims on nominal wealth are equal for residents of all countries, when expressed in terms of an arbitrary numéraire currency. The international allocation of *state-contingent* claims on nominal wealth is Pareto efficient if no individual can be made better off by a redistribution of state-contingent claims on nominal wealth and present consumption without making one or more individuals worse off.

A Pareto optimal allocation of state-contingent claims on nominal wealth is obtained by distributing state-contingent claims and present consumption to maximize a convex combination of the expected utility functions of all individuals in the economy subject to conservation equations. Relation (7) follows from the first-order condition for this maximization. It follows that in a complete international capital market, where the number of assets having linearly independent payoffs equal the number of states of the world, unrestricted international capital flows are sufficient for the international allocation of state-contingent claims on nominal wealth to be Pareto efficient.

Unrestricted flows of commodities and services across national boundaries are not a necessary condition for the allocation of state-contingent claims on nominal wealth to be efficient. However, imperfections in international commodimarkets are shown to require stronger conditions on the spanning of the state–space in order to achieve an efficient allocation of state-contingent claims on nominal wealth.

3. Closed-form valuation in an international capital market with commodity price uncertainty and unrestricted international trade

Assume international exchange of commodities and capital is unrestricted and costless and the state space spanned by the payoffs from existing assets permits a Pareto optimal international allocation of state-contingent claims on nominal wealth. To derive closed-form valuation equations for assets also assume that individuals have Von Neumann–Morgenstern utility functions multiplicative in consumption commodities and time–state independent in total time–state consumption,

$$U(\cdot) = \alpha_0 \left(\delta + \prod_i c_{i0}^{\beta_i} \right)^\gamma + \alpha_1 \left(\delta + \prod_i c_{is}^{\beta_i} \right)^\gamma, \tag{8}$$

where

$$\sum_i \beta_i = 1 \quad \text{and} \quad \gamma < 1 \quad \text{and}$$

$$\alpha_t > 0 \quad \text{where} \quad \gamma \geqq 0 \quad \text{for} \quad t = 0, 1, \quad \textit{or}$$

$$\alpha_t < 0 \quad \text{where} \quad \gamma < 0 \quad \text{for} \quad t = 0, 1.$$

This utility function is state independent in the sense of zero complementarity of consumption claims across states or 'no regret'. In other words, the utility of a given consumption sequence does not depend on what the individual's consumption sequence might have been had another state occurred. State independent utility is necessary to derive the expected utility rule and is implied by the strong independence axiom. The homotheticity of the multiplicative utility function is necessary to solve the price index problem, as noted by Samuelson and Swamy (1974). The time additive property (or zero complementarity of consumption claims over time) and the specification of $\beta_{i0} = \beta_{i1} = \beta_i$ and $\gamma_0 = \gamma_1 = \gamma$ in the utility function above are for notational convenience. A more general formulation would not alter the main analytical results. When $\delta \gtreqless 0$, then the utility function displays increasing, constant or decreasing relative risk aversion, respectively. For non-zero δ individuals may borrow or lend. As will be shown subsequently, heterogeneity with respect to δ among countries may be viewed as one source of international borrowing and lending.

From the multiplicative utility function (8) an induced utility function for the hth ($h \in n$) individual defined over consumption expenditure in period 0 and state-contingent real wealth may be derived,[1]

---

[1]Derivation of the induced utility function follows the recursive procedure outlined in section 2. Litzenberger and Grauer (1974) and Rubinstein (1974) provide a detailed derivation for similar utility functions. Stehle (forthcoming) derives valuation equations in international market equilibrium using the logarithmic utility function.

$$U_{sh}(\cdot) = [A_{hn} + c_{0hn}]^{\gamma} + (\alpha_{1h}/\alpha_{0h})[A_{hn} + I_{shn}^{-1}w_{shn}]^{\gamma}, \qquad \forall\, s, h, \qquad (9)$$

where $(\alpha_{1h}/\alpha_{0h})$ is the hth individual's "impatience" factor, and

$$A_h \equiv \delta_h \left[\left(\prod_i \beta_{ih}^{\beta_{ih}}\right)\left(\prod_i P_{i0n}^{-\beta_{ih}}\right)\right]^{-1}, \qquad I_{shn} \equiv \prod_i \left[\frac{P_{isn}}{P_{i0n}}\right]^{\beta_{ih}}.$$

Note that $\beta_{ih} = P_{isn}c_{ish}w_{shn}^{-1}$ is the hth individual's average propensity to consume commodity i.[2] This geometric price index may be viewed as a payoff from an 'indexed' or 'purchasing power parity' bond, whose state-contingent payoff, if held as the individual's sole source of nominal wealth in period 1, would leave the individual just indifferent between facing state s commodity prices and facing some other state θ commodity prices denominated in the nth country's unit of account.

Assume individuals share identical probability assessments, β_i's, and γ's. Since international commodity trade is unrestricted and costless, residents of different countries face the same relative prices of commodities thus, using the law of corresponding addition, the world's commodity price index may be expressed as follows:

$$I_{sn} \equiv \prod_i \left\{\left[\frac{P_{isn}}{P_{i0n}}\right]^{(P_{isn}C_{is})^{\frac{1}{2}}(P_{i0n}C_{0n})^{\frac{1}{2}}}\right\} W_{sn}^{-\frac{1}{2}}C_{0n}^{-\frac{1}{2}}$$

$$= (\Omega_{snm}/\Omega_{0nm})\, I_{sm},$$

$C_{i0} \equiv \sum_m \sum_{h\in m} c_{i0h}$ is aggregate international consumption of commodity i in period 0 (note that c_{i0h} is the hth resident's of the mth country consumption of commodity i in period 0);

$C_{is} \equiv \sum_m \sum_{h\in m} c_{ish}$ is aggregate international consumption of commodity i in state s;

$C_{0n} \equiv \sum_m \sum_{h\in m} \sum_i P_{i0m} c_{i0h}\Omega_{0nm}$ is aggregate international consumption expenditure in period 0 denominated in the nth country's unit of account;

$W_{sn} \equiv \sum_m \sum_{h\in m} w_{shm}\Omega_{snm}$ is aggregate international nominal wealth in state s denominated in the nth country's unit of account.

This geometric price index was introduced in a discussion of the statistical properties of index numbers by Walsh (1901) and later discussed by Fisher (1927). While the index is unique to the multiplicative utility function, no other

---

[2]As the differencing interval approaches zero asymptotically, geometric and arithmetic rates of return converge to the same value. Thus an empirical proxy for a geometric commodity price index in discrete time would be a Laspeyre or Paasche index.

F.L.A. Grauer et al., International capital market equilibrium   239

utility function is known to induce an exact symmetric closed-form representation of prices in the aggregate. From identity of consumption preferences and free trade, $I_{shn} = I_{sn}$ for all h in all countries. Using utility function (9) in relation (4), the individual's marginal rate of substitution between consumption expenditures in period 0 and nominal wealth contingent on state s is derived from the first-order conditions for optimality,

$$\frac{\partial c_{Ohn}}{\partial w_{shn}}\bigg|_U = \frac{\pi_s\{A_{hn}+I_{sn}^{-1}w_{shn}\}^{\gamma-1}I_{sn}^{-1}}{(\alpha_{Oh}/\alpha_{1h})\{A_{hn}+c_{Ohn}\}^{\gamma-1}}. \tag{10}$$

Since the marginal rate of substitution between consumption expenditure in period 0 and nominal wealth contingent on state s in equilibrium equals a constant across individuals, the law of corresponding addition and the market-clearing condition $W_{sn} = \sum_m \sum_{h\in m} w_{shm}\Omega_{snm}$ for all s may be used to write relation (10) as follows:

$$\frac{\partial c_{Ohn}}{\partial w_{shn}}\bigg|_U = \frac{\pi_s\{A_n+I_{sn}^{-1}W_{sn}\}^{\gamma-1}I_{sn}^{-1}}{\sum_m \sum_{h\in m}(\alpha_{Oh}/\alpha_{1h})\{A_{hn}+c_{Ohn}\}^{\gamma-1}}, \qquad \forall s, \tag{11}$$

where $A_n \equiv \sum_m\sum_{h\in m}A_{hn}$. Substituting relation (11) into relation (5), the price ratio in international market equilibrium denominated in the nth country's currency of the jth and lth assets is

$$\frac{V_{jn}}{V_{ln}} = \frac{E[(A_n+\tilde{I}_n^{-1}\tilde{W}_n)^{\gamma-1}\tilde{I}_n^{-1}\tilde{X}_{jn}]}{E[(A_n+\tilde{I}_n^{-1}\tilde{W}_n)^{\gamma-1}\tilde{I}_n^{-1}\tilde{X}_{ln}]}, \qquad \forall j, \tag{12}$$

where the tilde ($\sim$) denotes a random variable and E is a mathematical expectation operator.

Let the lth asset be the nth country's nominal bonds, having a payoff, $X_{lns} = 1$, for all s. The value of the jth asset may be expressed then in terms of the nominal interest rate in the nth country,

$$V_{jn} = \frac{E[(A_n+\tilde{I}_n^{-1}\tilde{W}_n)^{\gamma-1}\tilde{I}_n^{-1}\tilde{X}_{jn}]}{R_N E[(A_n+\tilde{I}_n^{-1}\tilde{W}_n)^{\gamma-1}\tilde{I}_n^{-1}]}, \qquad \forall j, \tag{13}$$

where $V_{ln} \equiv R_N^{-1}$, the inverse of unity plus the nominal rate of interest. A real bond denotes an asset whose payoff is indexed to provide a constant real return across states. Let the lth asset be real bonds, having a state-contingent payoff, I_{sn}, denominated in the nth country's currency. The value of the jth asset may be expressed in terms of the real interest rate,

$$V_{jn} = \frac{E[(A_n+\tilde{I}_n^{-1}\tilde{W}_n)^{\gamma-1}\tilde{I}_n^{-1}\tilde{X}_{jn}]}{rE[(A_n+\tilde{I}_n^{-1}\tilde{W}_n)^{\gamma-1}]}, \qquad \forall j, \tag{14}$$

where $V_l \equiv r^{-1}$, the inverse of unity plus the real rate of interest. From the definition of covariance relations (13) and (14) may be expressed as follows in either nominal terms:

$$V_{jn} = \frac{1}{R_n}\left[E(\tilde{X}_{jn}) + \frac{\text{cov}\,[\tilde{X}_{jn},\,(A_n + \tilde{I}_n^{-1}\,\tilde{W}_n)^{\gamma-1}\tilde{I}_n^{-1}]}{E[(A_n + \tilde{I}^{-1}\,\tilde{W}_n)^{\gamma-1}\tilde{I}_n^{-1}]}\right], \qquad \forall j, \quad (15)$$

or real terms:

$$V_{jn} = \frac{1}{r}\left[E(\tilde{X}_{jn}\tilde{I}_n^{-1}) + \frac{\text{cov}\,[\tilde{X}_{jn}\tilde{I}_n^{-1},\,(A_n + \tilde{I}_n^{-1}\,\tilde{W}_n)^{\gamma-1}]}{E[(A_n + \tilde{I}^{-1}\,\tilde{W}_n)^{\gamma-1}]}\right], \qquad \forall j. \quad (16)$$

Asset values established in an international capital market depend not only on the payoff from the asset, X_{jn}, and R_n, but also on a relative real risk measure, $\text{cov}\,[\tilde{X}_{jn},\,(A_n + \tilde{I}_n^{-1}\,\tilde{W}_n)^{\gamma-1}\tilde{I}_n^{-1}]$, defined over the marginal utility of aggregate world real wealth and asset payoff. International asset pricing in contradistinction to domestic asset pricing involves economic variables determined in a world economic setting. In general, the set of relative prices established in a world competitive equilibrium differs from the set established in competitive equilibrium in internationally segmented markets. International asset pricing relations (15) or (16) define then a set of asset prices dependent on their real payoffs in a world economic equilibrium.

4. International Sharpe–Lintner asset pricing in rate of return form

The Sharpe (1964)–Lintner (1965) capital asset pricing model, which does not state explicitly the level of aggregation in market equilibrium, is viewed traditionally in the context of a domestic economy with commodity price certainty. Relations (15) or (16) may be used to derive an international Sharpe–Lintner asset pricing model.

Write relations (15) and (16) in nominal excess rates of return,

$$E(\tilde{R}_{jn}) - R_n = [E(\tilde{R}_{Mn}) - R_n]\left\{\frac{\text{cov}\,[\tilde{R}_{jn},\,(B + \tilde{I}_n^{-1}\tilde{R}_{Mn})^{\gamma-1}\tilde{I}_n^{-1}]}{\text{cov}\,[\tilde{R}_{Mn},\,(B + \tilde{I}_n^{-1}\tilde{R}_{Mn})^{\gamma-1}\tilde{I}_n^{-1}]}\right\},$$
$$\forall j, \qquad (17)$$

or in real excess rates of return,

$$E(\tilde{r}_j) - r = [E(\tilde{r}_M) - r]\left\{\frac{\text{cov}\,[\tilde{r}_j,\,(B + \tilde{r}_M)^{\gamma-1}]}{\text{cov}\,[\tilde{r}_M,\,(B + \tilde{r}_M)^{\gamma-1}]}\right\}, \qquad \forall j, \qquad (18)$$

$R_{jn} \equiv X_{jn}V_{jn}^{-1}$ is unity plus the nominal rate or return on the jth asset denominated in the nth country's unit of account;

$R_{Mn} \equiv W_n(\sum_j V_{jn})^{-1}$ is unity plus the nominal rate of return on the international market portfolio of assets denominated in the nth country's unit of account;

$r_j \equiv X_{jn}I_n^{-1}V_{jn}^{-1}$ is unity plus the real rate of return on the jth asset;

$r_M \equiv W_nI_n^{-1}(\sum_j V_{jn})^{-1}$ is unity plus the real rate of return on the international market portfolio of assets;

$B \equiv A_nW_{0n}^{-1}$ is invariant with respect to the numéraire.

Without loss of generality, the nominal rate of return on asset j may be decomposed into a component correlated with the rate of return on the international market portfolio and a component uncorrelated with the rate of return on the market portfolio. Without loss of generality the nominal return generating process on the jth asset may be decomposed into a component perfectly correlated with the nominal rate of return on the international market portfolio and a component uncorrelated with the nominal rate of return on that portfolio,

$$\tilde{R}_{jn} = \alpha_{jn} + \beta_{jn}\tilde{R}_{Mn} + \tilde{u}_{jn}, \qquad \forall j, \tag{19}$$

where $\beta_{jn} = \text{cov}(\tilde{R}_{jn}, \tilde{R}_{Mn})/\text{var}(\tilde{R}_{Mn})$ and $\alpha_{jn} = E(\tilde{R}_{jn}) - \beta_{jn}E(\tilde{R}_{Mn})$. By construction, $E(\tilde{u}_{jn}) = 0$ and $\text{cov}(\tilde{u}_{jn}, \tilde{R}_{Mn}) = 0$. Using relation (19) to substitute for R_{jn} in relation (17), and simplifying, the expected nominal excess rate of return on an asset may be rewritten as

$$E(\tilde{R}_{jn}) - R_n = [E(\tilde{R}_{Mn}) - R_n]\left[\beta_{jn} + \frac{\text{cov}\left[\tilde{u}_{jn}, (B + \tilde{R}_{Mn}\tilde{I}_n^{-1})^{\gamma-1}\tilde{I}_n^{-1}\right]}{\text{cov}\left[\tilde{R}_{Mn}, (B + \tilde{R}_{Mn}\tilde{I}_n^{-1})^{\gamma-1}\tilde{I}_n^{-1}\right]}\right],$$
$$\forall j. \tag{20}$$

A sufficient condition for equivalence of relation (20) and the Sharpe–Lintner capital asset pricing model is that $\text{cov}\left[\tilde{u}_{jn}, (B + \tilde{R}_{Mn}\tilde{I}_n^{-1})^{\gamma-1}\tilde{I}_n^{-1}\right] = 0$. This case arises whenever the distributions of u_{jn} and R_{Mn} are independent and either $\gamma = 0$ (the case of logarithmic utility) or the distributions of u_{jn} and I_n are independent. If u_{jn} and I_n are independently distributed then that component of a security's return which is uncorrelated with the international market portfolio does not provide protection against changes in commodity prices, that is, against changes in the purchasing power of the nominal payoffs of risk assets. In general, however, $\text{cov}\left[\tilde{u}_{jn}, (B + \tilde{R}_{Mn}\tilde{I}_n^{-1})^{\gamma-1}\tilde{I}_n^{-1}\right] \neq 0$ thus risk assets provide some protection against changes in commodity prices.

Again, without loss of generality, the real rate of return on the jth asset may be decomposed into a component perfectly correlated with the real rate of return on the international market portfolio and a component uncorrelated with the real rate of return on that portfolio,

$$\tilde{r}_j = a_j + b_j\tilde{r}_M + \tilde{e}_j, \qquad \forall j, \tag{21}$$

where $b_j = \text{cov}(\tilde{r}_j, \tilde{r}_M)/\text{var}(\tilde{r}_M)$, the real 'beta' of the jth asset, and $a_j = E(\tilde{r}_j) - b_j E(\tilde{r}_M)$. By construction, $E(\tilde{e}_j) = 0$ and $\text{cov}(\tilde{e}_j, \tilde{r}_M) = 0$. The expected real excess rate of return on the jth asset may be rewritten as

$$E(\tilde{r}_j) - r = [E(\tilde{r}_M) - r]\left[b_j + \frac{\text{cov}[\tilde{e}_j, (B + \tilde{r}_M)^{\gamma-1}]}{\text{cov}[\tilde{r}_M, (B + \tilde{r}_M)^{\gamma-1}]}\right]. \tag{22}$$

On the assumption of independence between e_j and r_M, relation (22) reduces to an international Sharpe–Lintner capital asset pricing model in real rates of return.[3]

5. The relationship between the forward foreign exchange rate and the expected future spot rate

A forward foreign exchange contract is an agreement to exchange a fixed amount of the currency of one country for a fixed amount of the currency of another country at a specified future date. The forward exchange rate is implicit in the contract, being the ratio of the fixed amounts of currency in the exchange. In a two-period model foreign exchange contracts are written in period 0 and executed in period 1.

Equivalently, a forward foreign exchange contract is a complex security whose payoff is Ω_{snm} in state s denominated in the currency of the nth country. To enter into a forward foreign exchange contract requires only the posting of a performance bond on which the opportunity cost, R_n, is paid and payment upon settlement in period 1. The settlement price of a forward exchange contrast between currencies n and m, F_{mn}, is, therefore, $\sum_s (\partial c_{0hn}/\partial w_{shn}) R_n \Omega_{snm}$. Substituting from relation (10) into the definition of F_{nm}, summing over all states s and using the definition of covariance, the settlement price on a forward foreign exchange contract may be written in nominal terms as

$$F_{nm} = E(\tilde{\Omega}_{nm}) + \text{cov}\frac{[\tilde{\Omega}_{nm}, (B + \tilde{W}_n \tilde{I}_n^{-1})^{\gamma-1}\tilde{I}_n^{-1}]}{E[(B + \tilde{W}_n \tilde{I}_n^{-1})^{\gamma-1}\tilde{I}_n^{-1}]}. \tag{23}$$

Thus the forward foreign exchange rate between currencies n and m diverges

---

[3]If real returns are generated by a continuous time Weiner process, as the spacing interval between trades approaches zero, the assumption of independence of e_j and r_m is asymptotically valid, thus $E(\tilde{r}_j) - r = [E(\tilde{r}_M) - r]b_j$. Although the present model allows international trade the equilibrium result is similar to that derived by Solnik under no trade and money illusion. Consider Roll–Solnik's (1975) interpretation of Solnik (1974) that each country produces a single commodity whose price is constant in its unit of account, and returns and exchange rates are generated by a Weiner process. Since under these conditions exchange rates reflect relative prices, the real rate of interest is equal to the rate on Solnik's international bond portfolio where the weights reflect the relative gross national product of each country. $r = \sum_m \beta_m R_m$, where β_m is the mth the country's average prosperity to consume.

from the expected future spot foreign exchange rate as a function of the dependence between the future spot exchange rate and real gross world product plus B raised to the negative of the world's relative risk tolerance and scaled by the world commodity price deflator. Relation (23) may be interpreted traditionally in terms of backwardation (sgn cov < 0) or contango (sgn cov > 0). Alternatively, the forward foreign exchange rate may be written in real terms,

$$F_{nm} = \frac{R_n}{r} \left[E(\tilde{\Omega}_{nm} \tilde{I}_n^{-1}) + \frac{\text{cov } [\tilde{\Omega}_{nm} \tilde{I}_n^{-1}), (B + \tilde{I}_n^{-1} \tilde{W}_n)^{\gamma-1}]}{E(B + \tilde{I}_n^{-1} \tilde{W}_n)^{\gamma-1}} \right]. \tag{24}$$

6. Interest rate and purchasing power parity interpreted

Keynes (1923)–Einzig (1937) interest rate parity utilizes an arbitrage argument to establish the following parity relation:

$$R_m/R_n = F_{nm}/\Omega_{0nm}, \tag{25}$$

where R_m and R_n are unity plus the nominal rates of interest in the mth and nth countries, respectively. This relation can be interpreted in terms of the preceding discussion. Substituting for the forward foreign exchange rate,

$$\frac{R_m}{R_n} = \frac{E[(B + \tilde{I}_n^{-1} \tilde{W}_n)^{\gamma-1} \tilde{I}_n^{-1} \tilde{\Omega}_{nm}]}{\Omega_{0nm} E[(B + \tilde{I}_n^{-1} \tilde{W}_n)^{\gamma-1} \tilde{I}_n^{-1}]}, \tag{26}$$

or alternatively,

$$\frac{R_m}{R_n} = \frac{E(\tilde{\Omega}_{nm})}{\Omega_{0nm}} + \frac{\text{cov } [\tilde{\Omega}_{nm}, (B + \tilde{I}_n^{-1} \tilde{W}_n)^{\gamma-1} \tilde{I}_n^{-1}]}{\Omega_{0nm} E[(B + \tilde{I}_n^{-1} \tilde{W}_n)^{\gamma-1} \tilde{I}_n^{-1}]}. \tag{27}$$

Thus, nominal rates of interest in different countries may differ even though the exchange rates are not expected to change [that is, $E(\tilde{\Omega}_{nm}) = \Omega_{0nm}$], or conversely, different nominal rates of interest between two countries do not necessarily imply an expected change in exchange rates between two units of account. Rather the sign of covariation between B plus real wealth (raised to the relative risk tolerance of the world) and the future spot rate determines whether or not the interest rate differentials between countries are larger or smaller than the expected change in exchange rates between countries.

Cassel's (1918) purchasing power parity also relies on an arbitrage argument which typically assumes a world of identical preferences and production functions under free trade and factor mobility. Purchasing power parity is usually expressed as an *ex post* relation,

$$I_{sm}/I_{sn} = \Omega_{nm}/\Omega_{0nm}, \tag{28}$$

where the subscript s denotes the state that actually occurs.

An *ex ante* analogue of purchasing power parity could be expressed as follows:

$$E(\tilde{I}_m/\tilde{I}_n) = E(\tilde{\Omega}_{nm})/\Omega_{0nm}, \tag{29}$$

which may be alternatively expressed as,

$$E\left(\frac{\tilde{I}_m}{\tilde{I}_n}\right) = \frac{R_m}{R_n} - \frac{\text{cov}\,[\tilde{\Omega}_{nm}, (B+\tilde{I}_n^{-1}\,\tilde{W}_n)^{\gamma-1}\tilde{I}_n^{-1}]}{\Omega_{0nm}E[(B+\tilde{I}_n^{-1}\,\tilde{W}_n)^{\gamma-1}\tilde{I}_n^{-1}]} .$$

Thus the expected ratio of the indices of the two countries equals the ratio of nominal rates of interest in the two countries and a risk–return measure. Even though the nominal rates of interest in the two countries may be equal, the expected ratio of commodity price indices in the two countries may differ from one.

7. International capital flows with and without barriers to trade

7.1. No barriers to trade

International capital flows may be decomposed into flows of risk and riskless capital. And international sharing rules may be derived for all countries which represent for each country its net demand for risk and riskless capital. Heterogeneous preferences and beliefs and/or barriers to the international exchange of commodities change the set of sharing rules that must be feasible in order for the exchange of contingent financial claims to be Pareto efficient and may be viewed as additional sources of international capital flows.

A country is an aggregation of individuals sharing a common unit of account and residency (usually defined as a common geo-political boundary). Assume all trade within a country is free and all residents of a country share preferences and beliefs. Further assume initially that individuals in all countries share identical beliefs, consumption preferences and cautiousness (i.e., π's, β's and γ's) but have different δ's and that international exchange of claims and commodities is unrestricted. Then, given the existence of real bonds, the equilibrium allocation of state-contingent claims is Pareto efficient and from relation (10), the marginal rate of substitution between states s and 0 for all residents of the mth country is

$$\frac{\partial w_{\theta mn}}{\partial w_{smn}} = \frac{\pi_s \{A_{mn} + I_{sn}^{-1} w_{smn}\}^{\gamma-1} I_{sn}^{-1}}{\pi_\theta \{A_{mn} + I_{0n}^{-1} w_{0mn}\}^{\gamma-1} I_{0n}^{-1}}, \qquad \forall\, m, s, \tag{30}$$

where

$$A_{mn} \equiv \sum_{h \in m} A_{hn},$$

and

$$w_{\theta mn}, w_{smn} \equiv \sum_{h \in m} w_{\theta hn}, \sum_{h \in m} w_{sn}$$

is the gross national income of the mth country in state θ and s, respectively, denominated in the numeraire (n) unit of account.[4]

Relation (30) induces the following Pareto optimal international sharing rule:

$$w_{smn} I_{smn}^{-1} = A_n \left(\frac{r H_{0mn} + A_{mn}}{r H_{0n} + A_n} \right) - A_{mn} + \frac{r H_{0mn} + A_{mn}}{r H_{0n} + A_n} W_{sn} I_{sn}^{-1},$$

$$\forall m, s, \qquad (31)$$

where

$$H_{0mn} \equiv \sum_s \frac{\partial c_{0hn}}{\partial w_{shn}} w_{smn}$$

is the market value of the mth country's holding of securities, and

$$H_{0n} \equiv \sum_m H_{0mn}$$

is the total market value of all securities in the world in period 0.

The intercept of the linear function (31) is a state-independent constant representing a constant amount of real wealth demanded in all states of the world and determines the amount of real bonds·residents of different nations demand (positive intercept) or supply (negative intercept). If all countries have constant relative risk aversion, then A_n and A_{mn} are zero – the mth country neither borrows or lends. The mth country, therefore, invests solely in risk capital, demanding a constant share across states of state-contingent real gross world product, proportional to the market value of its holdings of securities in the

---

[4]Using the definition of a real bond and relation (29), summing over all states θ, a country's real gross national income contingent on state s equals

$$w_{smn} I_{sn}^{-1} = (r I_{sn} \pi_s^{-1} (\partial c_{0hn}/\partial w_{shn}))^{1/(\gamma-1)} K_{mn}^{1/(\gamma-1)} - A_{mn}, \qquad \forall m, s, \qquad (i)$$

where $K_{mn} \equiv E\{[A_{mn} + I_{sn}^{-1} w_{smn}]^{\gamma-1}\}$. By rearranging (29) and aggregating over all m, a similar relation may be derived for the world economy,

$$W_{sn} I_{sn}^{-1} = (r I_{sn} \pi_s^{-1} (\partial c_{0hn}/\partial w_{shn}))^{1/(\gamma-1)} K_n^{1/(\gamma-1)} - A_n, \qquad \forall s, \qquad (ii)$$

where $K_n \equiv E\{[A_n + I_{sn}^{-1} W_{sn}]^{\gamma-1}\}$. Relations (i) and (ii) may be equated through their common factors and a linear sharing on real gross world product contingent on state s thus derived,

$$w_{smn} I_{sn}^{-1} = \{A_n [K_{mn}/K_n]^{1/(\gamma-1)} - A_{mn}\} + [K_{mn}/K_n]^{1/(\gamma-1)} W_{sn} I_{sn}^{-1}, \qquad \forall m, s. \quad (iii)$$

Multiplying both sides of (iii) by $\partial c_{0hn}/\partial w_{shn}$, relation (iii) may be solved for $[K_{mn}/K_n]^{1/(\gamma-1)}$ in terms of H_{0mn} and H_{0n}, defined subsequently, and rewritten as relation (30).

E

world market portfolio of securities. If the mth country alone has constant re-lative risk aversion, however, the mth country may either borrow or lend and allocates its risk capital other than in proportion to the market value of its security holdings in the world market portfolio of securities, depending on the sign of A_n and whether $rH_{0n} \gtreqless A_n$ given $A_n < 0$ [note if $A_n < 0$ then relation (31) is undefined when $A_n = rH_{0n}$]. Countries lend (borrow) more *ceteris paribus* the larger (smaller) the total market value of their holding of securities is relative to the market value of all securities. Similarly, countries allocate more (less) to risky assets the larger (smaller) the relative market value of their holding of securities. Thus a country's optimal holding of risk and riskless capital de-pends on not only the risk preferences of its residents, but also the risk pre-ferences of other countries, the real rate of interest and the market value of its holdings of securities relative to the market value of all securities. The sign of the intercept unambiguously establishes the net creditor–net debtor status of a nation. The sign and size of the slope coefficient establishes the size and composition of the risk asset portfolio of a nation.

Note that in the world economy net private borrowing at the real rate of interest is zero. Equivalently, the equilibrium real rate of interest equates total riskless borrowing and lending in real terms. Thus, the equilibrium real rate of interest in relation (3) clears the market in real bonds, that is, the sum over all m of the intercept is zero. Under uncertainty, the equilibrium real rate of interest cannot be equated exclusively with the marginal rate of social time preference (as in the certainty paradigm of Fisher) but impounds not only time preferences but also risk attitudes and the distribution of investable wealth.

Using a comparative statics approach, the partial equilibrium effect of a change in the real rate of interest on the mth country's demand for risky and riskless assets is

$$\frac{\partial(w_{smn}I_{sn}^{-1})}{\partial r} = \frac{H_{0mn}A_n^2 - H_{0n}A_{mn}A_n}{(rH_{0n} + A_n)^2} + \frac{H_{0mn}A_n - H_{0n}A_{mn}}{(rH_{0n} + A_n)^2} W_{sn}I_{sn}^{-1},$$

$$\forall\, s, m. \qquad (32)$$

The sign of the intercept determines whether the mth country's demand for real bond varies directly or inversely with a change in the real rate of interest. A necessary condition for the mth country's demand for bonds to be inversely related to the real rate of interest is that A_{mn} and A_n have the same sign. Simi-larly, the sign of the slope coefficient determines whether the mth country's demand for risk assets varies directly or inversely with a change in the real rate of interest. Only if A_{mn} and A_n have different signs can the effect of a change in the real rate of interest on the demand for risk assets be determined solely on the basis of risk preference, otherwise the international distribution of investable wealth is a determinant.

7.2. Barriers to trade

Restrictions on commodity markets can result in international differences in relative commodity prices which may be represented by means of commodity price indices. Under the assumption of multiplicative multi-commodity utility functions, the effect of these restrictions on the valuation of risk assets may be analyzed.

Assume, as before, that all individuals within a country face the same commodity and asset prices and have identical preferences and beliefs. The commodity price index for the mth country is an aggregation over all residents of that country of their individual price indices defined in relations (9),

$$I_{smn} = \prod_i [P_{ismn}/P_{i0mn}]^{\beta_{im}}, \qquad \forall\, m, s,$$

where P_{ismn} and P_{i0mn} are the prices of the ith commodity inclusive of taxes and transportation costs for residents of the mth country in state s and period 0, respectively, denominated in the numeraire unit of account. β_{im} is the mth country's aggregate average propensity to consume the ith commodity.

Assume for convenience that individuals in *all* countries have identical probability beliefs, time preference, cautiousness and constant relative risk aversion ($\delta = 0$). In general, $P_{ismn} \neq P_{isqn}$ for all i and m, implying commodity trade is restricted. Relation (10) may be solved for the aggregate demand of residents of the mth country for state-contingent claims,

$$\frac{W_{smn}}{W_{sn}} = \left[\frac{C_{0mn}}{C_{0n}}\right]\left[\frac{I_{smn}}{I_{sn}^*}\right]^{\gamma/\gamma - 1}, \qquad \forall\, m, s, \tag{33}$$

where

$$I_{sn}^* \equiv \left[\sum_m \frac{C_{0mn} I_{smn}^{\gamma/\gamma-1}}{C_{0n}}\right]^{\gamma-1/\gamma}$$

is a weighted average of country geometric relative price indices where the weights are relative consumption shares in period 0 evaluated in terms of each country's prices in period 0;

$$W_{smn} \equiv \sum_{h \in m} W_{shn}$$

is the gross national income of the mth country in state s denominated in the numeraire unit of account;

$$C_{0mn} \equiv \sum_{h \in m} \sum_i P_{i0mn} c_{i0h}$$

is the total consumption expenditure in the mth country in period 0 denominated in the numeraire unit of account;

$$C_{0n} \equiv \sum_{m} c_{0mn}$$

is total world consumption expenditure in period 0 denominated in the numeraire unit of account;

$$W_{sn} \equiv \sum_{m} w_{smn}$$

is gross world product in state s denominated in the numeraire unit of account.

Since commodity prices in different countries for the same commodity are in general different, $I_{smn} \neq I_{sqm}$ and $w_{smn}/W_{sn} \neq w_{sqn}/W_{sn}$, even though preferences and beliefs have been assumed identical. Note that the equilibrium relative asset prices when commodity trade is restricted (or costly) are precisely those established in relations (11) and (12) where I_{sn}^{*} is substituted for I_{sn}. In general, I_{sn}^{*} and I_{sn} would differ, so the set of relative asset prices in the presence of commodity trade restrictions would also differ from the set in the absence of barriers to trade. Note that residents of different countries would hold different investment portfolios because they face different sets of state-dependent relative prices, not because the numeraire currency changes as a function of their respective countries of residence.

To illustrate, assume all commodity taxes are *ad valorem* and there are no transportation costs, national governments distribute all commodity tax revenues by lump-sum transfer payments to their residents, all governments have balanced budgets, and each country produces a unique set of goods (see appendix for a formal statement of the individual choice problem and market clearing conditions). Under these conditions, $P_{ismn} \equiv (1+t_{ism})P_{isn}$ and $P_{i0mn} \equiv (1+t_{i0m})P_{i0n}$ where t_{ism} and t_{i0m} are *ad valorem* taxes paid by residents of the mth country on the ith commodity in state s and period 0, respectively, and P_{isn} and P_{i0n} are prices of the ith commodity in its country of origin in state s and period 0, respectively. Therefore, the national price index may be decomposed as follows:

$$I_{smn} \equiv \prod_{i} \left[\frac{P_{isn}}{P_{i0n}}\right] \prod_{i} \left[\frac{1+t_{ism}}{1+t_{i0m}}\right]^{\beta_{im}}, \qquad \forall\, s, m. \tag{34}$$

In the limit as the *ad valorem* tax on a given commodity paid by residents of a country approaches infinity the demand for that commodity is zero. Given identical consumption preferences and a unique set of commodities pro-

F.L.A. Grauer et al., International capital market equilibrium   249

duced by each country relation (33) may be rewritten as

$$\frac{w_{smn}}{W_{sn}} = \frac{c_{0mn}}{C_{0n}} \left[\frac{T_{sm}}{T_s} \right]^{\gamma/\gamma - 1}, \qquad \forall\, s, m. \tag{35}$$

where

$$T_{sm} = \prod_i \left[\frac{1 + t_{ism}}{1 + t_{i0m}} \right]$$

is a geometrically weighted average of *ad valorem* commodity taxes incurred by residents of the *m*th country; and

$$T_s = \left[\sum_m \frac{c_{0mn} (T_{sm})}{C_{0n}} \right]^{\gamma - 1/\gamma}$$

is a weighted average of *ad valorem* commodity taxes incurred by all individuals in the world.

The fractional claim on state-contingent world wealth demanded by residents of the *m*th country is related to an index of change in relative tax burden, $T_{sm}T^{-1}$, which measures the change between period 0 and state *s* in proportional taxation of consumption for residents of the *m*th country relative to residents of all other countries. The fractional claim demanded may decrease, remain the same, or increase with an increase in the index of change in relative tax burden, depending on the sign of γ, the elasticity of the marginal utility of wealth. When $0 < \gamma < 1$, individual utility functions display multivariate risk-loving[5] and demand for fractional claims on state-contingent wealth of residents of the *m*th country varies inversely with the index of change in relative state-dependent tax burden. Hence residents of the *m*th country would allocate their holdings of securities in larger (smaller) than market value proportions to states in which their index of change in relative state-dependent tax burden is less (greater) than unity. When $\gamma = 0$, individual utility functions display multivariate risk neutrality and national portfolio allocations are unaffected by the index of change in relative tax burden. When $\gamma < 0$, individual utility functions display multivariate risk aversion and demand for fractional claims of residents of the *m*th country varies directly with the index of change in relative state-dependent tax burden. Hence residents of the *m*th country would allocate their

---

[5]See Richard (1973). Multivariate risk preference is a property of the cross-partials of the utility function. For example (from Richard), consider two lotteries on the following x_0, x_1, y_0 and y_1, where $x_0 < x_1$ and $y_0 < y_1$. Lottery one (L_1) pays off (x_0, y_0) with probability 0.5, and (x_1, y_1) with probability 0.5. Lottery two (L_2) pays off (x_0, y_1) with probability 0.5, and (x_1, y_0) with probability 0.5. Multivariate risk aversion implies that $L_2 \geq L_1$ for all x_0, x_1, y_0 and y_1, and $L_2 > L_1$ for some x_0, x_1, y_0, y_1. Multivariate risk neutrality implies that $L_1 \sim L_2$ for all x_0, x_1, y_0 and y_1. Multivariate risk-loving implies $L_1 \geq L_2$ for all x_0, x_1, y_0 and y_1, and $L_1 > L_2$ for some x_0, x_1, y_0, y_1.

holdings of securities in larger (smaller) than market value proportions to states in which their index of change in relative state-dependent tax burden is greater (less) than unity. Changes in relative state-dependent tax burdens induce international capital flows, therefore, whenever individuals have non-neutral multivariate risk preferences.[6] Since γ is assumed identical across individuals, all individuals are either multivariate risk-loving, multivariate risk-neutral or multivariate risk-averse. Individuals face, however, different effective commodity prices (bear different relative state-dependent tax burdens) thus residents of different countries may demand assets in other than market value proportions though they share the same multivariate risk preference. Denoting $T_s^* \equiv T_{sm}T_s^{-1}$ and substituting for I_{sn} in relations (11) and (12) the set of relative asset prices in market equilibrium with proportional frictions in international commodity markets is defined.

The set of optimal proportional sharing rules for a world economy characterized by identical beliefs, consumption, time and risk preferences and proportional frictions is defined by

$$w_{smn} = \left[\frac{c_{0mn}}{C_{0n}} \right]\left[\frac{T_{sm}}{T_s} \right]^{\gamma/\gamma - 1} W_{sn}, \qquad \forall \, s, m. \tag{36}$$

For an allocation of state-contingent claims to be a Pareto optimum the feasibility of relation (36) is both necessary and sufficient, that is, for residents of the mth country (for all m) there must exist a state-contingent payoff, w_{smn}, which is a linear combination of existing securities.

For the special case of state-independent *ad valorem* import and export taxes for residents of all countries, $T_{sm}T_s^{-1}$ is constant across all states thus all individuals would hold the market portfolio. A state independent proportional *ad valorem* commodity tax changes the price index by the same proportion across all states. Under constant relative risk aversion a state-independent proportional increase in the price index does not affect the relative demand for state-contingent claims on nominal wealth. Thus if the market portfolio was optimal before the introduction of state-independent commodity taxes, the market portfolio must be optimal after their introduction [from relations (33) and (36), by inspection]. Note that since nominal state-contingent claims economize on markets relative to contingent claims on real goods [Arrow (1971)], individuals would demand a market portfolio of nominal contingent claims, whether or not taxes are state-independent.

While some may view import and export taxes as approximately state-independent, transportation costs would be expected to be state-dependent since they are a function of state-dependent endowments and choices. Then

---

[6]Individuals may respond to this variation in real payoff by migrating. Spatial movement is defined to occur only over time, however, thus individuals cannot move from country to country *within* a period to maximize the real value of nominal payoffs.

t_{ism} and t_{i0m} may be reinterpreted as state-dependent *ad valorem* transportation costs and again residents of different countries would not in general hold identical risk asset portfolios.

Assume now that individuals in different countries have different consumption preferences, $\beta_{im} \neq \beta_{iq}$ for all i and m, hence from relation (33) prices do not cancel. The optimal proportion of total state-contingent wealth varies then not only with the index of change in relative state-dependent tax burden but also with relative inflation. Since consumption preferences are different, both price changes and tax changes between period 0 and state s affect relative shares demanded and in a way depending on the preferences of residents of different countries for the particular commodity whose price in country of origin is changing. For instance, assume $\gamma > 0$ then an increase in the price of rice (due to failure of the monsoon, say) in state s together with an increase in the *ad valorem* export tax on rice in the qth country in state s would, *ceteris paribus*, reduce more the relative share of total world wealth contingent on state s demanded by a rice-preferring country than by a wheat-preferring country. That is, the real payoff in state s would be relatively lower (and thus the state less desirable) for residents of the rice-preferring country.

Changes in relative tax burden (or transportation costs) and or/changes in world commodity prices in the presence of diverse consumption preferences generate international capital flows as residents of different countries adjust their risk asset portfolios to these changes. As hedgers or gamblers, individuals value the payoffs of risk assets in terms of their real purchasing power. International flows of risk capital reflect their individual portfolio responses to international variations in commodity prices and thus to variations in real payoffs from nominal claims.[7]

8. Exchange risk and money illusion

That the valuation of an asset does not depend on the numeraire currency of an individual's country of residence is a conclusion contrasting markedly with much of the literature on international financial investment.[8] Solnik, for example, contends that due to uncertain future exchange rates, the same asset must be evaluated differently by investors from different countries.

> When considering an international investment, a fundamental dimension should be added to the analysis: the exchange risk. Anyone investing abroad will bear not only the risk due to the real characteristics of the investment, but also an exchange risk .[Solnik (1973, p. 8)]

To clarify the issue, consider a resident of the nth country who invests in the

[7]Diverse beliefs define a different set of optimal sharing rules and are derived in Litzenberger and Grauer (1974).

[8]A notable exception is Heckerman (1972), who, in the context of a two-country, two-good model, heuristically develops the notion of 'exchange illusion' substantially the same as that discussed below.

nominally riskless asset of the mth country. The nominal proceeds of this investment expressed in the nth country's currency will fluctuate as the exchange rate between the nth and mth currencies fluctuates. However, with free trade the real proceeds accruing to an investor with the same preferences residing in the nth country will be identical to the real proceeds accruing to an investor with the same preferences residing in the mth country, who invests in the same nominally riskless asset. Since, by assumption, investors evaluate alternative investments in real terms, the currency in which they express their choice problem, the numeraire currency, does not affect consumption or asset choices of individuals.

More formally, a model of pure exchange determines only relative prices. Given relative commodity prices, the absolute price levels in different countries and corresponding exchange rates must be determined exogenously. The absolute price levels in different countries do not affect an individual's contracts for real payoffs, that is, given relative commodity prices, individuals will be indifferent to changes in absolute price levels and corresponding fluctuations in exchange rates.[9] This suggests that exchange rate fluctuations may be divided into two components: one component of the exchange rate reflects variation in relative prices across states of the world which affects consumption–asset choices of individuals, while the other component reflects variations in absolute price across states of the world and does not affect consumption–asset choices. Exchange risk attributable to the variation in relative prices across states of the world is redundant, however, since the variation in relative prices across states is a causal factor determining asset and consumption choices. Since fluctuating relative prices are encountered in international, as well as segmented, capital markets, there is no added dimension to international investment which creates a new type of risk for individual investors, hence, given our assumptions, exchange risk has no independent identity.

Agmon (1974) recognizes that the mere existence of multiple currencies does not affect individual asset choice. He speculates, however, that barriers to international trade (imperfections) introduce exchange risk. When the international trade of commodities is subject to proportional imperfections such as *ad valorem* export or import taxes or transportation costs, identical individuals in different countries may value the same asset differently. However, this different valuation is caused solely by the different sets of relative commodity prices which investors in different countries face and not by the component of exchange rate fluctuation that is independent of variations in relative prices. Equilibrium determines only relative prices, absolute price levels are determined outside the system. Of

[9]Note that different absolute price levels in different states of nature appear to change the real characteristics of securities, for example, of equities of levered firms or bonds. Different absolute price levels will therefore induce individuals to hold different portfolios if we define portfolios in terms of the numbers of particular securities they contain. However, given relative commodity prices, an individual will hold the same portfolio regardless of the absolute price level, once portfolios are defined in terms of their real payoff.

course, each possible set of absolute price levels in different countries implies a different set of exchange rates, but relative prices of assets are not affected. Thus proportional imperfections in international commodity trade add no new dimension to foreign exchange risk.[10]

Solnik's conclusion that exchange rate fluctuations affect relative prices of assets is based on his model of an international capital market in which individuals' utility functions are defined over a single consumption good that differs by country of residence. Since a given country's consumption good has zero marginal utility to residents of other countries, under pure exchange, there is no international price competition for goods. Exchange ratios (or relative prices) will adjust so that the total endowment each country has of foreign consumption goods exchanges for the total endowment all other countries have of its consumption good. For example, consider a two-country world where Americans consume corn and French consume wine. The relative price of corn and wine would be the ratio of the number of litres of wine held in the American endowment to the number of kilos of corn held in the French endowment. Each country's real wealth is, therefore, determined solely by the worldwide endowment of its national consumption good. Unlike a domestic capital market where returns on financial assets determine relative purchasing power and hence the real wealth of individuals, the international exchange of financial assets in Solnik's model cannot affect the real wealth of different countries. Note that in the Solnik model, if each country produces only their domestic consumption good, the international transfer of goods is precluded and exchange ratios do not exist.[11]

Since a country's holdings of financial assets cannot affect its ability to acquire foreign holdings of its domestic consumption goods, a country's total end-of-period real wealth is unaffected by the international exchange of financial assets. However, if the domestic allocation of state-contingent claims is Pareto optimal (for example, the number of linearly independent payoffs from domestic assets equals the number of states of the world), then the international exchange of financial claims does not affect the allocation of consumption across states achieved by residents of that country, hence does not lead to Pareto superior allocations.[12] Solnik does not recognize the money illusion in his model because

---

[10]Proportional imperfections are assumed in order to assure existence of an equilibrium. See Shoven (1974). Non-convex imperfections may be introduced through the same mechanism as in section 8, an equilibrium may not exist, however. Note that when real export and import taxes are a function of the absolute price level in a country, the level of absolute prices chosen by the monetary authority may affect the set of relative prices of commodities. In this particular case, relative price variation is induced by the monetary authority, but as previously argued such variation should not be construed as foreign exchange risk.

[11]Roll and Solnik (1975, p. 3) interpret the Solnik (1974) model to mean that each country produces only its domestic consumption good, thus simultaneously precluding international exchange of both commodities and financial claims.

[12]The real benefit of international diversification results from the opportunity to affect the pattern of state-contingent payoffs which could not be achieved by a system of domestic side bets.

he incorrectly assumes that exchange rates are exogenously determined. However, if a conservation relationship is included, recognizing that prices of goods are determined in equilibrium, the implicit assumption of a money illusion is apparent.

Money illusion is a phenomenon common to many models of the international pricing of financial claims; for example, Adler and Dumas (1975). Black (1974) introduces international barriers to investment in a valuation model that avoids money illusion if interpreted in a single-good world where the absolute price level is known for certain in all countries.

9. Summary

Exchange rate fluctuations that reflect differential changes in absolute price levels in different countries do not affect the allocation of real goods, services and capital, and therefore do not create exchange risk for rational investors. It has been shown that the set of relative asset prices under pure exchange in international capital markets depends on the real purchasing power of nominal payoffs under uncertainty – specifically, in international capital market equilibrium, given multiplicative, multi-commodity utility functions, the relative price of equities, nominal bonds and forward foreign exchange contracts all depend on the relation of their real return to the return on aggregate real wealth. In other words, the set of *relative* assets prices in a multi-commodity world is no different from that arising in capital market equilibrium with a single international currency, since the stochastic characteristics of real wealth are unaffected by the introduction of more than one currency. The valuation equations derived for risky assets, on the assumption of multiplicative multi-commodity utility functions and unrestricted commodity and asset flows across national boundaries, reduce, on the further assumption of a linear relation between real (nominal) rates of return on assets and the world market portfolio of assets, to a Sharpe–Lintner type capital asset pricing model in international capital market equilibrium. The presence of state-independent proportional *ad valorem* commodity taxes and/or transportation costs does not modify the asset pricing relations derived.

International exchange involves the exchange of financial claims denominated in different currencies. In the context of international capital market equilibrium, it has been shown that the difference between the settlement price of a forward foreign exchange contract and its expected future spot price of foreign exchange is a function of the dependence between the future spot price of foreign exchange and real gross world product. This dependence may be viewed as a measure of the real systematic risk associated with the foreign exchange position.

Competitive arbitrage notions of interest rate parity under certainty have been re-interpreted under uncertainty and shown to imply that nominal interest rates in different countries may diverge even though foreign exchange rates are not expected to change, since the real systematic risk (if any) of foreign exchange positions cannot be arbitraged. Similarly, nominal interest rates in different countries may diverge even though the expected ratio of national indices of price change are the same.

Under uncertainty, when commodities and assets flow unrestricted across national boundaries, a country's demand for risk and riskless capital depends not only on the risk preferences of its residents, but also on the risk preferences of other countries, the world real rate of interest, and the market value of its holdings of securities relative to the market value of all securities. Barriers to trade can modify a country's demand for risk and riskless capital, however. The real purchasing power of nominal payoffs change as the structure of state-dependent tariffs or international state-dependent transactions costs change, thus changing equilibrium relative asset prices and the portfolio allocation of countries across assets.

Appendix

The individual choice problem with taxes and lump-sum transfers is

$$\text{Max} \sum_s \pi_s U_s(c_{10}, \ldots, c_0, c_{1s}, \ldots, c_s),$$

subject to

$$\sum_i c_{i0}(1+t_{i0})P_{i0n} + \sum_j \alpha_j V_j n \leq w_{0n} + \tau_{0n},$$

$$\sum_i c_{is}(1+t_{is})P_{isn} \leq \sum_j \alpha_j X_{jsn} + \tau_{sn}, \qquad \forall s,$$

where τ_{0n}, τ_{sn} are lump-sum transfers from the country of residence to a resident in period 0 and state s, respectively and w_{0n} and $\sum_j \alpha_j X_{jsn}$ constitute personal disposable income before transfer payments. Market clearing requires

(i) $$\sum_j \sum_m \sum_{h \in m} (\alpha_{jh} X_{jsn} + \tau_{0hn}) = W_{sn}, \qquad \forall s,$$

(ii) $$\sum_{h \in m} \sum_i P_{i0n} c_{i0h} t_{i0m}^{d(m)} + \sum_m \sum_{h \in m} \sum_i P_{i0n} c_{i0h} t_{i0m}^{x(m)} = \sum_{h \in m} \tau_{0hn}, \qquad \forall m$$

(iii) $$\sum_{h \in m} \sum_i P_{isn} c_{ish} t_{ism}^{d(m)} + \sum_m \sum_{h \in m} \sum_i P_{isn} c_{ish} t_{ism}^{x(m)} = \sum_{h \in m} \tau_{shn}, \qquad \forall m, s,$$

where $t_{i0m}^{d(q)}$ is an *ad valorem* import tax on commodity i in period 0 payable by residents of the mth country and imposed by the qth country and $t_{i0m}^{x(q)}$ is an *ad valorem* export tax on commodity i in period 0 payable by residents of the mth country and imposed by the qth country.

256   *F.L.A. Grauer et al., International capital market equilibrium*

References

Adler, M. and B. Dumas, 1975, Optimal international acquisitions, Journal of Finance 30, 1–19.
Agmon, T., 1974, Exchange risk – Conceptual framework and measurement, Alfred P. Sloan School of Management Working Paper no. 758–74 (Cambridge, MA).
Arrow, K.J., 1971, The role of securities in the optimal allocation of risk-bearing, in: Essays in the theory of risk-bearing, ch. 4 (Markham, Chicago, IL).
Black, F., 1974, International capital market equilibrium with investment barriers, Journal of Financial Economics 1, 337–352.
Cassel, G., 1918, Abnormal deviations in international exchanges, Economic Journal 28, 413–415.
Einzig, P., 1937, The theory of foreign exchange (Macmillan, London).
Fisher, I., 1927, The making of index numbers (Houghton–Mifflin, Boston).
Heckerman, D., 1973, On the effects of exchange risk, Journal of International Economics 3, 379–387.
Keynes, J.M., 1923, A tract on monetary reform (Macmillan, London).
Lintner, J., 1965, The valuation of risk assets and the selection of risky investments in stock portfolios and capital budgets, Review of Economics and Statistics 47, 13–37.
Litzenberger, R.H. and F.L.A. Grauer, 1974, A state preference model of the valuation of commodity futures contracts under uncertain commodity prices, Stanford Graduate School Research Paper no. 220 (Stanford, CA).
Richard, S., 1973, Multivariate risk aversion, utility independence and separable utility functions, Carnegie–Mellon Graduate School of Industrial Administration Working Paper no. 101 (Pittsburgh, PA).
Roll, R. and B.H. Solnik, 1975, A pure foreign exchange asset pricing model, CESA Working Paper no. 75–31 (Jouey-en-Josas, France).
Rubinstein, M., 1974, A discrete-time synthesis of financial theory: Part III – Extensions and prospective, Working Paper no. 26 (Berkeley, CA).
Samuelson, P.A. and S. Swamy, 1974, Invariant economic index numbers and canonical duality: Survey and synthesis, American Economic Review 64, 566–593.
Sharpe, W.F., 1964, Capital asset prices: A theory of market equilibrium under conditions of risk, Journal of Finance 19, 425–442.
Shoven, J., 1974, A proof of the existence of a general equilibrium with ad valorem commodity taxes, Journal of Economic Theory 8, 1–25.
Solnik, B.H., 1973, European capital markets (Lexington Books, Lexington, MA).
Solnik, B.H., 1974, Equilibrium in an international capital market, Journal of Economic Theory 8, 500–504.
Stehle, R., forthcoming, Dynamic equilibrium in a world economy (Stanford, CA).
Walsh, C.M., 1901, The measurement of general exchange-value (Macmillan, New York).

[4]

THE JOURNAL OF FINANCE • VOL. XXXVIII, NO. 3 • JUNE 1983

International Portfolio Choice and Corporation Finance: A Synthesis

MICHAEL ADLER and BERNARD DUMAS*

THE STRUCTURE OF THE theory of international finance largely mirrors that of domestic financial theory. Starting from a micro-theory of individual portfolio choice one obtains, via aggregation and market clearing, equilibrium pricing relationships and risk-return tradeoffs. These provide objectives for value maximizing firms from which decision rules can be computed. This analytical sequence is the same whether there is one or more capital markets. To distinguish between the domestic and international settings, one needs an economic concept of nationhood.

Alternative approaches to international economics differ essentially in their conception of what a nation is. Ricardian theory identifies countries by their technologies and consumption preferences. The Heckscher-Ohlin theory of international trade defines nations as zones within which physical factors of production are confined.[1] In monetary economics, individual economic units holding the same currency in their portfolios as a means of payments are recognized as belonging to the same nation, and currencies are distinguished from each other by the fact that they are issued by different central banks.[2]

In portfolio theory, two avenues have so far been explored in an attempt to capture the international dimension. Most of the recent literature stemming from Solnik [179] has been devoted to models where nations are defined as zones of a common purchasing power unit or, more precisely, as subsets of investors

* The authors are Professor of Business, Columbia University and Professor, C.E.S.A. (H.E.C., I.S.A., C.F.C.), respectively. The article was begun while Dumas was Visiting Professor at Columbia and completed while he was Visiting Professor at Berkeley. We are grateful to André Saurel, who helped supply part of the data base, and to Jean-Francois Dreyfus, who contributed to the data processing. We received valuable critical comments from Professors Bradford Cornell, Jeffrey Frankel, Bruce Lehmann, David Modest, Patrice Poncet, Richard Roll, Piet Sercu, Bruno Solnik, René Stulz and, especially, Michael Brennan. Errors may remain despite their efforts: they are our responsibility. We apologize to the authors whose work is not quoted. This is no indication of the quality of their work but only of our ignorance or of the limited scope of this survey.

[1] Generalizations of the Heckscher-Ohlin theory to economies with uncertain production and securities trading may be considered as belonging to the field of international finance but they will not be reviewed here. See Helpman and Razin [85, 86, 87], Baron and Forsythe [20], and Dumas [48, 49].

[2] This approach is germane to portfolio theory and originates from balance-of-payments analysis, especially since the latter took a very strong monetary orientation in the sixties under the influence of Mundell [145], and since the advent of the "portfolio-balance" approach: Branson [28]. The link with portfolio theory is, however, not complete since the latter is only today in the process of introducing money holdings into the portfolios of individual investors (for an early attempt, see Roll [159], Kouri [108], and more recently Fama and Farber [58], Hodrick [90], Poncet [151], and Dumas [49]). The device most commonly employed is the injection of real money balances as a separate argument of the utility functions.

925

who use the same price index in deflating their anticipated monetary returns. National groups of investors are delineated by deviations from Purchasing Power Parity (PPP) which cause them to evaluate differently the returns from the same security. As will be detailed below, these deviations may arise either from differences in consumption tastes or from differences in the prices of the various commodities to which investors have access. This heterogeneity in individuals' evaluation of returns plays havoc with the standard Separation, Aggregation, and Asset Pricing results of Portfolio Theory. A large part of this paper will be devoted to a review and extension of the several attempts made at restoring these results.[3] Resolving the problem of portfolio choice when investors' real returns differ is a necessary first step towards a truly international theory of finance.

In practice, nations may further be separated by such manifestations of sovereignty as taxes and border controls which constrain private financial transactions between countries. Financial economic theory does not deal easily with such imperfections which tend to segment international capital markets. We therefore relegate the problems associated with segmentation to a single section near the end. This leaves us free largely to adopt a unified world capital market as the paradigm for much of the rest. The survey can then be structured around the derivation of a mean-variance international asset pricing model (IAPM) in which the several nations feature as regions whose residents have different purchasing power indices. This organizing principle mirrors the state of the art in the field, enables us to identify both the contributions and misconceptions in the evolving literature, and leads to the following plan.

The first order of business is to determine whether, in empirical terms, nations can meaningfully be distinguished by PPP deviations. Accordingly, after reviewing briefly the conditions for the existence of price indices, Section I surveys empirical evidence on the stochastic behavior of inflation rates, exchange rates, and PPP deviations. This evidence strongly suggests that PPP deviations are significant as to size, that they last for lengthy but variable periods, and are highly random. It is therefore reasonable to suppose that investors residing in different countries have different yardsticks for measuring real returns and their risks. Consequently, one would expect the compositions of their portfolios also to differ.

Before developing a mean-variance theory, given that utility functions are not universally quadratic, it is further useful to know whether international rates of return are basically normally distributed. Section II addresses first the sketchy evidence concerning this question. Its provisional conclusion is that normality is not an untenable assumption. The section then proceeds to the wider issue of the correlation structure of nominal and real returns.

---

[3] Note that the PPP-deviations approach to international finance does not in principle presuppose the existence of several currencies. Because the PPP relationship is almost always stated in terms of an exchange rate relating two price levels expressed in two different currencies, the Purchasing "PPP" doctrine has been associated with the equilibrium theory of floating exchange rates. In fact, PPP deviations may very well occur, and typically would occur under fixed exchange rates, or indeed in a world with a unique currency; conversely PPP could conceivably prevail exactly everywhere, causing us to recognize but one "nation" in the world, in the presence of multiple currencies related by randomly fluctuating exchange rates. Empirically, however, we shall find below the most of the PPP deviations are linked to exchange rate movements during floating rate periods.

Section III turns to the problem of optimal portfolio choice in a unified world capital market with no taxes or transactions costs but where investors' consumption preferences are nationally heterogeneous. Every investor, regardless of nationality, has free access to the same menu of assets: all stocks, foreign and domestic, and one default-free, short-term bond per country. All bonds are risky in real terms. Investors are assumed to maximimize a time-additive, von Neumann-Morgenstern expected utility of life-time consumption function.[4]

Introducing random exchange rates for translating future returns in one currency into another raises a familiar technical problem. At one level it may be trivial: a change of measurement unit which leaves untouched the underlying economic reality.[5] Nonetheless, currency translation produces products of random variables whose probability distributions are hard to obtain. In particular, the product of two normal variates is not normal. We therefore adopt in Section III the continuous-time methodology of Merton [138, 139, 140] which to a large extent offers a way out of the difficulty. This technique basically justifies the mean-variance paradigm by the approximation reasoning of Samuelson [167] and, by employing Ito processes, effectually transforms products of random variables into sums.[6]

Sections IV and V focus on the international pricing of assets. Capital Asset Pricing Theories involving a multiplicity of measurement units, with the attendant translation problems, have been supplied by Fischer [62], Grauer, Litzenberger, and Stehle [GLS] [79], Friend, Landskroner, and Losq [FLL] [70] and Hodrick [90]. These CAPMs are restatements in terms of nominal returns of the traditional CAPM of Black [23] which dealt implicitly with real (i.e., deflated) returns. GLS assume a complete market and use a state-of-the-world formulation which avoids the problems connected with translation, since this operation can then be performed on a state-by-state basis. Fischer and FLL use the continuous-time methodology; they do not refer explicitly to several currencies but the manner in which they translate real rates of return into nominal ones and vice-versa can equally well be used to translate dollars into francs. Hodrick postulated the existence of one good traded worldwide at the same price and allows for non-stationary returns.

These CAPMs are applicable only when investors use the same price index in

---

[4] Time additive von Neumann-Morgenstern utility functions have a major drawback. The curvature of the instantaneous utility function ($U(\cdot)$ in the appendix) simultaneously plays the role of a risk aversion parameter and that of the elasticity of substitution between consumption of different points in time. For an attempt at disentangling these two aspects of preferences see Selden [171].

[5] *No matter what economic setting is chosen*, the decisions of rational economic units (investors, firms, etc.) should be invariant as one changes the unit of measurement or the currency of accounting, in which returns are expressed. This is a minimum criterion of rationality (which may admittedly not be passed by corporate treasurers concerned about the looks of their end-of-year accounting statements). To verify that this criterion is satisfied by a given decision method, one must translate from one currency into another using random exchange rates and check that the decisions obtained are unchanged. If so, the *principle of irrelevance of the measurement currency* is upheld and all is well with the theory at hand.

[6] The method does restrict at each instant the conditional distribution of instantaneous rates of return which must be normal. But rates of return on finite intervals of time are not so restricted since the parameters of the Ito process may themselves be variable.

deflating returns,[7] an assumption which is unrealistic at the international level. Nevertheless, even in this simple setting, one may derive an expression for the forward exchange rate[8] as a function of the distribution of the future spot exchange rate corresponding to the maturity of the forward contract. A strong conclusion emerges: the forward exchange rate generally ceases to be an unbiased predictor of the future spot rate. It differs from the expected value of the spot by two premia. One is the result of the risk aversion of investor-speculators. The other premium would exist under risk neutrality and it arises from the presence of random inflation. We shall obtain the same result, but in the more general setting where PPP is violated.

When PPP does not hold, the heterogeneity in portfolio-choice behaviors limits the aggregation of individual demands into a CAPM. Section IV rescues the standard CAPM to the extent it is possible, by limiting its scope to the pricing of some assets relative to the others. The number of these other assets is equal to the number of countries and, for practical purposes, they are identified with the local Treasury Bills. Section V then deals with the pricing of these remaining assets.

Section VI takes a closer look at the welfare problems that may be connected with the randomness of exchange rates. There has been much debate as to when and whether exchange risk is "nominal" or "real" and whether it matters or not. The issue is complex: it depends on such factors as how money is introduced into each economy and why it is held; on the completeness of capital markets; and on how the government raises revenues and uses the proceeds of money creation.

Progress can be made while ignoring capital market imperfections. Ultimately, however, these must be confronted, possibly more so in the international than in the purely domestic setting. Section VII therefore turns to the literature on segmentation. Some of the papers in this area aim to compute equilibrium conditions. Others discuss the welfare gains from bridging the investment barriers and the possibility for optimal corporate decisions. Empirically, the severity of the market imperfections which tend to produce segmentation and the extent of segmentation itself have yet to be measured. Resolving these matters remains a key challenge for future research.

Section, VIII, finally, turns to questions of corporate policy. It focuses mainly on foreign exchange risk avoidance, i.e., hedging policy. In a complete, perfect, and unified international capital market, corporate hedging would be irrelevant. The section then explores the difficulties of measuring exposure and the hedging decision in the circumstances in which it may matter.

This introduction owes its length to the necessity of setting the bounds of this survey. Apologies are due to authors who have contributed important insights into topics closely linked to those covered here. In particular, we shall discuss very few issues in macroeconomics. Empirical tests of the portfolio-balance

---

[7] In one part of their article, GLS do allow for PPP deviations but their investors must then have equal risk aversions. The GLS article contributed greatly to the focus on the role of PPP deviations and to the decomposition of exchange risk into a purely "nominal" and purely "real" component. A fuller discussion will be provided in Section VI.

[8] The forward exchange rate is the exchange rate specified in a contract to deliver a foreign currency at a future point in time. See Section V.

approach to capital flows initiated by Branson [28] have thrown some light on the validity of portfolio theory in international finance but we shall not have room to review them. The vast macroeconomic literature on the neutrality of money which is closely linked to the discussion of Section VI, will only be mentioned in passing. The literature on trade is totally omitted; furthermore, even for topics falling directly within the scope of this survey (e.g., the empirical literature on purchasing power parity and on forward rates as predictors of ensuing spot rates), when numerous papers have been published, only a few representative ones will be cited.

I. Purchasing Power Parity in International Finance

PPP has essentially two uses in capital market theory and international corporate finance. One is as a measure of the similarity of, or difference between, consumption opportunities in different countries. The other is as a possible influence on the cash flows generated by production or trade activities of firms. Our concern in this section is with the former aspect while the latter aspect will be discussed in Section VIII. Deviations from PPP, which our survey reveals to be the rule, serve to differentiate one nation from another. When PPP deviations exist, investors in different regions will measure their real returns differently and desire to hold generally different portfolios.

To fix ideas, let us first distinguish PPP from commodity price parity (CPP), also known as the law of one price. CPP is an instantaneous arbitrage condition which holds between the prices of identical traded goods in two locations in the absence of any barriers to trade. It may also hold between nontraded goods which are close substitutes for (or can be transformed into) traded goods.[9] In contrast, PPP is a relationship between weighted average price levels, not individual commodity prices. In practice, price levels are measured by indices which are calculated relative to some base period; writing the parity of price levels at two different instants and taking the ratio leads to the so-called "Relative PPP." If price levels are arbitrarily set to be equal in some base year, any change in the price of one good relative to the others, will suffice to create a PPP deviation in the ensuing years.

Let us dwell briefly on the conditions required for PPP to hold exactly. First, the consumer price indices computed by the world's national statistical institutes must be a valid representation of the consumption possibilities and preferences of their citizens. The Appendix details the assumptions required. If a nation's consumers are utility maximizers (with time additive utility), they will have a compositionally invariant price index in which budget shares reveal their tastes if their preferences are also homothetic. Given such homothetic preferences, published cost of living indices approximate exact indices and may reasonably be compared across countries.[10]

---

[9] CPP can be tested directly by comparing absolute prices after translation into a common currency. A second test is whether the relative price of two goods is the same everywhere.

[10] We know of no direct test of the homotheticity of preferences. If the homotheticity assumption is violated, *two variable* price indices (one reflecting "average" and the other "marginal" budget-

The Journal of Finance

For PPP to hold exactly, sufficient conditions include homothetic preferences, as above; CPP with respect to every good included in the index; and, in addition, identical tastes to guarantee that the compositions of different nations' indices will be identical. These conditions are not necessary; it is apparent from the debates of the 1920s that PPP could also emerge despite differences in tastes and the presence of nontraded goods, provided that there existed enough substitutability among goods in consumption and between traded and nontraded goods in production to produce high correlations between the prices of individual commodities. The details need not concern us here.

As noted, the importance of PPP deviations in international finance stems from the way in which investors compute the real returns from a given security. Consider a U.S. investor holding a Japanese security with a given (perhaps random) nominal return. If this nominal (or monetary) return is measured in yen,[11] he will first translate it into dollars and then deflate it using the U.S. Consumer Price Index or, better yet, his own index, expressed in dollars.[12] This generates the U.S. purchasing power of this foreign income. But, consider a Japanese investor holding the same security and expecting the same nominal (yen or dollar) nominal return. His real return is obtained by deflating the yen nominal return by his, or the Japanese, price index measured in yen. If PPP held exactly, i.e., if the two price indices were exactly in line with the exchange rate, the two investors would view the real return identically. Their notions of the real returns from the same security will differ to the extent that their price indices, expressed or translated into a common currency, are different, i.e., to the extent that PPP is violated.

This is not to say, however, that the deviations themselves enter any investor's calculus or, therefore, that they feature in any way as a separate source of risk. Each computes his real returns using his own index, irrespective of any comparison with a foreigner's index. For given distributions of nominal securities returns, the existence of PPP does not remove or alleviate the risk of a foreign investment absolutely or relatively to a home investment.[13]

---

shares) are necessary to model mean-variance portfolio choices. See the last section of Breeden [30]. See also Stulz [191].

[11] Starting from returns measured in Yen is of no importance. The end result, the real returns, is independent of that fact. If we had specified that the security, or its returns, is *denominated* in Yen, it would have been an indication as to the pay-off structure of the security, namely that the return in Yen is fixed ahead of time. Such a specification would apply to a deposit in a Japanese bank or to a Yen fixed income security. For other securities types, such as stocks, no matter what the currency of payment of the random dividends may be, there is no denomination a priori. But, based on the probabilistic payoff structure of the security, one may establish its implicit denomination. This is the object of exposure computations; see below, in Sections IV and VIII.

[12] Obviously cost-of-living indices given by national statistical institutes have a currency dimension (irrespective of the fact that they are usually quoted as a dimensionless number computed relative to a base year where the index is set at 100). They may accordingly be translated from one currency into the other. One may thus obtain the cost-of-living index of French households expressed in U.S. dollars.

[13] Nonetheless price discrepancies between trading areas will generally affect the trade and production activities of firms and therefore their returns as well as the general welfare (see Sections VI and VIII). But this is a separate issue. We are examining now portfolio choices with given securities returns. In this context, PPP deviations arise only when *comparing* the portfolio choices of different investors, not in examining the risk borne by any one of them.

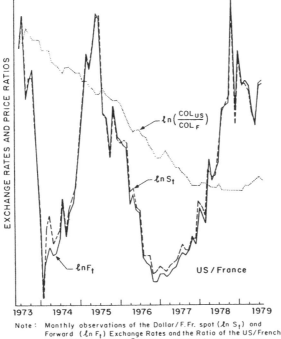

Note :   Monthly observations of the Dollar/F.Fr. spot ($\ell n\,S_t$) and
         Forward ($\ell n\,F_t$) Exchange Rates and the Ratio of the US/French
         Cost of Living Indices [$\ell n(COL_{US}/COL_F)$ (scaled to equal the
         spot exchange rate at the initial month)] June 1973 – July 1979.

Source :   J. A. Frenkel (68)

Figure 1.   U.S.–French PPP Deviations, 1973–1979

The empirical evidence regarding PPP deviations is important mainly for revealing that investors' real returns do differ and therefore that their portfolio compositions should differ. Figure 1 is typical of the empirical record: similar patterns are displayed by all the other major currencies. The clear implication is that PPP is violated. During the most recent period, PPP deviations have been large and cumulative in the sense that deviations in a given direction have lasted for lengthy but variable periods. Clearly, PPP is a questionable hypothesis for the short-run; is it better in the longer run? In terms of Figure 1, does the fact that the exchange rate seems to cycle irregularly around the price-index ratio mean that PPP deviations are ultimately self-reversing? Let us examine first the evidence regarding the two major causes of PPP deviations:[14] CPP deviations and differences in national consumption baskets.

CPP normally holds to within narrow transaction cost margins for homogeneous goods which are traded on organized auction markets such as commodities exchanges. Gold and other readily arbitrable metals are good examples. Since Cassel proposed the PPP hypothesis, however, other authors including most

[14] We shall not survey exhaustively the voluminous literation on PPP. It has been reviewed already by Balassa [18] and Officer [148] and in the May 1978 issue of the *Journal of International Economics*.

recently Isard [96], Kravis and Lipsey [112], and Richardson [156] have found evidence of persistent and large deviations from CPP (up to 5% during the fixed rate period and up to 20% under floating rates). Exhaustive empirical investigations have been conducted by Katseli-Papaefstratiou [101] and Crouhy-Veyrac et al. [38]. The combined sample includes most classes of traded goods; the deviations are largely unexplained. Their existence has been attributed to imperfections which prevent arbitrage such as taxes, tariffs, and transactions costs; asymmetric information; or monopoly and discriminatory pricing. In part they may be illusory. Goods within even narrow commodity trade classifications are not homogeneous. In addition, there may be measurement errors in prices, especially on long term contracts. All in all, however, CPP violations seem to be the rule rather than the exception.

As far as PPP is concerned, Kravis and Lipsey [112] quoting Kravis et al. [111] have produced comparisons of absolute price levels in 1970. Their Table 1 is reproduced here as our Table I. The comparison is performed in two ways: once using local national weights, and once using uniformly for all countries the same set of weights (*viz.* the U.S. weights) for the various commodity groups. Simple examination shows that deviations are wider when using different weights than when using the same weights. Differences in national consumption tastes therefore do contribute to PPP deviations.

There is a frequently stated view, however, that while PPP may fail at any instant, it is a good long-run hypothesis. This belief appears to be based on the notion that the average deviation, where the average is taken over long periods, seems to tend to zero for most countries. Gailliot [72] calculated the percentage deviations of wholesale price indices from purchasing power parity with the U.S. dollar, from the 1900–4 average to the 1963–7 average; they were, for Canada .04, France −.01, Germany .04, Italy −.11, Japan .26, Switzerland .14, and the United Kingdom .11 or .02, depending on which index he used. Aliber and Stickney [16] calculated annual PPP deviations and found that the average deviation declined

Table I

Relative Price Levels in 1970 (U.S. = 100)

	Own Weights			U.S. Weights		
	Price Levels			Price Levels		
Country	GDP	Traded Goods	Nontraded Goods	GDP	Traded Goods	Nontraded Goods
Kenya	34.9	58.5	22.3	74.2	96.7	48.9
India	24.0	46.8	10.3	47.6	74.4	17.3
Columbia	31.8	57.6	21.0	62.0	91.6	28.6
Hungary	44.7	62.7	30.7	66.0	95.0	33.0
Italy	66.2	84.0	50.4	82.9	107.0	55.5
Japan	61.1	82.5	46.4	76.4	95.3	55.0
United Kingdom	65.8	83.3	50.2	77.8	97.0	55.9
Germany, F.R.	79.8	99.2	60.9	95.4	114.5	73.5
France	73.8	83.4	63.4	89.1	105.9	70.4
United States	100.0	100.0	100.0	100.0	100.0	100.0

Source: I.B. Kravis, Z. Kenessey, A. Heston, and R. Summers [111].

as the number of annual observations was increased. Such results are to be expected if PPP deviations follow patterns usch as those reflected in Figure 1. The question is what they imply for the modeling of commodities price levels and exchange rates in the absolute, and relative to each other. Should we select stochastic processes for these quantities incorporating reversals towards PPP? The answer should, of course, come from a general equilibrium model, but at this stage, we can only discuss the elements of a reasonable formulation.

The available empirical evidence does not exhibit any tendency towards reversal (or non-zero serial correlation). Gailliot [72] claimed on the basis of casual observation that a positive 5-year-average deviation in one decade was followed by a negative deviation in the next, between 1903 and 1967. Such evidence does not seem strong. Roll [161] provided the first test of the existence of serial correlation in PPP deviations. Using monthly IMF data for twenty-three countries between 1957 and 1976, Roll found no evidence of serial correlations in his pooled-sample runs. However, some measure of serial correlation, both positive and negative, emerged for some countries, most notably Iran, Argentina, and Mexico. The individual country results were not analyzed in detail. Other tests by Rogalski and Vinso [158] reached similar conclusions. Adler and Lehmann [10], using distributed-lag regressions, tested the hypothesis that PPP deviations follow a martingale (and therefore exhibit no serial correlation). Various samples of monthly and annual data (for both "fixed" and flexible rate periods) and various durations of lags (up to ten years) all produce similar results: as a rule the martingale model is not rejected.[15]

These empirical results suggest that PPP is violated instantaneously and can be expected to be violated for any forecasting horizon. They therefore suggest the heterogeneity of national consumption tastes as a foundation for international finance.

The economic interpretation of the empirical success of the martingale process is not straightforward, however. A theoretically sound model of PPP deviations would incorporate both the action of costly commodities trading and that of almost costless information-efficient foreign exchange trading. Costly commodities trading would cause the law of one price (CPP) to be violated instantaneously (*ex post*) and would allow the exchange rate to fluctuate within a band (akin to the gold points of the previous century) on either side of its PPP level. On the other hand, costless information-efficient foreign exchange and bond trading causes the current spot exchange rate to be the best predictor of the future exchange rate adjusted for interest rates (see Section V) and further, since interest rates anticipate inflation, it also causes the current real exchange rate to be the best predictor of the future exchange rate adjusted for the anticipated inflation difference between the two countries. This last statement is what may be termed the *ex ante* PPP hypothesis and it leads to the martingale model.[16]

But it is not clear how the commodities and the foreign exchange markets

---

[15] I.e., the fact that a currency is below its PPP value is no indication that it will subsequently appreciate absolutely or even relative to price levels. Nevertheless, a number of commercial foreign exchange forecasting services sell forecasts based on PPP deviations.

[16] As was stressed by one referee, *ex post* PPP, and not just *ex ante* PPP, would be needed to remove the heterogeneity of perceived real returns across investors.

interact. If the martingale model held strictly, an absolute deviation taking place today would never tend to be corrected; this is surely an undesirable feature of this model.

For the present, all that can be safely said is that the actual behavior of PPP deviations cannot be statistically distinguished from a martingale. More specifically, under floating rates, PPP deviations behave approximately like the exchange rates themselves[17, 18] (see Genberg [73] and our Table II) and the latter more or less follow a martingale (Poole [152]).

II. The Empirical Structure of International Returns

Since much of the research in international finance involves either applications of statistical regression techniques or extensions of mean-variance portfolio theory, we should briefly review the little that is known about the probabilistic structure of international returns. Two separate aspects are covered in this section: one is the question of the probability distribution which best describes these returns; and the second is the matter of estimating empirically the scope for risk reduction through international diversification and, more generally, the validity of market regression models as descriptors of the risk structure of international asset prices. Let us take each in turn.

A. *The Probability Distribution of International Returns*

The first issue is whether the returns on international investment are normally distributed and, if they are not, what probability distribution best describes them. Unfortunately, no one yet has investigated the distributions of real returns. Farber, Roll, and Solnik [61] examined the distribution of $R = (S_{t+1}/S_t) [(1 + r_k)/(1 + r_n)] - 1$ where S is the spot exchange rate and r_k and r_n are the foreign and domestic nominal interest rates: R represents the nominal excess rate of return (over the domestic riskfree rate) on speculation in the money market.[19] For monthly data between 1964 and 1975, they discovered that the distribution of R departed from normality but less, apparently, than the distribution of the exchange rate change itself: the comparison was not made in great detail.

It is the distribution of exchange rate changes which has received the most attention. Besides Farber, Roll, and Solnik [61], investigations include those of Westerfield [202], Dooley and Shafer [42], Papadia [149] and, most recently, McFarland, Pettit, and Sung [135]. In all cases, severe departures from normality were discovered, generally more so for pre-1973 data than for the floating-rate period. Following the research of Granger and Morgenstern [77] and Fama and

---

[17] I.e., price levels fluctuate little in comparison to exchange rates. To some extent, this may be due to a diversification effect between commodities prices. See Cornell [35].

[18] This indicates that PPP deviations and the portfolio issues arising from them are properly raised within the context of a multi-currency world. PPP deviations also occur domestically (i.e., across one country) but they are probably less important and less random.

[19] Under interest rate parity (cf. Section V), R can be rewritten $R = S_{t+1}/F_t - 1$ where F_t is the forward rate: R is then also the nominal return to forward speculation for a contract size equal to one unit of domestic currency. If the domestic interest rate properly anticipates domestic inflation, it is also an estimate of the real rent from a foreign investment position (in excess of the domestic real interest rate).

Table II

Sources of Deviations from PPP: 1971
February–1979 December. Correlations
of eight exchange rates (against the
U.S. dollar) with their respective PPP
levels. 107 observations

The correlations are measured after
taking first differences on both sides.

Germany	.996
Belgium	.995
Canada	.923
France	.998
Japan	.938
Netherlands	.994
United Kingdom	.961
Switzerland	.983

Data Source: OECD main economic indicators,
various issues.

Roll [59], and the observation that the empirical exchange-rate distributions had fatter tails and greater kurtosis than the normal, further tests suggest that these distributions may be stable-paretian with characteristic exponent between 1.3 and 1.8. The currently prevailing hypothesis, then, is that the distributions of the exchange rates belong to the stable, infinite-variance class.[20]

Alternative views are, however, by no means excluded. One view is that the observed exchange rate variations are drawn from nonstationary normal distributions; i.e., that the exchange rates themselves follow a stochastic process with variable parameters. In order to account for the fat tails in exchange rate variations, this process should have a tendency to diverge or oscillate more widely than does a regular Brownian motion; i.e., the variance would have to grow faster than linearly with time.

One other view is that exchange rates, as a result of government intervention, or for some other reason, undergo discrete jumps. This could be modeled by means of combined Poisson and diffusion process, provided the mean frequency of these jumps is approximately constant. Kouri [107] calculated portfolio choices and some elements of the equilibrium (the forward premium) under the Poisson assumption. Both alternative views lack a good empirical analysis so far.

---

[20] As Granger [78] points out, it is, of course, difficult actually to prove that any sequence of observed random variables in fact has a stable, non-normal distribution. Strong indication but not proof is provided by tests of the stability of the characteristic exponent as increasing numbers of (log) price or exchange-rate changes are added together, both chronologically and in randomized order. Westerfield tested only the chronological sequences and found the characteristic exponents to be reasonably stable for sums of between one and ten weekly observations: characteristic exponents rose with the length of sequence but reached a maximum of 1.69. McFarland, Pettit, and Sung employ daily data between 1/75 and 7/79. Tests of chronological and randomized sequences both showed a tendency for characteristic exponents to rise slowly but to remain below 1.7 for sequences of up to 15. However, when the chronological sequences were lengthened to 25, at the cost of reduced sample size, the characteristic exponents of six out of eight exchange rates reached 2.00, the critical value for normality. The authors express little confidence in this comforting result.

The major question raised is whether these various distribution assumptions make mean-variance theory totally inapplicable. With regard to the infinite-variance hypothesis, one may note that, even if returns distributions are stable, they may be approximately normal within a finite range; if, further, utility functions are appropriately bounded, the expected utility integral computed over such a normal approximation may be approximately mean-variance. There is a clear need, at this point, for better theories of approximation. The nonstationarity hypothesis would create only minor complications at the theoretical level; the state variables which shift the parameters of the stochastic process must merely be made explicit. Mean-variance theory remains valid locally. The real difficulty is empirical; it would arise when attempting to identify the state variables and estimating the functional link between the parameters to the process and the state variables. Of course, the wider the class of permissible model formulations, the more hazardous the statistical task.[21] Similar comments may be made regarding the possibility of adding on some Poisson jumps.

B. *Correlations among International Returns and Diversification*

If national financial markets are not perfectly (positively) correlated, investors should be able to reduce their portfolio-variance-risk without sacrificing expected return by international diversification. This simple insight gave rise to a series of papers, including Grubel [80]; Levy and Sarnat [122], who computed also internationally-efficient combinations of stock market indices subject to a short-selling constraint; and Solnik [181] who demonstrated that the additional variance reduction could be obtained with a relatively small number of securities.

Table III illustrates, with data for nine stock markets during the 1971–9 period, the kind of correlation patterns which underlie these earlier studies. Panel A presents correlations between pairs of nominal returns which are not translated into U.S. dollars or adjusted for U.S. inflation: these seem quite similar to those presented in Lessard [117] for the period 1959–73. Translation and deflation do not exchange the coefficients very much: the correlations among real returns in U.S. terms appear in Panel B. The thing to notice about both panels is that the correlations are fairly small. The same pattern holds true for returns measured in other currencies and deflated by other indices.

One other method used to display the potential for risk reduction consists in regressions of individual stock returns or of national market indices on a world market index. This is the route taken by early writers such as Agmon [12], Solnik [180], and Lessard [118]. In Lessard's experiments, the residuals of regressions of the stock's national index or of its local industry index on the world market index proxy were introduced as additional orthogonal factors into the market model test.

In the actual event the fits produced by Agmon's single index, Lessard's multiple factor, and Solnik's "national" and "international" factor models were relatively weak. Generally, at least 40 percent of the variation was left unexplained. This result is not in itself surprising, given the low correlations between

---

[21] This is especially true when the results of the statistical estimation are to be fed into an optimization program. See the end of Section III.

Table III

Correlations of Monthly Price Relatives For Nine Major Stock Market Indices:
1/71–12/79

| | Panel A: Nominal Monthly Returns in Original Currency | | | | | | | | | | ST. |
	GER	BEL	CAN	FRA	JAP	NET	UK	SWI	USA	E.V.	DEV.
GER	1.00									0.005	0.041
BEL	0.48	1.00								0.008	0.038
CAN	0.24	0.45	1.00							0.011	0.051
FRA	0.44	0.60	0.34	1.00						0.009	0.070
JAP	0.35	0.29	0.26	0.13	1.00					0.013	0.050
NET	0.59	0.66	0.52	0.50	0.37	1.00				0.005	0.047
UK	−.03	0.06	−.01	−0.6	0.04	−.04	1.00			0.008	0.820
SWI	0.52	0.64	0.46	0.42	0.37	0.63	−.14	1.00		0.004	0.050
USA	0.28	0.49	0.69	0.34	0.34	0.52	−.005	0.53	1.00	0.005	0.046

| | Panel B: Real Monthly Returns in $US, Deflated by U.S. C.P.I. | | | | | | | | | | ST. |
	GER	BEL	CAN	FRA	JAP	NET	UK	SWI	USA	E.V.	DEV.
GER	1.00									0.011	0.090
BEL	0.51	1.00								0.012	0.085
CAN	0.25	0.40	1.00							0.004	0.053
FRA	0.41	0.59	0.40	1.00						0.018	0.144
JAP	0.47	0.40	0.28	0.26	1.00					0.011	0.059
NET	0.54	0.65	0.47	0.51	0.39	1.00				0.010	0.104
UK	0.11	0.09	0.66	−.02	0.06	0.12	1.00			0.071	0.764
SWI	0.56	0.70	0.46	0.55	0.48	0.60	−.07	1.00		0.007	0.058
USA	0.34	0.48	0.69	0.38	0.33	0.53	0.02	0.49	1.00	−.002	0.046

Sources: (a) Capital International, *Perspectives*, various issues; (b) OECD Main Economic Indicators.

the indices from various exchanges. It is consistent also with the earlier results of Blume [25] and King [103] for the U.S. market. The size of the firm-specific residual variances in any of these regressions, domestic or international, certainly seem to suggest that considerable scope exists for risk reduction from diversification. However, one should be careful about taking this conclusion much further.

The main limitation of this kind of analysis arises from the choice of the index or indices against which the regression is run. In domestic finance, regressing a security's return on any efficient-portfolio return produces residuals whose variance is easily interpreted as "diversifiable risk," since an investor choosing that portfolio would require no compensation for bearing that risk. Further, in a market which is at equilibrium and in which practically all investors do diversify, the market portfolio is one portfolio known to be efficient (Roll [160]). The normative implication is then fairly simple: diversifiable risk can be measured against the market portfolio. But, when investors' purchasing power units differ by nationality, as we allow below, they will in principle differ in their concept of what an efficient portfolio is (except if they all have logarithmic utilities: see Section III); and there will be no implication that at market equilibrium the market portfolio should be efficient in any sense or, *a fortiori*, that its nominal rate of return measured in any currency should serve as a benchmark for valuation. Any segmentation will compound this effect. As a result, there can be no simple way to infer the extent to which the gains from variance-risk reduction can be reaped by different nations' citizens merely from analyzing the structure of securities' markets data alone. The data themselves may be consistent with any number of models of portfolio selection and market equilibrium, with or without segmentation. The availability of risk reduction will depend upon which one is true. This point should put an end to all further attempts to base measures of such quantities as "risk reduction" or "diversifiable risk" on sample estimates of the means and variances of and correlations among market or industry indices. The covariance matrix also says nothing about the presence or absence of segmentation.[22]

Suppose, however, that we have an international CAPM where the market portfolio nominal rate of return is the proper benchmark, as is the case, for instance, in Solnik [179]. National or industry factors in this setting are theoretically irrelevant.[23] One may then regress individual stock returns on a single international market index. To an approximation, the residual risk may be diversified away.[24] One may, of course, introduce additional orthogonal factors such as the residuals from regressions of national indices on the world index or from regressions of industry indices on the world index. The expanded specification cannot produce any information regarding the relative benefits of international as opposed to interindustry or purely domestic diversification. This observation underscores the confusion surrounding the question of whether interindustry diversification within countries or international diversification across industries, or some combination of both, can be replicated by international diversification across national indices. This question, which no one has examined systematically, is of considerable practical interest.

In short, the main use of single or multiple-factor market models is probably, much as in Sharpe's [175] diagonal model, the reduction of data requirements for the computation of optimal portfolios. The variability of the world index combined with other factors, or alternatively, the variability of foreign market indices combined with orthogonal factors representing local industry groupings and the world market both leave large fractions of individual assets' variabilities unexplained. The potential for international diversification to reduce risk seems unquestionable. Beyond simplifying data requirements,[25]; however, the available

---

[22] See Adler and Dumas [3] and Section VII below. Two more criticisms may be leveled against these statistical descriptions. One is potentially devastating: rates of return may not be stationary so that it may not be legitimate to apply correlation or regression analysis to them. A second one may be less important empirically: most of the published work refers to U.S. current dollar returns when actually deflated returns should have been employed.

[23] This is not a critique of Solnik's [180] empirical procedure. Quite the opposite: he was precisely trying to verify that national factors (orthogonal to the world portfolio) received a zero price.

[24] See, however, Friend and Losq [71] who argued that a simple extension of the CAPM such as Agmon's [12] in which all investors worldwide hold only the world market portfolio, will tend to overstate the gains from international diversification.

[25] These statistics do have descriptive, if not normative, value, however, and they may lead to some more fundamental analysis: one could seek the sources of the correlations between financial markets and the origins and differences between means and variances of return. E.g., is there a connection between these and patterns of trade and specialization?

market-model results offer neither guidelines for the construction of optimally diversified international portfolios nor the basis for evaluating the benefits or value of such diversification. These matters are addressed next.

III. Portfolio Choice

In view of the fairly low correlation between national financial markets observed in the previous section, it is possible to reap important gains from international portfolio diversification. In the present section we seek the optimal portfolios of worldwide investments which maximize these gains.

Consider a world of $L + 1$ countries and currencies. Without loss of generality, we measure nominal returns in terms of the $L + 1$st currency. Nominal rates of return given in another currency can easily be translated by multiplying one plus the foreign-currency rate of return by the ratio of the end-of-period to the beginning-of-period exchange rate. There are N nominally risky securities, whose nominal price dynamics in terms of the measurement currency are given by stationary Ito processes (Brownian motions):[26]

$$dY_i/Y_i = \mu_i \, dt + \sigma_i \, dz_i \qquad i = 1 \cdots N \tag{1}$$

where

Y_i is the market value of security i in terms of currency $L + 1$;
μ_i is the instantaneous expected nominal rate of return on security i;
σ_i is the instantaneous standard deviation of the nominal rate of return
  on security i; and
z_i is a standard Wiener process and dz_i is the associated white noise.

We also define $\underline{\Omega}$ as the $N \times N$ matrix of instantaneous covariances $\sigma_{i,k}$ of the nominal rates of return on the various securities. Finally, there is one (the $N +$ 1st) security which is nominally riskless: an interest earning bank deposit or short-term bond denominated in the measurement currency. The instantaneous nominal rate of interest paid on this deposit is denoted r.

In some applications, it will be useful to distinguish two subsets among the nominally risky securities: the last L securities may be taken to be the nominal bank deposits denominated in the non-measurement currencies, while the first $n(n = N - L)$ would be stock securities paying a random dividend.[27] If we

---

[26] See the critique below.

[27] Formally Equation (1) only allows for income in the form of capital gains. A simple change of notation can incorporate dividends. Let a (constant return-to-scale) dividend dx be paid in an interval of time dt with

$$dx/Y = \mu_d \, dt + \sigma_d \, dz_d$$

and let the price actually behave as:

$$dY/Y = (\mu - \mu_d) \, dt + \sigma \, dz - \sigma_d \, dz_d \tag{1'}$$

then the total rate of return on the stock is given by Equation (1) in the text. Stock price behavior partition accordingly the covariance matrix $\underline{\Omega}$, its southeast block then contains the covariances of exchange rates.

There are $L + 1$ national investor types, each with homothetic utility functions.[28] The price index P^l of an investor of type l, expressed in the measurement currency, follows a stationary process:[29]

$$dP^l/P^l = \pi^l \, dt + \sigma_\pi^l \, dz_\pi^l \qquad l = 1 \cdots L + 1 \qquad (2)$$

where π^l and $\underline{\sigma}_\pi^l$ are the expected value and standard deviation of the instantaneous rate of inflation as seen by investor l. We call $\underline{\omega}^l$ the $N \times N$ vector of covariances $\sigma_{i,\pi}^l$ of the N risky securities returns with investor l's rate of inflation. The superscript l will be dropped whenever we consider one (generic) investor in isolation.

While they are not strictly inconsistent with the empirical evidence presented in Sections I and II above, one may nevertheless raise strong objections to the *a priori* specification of the functional forms ((1) and (2)) for the dynamics of stock and commodities prices when they should actually be endogenous. Lucas [129] can be interpreted as having shown that the stationary Brownian motion for asset prices in equation (1) is not consistent with the positive risk aversion of (time-additive von Neumann-Morgenstern utility endowed) investors. It would be consistent only with risk neutral investor behavior where μ would be the rate of time discount (applicable uniformly to all securities). Under risk aversion, asset prices multiplied by discounted marginal utilities must follow martingales and so discounted asset prices by themselves generally do not, in contradiction with equation (1). For further details, see Lucas [129]. Rosenberg and Ohlson [164] also pointed out that the portfolio choices (9) to be derived from the equations of motion (1) are unreasonable. In a domestic setting at least, these asset demands would imply that the prices of assets relative to each other would all be functions of one and the same random factor (the weighted average of risk tolerances α) and so would all be perfectly correlated.

These internal flaws can be corrected by introducing nonstationary Ito processes where the parameters μ and σ would be functions of a vector of state variables. The resulting portfolio choices would contain one more (hedge) fund per state variable, in addition to the two funds which appear in (9) below. See Merton [140] or Breeden [30], Stulz [191], and Hodrick [90]. The functions $\mu(\cdot)$ and $\sigma(\cdot)$ would in turn have to be endogenized at equilibrium. Procedures for so doing have been provided by Cox, Ingersoll, and Ross [37]. They amount essentially to interpreting the CAPM as a functional equation in these unknown factors, rather than as an algebraic equation giving the expected return on a security. This final step, so far, has only been performed for economies populated with *identical consumer-investors*.

(1′) is still a geometric Brownian motion because

$$(\sigma \, dz - \sigma_d \, dz_d)/(\sigma^2 + \sigma_d^2 - 2\rho\sigma\sigma_d)^{1/2}$$

is a Wiener process, for so long as σ and σ_d are constants (ρ stands here for the correlation between dz and dz_d.)

[28] See footnote 10 for references to the more general case.

[29] See the critique below.

For this reason, we are not prepared to propose a complete general-equilibrium model of international capital markets. The heterogeneity in consumption tastes which characterizes international finance would require as yet unknown procedures for computing equilibrium prices. State variables which will ultimately have to be introduced into the model could easily be handled in the portfolio computation below, in the manner of Merton [140] or Breeden [30], but this added complication would not speak to the specific feature of the field which is the heterogeneity in the purchasing power of money. In order to focus on that aspect and to illustrate its implications most vividly, we restrict ourselves to stationary Brownian motions; i.e., to constant μ's and σ's in Equation (1).

The equation of motion (2) can equally be criticized on the ground that commodities prices should be endogenized. In addition, it might have been preferable to start the analysis with the price dynamics of individual commodities rather than with that of a price index. Were individual prices to follow stationary Brownian motions, price indices generally would not, as expenditure shares fluctuate with relative prices (even if preferences are homothetic[30]). Only when expenditure shares are constant (Cobb-Douglas utility function) can both individual prices and indices simultaneously be Brownian. But we have no reason to favor one assumption over the other. Note that we leave unspecified the reason for the PPP deviations $(dP^l/P^l - dP^1/P^1)$; they may equally arise from differences in tastes (as in Stulz [191]) or from CPP deviations. If, as suggested by the empirical evidence of Section I, *ex ante* PPP holds and PPP deviations follow a martingale, the parameters of the stochastic process in (2) can be restricted accordingly.

Assuming homothetic direct utility functions, the material of the Appendix implies that we may express an investor's objective function as:[31]

$$\text{Max } E \int_t^T V(C, P, s) \, ds \qquad (3)$$

where C is the nominal rate of consumption expenditures, P is the price level index, and $V(\cdot)$ is a function homogeneous of degree zero in C and P expressing the instantaneous rate of indirect utility. Calling $w = \{w_i\}$, the $(N + 1) \times 1$ vector whose components sum to 1 and which indicates the investor's portfolio choice among the available investment opportunities, his wealth dynamics are:[32]

$$dW = [\textstyle\sum_{i=1}^N w_i(\mu_i - r) + r]W \, dt - C \, dt - \sum_{i=1}^N w_i \sigma_i \, dz_i \qquad (4)$$

where W is nominal wealth. Denoting by $J(W, P, t)$ the maximum value of (3) subject to (4), the Bellman principle states that this function must be stationary

---

[30] Homotheticity only guarantees that indices do not fluctuate with wealth, as relative prices are kept constant. If, in addition, utilities were not homothetic, recall from Breeden [30] and Stulz [191] that two indices (one based on average and the other on marginal expenditure shares) would be needed. A similar observation had been made by Adler and Dumas [6] in the more restrictive context of utilities assuming a quadratic form.

[31] Some bequest function could be added without modifying the results we wish to obtain. Income from sources other than security returns is ruled out.

[32] See Merton [138]. The last portfolio variable w_{N+1} has been eliminated on the basis of $\sum_{i=1}^{N+1} w_i = 1$.

or that its total expected rate of increase must be identically zero:

$$0 \equiv \underset{C,\underline{w}}{\text{Max}}[V(C, P, t) + J_t + J_W\{[\textstyle\sum_{i=1}^{N} w_i(\mu_i - r) + r]W - C\}$$

$$+ J_P P\pi + \tfrac{1}{2}J_{W,W}\textstyle\sum_{i=1}^{N}\sum_{k=1}^{N} w_i w_k \sigma_{i,k}W^2 + \tfrac{1}{2}J_{P,P}\sigma_\pi^2 P^2$$

$$+ J_{W,P}\textstyle\sum_{i=1}^{N} w_i\sigma_{i,\pi}WP] \tag{5}$$

The homogeneity of degree 0 of the function $V(C, P, t)$ implies that $J(W, P, t)$ and $C(W, P, t)$ which satisfy (5) must be homogeneous of degree zero in W and P. By Euler's theorem:

$$J_P \equiv -(W/P)J_W$$

and therefore:[33]

$$J_{P,W} \equiv -(1/P)J_W - (W/P)J_{W,W}$$

$$J_{P,P} \equiv -(W/P)J_{W,P} + (W/P^2)J_W$$

$$\equiv 2(W/P^2)J_W + (W/P)^2 J_{W,W}$$

Substituting into (5)

$$0 \equiv \underset{C,\underline{w}}{\text{Max}}[V(C, P, t) + J_t$$

$$+ J_W\{[\textstyle\sum_{i=1}^{N} w_i(\mu_i - r) + r - \pi + \sigma_\pi^2 - \sum_{i=1}^{N} w_i\sigma_{i,\pi}]W - C\}$$

$$+ \tfrac{1}{2}J_{W,W}\{\textstyle\sum_{i=1}^{N}\sum_{k=1}^{N} w_i w_k \sigma_{i,k} - 2\sum_{i=1}^{N} w_i\sigma_{i,\pi} + \sigma_\pi^2\}W^2]$$

The derivatives with respect to the decision variables C and w_i are set equal to zero:

$$V_C = J_W \tag{6}$$

$$0 = J_W(\mu_i - r - \sigma_{i,\pi}) + J_{W,W}(\textstyle\sum_{k=1}^{N} w_k\sigma_{i,k} - \sigma_{i,\pi})W \tag{7}$$

Defining: $\alpha = -J_W/J_{W,W}W$ as the investor's risk tolerance,[34] we can rewrite (7) in the form of a required nominal yield on security i:

$$\mu_i = r + \left(1 - \frac{1}{\alpha}\right)\sigma_{i,\pi} + \frac{1}{\alpha}\textstyle\sum_{k=1}^{N} w_k\sigma_{i,k}, \tag{8}$$

an equation we shall have occasion to refer to again. Solving for the optimal portfolio directly in vector notation, we get:

$$\underline{w} = \alpha\left(\frac{\Omega^{-1}(\underline{\mu} - r\underline{1})}{1 - \underline{1}'\Omega^{-1}(\underline{\mu} - r\underline{1})}\right) + (1 - \alpha)\left(\frac{\Omega^{-1}\underline{\omega}}{1 - \underline{1}'\Omega^{-1}\underline{\omega}}\right) \tag{9}$$

where $\underline{1}$ is an $N \times 1$ vector of ones and $\underline{1}'$ its transpose; $\underline{\mu}$ is the vector of

---

[33] This procedure has been used by Fischer [62] and Losq [127].

[34] This was not the only possible definition of risk tolerance. An alternative definition (Breeden [30]) is: $-V_C/V_{C,C}C$. The two are not equivalent, since the wealth elasticity of consumption is not generally equal to 1.

nominal expected returns, μ_i; $\underline{\Omega}$ is the $N \times N$ matrix of instantaneous covariances $\sigma_{i,k}$ of the nominal rates of return on the various securities; $\underline{\omega}$ is the $N \times 1$ vector of covariances $\sigma_{i,\pi}$ of the N risky securities returns with the investor's rate of inflation.

As has been pointed out by Kouri [107] and Losq [127], the optimal portfolio is the combination with weights α and $1 - \alpha$ of two component portfolios which we now interpret. As is well known,[35] the logarithmic utility function $((\rho)'\ln(C/P))$ implies $\alpha = 1$. The first component portfolio (with coefficient α) is therefore the portfolio of a logarithmic investor. The formula indicates that its composition is independent of the behavior of commodity prices. This is not a new result:[36] $\ln(C/P) = \ln C - \ln P$ and therefore commodities prices separate out in the objective function and have no influence on the decisions. As a result, the logarithmic component is the same for all investors, irrespective of nationality; a logarithmic investor would be nationless. Geometrically, this implies that the Markowitz efficient frontiers of all the investors have one point in common (where they are all tangent necessarily). Naturally, the composition is independent of the choice of the measurement currency.[37]

The second component portfolio (with weight $1 - \alpha$) is the portfolio of an investor with zero risk tolerance ($\alpha = 0$). It is therefore, for any given investor, his global minimum variance portfolio in real terms. The formula based on nominal rates of return bears out this interpretation: $\underline{\Omega}^{-1}\underline{\omega}$ is the vector of regression coefficients of the investor's rate of inflation on the various securities' returns. This portfolio is thus the one whose nominal rate of return is the most highly correlated with the investor's rate of inflation (in measurement currency); or, in other words, it is the best possible hedge against inflation. By Ito's lemma, the random part of real returns is nothing but the random part of nominal returns minus the random part of the rate of inflation. The regression just mentioned minimizes the variance of this difference which is the variance of the real portfolio return. Since this hedge portfolio involves the rate of inflation of commodities' prices, it is investor specific. Its composition is independent of expected nominal returns ($\underline{\mu}$) since the formula involves only covariances; this is appropriate, since this portfolio minimizes the variance without regard for profitability. The composition is also independent of the choice of measurement currency.

We summarize these results in the following formulae (describing investor l's portfolio) and a theorem:

$$\underline{w}^l = \alpha^l \underline{w}_{\log} + (1 - \alpha^l)\underline{w}_h^l \tag{10}$$

$$\underline{w}_{\log} = \begin{pmatrix} \underline{\Omega}^{-1}(\underline{\mu} - r\underline{1}) \\ 1 - \underline{1}'\underline{\Omega}^{-1}(\underline{\mu} - r\underline{1}) \end{pmatrix} \tag{11}$$

$$\underline{w}_h^l = \begin{pmatrix} \underline{\Omega}^{-1}\underline{\omega}^l \\ 1 - \underline{1}'\underline{\Omega}^{-1}\underline{\omega}^l \end{pmatrix} \qquad l = 1, \cdots L + 1 \tag{12}$$

---

[35] Merton [139].

[36] Hakansson [82].

[37] The incredulous reader may check in Sercu [174], Appendix A, where calculations are performed explicitly, using translation of returns, to verify that fact.

THEOREM.[38] (*Optimal portfolio strategy for the individual investor*). *Every investor in the world holds a combination of:*

— *the universal logarithmic portfolio with weight* α.
— *his personalized hedge portfolio which constitutes the best protection against inflation as he perceives it, with weight* $1 - \alpha$.

We have computed the logarithmic portfolio[39] as well as the hedge portfolios of U.S. and French investors as they would have been over the years 1971–9, based on *ex post* monthly rates of return. They are displayed in Table IV. The logarithmic portfolio exhibits large positive and negative weights, negative weights implying borrowing or short selling. This is the component portfolio which takes advantage of expected rate of return differentials. There are exact opposite entries in Canadian and U.S. dollar deposits, because, during this period, U.S. interest rates were above Canadian ones without offsetting exchange rate changes.[40] There is a similar pseudo-arbitrage between the Deutsche Mark on the one hand and the Belgian Franc and the Guilder on the other. When comparing stocks and bank deposits, there is a clear tendency for bank deposit entries to be negative in those currencies where the stock entry is positive and vice-versa, although the numbers are by no means exactly opposite. The reason is that exchange rate variations tend not to offset, and to be wider than, stock price variations; hence there is an incentive to hedge stock purchases against currency risk by means of local borrowing.

The hedge portfolios are even more striking. Although we have only shown the U.S. and French hedge portfolios, the pattern is the same for all nationalities.[41] An investor's hedge portfolio is almost entirely made up of a nominal bank deposit (or Treasury Bill or short-term bond) denominated in his home currency. The reason is that exchange rate fluctuations are much wider than price level (CPI) fluctuations, as we observed earlier in Section II. Also, contrary to a

---

[38] It is known since Black [23] that mean-variance investors who care only about real returns and who are confronted with nationality distinctions, only need (any) two efficient funds. The specific choice of the two funds made here is specially telling in the context of purchasing power differences across investors.

[39] All our statistics and portfolios are conditional. Nominal interest rates presumably contain some *ex ante* information on ensuing inflation rates, exchange rates and stock returns. We have therefore regressed all rates of return on the nine comcomitant interest rates of the various currencies and computed all statistics and portfolios from the residuals of the regression. This procedure amounts to treating nominal interest rates as pseudo state variables. As a result, the logarithmic portfolio composition is a (linear) function of the interest rates prevailing and it fluctuates from month to month. We show in Table IV the average portfolio over the entire decade. One referee objected to this statistical treatment on the grounds that it introduces errors in the variables. In practice, the procedure makes little difference: nominal interest rates simply "explain" very little of ensuing variations. It was introduced only in order to ensure that portfolio choices would be exactly invariant with respect to the choice of measurement currency.

[40] The same empirical result is obtained by Braga de Macedo [26] over the period October 1973 to April 1978. It arises, of course, from the strong correlation between the two currencies. But this multicollinearity itself renders unreliable the two figures −21.81 and 22.01. This and other critical statistical problems will be discussed below.

[41] The weights to be placed on their home-currency deposit by the ten national investor types are: for German investors, 1.009; for the Belgians, 1.029; for the Canadians, 0.983; for the French, 0.988; for the Japanese, 1.007; for the Dutch, 0.973; for the British, 1.030; for the Swiss, 1.021; and for U.S. nationals, 0.983.

popular belief, but full in line with the observations of Lintner [125] and Fama and Schwert [60], stocks are not good hedges against inflation, for various reasons. As a consequence, investors who are very risk averse prefer to bear fully their home inflation risk rather than to bear exchange rate uncertainty or stock price uncertainty. It is not clear whether the result would be modified if real estate or commodities such as rare metals were included in the array of possible investments.

The log-portfolio calculations, however, should not be taken at face value. They suggest improbably that investors individually and in the aggregate should short some securities and hold more than 100% of the available supply of others. Beyond the possibility that the calculated weights violate typical short selling constraints such a result, if sustained, would imply that international capital markets are not in equilibrium (a point on which the evidence will be reviewed in sections IV and V).

Moreover the estimates are plagued by major statistical problems which undermine their significance.[42] No statistical theory, to our knowledge, gives the sample distribution of the estimated $w_{\log}$ from equation (11). We are, therefore, unable to build confidence intervals for the optimal log-portfolio composition in Table IV. Simulation experiments using a single risky asset suggest that these confidence intervals are much wider than the hypothesized [0, 1] range. Had we run them with several risky assets, multicollinearity would have compounded the problem. Presumably, it would be possible to develop more efficient estimates of $w_{\log}$ than the one obtained simply by pre-multiplying the estimated average return vector by the inverse of the estimated covariance matrix. Bawa *et al.* [22] have worked on a Bayesian theory aimed in that direction but few applications have been made.

The hedge portfolio composition is, nonetheless, very clearcut and it is doubtful that, as long as one uses CPI's as indicators of inflation, any statistical problem could raise doubts about it. In fact, the small variability of CPI's relative to securities' returns and exchange rates in the countries we have considered provides a rationale for the early work of Solnik [179], generalized recently by Sercu [174],[43] where it is assumed that each investor ignores his home-currency inflation (or assumes it to be null) and therefore considers rates of return expressed in home currency units as being real returns. Quite evidently this is a case of deviation from PPP[44] since different people regard the same securities' returns differently. One consequence of the assumption is that the home currency bank deposit or Treasury Bill is seen as riskless in real terms by the national investors (and only by them). It is not difficult to verify on the basis of equation

---

[42] This is quite apart from the issue, which we leave aside, of the possible nonstationarity of the rate-of-return distribution.

[43] Solnik assumed independence of exchange rates and nominal local-currency stock returns, and he further made some (internally inconsistent) assumptions regarding exchange rate behavior. Sercu corrected these deficiencies. One referee pointed out that Solnik had produced an appendix to his work where independence was no longer assumed, but he had then reached no simple statement of portfolio strategy.

[44] One controversy arose from Solnik's assumption No. 7 which seemed to imply the absence of trade between countries! This assumption is actually unnecessary, for so long as there are several goods and different consumption tastes, PPP deviations could occur even if trade were unhampered.

The Journal of Finance

Table IV

Universal Logarithmic Portfolio and Investor Hedge Portfolios for
U.S. and French Investors, Computed from Nominal Rates of
Return February 1971 to December 1979

	Logarithmic Portfolio (weights sum to 1)	Hedge Portfolios	
		U.S. Investor	French Investor
Stocks			
Germany	−6.18	0.021	0.025
Belgium	6.15	0.000	−0.032
Canada	4.68	0.000	−0.028
France	−1.59	0.000	0.011
Japan	3.01	0.005	0.002
Netherlands	1.34	−0.011	0.014
United Kingdom	0.01	0.000	0.000
Switzerland	0.90	0.001	−0.022
United States	−6.75	−0.020	0.020
Bank Deposits			
Deutsche Mark	11.57	−0.029	−0.047
Belgian Franc	−9.22	−.003	0.059
Canadian Dollar	−21.81	0.034	0.046
French Franc	3.02	0.004	0.988
Japanese Yen	−0.68	0.034	−0.007
Guilder	−2.79	0.016	−0.009
British Pound	−4.10	−0.024	−0.005
Swiss Franc	1.43	−0.017	0.017
U.S. Dollar	22.01	0.983	−0.032

Data Source: Morgan Guaranty, *World Capital Markets* for one-month deposit rates; Capital International, *Perspectives* for stock price indexes and dividend rates; OECD, *Main Economic Indicators* for U.S. and French CPI's.

Warning: Monthly dividends are taken to be the last 12-month dividend divided by twelve.

(12) that in this case the hedge portfolio reduces to the home deposit. Consider the portfolio problem of an investor of country l; since he assumes that his rate of inflation measured in currency l is zero (or nonrandom), the same rate of inflation translated into the measurement currency $L + 1$ and to be introduced into the covariance vector φ^l, reduces to the rate of change of the $(L + 1/l)$th exchange rate; and since the translated rate of return on the currency l treasury Bill to be introduced into the covariance matrix $\underline{\Omega}$ is also equal, in its random part, to the same exchange rate change, the regression of inflation on securities which underlies formula (12) will produce a unit coefficient on the currency-l Bill and zeros on all other securities. Hence:[45]

---

[45] Solnik [179], in one of his separation theorems, had further split up the logarithmic portfolio into two: one whose return was independent of exchange rate changes and one which was fully dependent upon them (the latter being made up of bank deposits only). Sercu [174] did the same but only in order to show that Solnik could be generalized. While this procedure is always open (see also our Section VIII) even in the general case, there is really no point to it since the logarithmic portfolio in its entirety is held by all investors. If we split it into two parts, the two subportfolios will be held in the same proportion by all.

COROLLARY. (*Solnik*; *Sercu*)

When home inflation (measured in home currency and using home consumption weights) is zero (or nonrandom), every investor in the world holds a combination of:

— the universal logarithmic portfolio with weight α.
— his home currency Treasury Bill or bank deposit, with $1 - \alpha$.

Statements such as these generated considerable interest among macroeconomists (Kouri and de Macedo [110], Dornbusch [43], Krugman [113]) aiming to explain spot exchange rates and, more specifically, to find links between the current account and the exchange rate.[46] Portfolio balance theorists such as Branson [28], Girton and Henderson [75, 76], and Kouri [109] worked with postulated asset demand functions and assumed that investor's exhibited "home habitat" preference: they demand their home-currency denominated asset relatively more than foreigners do. A country's current account surplus which places more wealth in the hands of home investors consequently raises the demand for home currency assets and causes a rise in the value of the home currency.

The corollary above provides the microeconomic foundation for this reasoning: if a shift in wealth in favor of the home country leaves the world logarithmic demand more or less unchanged, it will usually raise the demand for the home Treasury bill. Braga de Macedo [26] and Krugman [113] suggested that the reasoning will be correct only if the home risk tolerance $\alpha < 1$ (i.e., home investors are holding the home bill rather than borrowing at that rate).[47] Strong further assumptions are required, however, to make this an exact equilibrium argument. These are detailed in the next section. One is tempted to accept Krugman's conjecture that the magnitude of the effect is small.

Actually, in much of this body of literature, the optimal portfolio strategy theorem has been specialized in another way which is often less favorable to the argument. Imagine that a country's *output* prices are fairly stable (or nonrandom) when expressed in the local currency. A given investor consumes in certain proportions goods produced in his home country which have a stable price and goods imported from various foreign countries whose translated prices fluctuate like exchange rates. He composes his purchasing power index accordingly. When, following formula (12), this index is regressed on the various securities' returns, including the translated returns on foreign Treasury Bills, which vary like exchange rates, the weights of the hedge portfolio obviously reconstruct the consumption mix. When the investor spends 10% of his consumption budget on goods imported from France, 10% of his hedge portfolio is devoted to French franc bank deposits as a hedge against the translated price of French imports.[48]

COROLLARY. (*Kouri and de Macedo*)

When the various countries' local-currency output prices are nonrandom, the weights falling on foreign currency Treasury Bills or bank deposits in an inves-

[46] We are grateful to Jeffrey Frankel for bringing this important insight to our attention.

[47] A frequently accepted value is $\alpha = \frac{1}{2}$ (risk aversion equal to 2).

[48] Kouri and de Macedo actually have a more general model where output prices are allowed to be random. But the theorem to be given, which is our responsibility, captures their contribution most strikingly.

tor's hedge portfolio replicate his consumption mix according to origin of the goods.[49]

The contrast between the two corollaries should serve to highlight the dependence of the hedge portfolio composition on the choice of the commodities price index: the CPI versus one which incorporates explicitly the prices of imports. The reason for this difference is to be found in the odd behavior of national CPI's: they do not seem to reflect immediately the variations in import prices arising from exchange rate changes. Why they do not is an open issue presumably linked to the behavior of importing firms and to the theory of commercial contracting.

IV. Partial Pricing: n Assets Priced Relative to $L + 1$ Other Assets

In the tradition of the Capital Asset Pricing Model (CAPM) of Sharpe [176], Lintner [124], and Mossin [143], equilibrium in the capital market is characterized by a relationship between the required yields on the various assets. The demand is assumed to originate from investors who hold optimal portfolios given by Equation (10) and the supply is assumed to be fixed. One asks the question: what return must this security bring relative to another security so that investors are willing to hold both in the proportion in which they are available? In the international context, the heterogeneous perceptions of real returns, due to PPP deviations, will prevent us from answering this question for every security; we shall have to take as given the expected rates of return of as many securities as there are countries $(L + 1)$ and price the other securities $(n = (N + 1) - (L + 1))$ relative to these.

The *nominal* yield required on the various securities by an individual investor in order for him to be willing to hold a given portfolio w is given to us by Equation (8) which we reproduce here for convenience, emphasizing with a superscript the terms which depend on the identity l of the investor:

$$\mu_i = r + (1 - 1/\alpha^l)\sigma_{i,\pi}^l + (1/\alpha^l) \sum_{k=1}^{N} w_k^l \sigma_{i,k}; \qquad i = 1 \cdots N \quad \text{(8 repeated)}$$

As we saw, this equation is equivalent to the formulation of portfolio demand (9) for given yields. It may be rewritten in the following form:[50]

$$\mu_i = r + \sigma_{i,\pi}^l + (1/\alpha^l) \sum_{k=1}^{N+1} w_k^l(\sigma_{i,k} - \alpha_{i,\pi}^l); \qquad i = 1 \cdots N \quad (13)$$

In this formula, the last term contains the covariance of the nominal return on security i with the nominal return on security k minus the covariance between the nominal return on security i with the rate of inflation; this difference is, in effect, the covariance between the nominal return on security i with the *real* return on security k; hence the summation is the covariance between the nominal return on security i and the real return on the investor's portfolio.

---

[49] Here is a comment by Braga de Macedo [26]: "That the effect of an increase in the relative demand for country 1 goods increases the relative demand for country 1 currency is similar to the condition for stablity in a flow view of the foreign exchange market, whereby the demand for currency is derived from the supply and demand for exports and imports." Some tests on the external demand for U.S. dollars were run by Dumas and Poncet [50].

[50] Recall that $\sum_{k=1}^{N+1} w_k = 1$ and that $\sigma_{i,N+1} = 0$ for all i since the last security is nominally riskless.

The intuitive meaning of (13) is therefore as follows. A security must bring a nominal return in excess of the nominal rate of interest, which is made up of two premia. The last one is a risk premium proportional to the covariance of the security's nominal rate with the investor's real portfolio return. A covariance with a portfolio is the usual measure in the CAPM literature of the risk contributed by a security to a portfolio (its marginal risk). When investors are concerned with their purchasing powers, they relate the required nominal yield on each asset to the real returns on their benchmark portfolio, much as one would expect.

The first premium in (13) is *not* a risk premium as it would exist even if the investor exhibited zero risk aversion ($1/\alpha = 0$). It reflects the fact that investors predicate their portfolio choices on real returns. The expected real return on a security depends on the expected value of the nominal return, the expected value of inflation, *and* the covariance between the nominal return and inflation. Deflation involving a product, it generates a covariance when computing expected values. We may perhaps call this the inflation premium.

Formulae (8) or (13), although valid for every investor, are unfortunately not usable directly to obtain, in an empirically meaningful fashion, the required yield on the various securities. This is because we cannot observe the individual portfolio holdings, w_k^l. The only portfolio which is directly observable by reading the prices in the newspaper is the aggregate one, given by the relative market capitalizations of all the securities on the market: the market portfolio[51] w^m with

$$w_k^m = \sum_l W^l w_k^l / \sum_l W^l$$

where the summation is taken over all the investors and W^l is investor l's nominal wealth. We must therefore transform (8) into an equation valid at the aggregate market level.

The operation of aggregation is typically performed by multiplying (8) by α^l and taking an average over all investors, where the weights are their relative wealths. But in the present case, with PPP deviations and with investor specific measures of inflation, the result will be disappointing:

$$\mu_i = r + (1 - 1/\alpha^m) \frac{\sum_l (1 - \alpha^l) W^l \sigma_{i,\pi}^l}{\sum_l (1 - \alpha^l) W^l} + (1/\alpha^m) \sum_{k=1}^N w_k^m \sigma_{i,k}$$

$$i = 1 \cdots N \quad (14)$$

where

$$\alpha^m = (\sum_l W^l \alpha^l)/(\sum_l W^l)$$

The disappointment is that the second term of (14) is now unobservable. Indeed, it contains the covariances of security i with the various investors' rate of inflation, weighted by their wealth *and* by one minus their risk tolerance. It is evidently out of the question to measure each individual's risk tolerance.[52] But

---

[51] Roll [160] objects that, in a world where the prices of most assets (e.g., real estate or human capital) are observed infrequently, if ever, the market portfolio itself is not observable. Worse yet, no proxy measure of this portfolio will work adequately in a test of the CAPM.

[52] This stumbling block is intrinsic to the international setting of heterogeneous investors' rate of inflation. No model known to us is capable of collapsing the wealth and risk-tolerance weighted

note that the problem may not be as large as it seems. The summation in the second term can be performed in two steps: once over all the individuals of the same nation who use the same deflator and therefore have the same $\sigma_{i,\pi}$; and then once again over the several nations, using the national wealth weighted average risk tolerances in lieu of the individual ones. We therefore have only a sum of $L + 1$ terms, one for each nation. The result is a CAPM containing $L + 1$ terms of covariance with inflation in addition to the intercept and the covariance with the market. This "multi-beta" CAPM may be tested directly for so long as the number of data points (i.e., securities) is sufficiently large ($N + 1 \gg L + 3$). The hypotheses to be tested are that the intercept is equal to the nominal measurement-currency interest rate, that the regression coefficients on all the covariance terms sum to one and that the coefficient on the covariance with the market is positive.

There exists, however, another procedure involving a prior analytic transformation of (14), which leads to a useful economic result. When the model is exact, this second approach is strictly equivalent to the previous one. It starts with the observation that the main difficulty arises from the $L + 1$ national weights (summing to one):

$$(1 - \alpha^l) W^l / \sum_l (1 - \alpha^l) W^l$$

which are not observable. In order to compute them, one may reverse the problem partially; i.e. take the expected yields on L nominally risky securities (e.g., the last L ones) as given, assume that they conform exactly to the model and use them to solve for the unknown weights. The weights so obtained can then be substituted back into (14) to compute the required yields on the other $n (n = N - L)$ securities. The effect of this procedure is to make the covariances between rates of return and inflation independent of investors or, equivalently, to set the covariances between rates of return and PPP deviations, which reflect the differences among investors, equal to zero.

To achieve the requisite transformation of (14), we introduce γ_i: this is the vector of regression coefficients from a regression of the returns of security $i (i \leq n)$, on the last L securities, so specified as to render the residuals independent of PPP deviations. For the given covariance matrix, the definition of γ_i emerges from:[53]

$$\sigma_{i,\pi}^l - \sum_{k=n+1}^{n+L} \gamma_{i,k} \sigma_{k,\pi}^l = \sigma_{i,\pi}^{L+1} - \sum_{k=n+1}^{n+L} \gamma_{i,k} \sigma_{k,\pi}^{L+1}; \quad i = i, \cdots, n,$$

$$l = 1, \cdots, L. \quad (15)$$

---

average rate of inflation into one observable number. The same problem arises, for instance, in the consumption CAPM of Breeden [30] and Stulz [191] when PPP is violated.

[53] The technique leading to (15) and (16) is an extension of Sercu [174] to the case with random domestic inflation rates. Pricing stocks relative to bonds requires partitioning and inverting the covariance matrix. The partition of the inverse corresponding to stocks can then be identified as the inverse of a matrix of the *residuals* from regressions of each stock on the set of bonds, so structured as to render these regression residuals themselves independent of PPP deviations. The γ_i emerge naturally as the *coefficients* of these regressions and represent the weights of a portfolio of bonds which immunizes stock i from the PPP deviations. A stock combined with its associated hedge portfolio is a hedged stock. Equation (15) defines the γ_i vector as the solution to setting the covariance between the hedged stock and PPP deviations equal to zero.

The suggested procedure then leads to the following CAPM:

$$\mu_i - \sum_{n+1}^{n+L} \gamma_{i,k}\mu_k = r(1 - \sum_{k=n+1}^{n+L} \gamma_{i,k}) + (1 - 1/\alpha^m)(\sigma_{i,\pi}^l - \sum_{k=n+1}^{n+L} \gamma_{i,k}\sigma_{k,\pi}^l)$$

$$+ (1/\alpha^m)[\sum_{j=1}^{N} w_j^m(\sigma_{i,j} - \sum_{k'=n+1}^{n+L} \gamma_{i,k'}\sigma_{k',j})]; \qquad i = 1, \cdots, n; \qquad \forall l; \quad (16)$$

where it will be noted that the right-hand side has the same value (by virtue of (15)) no matter which national rate of inflation ($l = 1, \cdots L + 1$) is used.

The economic interpretation of the above is clearest if one visualizes the γ_i's as side investments in the last L securities which would accompany negatively each unit investment in security i, ($i \leq n$). The purpose of these auxiliary investments is revealed by equation (15) which is a condition on the net nominal return from security i and its associated bundle of securities held short. The left-hand side is the covariance of this net return with investor l's purchasing power index and the right-hand side is the covariance with investor $L + 1$'s index. Taking the difference between the left and the right-hand sides, equation (15) says that the side investments associated with security i are chosen in such a way that the net return is linearly independent of the purchasing power deviation between investor l and investor $L + 1$ ($dP^l/P^l - dP^{L+1}/P^{L+1}$), and generally independent of all the L basic PPP deviations which may arise between $L + 1$ national investor groups. The side investments therefore constitute a hedge of security i against PPP deviations. It is natural to choose the L, non-measurement currency bonds as the hedging vehicles. The result is a CAPM which prices stocks relative to the L bonds, that is, which provides the expected returns on stocks only when all $L + 1$ nominal interest rates are given.

Consider, then, the following zero-investment bet:

— invest 1 measurement currency unit in security i,
— borrow (short sell) $\gamma_{n,k}$ units in securities $k = n + 1$ to $n + L$,
— borrow $1 - \sum_{k=n+1}^{n+1}\gamma_{i,k}$ units riskfree in the measurement currency.

The net expected return (in measurement currency) of this bet is the left-hand side of (16) minus the first term on the right-hand side. According to (16), this net expected return is linearly related to the covariance with inflation and the covariance with the market, exactly as in the nominal CAPM of, e.g., Friend, Landskroner and Losq [70]. Hence:

THEOREM. *The net nominal required yield on a security hedged against PPP deviations is given by the traditional nominal Capital Asset Pricing Model.*[54]

As noted, equation (15) specifies the γ's as coefficients of a regression of the first n securities on the last L ones, such that the residuals are independent of PPP deviations. We use the L nonmeasurement-currency bonds as the reference securities. These securities are nominally risky only because exchange rates are random. In practice, the regression can be estimated by instrumental-variables techniques, [100, p. 278], with the PPP deviations playing the role of

---

[54] The reader should carefully avoid a misunderstanding regarding the words "hedged against PPP deviations." The theorem means that we, as financial economists, know how to price a security by the standard CAPM once we have associated to it a combination of securities which constitutes a hedge against PPP deviations. There is no implication that PPP deviations are some kind of separate risk against which any one investor would want to hedge. See the remarks at the end of Section I and in Section VI below.

the instrumental variables. This is largely equivalent to a 2 SLS procedure. In the first stage, one regresses the exchange rates on the PPP deviations: in the second stage, one regresses the stock returns on the fitted values from the first stage. The coefficients in the second stage provide estimates of the γ_i vector; and by construction the residuals are independent of the PPP deviations.

In the Solnik-Sercu special case (see Section III) of zero local currency inflation as seen by local investors, PPP deviations are collinear with exchange rates. Hence, there is no distinction between the instrumental variables and the regressors, and the regression reduces to an ordinary least squares regression of the first n securities (stocks) on exchange rates. In that case, the regression coefficients γ may be interpreted as the sensitivities of the stocks with respect to exchange rates, or as their "exposures" to exchange risks. We shall return to this notion in our Section VIII on corporate policy. The theorem may thus be specialized:

COROLLARY No. 1 (*Solnik-Sercu*). *When local inflation rates are zero, the net nominal required yield on a security hedged against exchange risks by means of multi-currency borrowing and lending, is given by the traditional nominal[55] Capital Asset Pricing Model.*

There is actually an alternative way to derive and to state this corollary. We saw in Section III that, in this special case, the hedge portfolios are entirely made up to the investors' respective home Treasury bills. Stock securities, that is, receive a zero weight in the hedge portfolios and are therefore held by investors only as part of their logarithmic portfolio. Hence:

COROLLARY No. 2. *When local inflation rates are zero, the world market portfolio of stocks and the stock part of the logarithmic portfolio are proportional to each other. If, in addition, Treasury bills are in zero net supply, we have*

$$\alpha^m w_{i,\log} = w_i^m \qquad i = 1, \cdots, n$$

Substituting (11) into this relationship and partitioning out the elements corresponding to stocks would directly produce the CAPM alluded to in Corollary No. 1. The γ coefficients would appear as one partitions the inverse covariance matrix. One word of warning is in order: this corollary does not say that the market portfolio as a whole is efficient for anybody.

By way of illustration, we have computed the coefficients γ for the stock market returns included in our sample (described in Section II). This was done by regressing each market index (translated into dollars) on all exchange rates using the instrumental variables technique described above. Because exchange rates are so closely correlated with PPP deviations (cf. Table II), however, we may regard these coefficients as approximate exposures to exchange risk (i.e., OLS regressions on exchange rates). The numbers therefore are of great descriptive interest. They are displayed in Table V. It appears, from the diagonal elements of the array, that most European stock markets and Canada are

---

[55] In that case, it is immaterial whether one uses a nominal or real CAPM as the second term on the right-hand side of (16) (the covariance with inflation) is now equal to zero.

Table V

The coefficients γ or the deposit combinations needed to hedge one U.S. dollar invested in the national stock securities against PPP deviations. They are also approximately the exposures of the U.S. dollar rates of return on stocks to the national exchange rates

Deposits (i.e., Exchange Rates)

	Germany	Belgium	Canada	France	Japan	Netherlands	United Kingdom	Switzerland
Stocks								
Germany	1.540	−0.114	−0.205	0.071	−0.218	0.135	0.331	−0.483
	(0.057)	(0.077)	(0.253)	(0.040)	(0.126)	(0.055)	(0.131)	(0.107)
Belgium	−0.033	1.514	−0.311	0.071	−0.136	0.160	0.033	−0.404
	(0.048)	(0.064)	(0.212)	(0.034)	(0.106)	(0.047)	(0.110)	(0.090)
Canada	−0.057	0.081	1.931	0.188	−0.264	0.273	−0.048	0.068
	(0.095)	(0.128)	(0.420)	(0.067)	(0.210)	(0.092)	(0.218)	(0.177)
France	0.005	−0.115	−1.765	1.771	−0.057	0.099	0.207	−0.344
	(0.098)	(0.132)	(0.432)	(0.069)	(0.216)	(0.095)	(0.224)	(0.183)
Japan	0.276	−0.021	0.189	0.047	0.439	0.084	0.167	0.086
	(0.097)	(0.131)	(0.428)	(0.068)	(0.214)	(0.094)	(0.222)	(0.181)
Netherlands	0.064	−0.038	0.151	0.118	−0.140	1.576	0.138	−0.559
	(0.069)	(0.092)	(0.303)	(0.048)	(0.151)	(0.067)	(0.157)	(0.128)
United Kingdom	2.608	0.758	0.058	−1.673	−1.632	2.481	−9.220	2.621
	(1.652)	(2.223)	(7.289)	(1.162)	(3.644)	(1.600)	(3.78)	(3.087)
Switzerland	0.130	0.319	0.112	0.146	−0.250	0.209	0.407	0.269
	(0.079)	(0.106)	(0.347)	(0.055)	(0.173)	(0.076)	(0.180)	(0.147)
United States	0.078	0.168	0.803	0.074	−0.109	0.268	0.007	−0.244
	(0.084)	(0.113)	(0.373)	(0.059)	(0.184)	(0.082)	(0.194)	(0.158)

Note: "Exposure" to the U.S. dollar (the measurement currency) may be obtained by row complementation to one. E.g., exposure of the U.S. dollar is −0.045. See the text. Actually the array so completed is globally invariant to the choice of the reference currency, i.e., if everything had been measured in terms of francs instead of U.S. dollars, the U.S. dollar column (showing the very same numbers as the row complements to one) would have come out of the regression and the French franc column would have disappeared, but every other number would have been the same. Standard deviations are shown in parentheses.

Sources of data: See Table IV.

overexposed[56] to their respective currency. The United Kingdom, however, provides results which are difficult to rationalize. Japanese and Swiss stock are remarkably well diversified as far as their vulnerability to exchange rate changes are concerned. Finally, United States stocks are mostly exposed to the U.S./ Canada exchange rate but very little exposed to the overall posture of the U.S. currency. We cannot offer a theory which explains these results, but it is conceivable that an international extension of Fama [57] would provide one.

Specialized versions of the International Asset Pricing Model (15) have been submitted to empirical tests (Solnik [180] and Agmon [12]). The tests have been inconclusive both from a statistical standpoint and also in view of Roll's [160] general critique of such tests: the world market portfolio is an elusive entity which is probably badly proxied by any available index. In Solnik [180] the IAPM, which puts a price on the systematic risk measured against the world market portfolio, was tested against the alternative hypothesis that national factors (orthogonal to the world market portfolio) also receive a price. The absence of statistical significance was due to the large specific risks of individual securities and to the relatively small share of the variance of returns explained by national factors. For details on empirical tests, see Solnik [182] and the discussion by Dumas [45].

V. The International Structure of Interest Rates and the Forward Exchange Market

In a world of $L + 1$ nations, we have so far succeeded in pricing all assets except $L + 1$ of them, and we take these assets to be the $L + 1$ local currency bank deposits or Treasury bills. As far as these assets are concerned, we have no choice but to use Asset Pricing Model (14) which, as we have already observed, is not directly testable with the usual data. Letting exchange rates appear explicitly, we have

$$r_i + \theta_i = r_{L+1} + (1 - 1/\alpha^m)(\sum_l (1 - \alpha^l) W^l s_{i,\pi}^l)/\sum_l (1 - \alpha^l) W^l$$

$$+ (1/\alpha^m) \sum_{k=1}^{N} w_k^m s_{i,k}; \qquad i = 1, \cdots, L \quad (17)$$

where

r_i is the nominal interest rate on the currency i bank deposit;

θ_i is the expected value of the instantaneous rate of change of the exchange rate of currency i against the measurement currency $L + 1$;

r_{L+1} is the measurement currency interest rate, so far denoted simply r;

$s_{i,\pi}^l$ is the covariance of exchange rate i with national investor l's rate of inflation; and

$s_{i,k}$ is the covariance of exchange rate i with the translated return on asset k, including for $k = n + 1$ to N, the covariances with the exchange rates themselves.[57]

---

[56] One hundred percent exposure would be the case where the array contained ones in the diagonal and zeros everywhere else. Such was implicitly the assumption in the original Solnik [179] model where local-currency rates of return were assumed independent of exchange rates. A one-dollar investment in German stocks would then simply be hedged by borrowing one dollar's worth of Deutsche Marks.

[57] $s_{i,\pi}^j$ is another notation for $\sigma_{n+1,\pi}^j$ and $s_{i,k}$ another notation for $\sigma_{n+1,k}$.

Forward exchange contracts are redundant in our model.[58] Were they to exist then, in the absence of impediments to arbitrage, the forward rate would be set by interest rate parity (IRP). Calling f_i the percentage difference between the forward and spot rates (premium if positive, discount if negative), IRP implies

$$f_i = r_{L+1} - r_i \tag{18}$$

i.e., the forward premium equals the interest rate differential. As a result, at equilibrium we have the so-called "Fisher open" or "uncovered IRP" relationship:[59]

$$f_i = \theta_i - (1 - 1/\alpha^m)[(\textstyle\sum_l (1 - \alpha^l) W^l s^l_{i,\pi})/\sum_l (1 - \alpha^l) W^l]$$
$$- (1/\alpha^m) \textstyle\sum_{k=1}^{N} w^m_k s_{i,k} \tag{19}$$

or

$$f_i = \theta_i - [(\textstyle\sum_l (1 - \alpha^l) W^l s^l_{i,\pi})/\sum_l (1 - \alpha^l) W^l]$$
$$- (1/\alpha^m) \textstyle\sum_{k=1}^{N+1} w^m_k [s_{i,k} - (\textstyle\sum_l (1 - \alpha^l) W^l s^l_{i,\pi})/\sum_l (1 - \alpha^l) W^l] \tag{20}$$

Equations (19) and (20) imply that the forward rate is biased predictor of the ensuing spot. Repeating here a comment made previously in various contexts, the spread appearing in (20) between the forward rate and the expected spot is made up of two premia. One would exist even in the absence of risk aversion (1/$\alpha^m = 0$) but would disappear under nonrandom measurement-currency inflation and Purchasing Power Parity (i.e. nonrandom inflation for all when all rates are expressed in the measurement currency). The mathematical and economic reasons for its existence were given following Equation (13). Under risk neutrality, the expected value of the spot rate *deflated* must be equal to the forward rate also deflated.[60] The covariance between the spot rate and the deflator (deflators

---

[58] Selling francs forward is equivalent to selling borrowed francs spot and investing the proceeds in dollars. Hence the forward rate must be equal to the simultaneous spot rate corrected for the interest rate difference. Otherwise some arbitragers could reap instantaneous riskless profits (aside from default risk). We do not review here the evidence on the Interest Rate Parity relationships. See Frenkel and Levich [69], Herring and Marston [89] and, for a review, Kohlhagen [106] Section II. See also footnote 68 below.

[59] In the Solnik-Sercu special case of no local inflation as seen by local investors, we have:

$$s^l_{i,\pi} = s_{i,n+l}(= \sigma_{n+i,n+l})$$

i.e., translated nonmeasurement currency inflation rates behave like exchange rates.

[60] i.e.:
where

$FE(1/I) = E(S/I);$

    F = forward exchange rate (in measurement currency units per unit of foreign currency);

    S = future spot rate quoted the same way;

    I = price index expressed in measurement currency units; and

    E = expected value operator

Reasoning in real terms, as we do here, produces the inflation premium and also disposes of the so-called Siegel [177] paradox. Siegel argued that it is impossible simultaneously that $F = E(S)$ and, after changing measurement currency, that $1/F = E(1/S)$ since by Jensen's inequality, $E(1/S) > 1/E(S)$. The paradox was quickly dismissed as a trivial mathematical inconvenience without economic or empirical significance. Actually, in our formulation, there is no paradox. Note that in the above equation, the price index I has a currency dimension. If we switch currencies around, as Siegel did,

in the absence of PPP) is the source of this premium.[61] The second premium in
(20) is a plain risk premium and it is linked to the covariance of the exchange
rate with "the" real return on the world market portfolio. This real return is
computed using an average worldwide rate of inflation, where the weights in the
average are, as in the first premium, the national wealths times one minus
national risk tolerances. Again, the unobservability of the risk tolerance is the
reason for the nontestability of formulae (17), (19), and (20). The world market
portfolio composition is given as usual by the relative capitalizations of all the
assets. It contains, therefore, all the assets which are not globally in zero net
supply; Frankel [64] baptized these "outside assets." When all assets are "inside"
(all in zero net supply) and returns are stationary, there is no risk premium; i.e.
the formula reduces to what it would be if $1/\alpha^m = 0$.

This equilibrium model of the forward rate is useful in at least two respects.
First, it provides a focus for a short review of the empirical literature concerned
with the "efficiency" of the exchange markets. Second, it serves to reveal the
shortcomings of the so-called "Modern Theory" which features in the conventional account of the forward markets.

There are no direct tests of Equation (20) and it is unlikely that there will be
until the problem of estimating risk tolerance under diverse consumption preferences is solved. Roll and Solnik [163] tested a very special version in which the
second term of (20) was omitted and equal weights were used in the third. They
were unable to establish conclusively that risk premia exist. Frankel [65, 66]
must be credited for testing the hypothesis that the risk premium may fluctuate
with the supplies of "outside assets" and specifically with the supply of government debts (cumulated government deficits). But he was unable to produce
evidence of a significant link with these quantities.

What appears most frequently in the literature is time-series analyses of the
nominal difference between the (logarithms of the) forward and subsequent spot
rates, uncorrected for inflation. This difference reflects the nominal returns to
forward speculation (sell forward, buy at the future spot) or, equivalently, the
forecast error if one takes the forward rate as a predictor of the spot. The
literature asks two related questions: is the expected forecast error zero and are
forecast errors serially uncorrelated? Taken together, the hypothesis is that the

---

we must also translate the price index $(I \rightarrow I/S)$. Then we have:

$$(1/F)E(S/I) = E[(1/S)/(I/S)]$$

which is equivalent to the first equation. So there is no contradiction. To counter one referee's
misunderstanding, note that we are not arguing here that the inflation premium is unimportant;
quite the opposite; we say that it takes care of the Siegel paradox.

[61] Solnik [179] overlooked this premium because he was missing the term $1 \times \sigma^l_{i,\pi}$ in his version of
Equation (11). As a result, his comments regarding the weighting of the various assets in the overall
premium are incorrect. This is unfortunate: he had identified the weights with the net investment
position of each country. Under his restrictive set of assumptions (recall from footnote 43 that he
assumed not only absence of local inflation but also independence of exchange rates and local-
currency stock returns; so that: $s^l_{i,\pi} = s_{i,n+l}$ and $s_{i,k} = s_{i,n+k}$), his interpretation holds for the weights
appearing within the second premium of (23) only.

International Finance 957

forecast error follows a random walk.[62] This provides an indirect test of whether the premia in (20) are zero.

Evidence against the random walk hypothesis, which was at first the prevailing one, is mounting.[63] Levich [120] discovered biases which were of opposite sign depending on the direction of change of the spot rate. These he attributed not to risk premia, but to transaction costs which penalize speculation and keep the forward below the expected spot when the latter is rising and vice-versa. Cornell [34], Geweke and Feige [74], Hansen and Hodrick [83], and Cumby and Obstfeld [39] all found in floating rate data, both post-World War I and in the recent past, instances where the unconditional mean bias was significantly different from zero, and whether it was zero or not, other cases where forecast errors were serially correlated. These results do not, of course, imply anything about the efficiency of the forward exchange markets although some of the authors above motivated their tests by appeals to the efficient markets hypothesis.[64] They are, however, consistent with the existence of biases or premia, perhaps of the type described in (20), which fluctuate widely and in a serially correlated fashion. Indeed, Stockman [187] was able to find evidence of variable premia: when he split his sample into two subperiods, the premia which were not significantly different from zero in each subperiod were nevertheless significantly different from each other, for some currencies. There is need for a general equilibrium theory which would identify the exogenous determinants of the premia.

Equation (20) further enables us to confront Tsiang's [196] theory of the forward exchange market, subsequently baptized the Modern Theory (MT) by Stoll [189]. The MT apparently still enjoys currency in the thinking in central banks. In its later manifestations, the MT was used to account for deviations from IRP, to justify the forward rate as a predictor of the future spot, and as an underpinning for official intervention, often righteously termed "counter specu-lation." In the MT, forward transactions are contracted between two distinct and separate classes of traders. Speculators take open forward positions and link the forward rate to the expected future spot rate. Arbitragers demand forward contracts when the forward rate deviates from IRP and link the forward rate to

[62] Absence of serial correlation does not imply a random walk. But, since the hypothesis is usually couched in the form of a regression model, the assumption of stationarity of the residual term is needed anyway for statistical purposes. The random walk model is really the one being tested.

[63] See Kohlhagen [104] and Dufey and Giddy's [44] "submartingale" model. The literatures on the efficiency of the foreign exchange market prior to and until 1977 has been exhaustively surveyed by Kohlhagen [106]. There is no need to reproduce this work here. Also discussed there are some crucial macroeconomic questions which are related to the matter of efficiency but are too remote from our topic of international portfolio choice to be discussed here; these are: the impact of trade flows on the forward rate due to "hedging pressure" (Levin [121], Dooley [40]); the impact of official intervention (Kohlhagen [105]); and whether speculative activity can be destabilizing ("bandwagon" effects) and, if so, what measurement method would allow us to identify the periods where it is.

[64] By itself, market efficiency does not imply that the forward rate is equal to the expected spot. This used to be a frequent misconception. In the presence of risk aversion, or nonconstant required real returns, there is also no implication that market efficiency leads to serially uncorrelated returns. See Lucas [129]. But in practice, risk aversions are sufficiently low as to produce very low serial correlations. Witness the autocorrelations computed by Fama [56] on New York Stock Exchange data.

interest rates. Hedgers protecting previously-established exposures cannot be modeled in the MT. While their motives are akin to those of arbitragers, their calculations are like those of speculators and they are therefore lumped with the latter.

The key flaws in this specification are the assumed specialization of traders and the assumption that interest rates in the MT are purely exogenous, set by the whims of central bankers independently of expectations.[65] When IRP prevails, the equilibrium forward rate in the MT is therefore also exogenous. At IRP, the arbitrage demand is infinitely elastic. Any shift in speculators' expectations of the future spot, due say to government counter-speculation, leaves both the arbitrage schedule and the IRP forward rate unchanged. The arbitrage volume adjusts automatically to meet the speculative demand leaving the false impression that governments can successfully induce capital flows by forward intervention. Due to the exogeneity of interest rates, speculators' and arbitragers' demand curves for forward contracts are, implausibly, perfectly independent.

In contrast, there are no separate classes of traders in the theory leading to Equation (20). Investors are identifiable by their price deflators, not by their transactions motives. Their portfolio problem has been solved globally: their demand for forward exchange[66] is an indistinguishable component of their vector asset-demand function. Their motives may include arbitrage, speculation, and hedging when the latter is identified with the need to diversify. Any linear decomposition of forward transactions according to purpose is, however, essentially arbitrary.[67] The probability distribution of the exchange rate is simultaneously a determinant of both speculation and diversification. Because IRP holds, the arbitrage demand is potentially infinite but no arbitrage flows, accommodating or otherwise, will actually occur. More importantly, interest rates are endogenous. Equation (17) makes clear that, given expectations regarding future spot rates, interest rates in various currencies *cannot* be set independently: conversely, interest rate differentials reflect anticipations of future spot rates. The forward rate in (20) is therefore jointly at IRP and equal to the certainty equivalent of the future spot rate.

In the MT, the equilibrium forward rate generally falls between the exogenous IRP level and the expected future spot rate.[68] To forecast the future spot, all one

[65] There are others, quite aside from the difficulty with hedgers. First, speculators will not bet on the difference between the forward and expected spot rates unless they are risk neutral or, if they are risk averse, unless forward contracts are the only available risky asset. Second, in creating the link between the forward market and capital flows, the MT confusingly identified the spot transactions associated with covered interest arbitrage (borrow one currency, sell it spot, invest in a second) with "hot," interest-sensitive, short-term capital movements. In reality, these would not be covered by buying forward the borrowed currency and therefore, unlike arbitrage, will tend to be independent of the forward rate and of deviations from IRP.

[66] This is a figure of speech. As noted in footnote 58, forward contracts are redundant instruments when borrowing and lending is allowed in all currencies. Hence we never introduced (and could not have because of the perfect substitutability) a separate demand for forward exchange. In the present context the expression refers to the equivalent demands for bank deposits or loans. The situation will be different below when arbitrage becomes risky.

[67] Adler and Dumas [5 and 6] showed that the additive separation of the speculation and hedging purposes is possible with a quadratic utility function which generates a linear marginal utility function.

[68] To account for IRP deviations at equilibrium was one of the MT's design objectives. Nowadays,

does is to compare the concurrent actual and IRP forward rates. This demonstrably false proposition is the mechanical result of the MT's identification of forward equilibrium at the intersection of the speculator's inelastic demand curve (with its intercept at the expected spot) and the arbitragers' inelastic supply curve for forward contracts (with an intercept at IRP). The majority of the authors cited associated the finite elasticities of the two curves to traders' aversion to a notion of default risk which rises with market volume. To refute the MT's prediction, Adler and Dumas [5, 6] and Kouri [107] modeled the portfolio demand for forward exchange in the presence of an exogenous default risks on both forward conctracts and banking transactions, which made interest arbitrage risky. The results generalize Equation (20). Interest rates and the forward rate are endogenized: both are functions of spot rate expectations.[69] IRP may be violated due to the default risks. The demand for forward contracts cannot be decomposed additively among the motives: rather the arbitrage motive acts multiplicatively on the others. And above all, the forward rate need not be bracketed by the IRP rate and the expected spot.

Following the demise of the MT, the theory leading to Equation (20) has taken its place in the tool kit of macroeconomists. It produces as a special case the model, mentioned in Section III, which was used by Krugman [113] to suggest a link between exchange rates and the current account.[70] This link is directly apparent in Equation (17). Assume $1 - \alpha^i > 0$ and $\alpha^i = \alpha^{L+1}$ and take some wealth from country $L + 1$ and transfer it to country i. This modified situation may be the result of a history of large current account surpluses or smaller current account deficits for country i at the expense of country $L + 1$.[71] The (comparative-static) transfer induces a drop of the interest differential $(r_i - r_{L+1})$ in favor of currency i or a drop of its expected rate of appreciation (θ_i).[72] The

the daily press reveals that IRP holds to within very narrow transaction cost tolerances in the Eurocurrency interbank dealer market even during turbulent periods. Nevertheless, most of the papers in the area presume that IRP is violated. Many reasons have been given: transactions costs (Branson [27], Frenkel and Levich [69]; institutional constraints (Einzig [52], Sohmen [178], Canterbery [32]; interest rates functionally related to the volume of arbitrage (Prachowny [153], Frenkel [67] and Kenen [102]; default risk in arbitrage transactions (Stoll [189], Grubel [81]) or political risk (Aliber [14], Dooley and Isard [41]). Deviations from IRP are frequently observed in comparisons of domestic money market or local government T-bill rates. Internal markets may therefore be segmented while the offshore markets are not. IRP violations depend on where one looks.

[69] In one section of Kouri [107], interest rates are taken to be exogenous but then restrictions correctly follow on the expected behavior of spot rates. The fact that interest rates, as much as forward rates, reflect exchange rate anticipations have been noted before these formal models were constructed. See Branson, Katz, and Willett [29], Pippenger [150], and the literature reviewed in Kohlhagen [106], Section 11c.

[70] Via a wealth effect rather than an arbitrage effect.

[71] Larger wealth may also be the result of capital gains on country i's preferential holding of home-currency assets. These gains would, however, induce a current account deficit.

[72] This conclusion requires a world where local inflation rates are negligible so that $s_{i,\pi}^{L+1} = 0$ and $s_{i,\pi}^i = s_{i,n+i}$ is the variance of the exchange value of currency i and is therefore positive. Further the market portfolio of stocks is the stock component of the logarithmic portfolio $(w_k^m/\alpha^m = w_{k,\log}; k = 1 \dots n)$ which must be held constant. And, the market portfolio of bonds is zero if these are in zero net supply. Simple examination of Equation (17) then produces the stated result. Note, however, that the conclusion may be mitigated or strengthened by changes in the logarithmic portfolio induced by the lower value of $r_i + \theta_i - r_{L+1}$.

dynamics of wealth accumulation and exchange rates are yet to be worked out in keeping with this observation.[73]

VI. Some Welfare Questions Associated with Exchange Risk

The function of capital markets is the allocation of the bearing of risks. Among these, the risk arising from holding nominal assets is of special interest in international finance. To define terms, recall the development of Section I. A resident of a country holding a foreign security with a given probability distribution of foreign-currency rate of return would compute his real return by first translating into home currency and then deflating by means of the home price index. Consequently, the currency risk arising from holding a nominal asset denominated in foreign currency (i.e. paying a fixed amount of foreign money) is linked to the randomness of the exchange rate times the home purchasing power index. Exchange risk, which may be identified with the randomness of the exchange rate, is never borne alone but only in conjunction with home purchasing power uncertainty. The currency risk associated with holding a nominal security denominated in home currency is simply the randomness of the home purchasing power index, if any. The question is under what conditions these currency risks affect welfare and how they are allocated across individuals.

We first consider a world in which money is only a unit of account but is not held in the investors' portfolios and is issued by no one. Exchange rates are then arbitrary (random) numbers, exogenously given, translating one measurement unit into another. It should be clear that the multiplicity of benchmarks for value by itself has no impact on welfare. If there is a welfare issue, it arises from the presence in the financial markets of nominal securities, i.e., securities whose payoff is linked to the fluctuations in the purchasing power of one monetary unit of value. The issue, then, is in what circumstances would such securities be willingly held by investors at equilibrium; for, if they were not held, the randomness of exchange rates and price levels, holding constant the physical payoffs (outputs) on the other securities, could not possibly have an impact on welfare.

When the financial market allows individuals to trade risks and insurance in every conceivable dimension of their choice, the allocation of risk bearing is Pareto optimal. In that case, a strong assertion of financial theory is that all consumption risks are mutualized. Consider a random event which is to cause an individual to lose something to the benefit of another individual (a zero-sum risk). Then it would be optimal for these two risk-averse persons to precontract: the first person would buy insurance from the second one and pay him a fixed premium and, if the risk materializes, its effects would be cancelled by invoking the insurance policy. All personal risks would disappear in this manner and in the end individual consumption (assumed to be the only source of utility) would only be a function of aggregate consumption. Individual investors, that is, would only bear the impact of social (aggregative) risks. This function, relating individ-

---

[73] This current account argument may seem reminiscent of the "hedging pressure" theory wherein trade flows induced trading firms to hedge in the forward market, thereby affecting the equilibrium rate (Levin [121], Dooley [40]). But really it is not, as we are referring now to the accumulated current account and to the stock of wealth resulting from it rather than to trade flows.

ual and aggregate consumptions, is called an optimal sharing rule.[74] If there are several goods, each person's consumption of each good is a function of the aggregate consumption of all goods. If the investor's utility functions are of the von Neumann-Morgenstern type, the sharing rules are nonrandom functions.

Consider now a pure exchange economy (aggregate consumption of each good equals its aggregate exogenous output) endowed with a Pareto optimal capital market and where the various moneys are only units of account.[75] In this economy,[76] the only securities which would be held are those which achieve the optimal sharing rule, i.e., which serve to allocate the risks of aggregate output of the various goods. But, the various currency risks are not aggregate risk; they arise only in connection with the holding of nominal securities whose payoffs are linked to no underlying physical output.[77] For every borrower there is a lender. The gain of the one is the loss of the other. And, at equilibrium, there will be neither nominal borrower nor nominal lender; nominal securities *will not be held*.[78] This is an important conclusion and a fairly robust one provided one clarifies the phrase "nominal securities will not be held." If a nominal security is issued by a corporation and the proceeds are used to repurchase stock, it will, in the present setting, be bought by the stockholders of that corporation (Modigliani-Miller [141]). This is not to be seen as an exception to the above statement. If a government issues nominal bonds to purchase claims on future output, the bonds will be purchased and the claims on output sold (possibly short) by the taxpayers of that government (Wallace [200]).[79] This is not an exception to the above statement either. In both cases, stockholders or taxpayers will earn gains or losses on their dividends or on their tax bill which exactly offset their losses or gains on the holding of nominal bonds.

If we switch, however, to an exchange economy in which the capital market is not Pareto optimal because of restrictions in the array of tradable securities, then some personal risks will not be hedgable. In that case, capital market participants will look for proxies, i.e., securities which are correlated with the risks they wish to hedge. In general they will make up a portfolio of all the available securities and compose it in such a way as to achieve the best possible correlation. To the extent that nominal securities are available, they will be used for these purposes and will generally be held.[80] Increased currency risk could then reduce or improve welfare.

[74] See Rubinstein [165]. The concept is identical to the one of contract curves in an Edgeworth-box formulation where the edges of the box would represent consumption in the various states of nature.

[75] We must add the following purely technical assumption: there is no nominal security whose payoff in terms of one commodity is perfectly correlated with the aggregate consumption of that commodity. This is only meant to avoid indeterminacy.

[76] This is the kind of economy considered by Grauer, Litzenberger, and Stehle [79]. We do not introduce, however, their assumption of identical consumption tastes for all individuals, which leads to PPP holding exactly (i.e., *ex post*: see Section I).

[77] See *infra* the case of corporate or government bonds.

[78] Unless they are also real in the eyes of some investors, as in the Solnik-Sercu special case.

[79] The government budget deficit (on current account) bites into consumable output and as such constitutes a nonhedgable aggregative risk. The reasoning in the text keeps the deficit constant.

[80] In the model of Sections III, IV, and V the market was generally not Pareto optimal and nominal assets were indeed held at equilibrium. In the Solnik-Sercu special case the market became Pareto optimal but nominal assets also became real and were held for that reason.

Therefore, it appears that currency risks matter or do not matter depending on conditions in the capital market. This was the conclusion reached by Grauer, Litzenberger, and Stehle [79] but in the context of an economy where consumers had identical tastes for the various commodities and PPP prevailed. It should be clear that their conclusion owes nothing to this assumption.

What is crucial, however, to the reasoning is the assumption that, as one varies currency risks, one leaves unchanged the probability distributions of the consumable outputs which are the real aggregate risks to be borne by investors. This assumption may not be tenable in some settings. For instance, in the Solnik-Sercu special case, where local currency inflation in each country is zero but tastes differ, Grauer, Litzenberger, and Stehle make the valid point that, if CPP prevailed for each good, then exchange rates could not fluctuate and currency risks would not exist unless the relative prices between goods and their outputs fluctuated; and this in turn implies that one could not vary currency risks without varying output risks. In that case, currency risks may be said to matter, but only because they vary in step with output risks.[81]

The juxtaposition of the Grauer et al. model where PPP was assumed and currency risks did not matter, with the Solnik model where PPP did not prevail and currency risks mattered, led some astray. It is often stated in the literature (Aliber [15, p. 106], Jaffee [98], Cornell [36]) that, with PPP, exchange rates are not linked with relative commodities prices or that their variations are offset by price levels, so that exchange risk becomes a purely nominal uncertainty which matters to no one. The result is to identify the exchange risk which matters (sometimes called "real exchange risk") with deviations from PPP, and the exchange risk which does not matter ("nominal exchange risk") with fluctuations in the PPP level of exchange rates (i.e., the ratio of price indices). This seems wrong for the above reasons and also because the risk of PPP deviations is not a separate risk which is to be borne by anyone: the foreign deflator does not enter any domestic investor's risk calculus. PPP deviations, as distinct from variations in the purchasing power at home of domestic and foreign securities, will therefore not affect any investor's financial decisions.

At some point, one must stop thinking in terms of price levels and exchange rates reflecting only exogenous random changes in measurement units, and come to grips with the fact that moneys are held by households and issued by Central Banks. But, at that stage, one must also realize that the question of the relevance of exchange risk becomes ill-formulated since exchange rates and price levels are endogenous. The issue then becomes that of the welfare impact or non-neutrality of monetary policies in a multi-currency world. It is a very complex one, for which few statements remain valid outside a particular context or model formulation. The vast macroeconomic literature which addressed this issue recognized at least four channels of influence:[82]

(a) The rate of monetary expansion affects the nominal rate of interest which

---

[81] Two other instances of links between consumable output and nominal quantities will be encountered below and in Section VIII: monetary policy may have a real effect and the outputs and sales flows of firms may be affected by e.g., a change in the selling price abroad of the finished product, relative to the production cost at home.

[82] In addition, government's fiscal policy directly influences the amount of output available for consumption as the budget deficit (on current account) is a drain on real resources. The deficit may

influences real money balances, consumption, and the demand for securities (savings). If output is kept constant, a rise in the nominal rate of interest increases the cost of the liquidity services of money and lowers welfare (Bailey [17], Barro [21]). If output is allowed to vary, the conclusion depends on the setting chosen (Mundell [146], Fischer [63]);

(b) Monetary policy alters the relative stocks of available assets. As their prices adjust to maintain market equilibrium, the discrepancies which appear between the market prices of physical assets and their replacement costs affect aggregate demand and have therefore real effects (Tobin [194]). This argument is independent of the liquidity services of money. It deals only with the composition of the government's versus the private portfolios. Some irrelevance propositions are being developed (Wallace [200], Chamley and Polemarchakis [33]) which tend to invalidate it;

(c) Random monetary policies induce equivocation in price signals (Lucas [128], Sargent and Wallace [170], Santomero and Seater [169], Weiss [201]), leading to a short-term inflation-employment trade-off;

(d) Exchange rates affect export competitiveness and employment (Laursen and Metzler [115]).

Capital market theory is not, so far, capable of incorporating these effects into a general-equilibrium framework (see Lucas [130, 131] and Helpman and Razin [88]). Attempts at introducing moneys into portfolios have been made in the partial equilibrium context of the capital asset pricing model: Kouri [108], Stockman [187], Fama and Farber [58], Landskroner and Liviatan [114], Stapleton and Subrahmanyam [184], Poncet [151], and Dumas [49]. Some limited welfare issues are discussed in Fama and Farber [58] and Dumas [49]. In both of these, money is a separate argument in investors' utility functions and is held because it yields liquidity services. Fama and Farber [58] make the point that $1 of money and a nominal (short-term) bond paying $1 carry the same currency risk. Hence a "separation" exists between the decision to hold money versus nominal bonds and the decision as to the composition of the remainder of the portfolio. People may decide how much they want to hold of nominal assets in their overall portfolio and then divide this amount between money and bonds depending on the amount of liquidity services they wish to use (the cost is as usual the foregone nominal rate of interest). The implication is that the presence of money does not increase or reduce the amount of currency risks people have to bear, as compared to the situation where the government would only issue nominal bonds to finance its purchases. The point is quite general; but, in order to illustrate, consider the simplest case analyzed in Dumas [49] where financial markets are Pareto optimal and money is issued to make transfer payments (or reduce taxes). The random benefits to transfer recipients are exactly equal to the purchasing power losses of money holders. Pre-contracting between the two overlapping groups of households can occur: transfer recipients may borrow in a state-contingent way from money holders and, in exchange, remit the transfers to them later.[83] This possibility makes it unnecessary in this case for anyone to

---

be financed by money creation, thereby creating a link between consumable output on the one hand and prices and exchange rates on the other.

[83] If the amount of the transfers are fixed nominally, the market need not be a complete one: nominal bonds of maturities can be used for the purpose.

bear the purchasing-power risk of currencies.

While in full agreement with Fama and Farber on the matter of currency risk, Dumas [49] points out that they overlooked another risk of a monetary origin: the risk of fluctuations in the nominal rate of interest.[84] As has been recognized by macroeconomists (see the monetary channel of influence (a) above), the opportunity cost of holding money balances, measured by the nominal interest rate, is a determinant of aggregate welfare (along with aggregate consumption) and, of course, the next period's nominal interest rate is also a separate argument of the optimal sharing rules. Because nominal interest-rate randomness is an aggregate risk, it cannot be pre-contracted away and each investor must bear a share of it.

While the above discussion has de-emphasized PPP deviations as a measure of exchange risk (especially those arising from differnces in investors' consumption tastes), the matter may be different when CPP is violated and individual commodity prices are misaligned across the world. CPP deviations are symptomatic of barriers to free trade. It is then not clear how investors trading contingent claims in a supposedly integrated world capital market will take receipt or make delivery of the physical payoffs resulting from their bets. The notion that the world-wide aggregate amount of each good constitutes a pool of freely allocable resources must be called into question. The concepts of aggregate consumption and of sharing rules may well lose their meaning. To take the issue further requires a model capable of accounting for the CPP deviations. Anticipating the results of such a model, it will undoubtedly remain improper loosely to identify currency risks (or the part of them that matters) with CPP (or PPP) deviations. There is a presumption that the wider the CPP deviations, the larger will be the amount of welfare foregone as a result of insufficient or inefficient trading. But one can only speculate as to how widely-fluctuating, random CPP deviations will be linked empirically to variability in exchange rates or to their product with domestic price levels. Whether increased exchange or currency risks reduce welfare is an open question.

VII. Segmentation

Segmentations of the international commodities markets which produce CPP deviations may disturb the worldwide allocation of risk: because the goods market is partly segmented, so is the capital market.[85] Independently, however, capital markets may be separated along national lines owing either to investors' inhibitions or official restrictions. Investors may be inhibited by a lack of information, the fear of expropriation or, more generally, discriminatory taxation.[86] Official restrictions may include exchange and border controls which restrict foreigners'

---

[84] Technically, the reason they overlooked it is that they worked with an indirect utility function of current consumption, current balances, and end-of-period wealth. This is incorrect: when money is held, the indirect utility cannot be a function of future wealth alone; it also depends on the future nominal interest rate.

[85] The CPP deviations need not be random for this to happen. When investors encounter difficulty in collecting payoffs in consumable form, they may be deterred from investing in the first place.

[86] The randomness of exchange rates is not to be conceived as a source of segmentation since by proper hedging, repatriated payoffs may be rendered independent of exchange rates.

International Finance 965

access to local capital markets, reduce their freedom to repatriate capital and dividends, and limit the fraction of a local firm's equity that they may own. These manifestations of sovereignty serve in part to define nations as distinct segments of the international capital market.

As a phenomenon, segmentation is not unique to the international arena. It has received attention also at the domestic level, from Rubinstein [166] and, more comprehensively, from Lintner [126]. Capital market segments in these papers generally consist of groups of investors and of groups of securities which each investor class is allowed to trade. The multiplicity of possible groups of investors and securities led the authors to define gradations ranging from complete segmentation to partial segmentation with overlap.[87] The main objective and contribution of these models was to show that a sufficient amount of diversity among investors in different segments would lead to firms having optimal, value maximizing, interior capital structure decisions. The cost is that separation properties generally break down: portfolio separation for individuals and the independence of capital budgeting and financing decisions for firms. Lintner's encyclopedic treatment attempts parenthetically to establish conditions in which separation is restored. Neither paper questions the existence or uniqueness of equilibrium in segmented markets or whether the risk allocation will be Pareto optimal. Both assume that value maximization will be unanimously supported irrespective of the type of segmentation being postulated. Whether this last assumption can be maintained, at least to an approximation, is a question that continues to bedevil this strand of the literature.

Despite an absence of empirical justification, it is possible that segmentation can safely be ignored at the domestic level. Most authors do. Internationally it is harder to avoid if only because, from time to time and place to place, governments try to insulate their capital and goods markets from the rest of the world. To the extent that segmentation exists in practice, international corporations may be able to play an important role by recognizing the causes of the segmentation and by planning transactions to enable their stockholders to reap the welfare gains from integration.[88] When stock markets are segmented, for example, home-country firms can purchase shares in foreign firms and provide an indirect diversification as well as a rate-of-return arbitrage service. Adler [1] and Adler and Dumas [3] calculated the value-maximizing foreign acquisition and the resulting home and foreign market equilibria when both markets separately are described by a CAPM. They calculated that the value maximizing foreign acquisition would not be welfare maximizing from the viewpoint of home investors. This point was pursued by Lee and Sachdeva [116]. They pointed out that what produced the result was the implicit assumption that home firms had monopoly power in the home capital market. When these firms behave at home as pure competitors, as in Ekern and Wilson [53], home welfare is maximized

---

[87] Rubinstein further remarked that segmentation might not be an essential concept. Incomplete diversification of domestic portfolios can result from other causes such as nontraded assets, default risks in borrowing, taxes, and transaction costs. Internationally, however, such factors may operate to separate financial markets from each other. We do not therefore attempt any further distinction between segmentation and the imperfections that may cause it.

[88] The welfare gains from integration have been evaluated by Subrahmanyam [193].

while the welfare of investors in the host country is generally minimized. Their work contributed an essential insight. When conditions in the domestic market are those leading to the Modigliani and Miller theorem, there is no optimal foreign acquisition decision for any single, individual home-firm. What exists is an optimum for the total amounts of foreign shares to be acquired by all the firms in the home-market segment. The allocation of this total acquisition among home firms is irrelevant for investors holding a diversified home market portfolio.

Stapleton and Subrahmanyam [133] calculated numerically optimal decisions and capital market equilibrium in a variety of stock market settings. Adler and Dumas [4] established the principle that for each kind of segmentation there is a corresponding domestic value-maximizing decision for unrestricted home firms: when the bond market is segmented, there is an optimal foreign versus home borrowing decision; and there is an optimal forward contracting decision when stockholders' access to the forward exchange market is restricted. As before, these decisions will not be firm-specific if the domestic market is free of imperfections and bankruptcy costs.

The acquisitions of foreign shares that firms make for the purpose of providing their owners with international diversification should be distinguished clearly from private foreign direct investment (PFDI), although they might accidentally be so classified in the balance of payments statistics. For one thing, PFDI involves the purchases of control, a consideration excluded from the acquisition decisions discussed above. Segmentation among the financial markets does not seem particularly important in this connection.[89] Most explanations of MNC's behavior and of synergy, however, appeal to imperfections in, and segmentations of, not the financial markets but of the markets for products, factors, and technology. To paraphrase Kindleberger, direct investment falls more within the province of industrial organization and monopoly theories than financial theory.[90]

Nevertheless, the fact that MNC's foreign operations can be viewed as (more

---

[89] Ragazzi [154] offers an intriguing theory based on segmentation within countries which are financially underdeveloped. In such countries, he hypothesizes two capital markets, one for the trading of very large, controlling blocks of shares and one for the trading of minority holdings. Expected returns for a given level of risk would be higher in the market for control. Ragazzi suggests that MNC's might finance themselves in the minority market, repackage the funds, and enter the oligopolistic market for controlling interests, thus reaping the difference in rates of return.

[90] A full review of the determinants of PFDI is beyond the scope of this survey. Segmentation of product markets underlies Adler and Stevens's [10] analysis of MNC's exporting and investment decisions. Early accounts of the spread of international investment, summarized in Hufbauer and Adler [95] and elsewhere, emphasized the migration of labor-intensive industries to low wage countries: such investment bridges a segmentation in the factor market. By the same token, however, capital intensive industries should concentrate in, and preferably export capital intensive goods from, countries like the U.S. where the cost of capital may be relatively low. This proposition has proved empirically questionable. The failure of the factor proportions account led to the analysis of PFDI as a channel for the transfer of technology: Hufbauer [92, 93, 94] and Vernon [199]. The product life cycle account follows from the view that the market for technology is segmented and monopolistic. This notion also underlies the influential proposal by Johnson [99] and Magee [132] that MNC's be modeled as monopolistic producers, not of goods, but of information. Their efforts to appropriate the externalities tend to segment the information market between private information held by the innovating firms and public information. Other explanations of PFDI resort to economies of scale in the production of goods and information or in the ability of large firms to negotiate concessions from host governments. Few feature financial market segmentations as key contributing factors.

or less diversified) portfolios of controlling shares raised the hypothesis that they may offer a (partial) diversification service. Can one replicate true international diversification by purchasing a portfolio of MNC stocks? Agmon and Lessard [13] regressed the returns of 217 U.S. MNC's on the U.S. index and an international factor. In second pass regressions, they found the coefficient of the world factor to be correlated with a sales measure of MNC's international involvement and, therefore, suggested that perhaps one can. However, using a sample of 40 European and 23 U.S. firms between 1966 and 1974, Jacquillat and Solnik [97] concluded that one cannot. Basically, a multiple regression of MNC returns on various national indices showed that these firms correlate highly with their respective national indices and very little with foreign stock markets. These negative results were confirmed by Brewer [31] and Senschak and Beedles [173]. The issue is not easy to settle empirically, as noted in Adler [2]. If investors can diversify costlessly into the shares of foreign firms with equal access to the same projects as U.S. MNC's, geographical diversification of projects ceases to be a service that MNC's can valuably perform on behalf of their stockholders. It may be impossible to detect diversification benefits if MNC's operate in markets where individuals also can trade. If any "foreign investment" effect is to be observed then, based on the theory of PFDI, it is likely to be the result of MNC's monopoly advantages abroad. Errunza and Senbet [54] independently followed this reasoning. They found that a measure of MNC's monopoly returns, i.e., market value minus replacement cost, was significantly correlated with a sales measure of MNC's foreign involvement. The clear implication is that it is hard empirically to unravel the effects of monopoly from potential diversification benefits.

While segmentation within and among capital markets may not be central to explanations of PFDI, the possibility that it exists is important and perhaps crucial in connection with the analysis of corporate financial decisions. Unfortunately, there is as yet no definitive empirical method for determining whether and to what extent the international capital market is segmented. There appear to be four conceivable avenues of investigation, not all of which have been followed in the literature.

The first is misguided. Section II reviewed several studies of the correlations between national stock markets. A theme sometimes encountered in these papers is that low correlations indicate segmentation on the grounds that integrated national markets would tend to fluctuate together. This inference, however, is incorrect. There are national random factors (politics, etc.) which affect selectively the production activities of any one country. They are reflected in stock returns but this is no evidence of segmentation. Further, output mixes vary considerably among countries partly as a consequence of the specialization induced by international trade. Random shocks may affect selectively specific industrial sectors. They may, therefore, have a relatively heavy impact on those stock markets where these sectors are large but not in others. Small correlations among national stock market indices are generally consistent with perfect capital market integration.

Prospectively, a better approach for detecting segmentation is to analyze the correlations among national consumption rates. As was pointed out in Section

VI, consumption risks (as opposed to production risks) are mutualized in an integrated and Pareto optimal capital market. Consequently, small random (unanticipated) fluctuations in national consumption rates should in such a market be perfectly correlated with the aggregate random consumption rate. There are some difficulties in defining aggregate consumption risk when differences in tastes lead to PPP deviations. These are not impossible to overcome.[91] The problem of CPP violations may, however, be more severe for reasons already given at the end of the previous section.

The third possible method is, like the first, based on an analysis of securities' prices. Rather than trying to infer segmentation directly from the correlation structure, however, the idea is to derive competing capital asset pricing models, with and without segmentation, and to confront them with data to see which one fits best.[92] Stehle [195] attempted to test the hypothesis that the U.S. market is completely isolated against the null that it is completely integrated with the rest of the world. To avoid the problems associated with PPP deviations, he assumed a world of logarithmic investors ($\alpha^j = 1$ and, therefore, $\alpha^m = 1$ in Equation (17)). With complete segmentation, the proper market portfolio for U.S. investors would be represented by the U.S. index whereas under complete integration a world index would be appropriate. Unfortunately, his empirical evidence did not significantly discriminate between the two competing models.[93]

The last approach, which also relies on CAPM concepts, was initiated by Black [24]. A variation and extension was recently proposed by Stulz [190]. Rather than postulate the extremes of either complete segmentation or none at all, these papers employ a continuous parameter of segmentation in the form of a proportional tax. In Black, the tax is on an investor's net holdings (longs minus shorts) of risky foreign assets while in Stulz the tax on both long and short positions is positive. Borrowing at home and abroad is riskless and untaxed in both models. This apparently minor difference in specification, nevertheless, produces two quite different CAPMs with a common feature: the world portfolio will not be efficient for any investor in either one. The segmentation test in each case would essentially consist of fitting the derived CAPM to stock price data and either estimating the value of the implied tax rate or detecting its effects via security market line analysis. So far, this approach remains in the realm of theory.

---

[91] Breeden [30] is credited for pointing out that the mutualization of consumption risks implies the perfect correlation of consumption rates. Admittedly, (Stulz [191]) consumption mixes vary across the world, leading to PPP deviation, and destroying the perfect correlation. But examining correlations of consumption rates of *individual* goods would eliminate the problem. Such a route was not open to the authors who studied the stock market returns: examining industry rates of return would have resolved the specialized issue but would not have dealt with the issue of country-specific production risks (which are not supposed to be mutualized).

[92] An alternative method, in the same spirit, would use the Arbitrage Pricing Theory (Roll and Ross [162] and test whether random factors which are common to stocks of different countries receive the same price in the different national stock markets (an APT in the absence of PPP would be needed for this purpose). This suggestion was made by one referee. We are thankful to him.

[93] Solnik [182] following the Roll [160] methodology argues in favor of comparing actual and optimal portfolios (the latter computed on the basis of actual returns) rather than comparing the actual return statistics to their theoretical values (19). He claims that optimal aggregate portfolios under segmentation and under integration would not be sufficiently different (because of the low correlation of returns across countries) to permit a clear-cut conclusion.

VIII. International Corporate Financial Decisions: Hedging Policy

The discussion of the previous section clearly implies that the analysis of international corporate financial decisions rapidly becomes problematic once capital market imperfections and segmentations enter the picture. As these are often hard to ignore in practice, the literature in this sub-field is correspondingly slim. We shall therefore focus on the subject which has received the most attention, hedging policy, after the briefest of reviews of other decision problems.

A few papers address long-term decisions. Mehra [137] confirms that all the Modigliani and Miller (M & M) propositions continue to hold in a perfectly integrated, two country capital market with random exchange rates, identical investors but no (or identical) taxes and no inflaton. The capital budgeting criterion in such a world is independent of the choice of measurement currency, the nationality of the investing firm, and of the financing decision. The same conclusion regarding investment and financial decisions will also emerge, however, from any of the (quasi-) complete-market, tax-free international asset pricing models such as Solnik's [179], GLS's [79] or, for that matter, our own in Section IV above. Adler and Dumas [4] and Senbet [172] introduce different tax rates at home and abroad with the result that there emerges a value-maximizing foreign borrowing decision, the investment and financing decisions become interdependent and planning becomes a programming problem. Adding other sources of segmentation does not change this general picture but complicates it considerably. Exact solutions depend very much on the specific provisions of the assumed tax regime and on the specific constraints imposed by the assumed imperfections. Lessard [119] offers a pragmatic compromise which treats the decisions separately. One would like to know how good an approximation his procedure is.

Exchange rate variations can affect firms along several dimensions: through their impact on short and long-term monetary assets and liabilities and on physical assets; and via their effect on the volume of sales and the associated production plans. Exchange risk is but one of many environmental risks with which firms contend. Isolating its effects is a matter of decomposing the variability of some measure of the firm's results among the various risk sources. Once the extent of the firm's vulnerability to foreign currency risk is determined, it may readily be modified using financial hedging instruments such as forward contracts, swaps (borrowing one currency and lending the proceeds in another), and a variety of insurance schemes. Two questions then arise. Should a firm hedge at all? If there are circumstances in which it should, then by how much? While these issues are by no means completely settled, we may review the progress to date and the problems that remain.

In a perfectly integrated world capital market like that of Section IV, where the M & M propositions all hold, Baron [19] and Dumas [46] show that corporate hedging, like the choice of debt versus equity, is irrelevant *regardless* of the firm's exposure. In such a world, firms need not do what investors can do equally well for themselves. This irrelevance proposition is independent of the existence of risk and inflation premia in the relationship between the forward and expected future spot rates. The equilibrium forward rate in Equation (23) is set precisely at the level where no value is gained or lost by hedging. When a firm hedges, there is a change in its risk posture which is precisely offset by a value-preserving change in its expected return. What the proposition depends on, in other words, is the dual assumption of symmetric information and the (quasi-) completeness of the world's financial markets. Integration of the foreign exchange and stock markets guarantees that the same (linear) valuation functional is used in both. This allows the value additivity principle to be applied: the value of a firm with a forward contract is equal to the value of the same firm without a contract plus the value of a contract. In the absence of transactions costs, forward contracting involves no exchange of money between the parties: the forward rate adjusts until the value of the contract at the time it is entered is exactly zero. The values of the hedged and unhedged firms are therefore equal on the hedging-decision date.

We should emphasize that the market conditions which guarantee that this variant of the M & M theorem will hold are the only reasons for hedging to be irrelevant. Hedging is also claimed to be unnecessary by followers of Aliber [15] on the generally faulty ground that the net gain from it (equal to the forward rate minus the ensuing spot) is sometimes positive and sometimes negative and tends to zero over long periods. Aliber's own argument was empirical and more restrictive: he observed that the average deviation of the forward from the future spot rate tended towards zero as the number of observations included in the average increased.[94] He proceeded to deduce that long-term nominal foreign-currency assets are not exposed in the long run, and therefore that these assets, at least, need not be hedged. The argument is flawed for several reasons. The most important is that it ignores risks whose expected values are zero. It is wrong to base on reasoning dealing with averages the theoretical argument that risk avoidance is irrelevant.[95] There is no reason to suppose that stockholders or corporate managers are risk-neutral and care only about long-run expected values. If hedging is useless, it can only be for the reasons given in the previous paragraph.

As is the case with most financial decisions that do not matter in M & M's theory, practitioners do devote time and resources to hedging exchange risk. Even those who ignore balance sheet translation exposures substitute some other target. What accounts for this activity? One reason may be that the market is not as integrated as the theory requires. Segmentation and other imperfections, including bankruptcy costs in addition to the ones already mentioned, may be part of the explanation; but their impact is hard to measure. Information may not be symmetrically distributed. Firms do not publish their exposures by currency so treasurers must be better informed in this regard than investors. Perhaps there is room for managers to make hedging decisions for stockholders.[96]

---

[94] Note that the long term-average observation would only show that the expected value of the forward rate is equal to the expected value of the spot, *not* that the forward rate is equal to the conditional expected value of the spot.

[95] Also, when risk is considered, the exposure of long-term nominal foreign-currency assets is found to have little to do with deviations of the forward from the future spot rate: we discuss exposure below.

[96] Asymmetric information raises thorny problems. If managers attempt to enter forward trans-actions on behalf of shareholders, what should they assume regarding the forward contracting

International Finance 971

Organization and accounting theories may provide additional clues. Managers may not willingly further the interests of stockholders. Many of them in fact object to value maximization partly on the generally questionable grounds that it is unfair to evaluate their performances relative to market prices over which they have no control. Instead, they prefer or may be required to serve some accounting objective such as minimizing the exchange losses reported in financial statements. This last is reflected in Rodriguez's [157] survey and would account for the popularity of Aliber's averaging arguments. There is for the present no comprehensive theoretical framework for dealing convincingly with this issue. We can offer some preliminary notions as a step in that direction.

For a point of departure, let us postulate that "market-value stabilization" is the objective.[97] A firm's exposure to a given foreign exchange rate can then be defined as the sensitivity of the domestic real market value of the firm's equity, as of a *given future date*, to the concomitant random variations in the future domestic purchasing power of the foreign currency on that date. The measure of sensitivity is an amount of foreign currency: it is the amount deposited in the bank which would render the firm as vulnerable to foreign currency risk at the target date, as does its commercial activity. A perfect hedge consists of the forward transaction in foreign currency for the said maturity required to render the random variations in the *future* real domestic market price of the stock independent of the randomness of the future purchasing power of the foreign currency. As one performs this sensitivity measure vis à vis all currencies simultaneously,[98] the result is an equivalent portfolio of foreign (and also domestic) currencies which the firm is implicitly holding on account of its commercial activity. An optimal hedge is equal to the simple difference between the implicit pre-existing portfolio and some desired portfolio which meets the postulated objective.

To state a theoretical definition of exposure is to reveal also its practical limitations. Economic theory has not yet progressed to the point where it is possible in the case of a firm, security, or commodity accurately to associate a specific future market price and its probability with each possible level of the future exchange rate. Much of the managerial literature (Lietaer [123], Makin [133], Adler and Dumas [7] seeks to avoid the problems involved with market value objectives by relying on accounting numbers.[99] These suffer from at least

behavior of the stockholders themselves? The answer is especially difficult to provide when stockholders' nationalities differ. Asymmetric information is not the only rationale for corporate hedging: one referee pointed out that hedging entails fixed (information and transactions) costs which would become prohibitive if stockholders hedged on their own account on a day-to-day basis.

[97] Perhaps, this objective would be derived from the desire to minimize the probability of default (default being the circumstance where the value of equity is zero).

[98] If the postulated objective function can be put in the mean-variance form (as, for instance, when the market value of the equity is normally distributed), the exposures to the various currencies are coefficients of a multiple regression (across states of nature) of the market value of the equity on the purchasing powers of all foreign currencies (Dumas [46]). The same procedure applies, of course, to any asset or security. Approximate stock market exposures were displayed in Table V.

[99] Accountants themselves somewhat arbitrarily classify balance sheet items into exposed and nonexposed. Exposure is then simply the net amount of exposed assets minus liabilities in today's balance

one deficiency:[100] they do not incorporate the delayed effects of an exchange rate change on the firm's ensuing cash flows.[101] To remedy this limitation and to accommodate managerial concerns, Adler and Dumas [7] proposed that treasurers be concerned with the mean and variance of the consolidated net worth or the consolidated cash balance[102] (in the company's functional currency), measured at some cut-off date. This date would be chosen posterior to the target date at which the exchange rate changes being analyzed are to take place.[103] Either nominal objective may be justified as a signal of default risk. A firm is equally bankrupt when the real or nominal value of its equity reaches zero; and cash balances can be compared to their deficiency levels, irrespective of the measurement unit.

Equipped with such a mean-variance objective, the firm could proceed as before. Levels of the cut-off-date net worth or cash balance would be associated, perhaps by simulation, with levels of the target-date exchange rates after taking account of the responses the firm might plan to make in each state. Exposures to each currency will be represented by the coefficients in a regression (across states) of the target variable on the set of exchange rates.

The exposures measured in this way or on the basis of the earlier market-value reasoning will be global in the sense that they encompass the sensitivity of the firm as a whole to exchange rates. They can, however, be decomposed among components which represent the different kinds of influence that exchange rates can have. There are at least five categories of these: (1) the impact on short-term nominal net assets with maturity equal to the target date; (2) the impact on longer term nominal net assets with maturities falling beyond the target date; (3) the impact on the salvage value of existing physical assets and on the replacement cost or purchase price of physical assets to be replaced or acquired; (4) the impact on sales prices and unit costs; and (5) the indirect impact via sales prices on the volume of sales and consequently on the planned volume of production and other physical activities. Accounting measures of exposure have imperfectly dealt with only the first two of these effects. The fifth has so far been completely ignored. There is some confusion regarding the rest.

---

sheet: the time-dated forward-looking nature of exposure is lost. Under FASB 8 exposure was equal to foreign accounts receivable plus cash minus long-term debt, accounts payable, and short-term debt; it was generally negative. Under FASB 52, all items are considered exposed; exposure is then equal to net foreign assets and it is necessarily positive.

[100] One other deficiency is that accounting numbers are nominal in nature and no price index seems inherently satisfactory to deflate them as has been made clear by the endless debate on inflation accounting. For a questionable attempt at solving the firm's numeraire problem, see Eaker [51].

[101] These would have been included in a market-value based measure of exposure.

[102] This approximation, too, is ad hoc. It suffers from the same potential problems of non-optimality and inconsistency as any firm-specific quantity. It has, however, the major virtue of being able to bring all the potential effects of the exchange rate into the picture. There is little to choose between book net worth and the cash balance on this count. The former accommodates long-term debt while the latter focuses on treasurers' professed main concern, cash, and is independent of any accounting rule.

[103] The cut-off date only determines the precision of the measurement whereas the target date is an essential parameter of exposure measures.

Adler and Dumas [8] considered channel (2); i.e., nominal long-term, foreign currency bonds. The market values of such bonds may be exposed more or less than 100% in the sense that their exposures, and therefore the amount of shorter-term forward contracts required for a perfect hedge, may be larger or smaller than their face or redemption values. Whether they are over- or under-exposed depends on the degree of serial dependence in anticipated exchange rates (and not on the difference between the forward and ensuing spot exchange rates, as in Aliber [15]).

Aliber and Stickney [16] linked channels (3) and (4) to the existence of deviations from commodity price parity (CPP) between countries. Their specific contention was that physical assets are not exposed because the average deviation from purchasing power parity (relative to a base period) empirically tends to zero over the long haul. In Section (2), this evidence was seen to be consistent with the hypothesis that PPP deviations follow a martingale, hardly a situation of no risk. Their argument is also highly questionable for additional reasons. As far as channel (3) is concerned, it is clear that exchange rates may influence the reference currency *market* value of a physical asset located in any country once exchange rates and goods prices are correlated. Physical assets regardless of their location are indeed generally exposed to exchange risk. It is equally clear, however, that the issue of comparing the exposures of (identical) physical assets located in different countries does not arise when exposure is properly defined. Hence comparative prices (as in CPP) have no role to play. Traditional accounting trailed this red herring: the original cost book value of physical assets located at home does not fluctuate and is by definition not exposed. The CPP misconception presumably arose from an implicit comparison with home assets.

As for channel (4), it is clear that exchange rate variations may erode or improve the firm's competitiveness abroad. But note that a firm generally purchases goods and services in one country, transforms them, and may sell them in some other country. Except in the case of a pure shipping firm, the goods bought in one place and sold in another are never the same. Even if CPP held exactly, there remains the possibility that the prices of the output good and the input goods will have different exposures. Profitability and net cash flows would then be affected by exchange rates. It is small solace to know that on the average over the long run goods prices may be internationally linked. The firm should not be concerned with averages when it is planning its risk-bearing strategy.

IX. Conclusion

The best conclusion of a survey paper is undoubtedly one filled with directions for research prompted by the shortcomings of existing theory. The shortcomings have probably been apparent to the reader, but it may be useful to recapitulate.

Deviations from parity of individual commodities prices are a phenomenon about which existing microeconomics has very little to say. A model of international goods markets must be constructed before we can say anything serious regarding the financial side. We have mentioned that segmentation of the goods market can induce segmentation of capital markets. The manner in which the foreign exchange market reacts to CPP or PPP deviations (see Section I) can and will be properly analyzed only when the physical events (shipments, production, etc.) which are being anticipated by this market are themselves made explicit. Macroeconomists would also benefit from such models, since fluctuations in employment may be linked to the international competitiveness of a country's products.

Disregarding possible inconsistencies, we dealt with portfolio choices and asset pricing in a unified worldwide capital market with PPP deviations. As in much of finance theory so far, the functional form of the dynamics of securities prices was postulated *ab inito*, leaving only the cross-sectional relationship between risk and return parameters to be determined in market equilibrium. Following Lucas [129] and Cox, Ingersoll, and Ross [37], the stochastic process of asset prices should instead be fully endogenized by dynamic methods borrowed from functional analysis and by imposing an assumption of rational expectations.[104] Such a project would come at an auspicious time since balance-of-payments theorists, who have so far postulated *ad hoc* asset demands, have lately become interested in utility maximization (see Obstfeld [167]). The introduction of money balances in portfolios which we discussed briefly in Section VI would tie together the concerns of financial micro- and macroeconomists, which are becoming remarkably convergent. We are on the threshold of a true stochastic theory of the balance of payments. One difficulty, however, looms large. In a complete financial market with available instruments for all maturities and investors holding rational expectations, there is no need for portfolio revisions; prices adjust but not portfolios. One way to account for international capital flows under rational expectations is if there remain unhedgable or unexpected risks for at least some maturities. Other avenues for introducing portfolio revisions may prove fruitful. Delicate analytical choices will have to be made.

On the empirical side, tests and measures of the degree and specific sources of segmentation of international capital markets are becoming essential. It is almost impossible to progress without having some knowledge of the true meaning of national borders in finance. Initial tests should be based not on an analysis of securities prices, but on the principle that in integrated capital markets all consumption risks are mutualized. It is to be feared, however, that data on consumption behavior are not sufficiently reliable to be submitted to stochastic analysis. In particular, it may prove difficult to distinguish in a relatively stable fashion the expected and unexpected variations of consumption rates or to trace the effects of specific imperfections.

As far as policy implications are concerned, corporate financial behavior still awaits a proper paradigm which will have to be provided by general financial theory. In the meanwhile, some mean-variance portfolio choice will serve as a framework for exchange risk hedging decisions. The thrust should be towards practicality and towards a good understanding of the dynamics of the problem: should one hedge stocks or flows and how to long-term and short-term hedging instruments interact?

---

[104] In order for the theory to have content, the state variables upon which prices and decisions are contingent should be fully specified. Stulz [191] stopped short of this goal. In addition, the difficult problems associated with aggregating across investors' diverse preferences will have to be solved.

APPENDIX

Conditions for the Existence of Price Indices

As in standard portfolio theory, we assume that investors maximize a time-additive von Neumann-Morgenstern expected-utility of lifetime consumption function. But we introduce here several commodities so that there is some difficulty in defining what is meant by the consumption rate. The basic objective function of the investor must now be formulated as a function of the several consumption rates achieved for the various commodities:

$$\text{Max } E \int_t^T U(\underline{c}(s); s) \, ds \tag{1}$$

where

$E(\cdot)$ = the expected-value operator conditional on the information available at time t; and

$\underline{c}(s) = \{c_g(s); g = 1, \cdots G\}$ is the vector of consumption rates for the G goods at time s

Optimization of the consumption mix at each point in time leads to an equivalent objective in terms of the indirect utility function $V(\cdot)$:

$$\text{Max } E \int_t^T V(C(s); \underline{P}(s); s) \, ds \tag{2}$$

where

$C(s)$ is the rate of nominal consumption expressed in some arbitrary monetary unit per unit of time; and
$\underline{P}(s) = \{P_g(s); g = 1, \cdots G\}$ is the vector of prices for the G goods at time s, expressed in the same monetary unit, and

$$V(C; \underline{P}; s) \equiv \text{Max } U(\underline{c}; s) \quad s.t. \quad \underline{c}.\underline{P} = C, \quad \underline{c} \geq 0 \tag{3}$$

Assuming that the function $U(\cdot)$ is sufficiently well behaved for the function $V(\cdot)$ to exist, be unique and – for the purposes of later derivations – to be continuous and twice differentiable, the function $V(\cdot)$ satisfies a relationship known as Roy's identity (see Varian [198], page 93):

$$\underline{V}_p = -\underline{c} \, V_C \tag{4}$$

where

$\underline{V}_p$ is the $1 \times G$ vector of partial derivatives of V with respect to the price of goods;
$\underline{c}$ is here the $1 \times G$ vector of *optimal* consumption rates; and V_C is the partial derivative of V with respect to the consumption budget C.

The formulation (2) proves somewhat cumbersome when it comes to portfolio choices because all prices of consumption goods appear separately in the objective function. A more compact, albeit special, formulation is possible when the function $U(\cdot)$ is such that there exists an invariant price index, i.e., a compression of the price vector $\underline{P}$ into a single scalar leading to the same decisions and valid at all levels of the consumption budget C. Precisely:

DEFINITION. *There exists an invariant price index when the indirect utility function $V(\cdot)$ either satisfies the property*

$$V(C; \underline{P}; s) \equiv C(V(1; \underline{P}; s)) \tag{5}$$

or can be transformed by some monotonic transformation into a function which satisfies (5).

The condition to be satisfied by the direct utility function $U(\cdot)$ in order for there to exist an invariant price index was pointed out by Samuelson and Swamy [168]:

LEMMA. *A necessary and sufficient condition for the indirect utility function $V(\cdot)$ to satisfy property (5) is that the direct utility function $U(\cdot)$ be homogeneous of degree one with respect to the consumption rates $\underline{c}$.*

Proof: The proof is given in Varian ([198], pages 14 and 42) apropos cost and production functions exhibiting constant returns to scale.

A homothetic function is defined as the composition of a monotonic transform with a function homogeneous of degree one.

THEOREM (*Samuelson and Swamy*). *A necessary and sufficient condition for there to exist an invariant price index is that the direct utility function $U(\cdot)$ be homothetic with respect to the vector of consumption rates $\underline{c}$.*

Proof: It is obvious from the definition (3) of $V(\cdot)$ that applying a monotonic transformation to $U(\cdot)$ applies the same transformation to $V(\cdot)$ and vice versa.

When property (5) is satisfied, $V(1; \underline{P}; s)$ is evidently one over the invariant price index (or, it is the purchasing power index). It can be computed in practice only if one knows explicitly the function $V(\cdot)$. However, one may expect that for small percentage changes in prices, the local log-linear approximation of the function $V(\cdot)$ may be revealed by the consumer's budget allocation. Indeed, when (5) holds, one may write Roy's identity (4) as

$$C \underline{V}_p(1; \underline{P}; s) \equiv -\underline{c} V(1; \underline{P}; s) \tag{6}$$

so that, for each commodity g,

$$[P_g/V(1; \underline{P}; s)] V_{P_g}(1; \underline{P}; s) \equiv c_g P_g/C$$

PROPOSITION. *The elasticities of the index function with respect to prices are revealed by budget shares.*

This result is not affected if a monotonic transformation is applied to the function $V(\cdot)$, as the derivative of the monotonic transformation would only appear as a factor on both sides of Equation (6). In practice it means that percentage variations of the price index may be computed as an average of the percentage variations of individual commodity prices weighted by budget shares. This is, approximately, the way in which national statistical institutes across the world compute cost-of-living indices, a procedure which is valid under homothetic preferences only.

International Finance 977

References

1. M. Adler. "The Cost of Capital and Valuation of a Two-Country Firm." *Journal of Finance* 29 (March 1974), 119–33.
2. ———. "Investor Recognition of Corporate International Diversification: Comment." *Journal of Finance* 36 (March 1981), 187–91.
3. ——— and B. Dumas. "Optimal International Acquisitions." *Journal of Finance* 30 (March 1975), 1–20.
4. ———. "The Long-Term Financial Decisions of the Multinational Corporation." In E. J. Elton and M. J. Gruber (eds.), *International Capital Markets.* Amsterdam: North Holland, 1975.
5. ———. "Portfolio Choice and the Demand for Forward Exchange." *The American Economic Review* 66 (May 1976), 332–40.
6. ———. "Default Risk and the Demand for Forward Exchange." In H. Levy and M. Sarnat (eds.). *Financial Decision Making under Uncertainty.* New York: Academic Press, 1977.
7. ———. "Foreign Exchange Risk Management." In B. Antl (ed.). *Currency Risk and the Corporation.* London: Euromoney Publications, 1980: 145–158.
8. ———. "The Exposure of Long-Term Foreign Currency Bonds." *Journal of Financial and Quantitative Analysis* 15 (November 1980), 973–95.
9. ———. "Should Exposure Management Depend on Translation Accounting Methods?" *Euromoney* (June 1981), pp. 132–8.
10. M. Adler and B. Lehmann. "Deviations from PPP in the Long Run: A Random Walk?" Working paper, Columbia University, August 1982.
11. M. Adler and G. V. G. Stevens. "The Trade Effects of Direct Investment." *Journal of Finance* 29 (May 1974), 655–76.
12. T. Agmon. "The Relations Among Equity Markets in the United States, United Kingdom, Germany and Japan." *Journal of Finance* 27 (September 1972), 839–56.
13. ——— and D. R. Lessard. "Investor Recognition of Corporate International Diversification." *Journal of Finance* 32 (September 1977), 1049–56.
14. R. Z. Aliber. "The Interest Rate Parity Theorem: A Reinterpretation." *Journal of Political Economy* 81 (November/December 1973), 1451–9.
15. ———. *Exchange Risk and Corporate International Finance.* London: Macmillan, 1978.
16. ——— and C. P. Stickney. "Accounting Measures of Foreign Exchange Exposure: The Long and Short of It." *Accounting Review* 50 (January 1975), 44–57.
17. M. J. Bailey. "The Welfare Cost of Inflationary Finance." *Journal of Political Economy* 64 (April 1956), 93–110.
18. B. Balassa. "The Purchasing-Power Parity Doctrine: A Re-appraisal." *Journal of Political Economy* 72 (December 1964), 584–96.
19. D. P. Baron. "Flexible Exchange Rates, Forward Markets and the Level of Trade." *American Economic Review* 66 (June 1976), 253–66.
20. ——— and R. Forsythe. "Models of the Firm and International Trade under Uncertainty." *American Economic Review* 69 (September 1979), 565–74.
21. R. Barro. "Inflationary Finance and the Welfare Cost of Inflation. *Journal of Political Economy* 80 (September 1972), 978–1001.
22. V. S. Bawa, S. J. Brown, and R. W. Klein. *Estimation Risk and Optimal Portfolio Choice.* Amsterdam and New York: North Holland Publishing Co., 1979.
23. F. Black. "Capital Market Equilibrium with Restricted Borrowing." *Journal of Business* 45 (July 1972), 444–54.
24. ———. "International Capital Market Equilibrium with Investment Barriers." *Journal of Financial Economics* 1 (December 1974), 337–52.
25. M. E. Blume. "On the Assessment of Risk." *Journal of Finance* 26 (March 1971), 1–10.
26. J. Braga de Macedo. "Portfolio Diversification across Currencies." Working Paper, Princeton University, November 1980.
27. W. H. Branson. "The Minimum Covered Interst Differential Needed for International Arbitrage Activity." *Journal of Political Economy* 77 (November/December 1969), 1028–35.
28. W. H. Branson. "Asset Markets and Relative Prices in Exchange Rate Determination." IIES Seminar paper No. 66, Stockholm, December 1976.

29. ———, S. I. Katz, and T. D. Willett. "Exchange Rate Systems, Interest Rates, and Capital Flows." *Princeton Essays in International Finance*, No. 78, January 1970.

30. D. T. Breeden. "An Intertemporal Asset Pricing Model with Stochastic Consumption and Investment Opportunities." *Journal of Financial Economics* 7 (September 1979), 265–96.

31. H. L. Brewer. "Investor Benefits from Corporate International Diversification." *Journal of Financial and Quantitative Analysis* 16 (March 1981), 113–26.

32. E. R. Canterbery. "Foreign Exchange, Capital Flows and Monetary Policy." *Princeton Studies in International Finance*, Department of Economics, Princeton University, 1965.

33. C. Chamley and H. M. Polemarchakis. "Asset Markets, General Equilibrium and the Neutrality of Money." Working paper, Cowles Foundation, September 1981.

34. B. Cornell. "Spot Rates, Forward Rates and Exchange Market Efficiency." *Journal of Financial Economics* 5 (August 1977), 55–66.

35. ———. "Relative Price Changes and Deviations from Purchasing Power Parity." *Journal of Banking and Finance* 3 (September 1979), 263–79.

36.———. "Inflation, Relative Prices and Exchange Risk." *Financial Management* 9 (Autumn 1980), 30–34.

37. J. C. Cox, J. E. Ingersoll, Jr., and S. A. Ross. "Theory of the Term Structure of Interest Rates." *Econometrica*, forthcoming.

38. L. Crouhy-Veyrac, M. Crouhy, and Jacques Melitz. "More About the Law of One Price." *European Economic Review* 18 (July 1982), 325–44.

39. R. E. Cumby and M. Obstfeld. "A Note of Exchange Rate Expectations and Nominal Interest Differentials: A Test of the Fisher Hypothesis." *Journal of Finance* 36 (June 1981), 697–704.

40. M. P. Dooley. "A Model of Arbitrage and Short-term Capital Flows." *International Finance Discussion Papers*, No. 40 (January 1974), Division of International Finance, Board of Governors of the Federal Reserve System.

41. ——— and P. Isard. "Capital Controls, Political Risks, and Deviations from Interest-Rate Parity." *Journal of Political Economy* 88 (April 1980), 370–84.

42. ——— and J. R. Shafer. "Analysis of Short-Run Exchange Rate Behavior." Board of Governors of the Federal Reserve System, International Finance Discussion Papers, No. 76, February 1976.

43. R. Dornbusch. "Exchange Risk and the Macroeconomics of Exchange Rate Determination." In R. Hawkins et al., editors. *The Internationalization of Financial Markets and National Economic Policy.* Greenwich, CT: JAI Press, 1982.

44. G. Dufey and I. Giddy. "The Random Behavior of Flexible Exchange Rates: Implications for Forecasting." *Journal of International Business Studies* (Spring 1975), 1–32.

45. B. Dumas. "Discussion." *Journal of Finance* (May 1977), 512–15.

46. ———. "The Theory of the Trading Firm Revisited." *Journal of Finance* 33 (June 1978), 1019–29.

47. ———. "The Theorems of International Trade under Generalized Uncertainty." *Journal of International Economics* 10 (November 1980), 481–98.

48. ———. "Trade Theorems with Less than Perfectly Correlated Disturbances." CERESSEC Working Paper, 1980.

49. ———. "Trading Rules and Equilibrium in a Monetary Economy." In M. Sarnat (ed.). *Capital Markets and Inflation.* Cambridge, MA: Ballinger, 1982.

50. ——— and P. Poncet. "La Demande de Dollars des Personnes ne resident pas aux Etats-Unis." Working paper, 1980, *Archives de l'I.S.E.A.*, forthcoming.

51. M. R. Eaker. "The Numeraire Problem and Foreign Exchange Risk." *Journal of Finance* 36 (May 1981), 419–26.

52. P. A. Einzig. *A Dynamic Theory of Forward Exchange.* New York: Macmillan, 1961.

53. S. Ekern and R. Wilson. "On the theory of the Firm in an Economy with Incomplete Markets." *Bell Journal of Economics and Management Science* 5 (Spring 1974), 171–80.

54. V. R. Errunza and L. W. Senbet. "The Effects of International Operations on the Market Value of the Firm: Theory and Evidence." *Journal of Finance* 36 (May 1981), 401–18.

55. E. F. Fama. "The Behavior of Stock Market Prices." *Journal of Business* 38 (January 1965), 34–105.

56. ———. *Foundations of Finance.* New York: Basic Books, 1976.

57. ———. "Stock Returns, Real Activity, Inflation and Money." *American Economic Review* 71 (September 1981), 545–65.

58. ——— and A. Farber. "Money, Bonds and Foreign Exchange." *American Economic Review* 69 (September 1979), 639–49.

59. ——— and R. Roll. "Some Properties of Symmetric Stable Distributions." *Journal of the American Statistical Association* 63 (September 1968), 817–36.

60. E. F. Fama and G. W. Schwert. "Asset Returns and Inflation." *Journal of Financial Economics* 5 (November 1977), 115–46.

61. A. Farber, R. Roll and B. Solnik. "An Empirical Study of Risk Under Fixed and Flexible Exchange Rates." In K. Brunner and A. H. Meltzer (eds.). *Stabilization of the Domestic and International Economy.* Amsterdam: North Holland, 1977: 235–75.

62. S. Fischer. "The Demand for Index Bonds." *Journal of Political Economy* 83 (June 1975), 529–34.

63. ———. "Capital Accumulation on the Transition Path in a Monetary Optimizing Economy." *Econometrica* 47 (November 1979), 1433–9.

64. J. Frankel. "The Diversifiability of Exchange Risk." *Journal of International Economics* 9 (August 1979), 379–94.

65. J. Frankel. "A Test of Perfect Substitutability in the Foreign Exchange Market." *Southern Economic Journal* 48 (October 1982), 406–16.

66. J. Frankel. "In Search of the Exchange-Risk Premium: A Six-Currency Test Assuming Mean-Variance Optimization." *Journal of International Money and Finance* (December 1982), forthcoming.

67. J. A. Frenkel. "Elasticities and the Interest Parity Theory." *Journal of Political Economy* 81 (May/June 1973), 741–7.

68. ———. "Flexible Exchange Rates, Prices and the Role of News: Lessons from the 1970's." *Journal of Political Economy* 89 (August 1981), 665–705.

69. ——— and R. M. Levich. "Covered Interest Arbitrage: Unexploited Profits?" *Journal of Political Economy* (April 1975).

70. I. Friend, Y. Landskroner, and E. Losq. "The Demand for Risky Assets under Uncertain Inflation." *Journal of Finance* 31 (December 1976), 1287–98.

71. I. Friend and E. Losq. "Advantages and Limitations of International Portfolio Diversification." In M. Sarnat and G. P. Szego (eds.). *International Finance and Trade.* Cambridge, MA: Ballinger, 1979: 3–16.

72. H. J. Gailliot. "Purchasing Power Parity as an Explanation of Long Term Changes in Exchange Rates." *Journal of Money, Credit and Banking* 2 (August 1970), 348–57.

73. H. Genberg. "Purchasing Power Parity under Fixed and Flexible Exchange Rates." *Journal of International Economics* 9 (May 1978), 247–76.

74. J. Geweke and E. Feige. "Some Joint Tests of the Efficiency of the Markets for Forward Foreign Exchange." *Review of Economics and Statistics* 61 (August 1979), 334–41.

75. L. Girton and D. Henderson. "Central Bank Operations in Foreign and Domestic Assets under Fixed and Flexible Exchange Rates." In P. Clark, D. Logue, and R. Sweeney (eds.). *The Effects of Exchange Rate Adjustments.* Washington: U.S. Government Printing Office, 1976: 151–79.

76. L. Girton and D. Henderson. "Financial Capital Movements and Central Bank Behavior in a Two-Country, Short-run Portfolio Balance Model." *Journal of Monetary Economics* 2 (January 1976), 33–61.

77. C. W. J. Granger and O. Morgenstern. *Predictability of Stock Market Prices.* Lexington, MA: Heath-Lexington, 1970.

78. C. W. J. Granger. "A Survey of Empirical Studies on Capital Markets." In E. J. Elton and M. J. Gruber (eds.). *International Capital Markets.* Amsterdam: North Holland, 1975: 3–36.

79. F. L. A. Grauer, R. H. Litzenberger, and R. Stehle. "Sharing Rules and Equilibrium in an International Capital Market under Uncertainty." *Journal of Financial Economics* 3 (June 1976), 233–56.

80. H. G. Grubel. "Internationally Diversified Portfolios: Welfare Gains and Capital Flows." *American Economic Review* 58 (December 1968), 1299–1314.

81. ———. *Forward Exchange, Speculation and the International Flow of Capital.* Stanford: Stanford

University Press, 1966.

82. N. H. Hakansson. "On the Relevance of Price-Level Accounting." *Journal of Accounting Research* 7 (Spring 1969), 22–31.

83. L. P. Hansen and R. J. Hodrick. "Foward Exchange Rates as Optimal Predictors of Future Spot Rates: An Econometric Analysis." *Journal of Political Economy* 88 (October 1980), 828–53.

84. D. Heckerman. "On the Effects of Exchange Risks." *Journal of International Economics* 3 (November 1973), 379–88.

85. E. Helpman and A. Razin. "Uncertainty and International Trade in the Presence of Stock Markets." *Review of Economics Studies* 45 (June 1978), 239–50.

86. ———. "Welfare Aspects of International Trade in Goods and Securities." *Quarterly Journal of Economics* 92 (August 1978), 489–508.

87. ———. *A Theory of International Trade under Uncertainty.* New York: Academic Press, 1980.

88. ———. "Comparative Dynamics of Monetary Policy in a Floating Exchange Rate Regime." Working paper, Tel-Aviv University, 1981.

89. R. J. Herring and R. C. Marston. "The Forward Market and Interest Rates in the Eurocurrency and National Money Markets." In Carl H. Stein, John H. Makin, and Dennis E. Logue (eds.). *Eurocurrencies and the International Monetary System.* Washington: American Enterprise Institute, 1976.

90. R. Hodrick. "International Asset Pricing with Time-varying Risk Premia." *Journal of International Economics* 11 (November 1981), 573–7.

91. D. Hsu, R. B. Miller, and D. W. Wichern. "On the Stable Paretian Behavior of Stock Market Prices." *Journal of the American Statistical Association* 69 (March 1974), 108–13.

92. G. C. Hufbauer. *Synthetic Materials and the Theory of International Trade.* Cambridge, MA: Harvard University Press, 1966.

93. ———. "The Impact of National Characteristics and Technology on the Commodity Composition of Trade in Manufactured Goods." In R. Vernon (ed.). *The Technology Factor in International Trade.* New York: Columbia University Press, 1970: 145–232.

94. ———. "The Multinational Corporation and Direct Investment." In P. B. Kenen (ed.). *International Trade and Finance: Frontiers for Research.* New York: Cambridge University Press, 1975: 253–320.

95. G. Hufbauer, and M. Adler. *Overseas Manufacturing Investment and the Balance of Payments.* Washington, D.C.: Government Printing Office, 1968.

96. P. Isard. "How Far Can We Push the Law of One Price?" *American Economic Review* 67 (December 1977), 942–8.

97. B. Jacquillat and B. Solnik. "Multinationals are Poor Tools for Diversification." *Journal of Portfolio Management* (Winter 1978).

98. D. M. Jaffee. Comment on R. Z. Aliber: "The Firm under Pegged and Floating Exchange Rates." *Scandinvaian Journal of Economics* 78:2 (1976), 323–6.

99. H. G. Johnson. "The Efficiency and Welfare Implications of the International Corporation." In Kindleberger (ed.). *The International Corporation.* Cambridge, MA: MIT Press, 19: 35–36.

100. J. Johnston. *Econometric Methods.* New York: McGraw Hill, 1972.

101. L. Katseli-Papaefstratiou. "The Reemergence of the Purchasing Power Parity Doctrine in 1970's." *Special Paper in International Economics* No. 13 (December 1979), Princeton.

102. P. B. Kenen. "Trade, Speculation and the Forward Exchange Rates." In R. E. Baldwin et al. (eds.). *Trade, Growth and the Balance of Payments.* Chicago: Rand MacNally, 1965.

103. B. F. King. "Market and Industry Factors in Stock Price Behavior." *Journal of Business* 39 (January 1966), 139–90.

104. S. W. Kohlhagen. "The Forward Rate as an Unbiased Predictor of the Future Spot Rate." University of California, Berkeley, 1976.

105. ———. "'Rational' and 'Endogenous' Exchange Rate Expectations and Speculative Capital Flows in Germany." *Weltwirtschaftsliches Archiv* 113 (December 1977), 624–44.

106. ———. *The Behavior of Foreign Exchange Markets—A Critical Survey of the Literature.* NYU Monograph Series, 1973.

107. P. Kouri. "The Determinants of the Forward Premium." IIES Seminar Paper 62, University of Stockholm, August 1976.

108. ———. "International Investment and Interest Rate Linkages under Flexible Exchange Rates."

In R. Aliber (ed.). *The Political Economy of Monetary Reform.* London: Macmillan & Co., 1977.

109. ———. "The Exchange Rate and the Balance of Payments in the Short Run and in the Long Run: A Monetary Approach." *Scandinavian Journal of Economics* 78:2 (1976), 280–304.

110. P. Kouri and J. Braga de Macedo. "Exchange Rates and the International Adjustment Process. *Brookings Papers* (1:1978), 111–150.

111. I. B. Kravis, Z. Kenessey, A. W. Heston, and R. Summers. *A System of International Comparisons of Gross Product and Purchasing Power.* Baltimore: Johns Hopkins University Press, 1975.

112. I. B. Kravis and R. E. Lipsey. "Price Behavior in the Light of Balance of Payments Theory." *Journal of International Economics* 8 (May 1978), 193–246.

113. P. Krugman. "Consumption Preferences, Assets Demands, and Distribution Effects in International Financial Markets." Working Paper No. 651, National Bureau of Economic Research, March 1981.

114. Y. Landskroner and M. Liviatan. "Risk Premia and the Sources of Inflation." *Journal of Money, Credit and Banking* 13 (May 1981), 205–14.

115. S. Laursen and L. Metzler. "Flexible Exchange Rates and the Theory of Employment." *Review of Economics and Statistics* 32 (November 1950), 281–99.

116. W. Y. Lee and K. S. Sachdeva. "The Role of the Multinational Firm in the Integration of Segmented Capital Markets." *Journal of Finance* 32 (May 1977), 479–92.

117. D. R. Lessard. "World, National and Industry Factors in Equity Returns. *Journal of Finance* 29 (May 1974), 379–91.

118. ———. "World, Country and Industry Relationships in Equity Returns: Implications for Risk Reduction through International Diversification." *Financial Analysts Journal* (January/February 1976), 2–8.

119. ———. "Evaluating Foreign Projects: An Adjusted Present Value Approach." In D. R. Lessard (ed.). *International Financial Management.* Boston, MA: Warren, Gorham & Lamont, 1979: 577–92.

120. R. M. Levich. "Tests of Forecasting Models and Market Efficiency in the International Money Market." In J. A. Frenkel and H. G. Johnson (eds.). *The Economics of Exchange Rates.* Reading, MA: Addison-Wesley, 1978.

121. J. H. Levin. *Forward Exchange and Internal-External Equilibrium.* Ann Arbor: Michigan International Business Series, No. 12, 1970.

122. H. Levy and M. Sarnat. "International Diversification of Investment Portfolios." *American Economic Review* 60 (September 1970), 668–75.

123. B. A. Lietaer, *Financial Management of Foreign Exchange: An Operational Technique to Reduce Risk.* Cambridge, MA: M.I.T. Press, 1971.

124. J. Lintner. "The Valuation of Risk Assets and the Selection of Risky Investments in Stock Portfolios and Capital Budgets." *Review of Economics and Statistics* 47 (February 1965), 13–37.

125. ———. "Inflation and Security Returns." *Journal of Finance* 30 (May 1975), 259–80.

126. ———. "Bankruptcy Risk, Market Segmentation and Optimal Capital Structures." In I. Friend and J. Bicksler (eds.). *Risk and Return in Finance, Vol. 11.* Cambridge, MA: Ballinger Publishing Co., 1977: 1–128.

127. E. Losq. "Commodity Price Uncertainty and Capital Market Equilibrium." McGill University, mimeo, 1977.

128. R. E. Lucas. "Some International Evidence on Output-Inflation Trade-offs." *American Economic Review* 63 (June 1973), 326–34.

129. ———. "Asset Prices in an Exchange Economy." *Econometrica* 46 (November 1978), 1429–46.

130. ———. "Equilibrium in a Pure Currency Economy." *Economic Inquiry* 18 (April 1980), 203–20.

131. ———. "Interest Rates and Currency Prices in a Two-country World." Working paper, University of Chicago, July 1981.

132. S. Magee. "Multinational Corporation, the Industry Technology Cycle and the Transfer of Technology to Developing Countries." *Journal of World Trade Law*, 1978.

133. J. H. Makin. "Portfolio Theory and the Problem of Foreign Exchange Risk." *Journal of Finance* 33 (May 1978), 517–34.

134. J. Mayshar. "Transaction Costs and the Pricing of Assets." *Journal of Finance* 36 (June 1981),

583–98.

135. J. W. McFarland, R. R. Pettit, and S. K. Sung. "The Distribution of Foreign Exchange Price Changes: Trading Day Effects and Risk Measurement." *Journal of Finance* 37 (June 1982), 693–716.

136. R. I. McKinnon. "The Exchange Rate and Macroeconomic Policy: Changing Postwar Perceptions." *Journal of Economic Literature* 29 (June 1981), 531–57.

137. R. Mehra. "On the Financing and Investment Decisions of Multinational Firms in the Presence of Exchange Risk." *Journal of Financial and Quantitative Analysis* 13 (June 1978), 227–44.

138. R. C. Merton. "Lifetime Portfolio Selection under Uncertainty: The Continuous-Time Case." *Review of Economics and Statistics* 51 (August 1969), 247–57.

139. ———. "Optimum Consumption and Portfolio Rules in a Continuous-Time Model." *Journal of Economic Theory* 3 (December 1971), 373–413.

140. ———. "An Intertemporal Capital Asset Pricing Model." *Econometrica* 41 (September 1973), 867–87.

141. E. Modigliani and M. H. Miller. "The Cost of Capital, Corporation Finance and the Theory of Investment." *American Economic Review* 48 (April 1958), 261–97.

142. Moon Ho Lee. *Purchasing Power Party.* New York: Marcel Dekker, Inc., 1976.

143. J. Mossin. "Equilibrium in a Capital Asset Market." *Econometrica* 34 (October 1966), 768–83.

144. ———. *The Economic Efficiency of Financial Markets.* Lexington, MA: D. C. Health, 1977.

145. R. A. Mundell. *International Economics.* New York: Macmillan, 1968.

146. ———. *Monetary Theory: Inflation, Interest and Growth in the World Economy.* New York: Goodyear Publishing Company, 1971.

147. M. Obstfeld. "Macroeconomic Policy and World Welfare under Flexible Exchange Rates." Working paper, Columbia University, March 1980.

148. L. H. Officer. "The Purchasing Power Theory of Exchange Rates: A Review Article." *I.M.F. Staff Papers* 23 (March 1976), 1–60.

149. F. Papadia. "Forward Exchange Rates as Predictors of Future Spot Rates and the Efficiency of the Foreign Exchange Market." *Journal of Banking and Finance* 5 (June 1981), 217–40.

150. J. E. Pippenger. "Spot Rates, Forward Rates, and Interest Rate Differentials." *Journal of Money, Credit and Banking* 4 (May 1972), 375–83.

151. P. Poncet. "Optimum Consumption and Portfolio Rules with Money as an Asset." Working paper, ESSEC, Department of Finance, November 1979.

152. W. Poole. "Speculative Prices as Random Walks: An Analysis of Ten Time Series of Flexible Exchange Rates." *Southern Economic Journal* 83 (1966).

153. M. F. Prachowny. "A Note on Interest Parity and the Supply of Arbitrage Funds." *Journal of Political Economy* 78 (May/June 1970), 540–5.

154. G. Ragazzi. "Theories of the Determinants of Direct Foreign Investment." *I.M.F. Staff Papers* 20 (July 1973), 471–98.

155. S. F. Richard and M. Sundaresan. "A Continuous Time Equilibrium Model of Forward Prices and Future Prices in a Multigood Economy." *Journal of Financial Economics* 9 (December 1981), 347–72.

156. J. D. Richardson. "Some Empirical Evidence on Commodity Arbitrage and the Law of One Price." *Journal of International Economics* 8 (May 1978), 341–52.

157. R. M. Rodriguez. *Foreign-Exchange Management in U.S. Multinationals.* Lexington, MA: D.C. Heath, 1980.

158. R. Rogalski and J. D. Vinso. "Price Level Variations as Predictors of Flexible Exchange Rates." *Journal of International Business Studies* (Spring/Summer 1977), 71–81.

159. R. Roll. "Interest Rates on Monetary Assets and Commodity Price Index Changes." *Journal of Finance* 27 (May 1972), 251–77.

160. ———. "A Critique of the Asset Pricing Theory's Test; Part I: On Past and Potential Testability of the Theory." *Journal of Financial Economics* 4 (March 1977), 129–76.

161. ———. "Violations of Purchasing Power Parity and their Implications for Efficient International Commodity Markets." In M. Sarnat and G. P. Szego (eds.). *International Finance and Trade.* Cambridge, MA: Ballinger Publishing Co., 1979.

162. ——— and S. Ross. "An Empirical Investigation of the Arbitrage Pricing Theory. *Journal of Finance* 35 (December 1980), 1073–1103.

163. R. Roll and B. Solnik. "A Pure Foreign Exchange Asset Pricing Model." *Journal of International Economics* 7 (May 1977), 161–80.

164. B. Rosenberg, and J. Ohlson. "The Stationary Distribution of Returns and Portfolio Separation in Capital Markets: A Fundamental Contradiction." *Journal of Financial and Quantitative Analysiss* 11 (September 1976), 393–402.

165. M. Rubinstein. "An Aggregation Theorem for Securities Markets." *Journal of Financial Economics* 1 (September 1974), 225–44.

166. ———. "Corporate Financial Policy in Segmented Securities Markets." *Journal of Financial and Quantitative Analysis* 8 (December 1973), 749–62.

167. P. A. Samuelson. "The Fundamental Approximation Theorem of Portfolio Analysis in Terms of Means, Variances and Higher Moments." *Review of Economic Studies* 37 (October 1970), 537–42.

168. ——— and S. Swamy. "Invariant Economic Index Numbers and Canonical Duality: Survey and Synthesis." *American Economic Review* 64 (September 1974), 566–93.

169. A. Santomero and J. Seater. "The Inflation-Unemployment Trade-off: A Critique of the Literature." *Journal of Economic Literature* 16 (January 1978), 499–544.

170. T. Sargent and N. Wallace. "Rational Expectations, the Optimal Monetary Instrument and the Optimal Policy Rule." *Journal of Policitcal Economy* 83 (April 1975), 241–54.

171. L. Selden. "An OCE Analysis of the Effect of Uncertainty on Saving under Risk Preference Independence." *Review of Economic Studies* 46 (January 1979), 73–82.

172. L. W. Senbet. "International Capital Market Equilibrium and the Multinational Firm Financing and Investment Policies." *Journal of Financial and Quantitative Analysis* 14 (September 1979), 455–80.

173. A. J. Senschak and W. L. Beedles. "Is Indirect International Diversification Desirable?" *Journal of Portfolio Management* 6 (Winter 1980), 49–57.

174. P. Sercu. "A Generalization of the International Asset Pricing Model." *Revue de l'Association Française de Finance* 1 (June 1980), 91–135.

175. W. F. Sharpe. "A Simplified Model for Portfolio Analysis." *Management Science* 9 (January 1963), 277–93.

176. ———. "Capital Asset Prices: A Theory of Market Equilibrium under Conditions of Risk." *Journal of Finance* 19 (September 1964), 425–42.

177. J. J. Siegel. "Risk, Interest and Forward Exchange." *Quarterly Journal of Econoics* 86 (May 1972), 303–9.

178. E. Sohmen. *Flexible Exchange Rates.* Chicago: University of Chicago Press, 1969.

179. B. H. Solnik. "An Equilibrium Model of the International Capital Market." *Journal of Economic Theory* 8 (August 1974), 500–24.

180. ———. "The International Pricing of Risk: An Empirical Investigation of the World Capital Market Structure." *Journal of Finance* 29 (May 1974), 48–54.

181. ———. "Why Not Diversify Internationally Rather than Domestically?" *Financial Analysts Journal* 30 (July/August 1974), 48–54.

182. ———. "Testing International Asset Pricing: Some Pessimistic Views." *Journal of Finance* 32 (May 1977), 503–11.

183. R. C. Stapleton and M. G. Subrahmanyam. "Market Imperfections, Capital Asset Equilibrium and Corporation Finance. *Journal of Finance* 32 (May 1977), 307–21.

184. ———. "Uncertain Inflation, Exchange Rates and Bond Yields." *Journal of Banking and Finance* 5 (March 1981), 93–107.

185. R. Stehle. "An Empirical Test of the Alternate Hypotheses of National and International Pricing and Risky Assets." *Journal of Finance* 32 (May 1977), 493–502.

186. G. V. G. Stevens. "Two Problems in Portfolio Analysis: Conditional and Multiplicative Random Variables." *Journal of Financial and Quantitative Analysis* 6 (December 1971), 1235–50.

187. A. C. Stockman. "Risk, Information and Forward Exchange Rates." In J. A. Frankel and H. F. Johnson (eds.). *The Economics of Exchange Rates.* Reading, MA: Addison-Wesley, 1978.

188. ———. "A Theory of Exchange Rate Determination." *Journal of Political Economy* 88 (August 1980), 673–98.

189. H. R. Stoll. "Causes of Deviations from Interest Rate Parity." *Journal of Money, Credit and Banking* 4 (February 1972), 113–17.

190. R. M. Stulz. "On the Effects of Barriers to International Investment." *Journal of Finance* 36 (September 1981), 923–34.

191. ———. "A Model of International Asset Pricing." *Journal of Financial Economics* 9 (December 1981), 383–406.

192. ———. "The Forward Exchange Rate and Macroeconomics." *Journal of International Economics* 12 (May 1982), 285–99.

193. M. G. Subrahmanyam. "On the Optimality of International Capital Market Integration." *Journal of Financial Economics* 2 (August 1975), 3–28.

194. J. Tobin. "A General Equilibrium Approach to Monetary Theory." *Journal of Money, Credit and Banking* 1 (February 1969), 15–29.

195. ——— and W. R. Brainard. "Asset Markets and the Cost of Capital." In B. Balassa and R. Nelson (eds.). *Economic Progress, Private Values and Public Policy: Essays in Honor of William Fellner.* Amsterdam: North-Holland Publishing Co., 1977.

196. S. C. Tsiang. "The Theory of Forward Exchange and the Effects of Government Intervention in the Forward Exchange Market." *I.M.F. Staff Papers* 7 (April 1959), 75–106.

197. R. B. Upson. "Random Walk and Forward Exchange Rates: A Spectral Analysis." *Journal of Financial and Quantitative Analysis* 7 (September 1972), 1897–1906.

198. H. R. Varian. *Microeconomic Analysis.* New York: Norton, 1978.

199. R. Vernon. "International Investment and International Trade in the Product Cycle." *Quarterly Journal of Economics* 80 (May 1966), 190–207.

200. N. Wallace. "A Modigliani-Miller Theorem for Open-Market Operations." *American Economic Review* 71 (June 1981), 267–74.

201. L. Weiss. "The Role for Active Monetary Policy in a Rational Expectations Model." *Journal of Political Economy* 88 (April 1980), 221–33.

202. J. M. Westerfield. "An Examination of Foreign Exchange Risk under Fixed and Floating Rate Regimes." *Journal of International Economics* 7 (May 1977), 181–200.

[5]

Journal of Financial Economics 9 (1981) 383–406. North-Holland Publishing Company

A MODEL OF INTERNATIONAL ASSET PRICING*

René M. STULZ

University of Rochester, Rochester, NY 14627, USA

Received May 1980, final version received May 1981

In this paper an intertemporal model of international asset pricing is constructed which admits differences in consumption opportunity sets across countries. It is shown that the real expected excess return on a risky asset is proportional to the covariance of the return of that asset with changes in the world real consumption rate. (World real consumption does not, in general, correspond to a basket of commodities consumed by all investors.) The model has no barriers to international investment, but it is compatible with empirical facts which contradict the predictions of earlier models and which seem to imply that asset markets are internationally segmented.

1. Introduction

Without a model showing how assets are priced in a world in which asset markets are fully integrated, it is impossible to determine whether asset markets are segmented internationally or not.[1] Many issues in financial economics cannot be dealt with unless an assumption is made about whether markets are segmented internationally or not. For instance, the widespread use, in all countries which have a stock market, of some proxy of the home-country market portfolio to test how home-country assets are priced can be justified only by an assumption that markets are internationally segmented. As another example, only if markets are fully integrated is it true that projects with perfectly correlated cash-flows are valued in the same way regardless of the country in which they are undertaken. As a final example, it is only when markets are fully integrated that it is always optimal, in a mean-variance framework, to diversify internationally.

Presently, there does not appear to exist conclusive evidence showing that

*This paper draws on Part I of my dissertation at M.I.T. I am grateful to Doug Breeden, Stan Fischer, Don Lessard, John Long, Pat Reagan, Eric Rosenfeld, Cliff Smith, Bill Schwert, Lee Wakeman, and especially Mike Jensen and my dissertation advisor Fischer Black, for useful discussions and comments. I also thank the referee, Scott Richard, for helpful comments. All remaining mistakes are my own. I acknowledge generous financial help from the Swiss National Research fund.

[1]In this paper, asset markets are said to be perfectly integrated internationally if two assets (existing or hypothetical) which have perfectly correlated returns in a given currency but belong to different countries have identical expected returns in that currency. Markets are said to be segmented if this condition does not hold.

the hypothesis of segmented national stock markets can be rejected.[2] It might well be the case that markets are indeed segmented.[3] One can, however, argue that the reason the hypothesis of market segmentation cannot be rejected is that the models used to test it offer an insufficient description of how assets are priced in a world in which markets are fully integrated and exchange rates are flexible.[4] Existing models of international asset pricing proceed from one of two assumptions; the world can be modeled as if there is only one commodity,[5] while countries have different rates of inflation, or it can be assumed that the terms of trade (i.e., the relative price of imports) are perfectly correlated with the exchange rate.[6] Such assumptions are unsatisfactory, as it is known that the terms of trade change stochastically through time and are not perfectly correlated with exchange rates. Those empirical facts about exchange rate dynamics imply that at each point in time, the consumption opportunity set of an investor depends on the country in which he resides.[7] The consumption opportunity set of an investor is defined here as the set of goods available for his consumption, the current prices and the distribution of the future prices of those goods. The fact that consumption opportunity sets differ today does not mean that investors believe they will differ forever. A vast body of empirical literature indicates that whenever consumption opportunity sets differ, international trade in commodities and international factor mobility will, over time, reduce differences between consumption opportunity sets. Existing models of international asset pricing, however, assume that consumption opportunity sets are the same across countries at any point in time.

Earlier models of international asset pricing make predictions which are not compatible with observed facts. Contrary to the prediction of those models, it does not seem to be the case that an asset whose suitably defined excess return has a covariance equal to zero with the return on some world

---

[2]Aliber (1978) and Solnik (1977) review the literature. Rodriguez and Carter (1979) summarize the evidence and conclude their discussion by implying that markets are segmented (see p. 498).

[3]Models with barriers to international investment are offered by Adler and Dumas (1975, 1976), Black (1979), Kouri (1976) and Stulz (1981).

[4]The model developed in this paper does not hold if exchange rates are fixed, except for adjustments at discrete intervals of time.

[5]See, for instance, Grauer, Litzenberger and Stehle (1976), Kouri (1978) and Fama and Farber (1979). In the following, the terminology of Holmes (1967) is used and the assumption that the world can be modeled as if there exists only one good is called the assumption of 'naive' purchasing power parity.

[6]See, for instance, Solnik (1974).

[7]There is a large literature on exchange rate dynamics. For a review of the literature on purchasing power parity, see Officer (1976) and Katseli-Papaefstratiou (1979). Genberg (1978) and the other papers in the same issue of the *Journal of International Economics* give empirical evidence on purchasing power parity during the seventies. Dornbusch (1978), Bilson (1979) and Isard (1978), among others, review current ideas on exchange rate dynamics.

market portfolio, will have an expected excess return equal to zero.[8] It has been argued that assets which have the same covariance with the world market portfolio have different excess returns if they belong to different home countries.[9] Finally, investors hold a much larger amount of risky assets of their home country than predicted by those models.[10]

One could claim that the fact that those predictions of earlier models of international asset pricing do not hold shows that markets are segmented internationally. In the present paper, a model of international asset pricing is developed on the assumption that markets are fully integrated. It includes earlier models as special cases. The model can hold even when the predictions of earlier models are contradicted by observed facts.

In the model developed in this paper, consumption opportunity sets can differ across countries. Section 2 describes the investment and consumption opportunity set of investors. Section 3 discusses the asset demands of investors and argues that investors with identical utility functions living in different countries can have different asset demands when consumption opportunity sets differ across countries. Section 4 derives the fundamental asset pricing equation of this paper, while section 5 discusses the economic implications of that equation. Section 5 shows that predictions of earlier models do not necessarily hold in a world in which markets are fully integrated but investors have different consumption opportunity sets. The same section also derives implications of the model for the risk premium incorporated in the forward exchange rate. Section 6 offers concluding remarks.

2. Consumption and investment opportunity sets

2.1. Consumption opportunity sets

It is assumed that a domestic investor can buy K different commodities. The path of the price $P(i)$ of the ith domestic commodity is described by a stochastic differential equation written as[11]

$$dP(i)/P(i) = \mu_{P(i)}(s, t)\,dt + \sigma_{P(i)}(s, t)\,dz_{P(i)}, \qquad i = 1, \ldots, k, \tag{1}$$

where s is an $S \times 1$ vector of state variables, $dz_{P(i)}$ is a Wiener process, $\mu_{p(i)}$ is the instantaneous mean and $\sigma_{p(i)}^2$ is the instantaneous variance of the

---

[8]See Stehle (1978).

[9]See references in Aliber (1978).

[10]Black (1978, p. 8) writes: 'What we have to understand is not why foreign investment occurs, but why it isn't much more common.'

[11]See Merton (1971) for an introduction to those equations. Additional references are given in Breeden (1979).

percentage rate of change of the price of the ith good. By assumption the state variables follow Ito processes. An intuitive way to understand eq. (1) is to look at it as a reduced-form equation for the rate of change of the price of commodities. The vector of state variables is understood to include all the state variables which affect at least one investor's expected intertemporal utility. Without loss of generality, it is assumed that there are two countries, and asterisks are used to designate prices of commodities and assets in the foreign country. (K^* commodities are available in the foreign country.)

The first K state variables in the vector s are taken to be the logarithms of the prices of the commodities available in the domestic country. The vector s^* is defined as the vector of state variables rearranged so that the first K^* state variables are the logarithms of the prices in foreign currency of the commodities available in the foreign country. Some of the other state variables which could belong in the vector s are specified later.

The functional relationships between the state variables and the instantaneous mean and variance of the rate of change of commodity prices do not need to be further restricted for the purpose of this paper. Markets are assumed to be always in equilibrium. The only important restriction on the path of the price of good i given by eq. (2) is that, in non-mathematical terms, it must be smooth. This restriction is important because it prevents our model from being used to study a world in which exchange rates are fixed, except for adjustments at discrete time intervals.[12]

Let the domestic price of one unit of foreign currency at time t be e_t. If there are no obstacles to international commodity arbitrage, in the sense that arbitrage can always be made instantaneously at zero costs, then for identical traded commodities, the law of one price holds exactly, i.e.,

$$P_t(j) = e_t P_t^*(j), \qquad \forall j \in G_t, \tag{2}$$

where $P_t^*(j)$ is the price in foreign currency of good j and G_t is the set of traded commodities at time t. The set of traded goods does not need to be constant through time, but it is assumed that the set of consumed goods in each country is constant. In this paper, it is always assumed that the law of one price, as stated in eq. (2), holds for all traded commodities.

There exists no theoretical or empirical reason to assume that eq. (2) holds all the time for all commodities.[13] For simplicity, a commodity for which the law of one price, as stated in eq. (2), does not hold at time t is viewed as a non-traded commodity at time t. If a commodity is non-traded at time t, this does not mean that that commodity will be non-traded forever. In fact, for

---

[12]Kouri (1976) has a model in which that restriction does not hold.
[13]See Kravis and Lipsey (1978) and Isard (1977) for good empirical evidence. Samuelson (1948) was among the first authors to stress the role of non-traded commodities.

most commodities, today's expectation of how the prices of those commodities will deviate from some version of the law of one price at some future date, not too close from today, is likely to be equal to zero.[14] A large number of studies have shown that short-run deviations from the law of one price, as stated in eq. (2), are not trivial.

It is assumed that the exchange rate follows an equation similar to the equation which describes the price dynamics of the ith domestic commodity,

$$de/e = \mu_e(s,t)dt + \sigma_e(s,t)dz_e, \tag{3}$$

where μ_e is the instantaneous mean and σ_e^2 is the instantaneous variance of the percentage rate of change of the exchange rate. The exchange rate dynamics, together with the price dynamics and the law of one price, yield the dynamics for the foreign currency price of the ith traded commodity, $P^*(i)$. Differentiate (2) using Ito's Lemma to get the dynamics of $P^*(i)$,

$$\frac{dP^*(i)}{P^*(i)} = -\frac{de}{e} + \frac{dP(j)}{P(j)} - \frac{de}{e}\frac{dP(j)}{P(j)} + \left(\frac{de}{e}\right)^2, \tag{4}$$

where $(de/e)dP(j)/P(j))$ is equal to the instantaneous covariance between the percentage rate of change of the exchange rate and the percentage rate of change of the domestic currency price of the jth commodity, and $(de/e)^2$ is equal to the instantaneous variance of the percentage rate of change of the exchange rate.

In a world with only one commodity, eq. (4) simply states that 'naive' purchasing power parity holds.[15] In the present paper, differences in tastes and consumption opportunity sets across countries make it impossible, in general, to model the world as if there is only one commodity.

2.2. Investment opportunity sets

All assets are assumed to be traded, i.e., the domestic price of a foreign asset is the price in foreign currency of that asset multiplied by the exchange rate. The return in domestic currency of a foreign asset is different from the return in foreign currency of the same asset because the return in domestic currency depends both on the change in the foreign currency price of the asset and on the change in the exchange rate. It is assumed that: (1) for each asset the returns accrue only in the form of capital gains; (2) there are no

---

[14]See Roll (1979) for the view that purchasing power parity (PPP) holds *ex ante* for some relevant period of time.

[15]'Naive' purchasing power parity is that version of PPP which states that a change in the domestic price level is immediately offset by a change in the exchange rate. See Holmes (1967).

transaction costs; (3) unlimited short-sales with full use of the proceeds are permitted; and (4) markets are always in equilibrium.

If the ith foreign asset is risky in the sense that its instantaneous return is stochastic, it is assumed that its price $I^*(i)$ follows a stochastic differential equation,

$$\frac{dI^*(i)}{I^*(i)} = \mu_{I^*(i)}(s,t)dt + \sigma_{I^*(i)}(s,t)dz_{I^*(i)}. \tag{5}$$

Eq. (5) gives the instantaneous rate of return in foreign currency for the ith foreign asset. Let $D(i)$ be the domestic price of the ith foreign asset, i.e., $eI^*(i)$. The dynamics of $D(i)$ are obtained by using Ito's Lemma,

$$\frac{dD(i)}{D(i)} = \frac{dI^*(i)}{I^*(i)} + \frac{de}{e} + \frac{de}{e}\frac{dI^*(i)}{I^*(i)}. \tag{6}$$

Inspection of eq. (6) shows that the return for a domestic investor on a foreign risky asset is different from the return on that asset for a foreign investor, because the exchange rate changes through time.

It is assumed that there are N securities which have risky nominal returns in both countries, and n of those securities are domestic securities. In each country, there is one nominal bond. Let $I(j)$ be the price in domestic money of a domestic risky asset. $I(j)$ follows a stochastic differential equation of the same form as the one followed by $I^*(i)$. Let B (B^*) be the price in domestic (foreign) currency of the domestic (foreign) nominal safe asset. The dynamics for B are given by

$$dB/B = R(s,t)dt, \tag{7}$$

where R is simply the instantaneous nominal rate of return on a safe domestic bond. R^* is the instantaneous nominal rate of return on the foreign default-free bond whose foreign currency price is given by B^*.

3. Properties of asset demand functions

3.1. Definition of excess returns

Define the instantaneous excess return of the ith foreign asset for a domestic investor as the instantaneous return of an investment of one unit of domestic currency in the ith foreign asset financed by borrowing abroad at the interest rate R^*. The instantaneous excess return of the ith foreign asset for a domestic investor, written $dH(i)/H(i)$, is

$$\frac{dH(i)}{H(i)} = \frac{dI^*(i)}{I^*(i)} + \text{cov}(d\ln I^*(i), d\ln e) - R^*dt. \tag{8}$$

The instantaneous excess return on the ith foreign asset for a domestic investor is perfectly correlated with the instantaneous return of that asset in foreign currency. The stochastic part of the change in the exchange rate (i.e., $\sigma_e dz_e$) does not enter the instantaneous excess return of a foreign asset and, consequently, the excess return on holdings of foreign assets is hedged against unanticipated changes in the exchange rate. To keep his holdings of foreign assets hedged through time, the investor must continuously adjust his borrowings so that his net investment in foreign risky assets is always equal to zero.

In the following, the return on an investment of one unit of domestic (foreign) currency in a risky asset i by a domestic (foreign) investor, financed by borrowing in the home-country of that asset, is called the excess return for a domestic (foreign) investor on the ith asset. For a foreign investor, the instantaneous excess return on the jth domestic asset is

$$\frac{dH^*(j)}{H^*(j)} = \frac{dI(j)}{I(j)} - \text{cov}(d\ln I(j), d\ln e) - R\,dt. \tag{9}$$

For all investors in a country, the excess return on each asset is the same. Because of the covariance terms in eqs. (8) and (9), the excess return for a domestic investor on a domestic asset is, in general, different from the excess return on the same asset for a foreign investor.

The excess return on the foreign safe nominal bond for a domestic investor is defined as the return on one unit of domestic currency invested in the foreign bond, financed by borrowing at the interest rate R in the domestic country, i.e.,

$$\frac{dH(B)}{H(B)} = R^*dt + \frac{de}{e} - R\,dt. \tag{10}$$

This equation implies that the excess return on a foreign safe nominal bond is perfectly correlated with the change in the exchange rate. For a foreign investor, the return on a domestic safe nominal bond is risky and its instantaneous excess return is given by

$$\frac{dH^*(B)}{H^*(B)} = R\,dt + \text{var}(d\ln e) - \frac{de}{e} - R^*dt. \tag{11}$$

Let μ be the $(N+1) \times 1$ vector of expected excess returns for domestic investors. The N-first elements of μ comprise the expected excess returns on assets which are risky in both countries, whereas the last element of μ is the expected excess return on a foreign bond. In the following, a vector is designated by a bold italic lower-case letter, whereas a matrix is designated by a bold roman capital letter. μ^* is the $(N+1) \times 1$ vector of expected excess returns for foreign investors. The last element of μ^* is the expected excess return on a domestic bond for foreign investors. The N-first elements of μ and μ^* correspond each to the expected excess return of identical assets which are held by investors belonging to different countries. The n domestic risky assets are the first n assets in μ and μ^*.

3.2. Asset demands

Let $[w^k \colon b^k]$ be the investments in risky assets of investor k, expressed as a fraction of his wealth, where w^k is an $1 \times N$ vector whose representative element w_i^k is the proportion of his wealth investor k invests in the ith asset, which is an asset risky in both countries. Let $b^k W^k$ be the investor's investment in foreign bonds in excess of his holdings of foreign bonds required to hedge his investments in foreign risky assets against exchange rate risks.[16] Finally, define V_{aa} ($V_{a^*a^*}$) as the $(N+1) \times (N+1)$ variance–covariance matrix of excess returns for domestic (foreign) investors and V_{as} ($V_{a^*s^*}$) as the covariance matrix of those excess returns with changes in the state variables in s (s^*). Assuming that each investor maximizes a well-behaved, state-independent von Neuman–Morgenstern expected utility function of lifetime consumption, the optimization problem of the investor is formally equivalent to the problem faced by an investor in Breeden (1979).[17] The optimal portfolio of domestic investor k is characterized by the following investments in risky assets:

$$[w^k \colon b^k]' = \left(\frac{T^k}{C_w^k W^k} \right) V_{aa}^{-1} \mu + V_{aa}^{-1} V_{as} \left(\frac{-C_s^k}{C_w^k W^k} + \left\{ \begin{matrix} \dfrac{C^k \alpha^k}{C_w^k W^k} - \dfrac{m^k T^k}{C_w^k W^k} \\ 0 \end{matrix} \right\} \right),$$

(12)

where $C^k(W,s,t)$ is the consumption expenditure function of investor k and $U^k(C(W,s,t),P,t)$ is the investor's indirect utility function of consumption

---

[16]To hedge his investments which are risky in the foreign country, the investor borrows abroad at the interest rate R^* an amount equal to $h^k = \sum_{i=n+1}^{N} w_i^k W^k$. To get the investor's *total* holdings of foreign bonds, one has to subtract h^k from $b^k W^k$. When investors hedge using bonds, $b^k W^k$ is the net foreign investment of domestic investor k.

[17]See Breeden (1979, sect. 7).

expenditures when the prices of the available commodities are given by the vector P. The partial derivatives of the consumption expenditure function with respect to the state variables form the $S \times 1$ vector C_s^k, whereas C_w^k is the partial derivative of the consumption expenditure function with respect to wealth. By convention, C^k is equal to $\sum_{i=1}^{k} P_i c_i^k$, where c_i^k is the number of units of commodity i consumed by investor k. α^k is the $K \times 1$ vector of average expenditure shares of the K goods available in the domestic country, i.e., $P_i c_i^k / C^k = \alpha_i^k$. m^k is the $K \times 1$ vector of marginal expenditure shares of the same goods, i.e., $P_i \partial c_i^k / \partial C^k = m_i^k$. Finally, T^k is the absolute risk tolerance of the investor, i.e., $-U_c^k / U_{cc}^k$, whereas 0 is an $(S-K) \times 1$ vector of zeros.

Let $[w^j : b^j]$ be the investments in risky assets of investor j, who is a foreign investor, expressed as a fraction of his wealth. Whereas w^j is the vector of fractions of the wealth W^j of the investor invested in assets which are risky in both countries, b^j is the fraction of the wealth of the investor invested in domestic safe bonds, in addition to his holdings of domestic safe bonds required to hedge his investments in risky domestic assets against foreign exchange risks. W^j is the wealth of the foreign investor in his home currency. The optimal portfolio of investor j is characterized by

$$[w^j : b^j]' = \left(\frac{T^j}{C_w^j W^j} \right) [\mathbf{V}_{a^*a^*}]^{-1} \boldsymbol{\mu}^* + [\mathbf{V}_{a^*a^*}]^{-1} \mathbf{V}_{a^*s^*}$$

$$\times \left(\frac{-C_{s^*}^j}{C_w^j W^j} + \left\{ \begin{array}{c} \dfrac{C^j \alpha^j}{C_w^j W^j} - \dfrac{m^j T^j}{C_w^j W^j} \\ 0 \end{array} \right\} \right), \tag{13}$$

where $C^j(W, s^*, t)$ is the consumption function of investor j in his home currency, α^j is his $K^* \times 1$ vector of average expenditure shares and m^j his $K^* \times 1$ vector of marginal expenditure shares on the K^* goods available in his country.

3.3. Comparison of asset demands

The domestic investor is indifferent between holding a linear combination of $S+1$ mutual fund portfolios and his portfolio of risky assets.[18] One mutual fund portfolio is the portfolio which corresponds to the point of tangency of the capital market line and the efficient frontier of portfolios of

---

[18]Merton is the first to have mentioned this result, for instance Merton (1973); formal proofs of the result and discussions of the properties of the mutual funds can be found in Breeden (1979), Richard (1979) and Merton (1981). To check the result, notice that (12) can be rewritten as a weighted sum of column vectors, where the column vectors do not depend on the preferences of investor k, whereas the weights do.

risky assets in the space of nominal expected returns and standard deviations of those returns for domestic investors. That portfolio will be called the tangency portfolio for domestic investors and written [*w* : *b*]. The *S* other mutual fund portfolios are portfolios which, among all feasible portfolios, have the highest possible correlation with the *S* state variables. The *S* + 1 mutual funds result also applies to foreign investors.

Note, however, that a mutual fund which is positively correlated with the exchange rate in the domestic country (i.e., *e*) is negatively correlated with the exchange rate in the foreign country (i.e., 1/*e*). If a mutual fund in the domestic country has an investment in an asset perfectly positively correlated with the domestic exchange rate, it is long in the foreign safe bond. Abroad, a mutual fund which holds an asset perfectly positively correlated with the exchange rate in the domestic country is short in the domestic safe bond. It follows that the composition of the *S* + 1 mutual fund portfolios held by foreign investors is (at least for some portfolios) different from the composition of the *S* + 1 mutual fund portfolios held by domestic investors. The tangency portfolio for foreign investors is written [*w** : *b**].

The relationship between the tangency portfolio for domestic investors and the tangency portfolio for foreign investors is given in the following proposition:

Proposition 1. The tangency portfolio held by domestic investors is different from the tangency portfolio held by foreign investors. However, the proportion in which two assets risky in both countries are held by domestic investors is the same as the proportion in which they are held by foreign investors.

Proof. See appendix.

Proposition 1 places no restrictions on the menu of assets available to domestic and foreign investors. One asset can be a foreign nominal bond with maturity at date *t'*, such that *t'* > *t* + d*t*. If a domestic investor holds such a bond to maturity, his return in domestic currency over the life of the bond will be perfectly correlated with the total change in the exchange rate over the life of the bond. Such a bond plays no special role in a mean-variance efficient portfolio. Notice that Proposition 1 does not depend on assumptions about the nature of the relationship between exchange rate changes and changes in commodity prices. Whether naive purchasing power parity holds or not has no impact on the composition of the mean-variance efficient mutual fund portfolio obtained by using nominal excess returns.

All domestic investors invest in the same 'hedge' mutual funds, i.e., the *S* mutual funds most highly correlated with state variables in the vector *s*. In the setting of this paper, two investors who have the same intertemporal utility function and identical wealth in domestic currency will invest in different 'hedge' mutual funds if they reside in different countries. This result is explained by the fact that consumption investment opportunity sets differ across countries. Suppose, for instance, that the dollar price of a haircut in Rome differs from the dollar price of a haircut in New York. Italian investors who want to hedge against unanticipated changes in the price of haircuts do not, in this example, hold the same portfolio as American investors who want to hedge against unanticipated changes in the price of haircuts, even if the utility function of all investors is the same. Differences in consumption opportunity sets *can* create meaningful differences in asset holdings across countries.

4. The asset pricing equation

In this section, an asset pricing relationship is obtained for a world of flexible exchange rates in which tastes and consumption opportunity sets differ across countries.

4.1. Aggregation within countries

Define $C(i)$ as the consumption expenditures of the ith domestic investor, i.e., $C(i) = C^i(W, s, t)$. Using Breeden (1979), eq. (12) can be transformed into

$$\mu - \mathbf{V}_{as}\begin{pmatrix} m^i \\ 0 \end{pmatrix} = (T^i)^{-1}\left\{ V_{aC(i)} - \mathbf{V}_{as}C(i)\begin{pmatrix} \alpha^i \\ 0 \end{pmatrix}\right\}, \tag{14}$$

where $V_{aC(i)}$ is the vector of covariances of home-country returns of risky assets with changes in consumption expenditures of investor i.

Let $Pm(i)$ be the price of a basket of commodities which contains $m^i_j P_k / m^i_k P_j$ units of commodity j, for all j's, where m^i_j is the marginal expenditure share of commodity j for the ith investor. Define $P\alpha(i)$ as the price of a basket of commodities which contains $\alpha^i_j P_k / \alpha^i_k P_j$ units of commodity j, for all j's, where α^i_j is the average expenditure share of commodity j for investor i. $Pm(i)$ ($P\alpha(i)$) is the price of a basket of commodities normalized so that it contains exactly one unit of commodity k and so that the expenditure on each commodity in the basket is equal to $m^i_j Pm(i)$ ($\alpha^i_j P\alpha(i)$). No generality is lost by assuming that there exists a traded commodity k which is consumed by all investors. As the first K state variables are the logarithms of the prices of the commodities available to a domestic investor, eq. (14) is equivalent to

$$\mu - V_{aPm(i)} = (T^i)^{-1}\{V_{aC(i)} - C(i)V_{aP\alpha(i)}\}, \tag{15}$$

where $V_{aP\alpha(i)}$ is the $(N+1) \times 1$ vector of covariances of excess returns for domestic investors with $d\ln P\alpha(i)$, and $V_{aPm(i)}$ is the vector of covariances of excess returns with $d\ln Pm(i)$.

Adding eq. (15) across all domestic investors yields

$$\mu - V_{aPm(D)} = (T^D)^{-1}\{V_{aC(D)} - V_{aP\alpha(D)}C(D)\}, \qquad (16)$$

where, if $\sum_D$ indicates the operation of summing across all domestic investors, $T^D = \sum_D T^i$, $C(D) = \sum_D C(i)$, $P\alpha(D) = \sum_D (C(i)/C(D))P\alpha(i)$, and $Pm(D) = \sum_D (T^i/T^D)Pm(i)$. $P\alpha(D)$ is the price of a basket of commodities which contains $\alpha_j(D)P_k/\alpha_k(D)P_j$ units of the jth commodity, where $\alpha_j(D)$, for all j's, is the fraction of domestic consumption expenditure spent on the jth commodity. $Pm(D)$ is the price of a basket of commodities which contains $m_j(D)P_k/m_k(D)P_j$ units of the jth commodity, such that $m_j(D)$ is a risk tolerance weighted average of the marginal expenditure share of the jth commodity for all domestic investors.

$1/Pm(D)$ is a locally accurate measure of the real value of a marginal increase in domestic consumption expenditure due to a change in the value of the investment of domestic investors in their tangency portfolio. The asset demand functions imply that the increase in consumption expenditures of an investor i due to a change in the value of the tangency portfolio is equal to the ratio of the risk-tolerances of investor i and j, i.e., T^i/T^j, times the increase in consumption expenditures of investor j due to the same cause. Suppose $T^i/T^j = 2$ and $C_w^j W^j = C_w^i W^i$. In this case, investor i invested twice as much as investor j in the tangency portfolio, and an unanticipated increase in the value of the tangency portfolio increases his consumption expenditures twice as much as it increases the consumption expenditures of investor j. The basket of commodities which is bought if consumption expenditures increase in the domestic country due to an increase in the value of the tangency portfolio reflects the fact that the increase in consumption expenditures of investor i is twice as large as the increase in consumption expenditures of investor j.

An equation similar to eq. (16) is obtained for the foreign country,

$$\mu^* - V_{a \cdot P^* \cdot m(F)} = (T^{*F})^{-1}\{V_{a \cdot C^*(F)} - V_{a \cdot P^* \cdot \alpha(F)}C^*(F)\}. \qquad (17)$$

The asterisks in (17) indicate that everything is computed from the perspective of foreign investors who use their home currency. For instance, μ^* stands for the vector of expected excess returns for foreign investors and $P^*\alpha(F)$ stands for the price in foreign currency of a basket of commodities which contains $\alpha_j(F)P^*(k)/\alpha_k(F)P^*(j)$ units of commodity j, where $\alpha_j(F)$ is the fraction of foreign aggregate consumption spent on the jth foreign commodity. The capital letter F indicates that eq. (17) is obtained by summing asset demand equations across all foreign investors.

Because nominal variables in eq. (16) are in domestic currency and excess returns are viewed from the perspective of a domestic investor, whereas nominal variables in (17) are in foreign currency and viewed from the perspective of a foreign investor, it is not possible to obtain a meaningful relationship for expected excess returns by simply summing eqs. (16) and (17).

4.2. Aggregation across countries

If the equation which describes equilibrium expected returns for foreign investors is multiplied by the exchange rate, it contains foreign aggregate consumption in domestic currency, i.e.,

$$\mu^* - V_{a \cdot P^* m(F)} = (T^F)^{-1} \{ e V_{a \cdot C^*(F)} - V_{a \cdot P \cdot \alpha(F)} C(F) \}, \tag{18}$$

where $C(F)$ is foreign consumption expenditure in domestic currency and $T^F = eT^{*F}$. $C(F)$ is equal to $eC^*(F)$, which implies that $V_{a \cdot C^*(F)}$, i.e., the vector of covariances of excess returns with changes in foreign aggregate consumption in foreign currency, is equivalent to $V_{a^*(1/e)C(F)}$. Using Ito's Lemma, $V_{a^*(1/e)C(F)}$ is equal to

$$V_{a^*(1/e)C(F)} = \frac{1}{e} (V_{a \cdot C(F)} - V_{a \cdot e} C(F)), \tag{19}$$

where $V_{a \cdot e}$ is the vector of covariances between home currency returns and $d \ln e$. The same transformation, applied respectively to $C(F)V_{a \cdot P \cdot \alpha(F)}$ and $T^F V_{a \cdot P^* m(F)}$, yields

$$C(F)V_{a \cdot P \cdot \alpha(F)} = (C(F)V_{a \cdot P\alpha(F)} - C(F)V_{a \cdot e}), \tag{20}$$

$$T^F V_{a \cdot P^* m(F)} = T^F (V_{a \cdot Pm(F)} - V_{a \cdot e}). \tag{21}$$

In the domestic country, it is not possible, in general, to buy the basket of commodities whose price abroad is $P^* \alpha(F)$ at the domestic currency price $P\alpha(F) = eP^* \alpha(F)$. In that sense $P\alpha(F)$ is not observable in the domestic country and neither is $Pm(F) = eP^* m(F)$. In principle, $P^* m(F)$ and $P^* \alpha(F)$ are observable in the foreign country.

Note that the excess return abroad of a security which is not a bond with a safe instantaneous return differs from the excess return at home of the same security by a non-stochastic term [see, for instance, eq. (9)]. The excess return abroad on the domestic bond which has a safe instantaneous return is equal to the excess return at home of the foreign bond with a safe instantaneous return multiplied by minus one plus a non-stochastic term [see eqs. (10) and (11)]. Using these facts, it can easily be shown that

$$\mathbf{L}\mu^* = \mu - V_{a \cdot e}, \tag{22}$$

where $\mathbf{L}$ is a diagonal matrix with ones everywhere along the diagonal except for minus one in the last row. Furthermore, if x is a stochastic variable,

$$V_{ax} = \mathbf{L}V_{a \cdot x}. \tag{23}$$

Premultiply (18) by $T^F \mathbf{L}$ to get

$$T^F(\mathbf{L}\mu^* - \mathbf{L}V_{a \cdot P \cdot m(F)}) = \mathbf{L}eV_{a \cdot C \cdot (F)} - \mathbf{L}V_{a \cdot P \cdot \alpha(F)}C(F). \tag{24}$$

Substitute into (24) eqs. (19) through (22) and use the result given by (23) to obtain

$$\mu - V_{aPm(F)} = (T^F)^{-1}\{V_{aC(F)} - C(F)V_{a P\alpha(F)}\}. \tag{25}$$

Summing eqs. (16) and (25) yields

$$\mu - V_{aPm} = (T^W)^{-1}\{V_{aC} - V_{aP_\alpha}C\} \quad \text{where} \quad T^W = T^F + T^D. \tag{26}$$

Here μ is the vector of expected excess returns for domestic investors. The excess return of an asset for a domestic investor is defined as the return in the domestic country of a portfolio with a long holding of that asset financed by selling the nominal safe bond of the home-country of the asset. T^W is a measure of world risk-tolerance. V_{aC} is the vector of covariances between home-country returns of risky assets and changes in world consumption in domestic currency. V_{aPm} and $V_{aP\alpha}$ are the vectors of covariances of home-country returns with $d \ln Pm$ and $d \ln P\alpha$. An increase in Pm means a decrease in the real value of a marginal dollar of consumption expenditures, whereas an increase in $P\alpha$ means a fall in the real value of total consumption expenditures. Eq. (26) is the fundamental pricing equation of this paper.

The left-hand side of eq. (26) can be interpreted as the vector of expected excess *real* returns of risky assets. An unanticipated increase in the value of the investors' tangency portfolios induces an increase in aggregate consumption expenditures which is distributed among investors in proportion to their risk tolerances.

Each investor spends his increase in consumption expenditures on a basket of commodities defined by his vector of marginal expenditure shares. The risk tolerance weighted average of marginal expenditure shares for a commodity gives the fraction of the increase in world consumption expenditures spent on that commodity when those expenditures increase because of an increase in the value of the tangency portfolios. (Remember that the tangency portfolio of domestic investors is different from the tangency portfolio of foreign investors.)

The risk tolerance weighted average of the vectors of marginal expenditure shares yields a commodity basket whose price is *Pm*. By construction, therefore, the basket of commodities whose price is *Pm* is the basket of commodities bought by the world as a whole when world consumption expenditure increases due to an increase in the value of the tangency portfolios. Applying Ito's Lemma, it immediately follows that the left-hand side of the asset pricing equation corresponds to the vector of expected excess returns of risky assets measured in units of the basket of commodities with price *Pm*.

The vector in curly brackets on the right-hand side of the asset pricing equation is easier to interpret. $1/P\alpha$ is a locally accurate measure of the real value of one dollar of consumption expenditures spent in exactly the same way as world consumption expenditures are spent. Let c be real consumption, i.e., $C/P\alpha$. It is easy to verify that $P\alpha V_{ac} = V_{aC} - C V_{aP\alpha}$, which is the term in curly brackets in eq. (26). The following proposition must now hold:

Proposition 2. The expected excess real return of a risky asset is proportional to the covariance of the home currency return of that asset with changes in world real consumption rate.

Two facts are the key to understanding Proposition 2. First, the higher the covariance of an asset's payoffs with marginal utility of consumption expenditure, the more valuable that asset is. A continuous function of a variable which satisfies a stochastic differential equation of the Ito-type is perfectly correlated with that variable. This fact makes it possible to state that the expected real return an investor requires on a risky asset is proportional to its covariance with changes in the real consumption expenditure of the investor. In equilibrium, however, what is relevant for the pricing of an asset is how much that asset is correlated with the common non-diversifiable part of the changes in consumption expenditure of all investors.

The second important fact is that, because investors can form a portfolio of common stocks whose return does not depend directly on unanticipated changes in the exchange rate, they will not be rewarded for bearing the exchange rate risks. If a domestic investor holds a foreign stock hedged against exchange rate risks, the return on that stock is perfectly correlated with the return on the same common stock for a foreign investor.

5. Economic implications

5.1. The pricing of common stocks

Earlier models of international asset pricing yield the result that suitably defined expected excess returns on common stocks are proportional to the covariance of those returns with the return on some suitably defined market portfolio.[19] The predictions of the model presented here can be made equivalent to the predictions of earlier models by making additional assumptions which imply that changes in world real consumption are perfectly correlated with the return on some world market portfolio. The world market portfolios implied by various earlier models are so highly correlated that it is not clear that those models are empirically distinguishable.[20]

The main use of those earlier models of international asset pricing has been to test the hypothesis that asset markets are segmented internationally. The segmentation hypothesis means that two assets which belong to different countries but have the same risk with respect to some model of international asset pricing without barriers to international investment have different expected excess returns. No study has successfully rejected the hypothesis that markets are segmented using earlier models of international asset pricing. If changes in world real consumption are not perfectly correlated with the return on some world market portfolio used by earlier studies, the measure of risk for assets used here is not equivalent to the measure used in earlier studies. This implies that it is possible for a test of the segmentation hypothesis which uses an earlier model of international asset pricing to fail to reject the hypothesis when in fact there are no barriers to international investment and expected returns satisfy the asset pricing equation developed in this paper. Since the revealed preference of investors for home-country assets is compatible either with the existence of barriers to international investment or with the fully integrated markets model presented here, more sophisticated tests of the segmentation hypothesis are required.

It should now be clear that one has to be careful about capital budgeting in open economies. If earlier asset pricing models hold, it does not matter where a firm produces. A scale-expanding project would not change the discount rate of a firm even if the scale-expanding project is located in a foreign country. With the model presented here, the location of a project matters if that project uses non-traded goods as inputs or produces non-traded goods. The discount rate of a project, in general, depends on where it is located even in a world without barriers to international investment.

---

[19]See references given in section 1.
[20]See Solnik (1978).

5.2. The pricing of bonds

Let $f(t, dt)$ be the forward exchange rate for a contract expiring at date $t+dt$ agreed upon at time t. Define $\ln\{f(t, dt)/e(t)\} = \mu_f dt$, where $e(t)$ is the exchange rate today. The interest rate parity theorem[21] states that if R is the rate of return on a domestic safe nominal bond and if R^* is the rate of return on a safe foreign nominal bond,

$$\mu_f = R - R^*. \tag{27}$$

Ceteris paribus, the lower μ_e, i.e., the expected rate of change of the exchange rate, the higher the forward exchange rate with respect to the expected future spot exchange rate. If the expected future spot exchange rate is higher than the forward exchange rate, the expected return on investing in a foreign nominal bond is higher uncovered than covered (i.e., hedged against exchange rate risks). It follows that the investor must pay a risk premium to hedge his investment against exchange rate risks. Using the asset pricing model developed in this paper, the relationship between μ_f and μ_e is given by

$$R - R^* = \mu_f = \mu_e - V_{ePm} - (\beta_{ec}/\beta_{Mc})[\mu_M - V_{MPm}], \tag{28}$$

where β_{Mc} is the covariance of changes in real consumption with the return of portfolio M, which can be any observable portfolio, μ_M is the expected excess return of that portfolio, and V_{MPm} is the covariance of the return of that portfolio with $d \ln Pm$, where Pm is the price of a commodity basket identified earlier.

The key point of eq. (28) is stated in the following proposition:

Proposition 3. Ceteris paribus, an increase in the covariance between changes in the exchange rate and changes in the world real consumption rate decreases the forward exchange rate.

The risk premium incorporated in the forward exchange rate, as given by eq. (28), can be different from zero when other models imply it should be zero and vice versa.[22] For instance, the empirical fact that the exchange rate is correlated with the terms of trade can be sufficient, by itself, to create a risk premium. It has been argued that if safe nominal bonds belong to the

---

[21]See, for instance, Officer and Willet (1970).

[22]Discussions of the risk premium incorporated in the forward exchange rate can be found, for instance, in Solnik (1974), Roll and Solnik (1977), Kouri (1976, 1978), Fama and Farber (1979), Frankel (1979) and Grauer, Litzenberger and Stehle (1976). For good empirical evidence that the forward exchange rate is not an unbiased predictor of the future spot exchange rate, see, for instance, Hansen and Hodrick (1980).

market portfolio, i.e., if there are 'outside' nominal assets like government bonds, there is a risk premium. The argument can be stated in this way: if some assets in the market portfolio have real returns negatively correlated with the rate of change of the price level, the exchange rate will, in general, have a non-zero beta, since it will be correlated with those assets. Safe nominal bonds have real returns perfectly negatively correlated with the rate of change of the price level. This fact is then interpreted to mean that a positive supply of so-called 'outside' assets is a sufficient condition for the existence of a risk premium.[23] (Note however, that there exist the theoretical possibility that the effect on beta of the correlation of the exchange rate with the real value of other assets offsets the effect on beta of its correlation with the real return of nominal bonds.) In the model presented in this paper, a change in the supply of government bonds does not necessarily affect the risk premium incorporated in the forward exchange rate. Many papers have been devoted to the fact that a change in the supply of so-called 'outside' assets does not leave the budget constraint of the government unchanged.[24] Unless one specifies exactly how the government budget constraint is affected by a change in the supply of outside assets, it is not possible to say, on theoretical grounds, how a change in the supply of 'outside' assets affects the risk premium incorporated in the forward exchange rate.

The generality of eq. (26) needs to be stressed. Earlier models which yield a formula for the risk premium incorporated in the forward exchange rate require a constant expected rate of change for the exchange rate (or, alternatively, that no asset has a return correlated with the expected rate of change of the exchange rate). Such an assumption leads to models which cannot account for the empirical fact that the risk premium incorporated in the forward exchange rate seems to change through time. It must also be noted that the asset pricing equation which leads to eq. (24) can be used to price the forward exchange rate for forward contracts for all maturities.

5.3. Correlation of consumption across countries

Assume that, for all prices, all investors consume some positive quantity of each good available in their home country. With this assumption, the following result holds:

Proposition 4. If (a) *markets are complete* (*in the sense that an unconstrained Pareto-optimal equilibrium is achieved*) *and* (b) *consumption opportunity sets differ across countries, then changes in the real consumption rates are not perfectly correlated across countries.*

---

[23]See Frenkel (1979) and also Kouri (1977) and Fama and Farber (1979).
[24]See, for instance, Barro (1974).

To prove Proposition 4, choose the $(K + K^* - G)$ first state variables to be the logarithms of the prices in domestic currency of commodities available in at least one country. Let all vectors of average and marginal expenditure shares have dimension $(K + K^* - G) \times 1$ and $\mathbf{V}_{ss}$ be the $S \times S$ variance–covariance matrix of state variables. $\boldsymbol{\mu}_s$ is the vector of excess expected returns on assets perfectly correlated with state variables. It is shown in the appendix that the covariance between changes in the consumption of the ith domestic investor and changes in the domestic currency consumption of the jth foreign investor is

$$
\mathrm{cov}\,(C^i, eC^j) = e\left[T^i \boldsymbol{\mu}_s - \mathbf{V}_{ss}\binom{\boldsymbol{m}^i}{\boldsymbol{0}} T^i \right]' \mathbf{V}_{ss}^{-1}\left[T^j \boldsymbol{\mu}^j - \mathbf{V}_{ss}\binom{\boldsymbol{m}^j}{\boldsymbol{0}} T^j \right]
$$

$$
+ eC^i\binom{\boldsymbol{\alpha}^i}{\boldsymbol{0}}'\left[T^j \boldsymbol{\mu}_s - \mathbf{V}_{ss}\binom{\boldsymbol{m}^j}{\boldsymbol{0}} T^j \right]
$$

$$
+ \left[T^i \boldsymbol{\mu}_s - \mathbf{V}_{ss}\binom{\boldsymbol{m}^i}{\boldsymbol{0}} T^i \right]' eC^j\binom{\boldsymbol{\alpha}^j}{\boldsymbol{0}} + C^i\binom{\boldsymbol{\alpha}^i}{\boldsymbol{0}}' \mathbf{V}_{ss}\binom{\boldsymbol{\alpha}^j}{\boldsymbol{0}} eC^j. \qquad (29)
$$

Changes in the domestic currency consumption of investor i and investor j can be perfectly correlated only if $\mathrm{cov}\,(C^i, eC^j)$ is equal to the product of the standard deviations of changes in C^i and eC^j. It is easy — but cumbersome — to show that this happens *only* if the investors are the same (except for their risk tolerance if utility functions are homothetic) and consumption opportunity sets do not differ. It follows that only if 'naive' purchasing power parity holds are changes in real consumption perfectly correlated across countries. This result is important because it allows one to understand the assumption required to price domestic assets using only domestic data, i.e., the assumption of 'naive' purchasing power parity. If this assumption is not correct, domestic risky assets will be priced differently if they are correlated with foreign consumption than if they are not.

5.4. Empirical research

The analysis conducted so far suggests some new directions for empirical research in international finance. The most important question which emerges from this paper is: are the real expected excess returns of risky assets proportional to their covariances with changes in world real consumption? Some of the problems associated with testing this hypothesis are briefly discussed in this section.

One important advantage of the approach developed here is that consumption data are easily available for most countries, whereas no data are available on the value of invested wealth in most countries.

Unfortunately, consumption data are never computed in a way which is ideally suited for economic analysis. For instance, consumption data nearly always include purchases of durable goods, rather than the value of the services provided by the existing stock of durable goods.

The empirical relevance of international asset pricing considerations depends here on the correlation of changes in real consumption in various countries with changes in world real consumption. This suggests that a useful preliminary test would be to look at whether or not changes in U.S. real consumption have a correlation coefficient with changes in world real consumption that is statistically different from one. If this correlation coefficient is not statistically different from one, using U.S. data on consumption when measuring the risk of an asset could be an acceptable procedure. Furthermore, such a result would indicate that differences in consumption opportunity sets are not likely to matter very much for studies of international asset pricing.

If changes in U.S. real consumption are not too highly correlated with changes in world real consumption, it is theoretically possible to test the hypothesis that the risk of a U.S. asset is measured by the covariance of its return with changes in world real consumption rather than with changes in U.S. real consumption. The problem which arises in practice with such a test is that consumption betas are not likely to be stable over time. If those non-stationarities turn out to be important, the full vector of state variables must be identified and observable to test the hypothesis. In this case, the informational requirements of a test of the asset pricing equation are not smaller than those of a test of an international version of Merton's multi-beta asset pricing equation.[25]

It is well-known that investors hold portfolios heavily weighted towards assets of their home country. One explanation advanced for that fact is that there are barriers to international investment. In section 3 of this paper, it is argued that another possible explanation is that home country assets form better hedges against state variables which affect the intertemporal expected utility of investors of a given country. It is possible to examine empirically whether a portfolio highly correlated with changes in the real consumption of a given country contains a relatively large proportion of assets of that country. Notice, however, that state variables which are relevant for investors in a particular country need not affect expected excess returns significantly.

6. Concluding remarks

In this paper, a model of international asset pricing which admits differences — albeit temporary — in consumption opportunity sets has been

---

[25]See Merton (1973). Cornell (1981) makes this point with respect to Breeden (1979). Richard (1979) has discussed the conditions under which a multi-beta model has stationary betas.

constructed. It has been shown that such a model yields a simple asset pricing equation, which states that the real expected return of a risky asset is proportional to the covariance of the home country return of that asset with changes in world real consumption rate. The model contains earlier models of international asset pricing as special cases and is compatible with some empirical facts which seem to contradict the predictions of earlier models of international asset pricing.

While this paper does not model differences in consumption opportunity sets across countries, it seems that an interesting extension of the present work would be to look at a more simple model in which differences in consumption opportunity sets would be studied explicitly. For instance, a model with transportation costs which are a decreasing function of time would generate interesting differences in consumption opportunity sets and would introduce an explicit role for the current account (i.e., net foreign investment) in a model of international asset pricing.

The present model does not take money into account explicitly. However, the nature of the process followed by the money supply in both countries is likely to affect the risk premium incorporated in the forward exchange rate. A possible extension of the present work would be to construct an explicit model of the money market equilibrium in both countries.

Appendix

A.1. *Proof of Proposition 1*

Let λ be a scalar, $\mathbf{V}_{II}$ the $N \times N$ variance–covariance matrix of excess returns of assets which are not bonds with instantaneous maturity, $\mathbf{V}_{Ie}$ the $N \times 1$ vector of covariances of the excess returns of these risky assets with the exchange rate, V_{ee} the variance of the exchange rate, μ^I the $N \times 1$ vector of expected excess returns on these risky assets. Using the definition of w and w^*,

$$w = \lambda (\mathbf{V}_{II} - V'_{eI} \mathbf{V}_{II}^{-1} V_{Ie})^{-1} [\mu^I - V_{Ie} V_{ee}^{-1} (R^* + \mu_e - R)], \tag{A.1}$$

$$w^* = \lambda^* (\mathbf{V}_{I^*I^*} - V_{eI^*} (\mathbf{V}_{I^*I^*})^{-1} V_{I^*e})^{-1} [\mu^{I^*} + V_{I^*e} V_{ee}^{-1} (R + \sigma_e^2 - \mu_e - R^*)]. \tag{A.2}$$

Asterisks used as superscripts in (A.2) indicate that excess returns for foreign investors are used.

First, the terms in square brackets are compared. Let $\mathbf{I}^f$ be an $N \times N$ diagonal matrix with zeros everywhere except for ones in the last $N - n$ diagonal elements. $\mathbf{I}$ is an $N \times N$ identity matrix. μ^I is the $N \times 1$ vector of home-currency excess returns of risky assets which are not bonds with instantaneous maturity. μ is an $N \times 1$ vector which has R in its first n elements and R^* everywhere else. Then

$$[\mu^{I^*} + V_{I^*e} V_{ee}^{-1}(R + \sigma_e^2 - \mu_e - R^*)]$$

$$= \mu^I - (\mathbf{I} - \mathbf{I}^f) V_{I^*e} - \mu - V_{I^*e} V_{ee}^{-1}(R^* - \sigma_e^2 + \mu_e - R)$$

$$= \mu^I + \mathbf{I}^f V_{I^*e} - \mu - V_{I^*e} V_{ee}^{-1}(R^* + \mu_e - R). \tag{A.3}$$

If $V_{I^*e} = V_{ie}$, the last line of (A.3) is equal to the term in square brackets of (A.1). A typical element of V_{I^*e} is

$$E\left\{\left(\frac{dI_i}{I_i} - \frac{de}{e}\frac{dI_i}{I_i} - Rdt\right)\frac{de}{e}\right\} = E\left\{\frac{de}{e}\frac{dI_i}{I_i}\right\}, \qquad i \leqq n. \tag{A.4}$$

It immediately follows that $V_{I^*e} = V_{Ie}$. A typical element of V_{II} is equal to the product of two terms of the same form as the term in parentheses in (A.4). The term in parentheses depends on the residence of the investor only because of the covariance term, which vanishes in products. It follows that $V_{II} = V_{I^*I^*}$. This means that the terms in the first parentheses of (A.1) are equal to those of the first parentheses of (A.2), which completes the proof.

A.2. Proof that eq. (27) holds

Proposition 4 holds only if markets are complete. If markets are complete, it is possible to construct portfolios which are perfectly correlated with the S state variables. Let V_{ss} be the $(S+1) \times (S+1)$ variance–covariance matrix of the returns of those S portfolios and the market portfolio, whereas w_s^i is the $(S+1) \times 1$ vector of proportions of wealth invested in those $S+1$ portfolios by investor i. Using Ito's Lemma and the assumption of complete markets [as in Breeden (1979)], it follows that

$$\text{cov}(eC^i, C^i) = C_w^i w_s^{i\prime} V_{ss} w_s^i W^i W^i eC_w^i + eC_w^i w_s^{i\prime} V_{ss} C_s^i W^i$$

$$+ eC_w^j w_s^{j\prime} V_{ss} C_s^i W^j + C_s^{i\prime} V_{ss} C_s^j e. \tag{A.5}$$

To obtain $\text{var}(C^i)$ let $e = 1$ in (A.5), whereas to obtain $\text{var}(eC^j)$, let $C^i = eC^j$ in (A.5). $\text{Cov}(eC^j, C^i)$ is the sum of four terms, where each term can be written in terms of the distribution of asset returns and the utility function of investors by substituting out w_s^i and w_s^j in (A.5) from the asset demand functions. Let μ_s be the vector of expected excess returns on the $S+1$

portfolios. The asset demands for investor i can be written, using (12), as

$$w_i^s = \left(\frac{T'}{C_w^i W^i}\right) \mathbf{V}_{ss}^{-1} \boldsymbol{\mu}_s + \left(\frac{-C_s^i}{C_w^i W^i} + \left\{ \begin{matrix} \dfrac{C^i \boldsymbol{\alpha}^i}{C_w^i W^i} - \dfrac{m^i T^i}{C_w^i W^i} \\ 0 \end{matrix} \right\} \right). \qquad (A.6)$$

Using (A.6), the first term on the right-hand side of (A.5) can be rewritten as

$$C_w^i w_s^{i\prime} \mathbf{V}_{ss} \mathbf{V}_{ss}^{-1} \mathbf{V}_{ss} w_s^j e C_w^j W^i W^j$$

$$= \left[T^i \boldsymbol{\mu}_s - \mathbf{V}_{ss} C_s^i + \mathbf{V}_{ss} C^i \begin{pmatrix} \boldsymbol{\alpha}^i \\ 0 \end{pmatrix} - \mathbf{V}_{ss} \begin{pmatrix} m^i \\ 0 \end{pmatrix} T^i \right]'$$

$$\times \mathbf{V}_{ss}^{-1} \left[e T^j \boldsymbol{\mu}_s^* - \mathbf{V}_{ss} e C_s^j + \mathbf{V}_{ss} e C^j \begin{pmatrix} \boldsymbol{\alpha}^j \\ 0 \end{pmatrix} - \mathbf{V}_{ss} \begin{pmatrix} m^j \\ 0 \end{pmatrix} e T^j \right]. \qquad (A.7)$$

Using (A.6), the second term on the right-hand side of (A.5) can be rewritten as

$$C_s^{i\prime} \mathbf{V}_{ss} w_s^i e C_w^i = C_s^{i\prime} \left[e T^i w_s^i - \mathbf{V}_{ss} e C_s^i + \mathbf{V}_{ss} e C^i \begin{pmatrix} \boldsymbol{\alpha}^i \\ 0 \end{pmatrix} - \mathbf{V}_{ss} \begin{pmatrix} m^j \\ 0 \end{pmatrix} T^i e \right].$$

$$(A.8)$$

The third term on the right-hand side of (A.5) can be obtained from (A.8) by letting investor i be the foreign investor and investor j be the domestic investor. This implies that all terms in square brackets in (A.8) are in this case expressed in domestic currency, whereas C_s^i is replaced by $e C_s^j$.

From (A.5), (A.7) and (A.8) it is straightforward to obtain eq. (27).

References

Adler, M. and B. Dumas, 1975, Optimal international acquisitions, Journal of Finance 30, no. 1, 1–19.

Adler, M. and B. Dumas, 1976, Portfolio choice and the demand for forward exchange, American Economic Review 66, 332–339.

Aliber, R.Z., 1978, The integration of national financial markets: A review of theory and findings, Weltwirtschaftliches Archiv 114, 448–480.

Bilson, J.O., 1979, Recent developments in monetary models of exchange rate determination,

Barro, R.J., 1974, Are government bonds net wealth?, Journal of Political Economy 82, 1095–1117.

IMF Staff Papers 26, 201–223.

Black, F., 1974, International capital market equilibrium with investment barriers, Journal of Financial Economics 1, 337–352.

Black, F., 1978, The ins and outs of foreign investment, Financial Analysts Journal, May–June, 1–7.

Breeden, D.T., 1979, An intertemporal asset pricing model with stochastic consumption and investment opportunities, Journal of Financial Economics 7, 265–296.

Cornell, B., 1981, The consumption based asset pricing model: A note on potential tests and applications, Journal of Financial Economics 9, 103–108.

Dornbusch, R., 1979, Monetary policy under exchange rate flexibility, in: Managed exchange rate flexibility, Conference vol. no. 20 (Federal Reserve Bank of Boston, Boston, MA).

Fama, E.F. and A. Farber, 1979, Money, bonds and foreign exchange, American Economic Review 69, 639–649.

Frankel, F., 1979, The diversifiability of exchange risk, Journal of International Economics 9, 379–393.

Genberg, H., 1978, Purchasing power parity under fixed and flexible exchange rates, Journal of International Economics 8, 247–276.

Grauer, F.L.A., R.H. Litzenberger and R.E. Stehle, 1976, Sharing rules and equilibrium in an international capital market under uncertainty, Journal of Financial Economics 3, 233–256.

Hansen, L. and R. Hodrick, 1980, Forward exchange rates as optimal predictors of future spot rates: An econometric analysis, Journal of Political Economy 88, 829–853.

Holmes, J.M., 1967, The purchasing power parity theory: In defence of Gustav Cassel as a modern theorist, Journal of Political Economy 75, 686–695.

Isard, P., 1977, How far can we push the 'law of one price', American Economic Review 67, 942–948.

Isard, P., 1978, Exchange rate determination: A survey of popular views and recent models, Princeton studies in international finance, no. 42 (Princeton University, Princeton, NJ).

Katseli-Papefstratiou, L.T., 1979, The re-emergence of the purchasing power parity doctrine in the 1970's, Special papers in international economics, no. 13 (Princeton University, Princeton, NJ).

Kouri, P.K., 1976, The determinants of the forward premium, Mimeo. (Institute for International Economic Studies, Stockholm).

Kouri, P.K., 1977, International investment and interest rate linkages under flexible exchange rates, in: R.Z. Aliber, ed., The political economy of monetary reform (New York).

Kravis, I.B. and Robert E. Lipsey, 1978, Price behavior in the light of balance of payments theories, Journal of International Economics 8, 193–246.

Merton, R.C., 1971, Optimum consumption and portfolio rules in a continuous-time model, Journal of Economic Theory 3, 373–413.

Merton, R.C., 1973, An intertemporal capital asset pricing model, Econometrica 41, 867–887.

Merton, R.C., 1981, On the microeconomic theory of investment under uncertainty, in: R.J. Arrow and M.D. Intriligator, eds., Handbook of of mathematical economics (North-Holland, Amsterdam).

Officer, L., 1976, The purchasing power parity theory of exchange rates: A review article, IMF Staff Papers 23, 1–61.

Officer, L.H. and T.O. Willet, 1970, The covered arbitrage schedule: A critical survey of recent developments, Journal of Money, Credit and Banking 2, 247–257.

Richard, S.F., 1979, A generalized capital asset pricing model, in: E.J. Elton and M.J. Gruber, eds., Portfolio theory 25 years after: Essays in honor of Harry Markovitz (North-Holland, Amsterdam).

Rodriguez, R.M. and E.E. Carter, 1979, International financial management (Prentice-Hall, Englewood Cliffs, NJ).

Roll, R., 1979, Violations of purchasing power parity and their implications for efficient international commodity markets, in: M. Sarnat and G. Szegö, eds., International finance and trade, Vol. I (Ballinger, Cambridge, MA).

Roll, R. and B. Solnik, 1977, A pure foreign exchange asset pricing model, Journal of International Economics 7, 161–180.

Samuelson, P.A., 1948, Disparity in postwar exchange rates, in: S. Harris, ed., Foreign economic policy for the United States (Harvard University Press, Cambridge, MA).

Solnik, B., 1973, European capital markets (Lexington Books, Lexington, MA).

Solnik, B., 1977, Testing international asset pricing: Some pessimistic views, Journal of Finance 38, 503—512.

Stehle, R., 1977, An empirical test of the alternative hypotheses of national and international pricing of risky assets, Journal of Finance 38, 493–502.

Stulz, R., 1981, On the effects of barriers to international investment, Journal of Finance, forthcoming.

[6]

THE JOURNAL OF FINANCE • VOL. XXXVIII, NO. 2 • MAY 1983

International Arbitrage Pricing Theory

BRUNO SOLNIK*

INTERNATIONAL ASSET PRICING (IAPM) has been the object of an intense controversy due to different assumptions on utility functions, sources of price uncertainty, and market imperfections. Some models assumed that all investors consume the same good, with different stochastic national inflation rates,[1] while others model a world in which exchange rates reflect relative price changes (deviation from purchasing power parity) with non stochastic inflation and different consumption tastes across countries.[2] Stülz (14) proposed a fairly complete consumption based model with nominal riskless bonds in every country, while a survey by Adler and Dumas (1) offers the most comprehensive and clarifying analysis of the IAPM.

A general conclusion is that the world market portfolio will not be optimal in the sense that investors will hold different portfolios, especially "hedge" portfolios (Solnik (10), Stülz (14), Adler and Dumas (1)). Since the composition of these portfolios depends on the covariance of asset returns with state variables, it is hard to identify such portfolios in order to test the theory. The attractive and simple domestic CAPM conclusion that a well identified market portfolio is efficient does not exist in the international framework, so that the IAPM does not yield operational (and easily testable) conclusions.

The Arbitrage Pricing Theory formulated by Ross (8, 9) provides a fruitful alternative to these utility based models. International Arbitrage Pricing Theory (IAPT) only requires perfect capital markets. It is shown below that the numeraires used by investors to measure (real) returns do not have to be specified[3] so long as they believe (homogeneously) that nominal asset returns follow a m-factor generating model. In other words, the differences between national investors need not be modeled.

As stressed by Ross, the m-factor assumption replaces the multivariate normal or Ito-Wiener asset return distribution assumption of the IAPM. In asset pricing models, "mathematical" difficulties arise when asset demands are aggregated over people using different numeraires to measure returns; such a problem is not present with APT because common factors are not constrained to be weighted "averages" of individual assets as are portfolios.

While IAPM uses the international parlance, it should be stressed that the analysis differs from the traditional CAPM by the introduction of differences in

---

* Centre D'Enseignement Superieur des Affaires, 78350 Jouy en Josas, France.

[1] See for instance Grauer, Litzenberger and Stehle (4), Kouri (5) and Fama and Farber (3).

[2] See for instance Solnik (10) and (11).

[3] All that is required is that investors be able to define some real deflator to apply to nominal returns.

consumption tastes and relative price uncertainty.[4] The IAPM is actually a multi-consumption real CAPM. Similarly, the IAPT results derived here could be regarded as an extension of the nominal APT to accommodate diverse consumption tastes and relative price uncertainty. While the international framework will be used throughout this paper, the reader should be aware that all the results could be stated in terms of real vs nominal rather than international vs domestic.

1—*The Usual APT on Nominal Returns*

Let's assume that there exist $n + 1$ currencies, and $N + 1$ assets with N much larger than n. One currency, say the U.S. Dollar, is arbitrarily chosen as the nominal numeraire and numbered 0. For the time being, assume that the first $n + 1$ assets are national bills, riskless in local currency terms; the asset subscripted 0 is the nominal riskfree asset in currency 0 (dollar). Investors are assumed to believe that the random returns on the set of assets are governed over short intervals of time by a m-factor generating model of the form:[5]

$$\tilde{r}_i = E_i + b_{i1}\tilde{\delta}_1 + \cdots + b_{im}\tilde{\delta}_m + \tilde{\epsilon}_i$$

$$i = 1, \cdots, N \tag{1}$$

where E_i is the expected return on the ith asset. The m zero mean common factors δ capture all systematic risks while the noise term ϵ_i is idiosyncratic to asset i. The ϵ's reflect all information unrelated to other assets and therefore are assumed to be independent of each other as well as unrelated to the common factors δ:

$$E(\tilde{\epsilon}_i \,|\, \tilde{\delta}_k) = 0 \quad \text{for all } i \text{ and } k.$$

We further assume that the number of common factors is much smaller than the number of assets.

The usual derivation of the nominal APT can now be performed for an investor who cares about U.S. dollar returns. To determine a pricing relation, one can build a well diversified arbitrage portfolio with weights x_i invested in asset i so that:

$$\sum_i x_i = \underline{X1} = 0$$

$$\sum_i x_i b_{ik} = \underline{Xb_k} = 0 \quad k = 1, \cdots, m$$

$$\sum x_i \tilde{\epsilon}_i = \underline{X\epsilon} \sim 0 \tag{2}$$

where $\underline{X}$ is a row vector and $\tilde{r}, \underline{E}, \tilde{\epsilon}, \underline{b_k}, \underline{1}$ are column vectors of size N.

This arbitrage portfolio is constructed as well diversified in the sense that the residual risk is negligible. The return on this arbitrage portfolio is equal to:

$$\underline{X}\tilde{r} = \underline{XE} + \sum_k \underline{Xb_k}\tilde{\delta}_k + \underline{X\tilde{\epsilon}} \sim \underline{XE} \tag{3}$$

---

[4] At least, the more comprehensive theories allowing for different consumption goods.

[5] For a more detailed description of the now well-known assumptions and implications of APT, see Ross (8, 9) and Roll and Ross (7).

This portfolio is almost riskless and, since it has a zero capital investment, it should also have a zero return (so that $\underline{X}E = 0$). As pointed out by Ross, this implies that the vector of expected return $\underline{E}$ must be a linear combination of the constant vector $\underline{1}$ and the $\underline{b}_k$ vectors, i.e., there exists $m + 1$ scalar constants λ_0 $\cdots \lambda_m$, such that:

$$\underline{E} = \lambda_0 + \lambda_1 \underline{b}_1 + \cdots + \lambda_m \underline{b}_m \qquad (4)$$

Since there exists a U.S. riskfree asset, its return r_0 is equal to λ_0.

We will now derive the equivalent of relation (4) for a foreign investor and aggregate it to a testable market relationship.

2—*International APT*

Investors of different countries measure (or care about) returns in different units, i.e. currencies; they are assumed to adjust nominal (dollar) returns by a random variable $\tilde{s}$. To use the international terminology, we will call this an exchange rate adjustment but this formulation also applies to the case where any investor j observes nominal returns and adjusts them by a specific inflation deflator $\tilde{s}_j$.

At first, one would not expect differences in utility functions to affect Arbitrage Pricing results as long as investors hold homogeneous expectations on the return generating model in nominal terms.[6] However, while APT is not a utility based approach, it does require the definition of a riskless investment. For example, if all investors are subject to stochastic inflation, they will not regard a nominal riskless portfolio as riskfree (i.e. in real terms) and the arbitrage argument applied in Section 1 to derive the pricing relation (4) might not be valid. So we will *first* show that, if asset returns are believed to follow (1), then any *arbitrage* portfolio which is nominally riskless will be riskless for any foreign investor. A *second* and more important question lies in the internal consistency of the m-factor model assumption in an international framework. To be a viable theory, it must be independent of the numeraire arbitrarily chosen to identify the model so that the m-factor model holds from any other currency viewpoint. For example, the m-factor model might hold true in terms of Poupou dollars (a small island on Mars) but, if no investors live in Poupou, it does not do us much good except if a similar m-factor model governs returns measured in other currencies. In other words, the dollar returns of Japanese, French and American stocks should exhibit the same structure as the returns of the same stocks computed in other currencies (Japanese Yen, French Franc or British Pound) and not be an artefact due to the return translation in some particular currency. Let's now prove these two points.

If P_i is the dollar price of asset i and S_{j0} the exchange rate of currency j in units of currency 0, the currency j price of asset i is equal to P_i/S_{j0} and the return

---

[6] For example, if all investors agree on the dollar factor generating model, and one investor cares about nominal dollar returns, the pricing relation (4) will hold for him as well as all other investors since, by assumption, expectations are homogeneous.

of asset i measured in currency j, for very short time interval,[7] will be equal, by Ito's lemma, to:

$$\tilde{r}_i^j = \tilde{r}_i - \tilde{s}_j - \tilde{r}_i\tilde{s}_j + \sigma_j^2 \tag{5}$$

where σ_j^2 is the variance of $\tilde{s}_j$ the random variation of S_j and $\tilde{r}_i\tilde{s}_j = C_{ij}$ is the covariance between $\tilde{r}_i$ and $\tilde{s}_j$.

Combining relation (1) and (5) yields the expression of the return on asset i in currency j as:

$$\tilde{r}_i^j = E_i + \sigma_j^2 - \tilde{s}_j + \sum_k b_{ik}(\tilde{\delta}_k - \tilde{\delta}_k\tilde{s}_j) + \tilde{\epsilon}_i - \tilde{\epsilon}_i\tilde{s}_j$$

Let's now compute the currency j return of an arbitrage portfolio which verifies conditions (2):

$$\underline{X}\tilde{r}^j = \underline{X}E + \underline{X}1(\sigma_j^2 - \tilde{s}_j) + \sum_k \underline{X}b_k(\tilde{\delta}_k - \tilde{\delta}_k\tilde{s}_j) + \underline{X}\tilde{\epsilon} - \underline{X}.\tilde{\epsilon}\tilde{s}_j$$

From (2), this reduces to:

$$\underline{X}\tilde{r}^j = \underline{X}E - \underline{X}.\tilde{\epsilon}\tilde{s}_j \tag{6}$$

The real return on this portfolio differs from its nominal return given in (3), if the last term cannot be diversified away because of systematic correlation between $\tilde{\epsilon}_i$ and currency j fluctuations. However by assumption, all $\tilde{\epsilon}_i$ are uncorrelated to other assets return including asset j which is the currency j riskfree bill.[8] In dollars, this asset return stochastic component is equal to the random exchange rate movement $\tilde{s}_j$, so that each $\tilde{\epsilon}_i$ is independent of $\tilde{s}_j$. Equation (6) therefore reduces to:

$$\underline{X}\tilde{r}^j = \underline{X}E$$

So, even in real or foreign terms, this arbitrage portfolio bears no risk, so that $\underline{X}E$ must be equal to zero in equilibrium and pricing relation (4) must hold for every investor.

Let's now show that the m-factor framework is invariant to the currency used to express the returns.

The riskfree bill in currency j is one of the assets whose dollar return r_j follows relation (1); its stochastic component is equal to $\tilde{s}_j$ when measured in dollars. This implies that $\tilde{s}_j$ also follows a m-generating factor model[9]:

$$\tilde{s}_j = E(\tilde{s}_j) + \sum_k b_{jk}\tilde{\delta}_k + \tilde{\epsilon}_j \tag{7}$$

Replacing in (5) $\tilde{r}_i$ and $\tilde{s}_j$ by their m-factor expression gives:

$$\tilde{r}_i^j = E_i - E(\tilde{s}_j) - C_{ij} + \sigma_j^2 + \sum_k (b_{ik} - b_{jk})\tilde{\delta}_k + \tilde{\epsilon}_i - \tilde{\epsilon}_j \tag{8}$$

---

[7] The m-factor generating model is required to hold over the shortest trading interval. The product of two rates of return will be zero (second order) if they are uncorrelated; this will be the case for $E_i\tilde{s}_j$ because E_i is non stochastic, but generally not for $\tilde{\delta}_k\tilde{s}_j$ which will be equal to $\mathrm{cov}(\tilde{\delta}_k, \tilde{s}_j)$. Note that this short time interval assumption is also required by the standard APT as stressed by Roll and Ross (7).

[8] The case where no riskfree bills exist and currency fluctuations do not follow the m-factor model is studied in the appendix.

[9] $\tilde{s}_j$ differs from $\tilde{r}_j$ by a constant term, the currency j interest rate λ_0^j.

Taking the expected value of $\tilde{r}_i^j$ in equation (5) shows that the constant term on the RHS of (8) is equal to $E(\tilde{r}_i^j)$ which will be denoted as E_i^j. Equation (8) might be rewritten as:

$$\tilde{r}_i^j = E_i^j + \sum_k b_{ik}^j \tilde{\delta}_k + \tilde{\mu}_i \tag{9}$$

with $b_{ik}^j = b_{ik} - b_{jk}$ the new factor loading and

$$\tilde{\mu}_i = \tilde{\epsilon}_i - \tilde{\epsilon}_j$$

Note that all the assumptions of the m-factor model are verified. The noise terms are mutually independent, and uncorrelated to the common factors, since this property holds for $\tilde{\epsilon}_i$ and $\tilde{\epsilon}_j$. The riskfree asset of currency now replaces the currency 0 riskfree asset which becomes risky in terms of currency j. In other words, the decomposition in m-factors plus a noise term is invariant to the currency chosen to compute the returns on this makes the IAPT an attractive and operational framework.[10] A pricing relation such as (4) will hold for returns determined in currency j or any other currency:

$$\underline{E^j} = \lambda_0^j + \lambda_1^j \underline{b_1^j} + \cdots + \lambda_m^j \underline{b_m^j} \tag{4'}$$

where λ_0^j is the currency j riskfree rate.

Without giving tedious mathematical derivations, it should be clear that while the *form* of the relation is invariant, the coefficients $\underline{b}_k^j$ and λ_k^j vary with j. Taking the difference between the two pricing equations, it can be shown that they are linked by the relation:

$$C_{ij} = (\lambda_i - \lambda_1^j)b_{i1} + \cdots + (\lambda_m - \lambda_m^j)b_{im}$$

or:

$$\underline{C_j} = (\lambda_1 - \lambda_1^j)\underline{b_1} + \cdots + (\lambda_m - \lambda_m^j)\underline{b_m} \tag{10}$$

in particular:

$$\sigma_j^2 = (\lambda_1 - \lambda_1^j)b_{j1} + \cdots + (\lambda_m - \lambda_m^j)b_{jm}$$

In a sense, relation (10) is a pricing relationship à la (4), where the coefficients $(\lambda - \lambda^j)$ indicate the price implication of the covariance structure between asset returns and investor J numeraire. If $\underline{C_j} \equiv 0$, then the risk premia will be identical in both currencies. Note that the assumption of only m common factors and independent residuals imply severe constraints on the currency-asset covariance matrix.

The differences in interest rates on two currencies can easily be derived from the pricing relations. In (4), the expected return on the currency j riskfree asset is:

$$\lambda_0^j + E(\tilde{s}_j) = \lambda_0 + \lambda_1 b_{j1} + \cdots + \lambda_m b_{jm} \tag{11}$$

This implies that the interest rate differential (or forward premium), $\lambda_0 - \lambda_0^j$,

---

[10] Again this attractive result comes partly from the fact that, contrary to portfolio returns, factors do not have to be translated into foreign currencies when investors measure returns differently. To understand this think of factors such as world real growth, etc. . .

is equal to the expected currency fluctuation, $E(\tilde{s}_j)$, plus a risk premium. This risk premium depends on the covariance of the currency fluctuations with the same common factors. This result is analogous to the traditional findings of the IAPM.

The case where riskless assets do not exist is discussed in the appendix. This is a situation where asset returns follow the m-factor model but currency fluctuations do not. However a simple riskless arbitrage argument can still be developed based on the construction of riskless portfolios in every currency.

The invariance property of the m-factor model will generally not hold in the absence of riskfree assets in each currency, but simple results still obtain. In a sense, the problem might be bypassed by adding individual currencies as common factors (with factor coefficients possibly equal to zero for many or all assets).[11] Since there exists a large number of assets in every country, the total number of assets will still be much larger than that of common factors. Furthermore, the total number of currencies might be reduced to a smaller set of common (currency) factors.

3—*Conclusions*

In this paper, we have provided an analysis of the international extension of arbitrage pricing theory, where investors value returns of the same asset differently; the same analysis could be applied to a domestic framework with heterogeneous consumption tastes. The technical problems posed by currency translation and aggregation in the international CAPM do not arise in APT since factors are not constrained to be portfolios of the original assets. While APT is not utility based, it requires the definition of a riskless portfolio, hence the numeraire used to measure (real) returns matters. This paper shows that, if a factor model is believed to hold when asset returns are expressed in some arbitrarily chosen currency, this factor structure, as well as its major conclusions, is invariant to the currency chosen. The relation between factor coefficients when measured in different currencies has been investigated, as well as the pricing of the forward exchange rates (or national interest rate differentials) which depend on the covariance of the currency fluctuations with the same common factors.

If investors hold homogeneous expectations as measured in some currency, the same m-factor model and pricing relation will apply for everyone and we can aggregate the ex ante specification to a market testable ex post relation. It follows that, whatever the numeraire used, the pricing relation (5) might be subjected to empirical scrutiny. Again, note that the IAPT says nothing about the size of the risk premia λ_k, nor the number or origin of the common factors, but only specifies the *linearity* of the pricing relation.

---

[11] Similarly, in the domestic real nominal framework, it would be sufficient to introduce the inflation rate as an additional common factor to maintain the same pricing relation on real return. However, if each investor has different consumption tastes with relative price uncertainty, the problem is serious because the number of investors (different inflation rates) is probably larger than that of assets. We are back to the situation of heterogeneous (real) anticipations discussed in Ross (8). Note, however, that as long as investors believe that *nominal* returns are governed by the m-factors generating model, pricing equation (4) will still hold.

Tests of international asset pricing models have so far been scarce and inconclusive (e.g. Solnik (12), Stehle (13)). Major limitations come from data availability, but also from the technical problems involved in the exact identification of the ex ante efficient portfolios as stressed by Roll (6). Consumption based CAPM are not void of similar types of problems as shown by Cornell (2). When the composition of efficient international portfolios suggested by the IAPM depends on utility functions parameters, the empirical task would even seem hopeless. If international markets segmentation plays a significant role, IAPM hardly provide any useful conclusions. In its more heuristic approach, arbitrage pricing theory seems to offer an attractive alternative.

To be a viable and useful theory, the number of common factors in an IAPT must be small compared to the number of assets. The most simple structure would consist of a few international factors common to all assets. Another extreme would be if the sets of common factors strictly differed across national markets. International factors could also be common within specific types of markets (e.g. all bond markets or all stock markets). A likely situation might be the combination of international factors common to all or specific types of assets plus national factors affecting only domestic assets. Of course if the number of factors is too large, the testability and operationality of IAPT is greatly reduced.[12]

APPENDIX

First, it should be stressed that the strong assumption of APT is that the stochastic return process ($\tilde{r}_i$) of a large number of assets can be reduced to *independent* residuals ($\tilde{\epsilon}_i$) by subtracting a linear combination of a small number of common factors ($\tilde{\delta}_k$). The independence assumption of $\tilde{\epsilon}_i$ and $\tilde{\delta}_k$ is not called for by the theory and is only a simple transformation made for economic interpretation purposes.

Let's now assume that the m-factors generating model is believed to hold in currency 0 but that there do not exist riskless bills in the various currencies. Then pricing equation (4) still holds but not relation (7). Fur convenience, let's write the random process of exchange rate fluctuation $\tilde{s}_j$ as:

$$\tilde{s}_j = E(\tilde{s}_j) + \tilde{\nu}_j \tag{A1}$$

Then, the return of asset i expressed in currency j for continuous time diffusion process described in (5) will be:

$$\tilde{r}_i^j = E_i - E(\tilde{s}_j) - C_{ij} + \sigma_j^2 + \sum_k b_{ik}\tilde{\delta}_k + \tilde{\epsilon}_i - \tilde{\nu}_j$$

$$= E_i^j + \sum_k b_{ik}\tilde{\delta}_k + \tilde{\epsilon}_i - \tilde{\nu}_j \tag{A2}$$

A straightforward application of the arbitrage portfolio method developed in equation (2) and (3) leads to a pricing relation similar to (4):

$$\underline{E}^j = \lambda_0' + \lambda_1'\underline{b_1} + \cdots + \lambda_m'\underline{b_m} \tag{A3}$$

---

[12] From a practical viewpoint, note that if the same international factors are common to all assets, the international risk diversification may be achieved by restricting its investments to domestic assets. This would not be the case if factors are segmented along national boundaries.

where $\underline{E}^j$ is the vector of expected returns in units of currency j and the factors coefficients b are exactly the same as before, i.e. computed ın currency 0. Intuitively, this "strange" mix comes from the fact that the "currency factor" $\tilde{\nu}_j$ appears with a coefficient equal to 1 in relation (A2) for every asset; this vector of coefficients is identical to the constant vector (one) in the arbitrage portfolio construction and therefore does not increase the vector space. While $\tilde{\nu}_j$ is not orthogonal to $\tilde{\epsilon}_i$, this is not required to establish the pricing equation as was mentioned above. Also note that relation (A3) imposes severe constraint on the covariance structure of asset and currency fluctuations C_{ij}. Given the definition of E^j_i, and substracting (A3) from (4) implies that the vector C_{ij} is a linear combination of the coefficients b_{ik}:

$$\underline{C}_j = \gamma_0 + (\lambda_1 - \lambda_1')\underline{b}_1 + \cdots + (\lambda_m - \lambda_m')\underline{b}_m \qquad (A4)$$

with

$$\gamma_0 = \lambda_0 - \lambda_0' + E(\tilde{s}_j) - \sigma_j^2$$

In other words the C_{ij}'s cannot be exogeneous; the number of factors postulated for assets sets the number of degrees of freedom on the covariance structure. If relation (A4) was violated, an investor in country j could build arbitrage portfolios to take advantage of it. Note that, to a constant term, this relation is similar to that found where riskless assets existed (equation (10)). In a sense, investors from country j views the return generating process of all asset returns expressed in their own currency as an $m + 1$ factors model with the additional factor being the random fluctuation in exchange rate $\tilde{\nu}_j$. In equation (A2) this could be formalized by replacing $\tilde{\epsilon}_i$ by the results of its regression on $\tilde{\nu}_j$ conditional on all the other factors.

REFERENCES

1. Adler, M. and B. Dumas "International Portfolio Choice and Corporation Finance: A Survey," *The Journal of Finance*, forthcoming, (1983).
2. Cornell, B. "The Consumption based Asset Pricing Model: A Note on Potential Tests and Applications," *Journal of Financial Economics*, 9, (March 1981), 103–109.
3. Fama, E. F. and A. Farber "Money, Bonds and Foreign Exchange," *The American Economic Review*, 69, (September 1979), 636–649.
4. Grauer, F. L., R. H. Litzenberger and R. Stehle, "Sharing Rules and Equilibrium in an International Capital Market Under Uncertainty," *Journal of Financial Economics*, 3, (June 1976), 233–256.
5. Kouri, P. J. K. *Essays on the Theory of Flexible Exchange Rates*, Ph.D. dissertation, MIT (1975).
6. Roll, R. "A Critique of Asset Pricing Theory's Tests," *Journal of Financial Economics*, 4, (March 1977), 129–176.
7. Roll, R. and S. A. Ross "An Empirical Investigation of the Arbitrage Pricing Theory," *The Journal of Finance*, 35, (December 1980), 1073–1104.
8. Ross, S. A. "The Arbitrage Theory of Capital Asset Pricing," *Journal of Economic Theory*, 13, (December 1976), 341–360.
9. Ross, S. A. "Return, Risk and Arbitrage," in Irwin Friend and James Bicksler, eds. *Risk and Return in Finance*, 1, 189–218, Cambridge; Ballinger, 1977.
10. Solnik, B. H. *European Capital Markets*, Lexington, D.C. Heath, 1973.
11. Solnik, B. H. "An Equilibrium Model of the International Capital Market," *Journal of Economic Theory*, 8, (July/August, 1974), 500–524.

International Arbitrage Pricing   457

12. Solnik, B. H. "International Pricing of Risk: An Empirical Investigation of the World Capital Market Structure," *Journal of Finance*, 29, (May 1974), 365–378.

13. Stehle, R. "An Empirical Test of Alternative Hypotheses of National and International Pricing of Risky Assets," *Journal of Finance*, 32, (May 1977), 493–502.

14. Stülz, R. M. "A Model of International Asset Pricing," *Journal of Financial Economics*, 9, (December 1981), 383–406.

Part II
Empirical Evidence on International Asset Pricing Models

[7]

THE JOURNAL OF FINANCE · VOL. XXXII, NO. 2 · MAY 1977

AN EMPIRICAL TEST OF THE ALTERNATIVE HYPOTHESES OF NATIONAL AND INTERNATIONAL PRICING OF RISKY ASSETS

RICHARD STEHLE*

INTRODUCTION

THEORETICALLY, IF THERE WERE NO BARRIERS to international capital flows, all assets in all countries should be priced according to a model of an integrated world capital market. On the other hand, if financial transactions were not possible on the international level, a model of segmented capital markets would be more appropriate. In reality, during the post World War II period, there were more formal and informal barriers to capital transactions on an international than on a domestic level. But what level of international capital market imperfection is needed to induce strictly local pricing of risk assets? As the quality of a positive theory of valuation should be judged by its predictive ability, the crucial question is whether a valuation model assuming no barriers to international capital flows predicts rates of return better than a model that assumes complete market segmentation.

The answer to this question is of great importance to individual investors and to corporations making capital budgeting decisions. National and international risk pricing imply different criteria for corporate capital budgeting decisions. The type of benefits attainable by international portfolio investment depends on the level of international capital market integration.

Prior studies have tested either the hypothesis that assets are priced in segmented capital markets against the null-hypothesis of no relationship [3, 4, 13] or have tested the hypothesis that assets are priced in integrated capital markets against the null hypothesis of no relationship [15]. However, the question whether assets are priced in segmented or integrated capital markets cannot be answered by comparing the results of two cross-sectional regressions using the alternative risk measures as the single independent variable. In the regression using the incorrect risk measure, the residual is not independently distributed from the independent variable. As a consequence, least squares estimates will be inconsistent.[1] By identifying those parts of the total rate of return variations that represent a

* Universität Mannheim. This paper is adapted from a section of my Ph.D. dissertation at the Graduate School of Business, Stanford University. Comments by K. Ramaswamy, W. F. Sharpe and especially by R. H. Litzenberger improved the quality of this paper. The financial support from the Ford Foundation during my doctoral studies is gratefully acknowledged.

1. None of Solnik's [15] tests can answer the question which hypothesis is correct. His tests are not efficient and contain serious statistical problems. To avoid the problems caused by errors-in-measurement [see footnote 10], Solnik used grouping procedures similar to those of Black/Jensen/Scholes [3]. BJS minimized the loss in efficiency by grouping according to an instrumental variable (historical β_{iD}) that is highly correlated with the (single) independent variable. Solnik grouped by the same instrumental variable as BJS did. Since he used different independent variables than BJS, the loss in efficiency is not minimized (see f. ex. [8], p. 231). By using different portfolio sizes, Solnik violated the

The Journal of Finance

diversifiable risk in a segmented but not in an international capital market (and those, which represent a diversifiable risk in an international but not in a segmented capital market), tests will be proposed which focus on the differences between the alternative hypotheses and which are not misspecified in either case.

Whether the stocks traded on the New York Stock Exchange were priced nationally or internationally during the time period January 1956 until December 1975 will be tested.[2] The tests will utilize monthly security data from the CRSP tape and stock price indices for Belgium, Canada, France, Germany, Italy, Japan, the Netherlands, Switzerland, the United Kingdom, and the United States.[3]

The risk characteristics of securities cannot be measured without error. To insure asymptotic unbiasedness in the presence of measurement errors, instrumental variables or grouping techniques may be used. The relative efficiencies of both methods will be discussed. The sacrifice in efficiency involved by either method must not be made in a way that favors either hypothesis.[4] By doing two different regressions to test the same hypotheses, this study will insure that the increase in sampling variances only increases the chances of obtaining inconclusive results. Generalized least squares will be used since the residuals are heteroscedastic.

THE MODEL

Theories of capital market equilibrium usually limit consumption to a single good. By further assuming homogeneous expectations, commodity price stability, and that investors utility depends only on the first two moments of a portfolio's rate of return distribution, Sharpe [14] and Lintner [11] derive the following relationship:

$$E\left(\tilde{R}_i\right)=R_f+\beta_{iM}\left[E\left(\tilde{R}_M\right)-R_f\right] \tag{1}$$

where $\beta_{iM}=\mathrm{cov}(\tilde{R}_i,\tilde{R}_M)/\mathrm{var}(\tilde{R}_M)=$ the systematic risk of security i;

OLS assumption of homoscedastic error terms. By using overlapping portfolios, he violated the OLS assumption of uncorrelated error terms even more than in the case of non-overlapping portfolios. Standard OLS procedures must be adjusted for the artificial increase in observations when using overlapping portfolios, which Solnik does not seem to do and which is probably the most serious statistical problem in his procedures.

2. In a two-country world, the hypotheses of national and international pricing of risk would be well specified. In an N-country world, every possible subset of countries can constitute an international capital market. This creates the problem of the empirical definition of the international capital market. In this study it will be assumed that if NYSE securities should be priced in an international capital market, this market consists of the 10 countries mentioned.

3. The following data is used: monthly rates of return on securities are taken from the CRSP tape. An equally weighted average of all securities is used as the rate of return on the U.S. market portfolio. End-of-month values of the 'Capital International Perspective' indices for the other countries for the time period Dec. 1958 to Dec. 1975 are combined with various other country indices to obtain an end-of-month stock index for each country starting Jan. 1952. Using the end-of-month exchange rates listed in the IMF Financial Statistics, all indices are converted to the numeraire currency, the dollar. Following Solnik, the rate of return on the international market portfolio is based on GNP weights.

4. Fama/McBeth [4], for example, by grouping according to historical β_{iD} use an extremely inefficient grouping procedure with respect to the coefficient of non-market risk and, possibly as a consequence, cannot reject the hypothesis of the Sharpe-Lintner model with respect to the effect of non-market risk on the expected rate of return (see footnote 10).

Empirical Test of Alternative Hypotheses of National/International Pricing 495

$\tilde{R}_i$ = the (real) rate of return on asset i; tildes denote random variables, E is the expected value operator;

R_f = the rate of return on the asset which yields a certain (real) return;

$\tilde{R}_M$ = the (real) rate of return on a portfolio, which includes all assets in proportion to their market value.

Although Sharpe and Lintner did not interpret their model with respect to the existing markets for financial assets, most of the subsequent literature concludes, that, from a theoretical viewpoint, not only stocks and bonds, but also real estate, insurance policies, durable goods, and human capital ought to be included in the portfolio of all assets (f.ex. [5]). As foreign assets (assets that are denominated in other currencies) are only mentioned in analyses that point out the benefits of international diversification (f.ex. [10]), or in the context of models of international capital asset pricing (f.ex. [15]), the literature seems to imply, that the Sharpe-Lintner model holds only for a capital market with a single currency which is totally separated from all capital markets with different currencies.

Note however, that the Sharpe-Lintner model is compatible with one or many currency areas, provided that the single consumption good is exchanged freely and an asset that is riskless in real terms exists. The rates at which currencies exchange in such a model, do not affect an investor's behavior. The investor's portfolio decision only depends upon the real rates of return, which are identical for all investors, regardless of the currency area in which they live. In a single commodity world exchange rate changes only reflect different inflation rates, that is, different monetary policies.

While the Sharpe-Lintner model may be interpreted as a model of segmented or integrated capital markets, a multi-commodity model of an international capital market is more appropriate, since exchange rate fluctuations may be accompanied by both, changes in the absolute price level and changes in the relative prices of commodities. Grauer/Litzenberger/Stehle [6], using the power utility function, present a model of an international capital market in which investor's portfolio decision depends on the non-diversifiable fluctuations of relative commodity prices. But neither the Sharpe-Lintner model nor a model in which relative price fluctuations affect an individual's asset choice behavior is ideally suited for an empirical test, since both would require data on the real rates of return on assets. Hakansson [7] has noted that individuals with logarithmic utility functions do not hedge against changing relative prices. Since individuals with logarithmic utility functions display the desirable properties of decreasing absolute and constant relative risk aversion in their asset choice, this utility function seems ideally suited as the basis for a testable model in the presence of fluctuating relative prices.[5]

$$U(c_{1t}, \ldots, c_{nt}, \ldots, c_{1T}, \ldots, c_{nT} / S_T = s_T) = \sum_h d_h \sum_j a_{jhs} \log c_{jh}$$

where c_{jh} = amount of good j that the individual consumes in period h;

$S_h(s_h)$ = the (specific) state of nature in period h;

---

5. Arrow [1] argues (page 98) that "relative risk aversion must hover around 1."

$d_h(a_{jhs})$ = a nonnegative preference parameter associated with total consumption in period h (consumption of good j in period h if the state of nature in period h is s); ratios of d_h may be interpreted as relative rates of impatience for consumption in different time periods.

Budget constraints limit the net present value of present and future consumption to the net present value of present and future income. The form of the budget constraints is the same for all individuals in all countries (the budget constraints are, however, expressed in different currencies for residents or different countries). At the beginning of any time period t, the individual maximizes the expected utility of present and future consumption by allocating his wealth between current consumption and investment in securities, whose market value at the beginning of period $t+1$ is his total wealth at that time. Stehle [16] solves the multiperiod decision problem of the individual and derives his demand for the various primitive securities.[6]

In the absence of restrictions on international capital movements, the following arbitrage relationship must hold in equilibrium between the prices of primitive securities that are denominated in different currencies:

$$1/\phi_{sk} = [1\phi_{sm}][r_{skm}/r_{tkm}] \qquad \text{for all } s,t,k,m$$

where ϕ_{sk} = the price in currency k of a primitive security that pays one unit of currency k at $t+1$ contingent on the occurance of state s;

$r_{tkm}(r_{skm})$ = the present exchange rate (exchange rate at $t+1$, should state s occur) between currencies k and m: the number of units of currency k that exchange for one unit of currency m.

This arbitrage relationship permits us to choose an arbitrary numeraire currency and aggregate the supply and demand for all securities, which pay off in the same state of nature, regardless of the currency in which they are denominated, to obtain the equilibrium prices for primitive securities. Alternatively, the equilibrium relationship may be expressed in rate of return notation:

$$E(\tilde{R}_{im}) = R_{fm} + \left[\text{cov}(\tilde{R}_{im}\cdot\tilde{R}'_{Wm})/\text{cov}(\tilde{R}_{Wm}\cdot\tilde{R}'_{Wm})\right]\left[E(\tilde{R}_{Wm}) - R_{fm}\right] \qquad (2)$$

where $\tilde{R}_{im}$ = unity plus the nominal (random) rate of return on security i, expressed in the numeraire currency m;

R_{fm} = unity plus the nominally riskless rate in the numeraire currency;

$\tilde{R}_{Wm}$ = unity plus the nominal rate of return of the international market portfolio, expressed in the numeraire currency; $\tilde{R}'_{Wm} = (\tilde{R}_{Wm} - R_{fm})$ / $\tilde{R}_{Wm}$.

In (2), expected values and covariances are based on the 'market probability assessment,' which is a weighted average of individuals' assessments of the probability of state s, using the values of their total investment in primitive securities as weights, with all the weights being expressed in the numeraire currency.

---

6. For a definition and discussion of primitive securities, see Arrow [1].

Empirical Test of Alternative Hypotheses of National/International Pricing 497

Kraus/Litzenberger [9] using a single good logarithmic utility, have derived a similar relationship for the case in which security i is traded in a completely segmented security market:

$$E(\tilde{R}_i) = R_f + \left[\text{cov}(\tilde{R}_i, \tilde{R}_D') / \text{cov}(\tilde{R}_D, \tilde{R}_D') \right] \left[E(\tilde{R}_D) - R_f \right] \tag{3}$$

where $\tilde{R}_D$ is unity plus the rate of return on the domestic market portfolio of the market in which security i is traded; R_f is unity plus the riskless rate in that market; and $\tilde{R}_D' = (\tilde{R}_D - R_f)/\tilde{R}_D$. When the currency of the market in which security i is traded is chosen as numeraire in (2), the implications of both hypotheses with regard to the pricing of security i may be compared. While both relationships state that the excess rate of return on a security is proportional to its non-diversifiable risk, the two models imply different definitions of security risk: In an international capital market the total of domestic and foreign securities will, in general, permit a greater degree of diversification than that available in a segmented capital market.

AN ALTERNATIVE STATEMENT OF THE EQUILIBRIUM RELATIONSHIPS

Given the multivariate probability distributions of $\tilde{R}_D$ and $\tilde{R}_W$, α_{WD} and β_{WD} may be calculated, where $\alpha_{WD} = E(\tilde{R}_W) - \beta_{WD} E(\tilde{R}_D)$; $\beta_{WD} = \text{cov}(\tilde{R}_W, \tilde{R}_D)/\text{var}(\tilde{R}_D)$. Using α_{WD} and β_{WD}, the rate of return on the international market portfolio, without loss of generality, may be broken down into a component perfectly correlated with the rate of return on the domestic market portfolio and a component uncorrelated with the rate of return on the domestic market portfolio (the currency subscript is omitted).

$$\tilde{R}_W = \alpha_{WD} + \beta_{WD}\tilde{R}_D + \tilde{v}_W \tag{4}$$

$\tilde{v}_W =$ the component of the international market portfolio's rate of return, which is uncorrelated with the rate of return on the domestic market portfolio. By construction, $E(\tilde{v}_W) = \text{cov}(\tilde{v}_W, \tilde{R}_D) = 0$.

The rate of return on risk asset i may be broken down into three components: the first component is perfectly correlated with the rate of return on the domestic market portfolio, the second component is perfectly correlated with $\tilde{v}_W$, and the third component is uncorrelated with either the international market factor or the rate of return on the domestic market portfolio.

$$\tilde{R}_i = \alpha_i + \beta_{iD}\tilde{R}_D + \gamma_i \tilde{v}_W + \tilde{u}_i \tag{5}$$

where $\gamma_i = \text{cov}(\tilde{R}_i, \tilde{v}_W)/\text{var}(\tilde{v}_W)$, $\beta_{iD} = \text{cov}(\tilde{R}_i, \tilde{R}_D)/\text{var}(\tilde{R}_D)$, $\alpha_i = E(\tilde{R}_i) - \beta_{iD}E(\tilde{R}_D)$.

By construction $E(\tilde{u}_i) = \text{cov}(\tilde{u}_i, \tilde{R}_D) = \text{cov}(\tilde{u}_i, \tilde{v}_W) = \text{cov}(\tilde{u}_i, \tilde{R}_W) = 0$. Relations (4) and (5) are perfectly general and do not make any assumption about the process generating rates of return.

Substituting (5) into (3) [into (2)] yields an alternative expression for the expected excess rate of return on risk asset i for the case of purely domestic [international] risk pricing, equation (6) [(7)]:[7]

$$E(\tilde{R}_i) - R_f = \beta_{iD}\left[E(\tilde{R}_D) - R_f\right] \tag{6}$$

$$E(\tilde{R}_i) - R_f = \beta_{iD}b_1 + \gamma_i b_2 \tag{7}$$

where $b_1 = E(\tilde{R}_D) - R_f$, $b_2 = [\text{cov}(\tilde{v}_W, \tilde{R}'_W)/\text{cov}(\tilde{R}_W, \tilde{R}'_W)][E(\tilde{R}_W) - R_f]$
$= [\text{cov}(\tilde{v}_W, \tilde{R}'_W)/\text{cov}(\tilde{R}_D, \tilde{R}'_W)][E(\tilde{R}_D) - R_f]$

The covariation of a security's rate of return with the rate of return on the domestic market portfolio represents a systematic risk not only when markets are segmented, but also in an international capital market, when the rates of return on the domestic and the international market portfolio are positively correlated. In addition a security's rate of return may be correlated with those components of the international market portfolio, which are uncorrelated with the domestic market portfolio. This second source of risk in an international capital market may be called the non-domestic international risk, and is measured by γ_i.

Clearly, in the case of risk pricing on an international level, a cross-sectional regression using only β_{iD} as an independent variable would be misspecified. On the other hand, a cross-sectional regression using both β_{iD} and γ_i as independent variables will not introduce a bias in the case of purely domestic risk pricing, since γ_i would only be an irrelevant variable in a well-specified regression. Such a regression will therefore be used to test the alternative models. Since the inclusion of an irrelevant variable increases the sampling variances of the coefficients, a regression using only β_{iD} as independent variables will be used to obtain the minimum-variance estimate of the coefficient of β_{iD} for the case of segmented capital markets.

Instead of using $\tilde{R}_D$ and $\tilde{v}_W$ to break down the rate of return on assets into the various components, $\tilde{R}_W$ and $\tilde{e}_D$ could have been used, where $\tilde{e}_D$ is defined by:

$$\tilde{R}_D = \alpha_{DW} + \beta_{DW}\tilde{R}_W + \tilde{e}_D \tag{8}$$

The rate of return on risk asset i may then be broken down into three components,

$$\tilde{R}_i = \alpha_i + \beta_{iW}\tilde{R}_W + \partial_i \tilde{e}_D + \tilde{u}_i \tag{9}$$

β_{iW} measures the total systematic risk of a security i in an international capital market; δ_i measures the risk that is diversifiable internationally but not domestically.

In the case of international risk pricing,[7]

$$E(\tilde{R}_i) - R_f = \beta_{iW}\left[E(\tilde{R}_W) - R_f\right], \tag{10}$$

---

7. In (6) it is assumed that v_W as well as u_i are uncorrelated with R'_D; in (7) it is assumed that u_i and R'_W are uncorrelated. In (10) and (11) similar assumptions are made.

while in the case of domestic risk pricing,

$$E(\tilde{R}_i) - R_f = \beta_{iW}c_1 + \delta_i c_2 \tag{11}$$

where $c_1 = [\text{cov}(\tilde{R}_W, \tilde{R}'_D)/\text{cov}(\tilde{R}_D, \tilde{R}'_D)][E(\tilde{R}_D) - R_f]$
$c_2 = [\text{cov}(\tilde{e}_D, \tilde{R}'_D)/\text{cov}(\tilde{R}_D, \tilde{R}'_D)][E(\tilde{R}_D) - R_f]$

In a regression based on (6) and (7) the segmented markets hypothesis will be rejected, if b_2 is significantly different from its theoretical value, zero. Since the theoretical value of b_2 in case of integrated markets is not known, but only a confidence region is available based on the sample observations, the integrated market hypothesis will only be rejected, if the confidence regions for the theoretical value of b_2 and its regression estimate do not overlap. In order not to bias our procedure against either hypothesis, and because the choice of either of the two reformulations would be arbitrary, regressions based on both will be used. Either theory will only be accepted, if the estimated parameters match (the estimates of) their theoretical values in both cross-sectional regressions.

EMPIRICAL TESTS

The theory developed in the previous sections relates the ex-ante expected excess rate of return on a security to its ex-ante covariances; both based on the market probability assessments. Since investor's subjective probability estimates and time preferences, as well as the distribution of wealth across investors, are not directly observable, it is necessary to extend the theory to include hypotheses relating unobservable ex-ante variables to the observable ex-post rates of return. Under the assumption of proportional stochastic growth in aggregate end-of-period wealth, $\tilde{R}_W/R_f$ is identically distributed over time, and $E(\tilde{R}_W/R_f)$ is an inter-temporal constant if the single world market hypothesis holds.[8] If all portfolio rates of return deflated by unity plus the riskless one period rate of interest are identically distributed over time, covariances among deflated portfolio rates of return will be constant over time. (Similarly, in the case of segmented capital markets, the assumption of proportional stochastic growth must hold domestically.) The ex-post values of the variables in the model are considered to be random outcomes of these stationary ex-ante probability distributions. Further it is assumed that the market probability assessments are efficient and unbiased estimates of the true underlying distributions. A justification of this assumption is given by Kraus/Litzenberger [9]. The expectational hypothesis suggests the following ex-post relationship:[9]

$$\tilde{r}_i = \alpha + b_1 \hat{\beta}_{iD} + b_2 \hat{\gamma}_i + w_i \tag{12}$$

---

8. For a more detailed description of the assumption of stochastic proportional growth, see Kraus/Litzenberger [9]. The 30-day Treasury Bill rate is used to calculate deflated excess rates of return.

9. Note that the β_{iD}'s and γ_i's cannot be estimated by a regression based on (5), because v_W cannot be measured without error. The common practice of using orthogonalized industry factors in regressions will, therefore, result in biased coefficients.

where $r_{it}(\bar{r}_i) = (R_{it} - R_{ft})/R_{ft}$ = the realized (mean) deflated excess rate of return on the ith portfolio for month t ($t = 1, \ldots, 240$);

$$\hat{\beta}_{iD} = \frac{\sum_t (r_{it} - \bar{r}_i)(r_{Dt} - \bar{r}_D)}{\sum_t (r_{Dt} - \bar{r}_D)^2}$$

$$\hat{\gamma}_i = \frac{\sum_t (r_{it} - \bar{r}_i)(r_{Mt} - \bar{r}_M)\cdot\sum_t (r_{Dt} - \bar{r}_D)^2 - \sum_t (r_{it} - \bar{r}_i)(r_{Dt} - \bar{r}_D)\cdot\sum_t (r_{Dt} - \bar{r}_D)(r_{Mt} - \bar{r}_M)}{\sum_t (r_{Mt} - \bar{r}_M)^2 \sum_t (r_{Dt} - \bar{r}_D)^2 - \left[\sum_t (r_{Dt} - \bar{r}_D)(r_{Mt} - \bar{r}_M)\right]^2}$$

Equation (12) is used to test, whether the stocks on the New York Stock Exchange were priced nationally or internationally from January 1956 until December 1975:

$$\bar{r}_i = \underset{(1.73)}{.00422} + \underset{(.27)}{.00117}\ \beta_{iD} + \underset{(.92)}{.00280}\ \gamma_i$$

(t-statistics are in parentheses)

$$\bar{r}_i = \underset{(2.28)}{.00446} + \underset{(.22)}{.00089}\ \beta_{iD}$$

Similarly, using the second reformulation:

$$\bar{r}_i = \underset{(1.97)}{.00437} + \underset{(.23)}{.00096}\ \beta_{iW} - \underset{(-.05)}{.00017}\ \delta_i$$

Portfolio observations were used instead of security observations, because of the possibility that security risk characteristics are non-stationary over time and because of the problems associated with the measurement errors in the independent variables.[10] Estimates of the coefficients were obtained by using generalized least squares, because the error terms (w_i) are heteroscedastic.[11]

---

10. Bogue [2] has found considerable evidence for the hypothesis that security risk characteristics change over time. Empirical tests using security risk characteristics as independent variables must take this non-stationarity into account in order to avoid biases.

When the independent variables in a regression are measured with error, the estimates of their coefficients will be inconsistent (see Johnston, page 281). Methods suggested to avoid the problems caused by measurement errors include the grouping of observations and the use of instrumental variables. When the groups are formed independently of the measurement errors, OLS based on the group means will produce consistent estimates (assuming that the number of groups is held constant and the number of observations per group goes to infinity).

In a two-variable linear regression the loss in efficiency due to grouping depends on the within group variation of the independent variable. Grouping by the size of the independent variable will minimize the loss in efficiency. Malinvaud ([12], p. 408) notes that grouping by a variable that contains a measurement error results in dependence between the groupings and the measurement errors and suggests that groupings be determined by an instrumental variable that is independent of the measurement error.

Another procedure to avoid the problems caused by measurement errors is the direct use of instrumental variables (Johnston, page 283). A major factor determining the relative efficiencies of both methods is whether the exact functional form of the relationship between the independent variable and

While neither of the two theories can be rejected in favor of the other, the slope coefficients have the sign predicted by the international model.[12] That is, all rate of return variations that are non-diversifiable in an international capital market (measured by β_{iD} and γ_i) command a higher mean rate of return, while the rate of return variations that are diversifiable internationally but not domestically (measured by δ_i) do not command a positive premium. However, the intercept is considerably higher than that predicted by either model. The international model partly explains why low beta securities have outperformed high beta securities on a beta adjusted basis. In our sample, β_{iD} and γ_i are negatively correlated, ($R = -.25$), that is, low beta firms tend to have higher non-domestic systematic risk than high beta stocks, and, therefore, command a higher risk premium than that predicted by a model of a segmented securities market. On the average, low beta firms are much larger than high beta firms and are, therefore, more likely to have international operations. As a consequence, they face more international risks. The utilities however, do not fit into this argument.

---

its instrument is known. The use of an incorrectly specified relationship reduces the efficiency of the instrumental variable method but will, in general, not affect the efficiency of the grouping method (see Stehle [16]).

Rosenberg/Marathe [13] argue heuristically, that when the exact form of the functional relationship is known, the direct use of instruments will always be asymptotically more efficient than an OLS regression based on grouped data. Stehle compares the asymptotic properties of both methods, assuming that the exact form of the functional relationship is known. The asymptotic properties of the grouping method depend on whether the number of observations per group or the number of groups is held constant. When the number of groups is held constant and the number of observations per group approaches infinity, both methods are consistent, but the direct use of instrumental variables is asymptotically more efficient. When the number of observations per group is held constant and the number of groups goes to infinity, the OLS estimate based on group means is asymptotically biased, but the asymptotic sampling variances of the coefficients is less than the asymptotic sampling variance of the instrumental variable estimate. In the latter case there exists a trade-off between asymptotic bias and asymptotic sampling variance. In this study the grouping method will be used because the exact functional form of the relationship between risk measures and their instruments is not known and because risk characteristics of portfolios chosen according to a stable selection rule would be expected to be more stationary than risk characteristics of securities.

In a three variable linear regression there are several grouping alternatives. Stehle [16] derives the optimal grouping procedure for a given group size. In a test based on equations (6) and (7), the magnitudes of the intercept and of the coefficient of γ_i are of crucial importance. When the independent variables are uncorrelated (here $R^2 = .06$), a minimum variance estimate of γ_i is obtained by maximizing the intergroup variation of the γ_i. To avoid the regression phenomena, grouping must be done by instrumental variables. Since past β_{iD} predict current β_{iD} better than past γ_i predict current γ_i, and since the magnitude of the intercept is also of crucial importance, each period 10 portfolios were formed according to historical β_{iD}'s and 10 according to historical γ_i's. In any given time period, each security is in only one portfolio.

11. Because realized monthly deflated excess rates of return on the ith risk asset, r_{it}, are assumed to be independent observations from the same population, the mean realized deflated excess rate of return, $\bar{r}_i$, is equal to its expectation, $E(r_i)$, plus a sampling error, w_i, $w_i = \bar{r}_i - E(r_i)$. Assuming that the independent variables are fixed variables observed without error, the coefficient in the ith row and the jth column of the variance-covariance matrix of the residuals of (12), Ω, is $\text{cov}(\bar{r}_i, \bar{r}_j)$. Ω_t, the variance-covariance matrix of the residuals in period t will be calculated using all portfolio rate of return observations with the exception of those in the current year.

12. Regression procedures: For each stock that was listed continuously from Jan. '52 to Jan. '56, β_{iD} and γ_i is calculated using the 48 monthly observations from Jan. '52 to Dec. '55. Stocks are ranked

REFERENCES

1. K. J. Arrow. *Essays in the Theory of Risk-Bearing* (Markham, Chicago, Ill. 1971).
2. M. Bogue. "The Estimation and Behavior of Systematic Risk," unpublished doctoral dissertation, (Stanford, Calif. 1973).
3. F. Black, M. C. Jensen and M. Scholes. "The Capital Asset Pricing Model: Some Empirical Tests," in: M. C. Jensen (ed.), *Studies in the Theory of Capital Markets* (Praeger, New York, N.Y. 1972).
4. E. F. Fama and J. D. Macbeth. "Risk, Return and Equilibrium: Empirical Tests," *Journal of Political Economy* 81, (1973) 607–636.
5. E. Fama and M. Miller. *The Theory of Finance* (Holt, Rinehart and Winston, New York, N.Y. 1972).
6. F. L. A. Grauer, R. H. Litzenberger and R. E. Stehle. "Sharing Rules and Equilibrium in an International Capital Market Under Uncertainty," *Journal of Financial Economics* 3 (1976), 233–256.
7. N. H. Hakansson. "On the Relevance of Price-Level Accounting," *Journal of Accounting Research* 7 (1969).
8. J. Johnston. *Econometric Methods* (Wiley, New York, N.Y. 1972).
9. A. Kraus and R. H. Litzenberger. "Market Equilibrium in a Multiperiod State Preference Model with Logarithmic Utility," *Journal of Finance* 30 (1975), 1213–1229.
10. H. Levy and M. Sarnat. "International Diversification of Investment Portfolios," *American Economic Review* 60 (1970), 668–675.
11. J. Lintner. "The Valuation of Risk Assets and the Selection of Risky Investments in Stock Portfolios and Capital Budgets," *Review of Economics and Statistics* 47 (1965), 13–37.
12. E. Malinvaud. *Statistical Methods of Econometrics* (Rand McNally, Chicago, Ill. 1966).
13. B. Rosenberg and V. Marathe. "Tests of Capital Asset Pricing Hypotheses," Working Paper No. 32, IBER, Research Program in Finance (Berkeley, Calif.) 1975.
14. W. F. Sharpe. "Capital Asset Prices: A Theory of Market Equilibrium Under Conditions of Risk," *Journal of Finance* 19 (1964), 425–442.
15. B. H. Solnik. *European Capital Markets* (Lexington Books, Lexington, Mass. 1973).
16. R. E. Stehle. "The Valuation of Risk Assets in an International Capital Market: Theory and Tests," unpublished doctoral dissertation (Stanford, Calif.) 1977.

according to the described criteria and 20 portfolios are constructed. This procedure is repeated for the time period Jan. '53 until Dec. '56 and so on, with the last selection period being Jan. '71 to Dec. '74. Monthly rates of return are calculated for the first set of portfolios for the time period Jan. '56 until Dec. '56, for the second set of portfolios for the time period Jan. '57 to Dec. '57 and so on. This results in 20 years of monthly rates of return on 20 portfolios. Risk assets existing at the beginning of any year are only excluded if they are delisted during the next 49 months. Using the raw portfolio returns and the T-Bill rate, deflated excess portfolio rates of return are calculated. Of the 2604 securities on the CRSP tape, 1790 were included in the sample. The minimum number of securities in a portfolio is 48.

Instead of estimating (12) directly, a time series of coefficients is calculated using the monthly deflated portfolio excess rates of return as dependent variable of the cross-sectional regressions (following [4]):

$$r_{it} = a_t + b_{1t}\hat{\beta}_{iDt} + b_{2t}\hat{\gamma}_{it} + w_{it} \qquad (t = 1, \ldots, 240)$$

While the average coefficients resulting from this procedure are identical to those that would result from a single regression based on mean returns, the time series of coefficients may be used to calculate an unbiased estimate of the sampling variance of the average coefficients: When $\hat{\Omega}$ is used as a substitute for the unknown Ω, the coefficients of a GLS-regression have the sampling variance (in matrix notation):

$$\text{var}(\hat{b}) = E\left[\left(X'\hat{\Omega}^{-1}X \right)^{-1} X'\hat{\Omega}^{-1}\Omega\hat{\Omega}^{-1}X \left(X'\hat{\Omega}^{-1}X \right)^{-1} \right]$$

which is not necessarily equal to the GLS-estimate of the sampling variances. To avoid possible spurious correlation, the calculation of period t's risk measures is based on all portfolio rates of return with the exception of those in period t.

[8]

Journal of Financial Economics 21 (1988) 177–212. North-Holland

SOME TESTS OF INTERNATIONAL EQUITY INTEGRATION*

Simon WHEATLEY

University of Washington, Seattle, WA 98195, USA

Received June 1986, final version received March 1988

This paper provides tests of international equity market integration. The tests use a simple version of the consumption-based asset pricing model which predicts there is an asset pricing line for each country that relates a representative individual's expected real return on each asset to the covariance of this return with growth in the individual's real consumption. Using monthly data from January 1960 to December 1985, tests provide little evidence against the joint hypothesis that equity markets are integrated internationally and that the asset pricing model holds.

1. Introduction

There are many restrictions on international investment. There are also many ways to avoid at least some of them. The extent to which asset markets are integrated or segmented internationally is an important empirical question that remains largely unanswered. In a recent survey, for example, Adler and Dumas (1983) state that 'empirically, the severity of the market imperfections which tend to produce segmentation and the extent of segmentation itself have yet to be measured ... resolving these matters remains a key challenge for future research'. Several issues in financial economics cannot be addressed without some assumption about whether asset markets are integrated or segmented internationally. For example, when they are segmented, the cost of capital for a project will generally depend on the country in which it is to be raised. As another example, how far an individual will wish to diversify his portfolio internationally will depend on the barriers to international invest-

*This paper is drawn from chapter 4 of my doctoral thesis at the University of Rochester. I would like to thank my dissertation committee, Charles Plosser (chairman), Peter Garber, Clifford Smith, and René Stulz for their guidance. I would also like to thank Douglas Breeden, Michael Jensen, John Long, Paul Malatesta, Richard Pettit, Edward Rice, Alan Stockman, Lee Wakeman, and two referees, Robert Hodrick and Robert Litzenberger, for their comments, and G. William Schwert (the editor) for his helpful suggestions at all stages of this research. Financial support was provided in part by the Earhart Foundation. Some of the data were provided by Capital International, S.A. (Geneva) and R.G. Ibbotson and Associates.

ment that he faces.[1] This paper provides some tests of international equity market integration that use a simple version of the consumption-based asset pricing model.

1.1. An outline of the tests

In this paper, asset markets are said to be integrated internationally if assets of equal risk that are not necessarily located in the same country yield equal expected returns in some common currency. To determine whether assets are of equal risk generally requires an asset pricing model.[2] Thus, a test of international equity market integration is generally a joint test of a model that prices assets in a world in which equity markets are integrated and of international equity market integration. The asset pricing model used in this paper is a discrete-time version of the consumption-based asset pricing model in Stulz (1981a). This model assumes that within each country a representative individual displays constant relative risk aversion. In addition, it is assumed that the marginal joint distribution of the continuously compounded growth in his real consumption and the continuously compounded real asset returns he faces is stationary and normal.[3] This assumption, however, does not imply that the distribution of real asset returns conditional on some set of state variables is unaffected by changes in those variables. Therefore, the investment opportunity set facing the individual can change through time. Also, in this model the consumption opportunity set facing the individual can change through time and deviations from relative purchasing power parity can arise from differences in both tastes and consumption opportunity sets across countries. Finally, individuals from different countries are allowed to hold different beliefs.

A testable implication of the model is that the expected real return that a representative individual faces on an asset is a linear function of the covariance of this real return with the growth in his real consumption.[4] Thus, the model predicts that there will be an asset pricing line for each country that relates the expected real return facing the country's representative individual

---

[1] In addition, the predictions of many macroeconomic models depend critically on whether or not asset markets are integrated internationally. For example, Mundell (1963) has shown that, within a simple model, monetary policy has real effects under fixed exchange rates and fiscal policy has real effects under flexible exchange rates only if asset markets are segmented internationally.

[2] A model that provides measures of asset risk is not required to determine that assets yielding certain returns in some common currency are of equal risk. Equities, however, generally do not yield certain returns in any currency.

[3] Throughout the paper, real returns and real consumption growth are continuously compounded unless otherwise stated.

[4] For convenience, throughout the paper, expected real returns refer to continuously compounded expected real returns and not to expected continuously compounded real returns.

on each asset to the covariance of this return with the growth in his real consumption. In this model, foreign data are not required to price domestic assets.[5] Therefore, tests of the model can be conducted, using only domestic data, that require no assumption about the integration of asset markets internationally. It is important to test the model at the domestic level because if it were to be rejected at this level it would not make sense to use it to test whether equity markets are integrated internationally.

In addition to restrictions on the unconditional means of the real returns facing a representative individual on a cross-section of assets, the model imposes restrictions on the serial dependence of a vector containing those returns and the growth in the individual's real consumption. Hansen and Singleton (1983) have tested this second set of restrictions and conclude that they can be rejected at conventional significance levels.[6] Wheatley (1988) uses simulations to show, however, that if real consumption is measured with error then these tests reject the model more frequently than the stated significance level. He also shows that estimates of a representative individual's relative risk aversion, computed under the second set of restrictions, are biased downward in finite samples when relative risk aversion is at least five. This holds whether or not real consumption is measured with error. Some of these cross-covariance restrictions can also be tested without using consumption data or a series of implicit price deflators. Hansen and Singleton test the model in this way under an additional distributional assumption. They assume that, for each asset, the covariance of the real return on that asset with real consumption growth, conditional on the change in the nominal return on a one-month Treasury bill, is constant over time. They test and reject the model under this distributional assumption. Similarly, Hansen and Hodrick (1983) test and reject the restrictions imposed by the model on the joint behavior of spot and forward exchange rates under a different distributional assumption. As Hansen and Hodrick emphasize, however, 'a reasonable explanation [for these rejections] is that the [distributional] assumption[s] ... [are] too strong'. That is, these rejections may represent rejections of the distributional assumptions made and not of the model. Wheatley conducts similar tests of the model used in this paper and is unable to reject it.[7]

---

[5]This is also true of the continuous-time model that Stulz develops, although he argues that, if relative purchasing power parity does not hold, then foreign data are required to price domestic assets. Inspection of eq. (16) in his paper, however, reveals that in his model the expected instantaneous return on a domestic asset can be determined using only domestic data whether or not relative purchasing power parity holds.

[6]Tests of the model under weaker distributional assumptions have been conducted by Hansen and Singleton (1982), Jagannathan (1985), and Mark (1985).

[7]The restrictions that Hansen and Singleton and Hansen and Hodrick test, without consumption data, are not imposed by the model used in this paper. This model implies that differences in nominal returns must be independent of the information set composed of past real returns and past rates of real consumption growth. Hansen and Singleton test whether these differences are

Wheatley (1988) has also tested the restrictions imposed by the model on the unconditional means of the real returns facing a representative individual. Using U.S. monthly data from February 1959 to December 1981, he found that real asset returns and real consumption growth are significantly correlated. In addition, his results indicate that expected real asset returns and the covariances of these returns with real consumption growth are significantly positively correlated. Finally, his tests provide little evidence to reject the model, although estimates of a representative individual's relative risk aversion he computes are high.

The test of international equity market integration is a test of whether, for each country, foreign equities plot along that country's asset pricing line. The joint hypothesis that equity markets are integrated internationally and that the asset pricing model holds is rejected when foreign equities plot significantly off this line. The distance by which a foreign equity plots off a country's asset pricing line represents the difference between the expected real return facing that country's representative individual on the asset and the expected real return he would require on a domestic asset of equal risk.

Foreign equities can plot off the asset pricing line for several reasons. For example, suppose that the representative individual of a country faces a tax rate on long positions he takes in an equity and a corresponding subsidy rate on short positions.[8] Then the distance by which the equity plots off that country's asset pricing line will equal this tax rate. On the other hand, suppose the individual faces a tax rate on both long and short positions he takes in some foreign equity. Then the distance by which the equity plots off the country's asset pricing line will be less than or equal to this tax rate.[9]

Tests of international equity market integration are conducted using monthly data from the U.S. and seventeen other countries from January 1960 to December 1985. The results provide little evidence against the joint hypothesis that equity markets are integrated internationally and that the asset pricing model holds. These tests, however, do not have sufficient power to reject this joint hypothesis when deviations from the null hypothesis are small. For example, the standard errors of the estimates of the distances by which

---

independent of changes in the nominal return on a one-month bill. Hansen and Hodrick test whether differences in the nominal returns facing a domestic individual on foreign and domestic nominally riskless assets are independent of forward premiums. However, neither the change in the nominal return on a one-month bill nor forward premiums are contained in the information set composed of past real returns and past rates of real consumption growth.

[8] This tax can be viewed as representing the various barriers to international investment that the individual faces. It is costly to determine the extent of some of these barriers. For example, it is costly to determine the extent of the political risk one faces when investing abroad. In principle, estimates of the differences between the expected real returns the domestic representative individual faces on foreign equities and the expected real returns he faces on domestic assets of equal risk could be used to measure market estimates of barriers to international investment.

[9] Deviations from the model at the international level can occur in other ways. For example, if the asset pricing model does not correctly price assets.

portfolios of non-U.S. equities plot off the U.S. asset pricing line are always at least 3.77% per annum.

1.2. A comparison with some alternative tests

Tests of international equity market integration like those outlined here can in principle be conducted with some version of the mean–variance capital asset pricing model (CAPM). However, those tests and the tests outlined here require different data, because risk is measured differently in each model. In the consumption-based asset pricing model used here, the representative individual of a country measures an asset's risk by the covariance of its real return with the growth in his real consumption. In mean–variance asset pricing models this individual measures an asset's risk by the covariance of its real return with the real return on his portfolio.[10] The composition of this portfolio will depend on the extent to which asset markets are integrated internationally. Each model predicts that there will be an asset pricing line for each country that relates the expected real return facing the country's representative individual on each asset to the risk of the asset for this individual. Thus, tests of mean–variance asset pricing models can be conducted at the domestic level. Whether or not foreign assets plot on the domestic asset pricing line can also be tested with these models. Both tests, however, require return data for the domestic representative individual's portfolio. These data are not available but could, in principle, be constructed, using estimates of domestic holdings of foreign assets. Accurate estimates of these holdings are, unfortunately, difficult to find. The tests conducted here, on the other hand, require domestic real consumption data. These data, although available, are measured with error.

Under the hypothesis that asset markets are integrated internationally, mean–variance asset pricing models typically predict that the world market portfolio will be mean–variance efficient. Return data for proxies for this portfolio are available, so that tests of the joint hypothesis that equity markets are integrated internationally and that some version of the mean–variance asset pricing model holds can be conducted.[11] As Wallingford (1974) and Solnik (1977) point out, however, any large internationally diversified portfolio of equities is likely to be close to mean–variance efficient, whether or not equity markets are integrated internationally. Thus, tests like these can be without power as tests of international equity market integration.[12]

---

[10] The portfolio he holds will generally not be his country's market portfolio.

[11] Roll (1977) discusses problems that can arise when proxies are used in tests like these.

[12] This does not imply that under these conditions the question of whether equity markets are integrated internationally is unimportant. If the world market portfolio is mean–variance efficient, but asset markets are segmented internationally, then the cost of capital for a project will nevertheless generally depend on the country in which the capital is to be raised. This is because when asset markets are segmented internationally no individual will hold the world market portfolio. Instead, in each country individuals will hold that country's market portfolio.

1.3. A review of related empirical work

Although there is evidence that some asset markets have not always been integrated, the empirical evidence to date on whether or not equity markets are integrated internationally is inconclusive.[13] Solnik (1974) tests an international asset pricing model in which deviations from relative purchasing power parity can occur while individuals choose portfolios that are mean–variance efficient.[14] He finds little evidence against the asset pricing model and thus against the hypothesis that equity markets are integrated. Stehle (1977), on the other hand, tests an international asset pricing model in which relative purchasing power parity holds and in which individuals again choose portfolios that are mean–variance efficient. Stehle is able to reject both this asset pricing model and a domestic version of the mean–variance CAPM in favor of an unspecified alternative.

More recently, Errunza and Losq (1985) have tested an international asset pricing model in which individuals choose portfolios that are mean–variance efficient. They are able to reject this model and also an alternative model in which U.S. residents are unable to hold equities traded on exchanges in a group of less developed countries.[15] Jorion and Schwartz (1986), on the other hand, have tested an asset pricing model in which Canadians choose portfolios of U.S. and Canadian equities that are mean–variance efficient with respect to equities traded on U.S. and Canadian exchanges. They test and are able to reject this model in favor of an alternative model in which Canadians choose portfolios of only Canadian equities.

Each of these tests is a joint test of the hypothesis that equity markets are integrated internationally and of some mean–variance asset pricing model. Rejection of a joint hypothesis of this kind can arise either because equity markets are not integrated internationally or because the asset pricing model chosen does not hold. This paper tests the hypothesis that equity markets are integrated using an asset pricing model in which individuals choose portfolios in a way that can differ substantially from the way they are chosen in mean–variance asset pricing models. Section 2 introduces the asset pricing

---

With the model used in this paper, tests of the hypothesis that equity markets are integrated internationally that use some measure of aggregate world real consumption are also likely to lack power, because deviations from the model at the individual country level can cancel out on aggregation across countries.

[13] Dooley and Isard (1980), for example, found that between 1970 and 1974, rates on domestic Deutsche mark money-market instruments differed substantially at times from those on their external counterparts.

[14] An international asset pricing model refers here to an asset pricing model that assumes that asset markets are integrated internationally.

[15] This conclusion differs from theirs. Their description of their empirical results, however, does not correspond closely to those results.

model and describes how deviations from it can arise, and section 3 presents results of some tests of international equity market integration. Section 4 provides some conclusions.

2. The model

2.1. The model with no barriers to international investment

The model is a version of the consumption-based asset pricing model. In this model, it is assumed that: (A.1) asset markets are perfect, (A.2) within each country individuals are homogeneous and their number is constant through time, and (A.3) the representative individual of the kth country chooses a consumption and investment plan to maximize the expected value of a time-additive utility function,

$$E\left[\sum_{s=0}^{\infty} e^{-s\delta_k} u_k(c_s^k)|I_0^k\right], \qquad k = 1, 2, \ldots, K, \tag{1}$$

where E is the expectations operator, I_0^k all information available to the individual at time 0, δ_k his rate of time preference, c_s^k a vector containing the quantities of goods he consumes at time s, and $u_k(.)$ a single period von Neumann–Morgenstern utility function that is increasing, strictly concave, and differentiable. It is also assumed that: (A.4) the direct utility function, $u_k(.)$, is homothetic, that is, a monotonically increasing, strictly concave, and differentiable transform of a linear homogeneous function. With this assumption the individual can be viewed as choosing a consumption and investment plan to maximize

$$E\left[\sum_{s=0}^{\infty} e^{-s\delta_k} U_k(C_s^k)|I_0^k\right], \tag{2}$$

where $U_k(.)$ is the individual's indirect utility function and C_s^k is his real consumption at time s, defined to be his expenditure on goods that he consumes at time s, deflated by an index of commodity prices in the kth country.[16,17] Throughout the paper, any nominal variable deflated by this

---

[16]See, for example, Grauer and Litzenberger (1979) or Jagannathan (1985). This index will depend on the linearly homogeneous part of $u_k(.)$. If, for example, this part is Cobb–Douglas, then the index will be an expenditure-weighted geometric average of commodity prices in the kth country.

[17]As Rubinstein (1974) shows, the assumption that within each country individuals are homogeneous can be relaxed. For example, if within each country individuals share the same beliefs and rate of time preference, consume the same bundle of goods, and display constant relative risk-averse preferences, but have different endowments, then the joint time-series behavior of asset returns, the index of commodity prices in that country, and aggregate real consumption in that country will be determined as if individuals were homogeneous.

index will simply be referred to as the corresponding real variable facing the individual.

In this model, representative individuals from different countries need not consume the same basket of commodities, nor does the law of one price necessarily hold for each good.[18] Thus, the model allows for deviations from relative purchasing power parity arising from differences in tastes across countries and from deviations from the law of one price. A representative individual will generally hold a portfolio that helps hedge against changes in the price that he faces of the bundle of goods he consumes. If domestic assets are better hedges than foreign assets against changes in the domestic price of the domestic consumption bundle, then, as Stulz (1981a) notes, an individual can choose to hold a portfolio heavily weighted with domestic assets. Hence, the observation that individuals tend to hold portfolios heavily weighted with domestic assets is consistent with the predictions of this model.[19]

Let W_t^k be the vector of the individual's asset demands at time t, P_t^k the vector of real asset prices at time t, and Y_t^k the real labor income he receives at time t. Feasible consumption and investment plans must satisfy the sequence of budget constraints,[20]

$$C_t^k + W_t^{k\prime} P_t^k \leq W_{t-1}^{k\prime} P_t^k + Y_t^k. \tag{3}$$

The maximization of (2) subject to (3) yields the following first-order necessary conditions:[21]

$$\mathrm{E}\left[e^{-\delta_k} P_{jt}^k U_k'\left(C_t^k \right) \big| I_{t-1}^k \right] = P_{jt-1}^k U_k'\left(C_{t-1}^k \right), \qquad j = 1, 2, \ldots, N, \tag{4}$$

where P_{jt}^k is the real price facing the individual on the jth asset and $U_k'(C_t^k)$ is his marginal utility of real consumption. Eq. (4) states that in equilibrium the marginal utility the individual would lose by foregoing consumption at time $t-1$ to purchase more of the jth asset, the right-hand side of (4), must equal the discounted marginal utility he would expect to gain by selling this at time t and consuming the proceeds, the left-hand side of (4).

---

[18] The existence of restrictions on trade between countries will generally not lead to the segmentation of international asset markets. If no goods can ever be traded, however, asset markets will be completely segmented internationally.

[19] Black (1978) states, for example, that 'what we have to understand is not why foreign investment occurs, but why it isn't much more common'.

[20] The choice between labor and leisure is ignored here. If the individual's indirect utility function is an additively separable function of his real consumption and the hours of labor he supplies, then ignoring this choice will not alter the analysis that follows. On the other hand, this implies that the individual makes his consumption and labor supply decisions independently of one another.

[21] See, for example, Lucas (1978).

To make (4) testable, an assumption must be made about the individual's preferences. This paper considers a set of assumptions about both the individual's preferences and the joint distribution of his real consumption and the real asset returns he faces. This set of assumptions together with (4) leads to an empirically tractable set of restrictions on the joint distribution of the individual's real consumption and the real asset returns he faces.

Let $r_{jt}^k \equiv \log(P_{jt}^k / P_{jt-1}^k)$, the continuously compounded real return that the individual faces on the jth asset, $r_t^{k\prime} \equiv (r_{1t}^k, r_{2t}^k, \ldots, r_{Nt}^k)$, and $x_t^k \equiv \log(C_t^k / C_{t-1}^k)$, the continuously compounded growth in his real consumption. It is assumed that

(A.5) $U_k(C_t^k) = C_t^{k(1-\theta_k)}/(1-\theta_k),$

and

(A.6) $z_t' \equiv (r_t^{1\prime}, x_t^1, r_t^{2\prime}, x_t^2, \ldots, r_t^{K\prime}, x_t^K)$ is a stationary normal process.

Assumption A.5 states that the individual displays constant relative risk aversion of θ_k.[22] Combining (4) and assumptions A.5 and A.6 yields[23]

$$\mu_{r_j^k} + \left(\sigma_{r_j^k}^2/2\right) = \psi_k + \theta_k \sigma_{r_j^k x_k}, \tag{5}$$

where

$$\psi_k = \delta_k + \theta_k \mu_{x_k} - \theta_k^2\left(\sigma_{x_k}^2/2\right)$$

and where $\mu_{r_j^k}$ and $\sigma_{r_j^k}^2$ are the mean and variance of the real return facing the individual on the jth asset, r_{jt}^k, conditional on the information $\Phi_{t-1} \subseteq (z_{t-s}: s > 0)$, μ_{x_k} and $\sigma_{x_k}^2$ are the mean and variance of x_t^k conditional on Φ_{t-1}, $\sigma_{r_j^k x_k}$ is the covariance between r_{jt}^k and x_t^k conditional on Φ_{t-1}, and ψ_k is the real return facing the individual on an asset, existing or hypothetical, whose real return for him is certain. Note that the left-hand side of (5), $\mu_{r_j^k} + (\sigma_{r_j^k}^2/2)$, is the continuously compounded expected real return on the jth asset.

Eq. (5) states that the expected real return facing the individual on an asset, less the risk-free real rate for this individual, is proportional to the covariance of this return with the growth in his real consumption. In addition, (5) imposes

---

[22]Assumption A.6 does not imply that the distribution of real asset returns conditional on the set of state variables is unaffected by changes in those variables. Thus, this assumption does not imply that the investment opportunity set is constant through time. However, assumption A.6 does limit the ways in which state variables can affect this opportunity set. For example, the assumption that z_t is stationary implies that the expected real return on an asset, conditional on some nonstationary state variable, cannot be a stationary linear function of that variable.

[23]See Hansen and Singleton (1983).

restrictions on the serial dependence of the vector z_t. The assumption that z_t is a stationary normal process implies that $\sigma_{r_j^k}^2$, $\sigma_{x_k}^2$, and $\sigma_{r_j^k x_k}$ do not depend on Φ_{t-1}. It follows from (5) that $r_{jt}^k - \theta_k x_t^k$ must be independent of Φ_{t-1}. Thus, the model implies that the serial dependence of the real returns the individual faces and the growth in his real consumption are closely related. Inspection of (5) also reveals that the model can price domestic assets without foreign data. Thus, tests of the model can be conducted at the domestic level that require no assumption about the extent to which asset markets are integrated internationally.

The remainder of this section shows how assets located outside the kth country can plot off that country's asset pricing line when barriers to international investment exist.

2.2. The model with barriers to international investment

Mean–variance asset pricing models with explicit barriers to international investment appear in Black (1974) and Stulz (1981b). While Black models barriers to international investment as taxes on long positions in foreign assets, with corresponding subsidies on short positions, Stulz models them as taxes on both long and short positions. These taxes are an admittedly imperfect way of representing the various barriers to international investment that individuals can face. These barriers can be modeled in a similar fashion here.

In what follows, it is assumed that the jth asset is located outside the kth country. Assume that: (A.7) τ_j^k is a continuously compounded tax (subsidy) rate on long (short) positions taken in the jth asset by the representative individual of the kth country, taxes are levied on the individual's position at the end of each period, they are paid at the end of each period, and asset markets are otherwise perfect. Thus, if W_{jt-1}^k denotes the number of units of the jth asset held by the individual at time $t-1$ and P_{jt}^k the real price, facing the individual, of this asset at time t, then the real tax paid on his position in this asset will be $(1 - e^{-\tau_j^k}) W_{jt-1}^k P_{jt}^k$. Assumptions A.2–A.7 together imply that[24]

$$\mu_{r_j^k} + \left(\sigma_{r_j^k}^2/2 \right) = \tau_j^k + \psi_k + \theta_k \sigma_{r_j^k x_k}. \tag{6}$$

After-tax foreign assets will still plot on the asset pricing line (5). Before-tax, however, these assets will generally plot above this line. The distance by which a foreign asset plots off this line will equal the tax rate the individual faces on long positions taken in this asset. As Black points out, with barriers to

---

[24] Proofs of (6) and (7) appear in Wheatley (1985).

international investment modeled in this way, the individual faced with a high tax rate on an asset will take a large short position in that asset. Thus, the model cannot be used to describe a world in which asset markets are completely segmented internationally.

Assume instead that: (A.8) τ_j^k is a continuously compounded tax rate on both long and short positions taken in the jth asset by the representative individual of the kth country, taxes are levied on the individual's position at the end of each period, they are paid at the end of each period and asset markets are otherwise perfect. Then, under assumption A.8, the real tax the individual pays on long positions in this asset will be $(1 - e^{-\tau_j^k})W_{jt-1}^k P_{jt}^k$ and on short positions in this asset $(1 - e^{\tau_j^k})W_{jt-1}^k P_{jt}^k$. Assumptions A.2–A.6 and A.8 together imply that

$$\mu_{r_j^k} + \left(\sigma_{r_j^k}^2/2 \right) = \pi_j^k + \psi_k + \theta_k \sigma_{r_j^k x_k}, \tag{7}$$

where if the individual holds the jth asset long (short), then $\pi_j^k = \tau_j^k \ (-\tau_j^k)$, whereas if he does not hold this asset, then $-\tau_j^k \leq \pi_j^k \leq \tau_j^k$. Under these conditions, foreign assets will generally plot off, but not necessarily above, the asset pricing line (5). $|\pi_j^k|$ represents the distance by which the jth asset plots off this line. If the individual holds the jth asset long, this asset will generally plot above the line and, again, the distance by which it does so will equal the individual's tax rate on positions in this asset. This model can be used to describe a world in which asset markets are completely segmented internationally, since taxes that are sufficiently high will discourage all foreign investment by domestic residents.

3. Tests of international equity market integration

Tests of international equity market integration are conducted using monthly data from January 1960 to December 1985. Thus, it is implicitly assumed that the representative individual makes his consumption and investment decisions at monthly intervals. These tests use series of asset returns, spot and forward exchange rates, a measure of U.S. real consumption, and its corresponding implicit price deflator. The sources of these data are described below. Because these tests use consumption data only from the U.S., all subscripts and superscripts indicating this are, for convenience, dropped.

3.1. The data

3.1.1. Asset returns

The tests use series of monthly returns on the one-month U.S. Treasury bill, a portfolio of U.S. government bonds, a portfolio of U.S. corporate bonds, twenty portfolios of U.S. securities sorted by prior five-year average returns, a portfolio of American Depository Receipts (ADRs), and stock indices from seventeen countries.[25]

The Treasury bill, the government bond, and corporate bond returns are from Ibbotson and Sinquefield (1986). The twenty portfolios of U.S. securities were formed in the following way. For each year from 1960 to 1985, securities listed on the CRSP (Center for Research in Securities Prices) tapes that were not ADRs for which monthly return data were available over the preceding five years were placed in one of twenty approximately equally sized portfolios on the basis of their average returns over that five-year period. Thus, for example, for 1960, securities were placed in portfolios on the basis of their average returns computed for the 1955–1959 period. In each year, the 5% of securities with the highest average returns over the preceding five-year period were placed in the first portfolio, the 5% with the next highest returns were placed in the second portfolio, and so on. In each portfolio an equal investment was made in each security. If a security was delisted during a year, it was sold at the beginning of the month in which it was delisted and the proceeds were reinvested equally among the remaining securities in the portfolio to which it belonged. Monthly returns on these twenty portfolios were computed from January 1960 to December 1985. This portfolio formation procedure was chosen to produce variation in expected real return among portfolios and thus, given the asset pricing model, variation in risk. On the other hand, since securities were placed in portfolios solely on the basis of average returns computed over previous months, this procedure produces no bias.[26] An equally weighted portfolio of ADRs was formed from all ADRs listed on the CRSP tapes. Monthly returns on this portfolio were also computed from January 1960 to December 1985.

The remaining seventeen non-U.S. stock indices used in the tests are the Capital International national indices for Australia, Austria, Belgium, Canada, Denmark, France, Germany, Hong Kong, Italy, Japan, the Netherlands, Norway, Singapore, Spain, Sweden, Switzerland, and the U.K. Capital International S.A. (Geneva) provided end-of-month market values from December 1959 to December 1985 for all indices but Hong Kong and Singapore, for which it provided these data from December 1969 to December 1985. It also provided dividend yields on most of these indices from January 1969 to

---

[25]American Depository Receipts are non-U.S. equities traded in the U.S. The certificates of ownership are typically deposited with a U.S. bank.

[26]A presumably very small bias could be introduced by the sale of securities in the month prior to their delisting. An alternative procedure would be to form portfolios on the basis of out-of-period estimates of consumption betas. However, because consumption betas are estimated imprecisely it is not clear that this procedure would lead to more powerful tests of the asset pricing model than those conducted here.

December 1985.[27] Using these data and dividend yields provided by R.G. Ibbotson and Associates for months where these yields had not been provided by Capital International, monthly with-dividend returns on the seventeen indices were computed.[28] These returns were computed from January 1960 to December 1985 for all indices but Hong Kong and Singapore, for which they were computed from January 1970 to December 1985.

3.1.2. Exchange rates

End-of-month spot exchange rates versus the U.S. dollar were either collected or computed from the International Monetary Fund's *International Financial Statistics* for all currencies except the Hong Kong and Singapore dollars from December 1959 to December 1985. These rates were computed from the same source for the Singapore dollar from December 1969 to December 1985. For the Hong Kong dollar they were taken from Pick's currency yearbook from December 1969 to December 1983 and from the *Financial Times* from January 1984 to December 1985.

End-of-month one-month forward exchange premiums versus sterling were collected from the *Financial Times* and the *Times* from December 1959 to November 1985 for the Austrian schilling, the Belgian franc, the Canadian dollar, the Danish krone, the Deutsche mark, the Dutch guilder, the French franc, the Italian lira, the Norwegian krone, the Swedish krona, the Swiss franc, and the U.S. dollar.

3.1.3. Consumption and prices

U.S. consumption and price series were taken from various issues of the *Survey of Current Business*. The measure of real consumption used is the real consumption of nondurables.[29] This series is seasonally adjusted and in constant 1972 dollars and was converted into per capita terms using popula-

---

[27]Before 1969, Capital International did not compute dividend yields on these indices.

[28]R.G. Ibbotson and Associates collected dividend yields from a variety of sources. These data are described in detail in Ibbotson, Carr, and Robinson (1982). Neither Capital International nor R.G. Ibbotson and Associates provided a dividend yield on the index of Hong Kong stocks from January 1970 to March 1970. Instead, the yield on this index for April 1970 was used as a proxy for this yield in each of these months.

[29]Hansen and Singleton (1983) note that the use of this measure corresponds to a test of an asset pricing model that differs somewhat from the model described in section 2. They show that if the representative individual's single-period utility is an additively separable function of some component of real consumption and of other components of real consumption, then a relation similar to (4) will hold for that component of real consumption. If, in addition, assumptions A.5 and A.6 are modified in an appropriate way, a relation similar to (5) will hold for that component of real consumption.

tion data from the Bureau of the Census.[30] Consumption of durables is excluded from the data, because of the difficulty of determining the flow of services yielded by the stock of durables.[31] Nominal returns are converted to real returns using the implicit price deflator for nondurables. This series of implicit price deflators is also seasonally adjusted.

3.2. Testing procedures

The assumption that z_t is a stationary normal process implies that

$$r_t = \alpha + \beta x_t + v_t, \tag{8}$$

where

$$\alpha' = (\alpha_1, \alpha_2, \dots, \alpha_N), \qquad\qquad \beta' = (\beta_1, \beta_2, \dots, \beta_N),$$

$$\beta_j = \sigma_{r_j x}/\sigma_x^2, \quad j = 1, 2, \dots, N, \qquad v_t' = (v_{1t}, v_{2t}, \dots, v_{Nt}),$$

$$E(v_t) = 0, \qquad\qquad E(v_t v_t') = \Omega,$$

and where, from here on, all means, variances, and covariances are unconditional. Tests are conducted of

$$\mathrm{H}_1: \quad \beta = 0,$$

$$\mathrm{H}_2: \quad \alpha_j = \tau_j + \psi - \left(\sigma_{r_j}^2/2\right) + \beta_j\left(\theta\sigma_x^2 - \mu_x\right), \quad j = 1, 2, \dots, N,$$

$$\tau_j = 0, \quad j = n + 1, n + 2, \dots, N,$$

$$\mathrm{H}_3: \quad \alpha_j = \psi - \left(\sigma_{r_j}^2/2\right) + \beta_j\left(\theta\sigma_x^2 - \mu_x\right), \quad j = 1, 2, \dots, N,$$

where assets are numbered so that the first n assets are located outside the U.S., while the remaining $N - n$ are U.S. assets. H_2 states only that U.S. assets satisfy the asset pricing model (5). H_3, on the other hand, states that all assets satisfy this model. The tests of H_3 reported here are tests of H_3 against the alternative H_2.

It is likely that the real consumption series is measured with error. Let the measured logarithm of the representative individual's real consumption be

---

[30] The use of a seasonally adjusted measure of real consumption also corresponds to a test of an asset pricing model that differs somewhat from the model described above. It can be shown to correspond to a test of a model in which the utility the representative individual derives from a particular level of real consumption depends on the season.

[31] Dunn and Singleton (1986) and Eichenbaum and Hansen (1987) test models in which durables yield an explicit flow of services.

given by

$$\log(\hat{C}_t) = \log(C_t) + \varepsilon_t,\tag{9}$$

where ε_t is a zero-mean normal white noise process that is independent of the information set Φ_s for all s. Then the measured growth in the individual's real consumption will be given by

$$\hat{x}_t = x_t + \varepsilon_t - \varepsilon_{t-1}.\tag{10}$$

Inspection of (5) reveals that the restrictions it imposes on the unconditional mean of the real return vector r_t continue to hold if measured real consumption growth $\hat{x}_t$ replaces true real consumption growth x_t. Thus, the actual and stated sizes of tests of the model's restrictions on the unconditional mean of r_t will be equal when real consumption is measured with random error. The presence of measurement error, however, does reduce the power of these tests.

From (10), the time series behavior of $\hat{x}_t$ and x_t will generally differ. Consequently, the actual sizes of tests of the model's restrictions on the serial dependence of the vector z_t, which use consumption data, will exceed the stated sizes of these tests when real consumption is measured with random error. However, under the assumption that the model holds and that real consumption is measured with random error, inferences can be made from the joint time series behavior of r_t and $\hat{x}_t$ about the time series behavior of x_t. Panel A of table 1 displays sample autocorrelation coefficients for measured real consumption growth and the real return on a value-weighted index of New York Stock Exchange stocks (hereafter, the U.S. market) and panel B of that table displays sample cross-correlation coefficients between these two series. Measured real consumption growth is significantly contemporaneously correlated with the real return on the U.S. market but the noncontemporaneous cross-correlations are generally insignificant. The model implies that, if r_t is uncorrelated with x_{t-s} for all $s > 0$, then x_t must be serially uncorrelated. Panel A of table 1 indicates that measured real consumption growth is not serially uncorrelated. However, if true real consumption growth is serially uncorrelated, but real consumption is measured with random error, then, from (10), measured real consumption growth will follow an MA(1) process. The sample autocorrelations reported in table 1 are consistent with this hypothesis.

More powerful tests of H_2 and H_3 can be produced by taking into account the presence of measurement error. It is assumed in what follows that true real consumption growth x_t is serially uncorrelated and real consumption is measured with random error. Measured real consumption growth $\hat{x}_t$, while given by (10), can alternatively be written as

$$\hat{x}_t = \mu_x + \eta_t - \phi\eta_{t-1},\tag{11}$$

Table 1

Panel A: Sample autocorrelations, means, standard deviations, and studentized ranges of U.S. real consumption growth and the real return on the U.S. market, measured by a value-weighted index of New York Stock Exchange stocks, computed using monthly data from January 1960 to December 1985. (Sample means and standard deviations are multiplied by 100. The standard error of the sample autocorrelations is about 0.06 under the hypothesis that the true autocorrelations are zero.)

Statistic	U.S. real consumption growth, $\hat{x}_t$	Real return on U.S. market, r_{mt}
Autocorrelation at lag:		
1	-0.36	0.08
2	-0.03	-0.03
3	0.13	0.04
4	-0.05	0.08
5	0.01	0.12
6	-0.05	-0.06
7	0.03	-0.09
8	0.01	-0.06
9	-0.04	0.05
10	0.02	-0.03
11	0.09	-0.03
12	-0.03	0.04
Mean	0.12	0.39
Standard deviation	0.86	4.31
Studentized range	7.02^a	6.68^a

Panel B: Sample cross-correlations between U.S. real consumption growth and the real return on the U.S. market, measured by a value-weighted index of New York Stock Exchange stocks, computed using monthly data from January 1960 to December 1985. (The standard error of the sample cross-correlations is about 0.06 under the hypothesis that the true cross-correlations are zero.)

Lag s	Cross-correlation between the real return on the U.S. market at lag s and U.S. real consumption growth	Lag s	Cross-correlation between the real return on the U.S. market at lag s and U.S. real consumption growth
-12	0.00	1	0.01
-11	0.01	2	0.03
-10	-0.12	3	0.11
-9	0.10	4	0.04
-8	0.07	5	0.04
-7	-0.05	6	-0.08
-6	-0.02	7	0.14
-5	-0.05	8	-0.06
-4	-0.01	9	0.02
-3	0.00	10	0.02
-2	-0.02	11	0.05
-1	-0.04	12	0.03
0	0.14		

Panel C: Estimated MA(1) model for U.S. real consumption growth using monthly data from January 1960 to December 1985. (L denotes the lag operator. Standard errors are in parentheses.)

$$\hat{x}_t = \underset{(0.0003)}{0.0012} + (1 - \underset{(0.0520)}{0.3953} \, L)\eta_t \qquad s(\eta_t) = 0.0079$$

---

^{a}Exceeds the 0.95 fractile of the distribution of the studentized range.

where ϕ is a function of the ratio $\sigma_x^2/\sigma_\epsilon^2$, σ_ϵ^2 is the variance of ϵ_t, and η_t is white noise. Let $a(L)$ be a two-sided infinite-order polynomial in the lag operator L. Appendix 1 demonstrates that the correlation coefficient between $\tilde{x}_t = a(L)\hat{x}_t$ and x_t will reach a maximum when $a(L) = (1 - \phi^2)[(1 - \phi L^{-1}) \times (1 - \phi L)]^{-1}$. Thus, the two-sided filter $\tilde{x}_t = (1 - \phi^2)[(1 - \phi L^{-1})(1 - \phi L)]^{-1}\hat{x}_t$ can be thought of as the best instrument for x_t. In practice, ϕ, and so $\tilde{x}_t$, has to be estimated. However, simulation evidence provided in appendix 2 indicates that the use of the maximum likelihood estimate of $\tilde{x}_t$ in place of $\hat{x}_t$ produces more efficient estimates of the model's parameters. Because of this evidence, only the results of tests of the model that use estimates of $\tilde{x}_t$ are reported. On the other hand, tests that used $\hat{x}_t$ were conducted and are discussed. An estimated MA(1) model for $\hat{x}_t$ appears in panel C of table 1. A series of estimates of $\tilde{x}_t$ was produced using the estimate of ϕ taken from this table.

As Hansen and Singleton (1983) note, the likelihood function for a sample $(r_t, x_t, \ t = 1, 2, \ldots, T)$, under H_2 and under H_3, cannot be concentrated, as α is a function of parameters in Ω. To avoid the computational burden involved in maximizing this likelihood function with respect to the parameters ψ, θ, β, μ_x, σ_x^2, and Ω, an alternate procedure is used to estimate these parameters and test H_2 and H_3. The details of this procedure are described in Wheatley (1985). Briefly, this procedure replaces variances in H_2 and H_3 with their sample counterparts and then estimates the parameters of the model and tests these restrictions using an iterative maximum likelihood procedure. This procedure is similar to an iterative scheme outlined, but not used, by Gibbons (1982). The standard errors of the estimates are produced under the assumption that the variances in H_2 and H_3 have been replaced by their true values, while the test statistics produced are compared with their theoretical asymptotic distributions under that assumption.

Appendix 2 reports the results of simulations conducted to investigate the properties of these estimators and test statistics. The results provide little evidence against the hypothesis that the estimators are unbiased. The results also indicate, however, that the mean asymptotic standard errors computed of the estimators of ψ and θ understate the simulated standard deviations of these estimators by about one-quarter when $T = 312$ and by about one-half when $T = 154$. On the other hand, the mean asymptotic standard errors computed of the estimators of the distance τ_j and its average across countries are close to the simulated standard deviations of these estimators. The likelihood ratio statistics for tests of H_2 and H_3 reject those hypotheses too often when critical values are based on their theoretical asymptotic distributions under the assumption that the variances in H_2 and H_3 have been replaced by their true values. This finding does not affect the interpretation of the results reported below, as these hypotheses cannot be rejected.

Table 2

Sample statistics for a series of real returns facing a representative U.S. individual on U.S. assets and on non-U.S. portfolios. These statistics are computed using monthly data from January 1960 to December 1985 for all assets except the Hong Kong and Singapore stock portfolios, for which they are computed using monthly data from January 1970 to December 1985.

Portfolio or asset j	Mean[a]	Standard deviation	Skewness	Kurtosis	Studentized range
Panel A: U.S. assets					
One-month Treasury bill	0.14	0.39	−0.04	4.43	6.75[b]
Govt. bonds	0.09	2.87	0.51	6.03	8.16[c]
Corp. bonds	0.13	2.78	0.52	6.29	8.26[c]
Panel B: U.S. stock portfolios ranked by prior five-year average return (portfolio 1 lowest, portfolio 20 highest)					
1	0.15	6.78	−0.21	3.84	6.86[b]
2	0.49	6.08	−0.47	4.23	7.08[c]
3	0.33	5.63	−0.50	4.11	6.36
4	0.51	5.44	−0.45	4.32	6.72[b]
5	0.58	5.30	−0.53	4.76	6.87[b]
6	0.62	5.22	−0.51	4.33	6.95[b]
7	0.76	5.07	−0.32	4.09	7.00[b]
8	0.65	5.16	−0.36	4.99	8.03[c]
9	0.71	4.87	−0.30	4.98	8.17[c]
10	0.69	4.79	−0.26	4.79	8.10[c]
11	0.62	4.85	−0.06	5.10	8.75[c]
12	0.73	4.78	0.24	6.57	8.95[c]
13	0.76	4.72	0.10	5.83	8.87[c]
14	0.77	4.80	−0.09	6.02	9.44[c]
15	0.83	4.97	0.19	6.91	9.73[c]
16	0.84	5.17	0.26	6.84	9.65[c]
17	0.82	5.24	0.52	8.88	10.70[c]
18	0.76	5.63	0.19	7.15	9.88[c]
19	0.91	6.15	0.73	7.89	9.97[c]
20	1.08	7.50	0.85	7.58	9.37[c]
Panel C: Non-U.S. stock portfolios					
ADR[d]	0.49	6.03	0.20	4.78	7.88[c]
Australia	0.26	6.47	−0.56	7.13	8.88[c]
Austria	0.45	4.19	1.10	9.08	8.90[c]
Belgium	0.55	4.65	−0.17	5.77	7.73[c]
Canada	0.36	5.20	−0.57	5.62	8.20[c]
Denmark	0.51	4.36	−0.11	5.65	8.52[c]
France	0.24	6.32	−0.23	4.89	7.92[c]
Germany	0.52	5.52	0.05	3.95	6.92[b]
Hong Kong	1.27	11.73	−0.66	6.24	8.47[c]
Italy	−0.01	6.87	−0.07	3.52	6.43
Japan	0.89	5.42	−0.10	3.66	5.99
Netherlands	0.53	5.21	−0.20	5.12	8.54[c]
Norway	0.49	6.60	−0.15	5.76	8.26[c]
Singapore	0.58	9.78	0.56	6.01	6.92[b]
Spain	0.27	5.11	−0.99	8.38	9.46[c]
Sweden	0.55	5.24	0.02	3.67	6.74[b]
Switzerland	0.53	5.62	−0.08	4.02	7.09[c]
U.K.	0.47	6.61	0.65	9.58	9.72[c]

[a] Means and standard deviations are multiplied by 100.
[b] Exceeds the 0.95 fractile of the distribution of the studentized range.
[c] Exceeds the 0.99 fractile of the distribution of the studentized range.
[d] An ADR is an American Depository Receipt.

S. Wheatley, Tests of international equity market integration 195

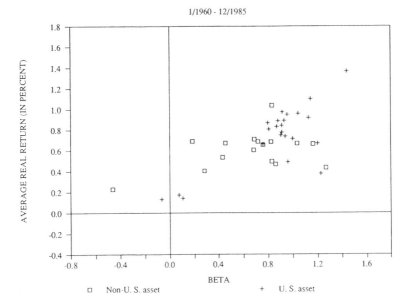

Fig. 1. Scatter plot of the average real return (in percent) facing the representative U.S. individual, $\hat{\mu}_{r_j} + (\hat{\sigma}_{r_j}^2/2)$, versus the estimate of beta, $\hat{\beta}_j$, for twenty U.S. stock portfolios, a one-month U.S. Treasury bill, a U.S. government bond portfolio, a U.S. corporate bond portfolio, and sixteen portfolios of non-U.S. stocks, where these estimates are computed using monthly data from January 1960 to December 1985.

3.3. The results

Table 2 presents summary statistics for the series of real returns facing the representative U.S. individual on U.S. assets and on non-U.S. portfolios. The sample means of the real returns vary substantially. For most of these series the studentized ranges are large enough that the hypothesis that each series was drawn from a normal distribution can be rejected at conventional significance levels. In addition, there appears to be a curious regularity: the real returns on portfolios of U.S. stocks with high historical average returns tend to be positively skewed, whereas the real returns on portfolios of stocks with low historical average returns tend to be negatively skewed.

Fig. 1 plots the estimate of the expected real return facing the representative U.S. individual $\hat{\mu}_{r_j} + (\hat{\sigma}_{r_j}^2/2)$ (hereafter, the average real return) against the estimate of beta computed using U.S. real consumption, $\hat{\beta}_j$ for the twenty U.S. stock portfolios, the one-month U.S. Treasury bill, the U.S. government bond portfolio, the U.S. corporate bond portfolio, and the sixteen portfolios of

Table 3

Likelihood ratio statistics for tests of the consumption-based asset pricing model and maximum likelihood estimates of the U.S. risk-free real return and a representative U.S. individual's relative risk aversion, computed using U.S. real consumption growth, a one-month U.S. Treasury bill, a U.S. government bond portfolio, a U.S. corporate bond portfolio, twenty U.S. stock portfolios, eighteen portfolios of non-U.S. stocks, and monthly data from January 1960 to December 1985. (P-values are in parentheses.)[a]

H_1: Real asset returns are uncorrelated with U.S. real consumption growth.
H_2: The consumption-based asset pricing model holds for U.S. assets.
H_3: The consumption-based asset pricing model holds for U.S. and non-U.S. assets.

| | Panel A | | Panel B | | Panel C | | Panel D | |
| | January 1960 to December 1985 | | January 1960 to February 1973 | | March 1973 to December 1985 | | Non-U.S. assets covered against exchange-rate changes January 1960 to December 1985 | |
	Statistic	Standard error of statistic	Statistic	Standard error of statistic	Statistic	Standard error of statistic	Statistic	Standard error of statistic
Likelihood ratio statistics for tests of the consumption-based asset pricing model								
For H_1[b]	69.846 (0.002)		56.405 (0.035)		56.515 (0.054)		65.306 (0.001)	
For H_2	18.567 (0.613)		21.727 (0.415)		11.815 (0.945)		18.567 (0.613)	
For H_3 against H_2	14.024 (0.597)		21.287 (0.168)		16.113 (0.585)		12.923 (0.375)	

Maximum likelihood estimates, under H_2 and H_3, of the U.S. risk-free real return ψ and a representative U.S. individual's relative risk aversion θ

U.S. risk-free real return ψ, under H_2 [c]	0.003 (0.483)	0.062	0.056 (0.147)	0.054	0.117	−0.063 (0.705)	0.003 (0.483)	0.062
A representative U.S. individual's relative risk aversion θ, under H_2 [d]	180.318 (0.000)	62.539	361.085 (0.000)	155.222	64.083	161.166 (0.000)	180.318 (0.000)	62.539
U.S. risk-free real return ψ, under H_3 [c]	0.058 (0.047)	0.035	0.047 (0.070)	0.032	0.055	0.059 (0.143)	0.066 (0.020)	0.032
A representative U.S. individual's relative risk aversion θ, under H_3 [d]	102.319 (0.000)	26.823	207.084 (0.000)	51.991	26.225	83.360 (0.000)	93.935 (0.000)	25.809

[a] The statistics in panels A and B are computed using sixteen non-U.S. stock portfolios, those in panel C are computed using eighteen non-U.S. stock portfolios, and those in panel D are computed using twelve non-U.S. stock portfolios.

[b] The likelihood ratio statistics for tests of H_1 are asymptotically χ^2_{39}, χ^2_{39}, χ^2_{41}, and χ^2_{35} in panels A, B, C, and D, for tests of H_2 they are asymptotically χ^2_{21} in all four panels, and for tests of H_3 against the alternative H_2 they are asymptotically χ^2_{16}, χ^2_{16}, χ^2_{18}, and χ^2_{12} in panels A, B, C, and D.

[c] Estimates of ψ and their standard errors are multiplied by 100. P-values in parentheses are for tests of the hypothesis that $\psi \le 0$.

[d] P-values in parentheses are for tests of the hypothesis that $\theta \le 0$.

non-U.S. stocks for which data were available from January 1960 to December 1985. The hypothesis H_2 states that the expected real return facing this individual on each U.S. asset will be a linear function of its consumption beta computed using U.S. real consumption. On the other hand, H_3 states that the expected real return the individual faces on every asset, whether U.S. or non-U.S., will be a linear function of its consumption beta computed using U.S. real consumption. This figure lends some support to these hypotheses. Average real returns on both U.S. and non-U.S. portfolios of equities appear to be positively related to their consumption betas.[32] Panel A of table 3 presents likelihood ratio statistics for tests of the asset pricing model and estimates of the U.S. risk-free real return and the representative U.S. individual's relative risk aversion, computed using these data. Panel A of table 4, on the other hand, presents estimates of the distances by which non-U.S. assets plot above the U.S. asset pricing line.[33] The results offer little evidence against the model. Non-U.S. portfolios do not plot significantly above or below the U.S. asset pricing line, either individually, as a group or on average. However, the standard errors of the estimates of the distances by which these portfolios plot off the U.S. asset pricing line are large; they lie between 0.35% and 0.81% per month. This implies that a single non-U.S. portfolio would need to plot off the asset pricing line by more than 0.68% per month, or 8.18% per annum, for the null hypothesis to be rejected at the 5% significance level.[34] The standard error of the distance by which non-U.S. portfolios plot on average above or below the U.S. asset pricing line is 0.30% per month. Thus, non-U.S. portfolios would need to plot on average above or below the U.S. asset pricing line by more than 0.59% per month, or 7.04% per annum, for the null hypothesis to be rejected at the 5% significance level.[35,36]

---

[32] The average real returns on the non-U.S. portfolios appear to be lower on average than those on the U.S. portfolios. In particular, the average real return on the portfolio of Italian stocks is close to that on the U.S. Treasury bill. On the other hand, estimates of the consumption betas of the non-U.S. portfolios appear to be lower on average than those of the U.S. portfolios, and the estimate of the consumption beta of the portfolio of Italian stocks is actually negative. Note, however, the U.S. portfolios are equally weighted while the non-U.S. portfolios are value-weighted. Consequently, this evidence should not be interpreted as an indication that non-U.S. equities are on average less risky for the representative U.S. individual than are U.S. equities.

[33] The residuals from each regression were checked for the presence of heteroskedasticity using White's (1980) procedure. For only one of the 39 regressions could the hypothesis of homoskedasticity be rejected at the 5% significance level. Similar results are found in subsequent tables.

[34] Alternatively, a single non-U.S. portfolio would need to plot above the asset pricing line by more than 0.57% per month, or 6.86% per annum, for the null hypothesis to be rejected in favor of the alternative that foreign assets plot above that line at the 5% significance level.

[35] Alternatively, non-U.S. portfolios would need to plot on average above the U.S. asset pricing line by more than 0.49% per month, or 5.91% per annum, for the null hypothesis to be rejected in favor of the alternative that foreign assets plot on average above that line at the 5% significance level.

[36] Note that the asymptotic standard errors of the estimators of θ depend on θ. The p-values reported for tests of the hypothesis that $\theta \leq 0$ are based on test statistics computed under the assumption that $\theta = 0$.

S. *Wheatley, Tests of international equity market integration* 199

Table 4

Maximum likelihood estimates of the distance by which each non-U.S. asset plots above the U.S. asset pricing line τ_j, computed using U.S. real consumption growth, a one-month U.S. Treasury bill, a U.S. government bond portfolio, a U.S. corporate bond portfolio, twenty U.S. stock portfolios, eighteen portfolios of non-U.S. stocks, and monthly data from January 1960 to December 1985. (Estimates and standard errors are multiplied by 100. *P*-values are in parentheses).

	Panel A		Panel B		Panel C		Panel D	
							Non-U.S. assets covered against exchange-rate changes	
	January 1960 to December 1985		January 1960 to February 1973		March 1973 to December 1985		January 1960 to December 1985	
Portfolio	Distance estimate	Standard error	Distance estimate	Standard error	Distance estimate	Standard error	Distance estimate	Standard error
ADR[a]	−0.377 (0.448)	0.497	−1.067 (0.334)	1.104	−0.112 (0.865)	0.660		
Australia	−0.314 (0.607)	0.611	−1.127 (0.365)	1.245	−0.050 (0.957)	0.916		
Austria	−0.030 (0.946)	0.441	0.500 (0.472)	0.696	−0.605 (0.396)	0.713	0.045 (0.896)	0.346
Belgium	−0.279 (0.545)	0.461	−1.017 (0.234)	0.854	−0.053 (0.939)	0.701	−0.310 (0.418)	0.383
Canada	−0.245 (0.481)	0.348	−0.209 (0.707)	0.556	−0.665 (0.229)	0.553	−0.164 (0.603)	0.314
Denmark	−0.233 (0.608)	0.455	−0.312 (0.701)	0.813	−0.285 (0.657)	0.643	−0.385 (0.369)	0.429
France	−1.088 (0.122)	0.704	−1.829 (0.161)	1.304	−1.220 (0.218)	0.991	−1.014 (0.096)	0.610
Germany	0.064 (0.903)	0.525	0.278 (0.796)	1.074	−0.106 (0.882)	0.717	0.150 (0.739)	0.450
Hong Kong					−3.216 (0.100)	1.954		
Italy	1.202 (0.139)	0.812	3.311 (0.085)	1.922	1.197 (0.288)	1.128	1.062 (0.173)	0.779
Japan	0.098 (0.860)	0.555	0.223 (0.851)	1.187	−0.214 (0.778)	0.758		
Netherlands	−0.593 (0.236)	0.500	−1.858 (0.103)	1.139	−0.403 (0.536)	0.652	−0.376 (0.380)	0.428
Norway	−0.119 (0.856)	0.655	0.406 (0.631)	0.844	−0.314 (0.761)	1.030	−0.082 (0.891)	0.600
Singapore					−1.479 (0.218)	1.201		
Spain	0.045 (0.930)	0.513	0.558 (0.461)	0.758	−0.372 (0.651)	0.822		
Sweden	0.653 (0.196)	0.504	0.339 (0.690)	0.850	0.953 (0.258)	0.843	0.726 (0.121)	0.468

continued overleaf

Table 4   (continued)

Portfolio	Panel A January 1960 to December 1985 Distance estimate	Panel A Standard error	Panel B January 1960 to February 1973 Distance estimate	Panel B Standard error	Panel C March 1973 to December 1985 Distance estimate	Panel C Standard error	Panel D Non-U.S. assets covered against exchange-rate changes January 1960 to December 1985 Distance estimate	Panel D Standard error
Switzerland	−0.335 (0.515)	0.514	−0.520 (0.644)	1.127	−0.535 (0.444)	0.698	−0.199 (0.643)	0.429
U.K.	−0.145 (0.810)	0.602	0.309 (0.745)	0.948	−0.318 (0.738)	0.951	−0.410 (0.459)	0.554
Average across countries	−0.106 (0.723)	0.299	−0.126 (0.790)	0.475	−0.433 (0.366)	0.480	−0.080 (0.739)	0.239

[a]An ADR is an American Depository Receipt.

The estimates of the representative U.S. individual's relative risk aversion are of the same order of magnitude as those produced by Hansen and Singleton (1983) under the restrictions imposed by the model on unconditional mean real returns. On the other hand, they are an order of magnitude higher than those produced by Friend and Blume (1975). However, Garber and King (1983) show that the first-order necessary condition for a representative producer can resemble (4). Thus, the tests in this paper could be interpreted as being based on that condition. Consequently, the estimates of relative risk aversion reported here may really be estimates of the reciprocal of the intertemporal elasticity of substitution in production and not consumption.

It is likely that the joint distribution of U.S. real consumption growth and real asset returns is not stationary over the entire period January 1960 to December 1985. In particular, it is likely that this distribution changed with the introduction of flexible exchange rates in March 1973. Let the subscript i denote the exchange rate regime. The likelihood ratio statistic for a test of the hypothesis $\Omega_i = \Omega$, $i = 1, 2$ (with α_{ij}, β_{ij} unrestricted), which is χ^2_{780} under this hypothesis, is 1,587.57 with a p-value of 0.00. On the other hand, the likelihood ratio statistic for a test of the hypothesis $\alpha_{ij} = \alpha_j$, $\beta_{ij} = \beta_j$, $i = 1, 2$, $j = 1, 2, \ldots, 39$ (with Ω_i unrestricted), which is χ^2_{78} under that hypothesis, is 82.90 with a p-value of 0.33. The estimates of the U.S. and non-U.S. assets' betas are quite stable. For example, among the sixteen non-U.S. assets that had return data available over both subperiods, in each subperiod the Italian index had the lowest estimated beta and the French and

S. Wheatley, Tests of international equity market integration   201

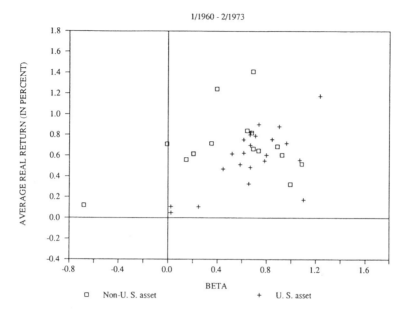

Fig. 2. Scatter plot of the average real return (in percent) facing the representative U.S. individual, $\hat{\mu}_{r_j} + (\hat{\sigma}_{r_j}^2/2)$, versus the estimate of beta, $\hat{\beta}_j$, for twenty U.S. stock portfolios, a one-month U.S. Treasury bill, a U.S. government bond portfolio, a U.S. corporate bond portfolio, and sixteen portfolios of non-U.S. stocks, where these estimates are computed using monthly data from January 1960 to February 1973.

Dutch indices had the highest pair of estimated betas. Because of the non-stationarity of the joint distribution of U.S. real consumption growth and real asset returns across the two subperiods, however, the model was tested separately in each subperiod.[37]

Figs. 2 and 3 plot average real returns facing U.S. residents against estimates of betas for these two subperiods. Fig. 2 does not appear to lend support to either H_2, the hypothesis that the asset pricing model holds for U.S. assets, or H_3, the hypothesis that the asset pricing model holds for U.S. and non-U.S. assets, for the 1960–1973 subperiod. Since expected real returns and betas have been estimated over a shorter period, however, the estimates of these parameters and of the distances by which assets plot off the asset pricing line are likely to have larger standard errors. On the other hand, fig. 3 lends some support for H_2 but less support for H_3 for the 1973–1985 subperiod.

---

[37]The model was also tested over the whole period, January 1960 to December 1985, allowing Ω_i to take on different values in each regime. The results of these tests are similar to those reported in tables 3 and 4.

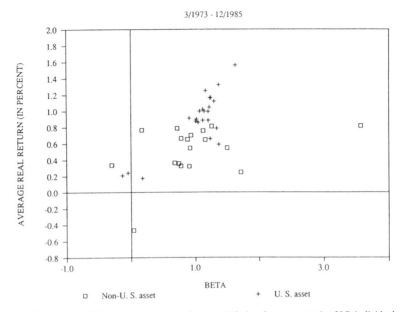

Fig. 3. Scatter plot of the average real return (in percent) facing the representative U.S. individual, $\hat{\mu}_{r_j} + (\hat{\sigma}_{r_j}^2/2)$, versus the estimate of beta, $\hat{\beta}_j$, for twenty U.S. stock portfolios, a one-month U.S. Treasury bill, a U.S. government bond portfolio, a U.S. corporate bond portfolio, and eighteen portfolios of non-U.S. stocks, where these estimates are computed using monthly data from March 1973 to December 1985.

Panels B and C of tables 3 and 4 present the results of tests of the asset pricing model over these subperiods. In the first subperiod the hypothesis that the Italian portfolio plots on the U.S. asset pricing line can be rejected at the 10% significance level, while in the second subperiod the hypothesis that the Hong Kong portfolio plots on the U.S. asset pricing line can also just be rejected at this level. Apart from this, however, non-U.S. portfolios do not appear to plot significantly above or below the U.S. asset pricing line, either individually or as a group. Again, however, the standard errors of the estimates of the distances by which these assets plot off the U.S. asset pricing line are large and are even larger than those in table 3 for the 1960–1985 sample period.

Test statistics for the hypothesis that non-U.S. assets plot on the U.S. asset pricing line over both subperiods can be formed from the results reported in panels B and C of table 4. Each test statistic is given by $\sum_{i=1}^{2}[\hat{\tau}_{ij}/s(\hat{\tau}_{ij})]^2$, where the subscript i again refers to the subperiod, $\hat{\tau}_{ij}$ is the maximum likelihood estimate of τ_{ij}, and $s(\hat{\tau}_{ij})$ is the standard error of this estimate. Under the null hypothesis this test statistic will be χ_2^2 distributed. None of

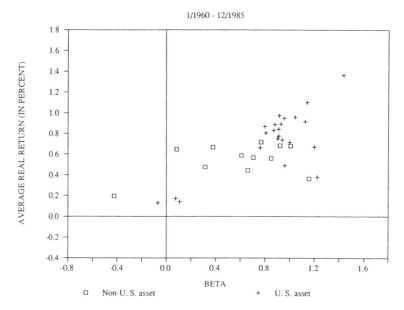

Fig. 4. Scatter plot of the average real return (in percent) facing the representative U.S. individual, $\hat{\mu}_{r_j} + (\hat{\sigma}_{r_j}^2/2)$, versus the estimate of beta, $\hat{\beta}_j$, for twenty U.S. stock portfolios, a one-month U.S. Treasury bill, a U.S. government bond portfolio, a U.S. corporate bond portfolio, and twelve portfolios of non-U.S. stocks covered against exchange-rate changes, where these estimates are computed using monthly data from January 1960 to December 1985.

these test statistics lead to a rejection of this hypothesis at less than the 10% significance level. Statistics can also be formed from the results in panels B and C of table 4 to test the hypothesis that each non-U.S. asset plots on the U.S. asset pricing line over both subperiods, against the alternative hypothesis that each non-U.S. asset plots off the U.S. asset pricing line, but in the same direction in each subperiod. Each of these test statistics is given by $[\sum_{i=1}^{2}\hat{\tau}_{ij}/s(\hat{\tau}_{ij})]/\sqrt{2}$. Under the null hypothesis this statistic will follow a standard normal distribution. Only two of these test statistics lead to a rejection of the null hypothesis at less than the 10% significance level. For France, the value of this test statistic is -1.86 with a p-value of 0.06; for Italy, it is 1.97 with a p-value of 0.05.

Possibly, more powerful tests of the model can be produced by using real returns on foreign portfolios covered against changes in exchange rates in place of real returns on uncovered foreign portfolios. Fig. 4 plots average real returns facing the representative U.S. individual against estimates of betas computed using U.S. real consumption and portfolios of non-U.S. equities that have been covered against changes in exchange rates. Each month, non-U.S. portfolios were covered by taking out one-month forward contracts to cover the amount of the initial investment. Although this procedure does not fully cover these portfolios against changes in exchange rates, forward contracts for amounts contingent on foreign portfolio returns are rarely used.

Panel D of table 3 and panel D of table 4 present tests of the model using these data. The results offer little evidence against the model. Non-U.S. portfolios do not plot significantly above or below the U.S. asset pricing line, either individually, as a group, or on average. In addition, the standard errors reported in panel D of table 4 are generally lower than their counterparts in panel A of the table. For example, the standard error of the distance by which the non-U.S. portfolios plot on average above or below the U.S. asset pricing line is 0.24% per month. Thus, non-U.S. portfolios would need to plot on average above or below the U.S. asset pricing line by more than 0.47% per month, or 5.63% per annum, for the null hypothesis to be rejected at the 5% significance level.[38] Unconditionally, foreign exchange positions appear to have close to zero consumption risk. Thus, for example, the estimates of the consumption betas of the covered non-U.S. portfolios are close to the estimates of these betas for their uncovered counterparts. On the other hand, covering non-U.S. portfolios against exchange-rate changes reduces the sample standard deviations of the real returns facing the representative U.S. individual on these portfolios. Thus, in these tests, covering these portfolios acts in the same way as reducing measurement error in a dependent variable.

The tests reported in tables 3 and 4 were also conducted using measured real consumption growth $\hat{x}_t$ in place of the two-sided filter $\tilde{x}_t$. Tests over the whole period produced results similar to those reported in panels A and D of tables 3 and 4. On the other hand, in line with the simulation evidence provided in appendix 2, tests over the two subperiods produced weaker results than those reported in panels B and C of these tables.

4. Conclusions

Several issues in financial economics cannot be addressed without some assumption about whether asset markets are integrated or segmented internationally. For example, if asset markets are segmented internationally, the cost of capital for a project will generally depend on the country in which the funds are to be raised, whereas if asset markets are integrated internationally, this cost will be independent of where the funds are raised. This paper provides

---

[38]Alternatively, non-U.S. assets would need to plot on average above the U.S. asset pricing line by more than 0.39% per month, or 4.72% per annum, for the null hypothesis to be rejected in favor of the alternative that foreign assets plot on average above that line at the 5% significance level.

tests of international equity market integration that use a discrete-time version of the consumption-based asset pricing model.

The model predicts there will be an asset pricing line for each country that relates the expected real return facing that country's representative individual on each asset to the asset's consumption risk computed using his real consumption. The test of international equity market integration is a test of whether, for each country, foreign equities plot along that country's asset pricing line. The joint hypothesis that equity markets are integrated internationally and that the asset pricing model holds is rejected when foreign equities plot significantly off this line.

Tests of international equity market integration are conducted using monthly data from the U.S. and 17 other countries from January 1960 to December 1985. The results provide little evidence against the joint hypothesis that equity markets are integrated internationally and that the asset pricing model holds. Thus, for example, this paper provides little evidence that the cost of capital for a project depends on where the funds are raised. The tests, however, do not have sufficient power to reject this joint hypothesis when deviations from the null hypothesis are small. This low power is probably in part a result of the weak, albeit statistically significant, relation between real consumption growth and real asset returns. One way to increase the power of tests like these would be to include in them only foreign equities for which there are *a priori* grounds to believe that effective barriers to ownership by domestic residents exist. On the other hand, it is difficult to determine for which foreign equities this is true, because, for every explicit barrier to international investment, there are usually many ways to get around it. This avenue of research is left for future work.

Appendix 1

This appendix demonstrates that, if $\hat{x}_t$ is given by (10) and x_t is serially uncorrelated, then the correlation coefficient between $\tilde{x}_t = a(L)\hat{x}_t$ and x_t, $\rho_{\tilde{x}x}$ will reach a maximum when $a(L) = (1 - \phi^2)[(1 - \phi L^{-1})(1 - \phi L)]^{-1}$. Note that $\tilde{x}_t$ can also be written in the form

$$\tilde{x}_t = \mu_x + \sum_{s=-\infty}^{\infty} b_s L^s (1 - \phi L)^{-1}(\hat{x}_t - \mu_x)$$

$$= \mu_x + \sum_{s=-\infty}^{\infty} b_s L^s \eta_t. \tag{A.1}$$

Note also that

$$\sigma_{\eta,x} = \phi^{-s}\sigma_x^2 \quad \text{for} \quad s \leq 0,$$
$$= 0 \qquad \text{for} \quad s > 0, \tag{A.2}$$

where $\sigma_{\eta,x}$ is the covariance between η_{t-s} and x_t.[39] From (A.1) and (A.2) it follows that

$$\sigma_{\tilde{x}}^2 = \sum_{s=-\infty}^{\infty} b_s^2 \sigma_{\eta}^2 \quad \text{and} \quad \sigma_{\tilde{x}x} = \sum_{s=-\infty}^{0} b_s \phi^{-s} \sigma_x^2,$$

where $\sigma_{\tilde{x}}^2$ is the variance of $\tilde{x}_t$ and $\sigma_{\tilde{x}x}$ is the covariance of $\tilde{x}_t$ and x_t. Consequently,

$$\rho_{\tilde{x}x} = \sigma_x \sum_{s=-\infty}^{0} b_s \phi^{-s} \Big/ \sigma_{\eta} \sqrt{\left(\sum_{s=-\infty}^{\infty} b_s^2 \right)}. \tag{A.3}$$

The first-order necessary conditions for maximizing $\rho_{\tilde{x}x}$ are satisfied when

$$b_s = \kappa \phi^{-s} \quad \text{for} \quad s \le 0,$$
$$ = 0 \qquad \text{for} \quad s > 0, \tag{A.4}$$

where κ is any positive constant. Substituting these results into (A.1) yields

$$\tilde{x}_t = \kappa \sum_{s=-\infty}^{0} \left(\phi^{-1} L \right)^s (1 - \phi L)^{-1} \hat{x}_t$$

$$= \kappa \left[(1 - \phi L^{-1})(1 - \phi L) \right]^{-1} \hat{x}_t. \tag{A.5}$$

Finally, note that if r_t is independent of x_{t-s} for all $s \ne 0$, then

$$\sigma_{r,\eta_s} = \phi^{-s} \sigma_{r,x} \quad \text{for} \quad s \le 0,$$
$$\phantom{\sigma_{r,\eta_s}} = 0 \qquad \text{for} \quad s > 0, \tag{A.6}$$

where σ_{r,η_s} is the covariance between r_{jt} and η_{t-s}. From (A.1) and (A.6) it follows that $\sigma_{r,\tilde{x}} = \kappa (1 - \phi^2)^{-1} \sigma_{r,x}$, where $\sigma_{r,\tilde{x}}$ is the covariance between r_{jt} and $\tilde{x}_t$. Thus, choosing $\kappa = (1 - \phi^2)$ ensures that estimates of relative risk aversion θ computed using the two-sided filter $\tilde{x}_t$ will be consistent.

Appendix 2

This appendix presents simulation evidence of the finite-sample properties of the likelihood ratio statistics used to test H$_2$ and H$_3$ and of the estimators of the model's parameters under each restriction. These simulations were

---

[39]All moments referred to in this appendix are unconditional.

conducted under the assumption that (10) holds and that x_t is serially uncorrelated.

For each simulation, 250 replications were performed with $N = 39$, $n = 16$, and $T = 312$ or 154. For each replication a vector white noise process $(v_t', x_t - \mu_x, \epsilon_t)'$ was produced with

$$\begin{pmatrix} v_t \\ x_t - \mu_x \\ \epsilon_t \end{pmatrix} \sim N\left(\begin{pmatrix} 0 \\ 0 \\ 0 \end{pmatrix}, \begin{pmatrix} \Omega & 0 & 0 \\ 0 & \sigma_x^2 & 0 \\ 0 & 0 & \sigma_\epsilon^2 \end{pmatrix} \right). \tag{A.7}$$

Parameter values were chosen to match estimates of the model's parameters computed using data from January 1960 to December 1985. First, note that if (10) holds and x_t is serially uncorrelated, then $\sigma_x^2 = (1 + 2\rho_{\hat{x}})\sigma_{\hat{x}}^2$, where $\rho_{\hat{x}}$ and $\sigma_{\hat{x}}^2$ are the first-order autocorrelation coefficient and variance of $\hat{x}_t$. Using estimates reported in panel A of table 1 and this relation, the following parameter values were chosen: $\mu_x = 0.12 \times 10^{-2}$ and $\sigma_x = 0.46 \times 10^{-2}$. On the other hand, the following values for ψ and θ were chosen: $\psi = 0.05 \times 10^{-2}$ and $\theta = 129.64$. These are estimates of ψ and θ computed, under H$_3$, using $\hat{x}_t$ and not $\tilde{x}_t$. Thus, they differ somewhat from the estimates reported in panel A of table 3. With $N = 39$, β and Ω together contain 819 distinct elements, so the values chosen for these are not reported here. However, β and Ω were chosen so that

$$\beta = \hat{\beta} \quad \text{and} \quad \Omega = \hat{\Xi} - \hat{\beta}\hat{\beta}'\hat{\sigma}_x^2, \tag{A.8}$$

where $\hat{\sigma}_x$ is the maximum likelihood (ML) estimate of σ_x and, from panel A of table 1, as noted, $\hat{\sigma}_x = 0.46 \times 10^{-2}$, where $\hat{\beta}$ is the unconstrained ML estimate of β, computed using $\hat{x}_t$ and where $\hat{\Xi}$ is the unconstrained ML estimate of the variance–covariance matrix of r_t. The estimate $\hat{\beta}$ was computed by regressing r_t on $\hat{x}_t$ and by then multiplying the resulting estimate of the slope coefficient vector by the ratio $\hat{\sigma}_{\hat{x}}^2/\hat{\sigma}_x^2$, where $\hat{\sigma}_{\hat{x}}^2$ is the ML estimate of $\sigma_{\hat{x}}^2$ and, from panel A of table 1, $\hat{\sigma}_{\hat{x}} = 0.86 \times 10^{-2}$. Thus, $\hat{\beta}$ is a consistent estimate of β. Using the parameter values chosen, each random sample $(r_t, t = 1, 2, \ldots, T)$ was chosen so as to satisfy (5) and (8). Finally, each sample $(\hat{x}_t, t = 1, 2, \ldots, T)$ was produced to satisfy (10) using the following parameter value: $\sigma_\epsilon^2 = -\hat{\rho}_{\hat{x}}\hat{\sigma}_{\hat{x}}^2$, where $\hat{\rho}_{\hat{x}}$ is the ML estimate of $\rho_{\hat{x}}$.

For each replication sixteen tax rates were estimated. Rather than report the simulation evidence for all sixteen estimators, one representative was chosen: the estimator of the tax rate on the Australian national index, which here is labeled τ_2. Table 5 shows the results of 250 replications that use measured real consumption growth $\hat{x}_t$, with $T = 312$ in panel A and $T = 154$ in panel B. In both panels the likelihood ratio statistics for tests of H$_2$ and H$_3$ reject those

Table 5

Results of simulations to investigate the properties of likelihood ratio statistics for tests of the consumption-based asset pricing model and estimators of its parameters, using measured real consumption growth $\hat{x}_t$. The number of U.S. and non-U.S. assets $N = 39$ and the number of non-U.S. assets $n = 16$. The results are based on 250 replications.[a]

H_1: Real asset returns are uncorrelated with U.S. real consumption growth.
H_2: The consumption-based asset pricing model holds for U.S. assets.
H_3: The consumption-based asset pricing model holds for U.S. and non-U.S. assets.

ψ = the U.S. risk-free real return, θ = a representative U.S. individual's relative risk aversion, τ_2 = the distance by which the Australian index plots above the U.S. asset pricing line, and $\bar{\tau}$ = the average distance by which the sixteen non-U.S. portfolios plot above the U.S. asset pricing line.

Panel A: $T = 312$

Likelihood ratio statistic for			Fraction rejected at 50% significance level[b]	Fraction rejected at 10% significance level	Fraction rejected at 5% significance level	Fraction rejected at 1% significance level
H_1			1.000	1.000	0.996	0.988
H_2			0.560	0.108	0.072	0.024
H_3 against H_2			0.640	0.212	0.116	0.036

Maximum likelihood estimator of	Mean	Median	Mean asymptotic standard error	Median asymptotic standard error	Simulated standard deviation	Studentized range
ψ, under H_2	0.043	0.051	0.039	0.036	0.058	7.865[d]
θ, under H_2	131.060	121.880	35.029	29.462	53.374	6.615[c]
τ_2	0.009	−0.001	0.491	0.470	0.457	5.792
$\bar{\tau}$	0.001	−0.003	0.227	0.216	0.239	7.248[d]
ψ, under H_3	0.046	0.049	0.034	0.032	0.047	6.937[c]
θ, under H_3	128.860	123.010	24.713	22.993	35.606	6.017

Panel B: $T = 154$

Likelihood ratio statistic for			Fraction rejected at 50% significance level[b]	Fraction rejected at 10% significance level	Fraction rejected at 5% significance level	Fraction rejected at 1% significance level
H_1			1.000	0.968	0.936	0.812
H_2			0.528	0.108	0.080	0.020
H_3 against H_2			0.644	0.308	0.180	0.056

Maximum likelihood estimator of	Mean	Median	Mean asymptotic standard error	Median asymptotic standard error	Simulated standard deviation	Studentized range
ψ, under H_2	0.056	0.066	0.058	0.045	0.102	10.235[d]
θ, under H_2	119.740	109.240	51.308	32.644	118.850	9.770[d]
τ_2	0.076	0.110	0.728	0.612	0.914	6.926[c]
$\bar{\tau}$	0.014	0.056	0.337	0.285	0.414	8.778[d]
ψ, under H_3	0.050	0.061	0.048	0.040	0.090	8.993[d]
θ, under H_3	124.710	115.130	34.278	25.646	95.765	8.575[d]

[a] Parameter values used in these simulations are $\psi = 0.05 \times 10^{-2}$, $\theta = 129.64$, $\tau_2 = 0$, and $\bar{\tau} = 0$. All statistics for estimators of ψ, τ_2, and $\bar{\tau}$, except the studentized range statistics, are multiplied by 100.
[b] Likelihood ratio statistics for tests of H_1, H_2, and H_3 against H_2 are compared to χ^2_{39}, χ^2_{21}, and χ^2_{16} distributions.
[c] Exceeds the 0.95 fractile of the distribution of the studentized range.
[d] Exceeds the 0.99 fractile of the distribution of the studentized range.

Table 6

Results of simulations to investigate the properties of likelihood ratio statistics for tests of the consumption-based asset pricing model, using the two-sided filter $\tilde{x}_t$. The number of U.S. and non-U.S. assets $N = 39$ and the number of non-U.S. assets $n = 16$. The results are based on 250 replications.[a]

H$_1$: Real asset returns are uncorrelated with U.S. real consumption growth.
H$_2$: The consumption-based asset pricing model holds for U.S. assets.
H$_3$: The consumption-based asset pricing model holds for U.S. and non-U.S. assets.

ψ = the U.S. risk-free real return, θ = a representative U.S. individual's relative risk aversion, τ_2 = the distance by which the Australian index plots above the U.S. asset pricing line, and $\bar{\tau}$ = the average distance by which the sixteen non-U.S. portfolios plot above the U.S. asset pricing line.

				Panel A: $T = 312$			
Likelihood ratio statistic for		Fraction rejected at 50% signif- icance level[b]		Fraction rejected at 10% signif- icance level		Fraction rejected at 5% signif- icance level	Fraction rejected at 1% signif- icance level
H$_1$		1.000		1.000		1.000	1.000
H$_2$		0.548		0.104		0.056	0.004
H$_3$ against H$_2$		0.588		0.172		0.112	0.024

Maximum likelihood estimator of	Mean	Median	Mean asymptotic standard error	Median asymptotic standard error	Simulated standard deviation	Student- ized range
ψ, under H$_2$	0.052	0.055	0.035	0.032	0.040	5.420
θ, under H$_2$	133.220	128.900	32.665	29.714	46.327	5.904
τ_2	0.014	0.064	0.442	0.426	0.439	5.396
$\bar{\tau}$	-0.017	-0.015	0.204	0.195	0.211	7.862[d]
ψ, under H$_3$	0.052	0.056	0.030	0.030	0.039	6.205
θ, under H$_3$	132.660	129.250	24.133	22.578	33.597	5.518

				Panel B: $T = 154$			
Likelihood ratio statistic for		Fraction rejected at 50% signif- icance level[b]		Fraction rejected at 10% signif- icance level		Fraction rejected at 5% signif- icance level	Fraction rejected at 1% signif- icance level
H$_1$		1.000		0.996		0.996	0.964
H$_2$		0.568		0.156		0.084	0.016
H$_3$ against H$_2$		0.692		0.268		0.176	0.068

Maximum likelihood estimator of	Mean	Median	Mean asymptotic standard error	Median asymptotic standard error	Simulated standard deviation	Student- ized range
ψ, under H$_2$	0.043	0.053	0.054	0.043	0.092	9.813[d]
θ, under H$_2$	144.010	126.500	51.745	36.673	105.690	9.547[d]
τ_2	-0.024	-0.019	0.658	0.580	0.735	6.589[c]
$\bar{\tau}$	0.010	0.027	0.307	0.275	0.347	6.403
ψ, under H$_3$	0.044	0.053	0.042	0.038	0.071	8.148[d]
θ, under H$_3$	142.090	131.350	33.750	29.170	65.811	7.697[d]

[a] Parameter values used in these simulations are $\psi = 0.05 \times 10^{-2}$, $\theta = 129.64$, $\tau_2 = 0$, and $\bar{\tau} = 0$. All statistics for estimators of ψ, τ_2, and $\bar{\tau}$, except the studentized range statistics, are multiplied by 100.

[b] Likelihood ratio statistics for tests of H$_1$, H$_2$, and H$_3$ against H$_2$ are compared to χ^2_{39}, χ^2_{21}, and χ^2_{16} distributions.

[c] Exceeds the 0.95 fractile of the distribution of the studentized range.

[d] Exceeds the 0.99 fractile of the distribution of the studentized range.

Table 7

Test statistics for the hypothesis that the standard deviation of each estimator from table 5 is less than or equal to the standard deviation of its counterpart from table 6. For each estimator, the test statistic is the ratio of the square of its simulated standard deviation from table 5 to the square of the simulated standard deviation of its counterpart from table 6. The hypothesis that the standard deviation of each estimator from table 5 is less than or equal to the standard deviation of its counterpart from table 6 is tested by comparing these statistics with critical values of the $F_{250, 250}$ distribution. (P-values are in parentheses.)

H_2: The consumption-based asset pricing model holds for U.S. assets.

H_3: The consumption-based asset pricing model holds for U.S. and non-U.S. assets.

ψ = the U.S. risk-free real return, θ = a representative U.S. individual's relative risk aversion, τ_2 = the distance by which the Australian index plots above the U.S. asset pricing line, $\bar{\tau}$ = the average distance by which the sixteen non-U.S. portfolios plot above the U.S. asset pricing line.

Maximum likelihood estimator of	$T = 312$	$T = 154$
ψ, under H_2	2.103 (0.000)	1.229 (0.052)
θ, under H_2	1.327 (0.013)	1.265 (0.032)
τ_2	1.084 (0.026)	1.546 (0.000)
$\bar{\tau}$	1.283 (0.025)	1.423 (0.003)
ψ, under H_3	1.452 (0.002)	1.607 (0.000)
θ, under H_3	1.123 (0.180)	2.117 (0.000)

hypotheses too often when critical values are based on their theoretical asymptotic distributions. The six estimators appear to be unbiased. Only for the estimator of ψ, under H_2, in panel A can the hypothesis that the estimator is unbiased be rejected at conventional significance levels. However, the mean asymptotic standard errors computed of the estimators of ψ and θ, under both H_2 and H_3, understate the corresponding simulated standard deviations of these estimators, particularly in panel B. On the other hand, the mean asymptotic standard errors of the estimators of τ_2 and the average distance by which non-U.S. assets plot above the U.S. asset pricing line $\bar{\tau}$ are closer to the corresponding simulated standard deviations of these estimators.

Table 6 shows the results of 250 replications that use the two-sided filter $\tilde{x}_t$, with $T = 312$ in panel A and $T = 154$ in panel B. The results are similar to those in table 5. However, the simulated standard deviations for all the estimators are below their counterparts in table 5. Note that the simulations reported in the four panels were conducted independently. Consequently, the hypothesis that the standard deviation of each estimator from table 5 is less than or equal to the standard deviation of its counterpart from table 6 can be easily tested. For each estimator, the test statistic given by the ratio of the square of its simulated standard deviation from table 5, to the square of the simulated standard deviation of its counterpart from table 6 can be compared to critical values of the $F_{250,250}$ distribution. Table 7 reports for each estimator this test statistic together with its p-value. The evidence provided by this table indicates that when (10) holds and x_t is serially uncorrelated, use of the two-sided filter $\tilde{x}_t$ in place of measured real consumption growth $\hat{x}_t$ produces more efficient estimates of the parameters of the model.

References

Adler, M. and B. Dumas, 1975, Optimal international acquisitions, Journal of Finance 30, 1–19.

Adler, M. and B. Dumas, 1983, International portfolio choice and corporation finance: A survey, Journal of Finance 38, 925–984.

Aliber, R.Z., 1978, The integration of national financial markets: A review of theory and findings, Weltwirtschaftliches Archiv 114, 448–480.

Black, F., 1974, International capital market equilibrium with investment barriers, Journal of Financial Economics 1, 337–352.

Black, F., 1978, The ins and outs of foreign investment, Financial Analysts Journal 34, May–June, 1–7.

Breeden, D.T., 1979, An intertemporal asset pricing model with stochastic consumption and investment opportunities, Journal of Financial Economics 7, 265–296.

Breeden, D.T., 1980, Consumption risk in futures markets, Journal of Finance 35, 503–520.

Brennan, M.J. and E.S. Schwartz, 1984, Asset pricing in a small economy: A test of the omitted assets model, Unpublished manuscript (University of British Columbia, Vancouver, BC).

Cornell, B., 1981, The consumption based asset pricing model: A note on potential tests and applications, Journal of Financial Economics 9, 103–108.

Dooley, M.P. and P. Isard, 1980, Capital controls, political risk, and deviations from interest-rate parity, Journal of Political Economy 88, 370–384.

Dunn, K. and K. Singleton, 1986, Modeling the term structure of interest rates under non-separable utility and durability of goods, Journal of Financial Economics 17, 27–56.

Eichenbaum, M.S. and L.P. Hansen, 1987, Estimating models with intertemporal substitution using aggregate time series data, NBER working paper no. 2181.

Errunza, V. and E. Losq, 1985, International asset pricing under mild segmentation: Theory and test, Journal of Finance 40, 105–124.

Friend, I. and M.E. Blume, 1975, The demand for risky assets, American Economic Review 65, 900–922.

Garber, P.M. and R.G. King, 1983, Deep structural excavation? A critique of Euler equation methods, NBER technical paper no. 31.

Gibbons, M.R., 1982, Multivariate tests of financial models: a new approach, Journal of Financial Economics 10, 3–27.

Grauer, F.L.A. and R.H. Litzenberger, 1979, The pricing of commodity futures contracts, nominal bonds and other risky assets under commodity price uncertainty, Journal of Finance 34, 69–83.

Grauer, F.L.A., R.H. Litzenberger, and R.E. Stehle, 1976, Sharing rules under uncertainty, and equilibrium in an international capital market, Journal of Financial Economics 3, 233–256.

Grossman, S.J. and R.J. Shiller, 1982, Consumption correlatedness and risk measurement in economies with non-traded assets and heterogeneous information, Journal of Financial Economics 10, 195–210.

Hall, R.E., 1978, Stochastic implications of the life cycle-permanent income hypothesis: Theory and estimation, Journal of Political Economy 86, 971–988.

Hansen, L.P. and R.J. Hodrick, 1983, Risk averse speculation in the forward foreign exchange market: An econometric analysis of linear models, in: Jacob A. Frenkel, ed., Exchange rates and international macroeconomics (University of Chicago Press, Chicago, IL).

Hansen, L.P. and K.J. Singleton, 1982, Generalized instrumental variables estimation of nonlinear rational expectations models, Econometrica 50, 1269–1286.

Hansen, L.P. and K.J. Singleton, 1983, Stochastic consumption, risk aversion, and the temporal behavior of stock market returns, Journal of Political Economy 91, 249–265.

Ibbotson, R.G., R.C. Carr, and A.W. Robinson, 1982, International equity and bond returns, Financial Analysts Journal 38, July–Aug., 61–63.

Ibbotson, R. and R.A. Sinquefield, 1986, Stocks, bonds, bills and inflation 1986 yearbook (Ibbotson Associates Capital Management Research Center, Chicago, IL).

Jagannathan, R., 1985, An investigation of commodity futures prices using the consumption-based intertemporal capital asset pricing model, Journal of Finance 40, 175–191.

Jorion, P. and E.S. Schwartz, 1986, Integration vs. segmentation in the Canadian stock market, Journal of Finance 41, 603–614.

Lucas, R.E., Jr., 1978, Asset prices in an exchange economy, Econometrica 46, 1426–1446.

Mark, N.C., 1985, On time-varying risk premia in the foreign exchange market: An econometric analysis, Journal of Monetary Economics 16, 3–18.

Mehra, R. and E.C. Prescott, 1985, The equity premium: A puzzle, Journal of Monetary Economics 15, 145–161.

Merton, R.C., 1973, An intertemporal capital asset pricing model, Econometrica 41, 867–887.

Mundell, R.A., 1963, Capital mobility and stabilization policy under fixed and flexible exchange rates, Canadian Journal of Economics and Political Science 29, 475–485.

Roll, R., 1977, A critique of the asset pricing theory's tests – Part 1: On past and potential testability of the theory, Journal of Financial Economics 4, 129–176.

Roll, R., 1979, Violations of purchasing power parity and their implications for efficient international commodity markets, in: M. Sarnat and G. Szego, eds., International finance and trade, Vol. I (Ballinger, Cambridge, MA).

Roll, R. and B. Solnik, 1977, A pure foreign exchange asset pricing model, Journal of International Economics 7, 161–180.

Rubinstein, M., 1974, An aggregation theorem for securities markets, Journal of Financial Economics 1, 225–244.

Rubinstein, M., 1976, The valuation of uncertain streams and the pricing of options, Bell Journal of Economics and Management Science 7, 407–425.

Solnik, B., 1973, European capital markets (Lexington Books, Lexington, MA).

Solnik, B., 1974, The international pricing of risk: An empirical investigation of the world capital market structure, Journal of Finance 29, 365–378.

Solnik, B., 1977, Testing international asset pricing: Some pessimistic views, Journal of Finance 32, 503–512.

Stehle, R., 1977, An empirical test of the alternative hypotheses of national and international pricing of risky assets, Journal of Finance 32, 493–502.

Stulz, R.M., 1981a, A model of international asset pricing, Journal of Financial Economics 9, 383–406.

Stulz, R.M., 1981b, On the effects of barriers to international investment, Journal of Finance 36, 923–934.

Wallingford, B.A., 1974, Discussion, Journal of Finance 29, 392–395.

Wheatley, S.M., 1985, Some tests of international equity market integration, Unpublished Ph.D. thesis (University of Rochester, Rochester, NY).

Wheatley, S.M., 1988, Some tests of the consumption-based asset pricing model, Journal of Monetary Economics 22, 193–215.

White, H., 1980, A heteroskedasticity-consistent covariance matrix estimator and a direct test for heteroskedasticity, Econometrica 48, 817–838.

THE JOURNAL OF FINANCE • VOL. XLI, NO. 2 • JUNE 1986

International Arbitrage Pricing Theory: An Empirical Investigation

D. CHINHYUNG CHO, CHEOL S. EUN, and LEMMA W. SENBET*

ABSTRACT

In this paper, we test the arbitrage pricing theory (APT) in an international setting. Inter-battery factor analysis is used to estimate the international common factors and the Chow test is used in testing the validity of the APT. Our inter-battery factor analysis results show that the number of common factors between a pair of countries ranges from one to five, and our cross-sectional test results lead us to reject the joint hypothesis that the international capital market is integrated and that the APT is internationally valid. Our results, however, do not rule out the possibility that the APT holds locally or regionally in segmented capital markets. Finally, the basic results of both the inter-battery factor analysis and the cross-sectional tests are largely invariant to the numeraire currency chosen.

NUMEROUS AUTHORS, NOTABLY SOLNIK [21], Grauer, Litzenberger, and Stehle [11], and Stulz [24] have derived various versions of the international asset pricing model (IAPM) under alternative views of the structure of international capital markets. However, only a few serious attempts have been made to test various versions of the IAPM. These tests are largely inconclusive (see Solnik [20] and Stehle [23]). Apart from the problem stressed by Roll [16] of identifying the world market portfolio, previous tests of the IAPMs suffer from the technical problem of aggregating assets of national investors using different numeraire currencies. Differences in the numeraire arise from differences in consumption baskets in an environment characterized by exchange rate uncertainty.

In a fruitful attempt to extend the arbitrage pricing theory (APT) of Ross [18] to an international setting, Solnik [22] derives an international arbitrage pricing theory which is largely devoid of the aforementioned difficulties and thus more amenable to empirical testing.[1] As shown by Solnik, testability of the APT in an

* Graduate School of Business, University of Wisconsin-Madison; College of Business and Management, University of Maryland; and Graduate School of Business, University of Wisconsin-Madison, respectively. The authors are grateful to Richard Roll, Mark Weinstein, Jay Shanken, Vihang Errunza, Alan Shapiro, and an anonymous referee for valuable comments and to Sung Oh for computational assistance. Cho is grateful for research support provided by the Graduate School of the University of Wisconsin-Madison. Senbet acknowledges support from Dickson-Bascom professorship. Earlier versions were presented at the 1984 American Finance Association meetings and the 1985 Western Finance Association meetings.

[1] The consumption-based IAPM of Stulz [24] is another model which seems to be more amenable to empirical testing. In the Stulz IAPM, the (world) market portfolio does not play an essential role. Empirical tests of the model, however, could be hampered by at least two difficulties. First, as pointed out by Cornell [5], the effects of the state variables are impounded in the consumption betas, implying that the consumption betas will be nonstationary if the state variables are random. Second, given that the national income accounts, the main source of aggregate consumption data, are subject to

international setting stems from the fact that, unlike asset returns, factors do not have to be translated from one currency to another. Furthermore, since the APT addresses relative pricing on any set of n assets following a particular return-generating process, it can be tested by examining only subsets of the universe of assets. Neither the international market portfolio nor a set of mean-variance efficient portfolios of the primary assets implied by the existing IAPMs play an essential role.

In fact, derivation of the asset pricing relationship via arbitrage consideration is not new in international finance. Let us consider an "arbitrage" portfolio which consists of: (i) borrowing a certain amount in U.S. dollars; (ii) lending the equivalent pound amount in the U.K.; and (iii) selling the proceeds of the pound investment forward. Clearly, this portfolio entails neither net investment nor (exchange) risk. To preclude arbitrage opportunities, such a portfolio should yield zero profit. From this arbitrage condition follows an international parity relationship stating that the interest rate differential should be equal to the forward exchange premium or discount. This, of course, is the well-known interest rate parity relationship (IRP). Thus, the IRP is akin in spirit to the APT. Unlike the APT, however, the IRP is incapable of pricing equities, the future payoffs of which are not fixed in any particular currency.

The purpose of this paper is to test the APT in an international setting (IAPT). Specifically, we address various issues as outlined in the following procedure:

(i) Extracting the number of international factors common to the universe of assets across national boundaries;
(ii) Testing the asset pricing relationship implied by the IAPT; and
(iii) Examining whether the factor structure and the asset pricing relationship are invariant to the numeraire chosen by using two major currencies, i.e., the U.S. dollar and the Japanese yen.

As will be discussed in detail, our test involves the joint hypothesis of the international capital market being integrated and the APT being valid internationally.

The rest of the paper is organized as follows. Section I briefly reviews the international arbitrage pricing theory. Section II discusses the test methodology and the hypotheses to be tested. Section III presents the empirical results. Section IV concludes the paper.

I. International Arbitrage Pricing Theory: A Review

Suppose there exist k factors in the world economy which generate the random returns on a set of n international assets in terms of a given numeraire currency,

---

errors and omissions, it would be a formidable task to measure the aggregate world real consumption rate without error. Recently, Shanken [19] has questioned the testability of APT itself. In response to this, Dybvig and Ross [7] specify certain testability restrictions and argue that these restrictions are reasonably satisfied by the real world economy.

International APT 315

say, the U.S. dollar:

$$\tilde{r}_i = E_i + b_{i1}\tilde{\delta}_1 + b_{i2}\tilde{\delta}_2 + \cdots + b_{ik}\tilde{\delta}_k + \varepsilon_i, \qquad i = 1, \cdots, n \qquad (1)$$

where E_i is the expected return on the ith asset, $\tilde{\delta}_j$'s are zero mean international common factors, b_{ij} is the sensitivity of the ith asset to the jth factor, and $\tilde{\varepsilon}_i$'s are the residual terms of the assets. As usual, it is assumed that $E(\tilde{\varepsilon}_i \mid \tilde{\delta}_j) = 0$ for $i = 1, \cdots, n, j = 1, \cdots, k, n > k$ and $E(\tilde{\varepsilon}_i^2) = \sigma_i^2 < \infty$.

Assuming that investors have homogeneous expectations concerning the k-factor generating process of Equation (1), we can derive the IAPT in terms of the U.S. dollar in the usual manner. Suppose that there is a sufficient number of assets so that a portfolio with the following characteristics can be formed:

$$\underline{x}^t \underline{1} = 0, \qquad (2a)$$

$$\underline{x}^t \underline{b}_j = 0, \qquad j = 1, \cdots, k \qquad (2b)$$

where $\underline{x}^t$ is an n-dimensional (row) vector of portfolio weights; $\underline{1}$ is an n-dimensional vector of ones; $\underline{b}_j$ is an n-dimensional vector of factor loadings b_{ij}'s. These portfolios entail neither net investment nor systematic risk. Further, the idiosyncratic risk of these portfolios should become negligible as the number of securities grows large. Consequently, in order to preclude arbitrage opportunities, these portfolios must earn zero profits, which in return implies the following relationship.

$$\underline{E} \simeq \lambda_0 + \lambda_1 \underline{b}_1 + \cdots + \lambda_k \underline{b}_k \qquad (3)$$

where $\underline{E}$ is an n-dimensional vector of E_i's.

The k weights, $\lambda_1, \cdots, \lambda_k$, can be viewed as risk premia. If a riskless asset exists with return, E_0, then $\lambda_0 = E_0$ and $\lambda_j = E^j - E_0$ where E^j is the expected return on portfolios with only systematic factor j risk. It is well known in the APT literature that the IAPT of Equation (3) holds only as an approximation, particularly in a finite economy, as shown by Ross [18] and others. In a large economy with infinitely many assets, the model holds as an exact equality under certain conditions (see Dybvig and Ross [7], for instance). However, the magnitude of mispricing due to the approximation should be mitigated in the international context by the fact that there are more assets in the world economy than in any particular national economy.

Although Equation (3) applies to a set of international assets, rather than a set of local assets as in the domestic APT, its structure is identical to the standard APT of Ross [18]. However, Solnik [22] demonstrates that the APT structure in Equation (3) is invariant to the currency chosen. Solnik shows that this invariance result is dependent upon two other invariance propositions he demonstrates, namely, (i) an arbitrage portfolio that is riskless in a given currency is also riskless in any other currency, and (ii) the factor structure in Equation (1) is also invariant to the choice of a currency in terms of decomposition into k factors and a residual. To derive the "invariance" propositions, Solnik requires that the exchange rates (like security returns) follow the k-factor model of Equation (1), with the assumption of mutually independent idiosyncratic terms.[2]

---

[2] For a detailed derivation and discussion of the invariance propositions, see Solnik [22].

II. Test Methodology and Hypotheses

In this section, we discuss the testing procedures, the hypotheses to be tested, and the data used in this study. We shall begin with a discussion of the joint nature of the hypothesis.

A. *International Market Integration and IAPT: Joint Hypothesis*

Our test involves a joint hypothesis like any other test of the asset pricing models. In the domestic setting, for instance, most of the studies test the joint hypothesis of the market being efficient and the underlying asset pricing model being valid. In an international setting, there is one additional hypothesis, i.e., the markets being integrated. International capital markets can be viewed as integrated if assets in various national markets are traded as though their prices are determined in a unified market so as to yield the same price in a given currency across countries.

Capital markets can be segmented along regional lines due to severe imperfections resulting from discriminatory border taxes, possibilities of expropriation, exchange controls, information gaps, etc. The existence of exchange rate uncertainty per se does not cause segmentation. Indeed, as we saw earlier, the IAPT was developed in an environment characterized by exchange rate fluctuations. We should also point out that, even if the IAPT fails to hold internationally, it can characterize a subset or a segment of international capital markets. This paper does not provide such regional tests of APT.

We cannot evaluate the extent of capital market integration between two countries by looking at the number of common factors. A strong single common factor may depict more integration than several weak factors. By the same token, we cannot judge capital market integration on the basis of economic integration. Two economies, the industrial bases of which are quite similar, could well have their capital markets segmented by virtue of the frictions that limit accessibility by foreign residents to domestic capital markets. The frictions that potentially segment capital markets are apparent, but their actual significance is an empirical matter. As mentioned earlier, we cannot infer capital market integration from factor structure or correlation structure. We must test if the factors are priced identically across markets, which should be the case if the IAPT is valid and capital markets are integrated. In this sense we seek to test a joint hypothesis.

B. *Estimation of Factor Loadings: Inter-Battery Factor Analysis*

Testing of the IAPT will be carried out in two parts. The first part involves estimation of the systematic risks, i.e., factor loadings for each asset, while the second part involves testing the pricing implications of the IAPT using cross-sectional regression analysis. Due to the well-known technological constraint, we adopted the group approach first used by Roll and Ross [17]. Unlike Roll and Ross, we grouped stocks according to their country membership, rather than, say, alphabetically. In view of the existing empirical findings indicating that there is a strong country factor influencing the return-generating process (see Eun and Resnick [10]), grouping stocks by their country membership is appropriate.

One of the major difficulties encountered in the group approach is the problem of comparing the factor structure across different asset groups. Granting that the factor structure is more likely to vary across countries than within a country, the problem of factor comparability becomes even more acute in an international setting. However, as Cho [4] shows, this problem can be substantially alleviated by using inter-battery factor analysis. Unlike traditional factor analysis, inter-battery factor analysis estimates the common factor loadings of two different groups of assets by examining only the inter-group sample covariance matrix rather than the entire sample covariance matrix. If two groups have the same set of factors, then it should be reflected in the inter-group covariance matrix. Conversely, the inter-group covariance matrix should reflect only those factors that are common between two groups and not those factors that are common for only one group.

Consider a pair of groups of assets whose returns are generated by the k-factor model:

$$\begin{bmatrix} \tilde{r}_J \\ \tilde{r}_K \end{bmatrix} = \begin{bmatrix} \underline{E}_J \\ \underline{E}_K \end{bmatrix} + \begin{bmatrix} \underline{b}_J \\ \underline{b}_K \end{bmatrix} \underline{\delta} + \begin{bmatrix} \tilde{\varepsilon}_J \\ \tilde{\varepsilon}_K \end{bmatrix}, \tag{4}$$

where J and K represent two different country groups of assets; $\underline{b}_H$, $H = J$ and K, are the $n_H \times k$ factor loading matrices; n_H is the number of securities in a group, H; $\underline{\delta}$ is the $k \times 1$ column vector of common factors; and $\tilde{\varepsilon}_H$ are the $n_H \times 1$ vectors of residual terms for $H = J$ and K. We assume that $\underline{\delta}$ and $\tilde{\varepsilon}_H$, $H = J$ and K, have zero means and $\tilde{\varepsilon}_H$ are orthogonal to $\underline{\delta}$. Furthermore, we assume that $\tilde{\varepsilon}_J$ and $\tilde{\varepsilon}_K$ are orthogonal to each other so that the covariance matrix of $[\tilde{\varepsilon}_J, \tilde{\varepsilon}_K]^t$ is block diagonal with covariance matrices of $\tilde{\varepsilon}_H$ being ψ_H for $H = J$ and K. Note that we allow more than k common factors within each group by not assuming ψ_H to be a diagonal matrix. For the sake of convenience, it is also assumed that the covariance matrix of $\underline{\delta}$ is an identity matrix. Then, the traditional factor analysis would find estimates $\hat{b}_H$ and $\hat{\psi}_H$ for $H = J$ and K in such a way that the estimated matrix, $\hat{V}$, closely replicates the sample covariance matrix, V, where

$$\hat{V} = \begin{bmatrix} \hat{b}_J \hat{b}_J^t + \hat{\psi}_J & \hat{b}_J \hat{b}_K^t \\ \hat{b}_K \hat{b}_J^t & \hat{b}_K \hat{b}_K^t + \hat{\psi}_K \end{bmatrix}, \tag{5}$$

$$V = \begin{bmatrix} V_{JJ} & V_{JK} \\ V_{KJ} & V_{KK} \end{bmatrix}. \tag{6}$$

On the other hand, the inter-battery factor analysis estimates $\hat{b}_J$ and $\hat{b}_K$ by relating their product $\hat{b}_J \hat{b}_K^t$ to V_{JK}.

There are several advantages to using inter-battery factor analysis rather than standard factor analysis. First, one can factor analyze a larger dimensional problem than is possible by traditional factor analysis. This is true because inter-battery factor analysis focuses only on the submatrix V_{JK} rather than the entire matrix V. Second, since the solution of the inter-battery factor analysis is in a closed form, a global optimal solution can be determined without going through an iteration procedure. Note that standard factor analysis does not guarantee a global optimal solution. Third, as we show later, inter-battery factor analysis does not appear as sensitive to the number of variables included in a sample as the standard factor analysis. Finally, inter-battery factor analysis estimates the factor loadings by constraining the factor structures between the two groups to be the same. This enables us to carry out the cross-sectional analysis in a more efficient manner using the Chow test.

C. Hypotheses Testing

Once we obtain estimates of international factor loadings, we can test the basic cross-sectional pricing relationship of the IAPT in Equation (3). Cross-sectional tests are performed by comparing the risk-free rate and the risk premia between two different country groups using the Chow test as was done in Brown and Weinstein [3]. Specifically, we test the following null hypotheses:[3]

(H1) the risk-free rate is the same between two country groups;
(H2) the risk premia are the same between two country groups;
(H3) both the risk-free rate and the risk premia are the same between two country groups.

Each of the above hypotheses will be tested using the U.S. dollar and the Japanese yen as the numeraire currency.

As previously mentioned, our test involves a joint hypothesis that the international capital market is integrated and that the APT is valid internationally. If the APT holds internationally, then none of the above hypotheses, H1–H3, should be rejected. If any of the hypotheses is rejected, then the APT does not hold internationally. It should be stressed, however, that, even if the APT does not hold internationally, it may hold locally in segmented capital markets.

Let us briefly provide the hypotheses testing procedure. If the APT holds, then the expected returns on assets must be linear combinations of the factor loadings:

$$E_H = [1 : b_H] \begin{bmatrix} \lambda_{0H} \\ \lambda_H \end{bmatrix}, \quad \text{for } H = J \text{ and } K \quad (7)$$

where λ_{0H} is the risk-free rate; and λ_H represents a column vector of the k risk premia for group H. Substituting Equation (7) into Equation (4), we obtain

$$\begin{bmatrix} \tilde{r}_J \\ \tilde{r}_K \end{bmatrix} = \begin{bmatrix} 1 : b_J : 0 : 0 \\ 0 : 0 : 1 : b_K \end{bmatrix} \begin{bmatrix} \lambda_{0J} \\ \lambda_J \\ \lambda_{0K} \\ \lambda_K \end{bmatrix} + \begin{bmatrix} \tilde{e}_J \\ \tilde{e}_K \end{bmatrix}, \quad (8)$$

where $\tilde{e}_H = b_H \tilde{\delta} + \tilde{\varepsilon}_H$ for $H = J$ and K.

---

[3] We also attempted to test for the effect of residual risk on international asset pricing, although this is not of direct interest to the paper. We do not report the results, because our tests are based on residuals extracted from the same sample, and hence there is bias toward rejecting the hypothesis that residual risk does not affect pricing. The bias is due to spurious correlation between sample mean and residual variation. Despite this bias, however, we do not reject the hypothesis on a data that excludes Japan and Australia. Consequently, we think our residual variance has negligible impact on international asset pricing if the bias were corrected for.

Noting that Equation (8) should hold for each time period and assuming the stationarity of factor loadings, we obtain the mean returns as follows:

$$
\begin{bmatrix} \tilde{r}_J \\ \tilde{r}_K \end{bmatrix} = \begin{bmatrix} 1\!: \underline{b}_J\!: 0\!: 0 \\ 0\!: 0 : 1\!: \underline{b}_K \end{bmatrix} \begin{bmatrix} \lambda_{0J} \\ \lambda_J \\ \lambda_{0K} \\ \lambda_K \end{bmatrix} + \begin{bmatrix} \bar{e}_J \\ \bar{e}_K \end{bmatrix},
\tag{9}
$$

where $\bar{r}_H = \sum_{t=1}^{T} \tilde{r}_{Ht}/T$; $\bar{e}_H = \sum_{t=1}^{T} \tilde{e}_{Ht}/T$ for $H = J$ and K; and T is the total number of time periods.

Equation (9) is the "unconstrained" regression equation. Now, by imposing each of the hypotheses on Equation (9), we can derive the "constrained" regression equations. The Chow test entails comparison of the constrained residual sum of squares (SSE_c) with the unconstrained residual sum of squares (SSE_u). A given hypothesis is not rejected when the two residual sum of squares are close in value. Furthermore, if df_c and df_u denote the degrees of freedom for the constrained and unconstrained regressions, respectively, then

$$
F = \frac{(SSE_c - SSE_u)/(df_c - df_u)}{SSE_u/df_u}
\tag{10}
$$

has an F-distribution with $(df_c - df_u)$ and df_u degrees of freedom. Note that one has to carry out the regressions using the Generalized Least Square methodology due to the correlations among residuals.[4]

D. Data

Our sample consists of 349 stocks representing 11 different countries, the monthly returns of which are available for the entire period of January 1973 through December 1983.[5] This sample period is roughly characterized by flexible exchange rates. Monthly return data for the U.S. and the foreign stocks were obtained, respectively, from the monthly version of the tape furnished by Center for Research in Security Prices (CRSP) of the University of Chicago and various monthly issues of *Capital International Perspective* (*CIP*). The returns were adjusted for dividends. The exchange rates, which were used in converting stock returns from one currency into another, were obtained from *CIP*.

The sample firms were divided into 11 groups according to their country membership:

1. United States (US: 60 stocks)
2. Canada (CA: 28 stocks)
3. France (FR: 24 stocks)
4. Germany (GE: 22 stocks)
5. Netherlands (NE: 26 stocks)
6. Switzerland (SW: 22 stocks)

---

[4] Readers are referred to Cho [4] for a detailed discussion of the inter-battery factor analysis and the test statistics.

[5] The period for the Canadian stocks was January 1975 through December 1983.

7. United Kingdom (UK: 48 stocks)
8. Australia (AU: 26 stocks)
9. Hong Kong (HK: 14 stocks)
10. Singapore (SI: 24 stocks)
11. Japan (JA: 55 stocks)

Thus, 4 Asia-Pacific, 5 European and 2 North American countries were represented in the sample. With the exception of Hong Kong, each country group contained at least 20 stocks and not more than 60 stocks. This was necessary to have large enough sample sizes in the second-stage cross-sectional regressions and to ease the calculation of the correlation matrices of the combined groups.

Table I presents the average correlation coefficients among country groups in terms of both the U.S. dollar and the Japanese yen. Since factors are derived from correlation matrices, it is worthwhile to briefly examine them. As expected in accordance with the existing literature, securities are found to be, on average, less positively correlated across countries than within a country. In fact, for our sample, the mean of the average inter-country correlations is 0.2336 (0.2029) in the U.S dollar (Japanese yen). This is compared with the mean of the average intra-country correlations, which is 0.5175 (0.4995) in the U.S. dollar (Japanese yen). It is also noted from comparing the two panels of Table I that the

Table I

Average Correlation Coefficients

	US	CA	FR	GE	NE	SW	UK	AU	HK	SI	JA
				Panel A: U.S. Dollar							
US	0.379										
CA	0.263	0.427									
FR	0.196	0.224	0.546								
GE	0.141*	0.150	0.290	0.539							
NE	0.189*	0.202	0.293	0.389	0.484						
SW	0.201	0.244	0.339	0.402	0.403	0.579					
UK	0.225	0.260	0.315	0.233	0.261	0.323	0.617				
AU	0.225	0.258	0.239	0.154	0.155	0.284	0.282	0.488			
HK	0.111*	0.139*	0.185	0.204	0.198	0.260	0.213	0.192	0.672		
SI	0.232	0.221	0.208	0.211	0.234	0.306	0.324	0.268	0.294	0.562	
JA	0.107*	0.134*	0.213	0.242	0.222	0.254	0.179	0.148	0.226	0.191	0.401
				Panel B: Japanese Yen							
US	0.463										
CA	0.332	0.451									
FR	0.206	0.205	0.514								
GE	0.192	0.146*	0.245	0.515							
NE	0.234	0.213	0.254	0.360	0.466						
SW	0.243	0.236	0.289	0.357	0.368	0.541					
UK	0.254	0.263	0.291	0.213	0.247	0.301	0.609				
AU	0.267	0.268	0.208	0.136	0.138	0.263	0.272	0.489			
HK	0.074*	0.103*	0.102*	0.108*	0.112*	0.160	0.160	0.132*	0.635		
SI	0.255	0.211	0.109	0.189	0.219	0.286	0.313	0.262	0.261	0.555	
JA	0.080*	0.062*	0.108*	0.125*	0.118*	0.120*	0.111*	0.070*	0.110*	0.131*	0.256

* Not significantly different from zero at 0.05 significance level.

international correlation structure is similar and varies only a little between the two currencies used to measure security returns.

III. Empirical Results

In this section, the inter-battery factor analysis is conducted to estimate the international common factors. Then, cross-sectional tests are performed in order to investigate the validity of the IAPT.

A. International Common Factors

All of the test samples were constructed by combining two different country groups. To be specific, each of the 11 country groups was combined with each of the remaining 10 country groups to generate 55 distinct samples. This procedure allows us to generate the greatest number of samples and test the validity of the IAPT across all groups of securities. We used the inter-battery factor analysis technique, which allowed us to constrain the factor structure between a pair of countries to be the same or common. Recall that this commonality is not ensured by the traditional factor analysis technique. On the other hand, our approach focuses only on common factors across countries and hence does not consider purely national factors. Nonetheless, it still allows us to test the pricing of common factors as predicted by the IAPT. This is, of course, the primary goal of the paper.

Results of the inter-battery factor analyses on the 55 samples, which are obtained using the significance level of 0.1, are summarized in Table II. Panel A and Panel B, respectively, present the number of factors to be used in subsequent analyses and their corresponding p-levels in terms of the U.S. dollar. Panel C and Panel D present the same in terms of the Japanese yen. It is interesting to note that the numbers in Panel A and Panel C are about the same. There are five cases in which Panel A has more factors, while there are six cases in which Panel C has more factors. In all of the 11 cases, however, the difference is only one factor. Thus, the factor structure is largely invariant to the numeraire currency chosen between the dollar and the yen. Hence, our discussion will be mainly focused on Panel A.

First, casual observation reveals that the samples that are paired with the U.S. group seem to have more factors than other samples. One apparent explanation might be that the U.S. group had more stocks than other groups. In traditional factor analysis, as was documented by Kryzanowski and To [13] and Dhrymes, Friend, and Gultekin [6], one should expect to find more factors as the number of variables in a sample increases.[6] Their studies show that the correlation coefficient between the number of factors and the size of samples is about 0.98. Our results, however, seem to indicate that we do not have as high a correlation.

---

[6] From a statistical point of view, we should note that χ^2 is positively related to the number of variables. Thus, adding a variable would, in general, increase χ^2 and, as long as this increase is more than that compensated by the increase in the degrees of freedom, one would tend to reject the hypothesis more often than not.

Table II

International Common Factors

	US	CA	FR	GE	NE	SW	UK	AU	HK	SI
				Panel A: Number of Factors (U.S. Dollar)						
CA	5									
FR	2	1								
GE	3	1	3							
NE	3	2	2	4						
SW	4	2	2	2	2					
UK	5	2	1	3	3	2				
AU	3	1	2	1	1	1	1			
HK	3	1	1	2	1	2	1	1		
SI	3	1	3	2	2	4	2	1	4	
JA	5	1	2	1	2	3	3	1	3	2
				Panel B: p-level (U.S. Dollar)						
CA	0.250									
FR	0.511	0.314								
GE	0.159	0.460	0.405							
NE	0.190	0.263	0.329	0.291						
SW	0.138	0.127	0.286	0.217	0.273					
UK	0.104	0.279	0.226	0.221	0.456	0.168				
AU	0.101	0.413	0.272	0.845	0.583	0.187	0.124			
HK	0.292	0.244	0.539	0.269	0.101	0.163	0.206	0.282		
SI	0.340	0.576	0.164	0.180	0.309	0.262	0.230	0.403	0.244	
JA	0.294	0.115	0.364	0.168	0.471	0.253	0.114	0.237	0.245	0.262
				Panel C: Number of Factors (Japanese Yen)						
CA	5									
FR	2	1								
GE	3	1	2							
NE	4	2	2	4						
SW	5	2	2	2	2					
UK	6	2	1	3	3	2				
AU	3	1	2	1	1	1	2			
HK	3	1	1	2	1	2	1	1		
SI	3	1	3	2	1	3	2	1	4	
JA	5	2	1	1	2	3	4	1	2	2
				Panel D: p-level (Japanese Yen)						
CA	0.200									
FR	0.407	0.445								
GE	0.228	0.467	0.114							
NE	0.436	0.444	0.335	0.311						
SW	0.278	0.135	0.346	0.238	0.288					
UK	0.487	0.322	0.165	0.202	0.370	0.173				
AU	0.144	0.369	0.308	0.804	0.577	0.231	0.426			
HK	0.225	0.308	0.552	0.331	0.231	0.247	0.313	0.263		
SI	0.285	0.592	0.168	0.366	0.105	0.151	0.210	0.285	0.354	
JA	0.224	0.512	0.128	0.165	0.488	0.440	0.465	0.256	0.152	0.224

For example, (HK, UK) has 62 stocks resulting in one factor, whereas (HK, SI) has 38 stocks resulting in four factors. In fact, the correlation coefficient between the number of factors and the size of samples is found to be about 0.45 in our tests. This clearly shows one of the advantages that inter-battery factor analysis

International APT   323

has over standard factor analysis. It should be noted, however, that our results may still be biased due to the differences in sizes across different samples.

Next, we observe that the number of factors ranges from one to five. In the domestic setting, Cho [4] finds that the number of factors ranges from two to nine. Thus, our results show that the number of factors fluctuates less in an international setting than in a domestic setting. However, we still observe a rather strong sampling fluctuation in the number of factors. It is not clear why we observe this fluctuation. However, as suggested by Cho [4], the observed fluctuations in the number of factors may reflect the homogeneity of the groups involved. For example, if two groups represent the same industry, then one should expect to find only those factors that are relevant to that industry. On the other hand, if two groups represent several different industries, then one should expect to find a wide range of factors that are relevant for the combined industries.

Against this backdrop, the number of factors reported in Table II may be interpreted as reflecting the complexity of the economic relationship between two countries. If two countries are integrated through many levels of economic activity (i.e., high "economic" integration), then we should expect to find more factors. Conversely, if two countries are integrated only through limited levels of economic activity (i.e., low "economic" integration), then we should expect to find a smaller number of factors.[7] This may also explain why fewer common factors were found in the international capital market than in the domestic capital market. In other words, economies are less integrated internationally than domestically. To the extent that the number of international common factors reflects the degree of economic integration, the United States can be said to be highly economically integrated with Canada, the United Kingdom and Japan, and least integrated with France.

Finally, Table III reports the average number of factors that each country has in common with the other countries. Suppose we want to estimate the average number of factors at an α significance level. Considering that the number of factors in Table II represents various p-levels, one cannot take a simple average of the number of factors in the table.[8] However, we can use a procedure similar to Roll and Ross [17]. By choosing an α significance level, we implicitly allow $100\alpha\%$ of our samples to reject the null hypothesis. Hence, we can estimate the average number of factors by identifying the smallest number of factors, say k, at which less than $100\alpha\%$ of our samples could reject the hypothesis that k factors are sufficient. For this procedure, we need p-level distributions for each factor, and an illustrative case is provided in Panel C of Table III for the United States.

Let us, for example, determine the average number of factors for the United States at the 0.1 significance level. As shown in Panel C of Table III, with three factors, there are four samples, namely, those paired with Canada, Switzerland,

---

[7] Economic integration discussed here in association with the number of factors should not be confused with the issue of capital market integration to be investigated later in this paper. Capital markets of two countries, which are characterized by high economic integration, may well be segmented from each other.

[8] For example, (US, FR) has two factors with a p-level of 0.5112 and (US, AU) has three factors with a p-level of 0.1009. Thus, if one takes the simple average of these two numbers of factors, one may not be able to calculate the p-level for the average number of factors.

Table III

Average Number of International Common Factors and p-Level Distribution of U.S. Common Factors

Panel A: U.S. Dollar

p-level	US	CA	FR	GE	NE	SW	UK	AU	HK	SI	JA	World
0.1	5	2	3	3	3	4	3	2	3	4	3	4
0.2	5	2	2	3	3	3	3	2	3	4	3	4
0.3	5	3	3	3	3	3	3	2	3	3	4	3
0.4	4	2	3	3	3	3	3	2	3	3	3	3
0.5	5	2	3	3	3	4	3	2	3	3	3	3

Panel B: Japanese Yen

p-level	US	CA	FR	GE	NE	SW	UK	AU	HK	SI	JA	World
0.1	5	2	2	3	4	3	4	2	3	3	4	4
0.2	5	2	2	3	3	3	3	2	3	4	3	3
0.3	6	2	2	3	3	3	3	2	3	4	3	3
0.4	4	2	3	3	3	3	3	2	3	3	3	3
0.5	5	2	3	3	3	3	3	2	2	3	3	3

Panel C: p-level Distributions of U.S. Common Factors (U.S. Dollar)

Factors	CA	FR	GE	NE	SW	UK	AU	HK	SI	JA
2	0.000	0.511	0.023	0.009	0.001	0.000	0.009	0.064	0.028	0.000
3	0.004	0.942	0.159	0.190	0.029	0.000	0.101	0.292	0.340	0.001
4	0.022	0.997	0.455	0.630	0.138	0.005	0.418	0.650	0.774	0.035
5	0.250	0.999	0.747	0.888	0.420	0.104	0.782	0.835	0.960	0.294

the United Kingdom, and Japan, that reject the hypothesis. With four factors, there are three samples, namely, those paired with Canada, the United Kingdom, and Japan, that reject the hypothesis. With five factors, there are no samples that reject the hypothesis. Since there are ten samples that contain the U.S. group, at most one sample (i.e., 10% of our samples) should be allowed to reject the hypothesis at the 0.1 significance level. Thus, we conclude that on the average, the United States has five factors in common with the other countries.

The results of Panel A and Panel B in Table III were obtained from the procedures illustrated above. Panel A and Panel B present the average number of factors in terms of the U.S. dollar and the Japanese yen, respectively. Notice that the results reported in the two panels are quite similar. Again, it seems that the international factor structure is largely invariant to the numeraire currency chosen between the two currencies. Also, the average number of international common factors is fairly consistent across different significance levels. If our results were biased due to the difference in sample sizes, then we should have observed marked differences in the number of factors across different p-levels.[9] Thus, the observed consistency in the number of factors seems to indicate that the possible bias due to the difference in sample sizes is not serious in our study. In summary, Table III indicates that, on average, there are about three or four worldwide common factors.[10] It also indicates that the United States and Singapore seem to be most highly economically integrated with the other countries, whereas Australia and Canada seem to be least integrated. A possible explanation for these results on this particular economic integration is the heavy emphasis on manufacturing industries by the U.S. and Singapore and on raw materials by Australia and Canada.

B. Tests of the International Arbitrage Pricing Theory

We investigate the validity of the IAPT by testing the three hypotheses enumerated in Section II.C, both in the U.S. dollar and the Japanese yen. In order to save space, we briefly summarize the results in the following paragraphs and report the test results only for the hypothesis (H3) in Table IV.[11] The hypothesis (H3) implies that both the intercept and risk premia are all equal between two country groups. In conducting these tests, the number of factors was not constrained to be the same across the entire sample; rather, it was allowed to vary as long as the significance level was similar across the entire sample.[12]

At the 0.05 significance level, the hypothesis (H1) of equal intercept (or the risk-free rate) between two country groups is rejected in three out of 55 total cases in terms of the U.S. dollar, which is 5.45% of the overall sample. In terms

---

[9] As mentioned in footnote 6, the p-levels at which a given number of factors is accepted depend on the sample sizes. We would not expect this kind of consistency in the number of factors across the different p-levels if the bias were serious.

[10] Worldwide common factors are estimated as above by examining all of the 55 samples.

[11] The test results for the hypotheses (H1) and (H2) are available upon request.

[12] Since we do not know the number of factors in the population, we allow our sampling fluctuation in the number of factors. This was done out of our desire not to overfit the model by considering more factors than necessary.

The Journal of Finance

Table IV

Cross-Sectional Test of Equal Intercepts and Risk Premia

	US	CA	FR	GE	NE	SW	UK	AU	HK	SI
Panel A: F-Statistics (U.S. Dollar)										
CA	3.804									
FR	18.422	18.331								
GE	1.662	0.075	4.603							
NE	3.611	7.149	9.495	1.587						
SW	8.915	2.887	0.370	3.056	5.357					
UK	15.600	4.697	1.942	7.448	5.817	4.068				
AU	2.386	8.388	3.330	0.327	0.329	0.205	4.569			
HK	4.441	4.424	0.110	1.626	5.223	1.035	3.631	0.449		
SI	1.516	2.910	0.767	1.593	0.675	3.735	2.658	3.406	1.218	
JA	13.198	2.891	3.752	5.973	6.148	5.295	25.582	0.444	4.014	0.752
Panel B: p-levels (U.S. Dollar)										
CA	0.002*									
FR	0.000*	0.000*								
GE	0.168	0.928	0.004*							
NE	0.009*	0.001*	0.000*	0.187						
SW	0.000*	0.046*	0.775	0.040*	0.003*					
UK	0.000*	0.005*	0.151	0.000*	0.001*	0.010*				
AU	0.058	0.001*	0.028*	0.723	0.721	0.816	0.014*			
HK	0.003*	0.019*	0.896	0.204	0.010*	0.391	0.033*	0.642		
SI	0.206	0.064	0.553	0.206	0.572	0.008*	0.056	0.042*	0.327	
JA	0.000*	0.061	0.015*	0.004*	0.001*	0.001*	0.000*	0.643	0.006*	0.525
Panel C: F-Statistics (Japanese Yen)										
CA	3.280									
FR	18.089	18.467								
GE	2.062	0.271	5.663							
NE	7.270	7.591	10.467	1.886						
SW	8.957	1.149	0.465	2.991	6.046					
UK	17.574	6.902	1.968	11.228	6.046	3.186				
AU	2.625	6.431	3.106	0.462	0.195	0.262	3.009			
HK	4.553	2.986	1.185	2.201	7.373	1.094	4.458	0.577		
SI	1.885	2.409	0.406	5.868	0.790	4.847	2.543	2.342	1.368	
JA	9.980	5.398	1.163	5.538	7.377	5.869	20.762	0.550	0.916	1.138
Panel D: p-levels (Japanese Yen)										
CA	0.006*									
FR	0.000*	0.000*								
GE	0.094	0.764	0.003*							
NE	0.000*	0.000*	0.000*	0.120						
SW	0.000*	0.340	0.709	0.043*	0.002*					
UK	0.000*	0.000*	0.148	0.000*	0.000*	0.030*				
AU	0.041*	0.003*	0.036*	0.633	0.824	0.771	0.036*			
HK	0.003*	0.063	0.318	0.109	0.002*	0.367	0.016*	0.567		
SI	0.122	0.101	0.803	0.002*	0.460	0.003*	0.006*	0.044*	0.266	
JA	0.000*	0.002*	0.318	0.006*	0.000*	0.000*	0.000*	0.580	0.438	0.340

* *p*-levels that are smaller than the significance level of 0.05.

of the Japanese yen, the hypothesis is rejected in two out of 55 cases, which is 3.64% of the entire sample. For the null hypothesis to be true at the 0.05 significance level, there should be at most two cases (5% of the entire sample) in which the hypothesis is rejected, if the samples are independent. Thus, our results indicate that the hypothesis should be rejected in terms of the dollar but not the yen. Considering, however, that our samples are not independent, and also that the normality assumption might have been violated, we are inclined not to reject H1 in terms of the dollar as well as the yen.

The hypothesis (H2) of the equal risk premia between two country groups is rejected in 30 out of 55 total cases in terms of both the dollar and the yen, which is about 55% of the entire sample. Table IV reports the F-statistics and p-levels for the hypothesis (H3). Again, at the 0.05 significance level, the hypothesis is rejected in 32 cases out of 55 cases in terms of both the dollar and the yen, which is about 58% of the entire sample. These empirical results lead us to reject both H2 and H3, irrespective of the numeraire currency chosen.

The empirical results presented above can be summarized as follows:

(H1) equal intercepts: not rejected.
(H2) equal risk premia: rejected.
(H3) equal intercepts and risk premia: rejected.

It should be pointed out that these results are invariant to the numeraire currency chosen. As previously mentioned, if the APT holds in an integrated international capital market, then all of the three hypotheses must not be rejected. Given that two of the hypotheses are rejected, the empirical results lead us to reject the joint hypothesis that capital markets are integrated and that the APT holds internationally.[13]

One caveat is that we have used the same data for factor estimation and testing the equality of the risk premia. This caveat is endemic to the tests conducted by Roll and Ross [17] as well. However, the bias would have worked in favor of the IAPT by increasing the test statistics associated with risk premia. Despite this, our tests reject the IAPT.[14] Still another caveat is that, due to the nature of testing the joint hypothesis, it is impossible to determine whether rejection of the joint hypothesis reflects the failure of the IAPT or segmentation of capital markets. If capital markets are segmented, then the APT cannot be valid internationally by definition, but can be valid locally or regionally. Thus, our results do not rule out the possibility of the APT being valid locally or regionally in segmented capital markets. For example, there are 20 (22) cases in terms of the dollar (the yen) out of 55 total cases, about 36% (40%) of the entire sample, in which none of the three hypotheses is rejected. This suggests the possibility that the APT holds locally or regionally in segmented capital markets. One

[13] The test results of H1, however, indicate that the risk-free rates "implicit" in the IAPT are equal in a given currency across countries. Our results thus seem to be consistent with the notion of an integrated international capital market for the risk-free assets (or the zero-beta assets) in which there exist no arbitrage opportunities across countries.

[14] We have also conducted a test of the effect of residual risk on international asset pricing. Our results are inconclusive and can be obtained from the authors upon request. See footnote 3 for further explanation.

328   *The Journal of Finance*

possible cause of market segmentation is an investment barrier in the form of differential tax regimes and border (or withholding) taxes across countries (see Black [2]). Of course, local tax asymmetry between capital gains and dividends may impact the structural form of APT even in the domestic setting, since the model is originally derived under competitive and frictionless capital markets. The analogy to this is the effect of taxes on capital asset pricing as in Litzenberger and Ramaswamy [15]. Obviously, these tax effects are more pronounced in an international setting so as to segment national or regional markets and hence possibly explain some of our results.

Thus, an interesting topic for future research would be to determine different regions or segments of the world in which security prices behave as if they are determined regionally. For example, the existence of a regional APT would be important in identifying those areas of the world that create an incentive for multinational firms to play a role in integrating the international capital market as argued by Errunza and Senbet [8, 9]. With more refined data on the degree of international involvement spanning geographic diversification and the corresponding "regionalization" of APT, one can study further the extent to which multinational firms provide valuable financial intermediation services through direct foreign investment.

IV. Conclusions

In this paper, we have provided an empirical investigation of the arbitrage pricing theory in an international setting. Inter-battery factor analysis was used to estimate the common factors between two country groups, and the Chow test was used in testing the validity of the APT.

Our inter-battery factor analysis results have shown that there are about three or four worldwide common factors and that the number of common factors between two countries ranges from one to five depending on the degree of their economic integration. These results are rather similar in terms of the U.S. dollar and the Japanese yen. We have also observed that the inter-battery factor analysis produces less bias concerning the effect of sample size on the number of factors extracted than the standard factor analysis.

Our cross-sectional test results led us to reject the joint hypothesis that the international capital market is integrated and that the APT is valid internationally. At present, we are unable to determine whether rejection of the joint hypothesis reflects segmentation of capital markets or the failure of the international APT. Resolution of this issue is left for future research. Our empirical results do not rule out the possibility of the APT being valid locally or regionally in segmented capital markets.

REFERENCES

1. M. Adler and B. Dumas. "International Portfolio Choice and Corporation Finance: A Synthesis." *Journal of Finance* 38 (June 1983), 925–84.
2. F. Black. "International Capital Market Equilibrium with Investment Barriers." *Journal of Financial Economics* 1 (December 1974), 337–52.

International APT   329

3. S. Brown and M. Weinstein. "A New Approach to Testing Asset Pricing Models: The Bilinear Paradigm." Journal of Finance 38 (June 1983), 711–43.

4. D. Cho. "On Testing the Arbitrage Pricing Theory: Inter-Battery Factor Analysis." *Journal of Finance* 39 (December 1984), 1485–1502.

5. B. Cornell. "The Consumption Based Asset Pricing Model: A Note on Potential Tests and Applications." *Journal of Financial Economics* 9 (March 1981), 103–8.

6. P. Dhrymes, I. Friend, and B. Gultekin. "A Critical Reexamination of the Empirical Evidence on the Arbitrage Pricing Theory." *Journal of Finance* 39 (June 1984), 323–46.

7. P. Dybvig and S. Ross. "Yes, the APT is Testable." *Journal of Finance* 40 (September 1985), 1173–88.

8. V. Errunza and L. Senbet. "The Effects of International Operations on the Market Value of the Firm: Theory and Evidence." *Journal of Finance* 36 (May 1981), 401–17.

9. ———. "International Corporation Diversification, Market Valuation and Size-Adjusted Evidence." *Journal of Finance* 39 (July 1984), 727–43.

10. C. Eun and B. Resnick. "Estimating the Correlation Structure of International Share Prices." *Journal of Finance* 39 (December 1984), 1311–24.

11. F. Grauer, R. Litzenberger, and R. Stehle. "Sharing Rules and Equilibrium in an International Capital Market under Uncertainty." *Journal of Financial Economics* 3 (June 1976), 233–56.

12. P. Kouri. "International Investment and Interest Rate Linkages under Flexible Exchange Rates." In R. Aliber (ed.), *The Political Economy of Monetary Reform*. London: Macmillan & Co., 1977.

13. L. Kryzanowski and M. To. "General Factor Models and the Structure of Security Returns." *Journal of Financial and Quantitative Analysis* 18 (March 1983), 31–52.

14. D. Lessard. "The Structure of Returns and Gains from International Diversification: A Multivariate Approach." In E. J. Elton and M. J. Gruber (ed.), *International Capital Markets*. New York: North-Holland, 1975.

15. R. Litzenberger and K. Ramaswamy. "The Effect of Personal Taxes and Dividends on Capital Asset Prices: Theory of Empirical Evidence." *Journal of Financial Economics* 7 (June 1979), 163–95.

16. R. Roll. "A Critique of the Asset Pricing Theory's Test; Part 1: On Past and Potential Testability of the Theory." *Journal of Financial Economics* 4 (March 1977), 129–76.

17. ——— and S. Ross. "An Empirical Investigation of the Arbitrage Pricing Theory." *Journal of Finance* 35 (December 1980), 1073–1103.

18. S. Ross. "The Arbitrage Theory of Capital Asset Pricing." *Journal of Economic Theory* 13 (December 1976), 341–60.

19. J. Shanken. "The Arbitrage Price Theory: Is It Testable?" *Journal of Finance* 37 (December 1982), 1129–40.

20. B. Solnik. "The International Pricing of Risk: An Empirical Investigation of the World Capital Market Structure." *Journal of Finance* 29 (May 1974), 48–54.

21. ———. "An Equilibrium Model of the International Capital Market." *Journal of Economic Theory* 8 (August 1974), 500–24.

22. ———. "International Arbitrage Pricing Theory." *Journal of Finance* 38 (May 1983), 449–57.

23. R. Stehle. "An Empirical Test of the Alternative Hypotheses of National and International Pricing of Risky Assets." *Journal of Finance* 32 (May 1977), 493–502.

24. R. Stulz. "A Model of International Asset Pricing." *Journal of Financial Economics* 9 (December 1981), 383–406.

[10]

An Empirical Investigation of International Asset Pricing

Robert A. Korajczyk
Northwestern University and University of Chicago

Claude J. Viallet
INSEAD

We investigate several asset pricing models in an international setting. We use data on a large number of assets traded in the United States, Japan, the United Kingdom, and France. The models together with the hypothesis of capital market integration imply testable restrictions on multivariate regressions relating asset returns to various benchmark portfolios. We find that multifactor models tend to outperform single-index models in both domestic and international forms especially in their ability to explain seasonality in asset returns. We also find that the behavior of the models is affected by changes in the regulatory environment in international markets.

In this article we evaluate the pricing performance of alternative domestic and international asset pricing models. The models are compared when pricing assets within national economies and, in their international versions, when pricing assets across economies. The pricing models together with the hypothesis of capital market integration imply testable restrictions on multivariate regression models relating asset returns to various benchmark portfolios. Conditional on capital market integration, the tests provide information on the

---

This research was completed thanks to the financial support of INSEAD, Northwestern University, and the Euro Asia Center. The authors thank Pascal Dumontier; Pierre Hillion; Bruce Lehmann; Alessandro Penati; Arthur Warga; an anonymous referee; the editors, Michael Gibbons and Michael Brennan; and seminar participants at Duke University, University of Illinois, INSEAD, and Ohio State University for helpful comments and discussions. Jay Wortman provided computational assistance. Address reprint requests to Robert A. Korajczyk, Kellogg Graduate School of Management, Northwestern University, 2001 Sheridan Road, Evanston, IL 60208-2006.

The Review of Financial Studies 1989, Volume 2, number 4, pp. 553–585
© 1990 The Review of Financial Studies 0893-9454/90/$1.50

The Review of Financial Studies / v 2 n 4 1989

validity of the model. Conversely, given that the assumed type of pricing model is correct, the tests provide information about integration across markets. We compare domestic and international versions of the capital asset pricing model (CAPM) and the arbitrage pricing theory (APT) where the pervasive factors are estimated by an asymptotic principal components technique.

We focus on three questions. First, we investigate whether the APT has greater explanatory power than the CAPM in a domestic as well as in an international setting. Second, we ask whether international versions of the asset pricing models outperform or underperform single-economy versions. Finally, we look for the influence of changes in the regulation of international financial markets on the deviations of returns from the predicted asset pricing relations. Our study, which covers the period 1969–1983, uses a large number of securities from the United States, Japan, the United Kingdom, and France both for factor estimation and hypothesis testing.

Asset pricing theories are commonly tested in a closed economy setting in which assets are priced relative to benchmark portfolios constructed from assets trading in the same economy. Fama and MacBeth (1973) and Roll and Ross (1980) are well-known examples of single-economy tests of the CAPM and APT, respectively. A variety of asset pricing anomalies have been uncovered by single-economy studies. In particular, seasonal, firm size, and dividend yield related mispricing have been documented.[1] Single-economy applications of the APT have had some success in explaining pricing anomalies.[2]

In related work, Cho, Eun, and Senbet (1986) reject an international version of the APT. Using a two-country version of the APT, Gultekin, Gultekin, and Penati (1989) find that the performance of the model is affected by changes in capital controls. We find that rejection of the international APT is sensitive to inclusion of sample periods with strict capital controls. Our study covers more countries than Gultekin, Gultekin, and Penati (1989) but fewer than Cho, Eun, and Senbet (1986). However, for the countries we study, we utilize many more securities.[3] The large number of cross sections allows more precise estimation of the factors. Also, the above studies do not address the issue of comparative performance across models (e.g., CAPM versus APT or international versus domestic).

[1] See, for example, Banz (1981) and Keim (1983) for evidence on U.S. exchanges, Kato and Schallheim (1985) for the Tokyo stock exchange, Corhay, Hawawini, and Michel (1987) for the London stock exchange, and Hawawini and Viallet (1987) for the Paris stock exchange.

[2] In the United States, Chen (1983) finds that the size anomaly becomes insignificant when the APT is used while Lehmann and Modest (1988) and Connor and Korajczyk (1988a) find a significant size effect remaining. Lehmann and Modest (1988) do find that the dividend yield anomaly is no longer significant. In the U.K., Beenstock and Chan (1984) find that the APT performs significantly better than the CAPM in explaining asset returns. Similar results are found by Dumontier (1986) using French stocks and Hamao (1986) using Japanese stocks.

[3] The minimum number of firms from our four countries is 4211 while the maximum number is 6692. The number of securities used in Cho, Eun, and Senbet (1986), by country, are United States (60), Japan (55), United Kingdom (48), and France (24) while the numbers used in Gultekin, Gultekin, and Penati (1989) are United States (110) and Japan (110).

The next section of the article contains a brief description of the alternative asset pricing models. In Section 2 we describe the data. The techniques used to estimate the pervasive factors and test the alternative models are described in Section 3, and the empirical results are given in Section 4. Section 5 comprises a summary and conclusions.

1. Alternative Asset Pricing Models

We investigate the pricing performance of domestic and international versions of the CAPM and APT. The CAPM or the APT implies that a particular benchmark portfolio or linear combination of a group of benchmark portfolios lies on the minimum-variance boundary of risky assets [e.g., see Roll (1977) or Huberman and Kandel (1987)]. The domestic and international versions of the models differ in that only securities traded on the local exchange are included in the benchmark portfolios for the domestic model while the benchmarks for the international versions include all the assets in the sample. Since the basic models are rather well known we will merely state the implications of the models and concentrate our discussion on the problems associated with implementing them.

The standard version of the CAPM postulates that the market portfolio is on the mean-variance efficient frontier, which, in turn, implies that the expected return on each asset is linearly related to its beta $[\beta_{iM} = \text{cov}(\tilde{r}_i, \tilde{r}_M)/\text{var}(\tilde{r}_M)]$. Assuming the existence of a real riskless asset with return r_F, we have

$$E(\tilde{R}_i) \equiv E(\tilde{r}_i) - r_F = \beta_{iM}[E(\tilde{r}_M) - r_F] \equiv \beta_{iM}E(\tilde{R}_M) \tag{1}$$

where $\tilde{r}_i$ and $\tilde{r}_M$ are the real returns on asset i and the market portfolio and $\tilde{R}_i$ and $\tilde{R}_M$ are returns in excess of the riskless return r_F. In a closed economy setting the market portfolio M is the portfolio of all domestic assets weighted by their respective proportionate values. Extending Equation (1) to an international setting generally involves more than replacing the domestic market portfolio with an international market portfolio. Exchange rate uncertainty and, particularly, potential deviations from strict purchasing power parity can lead to incremental hedging demands for assets (although hedging against shifts in the consumption-investment opportunity set is not peculiar to international models). Under admittedly restrictive conditions there will be no excess demand for hedging exchange risks and we can proceed with a relation like Equation (1).[4] Note that in both domestic and international applications one is never able to obtain the true market portfolio relevant for the particular model. Thus, tests of the pricing relation (1) for different proxies, M, amount to tests of mean-variance efficiency for these proxies.

---

[4] In addition to the usual assumptions needed for the CAPM [see Constantinides (1980)], assuming that strict purchasing power parity (PPP) holds (i.e., the law of one price must hold across national boundaries) would be sufficient for Equation (1) to hold internationally. Exchange rate uncertainty is not priced separately from market risk because the PPP assumption implies that changes in exchange rates do not change real relative prices. See, for example, Solnik (1974, pp. 514–518) and Stulz (1985, pp. 77–79).

The Review of Financial Studies / v 2 n 4 1989

As in many empirical investigations, we use the return on short-term U.S. Treasury bills as a proxy for the riskless rate of interest. Since these returns are not strictly riskless in real terms, we also test the restrictions implied by the Black (1972) zero-beta CAPM, assuming that the difference between the expected returns on the zero-beta portfolio and Treasury bills is a constant, λ. It follows that the expected returns, in excess of the Treasury-bill return, are determined by

$$E(\tilde{R}_i) = (1 - \beta_{iM}) \cdot \lambda + \beta_{iM} E(\tilde{R}_M) \tag{2}$$

A value of λ equal to 0 is consistent with the pricing relation (1).

As an alternative to the CAPM we consider the APT. An assumption underlying the APT is that asset returns follow a factor model:

$$\tilde{r}_i = \mu_i + b_{i1}\tilde{f}_1 + b_{i2}\tilde{f}_2 + \cdots + b_{ik}\tilde{f}_k + \tilde{\epsilon}_i$$

where b_{ij} is the sensitivity (beta) of asset i relative to factor j and $E(\tilde{f}_j) = E(\tilde{\epsilon}_i) = E(\tilde{f}_j\tilde{\epsilon}_i) = 0$ for all i and j. The number of assets in the economy is assumed to be sufficiently large and the correlation across the idiosyncratic returns (ϵ_i's) is assumed to be sufficiently small that the idiosyncratic risk can be eliminated in large portfolios.[5] Lack of arbitrage opportunities and existence of a riskless asset imply that

$$E(\tilde{R}_i) \approx b_{i1}\gamma_1 + b_{i2}\gamma_2 + \cdots + b_{ik}\gamma_k \tag{3}$$

Additional equilibrium conditions [as in Connor (1984)] can lead to the pricing relation (3) holding as an equality rather than an approximation. Our empirical work below tests Equation (3) as an equality. Ross and Walsh (1983) and Solnik (1983) extend the APT to an international setting. With the assumption that exchange rates follow the same factor model as asset returns, they find that the standard APT pricing relation (3) can be applied directly in an international setting. Thus, exchange rate uncertainty is priced to the extent that it represents pervasive factor risk. Also, the pervasive components of exchange rate risk will be reflected in the returns on our factor mimicking portfolios. We also estimate a zero-beta version of Equation (3), which we discuss in more detail below.

In Table 1 we present the particular models investigated. Two of them, the CAPM–EW and the CAPM–VW, are models in which the benchmark portfolios are equal-weighted and value-weighted portfolios of common stocks, respectively. The last two, the APT–5 and APT–10 factor models, use statistically estimated factors. Each of the four models (and their zero-beta alternatives) are tested in three versions. In the first version we test the mean/variance efficiency of domestic benchmark portfolios relative to domestic assets. In the second and third versions we test the mean-variance efficiency of international benchmark portfolios relative to both domestic

---

[5] Ross (1976) assumes that $E(\tilde{\epsilon}_i\tilde{\epsilon}_j) = 0$ (a strict factor model). Chamberlain and Rothschild (1983) and Ingersoll (1984) show that the APT can be derived under the weaker condition that the eigenvalues of the cross-sectional idiosyncratic covariance matrix are bounded as the number of assets grows large (an approximate factor model).

Investigation of International Asset Pricing

Table 1
Models and versions tested

Domestic/Domestic		Domestic/International		International/International	
R_i	P	R_i	P	R_i	P
US	US	US	International	International	International
JP	JP	JP	International		
UK	UK	UK	International		
FR	FR	FR	International		

Models used are CAPM–EW, CAPM–VW, APT–5, and APT–10. Models are tested by estimating the mispricing of size-ranked portfolios relative to various benchmark portfolios. CAPM–EW and CAPM–VW correspond, respectively, to the use of equal-weighted and value-weighted equity portfolios as the benchmarks. APT–5 and APT–10 use 5 and 10 factor-mimicking portfolios, estimated by the asymptotic principal components procedure, as benchmarks. Versions of the model are distinguished by the markets from which the size-based portfolios and benchmark portfolios are constructed. R_i identifies the source of the size-based portfolios while P identifies the source of the benchmark portfolios. US: United States, JP: Japan, UK: United Kingdom, FR: France, International: all four countries. Zero-beta variants of each model are also tested as are variants which use nominal and real returns.

assets (for each economy separately) and relative to an international set of assets.

2. Data Sources

The selected countries, markets, and data sources are shown in Table 2. We were able to obtain monthly stock return data for four countries spanning 15 years from January 1969 through December 1983. Our sample includes three major markets: the New York and American Stock Exchanges, the Tokyo Stock Exchange, and the London Stock Exchange. For these three countries our sample includes all assets traded on the exchanges. The Paris Bourse is added in order to introduce a country with severe foreign exchange controls. Unlike the major markets, our sample from this market includes only a subsample of the number of traded assets (approximately 20 percent). The four markets represented nearly 65 percent of the world equity market capitalization at the end of 1983. Returns from France, Japan, and the United Kingdom, adjusted for dividends and stock splits, are transformed into dollar returns using end-of-month exchange rates from the Data Resources Incorporated data file. Excess returns were computed using the short-term U.S. Treasury-bill return.[6] We perform our tests on both nominal and real returns. Nominal dollar returns are converted into real returns using inflation calculated at the percentage change in the U.S. consumer price index. The Treasury-bill returns and inflation series are from Ibbotson Associates (1985).

---

[6] We also test versions of the models denominated in each of the other three currencies. Excess returns are calculated relative to the short-term interest rates prevailing in each of the countries' currencies, which are obtained from the International Financial Statistics tables. We find that the test results are not significantly affected by the currency chosen. As a result we only present results using the U.S. dollar as *numeraire*.

557

The Review of Financial Studies / v 2 n 4 1989

Table 2
Exchange market data and sample data summary

	United States	Japan	United Kingdom	France	Total
Stock exchange	NYSE & Amex	Tokyo	London	Paris	
Market capitalization (12/ 83) ÷ world capitalization	43%	15%	6.1%	1%	65.1%
Number of listed firms (12/83)	2274	1441	2217	518	6450
Sample data					
Sample source	CRSP	Japan Securities Research Institute (JSRI)	London Share Price Data Base	Compagnie des Agents de Change	
Frequency of returns	Monthly	Monthly	Monthly	Monthly	
Number of sample firms:					
Minimum	2187	672	1138	112	4211
Maximum	2706	1420	2555	126	6692
Average	2457	1144	1874	121	5596

Source of market capitalization percentages and number of listed firms December 1983: *International Federation of Stock Exchange Statistics,* 1983.

3. Estimation of Pervasive Economic Factors and Hypothesis Tests

3.1 Estimation of pervasive factors

Our tests of the CAPM amount to specifying the benchmark portfolios whose mean-variance efficiency is being tested. However, the assumed linear factor structure that underlies the APT lends itself naturally to direct statistical estimation of the factors. In fact, most empirical tests of the APT, to date, use standard factor analytic techniques to estimate either the betas of assets or the factor realizations. For our factor models we use the asymptotic principal components technique of Connor and Korajczyk (1986, 1988b). An advantage of this procedure is its ability to utilize very large cross sections to estimate the pervasive factors. Also, while the number of time periods T has to be larger than the number of assumed factors k, it does not have to be larger than the number of assets n. While maximum-likelihood factor analysis is, in theory, more efficient than principal components, standard factor analysis packages cannot handle the number of securities analyzed here (e.g., the international APT uses between 4211 and 6692 securities to estimate the factors). A brief outline of the asymptotic principal components technique is presented below.

We assume that asset returns follow an approximate k-factor model [in the sense of Chamberlain and Rothschild (1983)], that exact multifactor pricing holds [i.e., Equation (3) holds as an equality], and that we observe the returns on n risky assets and the riskless interest rate over T time periods. Let R^n be the $n \times T$ matrix of excess returns; F be the $k \times T$ matrix of realized factors plus risk premia (i.e., $F_{jt} = f_{jt} + \gamma_{jt}$); and B^n be the $n \times k$ matrix of factor loadings. The estimation procedure allows the risk premia γ_{jt} to vary through time. Exact multifactor pricing implies that

$$R^n = B^n F + \epsilon^n \tag{4}$$

where $E(F\epsilon^{n\prime}) = 0$
$$E(\epsilon^n) = 0$$
$$E(\epsilon^n \epsilon^{n\prime}/T) = V^n$$

Let Ω^n be the $T \times T$ matrix defined by $\Omega^n = R^{n\prime} R^n/n$ and G^n be the $k \times T$ matrix consisting of the first k eigenvectors of Ω^n. Theorem 2 of Connor and Korajczyk (1986) shows that G^n approaches a nonsingular transformation of F as $n \rightarrow \infty$. That is, $G^n = L^n F + \phi^n$ where plim $[\phi^n] = 0$. The transformation L^n reflects the standard rotational indeterminacy of factor models. We assume that our sample size is sufficiently large that ϕ^n is the null matrix.

Note that, while we are working with cross sections as large as 6692, the factor estimation method only requires the calculation of the first k eigenvectors of a $T \times T$ matrix. In our work T is equal to 180 (15 years of monthly data). For the domestic versions of the APT, Ω^n is calculated over the assets traded on the domestic stock exchange and, for the international versions, over the entire sample. We use the extension of the principal components technique [from Connor and Korajczyk (1988b)], which does not require that assets have a continuous time series of returns. Because of this, our factor estimates are not contaminated by any survivorship bias.

A difficulty which arises in any application of the APT is the choice of the appropriate number of factors. A common approach, found in the factor analysis literature, tests whether V^n is diagonal after extracting k factors. This test is inappropriate when asset returns follow an approximate rather than a strict factor model since V^n need not be diagonal in the former case. We report the results of two tests, each of which takes a very different approach to the problem.

The asymptotic principal components procedure provides us with excess returns on factor-mimicking portfolios. We will consider the problem of testing a k_1-factor model versus a k_2-factor model $(k_2 > k_1)$. The first test is suggested by Kandel and Stambaugh (1987). It is based on the observation that if a k_1-factor model actually describes cross-sectional expected returns then the expected excess returns on the remaining $k_2 - k_1$ factor-mimicking portfolios should be described by the APT pricing relation (3), using the first k_1 factors. This test is more stringent than most approaches to determining the number of factors. While most tests only examine whether additional factors have explanatory power in time series, the approach of Kandel and Stambaugh (1987) tests whether the additional factors have risk that is not already priced by the first k_1 factors. Factors that have time-series explanatory power but that have a zero risk premium (i.e., $\gamma_j = 0$ for that factor) will not be identified as factors by this test.

Let P_{1t} denote the $k_1 \times 1$ vector of period t excess returns on the first k_1 factors and P_{2t} denote the $p \times 1$ vector $(p = k_2 - k_1)$ of period t excess

The Review of Financial Studies / v 2 n 4 1989

Table 3
Tests of k_1 factors versus the alternative of k_2 factors based on the mean/variance efficiency of k_1 factor portfolios relative to k_2 factor portfolios

		P-values				
k_1	k_2	United States	United Kingdom	Japan	France	International
0	1	.366	.074*	.003*	.368	.180
1	2	.349	.014*	.894	.400	.103
2	3	.328	.452	.745	.103	.032*
3	4	.771	.464	.730	.725	.292
4	5	.636	.138	.336	.623	.531
5	6	.445	.801	.932	.797	.511
1	5	.711	.050*	.882	.088	.068
5	10	.973	.986	.989	.414	.839
10	15	.872	.398	.588	.485	.937

The null hypothesis implies that the intercepts in a multivariate regression of the last $k_2 - k_1$ factors on the first k_1 factors equal 0. Factors are estimated by asymptotic principal components using monthly data from January 1969 through December 1983. *P*-values are the right tail area of the modified likelihood ratio (MLR) statistic for the restriction that intercepts equal 0.
* Significant at the 5 percent level.

returns on the remaining factors. The null hypothesis that k_1 factors are sufficient [from Equation (3)] implies that the $p \times 1$ vector of intercepts in a multivariate regression of P_2 on P_1 are equal to 0. That is, $a = 0$ in

$$P_{2t} = a + \beta P_{1t} + \eta_t \qquad (5)$$

To test $a = 0$ we use a modified likelihood ratio (MLR) statistic [see Rao (1973, p. 555)]. The MLR statistic for our hypotheses is given by

$$\left(\frac{|\hat{\Sigma}_N|}{|\hat{\Sigma}_A|} - 1 \right) \cdot \frac{T - k_1 - p}{p} \qquad (6)$$

where T is the number of time-series observations, $|\cdot|$ denotes determinant, and $\hat{\Sigma}_N(\hat{\Sigma}_A)$ are the maximum-likelihood estimates of $E(\tilde{\eta}_t \tilde{\eta}_t')$ assuming the null, $a = 0$ (the alternative, $a \neq 0$). Under the null hypothesis, the MLR statistic has an *F*-distribution with degrees of freedom equal to p and $T - k_1 - p$. An advantage of the MLR over alternative test statistics (such as the Wald or unmodified LR statistics) is that its exact small-sample distribution is known (when $\tilde{\eta}$ has a multivariate normal distribution).[7] We apply the above test to the factors estimated by the asymptotic principal components technique. The test results, which are reported in Table 3, do not seem to provide much power to discriminate against any hypothesized number of factors. In only two out of five cases are we able to reject the null hypothesis of no factors in favor of the alternative of one factor.

We suggest an alternative test, which, under certain conditions, will give us asymptotically (as the number of assets, n, increases) valid inferences

---

[7] Geometric interpretations of this test are provided in Gibbons, Ross, and Shanken (1986) and Kandel and Stambaugh (1987).

Table 4
Test of k_1 factors versus the alternative of k_2 factors based on the time-series explanatory power of the additional $k_2 - k_1$ factor portfolios

		P-values			
k_1	k_2	United States	United Kingdom	Japan	France	Inter-national
1	5	<.001*	<.001*	<.001*	<.001*	<.001*
5	10	.010*	.139	.001*	.005*	<.001*
10	15	<.001*	.060	<.001*	<.001*	.003*

The null hypothesis implies that the betas of an equal-weighted portfolio relative to factor $k_1 + 1$ through factor k_2 are equal to 0 asymptotically (as the number of assets in the equal-weighted portfolio increases). Factors are estimated by asymptotic principal components using monthly data from January 1969 through December 1983. P-values are the right tail area of the MLR statistic for the restriction that the betas of the equal-weighted portfolio relative to factors $k_1 + 1$ through k_2 are jointly zero.
* Significant at the 5 percent level.

regarding the number of factors for both strict or approximate factor structures. This test is different from the above approach in that it uses the usual criterion for pervasiveness, time-series explanatory power, and does not rely on pricing restrictions. Our test relies on a result from Ingersoll (1984) which states that the cross-sectional mean square of assets' betas relative to a *nonpervasive* factor must approach zero as n approaches infinity. That is, if the kth factor is nonpervasive then $B^{n'}_{.k}B^n_{.k}/n \to 0$ as $n \to \infty$, where $B^n_{.k}$ is the kth column of B^n in Equation (4). A necessary condition for the mean-square beta to approach zero is that the average beta must also approach zero since $B^{n'}_{.k}B^n_{.k}/n \to \sigma^2 + \bar{B}^2_k$ where σ^2 is the cross-sectional variance of betas and $\bar{B}_k$ is the average beta. We can estimate the average beta by regressing the excess return of an equal-weighted portfolio on the factors. Nonpervasive factors should have coefficients that are asymptotically zero as the number of assets in the equal-weighted portfolio approaches infinity. Thus, we can use a simple t-test for the null hypothesis that the equal-weighted portfolio has zero sensitivity to the kth factor. The test might indicate too few factors because it tests a necessary condition for nonpervasiveness. That is, it is possible for the mean beta to be zero while the limiting variance is not zero (e.g., the betas could alternate between 1 and -1). On the other hand, the test might indicate too many factors, in small samples, since the mean beta relative to a nonpervasive factor is only zero in the limit. The results of this test are reported in Table 4. They are diametrically opposed to the results of the first test. Only for the United Kingdom do we accept less than 15 factors. Given that the restriction being tested is only strictly valid for n equal to infinity, the apparently large number of factors should be interpreted with some caution.

Conflicting evidence about the number of factors is common in the empirical literature on the APT [e.g., Roll and Ross (1980), Dhrymes, Friend, and Gultekin (1984), and Trzcinka (1986)]. Since our tests do not provide an unambiguous picture, we use other grounds to choose the number of factors. If we wish to allow for the possibility that movements in exchange rates are a source of nondiversifiable risk, then it seems rea-

The Review of Financial Studies / v 2 n 4 1989

sonable to allow for at least four factors. The four factors might represent general market risk plus the risks associated with shifts in the three relative prices of the four currencies.[8] On the other hand, we do not wish to use many degrees of freedom through inclusion of too many factors. In some of our empirical work we allow for seasonality in betas and in mispricing. Since we have 15 years of data, use of more than 14 factors is not feasible. We have chosen to estimate multifactor models with 5 and 10 factors.

3.2 Tests of the asset pricing models

The alternative asset pricing models (1) and (3) each place testable restrictions on the relation between asset returns and the returns on the benchmark portfolios. If we let P denote the vector of excess returns on a generic benchmark proxy (i.e., the return on some market index for the CAPM or the return on either prespecified or estimated factors for the APT), then the intercept in the regression of any asset's excess returns on P should be 0. Thus, given a sample of m assets and the regressions

$$R_{it} = \alpha_i + b_i P_t + \epsilon_{it} \qquad i = 1, 2, \ldots, m; \ t = 1, 2, \ldots, T \qquad (7)$$

the pricing models imply the restriction

$$\alpha_1 = \alpha_2 = \cdots = \alpha_m = 0 \qquad (8)$$

We will refer to α_i as the mispricing of asset i relative to the benchmark P. We first test whether mispricing is nonzero across assets for each of our alternative benchmarks. This is a test for unconditional mean-variance efficiency of some linear combination of the benchmark portfolios P.

Because of the well-documented January seasonal patterns in asset returns, we also allow the mispricing of assets to differ in January from the mispricing common to all months.[9] This is done by estimating the regression

$$R_{it} = \alpha_{iNJ} + \alpha_{ij} D_{Jt} + b_i P_t + \epsilon_{it} \qquad (9)$$

where D_{Jt} is a dummy variable equal to 1 in January and 0 otherwise. Mispricing specific to January is measured by α_{ij} while mispricing which is not specific to January is reflected in α_{iNJ}.[10] The hypotheses regarding α_i, α_{iNJ}, and α_{ij} [e.g., as in Equation (8)] are tested using the MLR statistic described in Equation (6) above. Under the null, the test statistic has a

---

[8] Of course this ignores the fact that exchange rate movements relative to currencies not in our sample might also be a source of pervasive risk. We are only suggesting a lower bound.

[9] Some previous studies have reported January and April seasonality in stock returns in the United Kingdom [Corhay, Hawawini, and Michel (1987)]. Our tests show no significant April mispricing for the United Kingdom over our sample period. These results are not necessarily inconsistent since seasonality in risk premia need not imply seasonality in mispricing.

[10] The specification in Equation (9) incorporates variation in conditional means but assumes that conditional betas are constant. We also estimate a specification which incorporates variation in conditional betas by letting b_i be seasonal:

$$R_{it} = \alpha_{iNJ} + \alpha_{ij} D_{Jt} + b_{iNJ} P_t + b_{ij} D_{Jt} P_t + \epsilon_{it}$$

We find no substantive difference in the estimated mispricing between this specification and that of Equation (9). For this reason we report only the results from Equation (9).

central *F*-distribution with degrees of freedom equal to m (the number of assets in the sample) and $T - k - m$ (where k is the number of regressors, excluding the constant).

As discussed above, rejection of the null hypothesis in Equation (8) might be attributable to a difference between the expected return on the true zero beta asset and the return on our proxy for r_{Ft}. We allow for this by testing the restrictions implied by zero-beta forms of the models. Let $\tilde{r}_{zt}$ denote the return on a portfolio with zero covariance with the market. We assume that the expected excess zero-beta return, $\lambda = E(\tilde{r}_{zt}) - r_{Ft}$, is constant through time.

The restrictions implied by the zero-beta CAPM in Equation (2) on the multivariate regression (7) are given by

$$\alpha_i = (1 - b_i) \cdot \lambda \qquad i = 1, 2, \ldots, m \qquad (10)$$

This implication of the zero-beta CAPM is discussed in Black, Jensen, and Scholes (1972, equation 14) in a single-equation context. Gibbons (1982) derives and tests the nonlinear cross-equation restrictions implied by the zero-beta CAPM. Our restrictions in Equation (10) are of the same form as those tested in Gibbons (1982), although the interpretation is slightly different.[11]

There are a variety of asymptotically equivalent test statistics for hypothesis (10). We use the likelihood ratio (LR) test, which has a chi-square (χ^2) distribution, asymptotically, with degrees of freedom equal to $m - 1$ [see Gibbons (1982) and Gallant (1987, pp. 457–458)]. Unlike the MLR statistic for the linear multivariate regression case, we do not know the exact small-sample distribution of the LR test of restriction (10). The LR test tends to reject the null hypothesis too often in small samples. This is particularly true when the number of cross sections, m, is large relative to the number of time-series observations, T, as is shown in Stambaugh (1982), Shanken (1985), and Amsler and Schmidt (1985). We have also calculated the cross-sectional regression test (CSRT) statistic suggested in Shanken (1985) for the null hypothesis in Equation (10). An approximate small-sample distribution of this statistic is given by the Hotelling T^2-distribution. This approximation is better than the asymptotic χ^2 approximation [Shanken (1985) and Amsler and Schmidt (1985)]. For our sample, we find that there is very little difference between the inferences one would draw based on the LR test and the CSRT. Because of this, we only report the LR tests. The small difference between the two statistics is due mainly to the fact that our time-series sample of 180 observations is large relative to our cross section of 10 assets (portfolios) and is consistent with the simulation results of Amsler and Schmidt (1985).

We also test the restrictions implied by the zero-beta version of the APT.

---

[11] Gibbons uses returns rather than excess returns. In his case λ would equal $E(\tilde{r}_z)$. Since we use excess returns, λ should be interpreted as $E(\tilde{r}_{zt}) - r_{Ft}$. Note that mispricing relative to the zero-beta CAPM is measured by $[\alpha_i - (1 - b_i) \cdot \lambda]$.

The Review of Financial Studies / v 2 n 4 1989

We obtain particularly simple restrictions if we assume that our proxy for the riskless asset bears only factor-related risk.[12] In the Appendix we show that our estimates of the factors converge to the true factors plus risk premia relative to the true zero-beta return as long as the return r_{Ft} is well diversified. This implies that the intercepts in regression (7) are equal to λ when the benchmark portfolio proxies P are derived from the asymptotic principal components technique. Thus, mispricing relative to the zero-beta APT is measured by $(\alpha_i - \lambda)$.

Our hypotheses about α_i in Equations (7) and (10) are tests of unconditional mean-variance efficiency of the benchmark portfolios. When we allow the mispricing parameters to be seasonal we are testing a particular form of conditional mean-variance efficiency. The analysis of Hansen and Richard (1987) provides a framework for interpreting our tests of unconditional and conditional mean-variance efficiency. Note that our conditional tests use only a subset of information available to economic agents. Thus, we need to make the distinction between unconditional efficiency, efficiency conditional on a coarse (the econometricians') information set, and efficiency conditional on the full information set.[13] Hansen and Richard (1987) show that unconditional efficiency implies conditional efficiency but that the converse is not true.[14] Thus, failing to reject unconditional or limited conditional efficiency is consistent with the hypothesis of conditional efficiency. On the other hand, rejecting unconditional or limited conditional efficiency does not imply rejection of conditional efficiency. Rejection of limited conditional efficiency implies rejection of unconditional efficiency. Therefore, it may be possible to reject unconditional or limited conditional efficiency when the benchmarks are efficient conditional on the full information set. Panel A of Table 5 shows the parameter restrictions implied by the various models described above.

3.3 Tests of the effects of capital controls
The regulatory environment of international financial markets is likely to be an important determinant of capital market integration and asset pricing. Over our sample period there is a general trend toward deregulation marked by two major periods of change.[15] The first period of change took place at the beginning of 1974 when the interest equalization tax was eliminated in the United States (January) while other countries loosened restrictions on capital inflows (January–February). Also, the early 1974 period marks the completion of the transition from a regime of fixed exchange rates to

---

[12] Given that our proxy for the riskless asset is only riskless in nominal $U.S. returns, it is not necessarily a zero-beta asset in real terms. Thus, it is likely that the return on a portfolio with zero betas with respect to the international factors will differ from our Treasury-bill return.

[13] We will refer to these as unconditional, limited conditional, and conditional efficiency, respectively.

[14] The same logic shows that unconditional efficiency implies limited conditional efficiency but that the converse is also not true.

[15] In an unpublished appendix (available from the authors) we give a brief description of changes in capital controls over our sample period.

Investigation of International Asset Pricing

Table 5
Summary of parameter restrictions implied by asset pricing models

Null	Regression	Model
	Panel A: Regressions not adjusting for changes in capital controls	
1. $\alpha_i = 0$	$R_i = \alpha_i + b_i P + \epsilon_i$	CAPM, APT
2. $\alpha_{ij} = 0;\ \alpha_{iNJ} = 0$	$R_i = \alpha_{iNJ} + \alpha_{ij}D_j + b_i P + \epsilon_i$	CAPM, APT
3. $\alpha_{ij} = 0;\ \alpha_{iNJ} = 0$	$R_i = \alpha_{iNJ} + \alpha_{ij}D_j + b_{ij}D_j P + b_{iNJ}P + \epsilon_i$	CAPM, APT
4. $\alpha_i = (1 - b_i)\lambda$	$R_i = \alpha_i + b_i P + \epsilon_i$	CAPM zero-β
5. $\alpha_i = \lambda$	$R_i = \alpha_i + b_i P + \epsilon_i$	APT zero-β
6. $\alpha_{iNJ} = (1 - b_i)\lambda$	$R_i = \alpha_{iNJ} + \alpha_{ij}D_j + b_i P + \epsilon_i$	CAPM zero-β
7. $\alpha_{iNJ} = \lambda$	$R_i = \alpha_{iNJ} + \alpha_{ij}D_j + b_i P + \epsilon_i$	APT zero-β
8. $\alpha_{iNJ} = (1 - b_i)\lambda$	$R_i = \alpha_{iNJ} + \alpha_{ij}D_j + b_{ij}D_j P + b_{iNJ}P + \epsilon_i$	CAPM zero-β
9. $\alpha_{iNJ} = \lambda$	$R_i = \alpha_{iNJ} + \alpha_{ij}D_j + b_{ij}D_j P + b_{iNJ}P + \epsilon_i$	APT zero-β
	Panel B: Regressions adjusting for changes in capital controls	
10. $\alpha_i = 0;\ \alpha_{i74} = 0;\ \alpha_{i79} = 0$	$R_i = \alpha_i + \alpha_{i74}D_{74} + \alpha_{i79}D_{79} + b_i P + \epsilon_i$	CAPM, APT
11. $\alpha_{iNJ} = 0;\ \alpha_{iNJ74} = 0$; $\alpha_{iNJ79} = 0;\ \alpha_{ij} = 0$	$R_i = \alpha_{iNJ} + \alpha_{iNJ74}D_{74} + \alpha_{iNJ79}D_{79} + \alpha_{ij}D_j + b_i P + \epsilon_i$	CAPM, APT
12. $\alpha_{iNJ} = 0;\ \alpha_{iNJ74} = 0$; $\alpha_{iNJ79} = 0;\ \alpha_{ij} = 0$	$R_i = \alpha_{iNJ} + \alpha_{iNJ74}D_{74} + \alpha_{iNJ79}D_{79} + \alpha_{ij}D_j + b_{ij}D_j P +$ $b_{iNJ}P + \epsilon_i$	CAPM, APT
13. $\alpha_i = (1 - b_i)\lambda$	$R_i = \alpha_i + \alpha_{iNJ74}D_{74} + \alpha_{iNJ79}D_{79} + b_i P + \epsilon_i$	CAPM zero-β
14. $\alpha_i = \lambda$	$R_i = \alpha_i + \alpha_{iNJ74}D_{74} + \alpha_{iNJ79}D_{79} + b_i P + \epsilon_i$	APT zero-β
15. $\alpha_{iNJ} = (1 - b_i)\lambda$	$R_i = \alpha_{iNJ} + \alpha_{iNJ74}D_{74} + \alpha_{iNJ79}D_{79} + \alpha_{ij}D_j + b_{ij}P + \epsilon_i$	CAPM zero-β
16. $\alpha_{iNJ} = \lambda$	$R_i = \alpha_{iNJ} + \alpha_{iNJ74}D_{74} + \alpha_{iNJ79}D_{79} + \alpha_{ij}D_j + b_{ij}P + \epsilon_i$	APT zero-β
17. $\alpha_{iNJ} = (1 - b_i)\lambda$	$R_i = \alpha_{iNJ} + \alpha_{iNJ74}D_{74} + \alpha_{iNJ79}D_{79} + \alpha_{ij}D_j + b_{ij}D_j P +$ $b_{iNJ}P + \epsilon_i$	CAPM zero-β
18. $\alpha_{iNJ} = \lambda$	$R_i = \alpha_{iNJ} + \alpha_{iNJ74}D_{74} + \alpha_{iNJ79}D_{79} + \alpha_{ij}D_j + b_{ij}D_j P +$ $b_{iNJ}P + \epsilon_i$	APT Zero-β

The index $i = 1, \ldots, m$ refers to the dependent variables, which are size-based portfolios; P refers to the benchmark portfolios; D_j refers to a dummy variable with $D_j = 1$ in January and 0 otherwise; D_{74} and D_{79} refer to dummy variables with $D_{74} = 1$ until January 1974 and 0 afterward, $D_{79} = 1$ until November 1979 and 0 afterward. λ represents the average excess zero-beta return.

one of floating rates. The second important period is 1979 when the United Kingdom and Japan dismantled a number of controls.[16]

We investigate whether periods of more strict controls (ending in January 1974 and November 1979, respectively) are associated with greater deviations from the predictions of the asset pricing models than are periods of less stringent control. This is done by testing whether the size of mispricing is different during these periods. We construct two dummy variables D_{74t} and D_{79t} such that D_{74t} is equal to 1.0 before February 1974 and 0.0 afterward while D_{79t} is equal to 1.0 before December 1979 and 0.0 otherwise. We then test $\alpha_{i74} = 0$ and $\alpha_{i79} = 0$, for all i, in the regression

$$R_{it} = \alpha_i + \alpha_{i74}D_{74t} + \alpha_{i79}D_{79t} + b_i P_t + \epsilon_{it}$$
$$i = 1, 2, \ldots, m;\ t = 1, 2, \ldots, T \qquad (11)$$

We also estimate variants of Equation (11) that allow for a January seasonal in α_i and b_i as well as the zero-beta forms of the models. Mispricing that is invariant over the entire 15-year period is measured by α_i.[17] The use of

---

[16] In Japan, deregulation measures, announced in early 1979, were implemented in 1980.

[17] We also have estimated models that allow the sensitivities, b_n, to be period-dependent. The results are essentially the same as those with constant sensitivities.

The Review of Financial Studies / v 2 n 4 1989

dummy variables is an admittedly crude method of measuring the effects of capital controls. However, in the absence of a finer metric for the severity of controls, the dummy variable approach is a reasonable alternative. If the loosening of capital controls leads to a more integrated global market, we would expect that the performance of purely domestic models would deteriorate and the performance of international models improve in the periods with fewer controls.

In panel B of Table 5 we show our tests for the influence of capital controls.

3.4 Choice of dependent variables for hypothesis tests

As discussed above, the asset pricing models imply restrictions on the coefficients of a multivariate regression of asset returns on particular bench-mark portfolios. One would normally proceed in testing the hypothesis of zero mispricing by estimating the restricted null model [e.g., Equation (7) with the constraint $\alpha_i = 0$] and the unrestricted version [e.g., Equation (7) with the intercepts allowed to be nonzero]. Standard approaches to hypothesis testing involve investigating the increase in the generalized variance (determinant) of the residual covariance matrix, $\hat{V}$, due to additional restrictions (as in likelihood ratio tests) or calculating quadratic forms relative to $\hat{V}$. Large values of m [i.e., many assets on the left-hand side (LHS) of the regression] present some difficulties in hypothesis testing. In particular, when m is larger than T the generalized variances are uniformly zero and the estimated residual covariance matrix is singular. There are several alternative techniques designed to overcome this problem.

A common approach, which we adopt, is to group assets into portfolios on the basis of some instrumental variables. Thus, rather than having m individual assets on the LHS of the regressions, we have p portfolios (with $p \ll m$). This makes testing feasible, allows more precise estimates of the parameters, but also runs the risk of masking mispricing if the values of α_i are uncorrelated with the instruments. Thus, there is a trade-off between increased precision of our estimates and decreased heterogeneity in the sample.[18] The instrument used to form portfolios should be chosen to ensure heterogeneity across portfolios. The instrumental variable chosen here is the "size" of the firm.[19] We form five sets of ten size portfolios— one set per country plus a set which includes all assets. For each set we rank firms on the basis of market value of equity at the beginning of the period (December 1968) and form ten equal-weighted portfolios (the first portfolio containing the smallest 10 percent of the firms, etc.). A firm remains in its portfolio as long as there are observed returns for this asset. Assets are reallocated to size portfolios at five-year intervals (i.e., December 1973 and December 1978).

---

[18] The implications of this trade-off, in terms of the power of the tests, is analyzed in Gibbons, Ross, and Shanken (1986).

[19] The papers cited in note 1 indicate that size is a reasonable instrument in terms of ensuring heterogeneity across portfolios.

4. Empirical Results

The results reported below are robust to a variety of permutations in estimating the models. We estimate each model using both nominal and real
returns. The inferences we draw about the models are not dependent on
whether real or nominal returns are used. Because of this, we report our
results using nominal returns. Since we are assuming that various parameters are constant over our 15-year sample period, we check whether our
results are robust to allowing changes in the parameters. We do this by
estimating the models over three 5-year subperiods and aggregating the
subperiod results. The aggregated results did not yield different inferences
from the entire period. We report the results from the entire period.

4.1 The structure of factor returns

Before we proceed with the formal hypothesis tests, we discuss some
evidence on the covariance structure of asset returns across countries and
present evidence on the relation between market indexes and our estimated factors. The correlations across national common stock portfolios
range from .20 to .47 and are consistent with previous evidence. While
there are important common movements in the various indexes, there also
appear to be substantial country-specific components to the return series.
The correlation between equal-weighted and value-weighted indexes in
the same country are, as one would expect, high (from .87 to .98).

The international factors are estimated by the asymptotic principal components procedure from returns on every available asset. Over our 180-
month period, the monthly average number of firms with returns data is
5596. Regressions of the excess returns of the national indexes and percentage changes in exchange rates on the first five international factors are
reported in Table 6. The results indicate a very strong relation between
the estimated factors and the indexes for every country except France. Also,
each of the five factors generally has significant explanatory power across
all countries. These results and some extensive canonical correlation analysis not reported here, indicate that there are several common international
factors. The estimated mispricing of each index relative to these five benchmark portfolios (in percent per annum) is listed in the second column.
The estimated values of mispricing for the French indexes, $\hat{\alpha}_{FR}$, are (economically) very negative but are not measured with much precision. The
estimated mispricing relative to the 10-factor APT is generally smaller (in
absolute value). They are not reported in detail here in order to conserve
space.

The regressions of changes in exchange rates on the factors indicate that
exchange rates are related to the pervasive sources of risk in the equity
markets. For each of the three exchange rates there is a statistically significant (at the 5 percent level) relation with four of the five factors. The
factors explain between 30 and 53 percent of exchange rate variability.
Thus, exchange rate risk is, in part, pervasive and is reflected in the estimated factors.

The Review of Financial Studies / v 2 n 4 1989

Table 6
Regression of market index excess returns on five estimated international factors

$$R_{it} = \alpha_i + \beta_{i1}P_{1t} + \ldots + \beta_{i5}P_{5t} + \epsilon_{it}$$

Index	$\alpha_i \times 1200$	$\beta_{i1} \times 10$	$\beta_{i2} \times 10$	$\beta_{i3} \times 10$	$\beta_{i4} \times 10$	$\beta_{i5} \times 10$	R^2
US–EW	0.76	8.51	3.13	−0.02	0.29	0.45	0.99
	(1.19)	(121.91)	(44.76)	(−0.30)	(4.11)	(6.51)	
US–VW	−3.60	5.09	1.72	0.01	1.68	2.45	0.92
	(−2.78)	(36.05)	(12.16)	(0.05)	(11.93)	(17.47)	
UK–EW	1.78	6.76	−6.27	−1.25	0.26	−0.30	0.99
	(2.52)	(87.90)	(−81.38)	(−16.19)	(3.40)	(−3.87)	
UK–VW	−6.59	7.78	−6.19	−2.01	0.29	1.34	0.92
	(−3.15)	(34.02)	(−27.02)	(−8.73)	(1.27)	(5.89)	
JP–EW	1.69	2.75	−2.54	6.29	−0.46	0.66	0.96
	(1.75)	(26.13)	(−24.10)	(59.31)	(−4.41)	(6.26)	
JP–VW	−1.57	2.97	−2.12	5.22	−0.15	1.69	0.83
	(−0.77)	(13.26)	(−9.45)	(23.13)	(−0.69)	(7.59)	
FR–EW	−6.91	3.96	−2.56	1.62	0.16	2.23	0.35
	(−1.35)	(7.10)	(−4.58)	(2.88)	(0.29)	(4.01)	
FR–VW	−9.63	4.25	−2.57	1.55	0.35	2.36	0.35
	(−1.78)	(7.22)	(−4.34)	(2.61)	(0.59)	(4.02)	
Int'l–EW	0.03	6.70	−1.18	0.94	0.24	0.15	1.00
	(0.11)	(226.40)	(−40.06)	(31.40)	(8.00)	(5.04)	
Int'l–VW	−5.05	4.93	0.31	0.78	1.22	2.15	0.94
	(−5.31)	(47.40)	(3.02)	(7.49)	(11.82)	(20.73)	
UK–X	7.39	−0.94	1.67	−0.44	−0.59	0.00	0.35
	(3.83)	(−4.45)	(7.92)	(−2.07)	(−2.80)	(0.01)	
JP–X	3.39	−0.70	1.50	−2.30	0.04	−0.66	0.53
	(1.83)	(−3.46)	(7.41)	(−11.27)	(0.18)	(−3.28)	
FR–X	8.71	−0.64	1.55	−1.28	−0.36	−0.88	0.31
	(3.71)	(−2.49)	(6.06)	(−4.95)	(−1.42)	(−3.45)	

US, UK, JP, FR, and Int'l denote United States, United Kingdom, Japan, France, and International portfolios, respectively. EW denotes equal-weighted market portfolio, VW denotes value-weighted market portfolio, and X denotes the percentage change in the spot exchange rate (in units of foreign currency per dollar). R^2 denotes the coefficient of determination. t-statistics are in parentheses. Parameters are estimated using monthly returns over the period 1969–1983.

4.2 Multi-index versus single-index models

In this section we compare the performance of multi-index and single-index models using two criteria: first, whether or not the tests described in Section 3.2 reject the restrictions implied by the models and, second, whether the magnitudes of mispricing differ across models. The second criterion is useful in view of the nonnested nature of the models. For example, rejection of restriction (8) for one model and failure to reject (8) for a second model does not imply that the second model fits better. The mispricing parameters (α_i) of the first model might be closer to zero but measured with more precision. Thus a combination of the two criteria is more informative than either one alone.

When we assume that the U.S. Treasury-bill return is the appropriate riskless return, the asset pricing models imply that the intercepts (α_i) are zero in a multivariate regression of excess returns of size portfolios on particular benchmark portfolio returns. When we allow mispricing to be

Investigation of International Asset Pricing

Table 7
Modified likelihood ratio (MLR) tests of no mispricing for size-ranked portfolios

Panel A: CAPM

		CAPM-EW			CAPM-VW		
R_t	P	$\alpha_t = 0$	$\alpha_{INJ} = 0$	$\alpha_y = 0$	$\alpha_t = 0$	$\alpha_{INJ} = 0$	$\alpha_y = 0$
US	US	2.28*	2.20*	8.46*	1.65	1.58	11.06*
		(.016)	(.020)	(.020)	(.095)	(.118)	(<.001)
JP	JP	1.00	1.09	2.06*	1.64	1.37	2.56*
		(.447)	(.374)	(.031)	(.100)	(.198)	(.007)
UK	UK	4.39*	3.95*	0.57	4.71*	3.96*	1.64
		(<.001)	(<.001)	(.838)	(<.001)	(<.001)	(.100)
FR	FR	1.58	1.89*	1.45	1.58	1.89*	1.63
		(.115)	(.049)	(.155)	(.115)	(.049)	(.101)
US	Int'l	1.76	1.80	8.62*	1.51	1.57	10.93*
		(.072)	(.065)	(<.001)	(.139)	(.118)	(<.001)
JP	Int'l	1.61	1.57	2.71*	1.88	1.59	2.57*
		(.108)	(.120)	(.004)	(.051)	(.112)	(.006)
UK	Int'l	4.23*	3.92*	0.65	4.65*	3.89*	1.65
		(<.001)	(<.001)	(.770)	(<.001)	(<.001)	(.096)
FR	Int'l	1.69	1.92*	1.17	1.63	1.92*	1.87
		(.086)	(.045)	(.316)	(.101)	(.045)	(.121)
Int'l	Int'l	3.28*	3.14*	5.88*	3.64*	3.16*	8.31*
		(<.001)	(<.001)	(<.001)	(<.001)	(<.001)	(<.001)

Panel B: APT

		APT-5			APT-10		
R_t	P	$\alpha_t = 0$	$\alpha_{INJ} = 0$	$\alpha_y = 0$	$\alpha_t = 0$	$\alpha_{INJ} = 0$	$\alpha_y = 0$
US	US	5.60*	4.32*	1.48	6.37*	4.26*	1.51
		(<.001)	(<.001)	(.152)	(<.001)	(<.001)	(.140)
JP	JP	1.16	1.32	1.23	1.28	1.18	1.11
		(.323)	(.226)	(.274)	(.248)	(.307)	(.359)
UK	UK	4.03*	3.73*	0.69	3.93*	3.66*	0.50
		(<.001)	(<.001)	(.788)	(<.001)	(<.001)	(.865)
FR	FR	1.81	2.08*	1.31	1.95*	1.93*	0.88
		(.063)	(.028)	(.228)	(.042)	(.047)	(.898)
US	Int'l	2.69*	2.30*	2.18*	3.33*	2.92*	1.82
		(.004)	(.015)	(.021)	(.001)	(.002)	(.061)
JP	Int'l	1.14	0.88	0.98	1.35	1.58	0.38
		(.336)	(.551)	(.464)	(.205)	(.304)	(.952)
UK	Int'l	3.94*	3.67*	1.05	4.01*	3.03*	0.46
		(<.001)	(<.001)	(.401)	(<.001)	(<.001)	(.915)
FR	Int'l	1.56	1.79	1.65	1.53	1.76	1.68
		(.123)	(.066)	(.096)	(.135)	(.073)	(.089)
Int'l	Int'l	5.31*	5.12*	2.34*	5.79*	5.39*	1.53
		(<.001)	(<.001)	(.013)	(<.001)	(<.001)	(.134)

Modified likelihood ratio (MLR) test statistics from Equation (6) with p-values in parentheses. Under the null they have a central F-distribution (degrees of freedom equal to 10 and $170 - k$, where k is the number of nonconstant regressors). Tests are for zero mispricing across ten size-ranked portfolios given by restrictions 1 and 2 in Table 5. Parameters are estimated using monthly returns over the period 1969–1983. α_t, α_{INJ} and α_y are the estimates of mispricing, non-January mispricing, and January-specific mispricing over the 1969–1983 period. R_t identifies the market from which the size portfolios are constructed. P identifies the market from which the benchmark portfolios are constructed.

* Significant at the 5 percent level.

The Review of Financial Studies / v 2 n 4 1989

seasonal, both the seasonal and nonseasonal components of mispricing (α_{ij} and α_{iNJ}) should be zero. In Table 7 we present the results of the tests.

Each model has at least one rejection, at the 5 percent level of significance, of the null that nonseasonal mispricing is zero ($\alpha_i = 0$ or $\alpha_{iNJ} = 0$). The CAPM–VW model has the fewest rejections while the APT–10 model has the most. The null is always rejected for the United Kingdom and for international size portfolios but never rejected for Japanese portfolios. The hypothesis that January-specific mispricing is zero ($\alpha_{ij} = 0$) is never rejected by the APT–10 model and more often rejected by the CAPM than by the APT–5 model. Considering the three null hypotheses together: $\alpha_i = 0$, $\alpha_{iNJ} = 0$ and $\alpha_{ij} = 0$, it appears that there is some evidence against all of the models (with the exception of the APT for Japan). It appears that the CAPM does better in explaining returns that are not specific to January and the APT does better in explaining January-specific returns. Also, the pattern of rejections for the U.S. sample with domestic benchmarks is basically the same as that found by Connor and Korajczyk (1988a) and Lehmann and Modest (1988).

Test results for the zero-beta specifications of the models are presented in Table 8. With few exceptions (CAPM–EW model for the United Kingdom and the domestic APT–10 for France), whenever the null is rejected with the U.S. Treasury-bill rate as the zero-beta return, we also reject the zero-beta variant of the model. Thus, the rejections do not seem to be driven by our choice of the U.S. Treasury-bill return as the zero-beta return.

The tests reported in Tables 7 and 8 provide us with our first criterion for model evaluation. However, sole reliance on the p-values in those tables may be misleading because, among other things, the power of the tests may be different across models. The power of the above tests increases with the precision of our estimates of mispricing, ceteris paribus. Holding the level of mispricing constant, we would expect more precise estimates of mispricing for portfolios with larger numbers of securities (by diversification). The number of assets included in our size portfolios vary greatly across economies. For example, each of the 10 international size portfolios have 457 assets, on average, while the French size portfolios have only 12. Thus, a simple comparison of the test statistics may be insufficient to estimate the relative performance of each model and of each of their various versions across countries.

Hence, we present evidence of the relative magnitude of the mispricing of the alternative models. Space limitations prevent us from showing the entire set of figures corresponding to each possible permutation. We chose only four graphs that, along with Table 9, best illustrate the most important findings from a detailed comparisons of the models.

Figure 1 shows the mispricing for the four models using international size portfolios with international benchmarks. The graph plots the mispricing for each size portfolio, from the smallest (S1) to the largest (S10). Mispricing for small-size portfolios is larger than for large-size portfolios, whatever the model: actually none of the four models seems to fully explain

Investigation of International Asset Pricing

Table 8
Likelihood ratio tests of no mispricing for size-ranked portfolios (zero-beta models)

Panel A: CAPM

R_t	P	CAPM-EW		CAPM-VW	
		$\alpha_t = (1 - b_t)\lambda$	$\alpha_{t\eta} = (1 - b_t)\lambda$	$\alpha_t = (1 - b_t)\lambda$	$\alpha_{t\eta} = (1 - b_t)\lambda$
US	US	22.94*	19.49*	17.40*	16.16
		(.006)	(.021)	(.043)	(.064)
JP	JP	10.39	11.19	13.63	11.91
		(.320)	(.263)	(.136)	(.218)
UK	UK	17.96*	14.55	25.99*	16.97*
		(.036)	(.104)	(.002)	(.049)
FR	FR	15.94	19.13*	15.33	18.29*
		(.068)	(.024)	(.082)	(.032)
US	Int'l	18.47*	17.48*	16.06	15.70
		(.030)	(.042)	(.066)	(.073)
JP	Int'l	11.10	7.34	6.54	7.04
		(.269)	(.602)	(.685)	(.633)
UK	Int'l	18.20*	16.25	20.68*	17.63*
		(.033)	(.062)	(.014)	(.040)
FR	Int'l	16.93	19.97*	15.71	19.18*
		(.050)	(.018)	(.073)	(.024)
Int'l	Int'l	33.98*	30.25*	32.76*	28.67*
		(<.001)	(<.001)	(<.001)	(<.001)

Panel B: APT

R_t	P	APT-5		APT-10	
		$\alpha_t = \lambda$	$\alpha_{t\eta} = \lambda$	$\alpha_t = \lambda$	$\alpha_{t\eta} = \lambda$
US	US	52.38*	42.18*	60.26*	42.48*
		(<.001)	(<.001)	(<.001)	(<.001)
JP	JP	12.17	13.18	13.90	12.53
		(.204)	(.155)	(.126)	(.185)
UK	UK	39.46*	31.16*	39.66*	37.46*
		(<.001)	(<.001)	(<.001)	(<.001)
FR	FR	16.43	18.42*	15.09	20.65*
		(.058)	(.031)	(.088)	(.014)
US	Int'l	25.78*	22.92*	34.33*	30.54*
		(.002)	(.006)	(<.001)	(<.001)
JP	Int'l	11.15	9.02	12.71	10.29
		(.265)	(.435)	(.176)	(.328)
UK	Int'l	34.12*	33.99*	36.95*	29.48*
		(<.001)	(<.001)	(<.001)	(<.001)
FR	Int'l	14.23	20.07*	15.10	20.65*
		(.114)	(.017)	(.088)	(.014)
Int'l	Int'l	50.78*	47.69*	56.48*	53.00*
		(<.001)	(<.001)	(<.001)	(<.001)

Likelihood ratio test statistics with p-values in parentheses. Statistics are asymptotically χ^2 with 9 degrees of freedom. Tests are for zero mispricing across 10 size-based portfolios given by restrictions 4–7 in Table 5. Parameters are estimated using monthly returns over the period 1969–1983. For the CAPM, the estimates of mispricing and non-January mispricing are $\alpha_t - (1 - b_t)\lambda$ and $\alpha_{t\eta} - (1 - b_t)\lambda$, respectively. For the APT, the estimates of mispricing and non-January mispricing are $\alpha_t - \lambda$ and $\alpha_{t\eta} - \lambda$, respectively. Estimated difference between the zero-beta return and r_f is given by λ. R_t identifies the market from which the size portfolios are constructed. P identifies the market from which the benchmark portfolios are constructed.

* Significant at the 5 percent level.

The Review of Financial Studies / v 2 n 4 1989

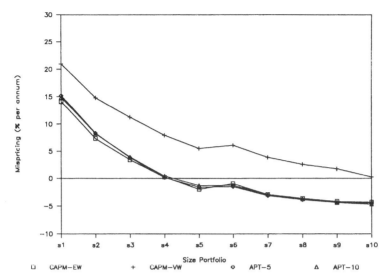

Figure 1
Mispricing, in percent per annum, for 10 international portfolios formed by ranking on firm size
Mispricing is estimated by the intercept in the regression of monthly portfolio excess returns on a constant and (*a*) monthly excess returns on a value-weighted portfolio of international stocks, denoted CAPM-VW (plus signs); (*b*) monthly excess returns on an equal-weighted portfolio of international stocks, denoted CAPM-EW (squares); (*c*) first five international factor estimates from the asymptotic principal components procedure, denoted APT-5 (diamonds); and (*d*) first 10 international factor estimates from the asymptotic principal components procedure, denoted APT-10 (triangles). Parameters are estimated using monthly returns over the period 1969-1983. S1 represents the portfolio of smallest firms while S10 represents the portfolio of largest firms. Size is defined as market value of common stock at the beginning of each five-year subperiod.

the size-related anomaly.[20] This finding holds for each of the four countries individually, using domestic as well as international benchmarks. A comparison of mispricing across countries is given in Figure 2 (CAPM using the value-weighted international market) and in Figure 3 (five-factor international APT). The United Kingdom shows the strongest size effect and France the weakest.[21] Again, the patterns of mispricing for the United States are similar to those shown in figures 1 to 3 of Connor and Korajczyk (1988a), although the levels of mispricing are slightly smaller. This may be due to the fact that we include all assets in our size portfolios while Connor and Korajczyk use a sample in which firms are required to have a continuous

---

[20] The size-related anomaly is apparent not only in the pattern of the mispricing but also by the fact that estimated mispricing is positive for all ten portfolios, relative to the value-weighted market (in Figure 1). This is due to the fact that the portfolios are equal-weighted and hence place more weight on smaller firms within each decile than would value-weighted portfolios.

[21] It is not surprising that France shows the weakest size effect. The 126 firms in the French sample are only a fraction of the firms traded on the Paris Bourse and represent the most frequently traded shares. As a consequence the sample comprises firms which are rather homogeneous in size.

Investigation of International Asset Pricing

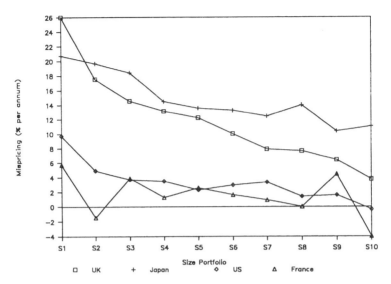

Figure 2
Mispricing of international CAPM across countries, in percent per annum
Mispricing is estimated by the intercept in the regression of monthly portfolio excess returns on a constant and monthly excess returns on a value-weighted portfolio of international stocks. S1 represents the portfolio of smallest firms while S10 represents the portfolio of largest firms. Parameters are estimated using monthly returns over the period 1969–1983. U.K. size portfolios are denoted by squares, Japanese size portfolios by plus signs, U.S. size portfolios by diamonds, and French size portfolios by triangles. Size is defined as market values of common stock at the beginning of each five-year subperiod.

trading history over five-year intervals. In Table 9 we present the average absolute mispricing of the size portfolios for the models as an estimate of the extent to which they deviate from zero mispricing. Mispricing is relatively large (in economic terms) for the CAPM–VW model and is systematically larger than any of the three other models whatever the version. Differences in mispricing between the factor models and the CAPM–EW model are minimal. There is a striking contrast between the frequency of rejection based on the test statistics and the level of mispricing. The CAPM–VW has the fewest number of rejections but the largest estimates of mispricing. Similarly the APT has more frequent rejections of the restrictions but fits the data better than the CAPM.

January mispricing for the same models and size portfolios are shown in Figure 4. As with average mispricing, January mispricing of small-size international portfolios is greater than for large-size ones. This finding also holds at the country level with the United States showing the strongest effect and France the weakest. However, the effect is clearly more pronounced for the CAPM, a finding that confirms the results of the statistical tests. This is also true for each country using domestic as well as international benchmarks. In other words, the APT models seem to include

573

The Review of Financial Studies / v 2 n 4 1989

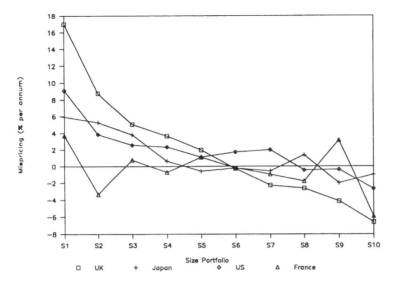

Figure 3
Mispricing of international five-factor APT, in percent per annum
Mispricing is estimated by the intecept in the regression of monthly portfolio excess returns on a constant and the first five international factor estimates from the asymptotic principal components procedure. Parameters are estimated using monthly returns over the period 1969–1983. S1 represents the portfolio of smallest firms while S10 represents the portfolio of largest firms. U.K. size portfolios are denoted by squares, Japanese size portfolios by plus signs, U.S. size portfolios by diamonds, and French size portfolios by triangles. Size is defined as market value of common stock at the beginning of each five-year subperiod.

seasonal factors not "picked up" by the alternative models. From Table 9, the CAPM–VW model, again, shows the largest average absolute mispricing of the four models, but contrary to the previous finding, the APT models and especially the APT–10 model show a much smaller mispricing than the CAPM–EW model.

To summarize, although the size effect is present when estimating each of the four models, the APT models tend to perform better than the CAPM models especially when comparing the magnitude of the January mispricing. The difference in performance between the two factor models is minimal. In particular, both seem to include seasonal factors that "explain" January-specific asset return behavior. Our results for domestic benchmarks are consistent with the single-economy applications of the APT cited in note 2. We know of no previous study which directly compares the international APT to the international CAPM.

4.3 Domestic versus international benchmarks
Most empirical studies of asset pricing models use securities and benchmark portfolios from a single country. While there undoubtedly exist some

Investigation of International Asset Pricing

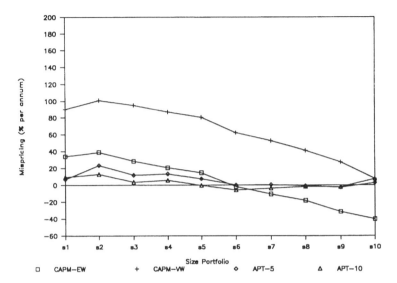

Figure 4
January-specific mispricing, in percent per annum, for 10 international portfolios formed by ranking on firm size
Mispricing is estimated by the slope coefficient on the January dummy variable in the regression of monthly portfolio excess returns on a constant, January dummy variable, and (*a*) monthly excess returns on a value-weighted portfolio of international stocks, denoted CAPM-VW (plus signs); (*b*) monthly excess returns on an equal-weighted portfolio of international stocks, denoted CAPM-EW (squares); (*c*) first five international factor estimates from the asymptotic principal components procedure, denoted APT-5 (diamonds); and (*d*) first 10 international factor estimates from the asymptotic principal components procedure, denoted APT-10 (triangles). Parameters are estimated using monthly returns over the period 1969–1983. S1 represents the portfolio of smallest firms while S10 represents the portfolio of largest firms. Size is defined as market values of common stock at the beginning of each five-year subperiod.

Table 9
Average absolute mispricing across size-ranked portfolios

		CAPM–EW		CAPM–VW		APT–5		APT–10	
R_i	P	A	AJ	A	AJ	A	AJ	A	AJ
US	US	1.40	34.49	4.76	72.74	2.58	5.21	2.63	4.69
JP	JP	1.98	15.04	13.88	35.05	1.81	5.43	1.78	5.76
UK	UK	6.14	3.18	12.63	73.15	3.31	2.14	3.35	2.36
FR	FR	2.21	8.70	3.15	21.89	2.46	9.44	2.14	7.53
US	Int'l	3.61	35.67	3.38	74.10	2.62	8.33	2.84	7.80
JP	Int'l	10.60	19.35	14.79	33.80	2.14	10.34	2.29	4.87
UK	Int'l	6.08	4.58	11.91	69.44	5.23	8.70	4.30	3.69
FR	Int'l	2.70	16.03	2.59	17.90	2.16	14.98	2.07	16.60
Int'l	Int'l	4.31	23.94	7.50	64.42	4.64	7.04	4.58	5.28

Average absolute mispricing across 10 size-ranked portfolios, in percent per annum, are given by $A = \Sigma |\alpha_i|/10$ and $AJ = \Sigma |\alpha_{ij}|/10$. α_i and α_{ij} are the estimates of mispricing and January-specific mispricing, respectively, from regressions 1 and 2 in Table 5. R_i identifies the market from which the size-ranked portfolios are constructed. P identifies the market from which the benchmark portfolios are constructed.

The Review of Financial Studies / v 2 n 4 1989

barriers to international investing, one might expect that increasing global diversification would lead to a greater role of international factors in asset pricing. In order to compare domestic versus international models, we consider the mispricing of the domestic size portfolios relative to the domestic and international benchmark portfolios, respectively. In terms of the frequency of rejection, there is not a clear difference between the use of domestic versus international benchmark portfolios. From Tables 7 and 8 the models with international benchmarks are rejected slightly less often than the domestic models. This lower frequency of rejection of the models with international benchmarks could be due to smaller levels of mispricing or to lower power of the tests. In Table 9 we provide estimates of the average absolute pricing error across models. On the basis of the magnitude of the estimated mispricing it appears that the domestic versions marginally outperform the international versions, except for the CAPM–VW model. Thus, at this stage the evidence does not unambiguously support the use of domestic or international benchmarks.

4.4 Effect of regulatory changes in international financial markets

Effect on model performance. If the changes in regulations do not influence international asset pricing, then we would expect the regime shift coefficients (α_{I74} and α_{I79}) in Equation (11) to equal 0.

Table 10, which is comparable to Table 7, shows the results of allowing mispricing to be regime-dependent. The hypotheses $\alpha = 0$ and $\alpha_{NJ} = 0$ are not rejected for any model, except for France where they are always rejected. The hypothesis $\alpha_I = 0$ is overwhelmingly rejected for the CAPM while it is seldom rejected for the APT (especially the 10-factor model). These results, which are quite different from those shown in Table 7 when no adjustment was made for changes in the international financial markets, are consistent with international regulatory influences on asset pricing.

The statistical significance of α_{I74} differs between the CAPM and APT. The coefficient tends to be significant for the APT but not for the CAPM. However, in the case of international size portfolios, α_{I74} is always statistically significant. The hypothesis that $\alpha_{I79} = 0$ is never rejected, except for France. These findings tend to show that the asset pricing model results are sensitive to the changes around early 1974 that include switching from fixed to floating exchange rates, the elimination of the interest equalization tax in the United States, and liberalization of capital controls on the part of other countries. The performance of the models does not seem to have been affected by the changes in 1979.

We present in Table 11 the tests of the zero-beta variants of the models. They are similar to those obtained when the U.S. Treasury-bill return is used as the zero-beta return. The restrictions implied by the zero-beta models cannot be rejected except for France, and they are also in sharp contrast with the results of the tests presented in Table 8, which do not allow for regime shifts in mispricing.

576

Because of the many different types of changes in international financial markets around 1974, it is not possible to attribute the apparent shift in pricing to particular changes in regulations or to the switch to floating from fixed exchange rates. Indeed, there may be other external reasons for the period-specific levels of mispricing since the purely domestic models also tend to perform well after adjusting for regime shifts. However, the fact that there are significant changes in the pricing of assets, relative to our benchmarks, around these regime shifts may indicate the importance of capital controls and exchange rate regimes for asset pricing.

Multi-index versus single-index models adjusting for regime shifts. The above results indicate that the APT tends to be rejected less often than the CAPM, especially relative to January mispricing. Figures 5 and 6 show our estimates of mispricing and January mispricing of international size portfolios when we include dummy variables for the 1974 and 1979 changes in the regulatory environment. The graphs show patterns that are similar to those in Figures 1 and 2. There is still a size effect for all models and a strong January effect for the CAPM models. However, the size effect is much less pronounced when the models are adapted for the regime changes. At the country level, the United States exhibits the strongest size effect and Japan and France the weakest. In none of the four countries is there any noticeable January effect for the APT. Estimates of average absolute mispricing are shown in Table 12. As before, CAPM–VW shows by far the largest mispricing and January mispricing of the four models (except for France). Differences are minimal between the CAPM–EW and the APT models except for the January mispricing that, again, is much lower with the APT. When compared to the estimates shown in Table 9, the APT's mispricing is systematically lower, except for France, while their January mispricing is comparable, again, except for France.

Domestic versus international models adjusting for regime shifts. The international version of the CAPM seems to outperform the domestic version in terms of both of our criteria. We reject the CAPM restrictions slightly more often for the domestic versions than the international versions (see Table 10). We also find that the CAPM has smaller pricing errors in its international version than in its domestic version (see Table 12).

We generally find the opposite results for the APT. Using domestic size portfolios we reject the APT restrictions slightly more often for the international benchmarks. From the levels of absolute mispricing in Table 12 the domestic versions of APT tend to outperform the international versions. However, when we use international size portfolios, the 10-factor APT is the only model which does not reject the absence of a January seasonal effect in pricing.

In summary, the analysis of the size of the mispricing confirms the finding of the statistical analysis: the four asset pricing models seem to be sensitive to changes in the regulatory environment of the international financial markets. The period from January 1969 (the beginning of our sample) to January 1974 causes many of the rejections of the model. Abstracting from

The Review of Financial Studies / v 2 n 4 1989

Table 10
Modified likelihood ratio (MLR) tests of no mispricing with capital control dummies

Panel A: CAPM

CAPM–EW

R_t	P	α_t	α_{J74}	α_{J79}	α_{WJ}	α_U	α_{WJ74}	α_{WJ79}
US	US	0.90 (.532)	2.76* (.004)	0.57 (.836)	0.79 (.641)	8.87* (<.001)	3.08* (.001)	0.57 (.839)
JP	JP	0.28 (.984)	1.26 (.258)	0.52 (.871)	0.39 (.950)	2.08* (.029)	1.29 (.240)	0.55 (.854)
UK	UK	1.24 (.267)	1.79 (.065)	1.04 (.408)	1.22 (.284)	0.58 (.830)	1.80 (.065)	1.05 (.403)
FR	FR	3.05* (.001)	0.91 (.522)	2.64* (.005)	3.42* (<.001)	1.99* (.037)	0.89 (.546)	2.68* (.005)
US	Int'l	0.38 (.952)	3.03* (.001)	0.54 (.860)	0.31 (.979)	8.92* (<.001)	3.31* (.001)	0.54 (.863)
JP	Int'l	0.26 (.988)	1.25 (.263)	0.42 (.937)	0.38 (.952)	2.86* (.003)	1.41 (.179)	0.48 (.899)
UK	Int'l	1.07 (.386)	1.30 (.235)	0.98 (.466)	1.12 (.353)	0.71 (.717)	1.36 (.205)	1.00 (.444)
FR	Int'l	3.27* (.001)	1.02 (.432)	2.80* (.003)	3.62* (<.001)	1.61 (.107)	0.97 (.473)	2.87* (.003)
Int'l	Int'l	0.42 (.937)	2.93* (.002)	0.68 (.739)	0.63 (.783)	5.92* (<.001)	2.98* (.002)	0.77 (.655)

Panel B: APT

APT-5

R_t	P	α_t	α_{J74}	α_{J79}	α_{WJ}	α_U	α_{WJ74}	α_{WJ79}
US	US	0.61 (.802)	2.45* (.009)	1.28 (.244)	0.43 (.930)	1.36 (.203)	2.28* (.016)	1.25 (.264)
JP	JP	0.31 (.978)	0.85 (.577)	0.41 (.942)	0.35 (.965)	1.31 (.231)	0.92 (.518)	0.41 (.942)
UK	UK	1.24 (.269)	2.11* (.026)	0.82 (.608)	1.19 (.298)	0.74 (.689)	2.15* (.024)	0.82 (.609)
FR	FR	1.98* (.038)	1.10 (.369)	2.32* (.014)	2.16* (.022)	1.33 (.217)	1.08 (.379)	2.31* (.015)
US	Int'l	0.38 (.956)	2.61* (.006)	0.68 (.746)	0.28 (.984)	2.04* (.032)	2.41* (.011)	0.64 (.774)
JP	Int'l	0.30 (.979)	2.39* (.011)	0.44 (.927)	0.34 (.969)	0.95 (.489)	2.38* (.012)	0.46 (.915)
UK	Int'l	1.14 (.334)	1.49 (.146)	0.93 (.509)	1.09 (.371)	1.38 (.194)	1.75 (.073)	0.91 (.527)
FR	Int'l	3.14* (.001)	1.08 (.379)	2.72* (.004)	3.82* (<.001)	1.83 (.059)	1.04 (.410)	2.95* (.002)
Int'l	Int'l	0.52 (.873)	3.05* (.001)	0.77 (.655)	0.77 (.653)	2.07* (.030)	2.79* (.003)	0.77 (.653)

Modified likelihood ratio (MLR) test statistics from Equation (6) with p-values in parentheses. Under the null they have a central F distribution (degrees of freedom equal to 10 and $170 - k$, where k is the number of nonconstant regressors). Tests are for zero mispricing across 10 size-ranked portfolios given by restrictions 10 and 11 in Table 5. Parameters are estimated using monthly returns over the period 1969–1983. Estimated mispricing throughout the 1969–1983 period is given by α_t. Estimated non-January mispricing

Investigation of International Asset Pricing

Table 10
Extended

Panel A: CAPM

CAPM-VW

α_I	α_{I74}	α_{I79}	α_{INJ}	α_J	α_{INJ74}	α_{INJ79}
0.49	3.10*	0.46	0.30	11.68*	3.54*	0.46
(.895)	(.001)	(.911)	(.980)	(<.001)	(<.001)	(.912)
0.27	1.13	0.41	0.36	2.59*	1.13	0.43
(.987)	(.340)	(.942)	(.964)	(.006)	(.342)	(.931)
1.51	1.33	1.35	1.33	1.95*	1.31	1.33
(.140)	(.217)	(.210)	(.217)	(.041)	(.230)	(.217)
3.05*	0.91	2.68*	3.42*	1.98*	0.88	2.72*
(.001)	(.529)	(.005)	(<.001)	(.039)	(.553)	(.004)
0.44	3.20*	0.46	0.28	11.05*	3.65*	0.46
(.925)	(.001)	(.911)	(.985)	(<.001)	(<.001)	(.911)
0.27	1.01	0.37	0.36	2.57*	1.04	0.40
(.988)	(.438)	(.957)	(.962)	(.006)	(.415)	(.944)
1.11	1.24	1.01	1.09	1.66	1.28	1.04
(.357)	(.271)	(.437)	(.374)	(.094)	(.247)	(.410)
3.27*	0.94	2.85*	3.71*	2.08*	0.91	2.90*
(.001)	(.501)	(.003)	(<.001)	(.029)	(.528)	(.002)
0.55	2.81*	0.56	0.65	8.83*	2.98*	0.67
(.850)	(.003)	(.848)	(.772)	(<.001)	(.002)	(.753)

Panel B: APT

APT-10

α_I	α_{I74}	α_{I79}	α_{INJ}	α_J	α_{INJ74}	α_{INJ79}
0.63	2.54*	1.25	0.42	1.34	2.38*	1.24
(.786)	(.007)	(.264)	(.933)	(.214)	(.012)	(.268)
0.41	0.76	0.50	0.39	1.20	0.84	0.50
(.943)	(.667)	(.891)	(.948)	(.297)	(.589)	(.888)
1.25	2.14*	0.90	1.21	0.55	2.14*	0.90
(.266)	(.024)	(.533)	(.286)	(.855)	(.024)	(.539)
1.98*	0.89	2.24*	2.13	0.89	0.89	2.23*
(.039)	(.543)	(.018)	(.025)	(.548)	(.547)	(.019)
0.45	2.93*	0.91	0.28	1.64	2.67*	0.84
(.919)	(.002)	(.528)	(.984)	(.100)	(.005)	(.593)
0.26	1.78	0.32	0.21	0.55	1.94*	0.31
(.989)	(.069)	(.976)	(.995)	(.854)	(.044)	(.977)
1.20	2.03*	1.08	1.10	0.49	2.05*	1.09
(.295)	(.034)	(.379)	(.364)	(.896)	(.031)	(.373)
2.80*	0.86	2.44*	3.45*	1.42	0.84	2.65*
(.003)	(.572)	(.010)	(<.001)	(.178)	(.587)	(.005)
0.41	2.89*	0.96	0.54	1.33	2.65*	0.91
(.943)	(.002)	(.484)	(.861)	(.220)	(.005)	(.529)

throughout the 1969–1983 period is given by α_{INJ}. Estimated January-specific mispricing is given by α_J. Estimated mispricing specific to the 1969–1974 and 1969–1979 periods is given by α_{I74} and α_{I79}, respectively. R_I identifies the market from which the size portfolios are constructed. P identifies the market from which the benchmark portfolios are constructed.

* Significant at the 5 percent level.

The Review of Financial Studies / v 2 n 4 1989

Table 11
Likelihood ratio tests of no mispricing for size-ranked portfolios (zero-beta models with capital control dummies)

Panel A: CAPM

R_i	P	CAPM-EW		CAPM-VW	
		$\alpha_i = (1 - b_i)\lambda$	$\alpha_{inj} = (1 - b_i)\lambda$	$\alpha_i = (1 - b_i)\lambda$	$\alpha_{inj} = (1 - b_i)\lambda$
US	US	8.44 (.490)	6.12 (.728)	5.12 (.824)	3.15 (.958)
JP	JP	2.01 (.991)	2.00 (.991)	2.07 (.990)	3.24 (.954)
UK	UK	10.37 (.321)	10.08 (.344)	15.61 (.075)	13.59 (.137)
FR	FR	31.89* (<.001)	29.34* (<.001)	32.07* (<.001)	36.01* (<.001)
US	Int'l	4.03 (.909)	3.09 (.961)	4.42 (.882)	2.96 (.966)
JP	Int'l	2.43 (.982)	3.48 (.942)	2.54 (.980)	3.70 (.930)
UK	Int'l	10.23 (.332)	10.86 (.285)	11.47 (.245)	11.33 (.254)
FR	Int'l	29.54* (<.001)	27.85* (.001)	32.41* (<.001)	35.44* (<.001)
Int'l	Int'l	4.29 (.891)	6.37 (.702)	5.83 (.756)	6.77 (.661)

Panel B: APT

R_i	P	APT-5		APT-10	
		α_i = constant	α_{inj} = constant	α_i = constant	α_{inj} = constant
US	US	5.52 (.787)	3.90 (.918)	6.65 (.673)	4.39 (.883)
JP	JP	3.36 (.948)	3.72 (.929)	4.51 (.875)	4.93 (.840)
UK	UK	13.10 (.158)	12.67 (.178)	13.54 (.140)	13.30 (.150)
FR	FR	20.46* (.015)	22.38* (.008)	20.90* (.013)	22.52* (.007)
US	Int'l	3.62 (.934)	2.84 (.256)	4.42 (.882)	2.98 (.965)
JP	Int'l	2.85 (.970)	3.30 (.951)	2.65 (.977)	2.39 (.984)
UK	Int'l	10.76 (.292)	10.69 (.297)	12.33 (.195)	11.72 (.230)
FR	Int'l	29.43* (<.001)	35.10* (<.001)	27.96* (<.001)	34.79* (<.001)
Int'l	Int'l	4.71 (.859)	6.28 (.712)	4.41 (.816)	5.85 (.799)

Likelihood ratio test statistics with *p*-values in parentheses. Statistics are asymptotically χ^2 with 9 degrees of freedom. Tests are for zero mispricing across 10 size-based portfolios given by restrictions 13–16 in Table 5. Parameters are estimated using monthly returns over the period 1969–1983. For the CAPM, the estimates of mispricing and non-January mispricing are $\alpha_i - (1 - b_i)\lambda$ and $\alpha_{inj} - (1 - b_i)\lambda$, respectively. For the APT, the estimates of mispricing and non-January mispricing are $\alpha_i - \lambda$ and $\alpha_{inj} - \lambda$, respectively. Estimated difference between the zero-beta return and r_f is given by λ. R_i identifies the market from which the size portfolios are constructed. P identifies the market from which the benchmark portfolios are constructed.

* Significant at the 5 percent level.

Investigation of International Asset Pricing

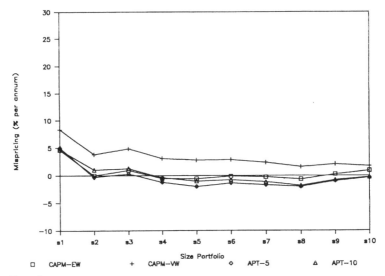

Figure 5
Mispricing (controlling for changes in capital controls) in percent per annum, for 10 international portfolios formed by ranking on firm size
Mispricing is estimated by the intercept in the regression of monthly portfolio excess returns on a constant, a dummy variable that is unity before February 1974, a dummy variable that is unity before December 1979, and (*a*) monthly excess returns on a value-weighted portfolio of international stocks, denoted CAPM–VW (plus signs); (*b*) monthly excess returns on an equal-weighted portfolio of international stocks, denoted CAPM–EW (squares); (*c*) first five international factor estimates from the asymptotic principal components procedure, denoted APT–5 (diamonds); and (*d*) first 10 international factor estimates from the asymptotic principal components procedure, denoted APT–10 (triangles). Parameters are estimated using monthly returns over the period 1969–1983. S1 represents the portfolio of smallest firms while S10 represents the portfolio of largest firms. Size is defined as market value of common stock at the beginning of each five-year subperiod.

the period prior to February 1974 we find that multi-index models continue to outperform the single-index models. Also, international versions of the CAPM outperform domestic versions while the opposite is generally true for the APT.

5. Conclusions

We compare domestic and international versions of several alternative asset pricing models. The empirical results indicate that

1. There is some evidence against all of the models, especially in terms of pricing common stock of small-market-value firms.

2. Multifactor models tend to outperform single-index CAPM-type models in both domestic and international forms. The value-weighted CAPM has much larger pricing errors than the APT. The equal-weighted CAPM performs about as well as the APT except in terms of explaining seasonality in asset returns.

The Review of Financial Studies / v 2 n 4 1989

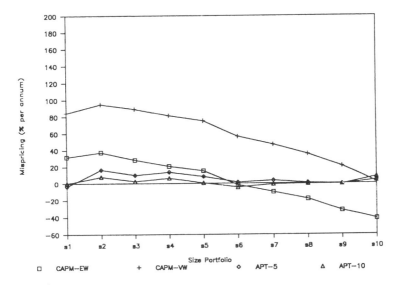

Figure 6
January-specific mispricing (controlling for changes in capital controls) in percent per annum, for 10 international portfolios formed by ranking on firm size
Mispricing is estimated by the slope coefficient on the January dummy variable in the regression of monthly portfolio excess returns on a constant, January dummy variable, a dummy variable that is unity before February 1974, a dummy that is unity before December 1979, and (*a*) monthly excess returns on a value-weighted portfolio of international stocks, denoted CAPM-VW (plus signs); (*b*) monthly excess returns on an equal-weighted portfolio of international stocks, denoted CAPM-EW (squares); (*c*) first five international factor estimates from the asymptotic principal components procedure, denoted APT-5 (diamonds); and (*d*) first 10 international factor estimates from the asymptotic principal components procedure, denoted APT-10 (triangles). Parameters are estimated using monthly returns over the period 1969–1983. S1 represents the portfolio of smallest firms while S10 represents the portfolio of largest firms. Size is defined as market value of common stock at the beginning of each five-year subperiod.

3. There is strong evidence that the behavior of the models in the period from January 1969 to January 1974 is different from their behavior after January 1974. We interpret this evidence as being consistent with a scenario in which some combination of capital control deregulation and the breakdown of the fixed exchange rate regime lead to pricing effects that are not well captured by models of either completely segmented or completely integrated markets.

4. Controlling for regime shifts in the level of capital controls, international versions of the CAPM outperform domestic versions while the opposite is true for the APT. The evidence is generally consistent with nontrivial international influences in asset pricing.

Appendix

Let $\tilde{r}_{zt}$ denote the return on a portfolio which has zero covariance with the benchmark portfolios. In most cases (particularly international models)

582

Investigation of International Asset Pricing

Table 12
Average absolute mispricing across size-ranked portfolios adjusting for changes in capital controls

R_i	P	CAPM-EW		CAPM-VW		APT-5		APT-10	
		A	AJ	A	AJ	A	AJ	A	AJ
US	US	12.71	77.41	14.83	86.35	1.30	4.95	1.23	4.72
JP	JP	1.22	29.02	6.56	33.94	1.58	5.43	1.54	5.90
UK	UK	3.19	21.57	6.17	79.41	2.27	2.17	2.29	2.42
FR	FR	12.82	23.24	13.18	21.82	4.77	9.15	4.48	7.47
US	Int'l	5.69	36.61	7.90	69.77	1.60	8.48	1.93	8.12
JP	Int'l	1.35	19.67	2.99	28.32	1.71	9.49	1.93	6.95
UK	Int'l	2.29	4.26	5.23	63.15	2.21	12.23	2.48	3.38
FR	Int'l	16.82	16.80	15.71	14.31	16.46	31.60	9.68	23.60
Int'l	Int'l	0.90	23.68	3.33	58.56	1.54	6.28	1.33	3.32

Average absolute mispricing across 10 size-ranked portfolios, in percent per annum, are given by $A = \Sigma \, |\alpha_i|/10$ and $AJ = \Sigma \, |\alpha_{ij}|/10$. α_i and α_{ij} are the estimates of mispricing and January-specific mispricing, respectively, from regressions 10 and 11 in Table 5. Parameters are estimated using monthly returns over the period 1969–1983. R_i identifies the market from which the size portfolios are constructed. P identifies the market from which the benchmark portfolios are constructed.

the U.S. Treasury-bill return is theoretically not the appropriate zero-beta return, that is, $r_{Ft} \neq E(\tilde{r}_{zt})$. In this Appendix we show that we need not assume that $r_{Ft} = E(\tilde{r}_{zt})$ or even that r_{Ft} is riskless in order to obtain valid estimates of the pervasive factors and their associated risk premia ($f_{jt} + \gamma_{jt}$). Although r_{Ft} is riskless in nominal U.S. dollar returns it is easy to see that it may not be riskless in real terms or relative to another currency. Under certain conditions we can use excess returns relative to any well-diversified asset or portfolio to obtain consistent estimates of ($f_{jt} + \gamma_{jt}$).

Let $\tilde{R}_{it} = \tilde{r}_{it} - \tilde{r}_{\delta t}$ (i.e., we are calculating excess returns relative to asset δ). We assume that $r_{\delta t}$ is well diversified and that calculating excess returns with respect to $r_{\delta t}$ does not alter the basic nature of the factor structure (i.e., calculating excess returns with respect to $r_{\delta t}$ does not turn a k-factor model into a q-factor model with $q < k$). That is,

(a) $r_{\delta t} = \mu_{\delta t} = \mu_{\delta t} + b_\delta f_t$
(b) $\|(B^{*n'}B^{*n})^{-1}/n\| \leq c < \infty$ for all n

where $B^{*n} = B^n - \iota b_\delta'$
     ι = an $n \times 1$ vector of 1s
     B^n is as defined in Equation (4)

Under these conditions, all of the assumptions required by Connor and Korajczyk (1986) hold and their theorem 2 can be applied to show that $G^n = L^n F + \phi^n$ with plim $[\phi^n] = 0$. Now the pricing model implies that $E(\tilde{r}_{it}) - E(\tilde{r}_{zt}) = b_i \gamma$ and, hence, that $E(\tilde{r}_{it}) - E(\tilde{r}_{\delta t}) = [E(\tilde{r}_{zt}) - E(\tilde{r}_{\delta t})] + b_i \gamma = \lambda_t + b_i \gamma$. Under the assumption that $\lambda_t = \lambda$, the intercept terms in Equation (7) should all equal λ as was stated in the text. If condition (b) does not hold then λ will include the risk premia for the $k - q$ factors that were eliminated.

The Review of Financial Studies / v 2 n 4 1989

References

Amsler, C. E., and P. Schmidt, 1985, "A Monte Carlo Investigation of the Accuracy of Multivariate CAPM Tests," *Journal of Financial Economics*, 14, 359–375.

Banz, R. W., 1981, "The Relationship Between Return and Market Value of Common Stocks," *Journal of Financial Economics*, 9, 3–18.

Beenstock, M., and K. Chan, 1984, "Testing Asset Pricing Theories in the U.K. Securities Market 1962–1981," Working Paper 66, The City University Business School, August.

Black, F., 1972, "Capital Market Equilibrium with Restricted Borrowing," *Journal of Business*, 45, 444–454.

Black, F., M. C. Jensen, and M. Scholes, 1972, "The Capital Asset Pricing Model: Some Empirical Tests," in M. C. Jensen (ed.), *Studies in the Theory of Capital Markets*, Praeger, New York, pp. 79–121.

Chamberlain, G., and M. Rothschild, 1983, "Arbitrage, Factor Structure, and Mean-Variance Analysis on Large Asset Markets," *Econometrica*, 51, 1281–1304.

Chen, N. F., 1983, "Some Empirical Tests of the Theory of Arbitrage Pricing," *Journal of Finance*, 38, 1393–1414.

Cho, D. C., C. S. Eun, and L. W. Senbet, 1986, "International Arbitrage Pricing Theory: An Empirical Investigation," *Journal of Finance*, 41, 313–329.

Connor, G., 1984, "A Unified Beta Pricing Theory," *Journal of Economic Theory*, 34, 13–31.

Connor, G., and R. A. Korajczyk, 1986, "Performance Measurement with the Arbitrage Pricing Theory: A New Framework for Analysis," *Journal of Financial Economics*, 15, 373–394.

Connor, G., and R. A. Korajczyk, 1988a, "Risk and Return in an Equilibrium APT: Application of a New Test Methodology," *Journal of Financial Economics*, 21, 255–289.

Connor, G., and R. A. Korajczyk, 1988b, "Estimating Pervasive Economic Factors with Missing Observations," Working Paper 34, Department of Finance, Northwestern University, May.

Constantinides, G. M., 1980, "Admissible Uncertainty in the Intertemporal Asset Pricing Model," *Journal of Financial Economics*, 8, 71–86.

Corhay, A., G. Hawawini, and P. Michel, 1987, "Seasonality in the Risk-Return Relationship: Some International Evidence," *Journal of Finance*, 42, 49–68.

Dhrymes, P. J., I. Friend, and N. B. Gultekin, 1984, "A Critical Reexamination of the Empirical Evidence on the Arbitrage Pricing Theory," *Journal of Finance*, 39, 323–346.

Dumontier, P., 1986, "Le Modèle d'Evaluation par Arbitrage des Actifs Financiers: Une Etude sur le Marché Financier Parisien," *Finance*, 7, 7–21.

Fama, E. F., and J. D. MacBeth, 1973, "Risk, Return, and Equilibrium: Empirical Tests," *Journal of Political Economy*, 71, 607–636.

Gallant, A. R., 1987, *Nonlinear Statistical Models*, Wiley, New York.

Gibbons, M. R., 1982, "Multivariate Tests of Financial Models: A New Approach," *Journal of Financial Economics*, 10, 3–27.

Gibbons, M. R., S. A. Ross, and J. Shanken, 1986, "A Test of the Efficiency of a Given Portfolio," Research Paper 853, Graduate School of Business, Stanford University; forthcoming in *Econometrica*.

Gultekin, M. N., N. B. Gultekin, and A. Penati, 1989, "Capital Controls and International Capital Markets Segmentation: The Evidence from the Japanese and American Stock Markets," *Journal of Finance*, 44, 849–869.

Hamao, Y., 1986, "An Empirical Examination of the Arbitrage Pricing Theory: Using Japanese Data," working paper, Yale University, June.

Hansen, L. P., and S. F. Richard, 1987, "The Role of Conditioning Information in Deducing Testable Restrictions Implied by Dynamic Asset Pricing Models," *Econometrica*, 55, 587–613.

Investigation of International Asset Pricing

Hawawini, G., and C. Viallet, 1987, "Seasonality, Size Premium and the Relationship Between the Risk and the Return of French Common Stocks," working paper, INSEAD, November.

Huberman, G., and S. Kandel, 1987, "Mean Variance Spanning," *Journal of Finance*, 42, 873–888.

Ibbotson Associates, 1985, *Stocks, Bonds, Bills, and Inflation*, 1985 yearbook.

Ingersoll, J. E., Jr., 1984, "Some Results in the Theory of Arbitrage Pricing," *Journal of Finance*, 39, 1021–1039.

Kandel, S., and R. F. Stambaugh, 1987, "A Mean-Variance Framework for Tests of Asset Pricing Models," Working Paper 219, CRSP, University of Chicago; forthcoming in *Review of Financial Studies*.

Kato, K., and J. S. Schallheim, 1985, "Seasonal and Size Anomalies in the Japanese Stock Market," *Journal of Financial and Quantitative Analysis*, 20, 243–260.

Keim, D. B., 1983, "Size Related Anomalies and Stock Return Seasonality: Further Empirical Evidence," *Journal of Financial Economics*, 12, 13–32.

Lehmann, B. N., and D. M. Modest, 1988, "The Empirical Foundations of the Arbitrage Pricing Theory," *Journal of Financial Economics*, 21, 213–254.

Rao, C. R., 1973, *Linear Statistical Inference and its Applications* (2d ed.), Wiley, New York.

Roll, R., 1977, "A Critique of the Asset Pricing Theory's Tests Part I: On Past and Potential Testability of the Theory," *Journal of Financial Economics*, 4, 129–176.

Roll, R., and S. A. Ross, 1980, "An Empirical Investigation of the Arbitrage Pricing Theory," *Journal of Finance*, 35, 1073–1103.

Ross, S. A., 1976, "The Arbitrage Theory of Capital Asset Pricing," *Journal of Economic Theory*, 13, 341–360.

Ross, S. A., and M. M. Walsh, 1983, "A Simple Approach to the Pricing of Risky Assets with Uncertain Exchange Rates," *Research in International Business and Finance*, 3, 39–54.

Shanken, J., 1985, "Multivariate Tests of the Zero-Beta CAPM," *Journal of Financial Economics*, 14, 327–348.

Solnik, B. H., 1974, "An Equilibrium Model of the International Capital Market," *Journal of Economic Theory*, 8, 500–524.

Solnik, B. H., 1983, "International Arbitrage Pricing Theory," *Journal of Finance*, 38, 449–457.

Stambaugh, R. F., 1982, "On the Exclusion of Assets from Tests of the Two-Parameter Model: A Sensitivity Analysis," *Journal of Financial Economics*, 10, 237–268.

Stulz, R. M., 1985, "Pricing Capital Assets in an International Setting: An Introduction," in D. R. Lessard (ed.), *International Financial Management: Theory and Applications* (2d ed.), Wiley, New York.

Trzcinka, C., 1986, "On the Number of Factors in the Arbitrage Pricing Model," *Journal of Finance*, 41, 347–368.

[11]

THE JOURNAL OF FINANCE • VOL. XLVI, NO. 1 • MARCH 1991

The World Price of Covariance Risk

CAMPBELL R. HARVEY*

ABSTRACT

In a financially integrated global market, the conditionally expected return on a portfolio of securities from a particular country is determined by the country's world risk exposure. This paper measures the conditional risk of 17 countries. The reward per unit of risk is the world price of covariance risk. Although the tests provide evidence on the conditional mean variance efficiency of the benchmark portfolio, the results show that countries' risk exposures help explain differences in performance. Evidence is also presented which indicates that these risk exposures change through time and that the world price of covariance risk is not constant.

IN A WORLD WITH increasingly integrated financial services, why do industrialized countries have much different average stock returns? Why have Japanese stocks done so well compared to all other countries through 1989 and so poorly recently? If we view countries as stock portfolios in a global market, asset pricing theory suggests that cross-sectional differences in countries' risk exposures should explain the cross-sectional variation in expected returns.

This paper tests whether conditional versions of the Sharpe (1964) and Lintner (1965) asset pricing model are consistent with behavior of returns in 17 countries. Country risk is defined as the conditional sensitivity (or covariance) of the country return to a world stock return. This risk is allowed to vary through time. The reward per unit of sensitivity is the world price of covariance risk. Conditional covariances are calculated for each country. The differences in the countries' conditional covariances should explain the differences in national performance if there is only one source of risk.

The empirical results indicate that the time-varying covariances are able to capture some, but not all, of the dynamic behavior of the country returns. This could be due to incomplete market integration, the existence of more than one source of risk, or some other misspecification. The world price of covariance risk is also calculated. This measure exhibits significant time

*Associate Professor of Finance, Duke University, Fuqua School of Business. I have benefitted from the comments and suggestions of Andrea Beltratti, Gene Fama, Wayne Ferson, Mike Hemler, Naoki Kishimoto, Robert Korajczyk, Tom Smith, an anonymous referee and seminar participants at Duke University, the Federal Reserve Bank at Cleveland, Helsinki School of Economics, MIT, Ohio State University, Princeton University, Queen's University, Washington University and conference participants at the American Finance Association meetings, the CRSP Fall Seminar and First International Conference of the Centre for Research in Finance—IMI Group. Arthur Evans provided valuable research assistance. I am especially indebted to René Stulz who provided many insights that greatly improve this paper.

variation, which indicates the investor's expected compensation per unit of country risk exposure changes through time in a partially predictable way.

My paper is organized as follows. In the first section, the econometric methodology is introduced that measures the conditional moments of the country and world stock returns. The data are documented in the second section. The empirical results are presented in the third section. Some concluding remarks are offered in the final part.

I. Methodology

A. An International CAPM with Time-Varying Moments

A number of studies have examined asset pricing relations with international data. The tests of the Sharpe (1964) and Lintner (1965) asset pricing model have been executed by Solnik (1974), Stehle (1977), and others.[1] Multifactor asset pricing models have been tested by Cho, Eun, and Senbet (1986), Hamao (1988), Gultekin, Gultekin, and Penati (1989), and Korajczyk and Viallet (1989). Finally, Wheatley (1988) tested the restrictions implied by the consumption-based capital asset pricing model. All of these studies assess unconditional moment restrictions implied by the models, i.e., do cross-sectional differences in *average* risk explain the differences in *average* returns?

This study focuses on *conditional* asset pricing restrictions. The conditional version of the Sharpe (1964) and Lintner (1965) capital asset pricing model restricts the conditionally expected return on an asset to be proportional to its covariance with the market portfolio. The proportionality factor is the price of covariance risk which is the expected compensation (expected return) that the investor receives for taking on a unit of covariance risk. The model is:

$$E\left[r_{jt} \mid \Omega_{t-1}\right] = \frac{E\left[r_{mt} \mid \Omega_{t-1}\right]}{\text{Var}\left[r_{mt} \mid \Omega_{t-1}\right]} \text{Cov}\left[r_{jt}, r_{mt} \mid \Omega_{t-1}\right], \tag{1}$$

where r_{jt} is the return on a portfolio of country j equity from time $t-1$ to t in excess of a risk free return, r_{mt} is the excess return on the world market portfolio, and Ω_{t-1} is the information set that investors use to set prices. The ratio of the conditionally expected return on the market index $E[r_{mt} \mid \Omega_{t-1}]$ to the conditional variance of the market index $\text{Var}[r_{mt} \mid \Omega_{t-1}]$ is the world price of covariance risk.

There are a number of issues that arise when applying the model to international data. For the Sharpe-Lintner model to hold internationally, Stulz (1981) demonstrates that some auxiliary assumptions must be made. A sufficient assumption is perfect correlation between the world market portfolio and world consumption. This assumption or equivalent distributional assumptions are implicit in this study's application of the Sharpe-Lintner

---

[1] See the references in Solnik (1977) and Stulz (1984).

model.[2] Alternatively, one can view the model as testing the mean-variance efficiency of the world market portfolio.

The empirical implementation of the model takes the view of a global investor whose returns are calculated in U.S. dollars. In other words, the investor is unhedged in exchange rates. Consistent with this assumption, the nominal return on the U.S. Treasury bill that is 30 days to maturity is conditionally risk-free. That is, when the investor buys a 30-day bill, the nominal return is conditionally known. Furthermore, the excess return is real because the U.S. inflation component in the stock return is cancelled out by the inflation component in the bill return.[3]

B. Econometric Specifications

Some additional structure must be imposed before equation (1) is testable. In particular, a model must be specified for the conditional first moments. Assume that investors process information using a linear filter:[4]

$$u_{jt} = r_{jt} - \mathbf{Z}_{t-1}\delta_j, \tag{2}$$

where u_{jt} is the investor's forecast error for the return on country j, $\mathbf{Z}_{t-1}$ are l information variables that are available to the investor, and δ_j is a set of time-invariant weights that the investor uses to derive the conditionally expected returns.

Given the assumption on the conditional first moments, we can rewrite (1):

$$\mathbf{Z}_{t-1}\delta_j = \frac{\mathbf{Z}_{t-1}\delta_m}{E[u_{mt}^2|\mathbf{Z}_{t-1}]} E[u_{jt}u_{mt}|\mathbf{Z}_{t-1}], \tag{3}$$

where u_{mt} is the investor's forecast error for the return on the world market portfolio. Notice that $E[u_{mt}^2|\mathbf{Z}_{t-1}]$ is the definition of conditional variance and $E[u_{jt}u_{mt}|\mathbf{Z}_{t-1}]$ is the conditional covariance. Also, equation (3) is conditioned on $\mathbf{Z}_{t-1}$ which is the subset of the true information set.[5] Next,

---

[2]Stulz's (1981) international capital asset pricing model assumes that representative investor has state-independent von Neuman-Morgenstern expected utility. Some recent research has considered non-von Neuman-Morgenstern utility. In particular, the assumption that the investor is indifferent about the resolution of uncertainty is dropped. Epstein and Zin (1988) and Giovannini and Weil (1988) provide a description of the conditions where the conditional Sharpe-Lintner model obtains.

[3]However, this does not imply that real returns are independent of inflation. Evidence on the relation between stock returns and inflation is presented in Gultekin (1983) and Solnik (1983).

[4]Sufficient distributional conditions that imply linear conditional expectations involve the joint distribution of the returns and the information variables falling into the class of spherically invariant distributions. This class of distributions is described in Vershik (1964) and Blake and Thomas (1968) and applied to conditionally expected stock returns in Harvey (1990).

[5]Since $\mathbf{Z} \subset \Omega$ (the true information set), the expectation of the true conditional covariance is not the covariance conditioned on $\mathbf{Z}$. Conditioning on the specified information, $E[\text{Cov}(r_{jt}, r_{mt}|\Omega_{t-1})|\mathbf{Z}_{t-1}] = \text{Cov}(r_{jt}, r_{mt}|\mathbf{Z}_{t-1}) - \text{Cov}(E[r_{jt}|\Omega_{t-1}], E[r_{mt}|\Omega_{t-1}]|\mathbf{Z}_{t-1})$. A similar result holds for the conditional variance (where $r_{jt} = r_{mt}$). As a result, equation (3) should be viewed as an approximation. The model conditioned upon Ω is untestable because Ω is not observable.

multiply both sides of (3) by the conditional variance:

$$E\left[u_{mt}^2 \mathbf{Z}_{t-1}\delta_j | \mathbf{Z}_{t-1} \right] = E\left[u_{jt}u_{mt}\mathbf{Z}_{t-1}\delta_m | \mathbf{Z}_{t-1} \right]. \qquad (4)$$

Notice that the conditionally expected returns on the market and the country portfolio are moved inside the expectation operators. This can be done because they are known conditional on the information $\mathbf{Z}_{t-1}$. The deviation from the expectation is:

$$h_{jt} = u_{mt}^2 \mathbf{Z}_{t-1}\delta_j - u_{jt}u_{mt}\mathbf{Z}_{t-1}\delta_m, \qquad (5)$$

where h_{jt} is a disturbance that should be unrelated to the information under the null hypothesis that the model is true. If h_{jt} is divided by the conditional variance of the world market return, it can be interpreted as the deviation of the country's return from the return predicted by the model. In other words, h_{jt} is a pricing error. A negative pricing error implies the model is overpricing while a positive pricing error indicates that the model is underpricing.

The econometric model to test the asset pricing restrictions is formed by combining equations (2) and (5):

$$\varepsilon_t = \begin{pmatrix} \mathbf{u}_t & u_{mt} & \mathbf{h}_t \end{pmatrix} = \begin{pmatrix} [\mathbf{r}_t - \mathbf{Z}_{t-1}\delta]' \\ [r_{mt} - \mathbf{Z}_{t-1}\delta_m]' \\ [u_{mt}^2 \mathbf{Z}_{t-1}\delta - u_{mt}\mathbf{u}_t \mathbf{Z}_{t-1}\delta_m]' \end{pmatrix}, \qquad (6)$$

where $\mathbf{u}$ is a $1 \times n$ (number of countries) vector of innovations in the conditional means of the country returns. The model implies that $E[\varepsilon_t | \mathbf{Z}_{t-1}] = 0$. With n countries, there are $n + 1$ columns of innovations in the conditional means ($\mathbf{u}$ and u_m) and n columns in $\mathbf{h}$. If there are l information variables, there are $[l \times (2n + 1)]$ orthogonality conditions. However, there are $[l \times (n + 1)]$ parameters to estimate, which implies there are $l \times n$ overidentifying conditions.[6]

Hansen's (1982) generalized method of moments (GMM) is used to estimate the parameters in equation (6). The GMM forms a vector of the orthogonality conditions $\mathbf{g} = vec(\varepsilon'\mathbf{Z})$ where ε is the matrix of forecast errors for T observations and $2n + 1$ equations, and $\mathbf{Z}$ is a $T \times l$ matrix of observations on thepredetermined instrumental variables. The parameter vector δ is chosen to make the orthogonality conditions as close to zero as possible by minimizing the quadratic form $\mathbf{g}'\mathbf{w}\mathbf{g}$ where the $\mathbf{w}$ is symmetric weighting matrix that defines the metric used to make $\mathbf{g}$ close to zero. The consistent estimate of $\mathbf{w}$ is formed by

$$\left[\sum_{t=1}^T (\varepsilon_t \otimes \mathbf{Z}_{t-1})'(\varepsilon_t \otimes \mathbf{Z}_{t-1}) \right]^{-1}.$$

However, ε depends on the parameters. As a result, the estimation proceeds in stages. An initial estimate of the parameters is obtained by using an

---

[6]This formulation is explored in the context of returns on the New York Stock Exchange by Harvey (1989) and Huang (1989).

identity matrix for **w**. These parameters are used to calculate ε and a new weighting matrix. The estimation procedure is repeated with this new weighting matrix. Hansen provides the conditions that guarantee that the estimates are consistent and asymptotically normal.

The minimized value of this quadratic form is distributed χ^2 under the null hypothesis with degrees of freedom equal to the number of orthogonality conditions minus the number of parameters. This χ^2 statistic, which is known as the test of the *overidentifying* restrictions, provides a goodness of fit test for the model. A high χ^2 statistic means that the disturbances are correlated with the instrumental variables. This is a symptom of model misspecification.

In a system of many equations, the test of the overidentifying restrictions does not tell us where the model is failing. One possible solution is to estimate equation (6) for individual countries. Even with one country, (6) provides a test of the model's restriction that the conditionally expected excess return on a country portfolio is proportional to its conditional covariance with the world return. However, the single country test does not impose the cross-country restriction that the proportionality factor (the world price of covariance risk) is the same for each country. The single country tests are weaker because fewer restrictions are being imposed. However, statistical rejections in the single country estimation may provide valuable insights as to where the model is failing. Another possibility is to examine subsets of the disturbances; in particular, the errors implied by the asset pricing model's restrictions **e**. An additional test is to regress the disturbances for a particular country portfolio on the set of instruments. If the model is correct, the R^2 should be zero.

C. World Price of Covariance Risk

In the framework of equation (6), all of the conditional moments—the means, variances, and covariances—are allowed to change through time. If some of these moments are constant, then more powerful tests can be constructed by imposing this additional structure.

Traditionally, asset pricing tests have focused on whether expected returns are proportional to the expected return on a benchmark portfolio. This restriction can be imposed and tested:

$$\mathbf{k}_t = \mathbf{r}_t - r_{mt}\beta, \tag{7}$$

where β is a n-vector of coefficients. This coefficient vector can represent the ratios of conditional covariances of the country excess returns to the conditional variance of the benchmark return.[7] The model implies that

---

[7]There is an alternative interpretation of equation (7). Since the coefficient is not restricted in the estimation to be the ratio of the conditional covariance of the country excess return to the conditional variance of the benchmark return, (7) can be interpreted as a single factor latent variables test [see Hansen and Hodrick (1983), Gibbons and Ferson (1985), and Ferson (1990)]. In this test, the coefficient represents the ratio of the covariance of the country's return and the single factor to the covariance of the benchmark's return and the single factor.

$E[\mathbf{k}_t | \mathbf{Z}_{t-1}] = 0$ where $\mathbf{k}_t$ is the pricing error associated with this implementation of the asset pricing model. There are $l \times n$ orthogonality conditions and n parameters to estimate leaving $l \times (n-1)$ orthogonality conditions to be tested. An advantage of equation (7) is that the models for conditional means need not be specified.

Another version of the model assumes that the reward to volatility ratio is constant. In our context, the reward to volatility is the world price of covariance risk. Imposing this restriction results in:

$$\mathbf{e}_t = \mathbf{r}_t - \lambda \mathbf{u}_t u_{mt}, \tag{8}$$

where λ is the ratio of the conditionally expected return on the market divided by the conditional variance, and $\mathbf{e}_t$ is the pricing error associated with the assumption of a constant price of covariance risk. In contrast to equation (7), it is necessary to have a model for the conditional means in (8). The system is:

$$\varepsilon_t = (\mathbf{u}_t \quad u_{mt} \quad \mathbf{e}_t) = \left(\begin{array}{c} [\mathbf{r}_t - \mathbf{Z}_{t-1}\delta]' \\ [r_{mt} - \mathbf{Z}_{t-1}\delta_m]' \\ [\mathbf{r}_t - \lambda(u_{mt}\mathbf{u}_t)]' \end{array} \right)'. \tag{9}$$

With n assets, there are $n+1$ columns in $\mathbf{u}$ and u_m and n columns in $\mathbf{e}$. If there are l instrumental variables, there are $[l \times (2n+1)]$ orthogonality conditions and $[1 + l \times (n+1)]$ parameters to estimate. As a result, there are $l \times n - 1$ overidentifying restrictions to be tested.[8]

It is possible to simplify the estimation in equation (9) by noting that $E[u_{mt}u_{jt}|\mathbf{Z}_{t-1}] = E[u_{mt}r_{jt}|\mathbf{Z}_{t-1}]$.[9] This allows us to drop the n equations for the conditional means of the country returns. The more parsimonious system is:

$$\eta_t = (u_{mt} \quad \mathbf{e}_t) = \left(\begin{array}{c} [r_{mt} - \mathbf{Z}_{t-1}\delta_m]' \\ [\mathbf{r}_t - \lambda(u_{mt}\mathbf{r}_t)]' \end{array} \right)'. \tag{10}$$

This system has $n+1$ equations and $l \times (n+1)$ orthogonality conditions. With $l+1$ parameters, there are $l \times n - 1$ overidentifying restrictions. This

---

[8]Using a different data set, Giovannini and Jorion (1989) provide maximum likelihood estimation of equation (8) where the covariance is parametered to be a non-stochastic function of the current information set.

[9]This follows from

$$E[u_{mt}u_{jt}|\mathbf{Z}_{t-1}] = E[u_{mt}(r_{jt} - \mathbf{Z}_{t-1}\delta_j)|\mathbf{Z}_{t-1}]$$
$$= E[u_{mt}r_{jt}|\mathbf{Z}_{t-1}] - E[u_{mt}\mathbf{Z}_{t-1}\delta_j|\mathbf{Z}_{t-1}]$$
$$= E[u_{mt}r_{jt}|\mathbf{Z}_{t-1}] - E[u_{mt}|\mathbf{Z}_{t-1}]\mathbf{Z}_{t-1}\delta_j$$
$$= E[u_{mt}r_{jt}|\mathbf{Z}_{t-1}],$$

since $E[u_{mt}|\mathbf{Z}_{t-1}] = 0$.

is the same number of restrictions as equation (9), and hence the systems (9) and (10) are asymptotically equivalent. However, in the context of the estimation, the dimensionality of the **w** matrix is much smaller in equation (10) and much more computationally manageable.

D. Time Variation in the Reward Per Unit of Risk

The constancy of the world price of covariance risk can be tested. The definition of a constant reward to volatility ratio is:

$$\frac{E[r_{mt}|\mathbf{Z}_{t-1}]}{E[u^2_{mt}|\mathbf{Z}_{t-1}]} = \lambda. \tag{11}$$

Multiply both sides by the conditional variance:

$$E[r_{mt}|\mathbf{Z}_{t-1}] = \lambda E[u^2_{mt}|\mathbf{Z}_{t-1}]. \tag{12}$$

This implies that the conditional mean of the market return is proportional to the conditional variance. To test this assumption, the following system can be estimated:

$$\xi_t = (u_{mt} \quad e_{mt}) = \left(\begin{matrix} [r_{mt} - \mathbf{Z}_{t-1}\delta_m]' \\ [r_{mt} - \lambda u^2_{mt}]' \end{matrix} \right)'. \tag{13}$$

This system has $l - 1$ overidentifying conditions.

It is also interesting to look at country-specific reward to volatility, i.e., the ratio of the country's conditionally expected return to its own conditional variance. If global markets are not financially integrated, then the ratio of country expected return to country variance is the relevant measure that transforms conditional covariance into expected return. This country-specific reward to volatility can be estimated by substituting the country returns into equation (13). The system also provides a test of whether the ratio is constant through time.

E. Country Performance

A country's performance is determined by its return in excess of the expected return given its riskiness. The pricing error is a measure of performance. A positive pricing error implies that the country earned more than expected given its level of risk. Of course, performance is measured under the null hypothesis that the model is correct. If the model is misspecified, then we cannot say which countries earned abnormal returns.

A useful measure of performance is the mean pricing error. In the context of system (9) which assumes a constant world price of covariance risk, this measure is defined as:

$$\text{Mean Error} = \frac{1}{T} \sum_{t=1}^{T} e_{jt}. \tag{14}$$

For Japan, if this measure is small or negative, then the results would indicate that the Japanese market has not done as well as is popularly believed. The patterns of the abnormal performance measure could also be examined in particular subperiods.

Another summary measure is the mean absolute pricing error:

$$\text{Mean Absolute Error} = \frac{1}{T} \sum_{t=1}^{T} |e_{jt}|, \tag{15}$$

where $|\cdot|$ is the absolute value operator. The mean pricing error indicates whether the performance is at the level of the expectations on average. Two countries may have the same mean error but very different performance through time. The mean absolute value captures the magnitude of the deviations from the mean. However, there is no reason to believe that the mean absolute error should be zero. This measure is included as a summary measure of the difference between the expected returns conditional on the model being correct and the actual returns.[10]

II. Data and Summary Statistics

A. *Data Sources*

Most of the data in this study are drawn from Morgan Stanley Capital International (MSCI). Monthly data on equity indices for 16 OECD countries and Hong Kong are available from December 1969 to May 1989.[11] These indices are value weighted and are calculated with dividend reinvestment. Morgan Stanley also calculates a value weighted world equity index which serves as the world market portfolio.

The MSCI international indices are composed of stocks that broadly represent stock composition in the different countries. Almost all the stocks (99%) can be readily purchased by non-nationals.[12] Although the MSCI indices are weighted towards larger capitalization stocks, the returns are similar to widely quoted country index returns. For example, there is a 99.1% correlation between the MSCI U.S. return and the New York Stock Exchange value-weighted return calculated by the Center for Research in Security Prices (CRSP) at the University of Chicago. For Japan, there is a 93.8%

---

[10]An alternative measure of the deviation is the root mean squared error. Since similar patterns were found in the mean absolute errors and the root mean squared errors, only the mean absolute errors are reported.

[11]The 16 OECD countries are Australia, Austria, Belgium, Canada, Denmark, France, Germany, Italy, Japan, the Netherlands, Norway, Spain, Sweden, Switzerland, the United Kingdom, and the United States. Morgan Stanley also has data on Finland and New Zealand but only since December 1987. Data is available for Singapore/Malaysia, but dividend data is not available for the full period. As a result, these countries are omitted from the empirical analysis.

[12]Cumby and Glen (1990) note that only 1% of the securities followed by Morgan Stanley Capital International are not available to non-nationals. This group is composed of Swedish bank stocks and some Swiss registered shares.

The World Price of Covariance Risk 119

Appendix Table A-I
The Composition of the Morgan Stanley Capital International Indices On March 31, 1989[a]

Country	Number of Companies Included	Weight in MSCI World Index	Market value of Companies billion U.S. $
Austria	15	0.1	5.6
Belgium	22	0.6	32.9
Denmark	27	0.3	15.1
Finland	21	0.3	13.2
France	83	2.6	132.9
Germany	57	2.7	141.7
Italy	68	1.4	73.8
Netherlands	24	1.3	70.0
Norway	18	0.2	12.7
Spain	31	1.0	50.0
Sweden	38	1.0	52.3
Switzerland	52	1.6	77.6
U.K.	136	8.4	438.6
Europe	592	21.4	1116.4
Australia	66	1.3	71.0
Hong Kong	21	0.9	44.7
Japan	265	42.9	2224.9
New Zealand	13	0.2	8.0
Singapore/Malaysia	53	0.6	29.3
EAFE	1021	67.3	3494.3
Canada	89	2.5	131.0
South African Gold Mines	21	0.2	10.3
U.S.	335	30.0	1555.5
World	1466	100.0	5191.1

[a]From Morgan Stanley Capital International *Perspective* First Quarter, 1989.

correlation between the MSCI return and the Nikkei 255 return.[13] An important difference between the MSCI indices and other national indices such as CRSP is the exclusion of investment companies and foreign domiciled companies. These stocks are excluded to avoid double counting. Appendix Table A-I provides a description of the number of companies included in the country indices and the market value of these companies as of March 31, 1989. The weight that each country commands in the MSCI world index is also reported.

[13]Over the 1970:2–1988:12 period, the mean return on the CRSP value weighted index is 0.40% per month with 4.83% standard deviation. Over the same period, the MSCI U.S. index has a mean return of 0.33% and standard deviation of 4.70%. The difference in mean return and standard deviation is due to the MSCI index using fewer small stocks. For Japan, the mean return on the Nikkei 225 is 1.13% with a standard deviation of 5.70%. The MSCI Japan index has an average return of 1.34% and a standard deviation of 6.09%.

McDonald (1989) and French and Poterba (1989) show that the MSCI world index gives too much weight to the Japanese stocks because of the large amount of cross-corporate ownership. I investigated an alternative index, the FT-Actuaries World Index which is compiled by *The Financial Times*, Goldman, Sachs and Co., and Country NatWest/Wood Mackenzie. Unfortunately, the FT-Actuaries index suffers from the same problem. In March 1989, Japan composed 42.9% of the MSCI index and as of June 1989, 40.7% of the FT-Actuaries index. The cross ownership problem is not restricted to Japan. Substantial intercorporate ownership is prevalent in other countries such as Germany.

All returns are calculated in excess of the U.S. Treasury bill that is closest to 30 days to maturity on the last trading day of the month. Data from 1970–1988 are drawn from the CRSP Government Bond File. The data for 1989 are from the *Wall Street Journal*. Holding period returns are calculated in the same way as Fama (1984).

The selection of conditioning information is an important step. The instrumental variables should approximate the information that investors use to set prices. Given that expected returns change through time, the instrumental variables should have the ability to predict returns.

The empirical strategy involves a prespecification of two categories of instrumental variables: common and local instruments. The common set of instruments consists of an identical set of instruments for all countries. In contrast, the local instruments include country-specific variables. According to the model, time variation in the conditionally expected country returns has three potential sources: variation in the world expected return, changes in the volatility of the world return, and time-varying conditional covariances of the country return with the world return. The common instrument set is important for the first two sources. Local information, in addition to the common instruments, may be important in detecting changes in the country's conditional covariances.

The specification of the common instrumental variables were drawn from studies of U.S. stock returns since there is little research on time-variation in international returns. The information set contains: the lagged world excess stock return, a dummy variable for the month of January, the dividend yield on the Standard and Poor's 500 stock price index, the U.S. term structure premia, and the U.S. default risk yield spread.

The first information variable is the lagged excess return on the world index. Many studies beginning with Fama (1965) have documented some degree of autocorrelation in returns. A dummy variable for the month of January is also included. Keim (1983) documents that U.S. returns in January are systematically higher. Gultekin and Gultekin (1983) find disproportionately large January returns in many industrialized countries.

The U.S. dividend price ratio is also included in the information set. Fama and French (1988, 1989) show that this is an important explanatory variable for U.S. stock returns. Cutler, Poterba and Summers (1989) show that many international stock returns are also influenced by the dividend yield. Following Harvey (1989), the dividend yield on the S&P 500 is expressed in excess of the 1-month bill rate.

A measure of default risk is the fourth information variable. Keim and Stambaugh (1986) and Fama and French (1989) show that the junk bond spread is able to predict returns. The junk bond spread is the difference in yields between Moody's Baa and Aaa rated bonds. A shorter maturity term structure variable is also included. Following Campbell (1987) and Harvey (1989), the excess return on a 3-month bill is included as the final information variable. Campbell and Hamao (1989) show that measures of the term structure are able to explain returns in Japan as well as the United States.

A number of local instruments are considered: the lagged own-country return, the country-specific dividend yields, foreign exchange rate changes, local short-term interest rates and local long-term to short-term interest rate spreads. In the model testing, three sets of instrumental variables are used. The first group is the common instruments. In the second set, *Local Instruments A*, the common instruments are augmented by the inclusion of the local dividend yields. In the third set, *Local Instruments B*, the common instruments are again augmented by the local dividend yield. In addition, the own-country lagged excess return replaces the lagged word excess return.

B. Summary Statistics

Unconditional means, standard deviations, and autocorrelations of the monthly returns are provided in Panel A of Table I. The highest mean excess return over the sample is from the Hong Kong market. Hong Kong also has the highest volatility. The United States has one of the lowest average returns. However, the volatility of the U.S. stock returns is lower than any other country.

While the first-order autocorrelation of the U.S. returns is not significant, there are some country returns that exhibit significant autocorrelation. High first-order autocorrelations are found in Austria, Belgium, Italy, Japan, Norway, and Spain. Significant seasonal autocorrelations are found in the returns of Austria and Denmark.

The world market portfolio is the value-weighted average of the country returns. The world portfolio has a lower standard deviation than any individual country.[14] Comparing the country portfolios to the world portfolio, there are seven countries (including the U.S.) that are unconditionally dominated by the world market portfolio. That is, given a choice between investing in one of these countries and the world portfolio, the world portfolio is a better investment for the risk-averse investor because it delivers a lower unconditional standard deviation and a higher unconditionally expected return.

---

[14]The differences in standard deviations across countries do not appear to be driven by the number of stocks included in the country indices. A cross-sectional regression (not reported) of the standard deviations on the number of firms included in each country index reported in Appendix Table A-I failed to detect a statistically significant relation.

Table I

Summary Statistics for the Country Returns and the Instrumental Variables

The statistics are based on monthly data from 1970:2–1989:5 (232 observations). The country returns are calculated in U.S. dollars in excess of the holding period return on the Treasury bill that is closest to 30 days to maturity. The dividend yields are the average (over the past year) monthly dividends divided by the current month price level. The returns and dividend yields are from Morgan Stanley Capital International. The instrumental variables are: the return for holding a 90-day U.S. Treasury bill for 1 month less the return on a 30-day bill (excess U.S. 3-month bill), the yield on Moody's Baa rated bonds less the yield on Moody's Aaa rated bonds (U.S. junk bond), and the dividend yield on the Standard and Poor's 500 stock index less the return on a 30-day bill (excess U.S. dividend yield).

Variable	Mean	Std. Dev.	ρ_1	ρ_2	ρ_3	ρ_4	ρ_{12}	ρ_{24}
A. Equity returns								
Australia	.00440	.08240	−.012	−.054	.012	.020	−.035	.011
Austria	.00554	.05382	.146*	.191*	.117	.015	.176*	.019
Belgium	.00867	.06018	.143*	.067	.044	.043	.078	.082
Canada	.00440	.05898	.017	−.104	.074	−.016	−.044	.034
Denmark	.00718	.05542	.065	.209*	.100	.121	−.177*	.088
France	.00647	.07362	.109	.045	.121	.029	−.008	−.011
Germany	.00502	.05984	.033	.057	.062	.073	.003	.025
Hong Kong	.01684	.12778	.062	−.035	−.007	−.050	−.001	−.043
Italy	.00221	.07774	.171*	−.031	.112	.089	.050	.028
Japan	.01341	.06094	.162*	.003	.110	.091	.081	−.024
Netherlands	.00767	.05562	.076	−.015	.048	−.107	.066	−.027
Norway	.00930	.08293	.186*	−.007	.152*	−.060	.009	.032
Spain	.00355	.06502	.156*	.029	−.037	.116	.044	.115
Sweden	.00938	.06217	.057	.015	.092	.056	.010	−.015
Switzerland	.00462	.05676	.080	−.023	.079	.044	.035	−.024
United Kingdom	.00736	.07925	.118	−.069	.099	.016	.001	.016
United States	.00373	.04695	.051	−.049	.004	.001	.065	−.055
World	.00533	.04175	.171*	−.026	.064	.027	.083	−.017

Table I—Continued

Variable	Mean	Std. Dev.	Autocorrelation					
			ρ_1	ρ_2	ρ_3	ρ_4	ρ_{12}	ρ_{24}
B. Dividend yields								
Australia	.00365	.00234	.973*	.945*	.916*	.887*	.644*	.265*
Austria	.00359	.00093	.940*	.892*	.856*	.803*	.391*	.024
Belgium	.00261	.00057	.977*	.957*	.931*	.910*	.718*	.444*
Canada	.00788	.00247	.985*	.966*	.948*	.931*	.783*	.537*
Denmark	.00362	.00150	.992*	.981*	.968*	.953*	.757*	.494*
France	.00427	.00139	.976*	.946*	.918*	.889*	.693*	.405*
Germany	.00357	.00084	.975*	.946*	.916*	.886*	.665*	.349*
Hong Kong	.00313	.00138	.957*	.899*	.840*	.783*	.471*	.069
Italy	.00231	.00065	.944*	.882*	.817*	.762*	.289*	−.107
Japan	.00168	.00092	.993*	.985*	.976*	.966*	.888*	.682*
Netherlands	.00491	.00108	.965*	.924*	.888*	.851*	.610*	.307*
Norway	.00298	.00108	.970*	.937*	.903*	.865*	.511*	.091
Spain	.00587	.00333	.992*	.983*	.975*	.966*	.870*	.675*
Sweden	.00331	.00113	.978*	.954*	.938*	.919*	.765*	.539*
Switzerland	.00225	.00038	.934*	.873*	.819*	.770*	.435*	.115
United Kingdom	.00426	.00107	.932*	.848*	.786*	.708*	.347*	.164*
United States	.00352	.00077	.981*	.952*	.923*	.895*	.642*	.425*
C. Other instrumental variables								
Excess U.S. 3 month bill	.00078	.00141	.276*	.014	.000	.001	−.096	.006
U.S. junk bond	.00108	.00037	.947*	.875*	.825*	.787*	.408*	.063
Excess U.S dividend yield	−.00243	.00183	.900*	.819*	.744*	.681*	.416*	.160*

*Significant at the 5% level based on an approximate standard error of $1/\sqrt{232} = .065$.

Interestingly, the world portfolio exhibits significant first-order autocorrelation, indicating that there is some predictable variation.

The unconditional means, standard deviations, and autocorrelations of the countries' dividend yields are provided in Panel B of Table I. Japan has, by far, the lowest dividend yield. Since the yield is an equally weighted 12-month moving average of dividends divided by the current month's price level, a high degree of autocorrelation is expected. The first 12 autocorrelations are significantly different from zero in all 17 countries.

Summary statistics are also provided for some of the common instrumental variables in Panel C of Table I. The excess returns on the 3-month Treasury bill have significant first order autocorrelation. Both the U.S. junk bond spread and the U.S. dividend yield spread show slower mean reversion. The U.S. junk bond spread autocorrelation drops to zero by the 24th lag. As already noted, the dividend yield is highly autocorrelated by construction. Notice that the mean dividend yield spread is negative, indicating that on average the bill rate is higher than the dividend yield on the S&P 500.

Unconditional correlations of the equity returns and the instrumental variables are provided in Table II. The first panel reveals that all stock returns move together on average. However, they may not move as closely together as one would expect. For example, the correlation between U.S. returns and U.K. returns is 49%; the correlation between U.S. and Japanese returns is only 27%.

The second panel shows that the dividend yields are not all positively correlated. The Australian dividend yield is negatively correlated with most other dividend yields. The U.S. and Japanese dividend yields are uncorrelated (-3%). The correlation of the U.S. and Canadian dividend yields is 84% which probably reflects the high degree of integration of the two economies.

To complement the summary statistics in Tables I and II, Figure 1 provides the traditional graph of mean return against variance. The unconditional minimum variance frontier calculated from the index returns is also plotted. Note that the returns are not excess returns. Unconditionally, the bill rate is not "risk free".

There are a number of interesting features to Figure 1. First, notice that Hong Kong is much different from the other portfolios—it has by far the highest volatility. Second, the two portfolios closest to the minimum variance frontier are the U.S. and Japan. Unconditionally, Japan does not dominate the United States. Third, the world market portfolio is the closest portfolio to the frontier.[15] Unconditional asset pricing tests would assess whether the world portfolio is far enough from the frontier to reject the restrictions of the asset pricing model. For example, Gibbons, Ross, and Shanken (1989) propose an exact F-statistic that tests the null hypothesis that the intercepts in the

---

[15] I also compared the minimum variance frontier based on 17 countries 1970:2–1987:12 to the minimum variance frontier based on 12 U.S. industry portfolios over the same period. The frontier based on the industry portfolios was always inside (less efficient than) the world frontier.

multivariate regression of the asset excess returns on the market excess return are jointly zero. When this test is executed on the 17 country portfolios, the probability value is 0.304.[16] Adler and Dumas (1983) provide an alternative specification where foreign exchange portfolios are included in the multivariate regression framework. The *p*-values are not substantially altered when this model is tested. Hence, these tests do not provide evidence against the hypothesis of unconditional mean variance efficiency. However, an examination of the individual regressions in both models reveals that Japan has a statistically significant intercept. So while the standard multivariate tests of the unconditional mean-variance efficiency do not provide evidence against the null hypothesis, these tests may not be very powerful.[17]

III. Empirical Results

A. The Predictability of Country Stock Returns with the Common Instruments

The predictability of the international equity returns using a common set of instruments is studied in Table III. The results indicate that there is significant time variation in most of the country returns. Furthermore, the value-weighted portfolio of all countries is the most predictable. The R^2 for the world market portfolio is 13.3%.

The results contrast with some other work on predicting international stock returns. For example, using country-specific dividend yields, Cutler, Poterba and Summers (1989) are only able to explain about 1% of the variance of the monthly returns over 1960–1988. They are able to account for 0.5% of the Japanese returns and 1.0% of the U.S. returns. This compares to 6.7% and 12.5% for the two countries, respectively, using the common information variables in Table III. Using a number of combinations of variables that include the U.S. and Japanese dividend yields, short-term rates, and long-term to short-term rate spreads, Campbell and Hamao (1989) report a 6.5% (largest) R^2 for Japan and a 10.0% (largest) R^2 for the U.S. over the 1971–1987 period.[18]

There are a number of interesting observations from Table III. For Japanese stock returns, the most important explanatory variable is the lagged world return.[19] The January dummy is more than one standard error from zero in

---

[16]The *F*-statistic for the same test with the Group of 7 (*G*-7) countries (Canada, France, Germany, Italy, Japan, United Kingdom, and United States) has a *p*-value of 0.103. The only country that has a significant intercept is Japan.

[17]Using a sample of 13 country indices and monthly data from 1982:1 to 1988:6, Cumby and Glen (1990) also cannot reject the null hypothesis of the mean-variance efficiency of the MSCI world index.

[18]Campbell and Hamao (1989) do not use the MSCI indices for Japan and the United States. They extend the index created by Hamao (1988) which is a value weighted index drawn from stocks listed in the first and second sections of the Tokyo Stock Exchange.

[19]I thought that this might be due to Japan being across the date line. The last trading day of the month for Europe and North America is only a few hours away from the first trading day of the month for Japan. However, when this regression is re-executed with the lagged Japanese return replacing the world index, the results are similar. Hamao, Masulis, and Ng (1990) also provide evidence of significant first-order autocorrelation in the Nikkei 225 return.

Table II
Unconditional Correlations of the Country Returns and the Instrumental Variables

The correlations are based on monthly data from 1970:2–1989:5 (232 observations). The country returns are calculated in U.S. dollars in excess of the holding period return on the Treasury bill that is closest to 30 days to maturity. The dividend yields are the average (over the past year) monthly dividends divided by the current monthly price level. The returns and dividend yields are from Morgan Stanley Capital International. The instrumental variables are: the excess return on the world index (rwd), the one month return for holding a 90-day U.S. Treasury bill less the return on a 30-day U.S. Treasury bill ($xustb3$), the yield on Moody's Baa rated bonds less the yield on Moody's Aaa rated bonds ($usjunk$), and the dividend yield on the Standard and Poor's 500 stock index less the return on a 30-day bill ($xusdiv$).

A. Equity returns

Portfolio	Aa	Au	Be	Ca	De	Fr	Ge	HK	It	Ja	Ne	No	Sp	Sw	Sz	UK	US
World	.57	.29	.62	.75	.47	.61	.54	.41	.42	.63	.74	.50	.41	.50	.68	.67	.86
Australia	–	.16	.32	.59	.28	.37	.28	.36	.24	.28	.40	.41	.32	.36	.42	.46	.47
Austria		–	.46	.18	.30	.43	.55	.21	.24	.25	.43	.28	.29	.27	.49	.23	.12
Belgium			–	.38	.45	.64	.63	.32	.42	.46	.65	.53	.40	.44	.67	.50	.41
Canada				–	.30	.44	.30	.29	.27	.28	.55	.45	.28	.35	.48	.52	.72
Denmark					–	.35	.39	.31	.26	.39	.45	.33	.30	.30	.44	.35	.33
France						–	.57	.24	.44	.41	.58	.47	.36	.33	.62	.52	.42
Germany							–	.28	.34	.42	.66	.37	.34	.39	.74	.38	.33
Hong Kong								–	.22	.32	.42	.29	.24	.27	.34	.35	.29
Italy									–	.38	.36	.25	.35	.30	.38	.34	.22
Japan										–	.45	.17	.35	.33	.43	.35	.27
Netherlands											–	.52	.38	.43	.73	.62	.56
Norway												–	.25	.38	.48	.40	.44
Spain													–	.31	.33	.30	.25
Sweden														–	.47	.39	.38
Switzerland															–	.55	.49
United Kingdom																–	.49
United States																	–

Table II—*Continued*

B. Dividend yields

Country	Aa	Au	Be	Ca	De	Fr	Ge	HK	It	Ja	Ne	No	Sp	Sw	Sz	UK	US
Australia	—	.33	-.50	-.24	-.33	-.20	-.29	.35	.19	-.50	-.10	.04	-.09	-.22	-.13	-.02	.01
Austria		—	.07	.41	.05	.58	.32	.74	.14	-.14	.70	.35	.23	.23	.73	.73	.60
Belgium			—	.47	.64	.63	.62	-.04	.19	.63	.52	.34	.36	.60	.47	.27	.40
Canada				—	.27	.86	.74	.41	-.08	.00	.73	.74	.81	.55	.71	.60	.84
Denmark					—	.41	.49	-.30	.19	.76	.51	.16	.03	.84	.33	.38	.28
France						—	.69	.38	.06	.20	.85	.68	.56	.64	.81	.67	.74
Germany							—	.22	-.20	.12	.77	.41	.63	.66	.70	.59	.76
Hong Kong								—	.04	-.41	.44	.31	.47	-.12	.56	.57	.58
Italy									—	.37	-.06	.14	-.08	.10	.02	-.06	.02
Japan										—	.16	-.00	-.22	.49	.12	.09	-.03
Netherlands											—	.54	.47	.68	.85	.81	.78
Norway												—	.64	.37	.42	.28	.66
Spain													—	.33	.41	.32	.79
Sweden														—	.49	.54	.54
Switzerland															—	.83	.74
United Kingdom																—	.69
United States																	—

C. Other instrumental variables

Variable	rwd	xustb3	usjunk	xusdiv
Excess world equity return	—			
Excess U.S. 3 month bill	.17	—		
U.S. junk bond	.19	.36	—	
U.S. Excess dividend yield	.22	-.16	-.31	—

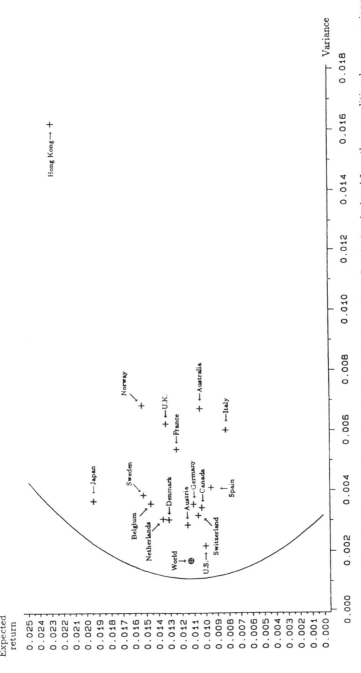

Figure 1. The unconditional minimum variance frontier. The minimum variance frontier is calculated from the unconditional means, variances, and covariances of 17 country returns. The returns are in U.S. dollars and are from Morgan Stanley Capital International. The data are from 1970:2–1989:5 (232 observations).

13 of the 17 countries. In Austria, there is a negative January effect. The excess return on the 3-month bill is two standard errors from zero in Australia, Belgium, Canada, the Netherlands, Switzerland, the United Kingdom, and the United States. The junk bond spread is more than two standard errors from zero in only two countries by 1.5 standard errors from zero in five additional countries. The dividend yield spread is more than two standard errors from zero in 12 of the 17 countries.[20]

The results in Table III can be interpreted as evidence against the hypothesis that the conditional mean returns in the countries are constant. Indeed, the examination of conditional asset pricing models is only well motivated if there is evidence of time-varying expected returns. An F-test shows that 15 of the 18 regressions are significant at the 10% level, 13 at the 5% level, and 10 at the 1% level.

B. The Predictability of Country Stock Returns with the Local Instruments

Table IV presents evidence on the predictability of international equity returns using both common and local information variables. The far left-hand column presents adjusted R^2 values using the common information variables. In some cases, they do not exactly match results reported in Table III because the sample may be slightly different.

Eight combinations of instrumental variables are used moving from the common information set (column 1) to a completely local information set (column 8). For comparison, the results of Cutler, Poterba and Summers (1989) and Campbell and Hamao (1989) are also reported. The local information variables include the country specific lagged return, the own dividend yield, the rate of change in the foreign exchange rate, the local short-term interest rate, and the long-term to short-term interest rate spread.

There are a number of interesting results in Table IV. First, the common information variables appear to capture the bulk of the predictable variation in the country returns. Comparing the common information regressions (column 1) to the completely local information regressions (column 8) only two countries show higher R^2 values using the local information. Explanatory power for Austria slightly increases from 5.6% to 5.9% when the local information variables are used. The R^2 for Norway increases from 1.9% to 4% with the local variables.

The other columns of Table IV show the effect of mixing the common information variables with the local information variables. Interestingly, the lagged U.S. dollar foreign exchange rate change has virtually no explanatory power. Only Norway and Sweden are affected by the change in the foreign exchange rate. Perhaps the most surprising result is the lack of importance of the local short-term interest rates and the long-term to short-term interest rate spread. Comparing columns 4 (common instruments with country-specific

---

[20] The regressions were re-estimated with own-currency returns rather than U.S. dollar returns. The explanatory power of these regressions was largely unaffected by using the own-currency returns. These results are available on request.

Table III
Regressions of Country Returns on the Common Set of Instrumental Variables

The regressions are based on monthly data from 1970:2–1989:5 (232 observations). The country returns are calculated in U.S. dollars in excess of the holding period return on the Treasury bill that is closest to 30 days to maturity. The equity data are from Morgan Stanley Capital International. t-statistics in brackets are heteroskedasticity consistent. The model estimated is:

$$r_{j,t} = \delta_{j,0} + \delta_{j,1} rwd_{t-1} + \delta_{j,2} jan_t + \delta_{j,3} xustb3_{t-1} + \delta_{j,4} usjunk_{t-1} + \delta_{j,5} xusdiv_{t-1} + \varepsilon_{j,t} \qquad (2)$$

The instrumental variables are: a constant, the excess return on the world index (rwd), a dummy variable for the month of January (jan), the return for holding a 90-day U.S. Treasury bill for 1 month less the return on a 30-day bill ($xustb3$), the yield on Moody's Baa rated bonds less the yield on Moody's Aaa rated bonds ($usjunk$), and the dividend yield on the Standard and Poor's 500 stock index less the return on a 30-day bill ($xusdiv$).

Portfolio	δ_0	δ_1	δ_2	δ_3	δ_4	δ_5	$\bar{R}^{2a}$
Australia	0.008	0.189	0.022	13.312	-1.131	6.306	0.073
	[0.499]	[1.267]	[1.013]	[3.160]	[-0.079]	[2.348]	
Austria	0.037	0.139	-0.034	2.352	-22.002	3.074	0.058
	[3.701]	[1.659]	[-2.873]	[1.044]	[-2.250]	[1.873]	
Belgium	0.017	-0.017	0.018	6.423	4.233	8.068	0.058
	[1.593]	[-0.169]	[1.536]	[2.303]	[0.391]	[3.594]	
Canada	0.004	0.035	0.017	12.598	2.911	5.871	0.107
	[0.351]	[0.379]	[1.052]	[3.730]	[0.253]	[2.595]	
Denmark	0.002	-0.148	0.016	0.923	19.047	6.831	0.032
	[0.180]	[-1.747]	[1.096]	[0.440]	[1.766]	[3.713]	
France	0.014	0.071	0.018	2.289	3.403	6.283	0.013
	[0.932]	[0.627]	[0.874]	[0.576]	[0.262]	[1.973]	
Germany	0.005	0.098	-0.006	2.490	11.088	5.579	0.021
	[0.435]	[0.913]	[-0.380]	[0.920]	[1.034]	[2.613]	

The World Price of Covariance Risk

131

Table III — *Continued*

Portfolio	δ_0	δ_1	δ_2	δ_3	δ_4	δ_5	$\bar{R}^2$ a
Hong Kong	0.026 [0.858]	0.305 [1.702]	0.065 [2.529]	4.368 [0.702]	-2.551 [-0.092]	6.756 [1.473]	0.029
Italy	0.006 [0.353]	0.210 [1.788]	0.027 [1.434]	1.379 [0.440]	-4.783 [-0.318]	1.057 [0.320]	0.005
Japan	0.016 [1.281]	0.287 [2.749]	0.005 [0.435]	-0.416 [-0.160]	9.191 [0.716]	5.822 [2.661]	0.067
Netherlands	0.001 [0.091]	-0.011 [-0.108]	0.026 [1.756]	6.205 [2.351]	15.940 [1.429]	7.154 [3.380]	0.076
Norway	0.033 [2.016]	0.083 [0.491]	0.044 [2.339]	5.398 [1.089]	-27.865 [-1.764]	0.932 [0.280]	0.020
Spain	0.019 [1.614]	0.172 [1.648]	0.017 [1.035]	3.757 [1.343]	-18.714 [-1.736]	0.329 [0.144]	0.009
Sweden	-0.013 [-0.974]	0.115 [0.974]	0.023 [1.540]	1.441 [0.486]	24.151 [1.805]	3.040 [1.160]	0.032
Switzerland	0.009 [0.853]	-0.049 [-0.463]	0.009 [0.586]	5.970 [2.335]	8.468 [0.759]	7.850 [3.606]	0.052
United Kingdom	-0.007 [-0.516]	-0.039 [-0.259]	0.044 [1.495]	9.103 [2.837]	25.052 [1.609]	9.432 [3.109]	0.079
United States	-0.014 [-1.550]	-0.092 [-0.913]	0.020 [1.682]	8.289 [3.080]	22.980 [2.735]	6.175 [4.137]	0.125
World	-0.005 [-0.664]	0.032 [0.455]	0.018 [1.751]	6.602 [3.495]	16.848 [2.256]	6.015 [4.448]	0.133

a Coefficient of determination adjusted for degrees of freedom.

Table IV

International Evidence on the Predictability of Equity Returns Using Common and Country Specific Instrumental Variables

The R^2 values are adjusted for degrees of freedom. The country returns are calculated in U.S. dollars in excess of the holding period return on the U.S. Treasury bill that is closest to 30 days to maturity. The equity data are from Morgan Stanley Capital International. The regressions are estimated with eight different sets of conditioning information. The instrumental variables are: excess world return (rwd_{t-1}), a January dummy (jan_t), the difference in returns on U.S. 3- and 1-month Treasury bills ($xustb3_{t-1}$), the spread between Moody's Baa and Aaa rated U.S. bonds ($usjunk_{t-1}$), the U.S. dividend yield in excess of the 1-month Treasury bill ($xusdiv_{t-1}$), the equity returns in each country ($r_{j,t-1}$), the dividend yields for each country ($div_{j,t-1}$), the return on the U.S. exchange rate for each country ($fx_{j,t-1}$), the level of short term interest rates in each country ($i_{j,t-1}$), and the difference between long term government bond yields and short term yields in each country ($term_{j,t-1}$).

Instruments → / Portfolio and (number of observations)	rwd_{t-1}, jan_t, $usjunk_{t-1}$, $xustb3_{t-1}$, $xusdiv_{j,t-1}$	$r_{j,t-1}$, jan_t, $usjunk_{t-1}$, $xustb3_{t-1}$, $xusdiv_{j,t-1}$	$r_{j,t-1}$, jan_t, $usjunk_{t-1}$, $xustb3_{t-1}$, $div_{j,t-1}$	$r_{j,t-1}$, jan_t, $usjunk_{t-1}$, $xustb3_{t-1}$, $xusdiv_{j,t-1}$, $div_{j,t-1}$	$r_{j,t-1}$, jan_t, $usjunk_{t-1}$, $xustb3_{t-1}$, $fx_{j,t-1}$	$r_{j,t-1}$, jan_t, $usjunk_{t-1}$, $xustb3_{t-1}$, $div_{j,t-1}$, $i_{j,t-1}$	$r_{j,t-1}$, jan_t, $usjunk_{t-1}$, $div_{j,t-1}$, $i_{j,t-1}$, $term_{j,t-1}$	$r_{j,t-1}$, jan_t, $div_{j,t-1}$, $i_{j,t-1}$, $term_{j,t-1}$	Cutler, Poterba, and Summers [1989]	Campbell and Hamao [1989]
Australia 70:2–89:1 (228)	.078	.070	.073	.087	.080	.070	.022	.011	.002	–
Austria 71:12–89:1 (216)	.056	.062	.049	.059	.050	.054	.057	.059	.017	–
Belgium[a] 70:2–89:5 (232)	.058	.062	.064	.080	.051	–	–	–	-.004	–
Canada 70:2–89:5 (232)	.107	.111	.082	.107	.084	.091	.028	.000	.001	–
Denmark 72:2–89:1 (204)	.035	.018	-.016	.013	-.004	.008	.013	.008	-.004	–
France[b] 70:2–89:5 (229)	.013	.020	.001	.019	-.004	.005	.007	.010	-.004	–

The World Price of Covariance Risk   133

Table IV—Continued

Instruments → Portfolio and (number of observations)	rwd_{t-1}, jan_t, $usjunk_{t-1}$, $xustb3_t$ $_{-1}$, $xusdiv_{t-1}$	$r_{j,t-1}$, jan_t, $usjunk_{t-1}$, $xustb3_{t-1}$, $xusdiv_{j,t-1}$	$r_{j,t-1}$, jan_t, $usjunk_{t-1}$, $xustb3_{t-1}$, $div_{j,t-1}$	$r_{j,t-1}$, jan_t, $usjunk_{t-1}$, $xustb3_{t-1}$, $div_{j,t-1}$	$r_{j,t-1}$, jan_t, $usjunk_{t-1}$, $xustb3_{t-1}$, $fx_{j,t-1}$	$r_{j,t-1}$, jan_t, $usjunk_{t-1}$, $xustb3_{t-1}$, $i_{j,t-1}$	$r_{j,t-1}$, jan_t, $usjunk_{t-1}$, $div_{j,t-1}$, $i_{j,t-1}$, $term_{j,t-1}$	$r_{j,t-1}$, jan_t, $div_{j,t-1}$, $i_{j,t-1}$, $term_{j,t-1}$	Cutler, Poterba, and Summers [1989]	Campbell and Hamao [1989]
Germany 70:2–89:5 (232)	.021	.017	−.007	.013	−.012	.003	.000	−.002	−.002	–
Hong Kong[a] 70:2–89:5 (232)	.029	.021	.008	.017	.007	–	–	–	.040	–
Italy 71:2–89:5 (220)	.001	.021	.021	.017	.016	.017	.018	.023	−.002	–
Japan 70:2–89:5 (232)	.067	.045	.006	.043	.003	.025	.029	.024	.005	.065
Netherlands 70:2–89:5 (232)	.076	.076	.029	.076	.025	.068	.087	.076	.001	–
Norway[c] 71:9–89:5 (213)	.019	.052	.056	.051	.062	.051	.045	.040	−.002	–
Spain[d] 74:1–89:5 (184)	.004	.013	.014	.010	.010	.018	–	–	−.003	–
Sweden 70:2–87:1 (204)	.022	.022	.013	.017	.034	.012	.020	.007	−.004	–
Switzerland 75:9–89:5 (175)	.046	.044	−.009	.041	−.015	.000	.000	.010	.002	–
United Kingdom 72:1–89:5 (208)	.078	.079	.082	.115	.078	.077	.071	.076	.006	–
United States 70:2–89:5 (232)	.125	.124	.077	.127	.076	.127	.076	.052	.010	.100

[a] Both short term and long term interest rates are not available.
[b] Excludes 1986:3–1986:6 when the interest rate data are not available.
[c] Excludes 1980:8–1980:9 when the interest rate data are not available.
[d] Long term interest rates are not available.

dividend yields and lagged returns) to columns 6–8, the explanatory power is marginally increased in only three countries: Spain (+0.8%), the Netherlands (+1.1%), and Italy (+0.6%). The local interest rate variables decrease the explanatory power of the regressions for the other countries.

The two local information variables that are the most important are the lagged own-country returns and the local dividend yields. The inclusion of the lagged own-country returns increases the explanatory power of the regressions (columns 1 and 2) in 8 of 17 countries and has a neutral effect on two other countries. The inclusion of the local dividend yields (in addition to the U.S. dividend yield) increases the explanatory power of the regressions (columns 1 and 4) in 9 of 17 countries and has a neutral effect on two countries.

While the lagged own-country return and the local dividend yield increase the explanatory power of some of the regressions, the overall improvement is small. In the countries that experience increased adjusted R^2 values, the average increment is only 1.7%. Most of the explanatory power is driven by the common variables. Cutler, Poterba and Summers (1990) state that "it seems unlikely that similar processes generate required returns . . ." in the international markets. The results in Table IV provide evidence against this claim. Expected returns in the individual countries appear to be generated by common world factors.

C. Conditional Asset Pricing with Time-Varying Moments

Table V provides tests of the general model that allows for time-varying expected returns, covariances, and variances. Tests of the asset pricing restrictions are provided for individual countries as well as multiple country systems.[21]

The χ^2 statistic provides a test of the model's restrictions. This statistic summarizes the departures from the null hypothesis—that the world market portfolio is conditionally mean variance efficient. Beside the χ^2 is the related but more intuitive R^2 statistic which is the adjusted coefficient of determination from a regression of the model errors on the common information variables. If the model fits well, the errors should be unrelated to the information, and the χ^2 and the R^2 should be small.

The asset pricing model in equation (6) can be tested using individual countries as well as multiple countries.[22] The test at the individual country level may not be powerful because the cross-asset restriction (identical conditionally expected world market return divided by conditional variance of the world market for each country) is not imposed. That is, if the model is *not* rejected at the individual country level, some caution should be exercised in

---

[21] For ease of exposition, beginning in Table V the countries are ordered by unconditional mean return.

[22] It is not computationally feasible to test equation (6) with all 17 countries. The dimensionality of the weighting matrix would be 210 which is much larger than any previously estimated GMM system. Furthermore, Hansen and Singleton (1982) warn that the quality of the consistent estimator of the weighting matrix may deteriorate with high dimensions.

interpreting the results—because not all of the CAPM's restrictions have been imposed. However, a *rejection* at the individual country level may provide valuable information about the model's failings. Using the common instrumental variables, Table V indicates that the model's restrictions are rejected at the 5% level for three of the 17 countries: Japan, Norway, and Austria. The model is rejected at the 10% level for the United States.

In the multiple country test using the returns of the Group of 7 countries, the model's restrictions are not rejected at standard levels of significance. The lack of rejection in this multivariate test reinforces the importance of testing at the individual portfolio level. The multivariate test is not powerful enough to reject the hypothesis of conditional mean-variance efficiency. However, the evidence at the individual country level (in particular for Japan) suggests that the world portfolio is not conditionally mean-variance efficient.

The last two columns provide test statistics for the model estimated using some local information variables. In the single country estimation, the inference is generally robust to the choice of the information set. Using the first local information set, the same four countries are rejected at the 10% level. Using the second local information set, three of those four countries are rejected at the 10% level. With this information set, Japan is no longer rejected. For Japan, the local information variables provide a less powerful test. This is perhaps not surprising given the results in Table IV which show that the maximum explanatory power for Japanese returns derives from the common information set.

Similar patterns arise when the local information variables are used in the multivariate test. Using the first local information set, the probability value of the test statistic is 13.7% which is somewhat lower than the 21.9% reported using the common instruments. With the second local information set, the *p*-value is 12.7%. Consistent with the previous results, this local information set fails to provide evidence to reject the null hypothesis at standard levels of significance.

Some additional information is provided in Table V. The average pricing errors and the average absolute pricing errors based upon estimation with the common instrumental variables are provided in the fourth and fifth columns. For Japan, the pricing error is positive, indicating that the actual return is on average higher than the expected return given the level of risk. A large positive pricing error is also found with the Hong Kong portfolio. The Austrian pricing error is negative, indicating that the average return is less than what is expected given the country risk. Interestingly, over this time period, both the mean error and the absolute pricing error for the United States are small.

The average conditional covariance is provided in the second column.[23] It is clear that the ordering of the average conditional covariances is not the

---

[23]This is not the unconditional covariance. It is the average value of the product of the innovations in the conditional mean of the country return and the world market return. This covariance is conditional on the common information set.

Table V

Estimates of a Conditional CAPM with Time Varying Expected Returns, Conditional Covariances, and Conditional Variances

Results based on monthly data from 1970:2–1989:5 (232 observations). The country returns $\mathbf{r}$ are calculated in U.S. dollars in excess of the holding period return on the Treasury bill that is closest to 30 days to maturity. The equity data are from Morgan Stanley Capital International. The following system of equations is estimated with the generalized method of moments:

$$\varepsilon_t = (\mathbf{u}_t \quad u_{mt} \quad \mathbf{h}_t) = \begin{pmatrix} [\mathbf{r}_t - \mathbf{Z}_{t-1}\boldsymbol{\delta}]' \\ [r_{mt} - \mathbf{Z}_{t-1}\delta_m]' \\ [u_{mt}^2 \mathbf{Z}_{t-1}\boldsymbol{\delta} - u_{mt}\mathbf{u}_t\mathbf{Z}_{t-1}\delta_m]' \end{pmatrix}, \qquad (6)$$

where r_m is the excess return on the world portfolio, $\boldsymbol{\delta}$ represents the coefficients associated with the instrumental variables, $\mathbf{u}$ is the forecast error for the country returns, u_m is the forecast error for the world market return, and $\mathbf{h}$ represents the deviation of the country return from the model's expected return. There are three sets of instrumental variables $\mathbf{Z}$ that are used in the estimation. The common set of predetermined instrumental variables are: a constant, the excess return on the world index, a dummy variable for the month of January, the 1-month return for holding a 90-day U.S. Treasury bill less the return on a 30-day bill, the yield on Moody's Baa rated bonds less the yield on Moody's Aaa rated bonds, and the dividend yield on the Standard and Poor's 500 stock index less the return on a 30-day bill. Local instrument set A is the common instrument set augmented with the country-specific dividend yield. Local instrument set B includes the country-specific dividend yield and the country-specific excess return in place of the world excess return.

Portfolio	Average Return	Average Conditional Covariance[a]	Average Error[b]	Average Absolute Error[c]	$\bar{R}^{2d}$	Common Instruments χ^{2e} [P-value]	Local Instruments A: χ^2 [P-value]	Local Instruments B: χ^2 [P-value]
Hong Kong	0.0168	1.8000	0.0037	0.0202	.022	8.14 [.228]	8.25 [.311]	7.91 [.340]
Japan	0.0134	1.4007	0.0013	0.0104	−.012	14.96 [.021]	13.95 [.052]	10.47 [.163]
Sweden	0.0094	1.0978	0.0014	0.0100	−.008	8.49 [.204]	8.60 [.282]	9.06 [.248]

The World Price of Covariance Risk

Table V — *Continued*

Portfolio	Average Return	Average Conditional Covariance[a]	Average Error[b]	Average Absolute Error[c]	$\bar{R}^{2d}$	Common Instruments χ^{2e} [P-value]	Local Instruments A: χ^2 [P-value]	Local Instruments B: χ^2 [P-value]
Norway	0.0093	1.6264	−0.0009	0.0162	.067	13.15 [.041]	12.49 [.085]	15.96 [.025]
Belgium	0.0087	1.3071	0.0004	0.0110	−.018	9.47 [.149]	10.74 [.150]	9.80 [.200]
Netherlands	0.0077	1.4351	0.0005	0.0081	−.020	6.30 [.391]	8.64 [.280]	8.43 [.296]
United Kingdom	0.0074	1.8155	−0.0007	0.0157	−.022	1.10 [.981]	4.97 [.663]	3.73 [.810]
Denmark	0.0072	0.9425	0.0006	0.0092	−.018	9.28 [.159]	9.93 [.193]	7.40 [.389]
France	0.0065	1.6901	−0.0011	0.0122	−.002	10.31 [.112]	11.80 [.107]	13.58 [.059]
Austria	0.0055	0.6339	−0.0033	0.0098	.163	20.50 [.002]	21.47 [.003]	22.57 [.002]
Germany	0.0050	1.1866	−0.0004	0.0112	−.020	3.47 [.748]	3.45 [.841]	4.29 [.746]
Switzerland	0.0046	1.3832	−0.0012	0.0093	−.004	10.25 [.115]	10.92 [.142]	9.91 [.194]
Australia	0.0044	1.5857	0.0014	0.0161	−.008	5.78 [.449]	6.87 [.442]	5.11 [.647]
Canada	0.0044	1.5231	−0.0004	0.0097	−.012	3.14 [.791]	3.13 [.873]	2.89 [.895]
United States	0.0037	1.4250	−0.0000	0.0043	−.016	10.75 [.096]	12.83 [.076]	11.19 [.131]
Spain	0.0036	1.0274	−0.0004	0.0138	.005	10.41 [.109]	11.28 [.127]	8.28 [.308]

continued overleaf

Table V — *Continued*

Portfolio	Average Return	Average Conditional Covariance[a]	Average Error[b]	Average Absolute Error[c]	$\bar{R}^{2d}$	Common Instruments χ^{2e} [P-value]	Local Instruments A: χ^2 [P-value]	Local Instruments B: χ^2 [P-value]
Italy	0.0022	1.2197	-0.0003	0.0125	.016	9.82 [.132]	9.89 [.198]	11.09 [.135]
G-7[f]						48.77 [.219]	59.91 [.137]	60.43 [.127]

[a] The average value of $u_i \times u_m$ multiplied by 1000 for country i based on single country estimation with the common instrument set.

[b] The average value of e_i for country i based on single country estimation with the common instrument set divided by the average conditional variance of the world market return.

[c] The average absolute value of e_i for country i based on single country estimation with the common instrument set divided by the average conditional variance of the world market return.

[d] The adjusted coefficient of determination from a regression of the model errors (e_{it}) on the common instrumental variables.

[e] The minimized value of the GMM criterion function. *P*-value is the probability that a χ^2 variate exceeds the sample value of the statistic. For single country systems with the common instrument set, there are 12 parameters and 18 orthogonality conditions leaving 6 overidentifying conditions. For the single country systems with local instrument sets, there are 14 parameters and 21 orthogonality conditions leaving 7 overidentifying restrictions. In the multiple equation system with the common instrument set, there are 48 parameters and 90 orthogonality conditions; this implies that there are 42 overidentifying restrictions to be tested. In the multiple equation system with the local instrument sets, there are 56 parameters and 105 orthogonality conditions; this implies that there are 49 overidentifying restrictions to be tested. The degrees of freedom in the test statistic correspond to the number of overidentifying restrictions.

[f] Japan, United Kingdom, France, Germany, Canada, United States, and Italy. These countries comprise 90% of the MSCI world index. In the tests with the local information variables, the local variables are used to get the forecasted country returns (equations 1 through 7). The common variables are used for the world expected return (equation 8). Orthogonality conditions are formed with the local information variables.

same as the ordering of the average returns. Nevertheless, it is interesting to note that Hong Kong has one of the highest average conditional covariances as well as the highest average return. However, the conditional asset pricing model does not restrict the 'average' conditional covariance to be positively related to the 'average' return. The average conditional covariance is provided only as bridge to unconditional asset pricing.

The results for the general formulation provides evidence against the asset pricing model's restrictions. Consistent with the results of tests of unconditional mean-variance efficiency, when many countries are examined there is little evidence against the model's restrictions. However, a country by country examination detects some significant departures from the null hypothesis. When Japan is examined, the restrictions are strongly rejected.

If some of the moments are constant, then it may be possible to construct more powerful tests. Two other formulations are examined: one that assumes constant conditional betas and another that assumes a constant world price of covariance risk. The constant conditional beta formulation is closely linked to unconditional formulations of the Sharpe-Lintner model. The constant world price of covariance risk is often interpreted as a measure of aggregate relative risk aversion.

D. Conditional Asset Pricing with Constant Conditional Betas

Table VI presents tests of the conditional version of the original Sharpe-Lintner formulation which implies that expected asset returns are proportional to the expected (mean-variance efficient) world market portfolio returns. Beta is the coefficient of proportionality. As with the previous table, single country as well as multiple country tests are presented. In most cases with the common set of instruments, the proportionality coefficients are more than two standard errors from zero. The highest beta is found with the Hong Kong portfolio.[24] The two smallest betas are estimated for Spain and Italy. These two countries have the smallest average returns.

The United States has a beta of 0.97 while Japan has a beta of 1.42. However, the difference in the betas does not explain the difference in the average excess returns of 0.37% per month for the United States and 1.34% per month for Japan. As with the general model presented in the previous table, the model's restrictions are rejected when the Japanese returns are examined. The results in Table VI indicate stronger evidence against the restrictions. The model is also rejected at the 5% level for Denmark as well as Austria. There is evidence against the model at the 10% level for Norway. The probability value for the United States is 0.103 which is slightly higher than the general model. Consistent with the results in Table V, there is little evidence against the restrictions in the multiple country system conditioning on the common information set.

---

[24] These betas are estimated under the null hypothesis that the model is true, i.e., no intercepts are included. An alternative formulation would specify intercepts in equation (7) and test whether they are significantly different from zero.

Table VI

Estimates of a Conditional CAPM with Time Varying Expected Returns and Constant Conditional Betas

Results are based on monthly data from 1970:2–1989:5 (232 observations). The country returns r are calculated in U.S. dollars in excess of the holding period return on the Treasury bill that is closest to 30 days to maturity. The equity data are from Morgan Stanley Capital International. Standard errors in parentheses are heteroskedasticity consistent. Generalized method of moments is used to estimate:

$$k_t = r_t - r_{mt}\beta \qquad (7)$$

where r_m is the excess return on the world market portfolio, β is the proportionality coefficient that relates the expected world excess return to the expected country return, and k represents the deviations from the country returns and the model's expected returns. There are three sets of instrumental variables Z that are used in the estimation. The common set of predetermined instrumental variables are: a constant, the excess return on the world index, a dummy variable for the month of January, the 1-month return for holding a 90-day U.S. Treasury bill less the return on a 30-day bill, the yield on Moody's Baa rated bonds less the yield on Moody's Aaa rated bonds, and the dividend yield on the Standard and Poor's 500 stock index less the return on a 30-day bill. Local instrument set A is the common instrument set augmented with the country-specific dividend yield. Local instrument set B includes the country-specific dividend yield and the country-specific excess return in place of the world excess return.

Portfolio	β_j	Average Return	Average Error[a]	Average Absolute Error[b]	$\bar{R}^{2c}$	Common Instruments χ^2 [P-value]	Local Instruments A: χ^2 [P-value]	Local Instruments B: χ^2 [P-value]
Hong Kong	2.0802 (0.4450)	.0168	.0058	.0841	.011	4.73 [.450]	4.95 [.551]	4.22 [.647]
Japan	1.4178 (0.2195)	.0134	.0059	.0386	.096	18.34 [.003]	18.27 [.006]	17.50 [.008]
Sweden	0.7281 (0.2086)	.0094	.0055	.0425	−.003	5.01 [.414]	5.24 [.514]	4.46 [.614]

The World Price of Covariance Risk   141

Table VI—*Continued*

Portfolio	$\hat{\beta}_J$	Average Return	Average Error[a]	Average Absolute Error[b]	$\bar{R}^{2c}$	Common Instruments χ^{2d} [P-value]	Local Instruments A: χ^2 [P-value]	Local Instruments B: χ^2 [P-value]
Norway	0.5742 (0.2859)	.0093	.0062	.0564	.021	11.02 [.051]	11.22 [.082]	16.61 [.011]
Belgium	1.0573 (0.1974)	.0087	.0030	.0357	.003	6.06 [.300]	7.76 [.256]	7.23 [.300]
Netherlands	1.0061 (0.1349)	.0077	.0023	.0291	−.013	2.64 [.755]	4.74 [.578]	4.73 [.579]
United Kingdom	1.3840 (0.2531)	.0074	−.0000	.0432	−.011	1.11 [.953]	2.93 [.817]	3.16 [.788]
Denmark	0.4908 (0.1411)	.0072	.0046	.0361	.013	12.56 [.028]	12.74 [.047]	7.79 [.254]
France	0.6937 (0.2426)	.0065	.0028	.0468	−.006	4.37 [.497]	5.60 [.470]	6.49 [.340]
Austria	0.1851 (0.1794)	.0055	.0046	.0353	.065	19.69 [.001]	19.99 [.003]	19.40 [.004]
Germany	0.7035 (0.2159)	.0050	.0013	.0388	−.001	4.78 [.443]	4.78 [.573]	4.93 [.579]
Switzerland	0.8293 (0.1624)	.0046	.0002	.0332	.003	5.86 [.320]	8.39 [.211]	7.89 [.246]
Australia	1.3949 (0.2622)	.0044	−.0030	.0532	−.001	5.78 [.328]	7.48 [.279]	6.42 [.378]
Canada	1.0466 (0.1539)	.0044	−.0012	.0300	.020	6.76 [.239]	6.98 [.323]	7.41 [.284]
United States	0.9656 (0.0939)	.0037	−.0014	.0176	.038	9.17 [.103]	9.53 [.146]	5.89 [.439]

continued overleaf

Table VI—Continued

Portfolio	β_j	Average Return	Average Error[a]	Average Absolute Error[b]	$\bar{R}^{2c}$	Common Instruments χ^{2d} [P-value]	Local Instruments A: χ^2 [P-value]	Local Instruments B: χ^2 [P-value]
Spain	0.3003 (0.2483)	.0036	.0020	.0460	.004	8.66 [.124]	8.90 [.179]	8.90 [.179]
Italy	0.4499 (0.2414)	.0022	−.0002	.0549	−.003	5.73 [.334]	5.73 [.454]	5.26 [.511]
G-7[e]						39.72 [.268]	45.96 [.312]	48.42 [.229]

[a]The average value of k_i for country i based on single country estimation with the common instrument set.
[b]The average absolute value of k_i for country i based on single country estimation with the common instrument set.
[c]The minimized value of the GMM criterion function. P-value is the probability that a χ^2 variate exceeds the sample value of the statistic. For single country systems with the common instrument set, there is one parameter and 6 orthogonality conditions leaving 5 overidentifying conditions. For single country systems with the local instrument sets, there is one parameter and 7 orthogonality conditions leaving 6 overidentifying conditions. In the multiple equation system with the common instrument set, there are 7 parameters and 42 orthogonality conditions; this implies that there are 35 overidentifying restrictions to be tested. In the multiple equation system with the local instrument sets, there are 7 parameters and 49 orthogonality conditions; this implies that there are 42 overidentifying restrictions to be tested. The degrees of freedom in the test statistic correspond to the number of overidentifying restrictions.
[d]The adjusted coefficient of determination from a regression of the model errors (k_{it}) on the common set of instrumental variables.
[e]Japan, United Kingdom, France, Germany, Canada, United States, and Italy. These countries comprise 90% of the MSCI world index. In the estimation with local instruments, orthogonality conditions are formed using the local instrumental variables.

Re-estimation of the models using the local information sets has virtually no impact on the inference. With the first set of local instruments, the restrictions are rejected at the 5% level for Japan, Denmark, and Austria and at the 10% level for Norway. These results are identical to those using the common information variables. With the second set of local instruments, the model's restrictions are rejected at the 5% level for Japan, Norway, and Austria. In contrast to the results in Table V, the inclusion of the local instruments does not increase the evidence against the model's restrictions when the multiple country system is estimated.

Table VI also reports pricing errors based upon the estimation with the common set of instrumental variables. The average error for Japan is 0.59%. This implies that the model is delivering an average expected return of 0.75% per month, and the average realized return is 1.34%. For the United States, the model is predicting a 0.51% return while only 0.34% is realized on average. The model appears to fit quite well for the United Kingdom with a less than 0.01% pricing error.

E. Conditional Asset Pricing with a Constant World Price of Covariance Risk

Table VII presents test of the formulation that allows for time-varying conditional covariances. The constant in the estimation is the expected compensation for world market volatility—or the world price of covariance risk. However, this parameter is not restricted to be the same across countries in the single country estimation.

The results in Table VII reveal more evidence against this formulation than the previous two tables. Using the common information set, the model's restrictions are rejected at the 5% level for Hong Kong, Japan, Sweden, Belgium, the Netherlands, the United Kingdom, Denmark, Austria, Switzerland, Australia, Canada, and United States.[25] The estimates with the local information sets provide similar evidence against the model's restrictions. The average pricing error for Japan is of the same magnitude as the constant conditional beta model. The pricing error for the United States is three times the size of the pricing error in the constant conditional beta formulation.

There is wide variation in the magnitude of the reward to risk ratio. For example, the expected compensation for world market volatility in the United States is 5.4. The same measure in Japan in 13.1. In a financially integrated global market with time-invariant reward to risk, this ratio should be the same across all countries. If the financial markets are not perfectly integrated or if the asset pricing model is misspecified, then there is no reason that the reward to risk ratios should be the same.

A formal examination of the differences in the reward to risk ratio across different countries is presented in the last two lines of Table VII. First, a seven country system is estimated with the reward to risk ratio constrained to be constant across all countries. This measure can be interpreted as the

---

[25]The results for the United States are consistent with the formulation tested in Campbell (1987) and Harvey (1989, 1990).

Table VII

Estimates of a Conditional CAPM with Time Varying Expected Returns and a Constant Price of Covariance Risk

The results are based on data from 1970:2–1989:5 (232 observations). The country returns **r** are calculated in U.S. dollars in excess of the holding period return on the Treasury bill that is closest to 30 days to maturity. The equity data are from Morgan Stanley Capital International. Standard errors in parentheses are heteroskedasticity consistent. Generalized method of moments is used to estimate the system:

$$\eta_t = (u_{mt} \quad e_t) = \left(\begin{array}{c} [r_{mt} - Z_{t-1}\delta_m]' \\ [r_t - \lambda(u_{mt}r_t)]' \end{array} \right), \tag{10}$$

where r_m is the excess return on the world portfolio, δ_m values are the coefficients associated with the instrumental variables for estimating the conditional mean of the world return, u_m is the forecast error in the conditional mean of the world return, and λ is the world price of covariance risk. In the estimation, the world price of risk (expected world excess return divided by the variance of world excess returns) is held constant through time. However, when (10) is estimated country by country, the cross-country restriction that the world price of risk is the same *in each country* is not imposed. The final line of the table tests whether the world price of risk is statistically different across the group of seven countries. There are three sets of instrumental variables **Z** that are used in the estimation. The common set of predetermined instrumental variables are: a constant, the excess return on the world index, a dummy variable for the month of January, the 1-month return for holding a 90-day U.S. Treasury bill less the return on a 30-day bill, the yield on Moody's Baa rated bonds less the yield on Moody's Aaa rated bonds, and the dividend yield on the Standard and Poor's 500 stock index less the return on a 30-day bill. Local instrument set A is the common instrument set augmented with the country-specific dividend yield. Local instrument set B includes the country-specific dividend yield and the country-specific excess return in place of the world excess return.

Portfolio	λ_j	Average Conditional Covariance[a]	Average Return	Aveage Error[b]	Average Absolute Error[c]	$\bar{R}^{2d}$	Common Instruments χ^{2e} [P-value]	Local Instruments A: χ^2 [P-value]	Local Instruments B: χ^2 [P-value]
Hong Kong	11.6735 (4.4172)	1.9589	.0168	−.0060	.0945	.029	18.05 [.003]	18.24 [.006]	10.62 [.101]
Japan	13.0803 (3.0075)	1.4792	.0134	−.0059	.0464	.045	16.18 [.006]	15.66 [.016]	11.66 [.070]

The World Price of Covariance Risk   145

Table VII—*Continued*

Portfolio	λ_j	Average Conditional Covariance[a]	Average Return	Aveage Error[b]	Average Absolute Error[c]	$\bar{R}^{2d}$	Common Instruments χ^{2e} [P-value]	Local Instruments A: χ^2 [P-value]	Local Instruments B: χ^2 [P-value]
Sweden	8.3814 (4.0166)	1.1494	.0094	−.0003	.0507	.037	11.40 [.044]	11.54 [.073]	11.28 [.080]
Norway	4.3466 (3.2699)	1.6953	.0093	.0019	.0653	.022	10.45 [.064]	11.04 [.087]	15.71 [.015]
Belgium	9.7415 (3.1100)	1.3983	.0087	−.0050	.0444	.067	17.76 [.003]	17.93 [.006]	16.50 [.011]
Netherlands	9.3435 (2.6487)	1.5527	.0077	−.0068	.0429	.070	15.26 [.009]	16.54 [.011]	14.55 [.024]
United Kingdom	8.8913 (2.1730)	1.9757	.0074	−.0102	.0566	.065	13.22 [.021]	13.52 [.035]	13.87 [.031]
Denmark	9.6631 (3.7602)	.9888	.0072	−.0024	.0419	.029	13.11 [.022]	13.13 [.041]	12.70 [.048]
France	3.6508 (2.7151)	1.7456	.0065	.0001	.0563	.017	8.82 [.116]	10.40 [.109]	9.96 [.126]
Austria	−0.2664 (3.9388)	.7291	.0055	.0057	.0367	.057	19.41 [.002]	19.93 [.003]	17.72 [.007]
Germany	1.4478 (2.9738)	1.2424	.0050	.0032	.0462	.025	10.91 [.053]	11.24 [.081]	10.61 [.101]
Switzerland	3.6684 (2.5421)	1.4785	.0046	−.0008	.0433	.059	14.66 [.012]	15.13 [.019]	14.85 [.021]
Australia	−3.7285 (2.6900)	1.7379	.0044	.0109	.0585	.063	20.62 [.001]	22.06 [.001]	20.47 [.002]
Canada	1.4885 (2.3548)	1.6587	.0044	.0019	.0438	.104	18.41 [.003]	14.68 [.023]	13.68 [.033]
United States	5.3716 (2.0917)	1.6159	.0037	−.0049	.0362	.086	18.20 [.003]	18.93 [.004]	18.97 [.004]

continued overleaf

Table VII—*Continued*

Portfolio	λ_j	Average Conditional Covariance[a]	Average Return	Aveage Error[b]	Average Absolute Error[c]	$\bar{R}^{2d}$	Common Instruments χ^{2e} [P-value]	Local Instruments A: χ^2 [P-value]	Local Instruments B: χ^2 [P-value]
Spain	0.9848 (3.8771)	1.0625	.0036	.0025	.0485	009	8.37 [.137]	8.32 [.216]	9.85 [.131]
Italy	0.6396 (3.8879)	1.2604	.0022	.0014	.0593	.006	7.23 [.204]	7.23 [.300]	8.37 [.212]
G-7[f]	11.4716 (1.8252)						48.42 [.198]	50.32 [.382]	48.47 [.454]
G-7[g]	$\lambda_j = \lambda$, $j = 1, \ldots, 7$						23.76 [.001]	32.72 [<.001]	22.74 [.001]

[a] The average value of $u_i \times u_m$ multiplied by 1000 for country i based on single country estimation.

[b] The average value of e_i for country i based on single country estimation.

[c] The average absolute value of e_i for country i based on single country estimation.

[d] The adjusted coefficient of determination from a regression of the model errors $(e_{i,t})$ on the common instrumental variables.

[e] The minimized value of the GMM criterion function. *P*-value is the probability that a χ^2 variate exceeds the sample value of the statistic. For single country systems with the common instrument set, there are 7 parameters and 12 orthogonality conditions leaving 5 overidentifying conditions. For single country systems with the local instrument sets, there are 6 parameters and 14 orthogonality conditions leaving 6 overidentifying conditions. In the multiple equation system with common instruments, there are 7 parameters and 48 orthogonality conditions; this implies that there are 41 overidentifying restrictions to be tested. In the multiple equation system with local instruments, there are 8 parameters and 56 orthogonality conditions; this implies that there are 48 overidentifying restrictions to be tested. The degrees of freedom in the test statistic correspond to the number of overidentifying restrictions.

[f] Japan, United Kingdom, France, Germany, Canada, United States, and Italy. These countries comprise 90% of the MSCI world index. In the estimation with the local instruments, the common variables are used for the conditional mean of the world return (equation 1). The orthogonality conditions are formed with the local variables in equations 2 through 8 and with the common variables in equation 1.

[g] The test statistic has 6 degrees of freedom.

world price of covariance risk. The estimate is 11.5 which is closer to the single country estimates of Japan and the U.K. than the other G-7 countries. The χ^2 test indicates that there is little evidence against the model's restrictions using common or local instrumentation. However, there is evidence at the single country level against the restrictions for four of the G-7 countries.

Intuitively, one would expect rejection in the multiple country system given strong rejections in three of the single country tests and a marginal rejection for another country. It has been argued that the multiple country test may lack power. An alternative test is presented in the final line of Table VII. In this estimation, the equality of the reward to risk ratios across the seven countries is explicitly tested. The test proceeds in two steps. Initially, a seven country system is estimated with country specific reward to risk ratios. The weighting matrix is saved from this unrestricted estimation as well as the final χ^2 statistic. Second, a seven country system is estimated with the reward to risk ratios restricted to be the same across the seven countries. However, in the estimation the weighting matrix is the saved matrix from the unconstrained estimation. The difference in the final χ^2 statistics is distributed χ^2 with six degrees of freedom.[26] The results in the final line of Table VII provide convincing evidence against the model's null hypothesis that the ratios are the same. This multivariate test is powerful enough to reject the model's restrictions.

F. Diagnostics

The asset pricing model implies that the coefficient λ which transforms conditional covariance with the world market portfolio into conditionally expected returns is the same for all countries. The evidence presented in Table VII provides sharp evidence against this hypothesis. In the country by country estimation, the routine was fitting different world prices of covariance risk in order to match the conditional covariances with the conditionally expected returns. For example, the Japanese conditional covariance was not high enough to account for the large conditionally expected returns. The routine fit a λ coefficient of 13.1, which is much higher than the average, to accommodate the higher expected returns.

Some authors including Merton (1980) have related the price of risk to the coefficient of relative risk aversion. It is tempting to interpret the results in Table VII as evidence of higher risk aversion in Japan. However, there are two important qualifications. First, the reward to risk ratio can only be linked to risk aversion if international markets are completely segmented. That is, in completely segmented markets, a country whose residents are more risk-averse will have a higher reward to risk ratio than other countries. However, few would argue that Japan is completely segmented. If a country is not completely segmented, then the relation between the reward to risk

---

[26]See Gallant and Jorgenson (1979), Newey and West (1987), Eichenbaum, Hansen, and Singleton (1988), and Eichenbaum and Hansen (1990) for discussions of this multivariate test.

ratio and risk aversion will depend on how domestic residents can access foreign markets and how foreign investors can access the domestic market.

Second, in a world of complete segmentation, the relevant reward to risk ratio is the conditionally expected own-country return divided by the own-country variance. This is not what is estimated in Table VII. To get an idea of the magnitude of the local reward to risk ratios, these are presented in Table VIII.

Two of the smallest reward to risk ratios are found in Italy and Spain—which have the smallest average returns. Interestingly, the highest reward to risk ratio is found in Japan. The magnitude of the measure is double that of the one found in the United States. Under the null hypothesis of complete segmentation, the differences in these ratios may account for the higher expected returns that Japan has experienced relative to the United States.

The table also provides tests of whether the ratio is constant through time. In 10 of the 17 countries, there is evidence at the 5% level of significance against the hypothesis that the ratio is constant through time. There is evidence against the hypothesis at the 10% level for two other countries. The inference and the parameter estimates are not sensitive to whether the common or local instruments are used.

The final line of Table VIII provides estimates of the world price of covariance risk. The evidence strongly suggests that the world price of covariance risk is not constant. These results may explain the rejections of the model tested in Table VII. That is, rejection of the model tested in Table VII could be caused by the inefficiency of the world portfolio and/or by incorrectly specifying the world price of covariance risk to be a constant. The results in the last line of Table VIII indicate that the world price of covariance risk is not constant.

The results in Table VIII consider reward to risk ratios for countries under the hypothesis of segmented markets. However, under complete segmentation, the U.S. dollar returns are no longer the relevant metric. In addition, excess returns should be calculated in excess of local short-term interest rates. Table IX re-estimates the reward to risk ratios using both own currency returns and local interest rates.

The results in Table IX are similar to those presented in Table VIII. Only four countries (Belgium, the Netherlands, Denmark, and Switzerland) have reward to risk ratios that are more than one standard error different from those presented in Table VIII. However, it should be noted that the sample is different for some of these countries because data on short-term interest rates are not available back to 1970 in some countries, e.g., the sample used for Switzerland contains 175 observations (75:9-89:5) in Table IX compared to 232 observations (70:2-89:5) in Table VIII. Also, there are two countries for which I could not obtain the short-term interest rates: Belgium and Hong Kong.

The χ^2 test of the constancy of the reward to risk ratio generally tells a similar story. However, when own-currency returns are considered, Italy,

The World Price of Covariance Risk   149

Table VIII

Test of Whether the Price of Risk is Constant

The results are based on monthly data 1970:2–1989:5 (232 observations). The country returns r_j are calculated in U.S. dollars in excess of the holding period return on the Treasury bill that is closest to 30 days to maturity. The equity data are from Morgan Stanley Capital International. Standard errors in parentheses are heteroskedasticity consistent. Generalized method of moments estimation of the following system of equations:

$$\eta_t = \left(u_{jt} \quad e_{jt} \right) = \left(\begin{array}{c} [r_{jt} - \mathbf{Z}_{t-1}\delta_j]' \\ [r_{jt} - \lambda_j^* u_{jt}^2]' \end{array} \right)',$$

where δ_j are coefficients associated with the instrumental variables that are used to obtain the conditional mean return for country j, u_j is the forecast error in the conditional mean of the country return, e_j is the deviation from the return and the model's expected return, and λ_j is the country-specific price of risk (expected return divided by variance of the returns). There are three sets of instrumental variables $\mathbf{Z}$ that are used in the estimation. The common set of predetermined instrumental variables are: a constant, the excess return on the world index, a dummy variable for the month of January, the 1-month return for holding a 90-day U.S. Treasury bill less the return on a 30-day bill, the yield on Moody's Baa rated bonds less the yield on Moody's Aaa rated bonds, and the dividend yield on the Standard and Poor's 500 stock index less the return on a 30-day bill. Local instrument set A is the common instrument set augmented with the country-specific dividend yield. Local instrument set B includes the country-specific dividend yield and the country-specific excess return in place of the world excess return.

Portfolio	λ^*	Common Instruments χ^{2a} [P-value]	Local Instruments A: χ^2 [P-value]	Local Instruments B: χ^2 [P-value]
Hong Kong	1.2539 (0.4926)	18.13 [.003]	18.49 [.005]	14.25 [.027]
Japan	5.0597 (1.0934)	18.10 [.003]	17.98 [.006]	13.63 [.073]
Sweden	2.9443 (1.0896)	8.97 [.110]	9.01 [.173]	9.02 [.173]
Norway	1.6027 (0.8033)	10.18 [.070]	10.79 [.095]	14.67 [.023]
Belgium	3.1584 (0.9994)	16.48 [.006]	16.67 [.011]	16.90 [.010]
Netherlands	4.2864 (1.1884)	16.00 [.007]	18.47 [.005]	15.96 [.014]
United Kingdom	2.5569 (0.6435)	11.60 [.041]	14.19 [.028]	14.44 [.025]
Denmark	3.4518 (1.1364)	13.66 [.018]	13.63 [.034]	11.89 [.064]
France	1.4355 (0.8928)	7.35 [.196]	8.53 [.202]	8.41 [.209]
Austria	2.7478 (1.0645)	14.32 [.014]	14.91 [.021]	14.51 [.024]
Germany	1.6569 (1.1074)	9.08 [.106]	9.56 [.144]	9.06 [.170]

150   *The Journal of Finance*

Table VIII—*Continued*

Portfolio	λ^*	Common Instruments χ^{2a} [P-value]	Local Instruments A: χ^2 [P-value]	Local Instruments B: χ^2 [P-value]
Switzerland	1.9780 (1.1413)	13.78 [.017]	14.41 [.025]	14.25 [.025]
Australia	1.1108 (0.8608)	17.17 [.004]	18.00 [.006]	17.32 [.008]
Canada	1.9765 (1.1897)	15.11 [.010]	15.06 [.020]	14.02 [.029]
United States	2.6655 (1.5090)	19.26 [.002]	15.59 [.030]	19.57 [.003]
Spain	0.8077 (1.0175)	7.80 [.168]	7.96 [.241]	9.65 [.140]
Italy	0.4034 (0.8384)	7.10 [.214]	7.10 [.312]	8.40 [.210]
World	5.7238 (1.8272)	21.06 [< .001]	–	–

[a]The minimized value of the GMM criterion function. *P*-value is the probability that a χ^2 variate exceeds the sample value of the statistic. In the estimation with the common instrumental variables, there are one parameter and 6 orthogonality conditions, leaving 5 overidentifying conditions. In the estimation with the local information variables, there are one parameter and 7 orthogonality conditions, leaving 6 overidentifying conditions.

Germany, and Sweden are added to the list of countries that have significant variation in the reward to risk ratios. With the local currency returns, we can no longer reject the constancy of the ratio of expected returns to volatility for Switzerland. There is little difference in the test results across the different sets of conditioning information.

G. Risk and Return in October 1987

Although the evidence suggests departures from conditional mean-variance efficiency, the asset pricing formulation may still be useful in explaining cross-sectional variation in returns. One phenomena that would be a challenge for the asset pricing model to explain is the cross-country variation of returns in October 1987. Some countries were hit much harder than others. For example, the excess return in the Australian market was – 45% and in Hong Kong – 44%. In contrast, the Danish return loss was only 8%.

For a given world price of covariance risk in October 1987, the asset pricing model suggests that the most severe losses should be associated with countries with the highest risk in October 1987. Using data for 1981–1987, Roll (1988) shows that the unconditional betas are important in explaining the cross-sectional returns in October. However, no one has examined the

The World Price of Covariance Risk   151

Table IX

Test of Whether the Price of Risk is Constant Using Returns Calculated in Local Currency and Country-Specific Short-Term Interest Rates

The country returns lr_j are calculated in local currency in excess of the holding period return on the country's Treasury bill or the call money rate. The equity data are from Morgan Stanley Capital International. Standard errors in parentheses are heteroskedasticity consistent. Generalized method of moments is used to estimate the following system of equations:

$$\eta_t = (u_{jt} \quad e_{jt}) = \left(\begin{array}{c} [lr_{jt} - \mathbf{Z}_{t-1}\delta_j]' \\ [lr_{jt} - \lambda_j^* u_{jt}^2]' \end{array} \right)',$$

where u_j is the forecast error in the conditional mean return for the country portfolio, and λ_j is the country-specific price of risk (or ratio of the expected return to the variance of returns). There are three sets of instrumental variables $\mathbf{Z}$ used in the estimation. The common set of predetermined instrumental variables are: a constant, the excess return on the world index calculated in U.S. dollars, a dummy variable for the month of January, the 1-month return for holding a 90-day U.S. Treasury bill less the return on a 30-day bill, the yield on Moody's Baa rated bonds less the yield on Moody's Aaa rated bonds, and the dividend yield on the Standard and Poor's 500 stock index less the return on a 30-day bill. Local instrument set A is the common instrument set augmented with the country-specific dividend yield. Local instrument set B includes the country-specific dividend yield and the country-specific excess return in local currency in place of the world excess return.

Portfolio and (number of observations)	λ^*	Common Instruments χ^{2a} [P-value]	Local Instruments A: χ^2 [P-value]	Local Instruments B: χ^2 [P-value]
Hong Kong[b] 70:2–89:5 (232)	1.9082 (0.5739)	19.56 [.002]	20.04 [.003]	17.08 [.009]
Japan 70:2–89:5 (232)	5.7076 (1.4382)	17.57 [.004]	17.57 [.007]	11.89 [.064]
Sweden 70:2–87:1 (204)	2.7887 (1.2409)	11.86 [.037]	14.20 [.027]	14.97 [.021]
Norway[d] 71:9–89:5 (213)	0.8359 (0.8624)	8.36 [.138]	8.98 [.175]	13.20 [.040]
Belgium[b] 70:2–89:5 (232)	7.4042 (1.4294)	14.25 [.014]	13.51 [.036]	13.99 [.030]
Netherlands 70:2–89:5 (232)	6.1320 (1.3633)	22.50 [< .001]	22.38 [.001]	21.63 [.001]
United Kingdom 72:1–89:5 (208)	3.5292 (0.8786)	10.67 [.058]	14.38 [.026]	14.72 [.023]
Denmark 72:2–89:1 (204)	1.8502 (1.3639)	14.96 [.010]	15.14 [.019]	16.94 [.012]
France[c] 70:2–89:5 (229)	1.1956 (1.0487)	8.02 [.155]	9.45 [.150]	8.66 [.193]
Austria 71:12–89:1 (216)	2.3982 (1.2800)	16.88 [.005]	18.09 [.006]	8.49 [.204]
Germany 70:2–89:5 (232)	1.4855 (1.3246)	11.92 [.036]	12.65 [.049]	12.31 [.055]

Table IX—*continued*

Portfolio and (number of observations)	λ^*	Common Instruments χ^{2a} [*P*-value]	Local Instruments A: χ^2 [*P*-value]	Local Instruments B: χ^2 [*P*-value]
Switzerland 75:9–89:5 (175)	6.1072 (2.4113)	5.98 [.309]	6.38 [.382]	7.05 [.316]
Australia 70:2–89:1 (228)	1.0063 (0.9840)	19.88 [.001]	22.13 [.001]	20.67 [.002]
Canada 70:2–89:5 (232)	1.4874 (1.2706)	15.17 [.010]	15.52 [.017]	13.76 [.032]
United States 70:2–89:5 (232)	2.6655 (1.5090)	19.26 [.002]	15.59 [.030]	19.57 [.003]
Spain 74:1–89:5 (184)	−0.1027 (1.1953)	6.93 [.226]	6.95 [.325]	8.64 [.195]
Italy 71:2–89:5 (220)	0.4415 (0.9056)	11.15 [.048]	11.62 [.071]	12.02 [.061]

[a]The minimized value of the GMM criterion function. *P*-value is the probability that a χ^2 variate exceeds the sample value of the statistic. In the estimation with the common instrumental variables, there are one parameter and 6 orthogonality conditions, leaving 5 overidentifying conditions. In the estimation with the local instrumental variables, there are one parameter and 7 orthogonality conditions, leaving 6 overidentifying conditions.

[b]Short term interest rates are not available. The returns are not excess returns.

[c]Excludes 1986:3–1986:6 when the interest rate data are not available.

[d]Excludes 1980:8–1980:9 when the interest rate data are not available.

conditional risk in October 1987.[27] To do this, conditional covariances were estimated for October 1987 based on the common information variables available in September 1987. Hence, the fitted conditional covariance is an out-of-sample forecast of the risk.

The fitted conditional covariances are plotted against the returns in October 1987 in Figure 2. Consistent with the asset pricing theory, there is roughly a linear relation between the returns and the conditional covariances. The slope of the relation is *negative*. However, this is reasonable because the out-of-sample world price of covariance risk is negative in October 1987. To ensure that this result is not a fluke, Figure 3 provides a plot of the same variables for October 1986. In that month, the forecasted world price of covariance risk is positive, and the relation between the returns and the conditional covariances is roughly positive.

In any given month, the world price of covariance risk is fixed. A cross-sectional regression of the October 1987 returns on the estimated conditional risk explains 41% of the variation. Hence, the differences in the countries'

---

[27]Ferson and Harvey (1991) argue that the rolling unconditional beta may be interpreted as a conditional risk measure. In fact, for October 1987 the correlation of Roll's 6-year betas and my conditional covariances is 67.3%.

The World Price of Covariance Risk   153

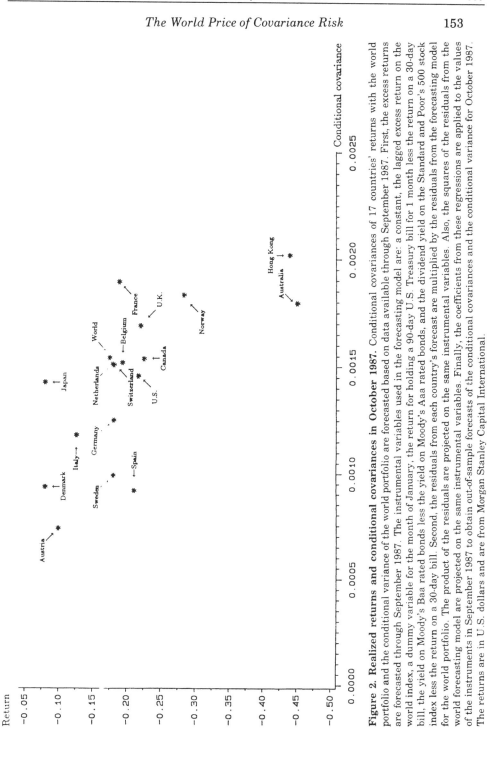

Figure 2. Realized returns and conditional covariances in October 1987. Conditional covariances of 17 countries' returns with the world portfolio and the conditional variance of the world portfolio are forecasted based on data available through September 1987. First, the excess returns are forecasted through September 1987. The instrumental variables used in the forecasting model are: a constant, the lagged excess returns on the world index, a dummy variable for the month of January, the return for holding a 90-day U.S. Treasury bill for 1 month less the return on a 30-day U.S. Treasury bill, the yield on Moody's Baa rated bonds less the yield on Moody's Aaa rated bonds, and the dividend yield on the Standard and Poor's 500 stock index less the return on a 30-day bill. Second, the residuals from each country's forecast are multiplied by the residuals from the forecasting model for the world portfolio. The product of the residuals are projected on the same instrumental variables. Also, the squares of the residuals from the world forecasting model are projected on the same instrumental variables. Finally, the coefficients from these regressions are applied to the values of the instruments in September 1987 to obtain out-of-sample forecasts of the conditional covariances and the conditional variance for October 1987. The returns are in U.S. dollars and are from Morgan Stanley Capital International.

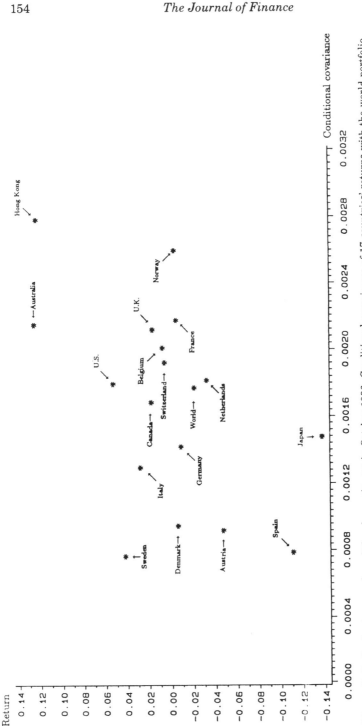

Figure 3. Realized returns and conditional covariances in October 1986. Conditional covariances of 17 countries' returns with the world portfolio and the conditional variance of the world portfolio are forecasted based on data available through September 1986. First, the excess returns are forecasted through September 1986. The instrumental variables used in the forecasting model are: a constant, the lagged excess return on the world index, a dummy variable for the month of January, the return for holding a 90-day U.S. Treasury bill for 1 month less the return on a 30-day bill, the yield on Moody's Baa rated bonds less the yield on Moody's Aaa rated bonds, and the dividend yield on the Standard and Poor's 500 stock index less the return on a 30-day bill. Second, the residuals from each country's forecast are multiplied by the residuals from the forecasting model for the world portfolio. The product of the residuals are projected on the same instrumental variables. Also, the squares of the residuals from the world forecasting model are projected on the same instrumental variables. Finally, the coefficients from these regressions are applied to the values of the instruments in September 1986 to obtain out-of-sample forecasts of the conditional covariances and the conditional variance for October 1986. The returns are in U.S. dollars and are from Morgan Stanley Capital International.

conditional covariances appear to account for a large portion of the differences in country performance.

IV. Conclusions

Tests of the conditional version of the Sharpe-Lintner capital asset pricing model are executed with country-specific stock portfolios. The tests assume that the representative investor only cares about U.S. dollar returns. Capital markets are also assumed to be fully integrated.

The tests allow for time-varying conditional moments. For most countries, a single source of risk appears to adequately describe the cross-sectional variation in returns across different countries. In an example, the differences in conditional covariances are able to account for a large portion of the different losses that countries experienced in October 1987. However, the model's restrictions are consistently rejected for Japan. Japan's covariance risk explains some—but not all—of its performance in the 1970:2–1989:5 sample.

However, all tests are joint tests of many hypotheses. An alternative hypothesis for the Japanese performance is that the market is not fully integrated. In this case, the Japanese covariance with the world market portfolio is not the relevant risk measure. Furthermore, the world price of risk is not the appropriate price of covariance risk. Evidence is presented that supports the hypothesis that the price of risk may be higher in Japan. This is consistent with the Japanese market performance over the sample.

REFERENCES

Adler, Michael and Bernard Dumas, 1983, International portfolio selection and corporation finance: A synthesis, *Journal of Finance* 46, 925–984.

Blake, Ian F. and John B. Thomas, 1968, On a class of processes arising in linear estimation theory, *IEEE Transactions on Information Theory* IT-14, 12–16.

Campbell, John Y., 1987, Stock returns and the term structure, *Journal of Financial Economics* 18, 373–400.

——and Yasushi Hamao, 1989, Predictable bond and stock returns in the United States and Japan: A study of long-term capital market integration, Working paper, Princeton University.

Cho, Chinhyung D., Cheol S. Eun, and Lemma W. Senbet, 1986, International arbitrage pricing theory: An empirical investigation, *Journal of Finance* 41, 313–330.

Cumby, Robert E. and Jack D. Glen, 1990, Evaluating the performance of international mutual funds, *Journal of Finance* 45, 497–521.

Cutler, David M., James M. Poterba, and Lawrence H. Summers, 1989, International evidence on the predictability of stock returns, Working paper, MIT.

——, James M. Poterba, and Lawrence H. Summers, 1990, Speculative dynamics, Working paper, MIT.

Eichenbaum, Martin S. and Lars P. Hansen, 1990, Estimating models with intertemporal substitution using aggregate time series data. *Journal of Business and Economic Statistics* 8, 53–69.

——, Lars P. Hansen, and Kenneth J. Singleton, 1988, A time series analysis of representative agent models of consumption and leisure choice under uncertainty, *Quarterly Journal of Economics* 103, 51–78.

Epstein, Larry G. and Stanley E. Zin, 1988, Substitution, risk aversion and the temporal behavior of consumption and asset returns: A theoretical framework. Working paper, University of Toronto.

Fama, Eugene F., 1965, The behavior of stock-market prices. *Journal of Business* 34-105.

——, 1984, The information in the term .structure, *Journal of Financial Economics* 13, 509-528.

——and Kenneth R. French, 1988, Dividend yields and expected stock returns, *Journal of Financial Economics* 22, 3-26.

——and Kenneth R. French, 1989, Business conditions and expected returns on stocks and bonds, *Journal of Financial Economics* 25, 23-50.

Ferson, Wayne E., 1990, Are the latent variables in time-varying expected returns compensation for consumption risk? *Journal of Finance* 45, 397-430.

——and Campbell R. Harvey, 1991, The variation of economic risk premiums, *Journal of Political Economy*, Forthcoming.

French, Kenneth R. and James M. Poterba, 1989, Are Japanese stock prices too high? Working paper, University of Chicago.

Gallant, A. Ronald and Dale W. Jorgenson, 1979, Statistical inference for a system of simultaneous, nonlinear, implicit equations in the context of instrumental variables estimation, *Journal of Econometrics* 11, 275-302.

Gibbons, Michael R. and Wayne E. Ferson, 1985, Tests of asset pricing models with changing expectations and an unobservable market portfolio. *Journal of Financial Economics* 14, 217-236.

——, Stephen A. Ross, and Jay Shanken, 1989, A test of the efficiency of a given portfolio, *Econometrica* 57, 1121-1152.

Giovannini, Alberto and Philippe Weil, 1988, Risk aversion and intertemporal substitution in the capital asset pricing model. Working paper, Columbia University.

——and Philippe Jorion, 1989, The time variation of risk and return in the foreign exchange and stock markets, *Journal of Finance* 44, 307-328

Gultekin, N. Bulent, 1983, Stock market returns and inflation: Evidence from other countries, *Journal of Finance* 38, 49-65.

Gultekin, Mustafa N. and N. Bulent Gultekin, 1983, Stock market seasonality: International evidence, *Journal of Financial Economics* 12, 469-481.

Gultekin, N. Bulent, Mustafa N. Gultekin, and Alessandro Penati, 1989, Capital controls and international capital market segmentation: The evidence from the Japanese and American stock markets, *Journal of Finance* 44, 849-869.

Hamao, Yasushi, 1988, An empirical examination of the arbitrage pricing theory: Using Japanese data, *Japan and the World Economy* 1, 45-61.

——, Ronald Masulis, and Victor Ng, 1990, Correlations in price changes and volatility across international stock markets, *Review of Financial Studies* 3, 281-307.

Hansen, Lars P., 1982, Large sample properties of generalized method of moments estimators, *Econometrica* 50, 1029-1054.

——and Robert J. Hodrick, 1983, Risk averse speculation in the forward foreign exchange market: An econometric analysis of linear models, in Jacob A. Frenkel, ed.: *Exchange Rates and International Macroeconomics* (University of Chicago Press, Chicago, IL).

——and Kenneth J. Singleton, 1982, Generalized instrumental variables estimation of nonlinear rational expectations models, *Econometrica* 50, 1269-1285.

Harvey, Campbell R., 1989, Time-varying conditional covariances in tests of asset pricing models, *Journal of Financial Economics* 24, 289-317.

——, 1990, On the linearity of conditionally expected market returns, Working paper, Duke University.

Huang, Roger D., 1989, Tests of the conditional capital asset pricing model with changing expectations, Working paper, Vanderbilt University.

Keim, Donald B., 1983, Size-related anomalies and stock return seasonality, *Journal of Financial Economics* 12, 13-32.

——and Robert F. Stambaugh, 1986, Predicting returns in the bond and stock market, *Journal of Financial Economics* 17, 357-390.

The World Price of Covariance Risk 157

Korajczyk, Robert and Claude Viallet, 1989, An empirical investigation of international asset pricing, *Review of Financial Studies* 2, 553-585.

Lintner, John, 1965, The valuation of risk assets and the selection of risky investments in stock portfolios and capital budgets, *Review of Economics and Statistics* 47, 13-37.

McDonald, Jack, 1989, The *Mochiai* Effect: Japanese corporate cross holdings, *Journal of Portfolio Management*, 90-94.

Merton, Robert, C., 1980, On estimating the expected return on the market: An exploratory investigation, *Journal of Financial Economics* 8, 323-362.

Newey, Whitney K. and Kenneth D. West, 1987, Hypothesis testing with efficient method of moments estimation, *International Economic Review* 28, 777-787.

Roll, Richard W., 1988, The international crash of October 1987, *Financial Analysts Journal* 44, 19-35.

Sharpe, William, 1964, Capital asset prices: A theory of market equilibrium under conditions of risk, *Journal of Finance* 19, 425-442.

Solnik, Bruno, 1974, The international pricing of risk: An empirical investigation of the world capital market structure, *Journal of Finance* 29, 48-54.

——, 1977, Testing international asset pricing: Some pessimistic views, *Journal of Finance* 32, 503-511.

——, 1983, The relationship between stock prices and inflationary expectations: The international evidence, *Journal of Finance* 38, 35-48.

Stehle, Richard, 1977, An empirical test of the alternative hypotheses of national and international pricing of risky assets, *Journal of Finance* 32, 493-502.

Stulz, René, 1981, A model of international asset pricing, *Journal of Financial Economics* 9, 383-406.

——, 1984, Pricing capital assets in an international setting: An introduction, *Journal of International Business Studies* Winter, 55-73.

Vershik, A. M., 1964, Some characteristic properties of Gaussian stochastic processes, *Theory of Probability and Its Applications* 9, 353-356.

Wheatley, Simon, 1988, Some tests of international equity integration, *Journal of Financial Economics* 21, 177-212.

[12]

THE JOURNAL OF FINANCE • VOL. XLVII, NO. 2 • JUNE 1992

Characterizing Predictable Components in Excess Returns on Equity and Foreign Exchange Markets

GEERT BEKAERT and ROBERT J. HODRICK*

ABSTRACT

The paper first characterizes the predictable components in excess rates of returns on major equity and foreign exchange markets using lagged excess returns, dividend yields, and forward premiums as instruments. Vector autoregressions (VARs) demonstrate one-step-ahead predictability and facilitate calculations of implied long-horizon statistics, such as variance ratios. Estimation of latent variable models then subjects the VARs to constraints derived from dynamic asset pricing theories. Examination of volatility bounds on intertemporal marginal rates of substitution provides summary statistics that quantify the challenge facing dynamic asset pricing models.

THERE IS NOW CONSIDERABLE evidence that excess returns on a variety of assets are predictable. In equity markets around the world, predictable returns have been documented using dividend yields, short-term interest rates, default spreads, and yields in the term structure of interest rates as predictors.[1] In foreign exchange markets, predictable returns have been documented using the forward premium as a predictor.[2] What has yet to be established is whether this predictability is evidence of market inefficiency or

*Bekaert is from the Department of Economics, Northwestern University, Evanston, IL. Hodrick is from the Department of Finance, Kellogg Graduate School of Management, Northwestern University. The authors gratefully acknowledge partial support of this research from the National Bureau of Economic Research (NBER) Committee on Dissertation Support Awards and the Kellogg Banking Research Center, respectively. We thank Laurie Bagwell, Tim Bollerslev, Robert Cumby, Robert Korajczyk, Bruno Solnik, René Stulz (the editor), Mark Watson, an anonymous referee and the participants in seminars at Carleton, Columbia, Florida, Georgetown, Illinois, McGill, Princeton, Rochester, and Yale and at the 1990 NBER Summer Institute and the 1991 Mid-West International Economics Conference for useful comments on the paper.

[1] For U.S. data, Fama and Schwert (1977) used nominal interest rates to predict stock returns. For recent uses of this instrument see Breen, Glosten and Jagannathan (1989) and Ferson (1989). Gultekin (1983) and Solnik (1983) extended the Fama and Schwert results to other countries. Dividend yields have been used as predictors of stock returns either alone or in conjunction with other instruments by Rozeff (1984), Shiller (1984), Keim and Stambaugh (1986), Fama and French (1988b), Campbell and Shiller (1988), Cochrane (1990), Campbell (1991), and Hodrick (1991), among others.

[2] Tryon (1979) and Bilson (1981) pioneered use of the foward premium in investigations of the efficiency of the foreign exchange market. See Hodrick (1987) for a survey of the empirical literature in this area. More recent contributions include Cumby (1988), Mark (1988), Kaminsky and Peruga (1990), Froot and Thaler (1990), and Bekaert and Hodrick (1991).

time-varying risk premiums in an efficient market. Although we do not resolve the issue here, our empirical analysis contributes to the debate in several ways. First, we characterize the predictability of returns in an integrated way. Second, we reject some simple models of market efficiency. Third, we provide a way of organizing the facts which demonstrates the challenge to the development of dynamic asset pricing models.

Our first purpose is to integrate the literature on the predictability of asset returns by characterizing the predictable components in excess returns in the equity markets of the U.S., Japan, the U.K., and Germany and in the foreign exchange markets of the dollar relative to the yen, the pound, and the Deutsche mark. We use dividend yields, forward premiums, and lagged excess returns as predictors.[3] Our innovation is to investigate the equity and foreign exchange excess returns with vector autoregressive techniques. This facilitates calculations of various long-horizon summary statistics. The importance of long-horizon predictability of equity returns in the debate on market efficiency has been stressed by Fama and French (1988a, b), Campbell and Shiller (1988), Poterba and Summers (1988), and in an international context by Cutler, Poterba, and Summers (1989).

The first part of our empirical analysis answers questions like the following: "What is the variability of expected returns in equity and foreign exchange markets at various horizons?" "Are equity markets characterized by mean reversion in stock prices?" "Do dividend yields predict long-horizon equity returns?" "Do exchange rates exhibit mean reversion at long horizons?" "Does a forward premium on the foreign currency predict appreciation of the domestic currency at all horizons?" Answers to questions such as these provide a useful characterization of the data. But, since return predictability is only inconsistent with the simplest model of market efficiency that postulates a constant required return, we conduct additional analysis.

Once excess return predictability is established, one would like to know if the predictability is due to time varying risk premiums. Asset pricing models typically predict that expected returns on assets move proportionately (with different betas) in response to movements in underlying factors, such as the return on the market portfolio in the CAPM. Hence, if markets are efficient and internationally integrated, a low dimensional factor structure may characterize the co-movements in excess returns. The second part of our analysis therefore investigates several latent variable models in an effort to determine the empirical plausibility of this argument.[4] Failure to reject such a

---

[3] Related papers include Giovannini and Jorion (1987, 1989), who examine models of risk premiums in several foreign exchange markets simultaneously with the risk premium in the U.S. stock market; Campbell and Hamao (1989) and Chan, Karolyi, and Stulz (1991), who examine excess equity returns in the U.S. and Japan; Cumby (1990), who examines real equity returns in the U.S., Germany, the U.K., and Japan; Solnik (1990), who examines out-of-sample predictability for eight countries' equity and bond returns; and Harvey (1991), who examines dollar denominated excess equity returns on seventeen countries.

[4] Hansen and Hodrick (1983) developed the latent variable model and applied it to the foreign exchange market. Gibbons and Ferson (1985) developed the model independently in an application to the stock market. In recent applications of the approach, Campbell and Hamao (1992) and Cumby (1990) examine integration of equity markets across countries.

model would be consistent with an efficient, integrated, world capital market in which the riskiness of an asset is determined by world market forces. Models with a single latent variable are strongly rejected, but the evidence against models with two latent variables is less strong.

Variation over time in expected returns poses a challenge for asset pricing theory because it requires an explicitly dynamic theory in contrast to the traditional static capital asset pricing model (CAPM). One way to quantify this challenge for a large class of models is to examine volatility bounds on the intertemporal marginal rate of substitution (IMRS) of investors. Hansen and Jagannathan (1991) derive such bounds nonparametrically by exploiting a duality between the mean-standard deviation frontier of returns and the mean-standard deviation frontier for the IMRS. Their most challenging volatility bounds arise when they use Treasury bill returns. We extend their analysis using dollar denominated excess returns on international investments and find even more restrictive bounds.

The paper is organized as follows. Section I contains a discussion of the data and some summary statistics. Section II provides the estimation of the vector autoregressions (VARs). In this section we also consider an alternative formulation of the VARs that uses the two nominal interest rates rather than the forward premium, which is the interest differential. The calculations of the long-horizon statistics are also reported here. Section III considers the latent variable models, and Section IV contains estimation of the Hansen-Jagannathan (1991) bounds. The last section contains concluding remarks.

I. Data and Summary Statistics

To facilitate the presentation and discussion of our empirical analysis, consider the following definitions. We subscript variables of the four countries with numbers: 1 for the U.S., 2 for Japan, 3 for the U.K. and 4 for Germany. Let the one-month nominal interest rate denominated in currency j that is set at time t for delivery at time $t + 1$ be i_{jt}. Define r_{jt+1} to be the continuously compounded one-month rate of return denominated in currency j in the equity market of country j in excess of i_{jt}. In the VARs we include the U.S. excess rate of return, r_{1t+1}, and a second country's excess equity rate of return denominated in currency j, r_{jt+1} for j equal to either 2, 3, or 4. Let the rate of return in dollars on an uncovered investment in the currency j money market in excess of the U.S. nominal interest rate be rs_{jt+1}, for $j = 2, 3, 4$. Including rs_{jt+1} in the VAR with r_{1t+1} and r_{jt+1} allows calculation of the excess rate of return on a country j equity investment from a dollar investor's perspective as $r_{jt+1} + rs_{jt+1}$.[5] Similarly, the currency j rate of return on a U.S. equity investment in excess of i_{jt} is obtained as $r_{1t+1} - rs_{jt+1}$.

[5]A focus on excess rates of return arises naturally in theoretical frameworks if returns are lognormally distributed. Use of gross excess returns in our empirical work would not change inference about return predictability, but it would complicate many of our calculations since they would no longer be linear.

To understand these calculations, consider the following analysis. Let S_{jt} be the dollar price of currency j. Then, the continuously compounded rate of depreciation of the dollar relative to currency j is $s_{jt+1} - s_{jt} = \ln(S_{jt+1}/S_{jt})$. The uncovered dollar return on a continuously compounded currency j money market investment is $\exp(i_{jt})(S_{jt+1}/S_{jt}) = \exp(i_{jt} + s_{jt+1} - s_{jt})$. Hence, the excess dollar rate of return on a currency j money market investment is:

$$rs_{jt+1} = i_{jt} + s_{jt+1} - s_{jt} - i_{1t}. \tag{1}$$

Analogously, if the continuously compounded rate of return denominated in currency j in the country j equity market is R_{jt+1}, the dollar return in this equity market is $\exp(R_{jt+1} + s_{jt+1} - s_{jt})$. Hence, the excess rate of return from the U.S. perspective on a foreign equity market investment is $R_{jt+1} + s_{jt+1} - s_{jt} - i_{1t}$. Using equation (1) and the fact that $r_{jt+1} = R_{jt+1} - i_{jt}$, the excess rate of return from the U.S. perspective on a foreign equity market investment is $r_{jt+1} + rs_{jt+1}$.

From interest rate parity, the dollar return on a foreign money market investment that is covered in the forward foreign exchange market to eliminate foreign exchange risk is the U.S. nominal return. Hence,

$$i_{1t} = i_{jt} + f_{jt} - s_{jt} \tag{2}$$

where $f_{jt} - s_{jt} = \ln(F_{jt}/S_{jt})$ is the continuously compounded forward premium on the foreign currency, which we denote fp_{jt}. Substituting from equation (2) into equation (1) notice that $rs_{jt+1} = s_{jt+1} - f_{jt}$. This is how we measure the excess money market rates of return, and we will refer to them as returns in the foreign exchange market.

Morgan Stanley Capital International (MSCI) constructs monthly equity returns, and we obtained our data from Ibbotson Associates, who report the total return, the capital appreciation, and an income return. While the capital appreciation is the actual percentage change in price, the reported income return is an estimate constructed from annualized dividends divided by the previous price. We use the MSCI total return denominated in the foreign currency in the construction of r_{jt+1}. Eurocurrency interest rates are subtracted from the equity returns to create excess returns. The Eurocurrency interest rate data are market-determined, end-of-month interest rates and are from Data Resources, Inc.[6] We also use the MSCI series to calculate dividend yields as annualized dividends divided by current price for the U.S., Japan, and the U.K. Observations on dividend yields were compared to data from the Financial Times Actuaries, and two outlier observations for the U.K. and two for Japan were corrected. The German dividend yield series is taken from various issues of the *Monthly Report of the Deutsche Bundesbank*, Section VI., Table 6, from the column labelled "yields on shares including tax credit." We chose this series because beginning in January 1977,

---

[6]We thank Bob Korajczyk for the eurocurrency interest rate data which were obtained at INSEAD and are used in Korajczyk and Viallet (1990).

domestic investors in German equities receive a tax credit for the corporate tax paid on dividends, which eliminates the double taxation of dividends. The dividend yield in country j is denoted dy_{jt}.

Daily bid and ask exchange rate data were obtained from Citicorp Database Services. The data are captured from a Reuter's screen and represent quoted market prices. We ran several filter tests on the data to check for errors, and we corrected several with observations from the *International Monetary Market Yearbook* or the *Wall Street Journal*. Exchange rate data are sampled at the end of the month, and we construct true returns for the foreign exchange markets by incorporating the market rules governing delivery on foreign exchange contracts. We also incorporate transactions costs by buying a currency at the bank's ask price and selling a currency at the bank's bid price for foreign exchange.[7]

Some summary statistics on the data are reported in Table I. The monthly data are scaled by 1200 to express returns in percent per annum. The means of the excess equity rates of return estimate the unconditional equity risk premiums in the different countries. The estimates are 5% for the U.S., 9% for the U.K., 10% for Germany, and 15% for Japan. The estimates of the unconditional means of the excess foreign exchange returns are -1% for the dollar-yen, -4% for the dollar-pound, and -3% for the dollar-DM.

The excess rates of return are quite variable. The standard deviations of the annualized monthly data range from 57% for both the U.S. and Japan to 68% for the U.K. and 71% for Germany. The comparable statistics for the foreign exchange market excess returns indicate slightly less variability with standard deviations between 42% and 46%.[8]

The estimated autocorrelations of the excess rates of return are all small, while the autocorrelations of the dividend yields are all quite large. The autocorrelations for the forward premiums and interest rates are also large. The standard deviations of the dividend yields, the forward premiums, and the interest rates are more than an order of magnitude smaller than those of the excess rates of return.

II. A Vector-Autoregressive Approach

One way to examine predictability of excess returns is to estimate VARs. We report two-country VARs for the United States and either Japan, the United Kingdom, or Germany. In each VAR we include the U.S. equity

---

[7]In Bekaert and Hodrick (1991), we explain the rules for delivery on forward contracts, and we compare proper and improper use of data, either through ignoring these rules or failing to account for bid-ask spreads, to determine whether previous inference about the predictive ability of the forward premium for foreign exchange returns is affected. We find essentially no differences in inference with monthly data.

[8]The reported standard deviations are not estimates of the standard deviation of the annual holding period return. If returns are i.i.d., the variance of the annual return is twelve times the variance of the one month return. To estimate the standard deviation of the annual holding period return, divide our reported numbers by $\sqrt{12}\,(=3.464)$.

Table I

Summary Statistics

The numerical subscripts denote countries: 1 for the U.S., 2 for Japan, 3 for the U.K. and 4 for Germany. The excess equity market rate of return in country j is r_{jt}, the excess dollar rate of return on a currency j money market investment is rs_{jt}, the dividend yield in country j is dy_{jt}, the forward premium on currency j in terms of U.S. dollars is fp_{jt}, and the interest rate on currency j is i_{jt}. The sample period is 1981 : 1 to 1989 : 12. The monthly data are scaled by 1200 to express returns in percent per annum. The standard error for the autocorrelations for the null hypothesis of no serial correlation is 0.096.

Variable	Mean	Standard Dev.	Autocorrelations			
			ρ_1	ρ_2	ρ_3	ρ_4
r_{1t}	4.969	56.937	0.081	−0.048	−0.061	−0.048
r_{2t}	15.420	57.003	0.016	−0.057	−0.036	−0.010
r_{3t}	8.744	68.276	−0.094	−0.082	−0.041	0.040
r_{4t}	10.188	71.246	0.125	−0.001	0.041	−0.006
rs_{2t}	−0.894	42.251	0.128	0.051	0.172	−0.024
rs_{3t}	−3.620	45.884	0.021	0.165	0.041	0.070
rs_{4t}	−2.740	43.644	0.059	0.133	0.086	0.039
dy_{1t}	4.346	0.934	0.964	0.932	0.901	0.864
dy_{2t}	1.070	0.508	0.970	0.938	0.912	0.894
dy_{3t}	4.434	1.148	0.949	0.909	0.876	0.846
dy_{4t}	3.887	1.054	0.922	0.879	0.823	0.787
fp_{2t}	4.166	2.629	0.897	0.833	0.758	0.694
fp_{3t}	−1.438	2.877	0.877	0.780	0.668	0.559
fp_{4t}	3.630	1.622	0.620	0.456	0.353	0.226
i_{1t}	9.683	3.167	0.935	0.878	0.835	0.756
i_{2t}	5.785	1.195	0.900	0.829	0.794	0.731
i_{3t}	11.320	2.023	0.893	0.791	0.688	0.597
i_{4t}	6.176	2.496	0.945	0.886	0.840	0.792

market excess return, the companion country equity market excess return, the relevant foreign exchange market excess return, the two dividend yields, and the forward premium. For example, the U.S.-Japan VAR contains $Y_t = [r_{1t}, r_{2t}, rs_{2t}, dy_{1t}, dy_{2t}, fp_{2t}]'$.

If Y_t follows a first-order VAR,

$$Y_{t+1} = \alpha_0 + A Y_t + u_{t+1}, \tag{3}$$

where α_0 is a vector of constants, A is a (6 by 6) matrix, and u_{t+1} is the vector of innovations in Y_{t+1} relative to its past history. Higher order systems can be handled in exactly the same way by stacking the VAR into first-order companion form as in Campbell and Shiller (1988). In Table II we report the values of the Schwarz (1978) criteria for the choice of lag length in the VAR. In all cases the minimized value of the criterion is associated with the first-order system.

We estimate equations (3) with ordinary least squares and report heteroskedasticity consistent standard errors for the parameters. We test

Table II

Values of the Schwarz Criteria for Vector Autoregressions of Excess Stock Returns, the Excess Foreign Exchange Return, Dividend Yields, and the Forward Premium

The appropriate lag length for the VAR minimizes the Schwarz (1978) criterion. The sample period is 1981 : 1 to 1989 : 12. The monthly data are scaled by 1200 to express returns in percent per annum.

	Lag 1	Lag 2	Lag 3	Lag 4
U.S.-Japan	12.228	13.249	14.275	15.270
U.S.-U.K.	16.256	17.149	18.427	19.481
U.S.-Germany	17.574	18.482	19.376	20.306

one-step-ahead predictability of excess returns with a joint test of the six coefficients in the appropriate row of A. We also report the Cumby and Huizinga (1992) l-tests for serial correlation in the error processes. In contrast to more traditional tests for serial correlation, this test allows for the facts that the regressors are lagged dependent variables and that the error processes are conditionally heteroskedastic.

Estimation of the parameters of the VAR completely characterizes the unconditional mean, variance and covariances of the Y_t process since the series are assumed to be covariance stationary. In this case, the moving-average representation of Y_{t+1} is:

$$Y_{t+1} = \mu_0 + \sum_{j=0}^{\infty} A^j u_{t+1-j}. \tag{4}$$

The unconditional mean of Y_t is $\mu_0 = (I - A)^{-1}\alpha_0$, where I is the six-dimensional identity matrix. If the innovation variance of u_t is V, the unconditional variance of the Y_t process can be derived from equation (4) to be $C(0) = \sum_{j=0}^{\infty} A^j V A^{j\prime}$, since u_t is serially uncorrelated.[9] The jth order autocovariance of Y_t can similarly be derived to be $C(j) = A^j C(0)$.

A. Implied Long-Horizon Statistics

There is considerable interest in the characteristics of asset prices and returns at long horizons. For example, Fama and French (1988a) and Poterba and Summers (1988) examine variances and covariances of long-horizon stock returns to determine whether there are mean-reverting components in stock prices. Huizinga (1987) performs analogous computations for real currency depreciations. These authors note that when using short horizon or high frequency data it is often difficult to reject the hypothesis of no serial

---

[9]In actual calculations we truncate the infinite sum in $C(0)$ at 255.

correlation in the logarithmic changes in asset prices, which are the primary part of an asset's return.[10]

One advantage of the VAR approach is that it uses additional variables that should be able to forecast returns under alternative hypotheses, which can improve the power of tests.[11] Furthermore, if there is long-horizon predictability in asset prices, there must be short-horizon predictability as well, since the long run is just a sequence of short runs. Characterizing long-run predictability can therefore be done with statistics that are functions of the autocovariances of the Y_t process. We consequently employ VAR methods to examine a number of implied long-horizon statistics.

The variance ratio for excess returns is defined to be the ratio of the variance of the sum of k one-period returns to k times the variance of the one-period return.[12] The variance ratio equals one if returns are serially uncorrelated; it is greater than one if returns are positively autocorrelated; and it is less than one if the returns are negatively autocorrelated.

Rather than calculate variance ratios using sample variances of the returns over various horizons k, we calculate an implied variance ratio. To determine an implied variance ratio, first consider the sum of k consecutive Y_t's. From equation (4) the variance of the sum of k Y_t's can be derived to be

$$V_k = kC(0) + (k-1)[C(1) + C(1)'] + \cdots + [C(k-1) + C(k-1)']. \quad (5)$$

Define ei to be a six element vector of zeros except for the ith element which is one. Consequently, the total variance of the sum of k consecutive U.S. excess returns is $e1'V_k e1$. The variance ratio for the U.S. excess rate of return is therefore

$$VR(k) = \frac{e1' V_k e1}{ke1' C(0) e1}. \quad (6)$$

The analogous variance ratios for the foreign country excess rate of return and the foreign exchange market excess return substitute $e2$ and $e3$, respectively, for $e1$ in equation (6).

We are also interested in variance ratios for dollar denominated rates of return to U.S. investors in the foreign equity markets and for foreign

---

[10] Poterba and Summers (1988) perform Monte Carlo experiments to examine the power of autocorrelation based tests. In the presence of highly serially correlated transitory components in prices, autocorrelation based tests have very low power. For example, such tests often incorrectly fail to reject the null hypothesis of no serial correlation in the changes in prices with probabilities of at least 0.8 when as much as 75% of the unconditional variance of the change in prices is due to transitory components.

[11] Kandel and Stambaugh (1988) and Campbell (1991) employ VAR methods to examine long-horizon equity returns, and Cumby and Huizinga (1990) employ the technique to examine long-horizon forecasts of real exchange rates. Hodrick (1991) reports Monte Carlo analyses of the VAR technique and finds that the asymptotic distribution theory works very well given that the order of the VAR is correct.

[12] See Cochrane (1988), Lo and MacKinlay (1988) and Poterba and Summers (1988) for discussions of variance ratios.

currency denominated rates of return to foreign investors in the U.S. equity market. As noted above in Section I, these excess rates of returns are just linear combinations of the elements of Y_t, the first uses $e7' = e2' + e3'$ and the second uses $e8' = e1' - e3'$. The final variance ratio we report is for depreciation of the dollar relative to the foreign currency, which is $e3' Y_{t+1} + e6' Y_t$.

Other long-horizon statistics can also be easily calculated. For example, Fama and French (1988b) regress long-horizon equity returns on the current dividend yield. The slope coefficient in such a regression is the covariance of the sum of returns from $t + 1$ to $t + k$ and the dividend yield at t divided by the variance of the dividend yield. Since a covariance involving a sum equals the sum of the covariances of the individual elements, an alternative estimator of this regression coefficient is

$$\beta_1(k) = \frac{e1'\big[C(1) + \cdots + C(k)\big]e4}{e4' C(0) e4}. \tag{7}$$

Analogous coefficients for regressions of long-horizon foreign equity market returns on the foreign dividend yield are found by substituting $e2$ for $e1$ and $e5$ for $e4$ in equation (7). We also calculate the implied coefficient in the regression of the long-horizon foreign exchange market excess return on the forward premium. This is found by substituting $e3$ for $e1$ and $e6$ for $e4$ in equation (7).

Although the R^2 in regressions of one-step-ahead returns on current information is often quite small, the R^2 in long-horizon studies is often quite large, which reflects the negative serial correlation in long horizon returns. The explanatory power of the VAR at long horizons can also be assessed by examining the ratio of the explained variance of the sum of k returns to the total variance of the sum of k returns. These long-horizon R^2 coefficients can be calculated as one minus the ratio of the innovation variance in the sum of k returns to the total variance of the sum of k returns.

The innovation variance of the sum of k consecutive Y_t's can be found from equation (4) to be

$$W_k = \sum_{j=1}^{k} (I - A)^{-1}(I - A^j)V(I - A^j)'(I - A)^{-1\prime}. \tag{8}$$

Hence, the implied long-horizon R^2 from the VAR for the U.S. equity return is

$$R^2(k) = 1 - \frac{e1' W_k e1}{e1' V_k e1}. \tag{9}$$

Analogous long-horizon R^2's can be produced for foreign excess equity returns and for the foreign exchange market by appropriate substitution for the indicator vector in equation (9).

B. Asymptotic Distributions for the Statistics

Each of the long-horizon statistics derived above is a function of the parameters of α_0, A, and V. Let η_0 represent the vector of these distinct parameters, and let η_T be an estimate of η_0 from a sample of size T. Estimation of the parameters of the VAR can be thought of as an application of Hansen's (1982) Generalized Method of Moments (GMM) and can be done as a just-identified system. We use 63 orthogonality conditions in a GMM estimation to obtain the asymptotic distribution of η_T. This is a just-identified system because there are 42 coefficients in α_0 and A and 21 distinct parameters in V. The first 42 orthogonality conditions are the usual ordinary least squares conditions that the residuals are orthogonal to the right-hand-side instruments, $E(u_{t+1} \otimes Z_t) = 0$, where $Z_t' = (1, Y_t')$. The last 21 orthogonality conditions are given by stacking the distinct elements of $E(u_{t+1}u_{t+1}' - V) = 0$ into a vector.

In constructing the GMM weighting matrix, we allow a Newey-West (1987) lag of three (the 0.25 root of the sample size) for all of the orthogonality conditions since the deviations of the cross-products of the residuals from the elements of V can be arbitrarily serially correlated. The asymptotic distribution theory of GMM implies that $\sqrt{T}(\eta_T - \eta_0) \sim N(0, \Omega)$, where $\Omega = (D_0' S_0^{-1} D_0)^{-1}$, D_0 is the expectation of the gradient of the orthogonality conditions with respect to the parameters, and S_0 is the spectral density of the orthogonality conditions evaluated at frequency zero.

Let $H(\eta_0)$ represent the true value of one of the implied long-horizon statistics. The asymptotic distribution of the estimated function can be derived from a Taylor's series approximation to be

$$\sqrt{T}\left[H(\eta_T) - H(\eta_0)\right] \sim N(0, \nabla H \Omega \nabla H'). \tag{10}$$

Numerical derivatives can be used to calculate the gradient of H evaluated at η_T, which is denoted ∇H.

C. Interpretation of the Results of the VARs

The estimated VARs are reported in Panels A-C of Table III. The sample period is January 1981 to December 1989 for 108 observations. We use this sample because of the deregulation of international capital markets that took place at the end of the 1970s and the beginning of the 1980s, particularly in the U.K. and Japan.[13]

We first analyze one-step-ahead predictability. A test that any of the excess returns is forecastable is a joint test that the six coefficients on the lagged variables are each zero. If we interpret the results of such tests as classical statisticians, we would reject the null hypothesis of no predictability if the value of the test statistic is greater than the prespecified critical value of a chi-square statistic with six degrees of freedom that is associated with a desired probability of a Type I error. Since we have no idea of the power of

---

[13]The sample corresponds to a sub-sample of Campbell and Hamao (1992) who describe the deregulation of Japanese financial markets.

these tests, and because Type II errors are also costly, we do not discuss the results in such terms. Instead, we report the confidence values of the test statistics which allows a quasi-Bayesian interpretation. We interpret large values of the test statistics as evidence against the hypothesis of no predictability.

Consider the results for the U.S.-Japan data in Panel A of Table III. For the U.S. equity market the test statistic is 24.245 with a confidence level of 0.999, for the Japanese equity market the test statistic is 13.955 with a confidence level of 0.970 and for the dollar-yen foreign exchange market the test statistic is 16.117 with a confidence level of 0.987. In each case there is some predictability of excess returns, but the returns are quite noisy, and the adjusted R^2's are not large. The lagged variables explain 6.3% of the U.S. excess equity return, 5.2% of the Japanese excess equity return, and 10.9% of the dollar-yen foreign exchange market return.

The Cumby-Huizinga (1992) l-tests generally provide no strong evidence against the hypothesis that the residuals are serially uncorrelated. There is also no strong evidence against the hypothesis that the coefficients on the three lagged returns in each of the equations are zero. These results are in the row labelled Ret. Tests. Nevertheless, there are several coefficients on lagged returns in the return equations that are large relative to their standard errors. The point estimates indicate that expected excess returns in the U.S. and Japan respond positively to lagged U.S. returns and negatively to lagged Japanese returns. The forward premium enters all excess return equations with a negative sign, and the dividend yields enter the equity return equations with positive signs in the own-country equation and negative signs in the cross-country equation.

The U.S.-U.K. data are investigated in Panel B of Table III, and the U.S.-German data are in Panel C. We view the results as qualitatively similar to those of the U.S.-Japan system. The confidence level of the test statistic that examines predictability of the excess return in the U.K. equity market is not as large as those of the U.S. and Japan, but the adjusted R^2 in this equation is comparable to the others, as are the coefficient estimates on the dividend yields and the forward premium. Similarly, the adjusted R^2 for the U.S. equity return in the U.S.-Germany VAR falls to zero, but the coefficient estimates on the dividend yields and the forward premium are very similar to the analogous coefficients in the other VARs, and the confidence level for the test of return predictability is 0.872. There is very strong evidence of predictability of the dollar-pound and dollar-mark excess returns. The confidence levels are never smaller than 0.999, and the adjusted R^2's are 17.2% and 17.8%, respectively.[14]

---

[14] Harvey (1991) reports a higher R^2 for the U.S. equity return, but he includes a term structure premium and a default premium. His R^2's for other countries are approximately the same as ours even though his are denominated in dollars and ours are denominated in foreign currency. The R^2's for dollar denominated returns on foreign equity investments using our data and our predictive variables are 12.6%, 13.0%, and 7.8% for Japan, the U.K., and Germany, respectively.

Table III

First Order Vector Autoregressions of Excess Stock Returns, the Excess Foreign Exchange Return, Dividend Yields, and the Forward Premium

The numerical subscripts denote countries: 1 for the U.S., 2 for Japan, 3 for the U.K. and 4 for Germany. The excess equity market rate of return in country j is r_{jt}, the excess dollar rate of return on a currency j money market investment is rs_{jt}, the dividend yield in country j is dy_{jt}, the forward premium on currency j in terms of U.S. dollars is fp_{jt}. The sample period is 1981 : 1 to 1989 : 12. The monthly data are scaled by 1200 to express returns in percent per annum. Heteroskedasticity consistent standard errors (SE) and associated confidence levels for the test that the coefficient is zero are below the estimates. A superscript a indicates that the coefficient estimate and its SE have been multiplied by 100. The $\chi^2(6)$ statistic tests the joint hypothesis that the six lagged variables have no predictive power. The $\chi^2(5)$ statistic is the Cumby-Huizinga (1992) t-test for serial correlation of the residuals. It is robust to conditional heteroskedasticity and lagged dependent variables. We test five correlation coefficients. The $\chi^2(3)$ statistic tests the joint hypothesis that the three lagged returns have zero coefficients in the forecasting equations.

Dependent Variables	Contant / SE / Confidence	r_{1t} / SE / Confidence	r_{2t} / SE / Confidence	rs_{2t} / SE / Confidence	dy_{1t} / SE / Confidence	dy_{2t} / SE / Confidence	fp_{2t} / SE / Confidence	R^2	$\chi^2(6)$ / Confidence	$\chi^2(5)$ / Confidence	$\chi^2(3)$ / Confidence
	Coefficients on Regressors										
	Panel A: U.S.-Japan										
r_{1t+1}	-60.95 / 54.12 / 0.74	0.13 / 0.12 / 0.72	-0.15 / 0.09 / 0.92	-0.02 / 0.12 / 0.14	31.17 / 17.46 / 0.93	-35.62 / 21.22 / 0.91	-6.97 / 2.37 / 0.99	0.063	24.25 / 0.99	3.59 / 0.39	4.70 / 0.81
r_{2t+1}	92.58 / 40.26 / 0.98	0.19 / 0.11 / 0.92	-0.12 / 0.10 / 0.78	0.05 / 0.14 / 0.30	-28.60 / 13.76 / 0.96	49.02 / 19.64 / 0.99	-1.08 / 2.43 / 0.34	0.052	13.96 / 0.97	3.50 / 0.38	3.12 / 0.63
rs_{2t+1}	60.26 / 26.05 / 0.98	-0.11 / 0.09 / 0.76	0.08 / 0.07 / 0.78	-0.04 / 0.09 / 0.38	-16.71 / 9.44 / 0.92	31.46 / 15.64 / 0.96	-5.48 / 1.97 / 0.99	0.109	16.12 / 0.99	7.13 / 0.79	2.16 / 0.46
dy_{1t+1}	0.35 / 0.20 / 0.92	-0.03^a / 0.05 / 0.46	0.06^a / 0.03 / 0.93	0.02^a / 0.05 / 0.36	0.85 / 0.07 / 0.99	0.15 / 0.08 / 0.95	0.03 / 0.01 / 0.99	0.950	2025 / 0.99	10.29 / 0.93	4.48 / 0.79

continued overleaf

Table III—Continued

Coefficients on Regressors

Dependent Variables	Constant	r_{1t}	r_{2t}	rs_{2t}	dy_{1t}	dy_{2t}	fp_{2t}	R^2	$\chi^2(6)$ Confidence	$\chi^2(5)$ Confidence	$\chi^2(3)$ Confidence
dy_{2t+1}	-0.10	-0.01^a	0.01^a	0.02^a	0.04	0.92	0.004				
SE	0.03	0.01	0.01	0.01	0.01	0.02	0.003	0.989	11807	4.11	4.52
Confidence	0.99	0.78	0.60	0.76	0.99	0.92	0.88		0.99	0.47	0.79
fp_{2t+1}	0.47	0.08^a	0.002	-0.001	-0.08	0.19	0.89				
SE	0.85	0.20	0.002	0.003	0.33	0.48	0.06	0.853	380.2	6.37	2.56
Confidence	0.42	0.34	0.68	0.38	0.18	0.31	0.99		0.99	0.73	0.54
Panel B: U.S.-U.K.											
r_{1t+1}	-79.84	0.13	-0.08	-0.16	27.55	-10.18	-7.22				
SE	48.88	0.16	0.13	0.10	17.50	12.96	2.24	0.041	18.67	6.12	2.89
Confidence	0.90	0.59	0.46	0.90	0.88	0.57	0.99		0.99	0.71	0.59
r_{3t+1}	-82.24	0.41	-0.32	0.01	12.74	6.62	-4.98				
SE	49.91	0.21	0.17	0.13	14.51	13.27	2.64	0.064	6.75	2.48	4.84
Confidence	0.90	0.95	0.95	0.08	0.62	0.38	0.94		0.66	0.22	0.82
rs_{3t+1}	-23.50	-0.12	-0.04	-0.15	4.12	-1.93	-8.15				
SE	27.94	0.10	0.08	0.11	12.11	9.37	2.48	0.172	28.20	9.43	7.98
Confidence	0.60	0.77	0.40	0.84	0.27	0.16	0.99		0.99	0.91	0.95
dy_{1t+1}	0.45	-0.03^a	0.03^a	0.06^a	0.84	0.06	0.03				
SE	0.19	0.06	0.05	0.04	0.09	0.06	0.01	0.949	2137	7.12	2.88
Confidence	0.98	0.42	0.53	0.87	0.99	0.70	0.99		0.99	0.79	0.59
dy_{3t+1}	0.33	-0.13^a	0.11^a	0.02^a	0.06	0.87	0.03				
SE	0.17	0.08	0.06	0.05	0.10	0.08	0.01	0.943	2031	3.31	3.53
Confidence	0.95	0.90	0.92	0.38	0.45	0.99	0.98		0.99	0.35	0.68
fp_{3t+1}	-1.39	-0.10^a	-0.05^a	0.20^a	0.44	-0.19	0.84				
SE	0.86	0.34	0.30	0.20	0.39	0.28	0.07	0.814	269	6.18	2.09
Confidence	0.89	0.22	0.13	0.72	0.75	0.51	0.99		0.99	0.71	0.45

Table III—*Continued*

Coefficients on Regressors

Panel C: U.S.-Germany

Dependent Variables	Contant SE Confidence	r_{1t} SE Confidence	r_{2t} SE Confidence	rs_{2t} SE Confidence	dy_{1t} SE Confidence	dy_{2t} SE Confidence	fp_{2t} SE Confidence	R^2	$\chi^2(6)$ Confidence	$\chi^2(5)$ Confidence	$\chi^2(3)$ Confidence
r_{1t+1}	-7.70	0.12	-0.08	0.02	17.66	-11.58	-5.04	-0.003	9.93	5.45	2.92
	34.36	0.11	0.08	0.11	12.26	7.29	3.70		0.87	0.64	0.60
	0.18	0.76	0.69	0.14	0.85	0.89	0.83				
r_{3t+1}	-7.14	0.26	-0.01	-0.30	13.42	-2.14	-9.39	0.052	13.60	0.69	5.88
	35.18	0.16	0.12	0.17	12.40	8.97	3.83		0.97	0.02	0.88
	0.16	0.90	0.08	0.92	0.72	0.19	0.99				
rs_{3t+1}	54.39	-0.20	-0.10^a	-0.14	6.30	-11.93	-10.07	0.178	38.92	4.28	12.40
	17.97	0.07	4.90	0.10	6.20	5.56	2.19		0.99	0.49	0.99
	0.99	0.99	0.02	0.83	0.69	0.97	0.99				
dy_{1t+1}	0.12	-0.03^a	0.04^a	-0.02^a	0.91	0.05	0.02	0.945	1488	7.56	2.94
	0.13	0.04	0.03	0.04	0.05	0.03	0.02		0.99	0.82	0.60
	0.64	0.58	0.77	0.36	0.99	0.91	0.83				
dy_{3t+1}	0.09	-0.07^a	0.04^a	0.11^a	0.04	0.89	0.04	0.902	935	10.41	3.71
	0.15	0.06	0.05	0.07	0.05	0.07	0.03		0.99	0.94	0.71
	0.46	0.82	0.50	0.90	0.63	0.99	0.79				
fp_{3t+1}	0.23	-0.13^a	0.16^a	-0.14^a	0.26	0.03	0.56	0.493	90.1	15.98	1.23
	0.50	0.19	0.14	0.32	0.26	0.21	0.12		0.999	0.99	0.26
	0.36	0.49	0.73	0.34	0.69	0.13	0.99				

Only for the dollar-DM forward premium does the Cumby-Huizinga (1992) l-test indicate strong evidence against the hypothesis that the residuals are serially uncorrelated. In contrast to the U.S.-Japan VAR, the tests for the significance of lagged returns as predictors indicate that past returns are useful for forecasting the dollar-pound and the dollar-DM foreign exchange market returns.

D. Sensitivity Analysis on the VARs

In the VARs reported above we employ the forward premium as a predictor. From equation (2) notice that the forward premium is the nominal interest rate differential between the U.S. and the other country. Fama and Schwert (1977) used the nominal interest rate to predict equity returns and found a negative coefficient. Here, we examine whether the VAR would be better specified if the two nominal interest rates are entered separately rather than being forced to enter with coefficients that are equal and opposite in sign. Several issues are worth noting.

First, if the true values of the coefficients are equal and opposite in sign, failure to impose a true constraint in a finite sample unnecessarily reduces degrees of freedom and lowers the power of tests. Even if the true values are different, the principle of parsimony (especially in a VAR) dictates imposition of a false constraint if the absolute values are not too different.

A second issue involves the persistence of the variables of the VAR. It is often argued that nominal interest rates are integrated processes (see King, Plosser, Stock, and Watson (1991)). From Table I it is clear that dividend yields are also highly persistent. If two interest rates are included with the two dividend yields, too many variables with near unit roots may be present in the VAR, which might negate the validity of the usual asymptotic distribution theory that we use to generate standard errors and test statistics.

A third issue involves cointegration of the interest rates. If the two nominal interest rates are each integrated processes but the forward premium is stationary, the two interest rates are cointegrated with a cointegrating vector of $(1, -1)$. If the levels of the two variables are included as regressors in an equation in which the dependent variable is stationary, their influence on the dependent variable will enter through the cointegrating relation. That is, the coefficients on the two interest rates will be equal but opposite in sign.

We address these issues in Table IV. Panels A-C report three sets of tests for the three VARs. Since our primary focus is return predictability, we discuss only the evidence for these equations. The first columns report coefficient estimates on the nominal interest rates for each of the three excess returns. The coefficient estimates for the U.S. interest rate are always negative, and the coefficients on the other country interest rate are always positive. The $\chi^2(1)$ statistics test the constraints that the coefficients are equal and opposite in sign. In the U.S.-Japan system there is no evidence against this constraint. In the other two-country systems, only in the U.S.

Table IV

Sensitivity Analysis of the Basic VARs

The numerical subscripts denote countries: 1 for the U.S., 2 for Japan, 3 for the U.K. and 4 for Germany. The VAR of Table III uses six variables: the excess equity market rates of return in the U.S, r_{1t}, and in country j, r_{jt}; the excess dollar rate of return on a currency j money market investment, rs_{jt}; the dividend yield in the U.S, dy_{1t}, and in country j, dy_{jt}; and the forward premium on currency j in terms of U.S. dollars, fp_{jt}. The sample period is 1981:1 to 1989:12. The monthly data are scaled by 1200 to express returns in percent per annum. The second and third columns report the coefficients and standard errors for the levels of the interest rate on the dollar, i_{1t}, and on currency j, i_{jt}, which replace the forward premium in the basic VAR. The fourth column tests the hypothesis that the coefficients on the interest rates are equal and opposite in sign. The fifth and sixth columns report the tests of return predictability, a $\chi^2(T)$, and the R^2. The quasi-differenced specifications enter dividend yields relative to a twenty-four month moving average, the interest differential and a variable constructed by subtracting 0.9 times the lagged interest rate from the current interest rate. The a columns use the quasi-differenced U.S. interest rate, and the b columns use the quasi-differenced foreign country interest rate. Only the statistics for the return equations are presented.

| | VARs with Nominal Interest Rates | | | | | | Quasi-Differenced Specifications | | | |
Dep. Var.	Coefficient i_{1t} (SE)	Coefficient i_{jt} (SE)	$\chi^2(1)$ Confidence	$\chi^2(T)$ Confidence	R^2		$\chi^2(T)^a$ Confidence	R^{2a}	$\chi^2(T)^b$ Confidence	R^{2b}
			Panel A: U.S.-Japan							
r_{1t+1}	-8.298 (2.670)	12.439 (6.447)	0.502 0.522	29.247 0.999	0.079		36.914 0.999	0.074	35.752 0.999	0.075
r_{2t+1}	-1.951 (2.489)	5.116 (8.063)	0.179 0.317	16.398 0.978	0.047		15.462 0.961	0.037	13.139 0.931	0.037
rs_{2t+1}	-4.837 (2.164)	9.657 (5.202)	0.979 0.678	14.056 0.950	0.092		13.933 0.948	0.084	12.800 0.933	0.083
			Panel B: U.S.-U.K.							
r_{1t+1}	-10.904 (2.873)	5.083 (2.613)	4.366 0.963	21.278 0.997	0.072		17.611 0.986	0.032	18.412 0.990	0.027

ctd. overleaf

Table IV — *Continued*

	VARs with Nominal Interest Rates					Quasi-Differenced Specifications			
Dep. Var.	Coefficient i_{1t} (SE)	Coefficient i_{jt} (SE)	$\chi^2(1)$ Confidence	$\chi^2(T)$ Confidence	R^2	$\chi^2(T)^a$ Confidence	R^{2a}	$\chi^2(T)^b$ Confidence	R^{2b}
r_{3t+1}	−6.431 (3.441)	2.607 (3.301)	1.052 0.695	6.613 0.530	0.058	5.890 0.447	0.024	5.793 0.436	0.025
rs_{3t+1}	−8.003 (9.430)	9.430 (2.774)	0.321 0.429	30.771 0.999	0.171	35.167 0.999	0.196	34.382 0.999	0.189
Panel C: U.S.-Germany									
r_{1t+1}	−10.732 (4.320)	4.237 (4.554)	5.648 0.983	21.386 0.997	0.040	14.333 0.954	0.030	13.139 0.931	0.017
r_{4t+1}	−8.493 (4.921)	3.274 (6.210)	1.483 0.777	13.074 0.930	0.035	10.016 0.812	0.038	9.910 0.806	0.042
rs_{4t+1}	−10.969 (2.813)	13.057 (2.951)	0.877 0.651	37.070 0.999	0.187	15.123 0.966	0.051	14.222 0.953	0.049

SE = standard error.

equity market equation is the test statistic sufficiently large to reject the restriction at the 5% level. The next columns report the $\chi^2(7)$ statistics testing overall predictability of returns and the adjusted R^2 statistics. The values of these statistics are not very different from their respective values in Table III. These statistics are all calculated under the assumption that interest rates are stationary.

In order to address the issue of highly persistent variables in the VARs, the last four columns of Table IV report a $\chi^2(7)$ statistic and an adjusted R^2 for two VARs in which the four highly persistent variables enter in a quasi-differenced form. For dividend yields we subtract a moving average of the past twenty-four months from the current dividend yield variable in both specifications. For nominal interest rates we enter the interest differential in both specifications and one quasi-differenced interest rate obtained by subtracting 0.9 times the previous interest rate from the current interest rate. Unless the results on the predictability of returns, reported above, are spurious, the quasi-differenced variables should continue to explain returns although perhaps not with the same explanatory power.

The results are qualitatively quite similar to the specifications reported in levels for the U.S.-Japan and U.S.-U.K. systems. For the U.S.-German system, there is a decline in the statistical significance in all three equations and a substantial reduction in the R^2 of the excess foreign exchange market return.

Given this evidence, we think that the original specification of the VAR is superior to the alternatives. Hence, the next section investigates long-horizon statistics calculated from the VARs of Table III.

E. Estimated Long-Horizon Statistics from the VARs

Tables V, VI, and VII report estimates of the implied long-horizon statistics derived in Section II.A with their associated asymptotic standard errors for the VARs of the U.S.-Japan, the U.S.-U.K., and the U.S.-Germany, respectively. Panel A of each table reports the implied unconditional means, standard deviations, and correlations of the series; Panel B reports several slope coefficients from implied OLS regressions; Panel C reports implied variance ratios; and Panel D reports implied R^2's.

The results for Panel A are very similar across the three sets of countries. The point estimates of the unconditional mean excess returns implied by the VAR are similar in magnitude to the unconditional means calculated directly, but their standard errors are very large.[15] The volatilities of the equity returns are larger than those of the foreign exchange market returns (between 50% and 70% for equities and between 40% and 50% for foreign exchange), and the correlations of the foreign exchange market returns with

---

[15]The large standard errors reflect imprecise estimation of the constant terms in the regressions and the near non-stationarity of the VAR caused by the inclusion of the highly serially correlated dividend yields and forward premiums.

Each Panel B of Tables V–VII reports implied slope coefficients, calculated analogously to equation (7), for the three sets of regressions. In the first two cases the own-country excess equity return compounded over various horizons is implicitly regressed on the own-country divided yield. In the third case, the compound excess foreign exchange return is implicitly regressed on the forward premium. Unfortunately, the large standard errors imply that the statistical significance of the estimates of the implied dividend yield coefficients is generally not as strong as that found in Hodrick (1991).[17] The point estimates reported here are approximately the same size or slightly smaller than their standard errors for the U.S., the U.K., and Germany, and they are generally smaller than their standard errors for Japan.

Interpretation of the point estimates from these implied regressions is facilitated by dividing by the time horizon. The resulting coefficient is the increase in an annualized expected excess return for a 100 basis point increase in a dividend yield. For example, the estimates imply that a 1% increase in the own country dividend yield forecasts an increase in expected returns over the next 48 months of 2% per annum for the U.S., 3% per annum for Japan, 3.5% per annum for Germany, and 4% per annum for the U.K. These results are comparable to those of Fama and French (1988b) whose coefficient estimates imply that U.S. real returns increase by 4% per annum during 48 months when the U.S. dividend yield increases by 1%.

The last sets of implied coefficients in Panel B of Tables V–VII are from the implicit regressions of long-horizon excess foreign exchange returns on the own-market forward premiums. These coefficients are quite significantly different from zero. The coefficients at the one-, three-, six-, and twelve-month horizons are two to five times their standard errors. To interpret these coefficients, remember that the exchange rates are expressed as dollars per foreign currency and the excess rates of return are for uncovered investments in the foreign currency money markets in excess of the U.S. interest rate.

The coefficients at the one-month horizon imply that a one percentage point increase in the forward premium is associated with a 6% per annum decrease in the expected excess rate of return to investing in yen or pounds and an 8% per annum decrease to investing in Deutsche marks. At the twelve-month horizon, the coefficients imply that a one percentage point increase in the forward premium is associated with a 4% per annum decrease in the compound expected excess return from investing in the yen money market. Similar coefficients are found for the other currencies as well.

Each Panel C of Tables V–VII reports the implied long-horizon variance ratios. For the U.S. and the U.K. the point estimates indicate mean

---

[17]Hodrick (1991) uses the three variable VAR of Campbell (1991) composed of real returns, dividend yields and the short-term Treasury bill rate relative to its one year moving average. For a sample of monthly data from 1952 to 1987, the coefficients from the implied OLS regression of returns on dividend yields for comparable horizons to those of Tables III–V are often five to eight times their standard errors. Presumably, both the larger number of variables in the VAR (six vs. three) and the smaller sample size (108 vs. 431 observations) of this paper conspire to increase the standard errors here.

486   *The Journal of Finance*

Table V

Implied Long Horizon Statistics from the U.S.-Japan VAR

The implied long-horizon statistics are functions of the parameters of the vector autoregression. The asymptotic standard errors are calculated as in equation (10) and are in parenthesis below the estimates. The sample period is 1981 : 1 to 1989 : 12. The monthly data are scaled by 1200 to express returns in percent per annum. Panel A reports implied unconditional means and a matrix with the standard deviations on the diagonal and the correlation coefficients on the off-diagonal (see equation (4)). Panel B reports implied slope coefficients from the regression of a compound return for a given horizon onto a particular forecasting variable (see equation (7)). Panel C reports the implied ratio of the variance of returns compounded over a given horizon k to k times the variance of the one period return (see equation (6)). Panel D reports the implied R^2 from the VAR at horizon k which is one minus the ratio of the innovation variance to the total variance (see equation (9)). The numerical subscripts denote countries: 1 for the U.S., 2 for Japan, 3 for the U.K. and 4 for Germany. The excess equity market rate of return in country j is r_{jt}, the excess dollar rate of return on a currency j money market investment is rs_{jt}, the dividend yield in country j is dy_{jt}, the forward premium on currency j in terms of U.S. dollars is fp_{jt}.

	Means						
		Panel A: Implied Means, Standard Deviations and Correlations					
		Standard Deviations and Correlation Matrix:					
		r_{1t}	r_{2t}	rs_{2t}	dy_{1t}	dy_{2t}	fp_{2t}
r_{1t}	6.436	55.677	0.402	-0.028	-0.208	0.019	-0.207
	(5.853)	(7.097)	(0.088)	(0.086)	(0.067)	(0.047)	(0.067)
r_{2t}	13.499		56.935	0.132	-0.259	-0.152	-0.128
	(8.558)		(4.768)	(0.086)	(0.058)	(0.036)	(0.073)
rs_{2t}	1.415			41.839	-0.216	-0.097	-0.382
	(9.115)			(4.054)	(0.113)	(0.101)	(0.150)
dy_{1t}	3.281				0.661	0.811	0.533
	(0.623)				(0.224)	(0.114)	(0.168)
dy_{2t}	0.371					0.304	0.222
	(0.325)					(0.108)	(0.262)
fp_{2t}	2.937						2.125
	(1.094)						(0.541)

Panel B: Implied Slope Coefficients								
Horizon: 1	3	6	12	24	36	48	60	∞
U.S. Return and U.S. Dividend Yield								
7.218	23.302	39.549	57.580	73.096	80.952	86.197	89.965	100.328
(7.325)	(25.357)	(44.156)	(65.789)	(89.815)	(105.431)	(116.315)	(123.897)	(140.084)
Japanese Return and Japanese Dividend Yield								
0.161	2.313	9.271	29.685	71.450	104.494	129.104	147.235	197.458
(13.428)	(38.832)	(73.902)	(135.131)	(228.942)	(294.165)	(338.816)	(368.947)	(423.126)
Forward Bias and Forward Premium								
-6.634	-18.807	-32.805	-49.211	-59.327	-60.572	-60.327	-59.626	-58.719
(1.843)	(5.348)	(10.272)	(18.891)	(31.339)	(39.789)	(46.048)	(50.858)	(64.827)

Characterizing Predictable Components in Excess Returns   487

Table V — *Continued*

Panel C: Implied Variance Ratios

	Means		Standard Deviations and Correlation Matrix:				
Horizon: 1	3	6	12	24	36	48	60
			U.S. Return				
1.000	1.023	0.919	0.768	0.625	0.559	0.521	0.496
(0.000)	(0.184)	(0.176)	(0.136)	(0.130)	(0.142)	(0.156)	(0.169)
			Japanese Return				
1.000	1.024	1.059	1.100	1.112	1.095	1.072	1.049
(0.000)	(0.102)	(0.175)	(0.288)	(0.425)	(0.504)	(0.557)	(0.597)
			Forward Bias				
1.000	1.246	1.594	2.114	2.679	2.936	3.068	3.145
(0.000)	(0.229)	(0.518)	(0.991)	(1.601)	(1.947)	(2.166)	(2.321)
			Dollar-Yen Depreciation				
1.000	1.186	1.460	1.872	2.317	2.513	2.608	2.660
(0.000)	(0.204)	(0.453)	(0.857)	(1.368)	(1.647)	(1.816)	(1.931)
			Dollar Return on Japanese Equity				
1.000	1.234	1.493	1.846	2.182	2.305	2.351	2.367
(0.000)	(0.197)	(0.418)	(0.770)	(1.213)	(1.463)	(1.623)	(1.738)
			Yen Return on U.S. Equity				
1.000	1.046	0.980	0.925	0.933	0.954	0.969	0.978
(0.000)	(0.223)	(0.279)	(0.369)	(0.532)	(0.633)	(0.697)	(0.741)

Panel D: Implied R^2's

Horizon: 1	3	6	12	24	36	48	60
			U.S. Return				
0.075	0.119	0.141	0.125	0.089	0.071	0.061	0.053
(0.044)	(0.079)	(0.100)	(0.101)	(0.100)	(0.100)	(0.098)	(0.094)
			Japanese Return				
0.103	0.128	0.151	0.142	0.093	0.063	0.048	0.039
(0.049)	(0.073)	(0.098)	(0.101)	(0.070)	(0.045)	(0.032)	(0.028)
			Forward Bias				
0.142	0.276	0.318	0.263	0.149	0.095	0.068	0.052
(0.100)	(0.165)	(0.172)	(0.149)	(0.105)	(0.077)	(0.061)	(0.050)

the equity returns are less than $\pm 14\%$ and are insignificantly different from zero.[16]

The dollar forward premiums on the foreign currencies are always negatively correlated with all excess returns. Dividend yields are almost always negatively correlated with all excess returns, and, unsurprisingly, the statistical significance of the correlation of dividend yields with returns is concentrated primarily, but not exclusively, in the own-country equity market. Dividend yields are highly positively correlated across countries (at least 78% in all cases), and they are always positively correlated with the forward premiums.

---

[16]This latter observation forms the basis of recent interest in hedged foreign investment strategies in which the principal on a long-term foreign equity or bond investment is sold in the short-term forward market.

Table VI

Implied Long Horizon Statistics from the U.S.-U.K. VAR

The implied long-horizon statistics are functions of the parameters of the vector autoregression. The asymptotic standard errors are calculated as in equation (10) and are in parenthesis below the estimates. The sample period is 1981:1 to 1989:12. The monthly data are scaled by 1200 to express returns in percent per annum. Panel A reports implied unconditional means and a matrix with the standard deviations on the diagonal and the correlation coefficients on the off-diagonal (see equation (4)). Panel B reports implied slope coefficients from the regression of a compound return for a given horizon onto a particular forecasting variable (see equation (7)). Panel C reports the implied ratio of the variance of returns compounded over a given horizon k to k times the variance of the one period return (see equation (6)). Panel D reports the implied R^2 from the VAR at horizon k which is one minus the ratio of the innovation variance to the total variance (see equation (9)). The numerical subscripts denote countries: 1 for the U.S., 2 for Japan, 3 for the U.K. and 4 for Germany. The excess equity market rate of return in country j is r_{jt}, the excess dollar rate of return on a currency j money market investment is rs_{jt}, the dividend yield in country j is dy_{jt}, the forward premium on currency j in terms of U.S. dollars is fp_{jt}.

Panel A: Implied Means, Standard Deviations and Correlations						
	Means	Standard Deviations and Correlation Matrix:				
		r_{1t}	r_{3t}	rs_{3t}	dy_{1t}	dy_{3t}	fp_{3t}
r_{1t}	4.386	56.297	0.700	−0.005	−0.191	−0.122	−0.187
	(6.112)	(5.918)	(0.066)	(0.088)	(0.052)	(0.065)	(0.063)
r_{3t}	3.173		68.083	0.024	−0.079	−0.106	−0.028
	(5.630)		(6.029)	(0.093)	(0.089)	(0.087)	(0.071)
rs_{3t}	6.592			45.303	−0.228	−0.219	−0.342
	(7.277)			(3.779)	(0.147)	(0.150)	(0.128)
dy_{1t}	3.646				0.875	0.925	0.685
	(0.661)				(0.356)	(0.064)	(0.162)
dy_{3t}	3.646					1.006	0.567
	(0.745)					(0.348)	(0.225)
fp_{3t}	−2.893						2.722
	(1.447)						(0.777)

Panel B: Implied Slope Coefficients								
Horizon: 1	3	6	12	24	36	48	60	∞
		U.S. Return and U.S. Dividend Yield						
2.127	8.715	19.736	41.226	75.000	96.536	109.722	117.728	130.034
(5.672)	(20.072)	(41.450)	(77.962)	(124.343)	(145.204)	(152.639)	(153.944)	(143.896)
		U.K. return and U.K. dividend yield						
8.594	23.262	45.482	84.735	140.433	174.187	194.608	206.972	225.966
(6.719)	(19.184)	(36.960)	(64.600)	(93.862)	(105.533)	(111.603)	(116.245)	(132.688)
		Forward Bias and Forward Premium						
−6.333	−16.786	−29.315	−47.250	−69.008	−81.491	−88.971	−93.491	−100.432
(1.160)	(3.363)	(7.188)	(16.215)	(35.035)	(51.556)	(64.736)	(74.673)	(97.602)

ctd. overleaf

Table VI—*Continued*

Panel C: Implied Variance Ratios

Horizon: 1	Means 3	6	Standard Deviations and Correlation Matrix: 12	24	36	48	60
			U.S. Return				
1.000	1.111	1.161	1.166	1.087	0.997	0.919	0.857
(0.000)	(0.187)	(0.242)	(0.263)	(0.308)	(0.377)	(0.435)	(0.477)
			U.K. Return				
1.000	0.880	0.847	0.792	0.700	0.630	0.577	0.537
(0.000)	(0.111)	(0.142)	(0.157)	(0.167)	(0.180)	(0.189)	(0.194)
			Forward Bias				
1.000	1.103	1.362	1.781	2.366	2.766	3.057	3.276
(0.000)	(0.191)	(0.429)	(0.861)	(1.587)	(2.175)	(2.657)	(3.054)
			Dollar-Pound Depreciation				
1.000	1.034	1.214	1.511	1.929	2.215	2.425	2.582
(0.000)	(0.159)	(0.344)	(0.680)	(1.236)	(1.681)	(2.042)	(2.338)
			Dollar Return on U.K. Equity				
1.000	0.872	0.927	1.014	1.084	1.108	1.119	1.125
(0.000)	(0.119)	(0.199)	(0.318)	(0.489)	(0.618)	(0.719)	(0.799)
			Pound Return on U.S. Equity				
1.000	1.178	1.217	1.221	1.211	1.202	1.196	1.190
(0.000)	(0.185)	(0.268)	(0.368)	(0.545)	(0.688)	(0.798)	(0.883)

Panel D: Implied R^2's

Horizon: 1	3	6	12	24	36	48	60
			U.S. Return				
0.074	0.093	0.096	0.082	0.074	0.075	0.074	0.071
(0.065)	(0.077)	(0.088)	(0.105)	(0.146)	(0.168)	(0.172)	(0.168)
			U.K. Return				
0.111	0.118	0.151	0.196	0.267	0.304	0.314	0.307
(0.102)	(0.112)	(0.151)	(0.215)	(0.305)	(0.341)	(0.346)	(0.339)
			Forward Bias				
0.198	0.319	0.391	0.397	0.331	0.268	0.219	0.181
(0.096)	(0.174)	(0.215)	(0.250)	(0.273)	(0.266)	(0.245)	(0.219)

reversion in stock prices at long horizons, with the U.S. evidence being the strongest in the U.S.-Japan VAR. The 48- and 60-month variance ratios fall to 0.50 or 0.60, which is consistent with the results of Poterba and Summers (1988) and Hodrick (1991). There is no evidence of mean reversion in Japanese or German excess returns. There is slight evidence that German excess equity returns are positively correlated at short horizons since the variance ratios rise to 1.2 at six months. For the excess returns in the foreign exchange market the point estimates indicate that returns are highly positively serially correlated. The variance ratios increase monotonically to above 2.9 for all currencies.

Each Panel D of Tables V–VII reports the implied long-horizon R^2 for the three excess returns. The U.S., Japanese and German excess returns show some predictability at long horizons, but the ratio of explained variance to total variance never rises above 15.1% for these countries. In contrast, the

Table VII

Implied Long Horizon Statistics from the U.S.-Germany VAR

The implied long-horizon statistics are functions of the parameters of the vector autoregression. The asymptotic standard errors are calculated as in equation (10) and are in parenthesis below the estimates. The sample period is 1981:1 to 1989:12. The monthly data are scaled by 1200 to express returns in percent per annum. Panel A reports implied unconditional means and a matrix with the standard deviations on the diagonal and the correlation coefficients on the off-diagonal (see equation (4)). Panel B reports implied slope coefficients from the regression of a compound return for a given horizon onto a particular forecasting variable (see equation (7)). Panel C reports the implied ratio of the variance of returns compounded over a given horizon k to k times the variance of the one period return (see equation (6)). Panel D reports the implied R^2 from the VAR at horizon k which is one minus the ratio of the innovation variance to the total variance (see equation (9)). The numerical subscripts denote countries: 1 for the U.S., 2 for Japan, 3 for the U.K. and 4 for Germany. The excess equity market rate of return in country j is r_{jt}, the excess dollar rate of return on a currency j money market in investment is rs_{jt}, the dividend yield in country j is dy_{jt}, the forward premium on currency j in terms of U.S. dollars is fp_{jt}.

	Means	Standard Deviations and Correlation Matrix					
		\multicolumn{6}{c}{Panel A: Implied Means, Standard Deviations and Correlations}					
r_{1t}	4.584	56.497	0.461	-0.046	-0.186	-0.126	-0.188
	(6.415)	(6.475)	(0.118)	(0.081)	(0.052)	(0.061)	(0.072)
r_{4t}	6.125		70.856	-0.101	-0.061	-0.177	-0.105
	(9.367)		(5.971)	(0.076)	(0.114)	(0.077)	(0.098)
rs_{4t}	6.826			42.602	-0.169	-0.222	-0.355
	(9.079)			(2.845)	(0.122)	(0.121)	(0.098)
dy_{1t}	3.660				0.877	0.776	0.510
	(0.807)				(0.386)	(0.161)	(0.205)
dy_{4t}	3.239					0.915	0.368
	(0.749)					(0.242)	(0.250)
fp_{4t}	2.988						1.537
	(0.740)						(0.391)

Panel B: Implied Slope Coefficients

Horizon:	1	3	6	12	24	36	48	60	∞
\multicolumn{10}{c}{U.S. Return and U.S. Dividend Yield}									
	2.538	9.881	20.191	39.010	67.890	87.105	99.686	107.895	123.269
	(6.472)	(22.990)	(46.300)	(85.844)	(138.777)	(166.844)	(180.436)	(186.183)	(180.468)
\multicolumn{10}{c}{German Return and German Dividend Yield}									
	3.202	13.467	29.098	59.700	109.612	143.626	166.007	180.626	208.014
	(5.568)	(18.210)	(37.702)	(74.659)	(130.985)	(164.804)	(184.399)	(196.070)	(217.750)
\multicolumn{10}{c}{Forward Bias and Forward Premium}									
	-8.096	-18.702	-29.336	-45.237	-67.905	-82.638	-92.236	-98.492	-110.206
	(1.918)	(6.183)	(12.772)	(25.865)	(50.230)	(71.238)	(102.146)	(102.146)	(140.820)

implied R^2 at the 60-month horizon for the U.K. is 31%. The excess returns in the foreign exchange market are more predictable. At the twelve-month horizon the implied R^2's are 26% for the yen, 40% for the pound, and 30% for the mark.

Table VII—*Continued*

Panel C: Implied Variance Ratios							
Means			Standard Deviations and Correlation Matrix				
Horizon: 1	3	6	12	24	36	48	60
U.S. Return							
1.000	1.089	1.089	1.062	0.982	0.907	0.845	0.794
(0.000)	(0.190)	(0.242)	(0.259)	(0.292)	(0.355)	(0.417)	(0.466)
German Return							
1.000	1.162	1.192	1.194	1.150	1.099	1.054	1.017
(0.000)	(0.161)	(0.232)	(0.276)	(0.283)	(0.268)	(0.254)	(0.242)
Forward Bias							
1.000	1.118	1.327	1.643	2.104	2.443	2.703	2.907
(0.000)	(0.173)	(0.346)	(0.643)	(1.151)	(1.586)	(1.960)	(2.282)
Dollar-DM Depreciation							
1.000	1.083	1.258	1.529	1.927	2.220	2.444	2.620
(0.000)	(0.161)	(0.311)	(0.571)	(1.014)	(1.390)	(1.713)	(1.990)
Dollar Return on Germany Equity							
1.000	1.081	1.190	1.308	1.421	1.479	1.515	1.540
(0.000)	(0.131)	(0.218)	(0.322)	(0.486)	(0.637)	(0.770)	(0.884)
DM Return on U.S. Equity							
1.000	1.136	1.143	1.135	1.110	1.089	1.072	1.058
(0.000)	(0.166)	(0.222)	(0.267)	(0.344)	(0.419)	(0.483)	(0.536)

Panel D: Implied R^2's							
Horizon: 1	3	6	12	24	36	48	60
U.S. Return							
0.039	0.055	0.065	0.068	0.067	0.068	0.067	0.065
(0.044)	(0.067)	(0.091)	(0.126)	(0.173)	(0.197)	(0.205)	(0.202)
German Return							
0.096	0.059	0.059	0.078	0.109	0.122	0.124	0.120
(0.081)	(0.075)	(0.104)	(0.164)	(0.232)	(0.252)	(0.250)	(0.238)
Forward Bias							
0.185	0.214	0.256	0.298	0.298	0.265	0.229	0.196
(0.075)	(0.128)	(0.173)	(0.220)	(0.257)	(0.265)	(0.257)	(0.241)

III. Latent Variable Models

This section examines several latent variable models that are constrained counterparts of the excess return equations of the VAR. As in Hansen and Hodrick (1983), we note that these models are not precise tests of a particular equilibrium theory of international asset pricing. Rather, they are best interpreted either as tests motivated by asset pricing theories with additional restrictions or simply as empirical investigations of parsimonious characterizations of the expected excess returns.[18] This analysis is also motivated by Campbell and Hamao (1992) who report latent variable models for the U.S.

---

[18] See Campbell (1987, pp. 394–396) for an extensive discussion relating theoretical intertemporal asset pricing models with additional auxiliary assumptions to empirical latent variable models. See Wheatley (1989) for a critique of the latent variable approach to testing asset pricing models.

and Japanese equity markets with returns denominated in dollars and yen. We include the dollar-yen money market as well.

Some intuition about latent variable models is the following. It is possible that there are K risks in the world economy that are priced and that the expected rates of returns on all assets depend linearly on these risk factors with constant betas. In this case each rate of return in the world economy would have the following representation:

$$E_t(r_{t+1}^i - r_{t+1}^f) = \sum_{k=1}^{K} \beta_{ik} E_t(r_{t+1}^k - r_{t+1}^f). \qquad (11)$$

In equation (11) the r_{t+1}^k are rates of return on portfolios that are perfectly correlated with the sources of risks and r_{t+1}^f is the risk free rate. If Θ is the (N by M) matrix of reduced form coefficients from regressions of N excess returns on M explanatory variables, the K-dimensional latent variable model is the restriction that the rank of Θ is K. The restriction arises because the explanatory power of a regressor must come through its ability to explain one of the K fundamental sources of risk.

Table VIII reports models with a single latent variable for each of the three country pairs, U.S.-Japan in Panel A, U.S.-U.K. in Panel B, and U.S.-Germany in Panel C. In each case, the three excess returns are the U.S. equity return, the foreign country equity return, and the relevant foreign exchange market return. In the VAR there are seven forecasting variables including a constant in each equation. Hence, there are twenty-one free coefficients in the three excess return equations. The single latent variable model constrains the explanatory power of the seven variables to be proportional across the three excess returns.

For example, with $Z_t' = (1, Y_t')$, the U.S.-Japan system is

$$r_{1t+1} = \alpha' Z_t + \varepsilon_{1t+1} \qquad (12)$$

$$r_{2t+1} = \beta_1 \alpha' Z_t + \varepsilon_{2t+1} \qquad (13)$$

$$rs_{2t+1} = \beta_2 \alpha' Z_t + \varepsilon_{3t+1} \qquad (14)$$

which results in nine free parameters or twelve constraints on the VAR coefficients. The nonlinear system of three equations is estimated with GMM using the 21 orthogonality conditions $E_t(\varepsilon_{it+1} Z_t) = 0$, for $i = 1\text{-}3$. Table VIII reports the estimated β as well as the constrained reduced form coefficients.

Models with two latent variables are reported in Table IX. These may be written as

$$r_{1t+1} = \alpha_1' Z_1 + \varepsilon_{1t+1} \qquad (15)$$

$$r_{2t+1} = \alpha_2' Z_t + \varepsilon_{2t+1} \qquad (16)$$

$$rs_{2t+1} = (\beta_1 \alpha_1' + \beta_2 \alpha_2') Z_t + \varepsilon_{3t+1} \qquad (17)$$

which allows sixteen free parameters with twenty-one orthogonality conditions. We report several chi-square statistics that examine the adequacy of the models. If the models are good representations of the data, the chi-square statistics that test the overidentifying restrictions should be small. On the other hand, since there is evidence that each of the excess returns is fore-castable in the unconstrained systems, the chi-square statistics for a particular equation that test the explanatory power of the constrained variables ought to be large.

For the U.S.-Japan system, a confidence level of 0.941 for the test of the overidentifying restrictions indicates evidence against the single latent variable model that is about as strong as the evidence in Campbell and Hamao (1992), who examine just the two excess equity returns. Hence, adding the foreign exchange market with its strong predictability did not strengthen the evidence against the model. Examination of the reduced form coefficients in Table III suggests one reason why the model is inconsistent with the data. In the unconstrained VAR, the own dividend yield enters the own country equity return equation with a positive coefficient and the foreign country excess return equation with a negative coefficient. Since the single latent variable model constrains all of the coefficients of a particular forecasting variable to be the same sign across equations, it clearly cannot fit the data.

In the models with two latent variables in Table IX, the evidence against the constrained U.S.-Japan system is essentially the same as found above, even though there are now only five constraints. The confidence level of the overall test is 0.92. The constrained reduced form coefficients now fit the pattern of the unconstrained system described above, but the explanatory power of the variables in the foreign exchange market equation is not as statistically significant as in the unconstrained system.

For the U.S.-U.K. single latent variable system, the dollar-pound foreign exchange market excess return is not well explained. In the constrained model, the beta for the foreign exchange market is essentially zero. The substantive evidence against the model from the confidence level of the overall test statistic of 0.988 appears to be driven by feedback effects from lagged returns to current returns present in the unconstrained model that cannot be captured in the constrained case.

The model with two latent variables for the U.S.-U.K. system works very well. The value of the chi-square statistic that tests the overidentifying restrictions is less than its mean. Notice that if equations (15) and (16) were estimated as unconstrained equations, β_1 and β_2 in equation (17) would measure the influence of predictable components of the U.S. and U.K. equity returns on the predictable part of the foreign exchange return. Because estimation of the system is done in a constrained way, this interpretation is not literally valid, but the positive β_1 and negative β_2 do suggest the following interpretation. Market forces that increase the U.S. equity risk premium also increase the risk premium on uncovered pound money market investments, and market forces that increase the U.K. equity risk premium also increase the risk premium on uncovered dollar money market invest-ments made with pounds. The statistical significance of the betas suggests that the former effect is more important than the latter.

For the U.S.-German data, the model with two latent variables also works better than the single latent variable model. In the unconstrained VAR there

Table VIII
Models With One Latent Variable

The numerical subscripts denote countries: 1 for U.S., 2 for Japan, 3 for the U.K. and 4 for Germany. The excess equity market rate of return in country j is r_{jt}, the excess dollar rate of return on a currency j money market investment is rs_{jt}, the dividend yield in country j is dy_{jt}, the forward premium on currency j in terms of U.S. dollars is fp_{jt}. The sample period is 1981:1 to 1989:12. The monthly data are scaled by 1200 to express returns in percent per annum. By definition, $Z'_t = [1, r_{1t}, r_{jt}, rs_{jt}, dy_{1t}, dy_{jt}, fp_{jt}]$. The single latent variable model imposes twelve cross equation constraints on the three excess return equations of the VAR as in the following:

$$r_{1t+1} = \alpha' Z_t + \varepsilon_{1t+1}$$
$$r_{jt+1} = \beta_1 \alpha' Z_t + \varepsilon_{2t+1}$$
$$rs_{jt+1} = \beta_2 \alpha' Z_t + \varepsilon_{3t+1}$$

The GMM estimation uses 21 orthogonality conditions; each of the 3 error terms should be orthogonal to the 7 elements of Z_t. The overall test of the model is therefore a $\chi^2(12)$ statistic. The reported parameter estimates are the quasi-reduced-form coefficients, which are β's multiplied by α's. The test of return predictability is the $\chi^2(6)$ statistic.

Dependence Variable	Consistent (SE) Confidence	r_{1t} (SE) Confidence	r_{jt} (SE) Confidence	rs_{jt} (SE) Confidence	dy_{1t} (SE) Confidence	dy_{jt} (SE) Confidence	fp_{jt} (SE) Confidence	$\chi^2(6)$ Confidence
Panel A: U.S.-Japan								
betas (SE)	$\beta_1 = 1.794$ (0.571)		$\beta_2 = 0.628$ (0.358)			$\chi^2(12) = 20.474$ Confidence = 0.941		
r_{1t+1}	54.812 (26.641) 0.960	0.047 (0.046) 0.699	−0.036 (0.040) 0.622	0.002 (0.059) 0.022	−13.947 (8.032) 0.918	23.357 (11.423) 0.959	−2.872 (1.242) 0.979	10.245 0.885
r_{2t+1}	98.323 (34.857) 0.995	0.085 (0.083) 0.691	−0.064 (0.069) 0.645	0.003 (0.105) 0.022	−25.019 (11.415) 0.972	41.899 (15.925) 0.991	−5.151 (1.972) 0.991	25.355 0.999
rs_{2t+1}	34.439 (17.113) 0.956	0.030 (0.032) 0.644	−0.022 (0.025) 0.624	0.001 (0.037) 0.022	−8.763 (4.987) 0.921	14.676 (7.743) 0.942	−1.804 (1.041) 0.917	5.167 0.360

ctd. overleaf

Table VIII—*Continued*

Dependence Variable	Consistent (SE) Confidence	r_{1t} (SE) Confidence	r_{jt} (SE) Confidence	rs_{jt} (SE) Confidence	dy_{1t} (SE) Confidence	dy_{jt} (SE) Confidence	fp_{jt} (SE) Confidence	$\chi^2(6)$ Confidence
Panel B: U.S.-U.K.	betas (SE)	betas (SE)	$\beta_1 = 1.319$ (0.231)	$\beta_2 = -0.003$ (0.246)	$\chi^2(12) = 25.554$ Confidence = 0.988			
r_{1t+1}	-92.228 (36.611) 0.988	0.179 (0.140) 0.799	-0.230 (0.116) 0.952	-0.065 (0.085) 0.557	28.764 (10.465) 0.994	-7.980 (9.607) 0.594	-5.790 (1.771) 0.999	18.833 0.997
r_{3t+1}	-121.615 (46.227) 0.991	0.236 (0.190) 0.786	-0.303 (0.152) 0.954	-0.086 (0.110) 0.563	37.929 (13.284) 0.996	-10.522 (12.685) 0.593	-7.635 (2.320) 0.999	20.043 0.997
rs_{3t+1}	0.300 (22.732) 0.011	-0.001 (0.044) 0.011	0.001 (0.057) 0.011	0.0001 (0.016) 0.010	-0.094 (7.085) 0.011	0.026 (1.963) 0.011	0.019 (1.428) 0.011	0.001 0.001
Panel C: U.S.-Germany	betas (SE)	betas (SE)	$\beta_1 = 2.856$ (1.178)	$\beta_2 = -1.369$ (0.826)	$\chi^2(12) = 16.183$ Confidence = 0.817			
r_{1t+1}	-10.608 (9.745) 0.724	0.119 (0.067) 0.925	-0.005 (0.026) 0.138	-0.070 (0.053) 0.814	4.937 (3.857) 0.799	-1.052 (2.479) 0.329	-1.130 (1.100) 0.696	4.409 0.268
r_{4t+1}	-30.733 (25.839) 0.759	0.341 (0.118) 0.996	-0.013 (0.076) 0.137	-0.200 (0.125) 0.891	14.103 (8.958) 0.885	-3.006 (6.783) 0.342	-3.227 (2.795) 0.752	21.361 0.997
rs_{4t+1}	14.519 (11.726) 0.784	-0.163 (0.057) 0.996	0.006 (0.036) 0.136	0.096 (0.065) 0.863	-6.758 (4.662) 0.853	1.440 (3.327) 0.335	1.546 (1.526) 0.689	11.385 0.877

SE = standard error.

496

The Journal of Finance

Table IX
Models With Two Latent Variables

The numerical subscripts denote countries: 1 for the U.S., 2 for Japan, 3 for the U.K. and 4 for Germany. The excess equity market rate of return in country j is r_{jt}, the excess dollar rate of return on a currency j money market investment is rs_{jt}, the dividend yield in country j is dy_{jt}, the forward premium on currency j in terms of U.S. dollars is fp_{jt}. The sample period is 1981:1 to 1989:12. The monthly data are scaled by 1200 to express returns in percent per annum. By definition, $Z_t' = [1, r_{1t}, r_{jt}, rs_{jt}, dy_{1t}, dy_{jt}, fp_{jt}]$. The model with two latent variables imposes five cross equation constraints on the three excess return equations of the VAR as in the following:

$$r_{1t+1} = \alpha_1' Z_t + \varepsilon_{1t+1}$$

$$r_{jt+1} = \alpha_2' Z_t + \varepsilon_{2t+1}$$

$$rs_{3t+1} = (\beta_1 \alpha_1' + \beta_2 \alpha_2') Z_t + \varepsilon_{3t+1}$$

The GMM estimation uses 21 orthogonality conditions; each of the 3 error terms should be orthogonal to the 7 elements of Z_t. The overall test of the model is the $\chi^2(5)$ statistic. The reported parameter estimates are the quasi-reduced-form coefficients, which are β's multiplied by α's. The test of return predictability is the $\chi^2(6)$ statistic.

Dependence Variable	Consistent (SE) Confidence	r_{1t} (SE) Confidence	r_{jt} (SE) Confidence	rs_{jt} (SE) Confidence	dy_{1t} (SE) Confidence	dy_{jt} (SE) Confidence	fp_{jt} (SE) Confidence	$\chi^2(6)$ Confidence
Panel A: U.S.-Japan								
	betas (SE)		$\beta_1 = 0.052$ (0.236)		$\beta_2 = 0.366$ (0.190)		$\chi^2(5) = 9.840$ Confidence = 0.920	
r_{1t+1}	-63.364 (47.969) 0.813	0.113 (0.113) 0.685	-0.137 (0.079) 0.918	-0.0001 (0.114) 0.001	32.113 (15.514) 0.962	-31.786 (18.805) 0.909	-8.533 (2.174) 0.999	31.786 0.999
r_{2t+1}	93.192 (39.039) 0.983	0.118 (0.103) 0.745	-0.037 (0.074) 0.379	-0.029 (0.116) 0.197	-28.146 (13.618) 0.961	54.880 (19.516) 0.995	-3.833 (2.322) 0.901	20.278 0.998
rs_{2t+1}	30.788 (23.536) 0.809	0.049 (0.047) 0.700	-0.021 (0.038) 0.415	-0.011 (0.044) 0.189	-8.620 (9.033) 0.660	18.420 (12.536) 0.858	-1.849 (1.710) 0.720	5.360 0.384

ctd. overleaf

Table IX—Continued

Dependence Variable	Consistent (SE) Confidence	r_{1t} (SE) Confidence	r_{jt} (SE) Confidence	rs_{jt} (SE) Confidence	dy_{1t} (SE) Confidence	dy_{jt} (SE) Confidence	fp_{jt} (SE) Confidence	$\chi^2(6)$ Confidence
Panel B: U.S.-U.K.	betas (SE)	betas (SE)	$\beta_1 = 1.973$ (0.758)	$\beta_2 = -0.669$ (0.505)		$\chi^2(5) = 3.347$ Confidence $= 0.353$		
r_{1t+1}	-43.575 (23.223) 0.939	0.091 (0.089) 0.695	-0.154 (0.085) 0.930	-0.094 (0.062) 0.873	10.142 (7.542) 0.821	-1.472 (6.016) 0.193	-6.242 (1.660) 0.999	17.988 0.994
r_{3t+1}	-70.814 (37.333) 0.942	0.373 (0.171) 0.971	-0.392 (0.140) 0.995	0.045 (0.114) 0.305	11.154 (12.644) 0.622	6.062 (10.980) 0.419	-4.497 (2.354) 0.944	10.447 0.893
rs_{3t+1}	-38.571 (26.695) 0.852	-0.070 (0.083) 0.601	-0.041 (0.072) 0.430	-0.216 (0.093) 0.980	12.543 (11.644) 0.741	-6.960 (8.023) 0.614	-9.304 (2.463) 0.999	27.180 0.999
Panel C: U.S.-Germany	betas (SE)		$\beta_1 = 4.308$ (4.402)	$\beta_2 = -1.593$ (1.743)		$\chi^2(5) = 5.300$ Confidence $= 0.620$		
r_{1t+1}	13.855 (15.547) 0.627	0.075 (0.073) 0.699	-0.027 (0.044) 0.454	-0.062 (0.063) 0.679	5.508 (4.905) 0.739	-3.886 (4.298) 0.634	-4.946 (2.697) 0.933	6.770 0.657
r_{4t+1}	8.448 (32.230) 0.207	0.310 (0.148) 0.964	-0.059 (0.120) 0.378	-0.121 (0.150) 0.578	10.138 (10.895) 0.648	-3.015 (8.469) 0.278	-7.442 (3.509) 0.966	15.881 0.986
rs_{4t+1}	46.229 (17.275) 0.993	-0.169 (0.066) 0.989	-0.021 (0.048) 0.339	-0.077 (0.094) 0.589	7.579 (5.836) 0.806	-11.937 (5.370) 0.974	-9.453 (2.159) 0.999	37.349 0.999

SE = standard error.

is strong positive feedback from U.S. equity returns to German equity returns but negative feedback from U.S. equity returns to the excess return in the foreign exchange market. This forces the betas in the single latent variable model to have opposite signs and causes the coefficient on the forward premium, which is negative in the unconstrained foreign exchange market equation to be positive in the constrained case. The model with two latent variables works quite well. The test statistics of the overidentifying restrictions has a confidence level of 0.62, and the joint statistical significance of the constrained reduced form coefficients is almost as large as in the unconstrained systems. The estimates of β_1 and β_2 are positive and negative, respectively, although neither is precisely estimated.

A. A Three-Country System

The results of two three-country latent variable models are reported in Table X (one latent variable in Panel A and two latent variables in Panel B). We include the three excess equity returns of the U.S., Japan, and the U.K., and the two foreign exchange market returns for a five equation system. We use a constant, the three dividend yields and the two forward premiums as the instruments in Z_t.[19] The single latent variable system is:

$$r_{1t+1} = \alpha' Z_t + \varepsilon_{1t+1} \tag{18}$$

$$r_{2t+1} = \beta_1 \alpha' Z_t + \varepsilon_{2t+1} \tag{19}$$

$$r_{3t+1} = \beta_2 \alpha' Z_t + \varepsilon_{3t+1} \tag{20}$$

$$rs_{2t+1} = \beta_3 \alpha' Z_t + \varepsilon_{4t+1} \tag{21}$$

$$rs_{3t+1} = \beta_4 \alpha' Z_t + \varepsilon_{5t+1} \tag{22}$$

Hence, there are thirty orthogonality conditions with ten free parameters in the single latent variable model.

The two latent variable model may be written as:

$$r_{1t+1} = \alpha_1' Z_t + \varepsilon_{1t+1} \tag{23}$$

$$r_{2t+1} = \alpha_2' Z_t + \varepsilon_{2t+1} \tag{24}$$

$$r_{3t+1} = (\beta_1 \alpha_1' + \beta_2 \alpha_2') Z_t + \varepsilon_{3t+1} \tag{25}$$

$$rs_{2t+1} = (\beta_3 \alpha_1' + \beta_4 \alpha_2') Z_t + \varepsilon_{4t+1} \tag{26}$$

$$rs_{3t+1} = (\beta_5 \alpha_1' + \beta_6 \alpha_2') Z_t + \varepsilon_{5t+1} \tag{27}$$

which allows eighteen free parameters with thirty orthogonality conditions.

There is evidence against the two models, since the confidence levels for the overall test statistics are 0.980 and 0.893. Nevertheless, in the two latent variable model there is also strong evidence of statistically significant

---

[19] We did not use the two German returns because we considered estimation of a model with seven returns using all dividend yields and all forward premiums as instruments in all equations to be inappropriate given our sample size.

Characterizing Predictable Components in Excess Returns   499

forecasting power for all excess returns but the U.K. equity market. Examination of the significance of the individual coefficients in the constrained reduced form in Panel B reveals an interesting pattern, which should also be interpreted with care given the high correlation of the instruments. Most of the coefficients on the forward premiums are negative, and these variables are important in forecasting the U.S. equity return and the two foreign exchange returns. The U.S. dividend yield has an important negative influence on the Japanese and the U.K. equity returns, but it is insignificant in the U.S. equity equation. The Japanese dividend yield enters all equations positively, and it is most important in the Japanese and U.K. equity equations.

IV. Hansen-Jagannathan (1991) Bounds

The linear predictability of equity and foreign exchange returns across countries documented above is not necessarily inconsistent with equilibrium asset pricing models, although there is currently no dynamic equilibrium model that has been shown to be consistent with it. One way to summarize the implications of this predictability for a rich class of dynamic models is to investigate volatility bounds on investors' IMRS as pioneered by Hansen and Jagannathan (1991).[20] The analysis builds on the observation that if time varying risk premiums are the source of the predictability, there must be volatility in an investor's IMRS.

To understand the derivation of these statistics, recognize that in models of rational maximizing behavior, investment decisions are dictated by intertemporal Euler equations that relate the loss in marginal utility from sacrificing a dollar at time t in purchasing an asset to the expected gain in marginal utility from holding the asset and selling it at time $t + 1$. Let Q_{t+1} be the intertemporal marginal rate of substitution of a dollar between period t and $t + 1$, and let R_{t+1} be a return at $t + 1$ on a dollar invested at t. The typical Euler equation is:

$$E_t(Q_{t+1} R_{t+1}) = 1. \tag{28}$$

Equation (28) is the foundation of many theoretical and empirical investigations of asset pricing. In the most basic representative agent model, e.g., Lucas (1982), the IMRS is

$$Q_{t+1} = \beta U'(C_{t+1}) \pi_{t+1} / U'(C_t) \pi_t, \tag{29}$$

which is the agent's discount factor times the ratio of the marginal utility of consumption at time $t + 1$ multiplied by the purchasing power of a dollar at time $t + 1$ to the product of these variables at time t.

---

[20] Snow (1991) extends the methodology of Hansen and Jagannathan (1991) to extract information about the IMRS from additional moments of the distribution of asset returns. He obtains bounds on moments of the IMRS other than its mean and variance, and he examines the information in returns on portfolios sorted by firm size.

Table X
U.S., Japan, U.K. Latent Variable Models

The five dependent variables are the three equity and two foreign money market excess returns. The instrumental variables for each equation are a constant, the three dividend yields and the two forward premiums. The GMM estimation uses thirty orthogonality conditions; each of the five error terms should be orthogonal to the six instruments. The reported parameter estimates are the quasi-reduced-form coefficients, which are β's multiplied by α's. The test of return predictability is the $\chi^2(5)$ statistic. The numerical subscripts denote countries: 1 for the U.S., 2 for Japan, and 3 for the U.K. The excess equity market rate of return in country j is r_{jt}, the excess dollar rate of return on a currency j money market investment is rs_{jt}, the dividend yield in country j is dy_{jt}, the forward premium on currency j in terms of U.S. dollars is fp_{jt}. The sample period is 1981 : 1 to 1989 : 12. The monthly data are scaled by 1200 to express returns in percent per annum.

Panel A: One Latent Variable

The model with one latent variable imposes twenty cross-equation constraints:

$$r_{1t+1} = \alpha' Z_t + \epsilon_{1t+1}$$
$$r_{2t+1} = \beta_1 \alpha' Z_t + \epsilon_{2t+1}$$
$$r_{3t+1} = \beta_2 \alpha' Z_t + \epsilon_{3t+1}$$
$$rs_{2t+1} = \beta_3 \alpha' Z_t + \epsilon_{4t+1}$$
$$rs_{3t+1} = \beta_4 \alpha' Z_t + \epsilon_{5t+1}$$

The overall test of the model is a $\chi^2(20)$ statistic.

Dependent Variables	Consistent (SE) Confidence	dy_{1t} (SE) Confidence	dy_{2t} (SE) Confidence	dy_{3t} (SE) Confidence	fp_{2t} (SE) Confidence	fp_{3t} (SE) Confidence	$\chi^2(5)$ Confidence
betas (SE)		$\beta_1 = 1.216$ (0.486)	$\beta_2 = 1.312$ (0.412)	$\beta_3 = 0.416$ (0.363)	$\beta_4 = -0.489$ (0.360)	$\chi^2(20) =$ Confidence =	35.019 0.980
r_{1t+1}	-26.848 (21.052) 0.798	8.331 (6.165) 0.823	-0.888 (16.004) 0.044	4.122 (7.147) 0.436	-4.725 (2.076) 0.977	0.221 (1.675) 0.105	9.050 0.893
r_{2t+1}	-32.650 (23.551) 0.834	10.132 (6.840) 0.861	-1.080 (19.449) 0.044	5.013 (8.666) 0.437	-5.749 (2.319) 0.987	0.268 (2.045) 0.104	15.048 0.990

ctd. overleaf

Table X—Continued

Dependent Variables	Consistent (SE) Confidence	dy_{1t} (SE) Confidence	dy_{2t} (SE) Confidence	dy_{3t} (SE) Confidence	fp_{2t} (SE) Confidence	fp_{3t} (SE) Confidence	$\chi^2(5)$ Confidence
betas (SE)		$\beta_1 = 1.216$ (0.486)	$\beta_2 = 1.312$ (0.412)	$\beta_3 = 0.416$ (0.363)	$\beta_4 = -0.489$ (0.360)	$\chi^2(20) =$ Confidence =	35.019 0.980

Panel A: One Latent Variable

Dependent Variables	Consistent (SE) Confidence	dy_{1t} (SE) Confidence	dy_{2t} (SE) Confidence	dy_{3t} (SE) Confidence	fp_{2t} (SE) Confidence	fp_{3t} (SE) Confidence	$\chi^2(5)$ Confidence
r_{3t+1}	-35.238 (26.296) 0.820	10.935 (7.650) 0.847	-1.166 (21.021) 0.044	5.410 (9.385) 0.436	-6.201 (2.473) 0.988	0.289 (2.201) 0.105	16.129 0.994
rs_{2t+1}	-11.169 (11.337) 0.675	3.466 (3.541) 0.672	-0.370 (6.608) 0.045	1.715 (3.007) 0.432	-1.965 (1.584) 0.785	0.092 (0.699) 0.104	1.784 0.122
rs_{3t+1}	13.136 (11.317) 0.754	-4.076 (3.303) 0.783	0.435 (7.749) 0.045	-2.017 (3.442) 0.442	2.312 (1.454) 0.888	-0.108 (0.801) 0.107	3.083 0.313

Panel B: Two Latent Variables

The model with two latent variables imposes twelve cross-equation constraints:

$$r_{1t+1} = \alpha_1' Z_t + \varepsilon_{1t+1}$$

$$r_{2t+1} = \alpha_2' Z_t + \varepsilon_{2t+1}$$

$$rs_{1t+1} = \left(\beta_1 \alpha_1' + \beta_2 \alpha_2'\right) Z_t + \varepsilon_{3t+1}$$

$$rs_{2t+1} = \left(\beta_3 \alpha_1' + \beta_4 \alpha_2'\right) Z_t + \varepsilon_{4t+1}$$

$$rs_{3t+1} = \left(\beta_5 \alpha_1' + \beta_6 \alpha_2'\right) Z_t + \varepsilon_{5t+1}$$

The overall test of the model is a $\chi^2(12)$ statistic.

The Journal of Finance

Table X — Continued

Dependent Variables	Consistent (SE) Confidence	dy_{1t} (SE) Confidence	dy_{2t} (SE) Confidence	dy_{3t} (SE) Confidence	fp_{2t} (SE) Confidence	fp_{3t} (SE) Confidence	$\chi^2(5)$ Confidence
betas (SE) Confidence	$\beta_1 = 0.351$ (0.401)	$\beta_2 = 0.464$ (0.209)	$\beta_3 = 0.901$ (0.489)	$\beta_4 = -0.109$ (0.277)	$\beta_5 = 2.064$ (0.883)	$\beta_6 = -0.519$ (0.519)	$\chi^2(12) = 18.29$ Confidence = 0.893
			Panel B: Two Latent Variables				
r_{1t+1}	5.363 (25.718) 0.165	2.370 (8.455) 0.221	22.905 (16.297) 0.840	-9.533 (6.694) 0.846	-0.171 (1.357) 0.100	-5.033 (1.730) 0.996	15.803 0.993
r_{2t+1}	101.477 (40.318) 0.988	-32.490 (12.415) 0.991	76.680 (33.145) 0.979	-5.839 (16.918) 0.270	-1.020 (3.371) 0.238	-3.653 (3.183) 0.749	17.617 0.997
r_{3t+1}	48.975 (33.766) 0.853	-14.248 (10.117) 0.841	43.616 (24.585) 0.924	-6.051 (9.895) 0.459	-0.533 (1.921) 0.219	-3.460 (2.617) 0.814	6.204 0.713
rs_{2t+1}	-6.260 (19.077) 0.257	5.678 (6.907) 0.590	12.256 (12.608) 0.669	-7.951 (5.049) 0.885	-0.042 (0.961) 0.035	-4.136 (1.565) 0.992	12.650 0.973
rs_{3t+1}	-41.663 (27.349) 0.872	21.765 (11.263) 0.947	7.464 (19.312) 0.301	-16.648 (8.750) 0.943	0.177 (1.922) 0.073	-8.493 (2.566) 0.999	26.623 0.999

SE = standard error.

Characterizing Predictable Components in Excess Returns   503

Hansen and Jagannathan (1991) use data on returns to compute bounds on the variability of an agent's real IMRS that any model implying an Euler equation like (28) must satisfy. Whereas Hansen and Jagannathan (1991) investigate real returns using only U.S. dollar assets, we consider the nominal IMRS and use dollar returns on domestic and international investments to see if this makes the bounds more restrictive. Below, we discuss the variability of the IMRS that is implied by parameterizing and simulating an international extension of equation (29) after we discuss the estimation of the bounds.

Bounds on the variability of Q_{t+1} using excess returns are derived as follows. Let x_{t+1} denote a vector of n excess returns. One can think of these excess returns as dollar payoffs on assets that have zero prices. From equation (28), by the law of iterated expectations, we know that

$$E(Q_{t+1}x_{t+1}) = 0. \tag{30}$$

Let P denote the space spanned by x_{t+1}, and let P^a be the space P augmented with a unit payoff. If Q_{t+1} were observable, we could run a regression of Q_{t+1} on a constant and x_{t+1} to recover the linear projection of Q_{t+1} onto P^a. The predicted part of Q_{t+1} would be $\alpha + \beta' x_{t+1}$. Because there will typically be a projection error, the variance of the nominal IMRS, which is the dependent variable in the regression, must be greater than $\beta' \Sigma \beta$, which is the variance of the explained part of Q_{t+1}, where Σ is the unconditional covariance matrix of x_{t+1}. From the algebra of least squares, we know that the true projection coefficient is:

$$\begin{aligned} \beta &= \Sigma^{-1}\big[E(Q_{t+1}x_{t+1}) - E(Q_{t+1})E(x_{t+1})\big] \\ &= -\Sigma^{-1}E(Q_{t+1})E(x_{t+1}). \end{aligned} \tag{31}$$

By substituting from equation (31) into $\beta' \Sigma \beta$, it is straightforward to derive a bound on the variance of Q_{t+1}:

$$\sigma^2(Q_{t+1}) > \big[E(Q_{t+1})\big]^2 E(x_{t+1})' \Sigma^{-1}E(x_{t+1}). \tag{32}$$

Since $E(Q_{t+1})$ is unobservable, we obtain a bound on the coefficient of variation of the nominal IMRS implied by the mean and the variance of excess dollar returns:

$$\frac{\sigma(Q_{t+1})}{E(Q_{t+1})} > \big(E(x_{t+1})' \Sigma^{-1}E(x_{t+1})\big)^{1/2}. \tag{33}$$

Notice that if only one excess return is used, the bound is immediately given by rewriting equation (30) as $\mathrm{cov}(Q_{t+1}, x_{t+1}) + E(Q_{t+1})E(x_{t+1}) = 0$ and using the Cauchy-Schwarz inequality. The bound then restricts the coefficient of variation of the nominal IMRS to be greater than or equal to the Sharpe ratio of the excess return, i.e., $|E(x_{t+1})|/\sigma(x_{t+1})$. The right-hand-side of equation (33) is similarly the Sharpe ratio of the return on a portfolio formed

The Journal of Finance

Table XI

Hansen-Jagannathan (1991) Bounds on the Coefficient of Variation of the Nominal Dollar Intertemporal Marginal Rate of Substitution

All returns are dollar denominated. The sample period is 1981 : 1 to 1989 : 12. The bound is the right-hand-side of equation (33). The unscaled bounds use excess returns. The scaled bounds use excess returns and pseudo excess returns generated by scaling an equity return with the lagged own dividend yield and a foreign exchange return with the lagged own forward premium. The cross-scaled bounds use both the excess returns and the scaled returns with additional pseudo returns generated by scaling an equity return with the lagged dollar-yen forward premium and a foreign exchange return with the lagged U.S. dividend yield. Standard errors are in parenthesis and are calculated using a Taylor's series approximation and three Newey-West (1987) lags.

Excess Returns Included in the Tests	Bound (unscaled) (SE)	Bound (scaled) (SE)	Bound (cross-scaled) (SE)
U.S. Equity	0.112 (0.153)	0.116 (0.100)	0.337 (0.086)
Japanese Equity	0.225 (0.210)	0.239 (0.095)	0.410 (0.069)
U.K. Equity	0.100 (0.107)	0.103 (0.093)	0.271 (0.064)
German Equity	0.128 (0.148)	0.183 (0.101)	0.381 (0.074)
Japanese Foreign Exchange	0.004 (0.111)	0.320 (0.082)	0.320 (0.082)
U.K. Foreign Exchange	0.060 (0.133)	0.394 (0.068)	0.405 (0.075)
German Foreign Exchange	0.045 (0.127)	0.319 (0.066)	0.337 (0.073)
U.S. Equity, Japanese Equity and Foreign Exchange	0.305 (0.098)	0.474 (0.097)	0.598 (0.093)
U.S. Equity, U.K. Equity and Foreign Exchange	0.181 (0.111)	0.474 (0.068)	0.579 (0.089)
U.S. Equity, German Foreign Exchange	0.181 (0.124)	0.384 (0.093)	0.519 (0.097)
Japanese, U.K. and German Foreign Exchange	0.077 (0.104)	0.477 (0.075)	0.479 (0.077)
U.S., Japanese, U.K. and German Equity	0.237 (0.105)	0.301 (0.089)	0.585 (0.080)
U.S. Equity, Japanese, U.K., and German Equity and Foreign Exchange	0.331 (0.111)	0.641 (0.088)	0.776 (0.083)

with the excess returns x_{t+1}, where the portfolio weights are given by the optimal portfolio in a mean-variance framework.

Table XI provides estimates of a variety of volatility bounds for the dollar IMRS calculated from our dollar denominated domestic and foreign excess returns. The column labelled (unscaled) contains bounds derived using only the raw excess returns listed in the first column. The bounds estimated only with foreign exchange investments are not very demanding (they are never larger than 0.07), nor are they precisely estimated. The volatility bound implied by all the equity market investments is 0.237. Using all of the foreign exchange returns with all of the equity market returns increases the bound to 0.331, which is not much larger than the bound implied by considering the Japanese foreign exchange and equity returns with the U.S. excess equity return.

Hansen and Jagannathan (1991) note that the payoff space can be increased by considering returns that are scaled by elements in the agents' information set. Essentially, scaling a return based on the realization of a random variable amounts to changing the investment in an asset as in a trading rule. The return from a trading rule is different from the return on the underlying asset. The empirical results from this paper suggest that incorporating conditioning information should be important because the returns are forecastable.[21]

The column of Table XI labeled (scaled) reports bounds generated from using the original unscaled excess returns and the scaled excess returns. The scaling factors are the own dividend yields for equity returns and the own forward premiums for the foreign exchange returns. The column labeled (cross-scaled) adds additional pseudo returns constructed by scaling the equity returns with the dollar-yen forward premium and the foreign exchange returns with the U.S. dividend yield.

For the scaled bounds, except for Germany, the use of dividend yields tends not to increase the volatility bounds, while the effect of using the forward premiums with the foreign exchange returns is dramatic. Whenever a foreign exchange return that is scaled by its forward premium is included in the analysis, the bound invariably exceeds 0.30 with a standard error less than 0.10. The volatility bound implied by all of our excess returns including the scaled ones is 0.641 with a standard error of 0.088.

Cross-scaling the equity returns with the dollar-yen forward premium tends to increase the volatility bounds quite substantially, but the effect of scaling the foreign exchange returns with the U.S. dividend yield is minimal. The volatility bound implied by all assets rises to 0.776 with a standard error of 0.083.

These bounds can be compared to some benchmarks provided by Bekaert (1991), who simulates a two country, general equilibrium, Lucas (1982) model using an estimated VAR of two money growth rates and two

---

[21]Gallant, Hansen, and Tauchen (1990) discuss efficient use of conditioning information using seminonparametric methods.

consumption growth rates to provide realistic exogenous processes.[22] Intertemporal preferences are separable across periods, and the period utility function is parameterized with constant relative risk aversion (CRRA) preferences. Equation (29) applies with consumption measured as a geometric average of foreign and home goods with equal weights on the two goods. For a risk aversion coefficient of 2, the coefficient of variation of Q_{t+1} is of the order 0.010. To obtain bounds on the coefficient of variation of Q_{t+1} of around 0.2, the CRRA coefficient must be increased to over 40. Obtaining a bound of 0.78 requires a CRRA coefficient over 140.

Hansen and Jagannathan (1991) report bounds that are less restrictive than the ones we report, except when they examine returns from the U.S. Treasury bill market. They argue that such restrictive bounds may be incorrectly estimated since Treasury bills may provide liquidity services to investors who hold them to maturity as cash substitutes. While this argument may apply to money market investments, we find bounds that are equally restrictive using only equity returns. The bound from the four equity returns, including the scaled and cross-scaled pseudo returns, is 0.585 with a standard error of 0.080.

V. Conclusions

In this paper we characterize the linear predictability of excess returns in major equity and foreign exchange markets. Variables such as dividend yields, that were known to predict excess equity returns, are demonstrated to have predictive power for excess returns in the foreign exchange market. Similarly, variables such as forward premiums, that were known to predict excess returns in the foreign exchange market, are demonstrated to have predictive power for excess equity returns. We establish these results in VAR that allow calculation of a variety of long-horizon statistics.

We find evidence of long-horizon mean reversion in stock prices in the U.S. and the U.K., but not in Japan or Germany. The excess returns in the foreign exchange market have strong positive persistence. This implies, for example, that a U.S. investor faces mean reversion in the U.S. equity market, but not in the dollar-denominated Japanese equity market, and from the Japanese perspective, there is no evidence of mean reversion in the Japanese equity market nor in the yen-denominated return on the U.S. equity market.

We investigate the implications of a change in the dividend yield for long-horizon equity returns finding that a 1% increase in dividend yields implies between a 2–4% per annum increase in expected returns over the next forty-eight months. Increases in the forward premium on foreign currencies imply large decreases in excess returns in the foreign exchange market

---

[22] Bekaert (1991) uses data from the U.S. and Japan. The consumption data are quarterly non-durables and services obtained from the OECD, and the money stocks are measures of M2 from International Financial Statistics.

that are quite significant at shorter horizons. The forecasting power of the forward premium (that appears so puzzling to some researchers in the foreign exchange market) is also present in the equity excess returns. Increases in the forward premium (dollars/foreign currency) forecast lower expected excess equity returns in all countries.[23] Latent variable models, which are constrained counterparts to the VAR analysis, require at least two latent variables to capture the covariance structure of excess returns, but even these models are not successful.

Our final results demonstrate that bounds on the nominal dollar IMRS derived from considering U.S. investments jointly with foreign money market and stock market investments with appropriate conditioning information are considerably higher than those obtained when attention is restricted only to the U.S. excess equity return. Whether the predictability of returns and the derived volatility bounds represent evidence of highly variable risk premiums, regime switching, peso problems, learning about policy changes, or market inefficiencies remains an open question.

REFERENCES

Bekaert, Geert, 1991, Exchange rate volatility and deviations from unbiasedness in cash-in-advance models, Working paper, Northwestern University.

—— and Robert J. Hodrick, 1991, On biases in the measurement of foreign exchange risk premiums, National Bureau of Economic Research Working Paper No. 3861.

Bilson, John F. O., 1981, The speculative efficiency hypothesis, *Journal of Business* 54, 433–451.

Breen, William, Lawrence R. Glosten, and Ravi Jagannathan, 1989, Economic significance of predictable variations in stock index returns, *Journal of Finance* 44 (December), 1177–1190.

Campbell, John Y., 1991, A variance decomposition for stock returns, *Economic Journal* 101, 157–179.

—— and Yasushi Hamao, 1992, Predictable stock returns in the United States and Japan: A study of long-term capital market integration, *Journal of Finance* 47, 43–69.

—— and Robert J. Shiller, 1988, The dividend-price ratio and expectations of future dividends and discount factors, *The Review of Financial Studies* 1, 195–228.

Chan, K. C., G. Andrew Karolyi, and René M. Stulz, 1991, Global financial markets and the risk premium on U.S. equity, Working paper, The Ohio State University.

Cochrane, John H., 1988, How big is the random walk component of GNP? *Journal of Political Economy* 96, 893–920.

——1990, Explaining the variance of price-dividend ratios, Working paper, University of Chicago.

Cumby, Robert E., 1988, Is it risk? Explaining deviations from uncovered interest parity, *Journal of Monetary Economics* 22, 279–300.

——, 1990, Consumption risk and international equity returns: Some empirical evidence, *Journal of International Money and Finance* 9, 182–192.

—— and John Huizinga, 1990, The predictability of real exchange rate changes in the short and long run, forthcoming in *Japan and the World Economy*.

—— and John Huizinga, 1992, Testing the autocorrelation structure of disturbances in ordinary least squares and instrumental variables regressions, *Econometrica*, 60, 185–195.

---

[23]See Froot (1990) for a recent investigation of short-term nominal interest rates as predictors of returns on a variety of assets. Froot argues that risk premiums cannot be the source of the predictive power because the nominal interest rates have similar predictive power for the forecast errors from surveys of expected returns.

Cutler, David M., James M. Poterba, and Lawrence H. Summers, 1989, International evidence on the predictability of stock returns, Working paper, Massachusetts Institute of Technology.

Fama, Eugene F. and Kenneth R. French, 1988a, Permanen and temporary components of stock prices, *Journal of Political Economy* 96, 246–273.

—— and Kenneth R. French, 1988b, Dividend yields and expected stock returns, *Journal of Financial Economics* 22, 3–26.

—— and G. William Schwert, 1977, Asset returns and inflation, *Journal of Financial Economics* 5, 115–146.

Ferson, Wayne E., 1989, Changes in expected security returns, risk, and the level of interest rates, *Journal of Finance* 44 (December), 1191–1217.

Froot, Kenneth A., 1990, Short rates and expected asset returns, Working paper, Massachusetts, Institute of Technology.

—— and Richard H. Thaler, 1990, Anomalies: Foreign exchange, *Journal of Economic Perspectives* 4, 179–192.

Gallant, A. Ronald, Lars Peter Hansen, and George Tauchen, 1990, Using conditional moments of asset payoffs to infer the volatility of intertemporal marginal rates of substitution, *Journal of Econometrics* 45, 141–179.

Gibbons, Michael R. and Wayne E. Ferson, 1985, Testing asset pricing models with changing expectations and an unobservable market portfolio, *Journal of Financial Economics* 14, 217–236.

Giovannini, Alberto and Philippe Jorion, 1987, Interest rates and risk premia in the stock market and in the foreign exchange market, *Journal of International Money and Finance* 6, 107–123.

—— and Philippe Jorion, 1989, Time variation of risk and return in the foreign exchange and stock markets, *Journal of Finance* 44, 307–326.

Gultekin, N. Bulent, 1983, Stock market returns and inflation: Evidence from other countries, *Journal of Finance* 38, 49–66.

Hansen, Lars Peter, 1982, Large sample properties of generalized method of moments estimators, *Econometrica* 50, 1029–1054.

—— and Robert J. Hodrick, 1983, Risk averse speculation in the forward foreign exchange market: An econometric analysis of linear models, in Jacob A. Frenkel, ed.: *Exchange Rates and International Macroeconomics* (University of Chicago Press, Chicago, IL).

—— and Ravi Jagannathan, 1991, Implications of security market data for models of dynamic economies, *Journal of Political Economy* 99, 225–262.

Harvey, Campbell R., 1991, The world price of covariance risk, *Journal of Finance* 46, 111–158.

Hodrick, Robert J., 1987, *The Empirical Evidence on the Efficiency of Forward and Futures Foreign Exchange Markets* (Harwood Academic Publishers, Chur, Switzerland).

——, 1991, Dividend yields and expected stock returns: Alternative procedures for inference and measurement, Finance Department Working Paper No. 88, Northwestern University.

Huizinga, John, 1987, An empirical investigation of the long-run behavior of real exchange rates, in Karl Brunner and Allan H. Meltzer, eds.: *Empirical Studies of Velocity, Real Exchange Rates, Unemployment and Productivity*, vol. 27, Carnegie-Rochester Conference Series on Public Policy (North-Holland Publishing, Amsterdam, The Netherlands).

Kandel, Shmuel and Robert F. Stambaugh, 1988, Modeling expected stock returns for long and short horizons, Working paper, University of Chicago.

Kaminsky, Graciela and Rodrigo Peruga, 1990, Can a time-varying risk premium explain excess returns in the forward market for foreign exchange? *Journal of International Economics* 28, 47–70.

Keim, Donald B. and Robert F. Stambaugh, 1986, Predicting returns in the stock and bond markets, *Journal of Financial Economics* 17, 357–390.

King, Robert G., Charles I. Plosser, James H. Stock, and Mark W. Watson, 1991, Stochastic trends and economic fluctuations, *American Economic Review* 81, 819–840.

Korajczyk, Robert A. and Claude Viallet, 1990, Equity risk premia and the pricing of foreign exchange risk, Finance Department Working Paper No. 758 Northwestern University.

Lo, Andrew W. and A. Craig MacKinlay, 1988, Stock market prices do not follow random walks: Evidence from a simple specification test, *The Review of Financial Studies* 1, 41-66.

Lucas, Robert E. Jr., 1982, Interest rates and currency prices in a two-country world, *Journal of Monetary Economics* 10, 335-360.

Mark, Nelson C., 1988, Time-varying betas and risk premia in the pricing of forward foreign exchange contracts, *Journal of Financial Economics* 22, 335-354.

Newey, Whitney K. and Kenneth D. West, 1987, A simple, positive semi-definite, heteroskedasticity and autocorrelation consistent covariance matrix, *Econometrica* 55, 703-708.

Poterba, James M. and Lawrence H. Summers, 1988, Mean reversion in stock prices: Evidence and implications, *Journal of Financial Economics* 22, 27-59.

Rozeff, Michael, 1984, Dividend yields are equity risk premiums, *Journal of Portfolio Management*, 68-75.

Shiller, Robert J., 1984, Stock prices and social dynamics, *Brookings Papers on Economic Activity* 2, 457-498.

Schwarz, G., 1978, Estimating the dimension of a model, *The Annals of Statistics* 6, 461-464.

Snow, Karl N., 1991, Diagnosing asset pricing models using the distribution of asset returns, *Journal of Finance* 46, 955-983.

Solnik, Bruno, 1983, The relation between stock prices and inflationary expectations: The international evidence, *Journal of Finance* 38, 35-48.

——, 1990, Predictability of foreign asset returns, Working paper, Groupe HEC-School of Management.

Tryon, Ralph, 1979, Testing for rational expectations in the foreign exchange market, Board of Governors of the Federal Reserve System, International Finance Discussion Paper No. 139.

Wheatley, Simon M., 1989, A critique of latent variable tests of asset pricing models, *Journal of Financial Economics* 23, 325-338.

[13]

Journal of Financial Economics 32 (1992) 137–167. North-Holland

Global financial markets and the risk premium on U.S. equity*

K.C. Chan, G. Andrew Karolyi, and René M. Stulz**

Ohio State University, Columbus, OH 43210, USA

Received August 1991, final version received February 1992

There is a significant foreign influence on the risk premium for U.S. assets. Using a bivariate GARCH-in-mean process, we find that the conditional expected excess return on U.S. stocks is positively related to the conditional covariance of the return of these stocks with the return on a foreign index but is not related to its own conditional variance. Further, we are unable to reject the international version of the CAPM. We present evidence for different model specifications, multiple-day returns, and alternative proxies for foreign stock returns.

1. Introduction

What drives the risk premium on U.S. equity? If the U.S. capital markets are segmented from foreign markets or if U.S. assets constitute most of the wealth traded internationally, the risk premium on U.S. assets should be determined solely in the U.S. Until the mid-1970s, these conditions seemed to prevail. Since

Correspondence to: G. Andrew Karolyi, Department of Finance, Ohio State University, 318 Hagerty Hall, Columbus, OH 43210-1309, USA.

*The authors thank participants in seminars at Concordia University, Queen's University, Vanderbilt University, the University of Western Ontario, Indiana University, the University of Chicago, Massachusetts Institute of Technology, the University of Minnesota, Ohio State University, Notre Dame University, the NBER Conference on International Asset Pricing in Philadelphia, the Western Economics Association meetings in Seattle, the European Finance Association meetings in Rotterdam, the Johnson Symposium at the University of Wisconsin, and the Pacific-Basin Capital Markets Research Conference in Seoul for useful comments. We are grateful to Warren Bailey, Tim Bollerslev, Stephen Brown, George Constantinides, Robert Cumby, Wayne Ferson, Stephen Foerster, Robert Hodrick, John Huizinga, Ravi Jagannathan, Patric Hendershott, Robert Korajczyk, Craig Lewis, Andrew Lo, Thomas McCurdy, Richard Roll, Paul Seguin, Lemma Senbet, Henri Servaes, Robert Stambaugh, Simon Wheatley, and especially the referee, Campbell Harvey, and editor, William Schwert. James Tompkins and Darrell Lee provided helpful research assistance. K.C. Chan and Andrew Karolyi thank the Dice Center for Financial Economics at Ohio State University for partial funding.

**René M. Stulz is also affiliated with the National Bureau of Economic Research, Cambridge, MA 02138, USA.

then, capital markets have become increasingly integrated internationally and the market value of U.S. assets has become a smaller fraction of world wealth. These developments suggest that the risk premium on U.S. assets may now be determined primarily on world capital markets. We investigate this issue and find empirical evidence of a significant foreign influence on the risk premium of U.S. assets.

The capital asset pricing model (CAPM) implies that the risk of the market portfolio is measured by the variance of its returns, so that the risk premium for the market portfolio increases with the variance of its returns. Further, with risk-averse investors, the addition of a mean-preserving spread to the distribution of the market portfolio return increases the risk premium, so that even if the CAPM does not hold, one would typically expect a positive relation between the risk premium and the variance of the market portfolio. Merton (1980) estimates the relation between the risk premium and volatility using contemporaneous variance estimates. Using a generalized autoregressive conditional hetero-skedasticity (GARCH) representation developed by Engle (1982) and Bollerslev (1986), French, Schwert, and Stambaugh (1987) provide evidence that the conditional expected excess returns on the market portfolio and the conditional variance of its returns are positively related. They use daily data from January 1928 to December 1984 for the excess returns on the market with Standard and Poor's (S&P) 500 index representing the market portfolio.

For most of the sample period studied by French, Schwert, and Stambaugh, foreign capital markets were substantially segmented from the U.S. capital markets and their capitalization value was much smaller. There is now substantial evidence that stock markets are reasonably well integrated. For instance, Cho, Eun, and Senbet (1986), Wheatley (1988), Korajczyk and Viallet (1989), Gultekin, Gultekin, and Penati (1989), Cumby (1990), Harvey (1991), Bekaert and Hodrick (1992), and Campbell and Hamao (1992) provide evidence of integration, especially during the 1980s, using a variety of asset pricing models with monthly data. Further, as fig. 1 indicates, the capitalization of U.S. stocks has become a smaller part of the capitalization of the world market portfolio of common stocks. These two developments suggest that the S&P 500 is unlikely to have been an adequate proxy for the world market portfolio over the last decade.

If we use the CAPM, the evidence that stock markets are fairly well integrated suggests that the risk premium on the market portfolio of U.S. assets depends on the covariance of its returns with the returns on the world market portfolio. This covariance is a weighted average of the variance of the market portfolio of U.S. assets and the covariance of the returns on the market portfolio of U.S. assets with the market portfolio of non-U.S. assets, where the weights are the proportions of U.S. and foreign stocks in the world market portfolio. Even if the CAPM does not hold, this covariance may be important in determining the risk premium on the U.S. market portfolio. For instance in Merton's (1973) intertemporal CAPM, the risk premium on a portfolio still increases with the covariance of the returns of that portfolio with the market portfolio.

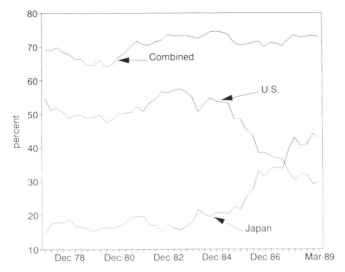

Fig. 1. Market capitalization of the U.S. and Japanese equity markets from 1978 to 1989 as proportion of total world equity market capitalization. The market values for the U.S. and Japanese stocks are drawn from various quarterly issues of Morgan Stanley's *Capital International Perspectives*.

In our empirical work, we model the daily excess returns of the S&P 500 and of a portfolio of non-U.S. assets jointly, using a bivariate GARCH-in-mean representation. We find that the conditional expected excess returns on the U.S. market portfolio are significantly related to the conditional covariance of the S&P 500 with Japan's Nikkei 225 index, but not significantly to the conditional variance of the S&P 500. We obtain a similar though weaker result if the market portfolio of foreign assets is approximated by the Morgan Stanley EAFE index (which is a value-weighted index comprising stocks from Europe, Australia, and the Far East) or the Morgan Stanley Japan index. We also show that this result is robust to a number of alternative econometric specifications as well as to different measurement intervals for the returns data. This result suggests that the impact of foreign stock markets on the risk premium of the U.S. market portfolio cannot be neglected.

When we impose the restrictions of the international version of the CAPM, we find that we cannot reject the model at the 5 percent significance level. Given the small number of assets in our tests, however, one might argue that this significance level is too low. At the 10 percent level, the model is rejected when we use the Nikkei indices, but not otherwise. Further, at that level of significance, we cannot reject a two-factor model that implies that Japanese and U.S.

market risks are priced identically across countries when the Nikkei or the EAFE indices are used. We view this evidence as supporting the notion of international integration among equity markets.

The paper proceeds as follows. The estimated model is introduced in section 2. Section 3 presents the main empirical results. Section 4 investigates the robustness of the results to alternative econometric specifications and returns measurement intervals, and section 5 presents concluding remarks.

2. The model

We assume that:

(A.1) Markets are internationally integrated.

(A.2) Investors are period-by-period mean-variance optimizers in a common numeraire, which we take to be the U.S. dollar.

(A.3) The aggregate relative risk aversion, $\lambda = \sum_{i=1}^{N} \lambda_{it} W_{it} / \sum_{i=1}^{N} W_{it}$, is constant, where λ_{it} is the ith individual's relative risk aversion, W_{it} is his wealth at time t, and N is the number of investors.

Assumption (A.1) implies that assets with the same risk have the same expected excess returns irrespective of where they are traded. Assumption (A.2) ensures that the CAPM holds. The assumption of a common numeraire implies that there are no preferred currency habitats for individual investors.[1] Assumption (A.3) implies that the risk premium changes only when the volatility of the market portfolio changes.

An alternative to assumption (A.2) used in some of our tests is:

(A.2') Investors use the currency of their home country as the numeraire.

Assumption (A.2') corresponds to a world in which the exchange rate reflects changes in the relative price of goods across countries and investors consume different baskets of goods in different countries. With this assumption, each stock position in the world market portfolio is financed in the country in which the stock is traded. Hence, the excess returns on a stock equal the returns of that stock in its own currency net of the returns of the risk-free asset in that currency. The interpretation of these own-currency returns is that they are equal to dollar returns hedged against currency risk with a hedge ratio of one: that is, one goes short one unit of foreign currency for each purchase of one unit of foreign

---

[1]See Alder and Dumas (1983) and Stulz (1983) for reviews of the literature on international asset pricing and discussions of the role of preferred currency habitats.

currency stock. This approach, pioneered by Solnik (1974), leads to a linear pricing relation between expected own-currency excess returns and their conditional covariance with the world market portfolio of own-currency excess returns.[2]

With these assumptions, we have

$$E(R_{mt+1} - R_{0t+1} | \Omega_t) = \lambda \mathrm{var}(R_{mt+1} - R_{0t+1} | \Omega_t),\tag{1}$$

where $E(\cdot)$ is the conditional expectation operator, Ω_t is the investors' information set at t, R_{mt+1} is the return on the world market portfolio from t to $t+1$, and R_{0t+1} is the risk-free rate for the same period of time. Var $(R_{mt+1} - R_{0t+1} | \Omega_t)$ is the conditional variance of the excess return on the world market portfolio for the period t to $t+1$ given the information set Ω_t. With assumption (A.2), all excess returns are computed in dollars, whereas with the preferred currency habitats assumption (A.2'), excess returns are own-currency returns, so that the excess return on the market portfolio is a weighted average of own-currency returns.

Using the CAPM and (1), we have

$$E(r_{dt+1} | \Omega_t) = \lambda \mathrm{cov}(r_{dt+1}, r_{mt+1} | \Omega_t)\tag{2}$$

where lower-case r denotes excess returns and $\mathrm{cov}(r_{dt+1}, r_{mt+1} | \Omega_t)$ is the conditional covariance of the excess returns on the U.S. domestic market portfolio with the excess return on the world market portfolio.

The return on the world market portfolio can be written as

$$r_{mt+1} = \omega_{dt} r_{dt+1} + (1 - \omega_{dt}) r_{ft+1},\tag{3}$$

where ω_{dt} is the capitalization of the U.S. market portfolio as a fraction of world wealth at time t, r_{dt+1} is the excess return on the U.S. domestic market portfolio, and r_{ft+1} is the excess return on the foreign market portfolio.

Using (3), we can rewrite (2) as

$$E(r_{dt+1} | \Omega_t) = \lambda [\omega_{dt} \mathrm{var}(r_{dt+1} | \Omega_t) + (1 - \omega_{dt}) \mathrm{cov}(r_{dt+1}, r_{ft+1} | \Omega_t)].\tag{4}$$

In this paper, we focus on the relation in (4). If the U.S. market portfolio equals the world market portfolio, the weights become $\omega_{dt} = 1$ for all t and (4) reduces to the relation examined by French, Schwert, and Stambaugh (1987).

---

[2]There is no theoretical reason for the hedge ratio of one to be the minimum-variance hedge. When it is not, Sercu (1980) shows that the appropriate returns are those of self-financing portfolios of stocks hedged against exchange rate risk using the minimum-variance hedge. Bailey, Ng, and Stulz (1992) provide evidence, however, that a hedge ratio of one cannot be improved on for the Nikkei 225 by using conditional minimum-variance hedge ratios.

Even if the returns of the U.S. market portfolio are not related to the returns of the market portfolio of non-U.S. assets, (4) still differs from that of French, Schwert, and Stambaugh (1987), since the conditional variance of the U.S. market portfolio is multiplied by the weight of the U.S. portfolio in the world portfolio.

With daily data from a single country, (4) has a straightforward interpretation because it corresponds to a portfolio strategy that can be easily implemented: buy the market portfolio at the close of trading and hold it until the next day's close. With daily data from several countries, the trading hours generally do not overlap in calendar time. Using close-to-close returns for each country, it is not possible to implement directly a portfolio strategy of buying the world market portfolio at the close of U.S. trading at time t and selling it at the close of U.S. trading at time $t + 1$, because the foreign markets typically close before the U.S. market. To reduce the problem created by nonsynchronous trading hours, one could use returns measured over longer periods, so that the nonoverlapping period becomes a smaller fraction of the measurement interval. We choose instead to use daily data and address the problem of nonsynchronous trading hours directly. We use daily data for two reasons. First, the period for which it is reasonable to investigate the effect of foreign stock markets on the U.S. risk premium is reasonably short, so our tests would lack power with infrequently sampled data. Since existing tests of international asset pricing models that focus on stock returns use monthly data, the use of daily data is a contribution to the international asset pricing literature.[3] Second, the results of French, Schwert, and Stambaugh (1987) that most strongly support the positive relation between conditional expected excess returns and conditional variances are obtained using daily returns.

In using daily returns, we consider an investor who makes his portfolio decisions at the close of trading in the U.S. markets. When the investor forms his portfolio, he uses expected returns and the variance–covariance matrix of returns conditional on information available at that time. If we had foreign returns computed from the close of the U.S. market to the next close of the U.S. market, we would use them as part of the information set. Since foreign returns measured over the same calendar time as U.S. returns are not available, we have to model the joint dynamics of the U.S. and foreign returns to reflect the nonsynchronism of trading hours. Specifically, at the close of the U.S. market the investor knows the return on the U.S. market and the return on the foreign market at its close earlier in the day. Since the U.S. market closes after most foreign markets, part of the next day's return of the foreign market has already accrued when the investor makes his portfolio decision. As long as contemporaneous returns on

---

[3]Engel and Rodriguez (1989) and Giovannini and Jorion (1989) use weekly data but test asset pricing models using returns on foreign currencies rather than on foreign stocks. Chang, Pinegar, and Ravichandran (1991) use daily returns in a study of the integration of European equity markets where the problem of nonsynchronous trading is not significant.

the domestic and foreign markets are correlated, the investor can use today's U.S. return to improve his forecast of tomorrow's foreign return. Our approach accounts explicitly for this correlation.

The information in the U.S. close-to-close return today about the next day's foreign return gives the appearance that foreign market returns can be predicted from the previous day's U.S. return. This predictability is spurious, however, since it cannot be exploited through a portfolio strategy if foreign markets are efficient. The foreign return does not contain similar information about the next-calendar-day U.S. return, since on the previous calendar day the foreign markets closed before the U.S. market and hence the information in the foreign returns is incorporated in the previous-day U.S. return.[4]

Since the lack of synchronism in trading hours affects our modeling strategy, it is important to make sure it does not bias our results. We therefore set up two further experiments. First, we know that as the measurement interval is lengthened, the lack of synchronism becomes less important. Our robustness tests indeed show that our finding of a significant foreign effect on the U.S. risk premium holds if we use longer measurement intervals for the returns. Second, we demonstrate that it holds if we use open-to-open U.S. returns and hence allow the investor to form his expectations at the open of U.S. markets.

In the following, we assume that the information set of investors, Ω_t, is approximated by a set of instruments that includes only past returns of the U.S. and the foreign portfolios for the sample period.[5] We therefore propose the parameterization

$$r_{dt+1} = a_d + \beta_{dt}\omega_{dt}h_{dt+1} + \beta_{dc}(1 - \omega_{dt})h_{ct+1} + \theta_{d1}\varepsilon_{dt} + \theta_{d2}\varepsilon_{dt-1}$$

$$+ \varepsilon_{dt+1}, \tag{5a}$$

$$r_{ft+1} = a_f + \beta_{ft}\omega_{ft}h_{ft+1} + \beta_{fc}(1 - \omega_{ft})h_{ct+1} + \theta_{f1}\varepsilon_{ft} + \theta_{f2}\varepsilon_{ft-1}$$

$$+ \phi_f\varepsilon_{dt} + \varepsilon_{ft+1}, \tag{5b}$$

where the conditional variances, h_{ft+1} and h_{dt+1}, and covariances, h_{ct+1}, depend only on past returns. The specification for each country allows the returns to depend on two lagged disturbances to incorporate the effects of infrequent

---

[4]If we had used the close of trading in foreign markets as the time when the investor makes his portfolio decision instead, today's foreign return would be useful to forecast the same-calendar-day U.S. return, but the U.S. return would not be useful to forecast tomorrow's foreign return. Hence, in this case, the returns dynamics would have to be modeled differently.

[5]This is in contrast of the instrumental variables approach of Harvey (1991), which conditions the market risk premium on a set of macroeconomic variables.

trading on the dynamics of the index returns[6]. We also allow the foreign returns to depend on one lagged disturbance of the domestic returns through ϕ_f to take into account the lack of synchronism in trading hours. As explained above, there should be no ϕ_d in the domestic returns equation.[7]

An important step in implementing the model empirically is specifying the dynamics of the conditional variances and covariances. We use a general specification drawn from the ARCH process originally proposed by Engle (1982), which allows the conditional covariance matrix to be related to its own past values and past squared disturbances. We posit the following general process:

$$\varepsilon_{t+1} \sim \mathrm{N}(0,\, \mathbf{H}_{t+1}) \quad \text{and} \quad \mathbf{H}_{t+1} = \begin{bmatrix} h_{dt+1} & h_{ct+1} \\ h_{ct+1} & h_{ft+1} \end{bmatrix}, \tag{6a}$$

$$\mathbf{H}_{t+1} = \mathbf{P}'\mathbf{P} + \mathbf{F}'\mathbf{H}_t\mathbf{F} + \mathbf{G}'\varepsilon_t\varepsilon_t'\mathbf{G}. \tag{6b}$$

where $\mathbf{H}_{t+1}$ denotes the 2×2 variance–covariance matrix conditional on information at time t and ε_{t+1} denotes the vector of disturbances from eqs. (5a)–(5b). $\mathbf{P}$ is an upper triangular matrix of coefficients, whereas $\mathbf{F}$ and $\mathbf{G}$ are free matrices of coefficients. This model was originally proposed by Baba, Engle, Kraft, and Kroner (1989) (BEKK). The important feature of this specification is that it builds in sufficient generality, allowing the conditional variances and covariances of the two stock markets to influence each other, and, at the same time, does not require us to estimate a large number of parameters (eleven for the bivariate system used here). Even more importantly, perhaps, the BEKK process guarantees that the covariance matrices in the system are positive definite. To see the level of generality we gain by implementing this specification, we can contrast it with the multivariate ARCH model adopted by Bollerslev, Engle, and Wooldridge (1988) (BEW), in which the conditional variances depend only on past squared residuals and covariances on past products of disturbances. The important cross-market effects, highlighted by Hamao, Masulis, and Ng (1990) for the national stock markets of the U.S., U.K., and Japan, are ignored in the BEW specification. A more general BEW process could be specified to capture these effects, but positive semi-definiteness of the

---

[6]Stoll and Whaley (1990) show how the effects of infrequent trading and bid–ask spreads can cause stock index returns to follow an ARMA-type process. See also Muthuswamy (1990).

[7]Our method of addressing this problem with nonsynchronous trading hours could be improved in future research, since we omit the covariance attributable to the unanticipated return on the foreign market between the close of that market and the close of the U.S. market because that return is unobservable. Instead, we implicitly assume that the true covariance is a constant proportion of the estimated covariance. If this assumption is incorrect, we would expect our results to be sensitive to alternative measurement intervals, but we show in section 4 that they are not.

conditional covariance matrix in that system is no longer assured. We discuss estimation results with alternative processes in section 4.

3. Description and interpretation of empirical results

3.1. Data

We use three indices for non-U.S. assets. The first is the Nikkei 225 Stock Average. The data for the Nikkei 225 index are collected from the *Asian Wall Street Journal* as are the exchange rates used to obtain dollar-denominated returns. The Nikkei 225 is a price-weighted index of stocks traded in the first section of the Tokyo stock market. For this index, we have data from January 3, 1978 to December 31, 1989. We also use two value-weighted indices published in Morgan Stanley's *Capital International Perspectives* that are available from January 3, 1980 to December 31, 1989. These are the Morgan Stanley Japan index in yen and the Morgan Stanley EAFE index in dollars. We use the indices only on calendar days when they are available in both countries and make no distinction between single- and multiple-day returns. The Morgan Stanley Japan index is the Japanese component of EAFE and hence is a value-weighted index. The EAFE index does not include all stocks for each market, since it generally ignores small-capitalization stocks. It is widely used by practitioners as a benchmark for the performance of non-U.S. stocks, however, and internationally-diversified index funds generally try to replicate the performance of that portfolio. It includes no adjustment for cross-holdings in Japan and other countries, so it may give more weight to Japan than is warranted, as argued by McDonald (1989) and French and Poterba (1991).

Table 1 provides summary statistics for the data, including the cross-correlations among the various portfolio excess returns. The U.S. index and dollar-denominated foreign equity index excess returns are obtained using the three-month U.S. Treasury bill yields; those for the yen-denominated Nikkei 225 index are computed with the three-month Gensaki interest rate. Panel A indicates that the excess returns series show significant negative skewness for the S&P 500 and the Nikkei yen excess returns and generally positive excess kurtosis. These results suggest that the returns distribution deviates from normality. The Kolmogorov D statistic and tests based on Bera and Jarque (1982) confirm this formally.

The autocorrelation coefficients are shown in panel B for the raw excess returns and squared returns series. The significant positive and declining auto-correlations for the squared series indicate some second-order dependence that the GARCH models in this study seek to capture.

Finally, the cross-correlations between the S&P 500 returns and those of the various foreign index returns are shown in panel C. The significant leading

Table 1

Summary statistics for daily U. S. and foreign equity market excess returns (in percent) from January 1978 to December 1989.

The U.S. equity index is Standard and Poor's 500 stock index and the foreign market indices are the U.S. dollar- and yen-denominated Nikkei 225 index, the Morgan Stanley Japan index (yen-denominated), and the Morgan Stanley EAFE (dollar-denominated) index. All dollar-denominated index returns are computed net of the three-month U.S. Treasury bill yield and the yen-denominated index returns are computed net of the three-month Gensaki interest rate. The returns associated with October 16, 19, 20, and 21, 1987 are omitted. The Kolmogorov–Smirnoff D statistic tests the null hypothesis of normality with critical values of 0.0256, 0.0281, and 0.0271 at the 5 percent significance level and 0.0307, 0.0337, and 0.0325 at the 1 percent significance level for 2819, 2338, and 2522 degrees of freedom, respectively. The Bera–Jarque B test statistic for normality is based on the excess skewness and kurtosis coefficients and is asymptotically distributed χ^2 with two degrees of freedom with critical values at the 5 percent significance of 5.99 and at the 1 percent significance level of 9.21. The tests for deviations from normality for the skewness and kurtosis statistics are based on D'Agostino, Belanger, and D'Agostino (1990). Cross-correlations are given between the S&P 500 index daily excess returns, r_t (and squared returns, r_t^2), and those of the index shown in the table.

Panel A: Distributional statistics

Statistic	S&P 500	Nikkei ($)	Nikkei (yen)	MS Japan	MS EAFE
Nobs.	2819	2819	2819	2338	2522
Mean	0.0254	0.0693	0.0619	0.0688	0.0495
Std. dev.	0.9760	1.0648	0.7658	0.9414	0.8917
Skewness	− 0.4409[a]	0.0535	− 0.2912[a]	0.1323	0.0327
Kurtosis	5.6594[a]	2.2764[a]	5.8208[a]	8.8262[a]	3.0575[a]
Kolmogorov D	0.0525[a]	0.0469[a]	0.0759[a]	0.0858[a]	0.0357[a]
Bera–Jarque B	72.576[a]	11.489[a]	75.706[a]	157.09[a]	19.570[a]

Panel B: Autocorrelations of daily excess returns

Statistic	S&P 500	Nikkei ($)	Nikkei (yen)	MS Japan	MS EAFE
			Series: r_t		
ρ_1	0.0552[a]	0.0975[a]	0.0934[a]	0.1229[a]	0.1059[a]
ρ_2	0.0077	0.0027	− 0.0604[a]	− 0.0646[a]	0.0258
ρ_3	− 0.0234	0.0246	− 0.0024	0.0051	0.0191
ρ_4	− 0.0042	0.0345	0.0134	0.0167	0.0300
ρ_5	− 0.0086	− 0.0295	− 0.0507[a]	− 0.0695[a]	0.0079
ρ_6	− 0.0047	− 0.0004	− 0.0379	− 0.0296	− 0.0100
			Series: r_t^2		
ρ_1	0.0675[a]	0.1492[a]	0.2617[a]	0.1156[a]	0.1493[a]
ρ_2	0.0792[a]	0.1025[a]	0.1826[a]	0.2121[a]	0.0619[a]
ρ_3	0.1641[a]	0.0600[a]	0.1853[a]	0.2134[a]	0.1009[a]
ρ_4	0.1227[a]	0.0451[a]	0.1003[a]	0.0466	0.1123[a]
ρ_5	0.0824[a]	0.0749[a]	0.1211[a]	0.1413[a]	0.0866[a]
ρ_6	0.1463[a]	0.0206	0.0966[a]	0.0711[a]	0.0219

Table 1 (continued)

Panel C: Cross-correlations of daily S&P 500 and foreign market excess returns

	Nikkei ($)		Nikkei (yen)		MS Japan		MS EAFE	
Lag	r_t	r_t^2	r_t	r_t^2	r	r_t^2	r	r_t^2
− 6	− 0.0167	0.0377	− 0.0394[a]	0.0689[a]	− 0.0263	0.0363	0.0034	0.0404[a]
− 5	0.0188	0.0567[a]	0.0177	0.0786[a]	0.0255	0.0418[a]	0.0061	0.0630[a]
− 4	− 0.0051	0.0487[a]	− 0.0153	0.0929[a]	− 0.0319	0.0783[a]	− 0.0022	0.1539[a]
− 3	0.0029	0.0609[a]	− 0.0144	0.1268[a]	− 0.0171	0.0782[a]	0.0390	0.0746[a]
− 2	0.0571[a]	0.0770[a]	0.0689[a]	0.1451[a]	0.1004[a]	0.1061[a]	0.0456[a]	0.0545[a]
− 1	0.1916[a]	0.1516[a]	0.2707[a]	0.2139[a]	0.2531[a]	0.1642[a]	0.3305[a]	0.1854[a]
0	0.0838[a]	0.1522[a]	0.1201[a]	0.2003[a]	0.1095[a]	0.1269[a]	0.1629[a]	0.2190[a]
1	0.0137	0.1021[a]	− 0.0033	0.2194[a]	− 0.0041	0.1999[a]	0.0062	0.0954[a]
2	0.0015	0.0754[a]	− 0.0164	0.1906[a]	− 0.0342	0.1806[a]	0.0099	0.0504[a]
3	0.0536[a]	0.0356	0.0411[a]	0.0747[a]	0.0422[a]	0.1556[a]	0.0195	0.0749[a]
4	− 0.0356	0.0675[a]	− 0.0471[a]	− 0.1129[a]	− 0.0281	0.0889[a]	− 0.0353	0.0555[a]
5	− 0.0206	0.0444[a]	− 0.0284	0.1274[a]	− 0.0483[a]	0.1036[a]	− 0.0288	0.0202
6	− 0.0044	0.0441[a]	− 0.0198	0.0647[a]	− 0.0044	0.0336	− 0.0001	0.0464[a]

[a]Significant at the 1 percent level.

correlations from U.S. to foreign stocks in the raw returns reflect the nonsynchronous trading hours for the respective markets. Eqs. (5a) and (5b) of the model proposed in the previous section attempt to control for this effect. More interestingly, the cross-correlations computed for the squared returns series suggest that what happens in one market affects the volatility of returns in another. Again, the dynamics of the conditional covariances applying the BEKK process of (6) can capture such cross-market dependence in the volatility of the returns.

Eqs. (5a) and (5b) require computation of market weights. We obtain these weights from Morgan Stanley's *Capital International Perspectives*. Since the weights are published quarterly, we use the beginning-of-quarter weights reported by Morgan Stanley and compute the weights within each quarter by adjusting the beginning-of-quarter weights dynamically, using the realized returns on the indices. For each quarter, we extend the interpolation to the beginning of the next quarter and compare our weights with those reported by Morgan Stanley. In this comparison, the reported weights are always very close to the predicted weights.

3.2. Empirical results

Panel A of table 2 reproduces estimates of (5a)–(5b) that use, respectively, the dollar-denominated excess returns on the Nikkei 225 index, the yen-denominated excess returns on the Nikkei 225 index and the Morgan Stanley Japan index, and the dollar-denominated excess returns on the EAFE index as the returns on the foreign market portfolio. The estimates are obtained using dummy variables in (5a)–(5b) for October 16, 19, 20, and 21, 1987, when it appears the distribution of returns differs dramatically from the distribution on the other days in our sample. The point estimates obtained without the dummy variables for the parameters of interest are quite similar to those reported here, but statistical inference becomes more complicated because of the serious departures from the normality assumption.

The estimates of the equation for U.S. returns with the dollar returns of the Nikkei 225 show that the conditional covariance of the U.S. returns with the Nikkei return has a significant positive effect on U.S. conditional expected returns, but that the conditional variance of the U.S. returns has no effect. This result holds whether we use standard t-statistics or the alternative t-statistics robust to departures from normality suggested by Bollerslev and Wooldridge (1990).[8] Hence, this result supports the hypothesis that the U.S. risk premium is determined on global markets during the sample period. The lack of significance of the coefficient on the variance is surprising. Since the conditional variance and covariance have a significant correlation (0.57 if we use the dollar-denominated Nikkei returns), one might be tempted to attribute the lack of significance of the conditional variance to multicollinearity. If we estimate a univariate model for the U.S. returns for our sample period, however, the coefficient on the variance is not significant either. A more plausible explanation is that, if the returns are measured with error, the error decreases the precision of our variance estimate more than the precision of our covariance estimate, since returns squared involve taking the square of the error, whereas products of domestic and foreign returns involve multiplying two errors that are imperfectly correlated. The estimates obtained with the yen-denominated excess returns of the Nikkei 225 are qualitatively similar to those obtained with dollar-denominated returns.

The estimates using the Morgan Stanley Japan index and EAFE as foreign market portfolios are consistent with those obtained using the Nikkei 225. In both equations, the covariance has a positive coefficient that is significantly different from zero using standard t-statistics. Using robust t-statistics, the covariance coefficient is significant at the 10 percent level for the Morgan Stanley Japan index, but is insignificant at the same level for the EAFE index. The point estimates of the covariance coefficients are almost the same for the equations using the Nikkei 225 and EAFE. The variance of the U.S. returns has a positive but statistically insignificant coefficient in both equations.

Table 2 also reports results for foreign excess returns. The results are not completely symmetric to those for the U.S. When we use the dollar excess returns on the Nikkei, the covariance with the U.S. returns has a positive but

---

[8]Because of the large sample size of this analysis, the appropriate criteria for statistical significance for sample statistics and estimated coefficients are unclear. Throughout the text and tables, we highlight critical values at conventional significance levels but caution the reader that a more conservative cutoff may be appropriate.

insignificant effect on the expected excess returns of the index, but the variance of the Nikkei has a significant positive coefficient. The same result holds for the equation estimated with the yen-denominated excess returns on the Nikkei, except that in this case the covariance has a significant positive coefficient with the standard t-statistic and an insignificant coefficient with the robust t-statistic. With the Morgan Stanley Japan and EAFE indices, the variance of the foreign index has an insignificant positive coefficient; the covariance has a negative insignificant coefficient for the EAFE but a positive significant coefficient for the Morgan Stanley Japan index at the 5 percent level using the standard t-statistic and at the 10 percent level using the robust t-statistic.

For all indices, we test the hypothesis that the expected returns are determined in the home country – i.e., that Japanese expected returns do not depend on the covariance of Japanese returns with U.S. returns and that U.S. expected returns do not depend on the covariance of U.S. returns with Japanese returns. Though the results are not reported, this hypothesis is easily rejected for all indices. Consequently, irrespective of the index used as a proxy for foreign stocks, the covariance of foreign stock returns with domestic stock returns has an important effect on the expected returns on domestic stocks.

Table 2 also measures the fraction of the total variation of returns captured by our explanatory variables. Whereas the fraction of the total variation explained for the U.S. returns, denoted R_1^2, is small but respectable, given the difficulty of forecasting daily returns, it would be virtually negligible if we ignored the international effect presented in this paper. For instance, if we set the coefficient on the conditional covariance equal to zero in the U.S. returns equation when the dollar return on the Nikkei 225 is used as the foreign return, the R_1^2 falls from 1.16 to 0.29 percent; in contrast, it falls to only 0.94 percent if we set the coefficient on the conditional variance equal to zero and to 0.25 percent if both coefficients on conditional variance and covariance equal zero. If the coefficients for the conditional variance and covariance are set at zero, the R^2 captures the proportion of the total variation that is due to the lagged moving average terms that are posited to capture the effects of nonsynchronous trading of the component stocks within each of the domestic and foreign market indexes. Further, the R^2 for the U.S. returns equation in this case is substantially larger than that for a simple univariate model (0.28 percent). Although the fraction of the total variation explained for the foreign returns, R_2^2, is much larger than the fraction explained for the U.S. return, it becomes comparable to the fraction explained for the U.S. return if ϕ_f is set equal to zero, as one would expect.

Figs. 2 and 3 plot the conditional expected excess returns and conditional variances and covariances for the U.S. when the foreign index uses dollar-denominated returns on the Nikkei 225; all the series exhibit substantial variation over time. For the U.S. returns, the conditional daily expected excess returns have a standard deviation of 0.09 percent and a mean of 0.04 percent, whereas the unconditional daily excess returns have a mean of 0.025 percent and

Table 2

Estimates from the bivariate model of daily expected excess returns for U.S. and foreign equity markets.

U.S. equity returns, r_{dt+1}, are given by Standard and Poor's 500 stock index and the foreign equity market returns, r_{ft+1}, by the U.S. dollar- and yen-denominated Nikkei 225 index (model 1 and 4), the Morgan Stanley Japan yen-denominated index (MSJP) (model 2), or the Morgan Stanley EAFE index (model 3). All dollar-denominated indices are computed net of the three-month U.S. Treasury bill yield; yen-denominated indices are computed net of the three-month Gensaki interest rate. The market-value weights, ω_{jt}, for each stock market j on day t, with $j=d$ for U.S. equity and $j=f$ for foreign equity markets, are daily interpolations from quarterly estimates published by Morgan Stanley's *Capital International Perspectives*. The market weights sum to unity in each regression. The number of observations for each model corresponds to that shown in table 1. R_1^2 and R_2^2 denote the ratio of the explained to total variation in the excess returns associated with the S&P 500 and foreign index markets. Standard t-statistics are presented in parentheses and robust t-statistics computed with quasi-maximum-likelihood methods are in brackets. The model parameters are given by the following system of equations:

$$r_{dt+1} = \alpha_d + \beta_{dt}h_{dt+1}\omega_{dt} + \beta_{dc}h_{ct+1}(1-\omega_{dt}) + \theta_{d1}\varepsilon_{dt} + \theta_{d2}\varepsilon_{dt-1} + \varepsilon_{dt+1}$$

$$r_{ft+1} = \alpha_f + \beta_{ft}h_{ct+1}(1-\omega_{ft}) + \beta_{fc}h_{ft+1}\omega_{ft} + \theta_{f1}\varepsilon_{ft} + \theta_{f2}\varepsilon_{ft-1} + \phi_f\varepsilon_{dt} + \varepsilon_{ft+1}$$

$$\begin{bmatrix} \varepsilon_{dt+1} \\ \varepsilon_{ft+1} \end{bmatrix} \sim N(0, \mathbf{H}_{t+1}) \quad \text{where} \quad \mathbf{H}_{t+1} = \begin{bmatrix} h_{dt+1} & h_{ct+1} \\ h_{ct+1} & h_{ft+1} \end{bmatrix} \quad \text{and} \quad \mathbf{H}_{t+1} = \mathbf{PP} + \mathbf{F'H_tF} + \mathbf{G'}\varepsilon_t\varepsilon_t'\mathbf{G}$$

Panel A: Conditional expected excess returns

Model	U.S. excess returns					Foreign excess returns						Log-likelihood
	α_d	θ_{d1}	θ_{d2}	β_{dt}	β_{dc}	α_f	θ_{f1}	θ_{f2}	ϕ_f	β_{ft}	β_{fc}	
1. Nikkei$ 1979–89	0.0362 (0.76) [1.16]	0.0516 (2.62)ᵃ [2.55]ᵃ	−0.0062 (−0.31) [−0.32]	−3.555 (−0.41) [−0.58]	87.38 (3.07)ᵃ [2.34]ᵃ	−0.0205 (−0.49) [−0.47]	0.0769 (3.82)ᵃ [3.42]ᵃ	0.0104 (0.53) [0.49]	0.2028 (10.92)ᵃ [8.95]ᵃ	27.57 (2.38)ᵃ [2.36]ᵃ	5.730 (0.25) [0.28]	18198.926 $R_1^2 = 1.16\%$ $R_2^2 = 4.52\%$
2. MSJP 1980–89	−0.0035 (−0.07) [−0.13]	0.0387 (1.85)ᵇ [1.81]ᵇ	−0.0057 (−0.27) [−0.29]	2.791 (0.32) [0.49]	56.01 (2.40)ᵃ [1.76]ᵇ	0.0335 (1.28) [1.37]	0.1453 (6.29)ᵃ [5.61]ᵃ	0.0232 (1.11) [0.88]	0.1692 (10.98)ᵃ [9.68]ᵃ	9.289 (1.08) [0.77]	53.44 (2.32)ᵃ [1.79]ᵇ	15559.932 $R_1^2 = 0.95\%$ $R_2^2 = 7.27\%$
3. EAFE 1980–89	0.0230 (0.47) [0.57]	0.0526 (2.63)ᵃ [2.74]ᵃ	0.0018 (0.09) [0.21]	1.722 (0.13) [0.16]	57.30 (2.57)ᵃ [1.60]	0.0329 (0.73) [0.76]	0.0735 (3.23)ᵃ [3.32]ᵃ	0.0252 (1.08) [1.24]	0.2871 (18.59)ᵃ [15.32]ᵃ	18.95 (1.52) [1.55]	−10.91 (−0.31) [−0.30]	16855.220 $R_1^2 = 0.67\%$ $R_2^2 = 11.1\%$
4. Nikkei yen 1979–89	−0.0060 (−0.12) [−1.65]ᵇ	0.0508 (2.65)ᵃ [2.56]ᵃ	−0.0047 (−0.24) [−0.24]	2.044 (0.24) [0.59]	72.93 (3.20)ᵃ [1.91]ᵇ	0.0196 (1.12) [1.05]	0.0801 (4.03)ᵃ [3.39]ᵃ	0.0026 (0.14) [0.11]	0.1694 (14.58)ᵃ [12.43]ᵃ	26.16 (2.55)ᵃ [2.12]ᵃ	35.33 (1.86)ᵇ [1.44]	19397.461 $R_1^2 = 0.56\%$ $R_2^2 = 6.13\%$

ctd. overleaf

Panel B: Conditional covariance dynamics

Model	P			G				F			
	P_{11}	P_{12}	P_{22}	G_{11}	G_{21}	G_{12}	G_{22}	F_{11}	F_{21}	F_{12}	F_{22}
1. Nikkei\$	0.1359 (10.6)[a] [5.08][a]	−0.0629 (−0.87) [−0.86]	0.4334 (14.4)[a] [9.17][a]	−0.1842 (−15.9)[a] [−6.57][a]	0.0136 (0.82) [0.90]	−0.1402 (−7.49)[a] [−3.87][a]	−0.3344 (−16.2)[a] [−10.6][a]	0.9707 (291.0)[a] [138.0][a]	0.0217 (1.96)[a] [3.29][a]	−0.0204 (−1.97)[a] [−1.41]	0.8332 (41.2)[a] [27.1][a]
2. MSJP	0.1184 (7.53)[a] [4.57][a]	−0.1182 (−3.09)[a] [−1.64][b]	0.1609 (6.19)[a] [2.29][a]	−0.1594 (−16.6)[a] [−5.67][a]	−0.0342 (−2.36)[a] [−3.25][a]	0.0664 (6.21)[a] [1.63]	−0.3869 (−23.7)[a] [−11.8][a]	0.9791 (292.0)[a] [169.0][a]	−0.0009 (−0.142) [−16.5][a]	0.0219 (4.37)[a] [1.61]	0.8966 (107.0)[a] [59.4][a]
3. EAFE	0.1043 (7.91)[a] [3.57][a]	0.0080 (0.178) [0.104]	0.2451 (10.5)[a] [8.45][a]	−0.1575 (−17.4)[a] [−4.23][a]	0.0134 (0.774) [0.545]	−0.0496 (−4.02)[a] [−1.42]	−0.3006 (−15.6)[a] [−8.76][a]	0.9792 (413.0)[a] [132.0][a]	0.0177 (2.15)[a] [1.25]	−0.0095 (−1.83)[b] [−0.763]	0.9060 (64.8)[a] [49.8][a]
4. Nikkei yen	0.1143 (7.29)[a] [4.09][a]	−0.0885 (−2.57)[a] [−1.46]	0.1619 (8.59)[a] [4.35][a]	−0.1627 (−15.5)[a] [−6.86][a]	−0.0671 (−3.92)[a] [−4.44][a]	0.0445 (4.22)[a] [1.97][b]	−0.4050 (−27.1)[a] [−12.7][a]	0.9786 (281.0)[a] [163.0][a]	−0.0139 (−1.57) [−4.63][a]	0.0170 (3.30)[a] [1.95][b]	0.8812 (119.0)[a] [49.5][a]

[a]Significant at the 5 percent level
[b]Significant at the 10 percent level

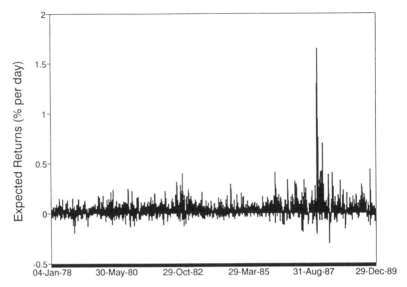

Fig. 2. Conditional expected risk premium on U.S. equity from 1978 to 1989. The fitted values for the expected risk premium of S&P 500 stocks are computed from estimates of the bivariate GARCH model using the dollar-denominated Nikkei 225 index returns as the foreign market (table 2, panel A). The figure excludes the four days around the October 1987 market crash (October 16, 19, 20, and 21).

a standard deviation of 0.97 percent. Further, the sample mean and standard deviation of the daily conditional variance are, respectively, 0.94 and 0.54, whereas for the covariance they are 0.09 and 0.22. As a measure of the economic significance of the international effect on the U.S. risk premium, our results suggest that a doubling of the conditional covariance from its mean value of 0.09 to 0.18 doubles the conditional expected excess return on the U.S. portfolio from 0.04 percent to 0.075 percent. A doubling of the conditional covariance is an increase of slightly less than half the standard deviation of the conditional covariance, indicating that such an increase is not unusual. Similarly, a doubling of the conditional risk premium is also an increase of slightly less than half its standard deviation.

Panel B of table 2 presents the estimates of the coefficients of the dynamics of the covariances from (6). The individual coefficient estimates are difficult to interpret, but the significance of the diagonal coefficients of the **F** and **G** matrices suggests that the GARCH effects are pervasive and strong. Moreover, most of the off-diagonal coefficients are also significant. This result confirms the evidence of Hamao, Masulis, and Ng (1990) that modeling the cross-market

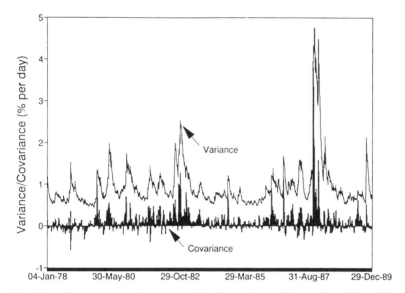

Fig. 3. Conditional variance and covariance of the risk premium on U.S. equity from 1978 to 1989. The fitted values for the conditional variance (*line*) and covariance (*solid bar*) of the risk premium of S&P 500 stocks are computed from estimates of the bivariate GARCH model using the dollar-denominated Nikkei 225 index returns as the foreign market (table 2, panel B). The figure excludes the four days around the October 1987 market crash (October 16, 19, 20, and 21).

dependence in the conditional volatility of U.S. and foreign stock returns is important.

Table 3 provides evidence on whether the coefficients on conditional variance and covariances of table 2 conform to the predictions of the international CAPM (ICAPM). The ICAPM implies that all the β coefficients of table 2 should be equal.[9] Table 3 presents estimates of the models of table 2 with the β coefficients constrained to be equal. Irrespective of the foreign portfolio used, the world price of risk is positive and significantly different from zero. With the ICAPM, the estimate for the price of risk corresponds to the representative investor's coefficient of relative risk aversion. The estimates for this coefficient vary from 9.6 to 18.1, depending on the foreign portfolio used. Although the estimate is high, it is not altogether unreasonable in light of the literature. For instance, although larger than the estimates obtained by Friend and Blume (1975) and Hansen and Singleton (1983), it is substantially smaller than those

---

[9]In footnote 7, we argue that our approach may yield measures that understate the true covariance. If it does, our test of the ICAPM is more conservative, because our estimate of the covariance effect, β_{dc}, is biased upward and hence away from the other β_{ij} coefficients.

Table 3

Tests of the international CAPM and alternative specifications using the bivariate model of daily expected excess returns for U.S. and foreign equity markets.

U.S. equity returns are given by Standard and Poor's 500 stock index and the foreign equity market returns by the U.S. dollar- and yen-denominated Nikkei 225 index (model 1 and 4), the Morgan Stanley Japan index (MSJP) (model 2), and the Morgan Stanley EAFE index (model 3). The following restrictions are tested:

$$\text{ICAPM model: } \beta_{dv} = \beta_{dc} = \beta_{fv} = \beta_{fc}$$

$$\text{Alternative 1: } \quad \beta_{dv} = \beta_{dc}, \quad \beta_{fv} = \beta_{fc}$$

$$\text{Alternative 2: } \quad \beta_{dv} = \beta_{fc}, \quad \beta_{fv} = \beta_{dc}$$

Alternative 1 assumes that the prices of risk in the U.S. and foreign market differ due to market segmentation; alternative 2 assumes a two-factor model with U.S. and foreign market risk as the respective loadings. Only the coefficient estimates for the conditional variance and covariance terms in the S&P 500 and foreign market excess returns equations are reported, with associated robust t-statistics computed with quasi-maximum-likelihood methods in brackets and χ^2 values of the likelihood ratio test of the restrictions.

Model	Specification	U.S. returns		Foreign returns		χ^2
		β_{dv}	β_{dc}	β_{fv}	β_{fc}	(p-value)
1. Nikkei $ 1979–89	Unrestricted	−3.555 [−0.58]	87.38 [2.34]^a	27.57 [2.36]^a	5.730 [0.28]	
	ICAPM	9.647 [1.90]^a	9.647	9.647	9.647	7.428 (0.0594)
	Alternative 1	7.912 [2.23]^a	7.912	12.54 [1.29]	12.54	7.202 (0.0273)
	Alternative 2	2.492 [0.06]	28.35 [2.50]^a	28.35	2.492	3.752 (0.1532)
2. MSJP 1980–89	Unrestricted	2.791 [0.49]	56.01 [1.76]^b	9.289 [0.77]	53.44 [1.79]^b	
	ICAPM	11.96 [2.01]^a	11.96	11.96	11.96	5.714 (0.1264)
	Alternative 1	8.853 [1.15]	8.853	14.33 [1.21]	14.33	5.294 (0.0709)
	Alternative 2	8.164 [0.86]	15.91 [1.53]	15.91	8.164	5.436 (0.0660)
3. EAFE 1980–89	Unrestricted	1.722 [0.16]	57.30 [1.60]	18.95 [1.55]	−10.91 [−0.30]	
	ICAPM	12.86 [1.75]^b	12.86	12.86	12.86	4.994 (0.1722)
	Alternative 1	17.87 [1.73]^b	17.87	6.820 [0.68]	6.820	3.904 (0.1420)
	Alternative 2	5.585 [0.45]	20.56 [1.73]^b	20.56	5.585	4.324 (0.1151)

Table 3 (continued)

Model	Specification	U.S. returns		Foreign returns		χ^2
		β_{dv}	β_{dc}	β_{fv}	β_{fc}	(p-value)
4. Nikkei yen 1979–89	Unrestricted	2.044 [0.59]	72.93 [1.91][a]	26.16 [2.12][a]	35.33 [1.44]	
	ICAPM	18.06 [2.91][a]	18.06	18.06	18.06	6.675 (0.0830)
	Alternative 1	12.09 [1.58]	12.09	23.02 [2.87][a]	23.02	4.984 (0.0827)
	Alternative 2	7.582 [1.41]	32.53 [2.92][a]	32.53	7.582	3.844 (0.1463)

[a]Significant at the 5% level.
[b]Significant at the 10% level.

presented by Wheatley (1988) and comparable to those of Harvey (1991) in tests of international asset pricing models.

The last column of table 3 presents χ^2 statistics that compare the unrestricted and restricted versions of the model. The restricted version cannot be rejected at the 5 percent level. One might argue that a more conservative approach is warranted, however, since we have only two assets. If we use the 10 percent significance level as our benchmark, we cannot reject the ICAPM when the foreign portfolio is EAFE or Morgan Stanley Japan; we can, however, reject the ICAPM if the foreign portfolio is the Nikkei, whether denominated in dollars or in yen. This limited success with the Nikkei may reflect the fact that the Nikkei is not a value-weighted index and hence gives more weight to small stocks. Hence, although our results support the ICAPM, the lack of rejection may also reflect the limited power of our tests.

4. Further tests

In this section, we first relate the results to earlier work. We then examine the robustness of the results and conclude with more tests of the international capital asset pricing model.

4.1. Relation to previous work

French, Schwert, and Stambaugh (1987) use a univariate GARCH-in-mean process to relate conditional expected returns on the S&P 500 index to the conditional volatility of the index and find a positive relation. Their test is not nested in the test discussed in section 3, since they estimate the process followed by the S&P 500 using U.S. data only. We replicated the French, Schwert, and Stambaugh study over our sample periods for the U.S. and Japan, but do not present the estimates here.[10] Their result does not hold for U.S. returns, as the conditional expected returns on the U.S. market portfolio are not significantly related to the conditional variance of the returns of that portfolio.[11] In contrast, however, there is evidence that the conditional expected returns of the foreign indices are related to their conditional volatility.[12] These results are consistent with the results obtained in table 2, since in that table the coefficient on the conditional volatility of the U.S. index in the U.S. returns equation was insignificant, whereas the coefficient on the conditional volatility of the foreign index in the foreign returns equation was significant for the Nikkei 225 whether denominated in yen or in dollars.

Bollerslev, Engle, and Wooldridge (1988) investigate a trivariate conditional CAPM that includes three portfolios: a portfolio of stocks, a portfolio of long-term bonds, and a portfolio of short-term bonds. Their approach is similar to ours in that they model the joint distribution of returns using a GARCH-in-mean process, but they posit dynamics for the variance–covariance matrix of returns that allow variances and covariances to depend only on their past values, in contrast to the dynamics we posit, which allow for additional cross-market dependence. They find a positive price of covariance risk, which is analogous to our finding of a positive price of risk in the equations estimated in table 3.

Existing research on international asset pricing has focused on unconditional returns. The most notable exception is Harvey (1991), who allows the price of risk to change over time in a pooled cross-sectional time-series test using monthly returns for a variety of countries. He models asset returns dynamics with instrumental variables and uses a generalized method-of-moments estimator to test the restrictions of the ICAPM. He finds evidence that the world price of covariance risk is not constant and rejects the hypothesis that Japanese stocks are priced according to the ICAPM.

4.2. Robustness and stability of the international effect

4.2.1. Nonsynchronous trading hours

As discussed in section 2, the use of daily data raises the issue of lack of synchronism in the returns measurement intervals across countries. There is no way to eliminate this lack of synchronism, but using longer measurement intervals should reduce its importance, since as the interval increases, the

---

[10]French, Schwert, and Stambaugh estimate a GARCH (1, 2) process, whereas the estimates reproduced in this paper are obtained for a GARCH (1, 1) process. None of the conclusions of this paper are affected if this alternative specification is introduced.

[11]Glosten, Jagannathan, and Runkle (1989) demonstrate the instability of the relation estimated by French. Schwert, and Stambaugh for different specifications of the conditional variance.

[12]See Chan and Karolyi (1991) for similar findings on the Nikkei 225 Stock Average index.

fraction of the interval for which returns are observed on both markets also increases. So, one way to evaluate the robustness of our results and the appropriateness of our approach for dealing with the nonsynchronous trading hours is to reestimate our equations on longer observation intervals. Results with the dollar-denominated Nikkei excess returns are reproduced in table 4 for two-day, three-day, and five-day returns. It is clear that our conclusion that the conditional U.S. expected excess returns are positively related to the conditional covariance of the U.S. excess returns with foreign-market returns still holds when we lengthen the observation interval. Importantly, as the returns are computed over longer periods, the apparent predictability of foreign returns from U.S. returns due to the overlapping of the measurement intervals disappears, as expected.[13]

The lack of synchronism in trading times leads to lower estimates of conditional covariances, since the same information can be incorporated in different indices on different calendar days. Although we try to estimate conditional covariances approximating those that would prevail if trading were synchronous across countries, our approach is imperfect. When returns are measured over longer horizons, the nonoverlapping part of the returns becomes a smaller fraction of the measurement interval, so that the conditional covariances should increase.[14] This difference between long-run and short-run conditional covariance does not affect our conclusion that there is an international effect on the U.S. risk premium, since that effect is robust to increases in the measurement interval. Although the coefficient β_{dc} falls when returns are measured over longer intervals, the decrease is not significant.

Another way to reduce the effects of the lack of synchronism in trading hours between the two countries is to use open-to-open U.S. returns with close-to-close Japanese returns. Transactions data of intraday quotes on the S&P 500 from the Chicago Mercantile Exchange were available to us for the 1984–89 subperiod. In table 4, we provide estimates of our model where U.S. returns are computed from prices one hour after the market opening. We use returns one hour after the opening because opening returns have different properties from other intraday returns.[15] These estimates fully support the conclusions drawn from the estimates that use the close-to-close returns. Interestingly, these estimates

---

[13]As the measurement interval is extended, however, one would expect the estimates to become less precise because the number of independent observations falls. Further, our regression framework becomes less appropriate, since longer-horizon returns may have different time-series properties than shorter-horizon returns. Nevertheless, in a regression not reproduced here, we extended the measurement interval to ten days and found that the β_{dc} coefficient estimate is also statistically significant with a value of 142.8.

[14]See Bailey and Stulz (1990) for evidence on how covariance estimates between U.S. and Japanese returns depend on the measurement interval because of the nonsynchronous trading hours.

[15]See Lin, Engle, and Ito (1991) for evidence of the importance of this distinction for the measurement of spillover effects across markets.

Table 4

Tests for robustness of estimates of the bivariate model of daily expected excess returns for U.S. and foreign equity markets.

U.S. equity returns are given by Standard and Poor's 500 stock index and the foreign market returns by the U.S. dollar-denominated Nikkei 225 index. The estimates for the covariance dynamics are not reported. Standard t-statistics are presented in parentheses and robust t-statistics computed with quasi-maximum-likelihood methods are in brackets. The model parameters are those for the system of equations displayed in table 2 and in the text.

Model	U.S. return equation					Foreign return equation						Log-likelihood
	x_a	a_{a1}	a_{a2}	β_{ia}	β_{da}	x_f	a_{f1}	a_{f2}	ϕ_f	β_{if}	β_{if}	
Two-day returns (1411 observations)	-0.0765 (-0.71) [-1.31]	0.0129 (0.42) [0.51]	-0.0271 (-1.02) [-0.95]	2.464 (0.29) [0.45]	80.59 (3.04)[a] [2.22][a]	-0.1309 (-1.21) [-0.87]	-0.0156 (-0.52) [-0.42]	0.0460 (1.52) [1.41]	0.1768 (5.87)[a] [5.51][a]	26.24 (2.68)[a] [2.14][a]	20.03 (0.99) [0.85]	7886.333
Three-day returns (941 observations)	-0.3307 (-1.69)[b] [-3.23][a]	-0.0358 (-0.96) [-1.11]	-0.0165 (-0.52) [-0.45]	11.87 (1.39) [1.93][b]	70.27 (1.99)[a] [2.14][a]	0.2231 (0.88) [0.98]	0.0044 (0.12) [0.11]	0.0176 (0.47) [0.52]	0.1259 (3.12)[a] [3.13][a]	6.450 (0.55) [0.65]	-11.88 (-0.58) [-0.52]	4820.689
Five-day returns (564 observations)	-0.3023 (-1.55) [-1.13]	-0.0347 (-0.81) [-0.90]	-0.0496 (-1.18) [-1.18]	10.26 (1.46) [1.16]	50.72 (1.86)[b] [1.85][b]	0.3786 (1.42) [1.42]	0.0567 (1.17) [1.32]	0.0796 (1.71)[b] [1.96][a]	0.0819 (1.74)[b] [1.62]	2.436 (0.21) [0.23]	4.438 (0.30) [0.28]	2671.088
Open-open U.S. returns (1984/08–1989/12) (1264 observations)	0.0793 (1.29) [0.77]	-0.0212 (-0.76) [-0.41]	0.0103 (0.35) [0.09]	-12.61 (-1.03) [-0.45]	87.49 (2.13)[a] [1.64][b]	0.0198 (0.27) [0.19]	0.1013 (3.34)[a] [2.96][a]	0.0555 (1.95)[b] [1.67][b]	0.1339 (4.88)[a] [3.84][a]	16.22 (1.04) [1.17]	49.78 (1.52) [1.34]	8115.645
Holiday/weekend dummy	0.0267 (0.56) [1.00]	0.0708 (3.59)[a] [3.73][a]	-0.0058 (-0.31) [-0.29]	3.014 (0.36) [0.54]	58.51 (2.58)[a] [1.59]	-0.0535 (-1.71) [-1.18]	0.0498 (2.32)[a] [2.09][a]	-0.0071 (-0.31) [-0.24]	0.2214 (12.6)[a] [9.86][a]	-2.875 (-0.17) [-0.12]	38.17 (4.54)[a] [3.13][a]	18150.384
No MA coefficients	0.0129 (0.29) [0.32]			0.556 (0.07) [0.12]	91.61 (4.29)[a] [3.04][a]	-0.0222 (-0.63) [-0.41]				28.46 (3.49)[a] [2.04][a]	-1.694 (-0.08) [-0.10]	18037.485
No market weights	0.0181 (0.38) [0.72]	0.0512 (2.59)[a] [2.52][a]	-0.0075 (-0.37) [-0.38]	-0.908 (-0.08) [-0.13]	66.99 (2.67)[a] [-2.22][a]	-0.0351 (-0.51) [-0.53]	0.0781 (3.85)[a] [3.48][a]	0.0111 (0.56) [0.53]	0.2036 (11.0)[a] [9.01]a	20.84 (1.47) [1.52]	19.94 (0.65) [0.59]	18197.939

[a]Significant at the 5 percent level.
[b]Significant at the 10 percent level.

correspond to a subperiod that approximates the second half of our sample of Nikkei data. Yet for this second half, the coefficient for the international effect is essentially the same as for the whole sample when we use close-to-close returns.

4.2.2. Conditioning information

The model estimated in table 2 includes lagged disturbances to account for the effects of nonsynchronous trading of component stocks in the index on the measurement of stock index returns. The significant positive effect of the first lagged disturbance is consistent with our infrequent trading motivation for the inclusion of these lagged disturbance terms.[16] Ignoring this lag structure may spuriously increase the importance of the international effect. This is shown in table 4, where we provide estimates of a version of our model that excludes the lagged disturbances. We also estimated the model with ϕ_f set equal to zero. These estimates, though not reproduced here, show a stronger international effect when ϕ_f is not included. Another alternative we examined but do not report was to roll back the investors' conditioning information by one day, so that ε_{t-1} replaced ε_t in (5) and (6); this approach still produced similar results. Rolling back the conditioning information set has three purposes. First, it is an attempt to see how the results change with changes in the information set.[17] Second, it shows the effect of removing the spurious predictability of foreign returns due to the lack of synchronism in trading hours. Finally, it shows that the covariance effect found for the U.S. expected excess returns is unlikely to be due to asynchronous trading in the S&P 500 stock index. When we roll back the conditioning information by one calendar day, the conditional covariance estimate does not incorporate information from the previous day and is not likely to be affected by information that may not have been fully incorporated into stock prices because of asynchronous trading. In summary, our results on the existence of an international effect are not sensitive to the lag structure included in the estimated models.

4.2.3. Day-of-the-week effects

The estimates in table 2 use trading time as the measurement unit for returns; i.e., all returns are computed from the end of a trading period to the end of the next trading period. In table 4, we provided model estimates where we allow different intercepts in the expected excess returns and the variance–covariance

---

[16]One would expect the foreign indices to have more evidence of infrequent trading, so the first lagged disturbance should have a greater effect on the foreign returns equations. It is puzzling, however, that the first lagged disturbance should have a greater effect in the foreign equation using the value-weighted Morgan Stanley index than on the equations using the price-weighted Nikkei 225.

[17]Our econometric models attempt to approximate (1). These models are approximations because we condition on an observed information set that is necessarily coarser than Ω_t, the true information set.

equations for multiple calendar days because of weekends or holidays. The results are similar, although the robust t-statistic on the international effect falls to 1.59. In this case, however, the coefficient on the first lagged disturbance becomes strongly significant for both countries and the coefficient in the Nikkei equation for the lagged U.S. return increases in value.

4.2.4. Alternative specifications

Multivariate GARCH is a full information maximum likelihood (FIML) estimation method. Although it is more efficient than conventional instrumental variables methods, its parameter estimates can be unstable if the model is misspecified. To investigate whether our inference about the foreign effect is sensitive to these estimation methods, we also use a two-pass procedure. We first estimate the model assuming constant conditional means to generate the conditional variance and covariance series and then regress the excess returns on the conditional variances and covariances using a seemingly unrelated regression (SUR) model. The conclusions are similar to those with the GARCH-in-mean approach. In particular, for the model with dollar-denominated Nikkei returns, using this two-pass approach, the coefficient β_{dc} is 54.02 with a heteroskedasticity-consistent t-statistic of 3.10.

Since the expression in (6) for the dynamics of the variance–covariance matrix is a projection equation without theoretical foundation, we also estimated our model using alternative specifications. One version uses (6) without imposing the BEKK constraints on the coefficient matrices. This unrestricted version, however, does not ensure that the variance–covariance matrix is positive semi-definite. With this version, the point estimates for the variance and covariance effects on the mean returns were similar to those from the BEKK process but less precise. The lack of precision was probably due to the larger number of parameters required for implementation. We also estimated the model using the constant correlation model of Schwert and Seguin (1990) and the Bollerslev, Engle, and Wooldridge (1988) process. The coefficients are again similar to those reported in table 2 except for the coefficient on the conditional covariance in the U.S. returns equation, which is 174 [with a standard (robust) t-statistic of 1.81 (1.40)] for the Bollerslev, Engle, and Wooldridge process and 284 [with a standard (robust) t-statistic of 1.44 (1.40)] for the Schwert and Seguin model. Though these additional formulations impose strong restrictions on the covariance dynamics – constant correlation in Schwert–Seguin and no cross-market spillover effects in BEW – the covariance effect is still important.

The market weights used in the estimation are constructed dynamically from quarterly observations provided by Morgan Stanley's *Capital International Perspectives*. We investigated the sensitivity of our results to the estimates for the market weights by reestimating the model assuming constant weights of 0.5.

These estimates are reproduced in table 3 and show that the international effect holds strongly with constant market weights.

4.2.5. Residual diagnostics

Table 5 reports some residual diagnostic tests for the bivariate and univariate models in this paper. Panel A presents the cross-sectional and time-series statistics for the scaled residuals of the bivariate models for the U.S. and foreign excess returns. The residuals are scaled by the square root of the conditional variance, $\hat{\varepsilon}_{it}/\sqrt{h_{it}}$. Tests indicate that the average standardized residuals are small compared with their standard deviation (using conventional t-statistics, they would not be significantly different from zero), suggesting that we should not be overly concerned that overfitting might lead to a bias in our estimates of the conditional means. The significant positive excess kurtosis and negative skewness observed for the raw returns in table 1 are reduced considerably, but the Kolmogorov D and Bera–Jarque test statistics for normality still indicate significant deviations from normality, suggesting that our focus on t-statistics robust to deviations from normality is warranted.[18] Panel C demonstrates that the cross-correlation patterns noted in the raw returns of table 1 are mostly absorbed by the bivariate model. In general, only contemporaneous correlations between the foreign and U.S. returns appear to be significantly different from zero.

4.3. Additional asset pricing tests

In table 3, we are unable to reject the ICAPM at the 5 percent level, but can do so at the 10 percent level for the Nikkei indices. A better way to understand our results is to compare them with tests of simple two-factor models. One can think of two possible such models in the context of this paper. First, there could be barriers to international investment that limit investors' abilities to benefit from international diversification. We refer to this version as the segmented model. Second, investors might not use a mean-variance framework, but rather hold securities also for the purpose of hedging against unanticipated changes in various state variables; we call this the hedging model. In the latter case, we posit the domestic and foreign market excess returns as factor-mimicking portfolios.

With segmented markets, the price of risk can differ across countries. In table 3, we report estimates of a model that allows for this variation. In this model, the coefficients on the weighted conditional variances and covariances are constrained to be the same within countries, but not across countries. This

---

[18]Nelson (1992) and Nelson and Foster (1991a,b) provide some conditions under which ARCH models may perform reasonably in estimating and even in forecasting conditional covariances even when some evidence of model misspecification (e.g., nonnormality in standardized residuals) remains.

Table 5

Residual diagnostics for bivariate GARCH models for daily U.S. and foreign equity market excess returns from January 1978 to December 1989. The corresponding model estimates are from table 2.

The U.S. equity index is Standard and Poor's 500 stock index and the foreign market is the U.S. dollar- and yen-denominated Nikkei 225 index, the Morgan Stanley Japan index, or the Morgan Stanley EAFE index. The Kolmogorov–Smirnoff D statistic tests the null hypothesis of normality with critical values of 0.0256, 0.0281, and 0.0271 at the 5 percent significance level and 0.0307, 0.0337, and 0.0325 at the 1 percent significance level for 2819, 2338, and 2522 degrees of freedom, respectively. The Bera–Jarque B test statistic for normality is based on the excess skewness and kurtosis coefficients and is asymptotically distributed χ^2 with two degrees of freedom with critical values at the 5 percent significance level of 5.99 and at the 1 percent significance level of 9.21. The tests for deviations from normality for the skewness and kurtosis statistics are based on D'Agostino, Belanger, and D'Agostino (1990). ρ_j denotes the autocorrelation coefficients of order j for both the raw and squared standardized residuals. Cross-correlations are given between the residuals from the S&P 500 index daily excess returns, $\hat{\varepsilon}_t$ (and squared returns, $\hat{\varepsilon}_t^2$), and those of the index shown in the table.

Panel A: Bivariate model standardized residuals

Statistic	Model 1		Model 2		Model 3		Model 4	
	S&P 500	Nikkei ($)	S&P 500	MS Japan	S&P 500	MS EAFE	S&P 500	Nikkei (yen)
Nobs.	2819	2819	2338	2338	2522	2522	2819	2819
Mean	-0.0148	-0.0124	-0.0082	-0.0327	-0.0154	-0.0233	-0.0044	-0.0335
Std. dev.	0.9915	0.9936	0.9916	0.9905	0.9956	0.9948	0.9886	0.9904
Skewness	-0.4119[a]	0.1256	-0.4523[a]	0.0479	-0.4529[a]	0.0608	-0.4274[a]	-0.3898[a]
Kurtosis	4.1108[a]	2.0331[a]	4.2673[a]	3.8949[a]	4.1796[a]	1.8164[a]	4.2162[a]	2.5917[a]
Kolmogorov D	0.0378[a]	0.0379[a]	0.0411[a]	0.0547[a]	0.0368[a]	0.0393[a]	0.0408[a]	0.0461[a]
Bera–Jarque B	38.886[a]	9.2839	38.336[a]	30.582[a]	38.270[a]	6.9354	40.940[a]	16.204[a]
				Series: $\hat{\varepsilon}_t$				
ρ_1	0.0327	0.0091	0.0326	0.0051	0.0199	0.0086	0.0292	0.0003
ρ_2	0.0153	0.0109	0.0179	-0.0002	0.0191	0.0099	0.0136	0.0056
ρ_3	-0.0094	0.0209	-0.0257	0.0071	-0.0145	0.0084	-0.0112	0.0088
ρ_4	-0.0085	0.0309	-0.0109	0.0019	-0.0268	0.0351	-0.0091	0.0053
ρ_5	0.0082	-0.0042	0.0021	-0.0242	-0.0123	0.0252	0.0066	-0.0129
ρ_6	-0.0003	0.0146	0.0022	-0.0009	-0.0013	0.0108	0.0018	-0.0077

K.C. Chan et al., Global influence on U.S. risk premium 163

Series: $\hat{\varepsilon}_t^2$

	Model 1 Nikkei ($)		Model 2 MS Japan		Model 3 MS EAFE		Model 4 Nikkei (yen)	
ρ_1	0.0015	0.0201	0.0111	-0.0029	0.0136	0.0079	0.0157	0.0308
ρ_2	0.0125	0.0020	0.0259	0.0191	0.0237	0.0028	0.0198	0.0252
ρ_3	0.0015	-0.0039	0.0201	0.0509ᵃ	0.0131	0.0195	0.0132	0.0145
ρ_4	0.0099	-0.0215	0.0258	-0.0413ᵃ	0.0326	-0.0094	0.0201	-0.0434ᵃ
ρ_5	-0.0134	0.0064	-0.0041	-0.0185	0.0084	0.0065	-0.0086	-0.0269
ρ_6	0.0282	-0.0342	0.0336	-0.0175	0.0019	-0.0292	0.0307	-0.0442ᵃ

Panel B: Cross-correlations of standardized residuals of bivariate models of S&P 500 and foreign market returns

Lag	Model 1 Nikkei ($)		Model 2 MS Japan		Model 3 MS EAFE		Model 4 Nikkei (yen)	
	$\hat{\varepsilon}_t$	$\hat{\varepsilon}_t^2$	$\hat{\varepsilon}_t$	$\hat{\varepsilon}_t^2$	$\hat{\varepsilon}_t$	$\hat{\varepsilon}_t^2$	$\hat{\varepsilon}_t$	$\hat{\varepsilon}_t^2$
-6	-0.0009	0.0018	-0.0018	-0.0085	0.0209	-0.0147	-0.0123	0.0005
-5	-0.0254	-0.0091	0.0421ᵃ	-0.0088	0.0169	0.0053	0.0227	-0.0084
-4	-0.0083	-0.0139	-0.0144	0.0116	0.0200	0.0186	-0.0073	-0.0089
-3	-0.0013	0.0005	-0.0102	0.0067	0.0223	0.0287	-0.0078	0.0257
-2	0.0457ᵃ	0.0136	0.0879ᵃ	0.0370	0.0356	0.0199	0.0571ᵃ	0.0449ᵃ
-1	-0.0003	0.0166	0.0366	0.0478ᵃ	0.0103	0.0523ᵃ	0.0263	0.0410ᵃ
0	0.0579ᵃ	0.0959ᵃ	0.0762ᵃ	0.0379	0.1349ᵃ	0.1315ᵃ	0.0747ᵃ	0.0686ᵃ
1	0.0072	0.0559ᵃ	0.0099	0.1350ᵃ	-0.0047	0.0346	0.0035	0.0687ᵃ
2	0.0086	0.0183	0.0060	0.0266	0.0285	0.0223	0.0157	0.0298
3	0.0549ᵃ	-0.0054	0.0371	-0.0160	0.0318	0.0281	0.0420ᵃ	-0.0195
4	-0.0174	0.0323	0.0052	0.0125	-0.0278	-0.0065	-0.0155	0.0158
5	-0.0143	0.0274	-0.0261	0.0611ᵃ	-0.0008	0.0078	-0.0205	0.0255
6	-0.0109	-0.0082	-0.0093	0.0151	0.0151	0.0172	-0.0264	0.0116

ᵃSignificant at the 1 percent level.

model does not appear to perform better than the ICAPM, so the weak performance of the ICAPM is apparently not due to barriers to international investment.

The hedging model does perform better than the ICAPM. With this model, the coefficients on the weighted domestic conditional variance (covariance) and the foreign weighted conditional covariance (variance) are constrained to be the same. At the 10 percent level, the hedging model is rejected only when we use the Morgan Stanley Japan index. These results suggest that more work on a multi-factor hedging model could lead to a better understanding of how risky assets are priced in an international setting. Evidence by Cumby (1990) and Wheatley (1988) on the Stulz (1981) international consumption asset pricing model supports this conjecture. Additional evidence is provided by Campbell and Hamao (1992) and Bekaert and Hodrick (1992) in their work showing that changes in expected returns can be captured by models with more than one latent variable.

So far, we have interpreted our tests of the ICAPM in terms of alternatives positing that an asset's risk is not measured simply by the conditional beta of its returns in relation to the world market portfolio. Since all our tests assume that the world relative risk aversion is constant, an alternative to the models in this section is one in which the world relative risk aversion changes over time.[19] Harvey (1991) pursues this approach using instrumental variables in a generalized method-of-moments framework. With daily data, an approach that models the dynamics for the price of risk explicitly will be difficult to implement because the instruments used in Harvey and related analyses are typically not observed daily. Nevertheless, in the spirit of Harvey we investigated the hypothesis that the price of risk changes during our sample period by allowing it to differ in the two halves of our sample when the index uses dollar-denominated returns on the Nikkei 225. We find that it is indeed significantly higher in the second half of the sample, suggesting that further research should model the time variation of the price of risk explicitly.

5. Concluding remarks

We find that there is a significant foreign influence on the time-varying risk premium for U.S. stocks. We investigate the relation between the conditional expected excess returns on the S&P 500 portfolio and its conditional risk as measured by its conditional volatility and its conditional covariance with the returns on some index of foreign stocks. We find that the conditional covariance of the S&P 500 returns with the returns of foreign stocks is significantly positively related to the conditional expected excess returns of the S&P 500 over

---

[19]McCurdy and Morgan (1991) employ a multivariate GARCH framework that allows for a CAPM-type specification with time variation in the conditional betas. They examine the risk premiums in deviations from uncovered interest rate parity in weekly spot currency prices.

the 1978–89 period, when the returns to foreign stocks are approximated by the returns of the Nikkei 225 index, Japan's Morgan Stanley index, or, to a lesser extent, by the EAFE index. This result holds whether the model is tested using dollar-denominated excess returns or the yen-denomianted excess returns for the Nikkei 225. In contrast, there is no significant relation between the conditional expected excess return on the S&P 500 and its conditional variance. We show that the international effect is economically significant, since an increase in the daily conditional covariance between U.S. and foreign returns that corresponds to half its sample standard deviation increases the daily U.S. risk premium by about 0.035 percent, or slightly less than one-half of its standard deviation.

We still find an international effect on the U.S. risk premium when we use alternative measurement intervals of the returns and alternative econometric specifications. The effect holds even if we use two-, three-, and five-day returns rather than daily returns and if we use open-to-open returns for the S&P 500 rather than close-to-close returns. Further, our results hold if the elements of the conditional variance–covariance matrix obtained from the GARCH approach are used as explanatory variables in a two-pass approach using seemingly unrelated regression models.

We are unable to reject the international CAPM at the 5 percent level of significance, but can reject it at the 10 percent level when the Nikkei 225 index is used as the foreign index. In general, a two-factor model in which the domestic and foreign indices stand for unspecified factors performs better than the ICAPM. In particular, this two-factor model cannot be rejected at the 10 percent level for the Nikkei indices. Our tests therefore support the hypothesis that markets are internationally integrated over the sample period we consider.

References

Adler, Michael and Bernard Dumas, 1983, International portfolio selection and corporation finance: A synthesis, Journal of Finance 46, 925–984.

Baba, Yoshihisa, Robert F. Engle, Dennis F. Kraft, and Kenneth F. Kroner, 1989, Multivariate simultaneous generalized ARCH, Working paper (University of California, San Diego, CA).

Bailey, Warren and René M. Stulz, 1990, Benefits of international diversification: The case of Pacific Basin stock markets, Journal of Portfolio Management, Summer, 57–62.

Bailey, Warren, Edward Ng, and René M. Stulz, 1992, Portfolio management and exchange rate risk: New theoretical and empirical perspectives on the hedging controversy, in: S. Khoury, ed., Recent developments in banking and finance (Basil Blackwell, Oxford).

Bekaert, Geert and Robert Hodrick, 1992, Characterizing predictable components in excess returns on equity and foreign exchange markets, Journal of Finance 47, 467–509.

Bera, Anil K. and Carlos M. Jarque, 1982, Model specification tests: A simultaneous approach, Journal of Econometrics 20, 59–82.

Bollerslev, Tim, 1986, Generalized autoregressive conditional heteroskedasticity, Journal of Econometrics 31, 307–327.

Bollerslev, Tim and Jeffrey M. Wooldridge, 1990, Quasi-maximum likelihood estimation and inference in dynamic models with time-varying covariances, Working paper (Northwestern University, Evanston, IL).

Bollerslev, Tim, Robert F. Engle, and Jeffrey M. Wooldridge, 1988, A capital asset pricing model
    with time-varying covariances, Journal of Political Economy 96, 116-131.
Campbell, John Y. and Yasushi Hamao, 1992, Predictable stock returns in the United States and
    Japan: A study of long-term capital market integration, Journal of Finance 47, 43-69.
Chan, K.C. and G. Andrew Karolyi, 1991, The volatility of the Japanese stock market: Evidence
    from 1977-90, in: Warren Bailey, Yasushi Hamao, and William Ziemba, eds., Japanese financial
    market research (Elsevier Science Publishers, Amsterdam).
Chang, Eric C., J. Michael Pinegar, and R. Ravichandran, 1991, Latent variables tests of the integra-
    tion of European equity markets, Working paper (Univeristy of Maryland, College Park, MD).
Cho, Chinhyung D., Cheol S. Eun, and Lemma W. Senbet, 1986, International arbitrage pricing
    theory: An empirical investigation, Journal of Finance 41, 313-330.
Cumby, Robert E., 1990, Consumption risk and international equity returns: Some empirical
    evidence, Journal of International Money and Finance 9, 182-192.
D'Agostino, Ralph, Albert Belanger, and Ralph D' Agostino, Jr., 1990, A suggestion for using
    powerful and informative tests of normality, The American Statistician 44, 316-321.
Engel, Charles and Anthony P. Rodriguez, 1989, Tests of international CAPM with time-varying
    covariances, Journal of Applied Econometrics 4, 119-138.
Engel, Robert, 1982, Autoregressive conditional heteroskedasticity with estimates of the variance of
    United Kingdom inflation, Econometrica 50, 987-1007.
French, Kenneth R. and James M. Poterba, 1991, Were Japanese stock prices too high?, Journal of
    Financial Economics 29, 337-364.
French, Kenneth R., G. William Schwert, and Robert F. Stambaugh, 1987, Expected stock returns
    and volatility, Journal of Financial Economics 19, 3-30.
Friend, Irwin and Marshall Blume, 1975, The demand for risky assets, American Economic Review
    65, 900-922.
Giovannini, Alberto and Philippe Jorion, 1989, The time variation of risk and return in the foreign
    exchange and stock markets, Journal of Finance 44, 307-326.
Glosten, Lawrence, Ravi Jagannathan, and David Runkle, 1989, The relationship between the
    expected value and the volatility of the nominal excess return on stocks, Working paper
    (Northwestern University, Evanston, IL).
Gultekin, N. Bulent, Mustafa N. Gultekin, and Alessandro Penati, 1989, Capital controls and
    international market segmentation: The evidence from the Japanese and American stock mar-
    kets, Journal of Finance 44, 849-869.
Hamao, Yasushi, Ronald Masulis, and Victor Ng, 1990, Correlations in price changes and volatility
    across international stock markets, Review of Financial Studies 3, 281-308.
Hansen, Lars and Kenneth Singleton, 1983, Stochastic consumption, risk aversion and the temporal
    behavior of asset returns, Journal of Political Economy 91, 249-266.
Harvey, Campbell R., 1991, The world price of covariance risk, Journal of Finance 46, 111-157.
Korajczyk, Robert and Claude Viallet, 1989, An empirical investigation of international asset
    pricing, Review of Financial Studies 2, 553-585.
Lin, Wen-ling, Robert Engle, and Takatoshi Ito, 1991, Do bulls and bears move across borders?,
    Working paper (University of Wisconsin, Madison, WI).
McCurdy, Thomas H. and Ieuan G. Morgan, 1991, Tests for a systematic risk component in
    deviations from uncovered interest rate parity, Review of Economic Studies 58, 587-602.
McDonald, Jack, 1989, The Mochiai effect: Japanese corporate cross-holdings, Journal of Portfolio
    Management, Fall, 90-94.
Merton, Robert C., 1973, An intertemporal capital asset pricing model, Econometrica 31, 867-887.
Merton, Robert C., 1980, On estimating the expected return on the market: An exploratory
    investigation, Journal of Financial Economics 8, 323-361.
Morgan Stanley, Capital International Perspectives, selected issues.
Muthuswamy, Jayaram, 1990, Nonsynchronous trading and the index autocorrelation problem,
    Ph.D. dissertation (Graduate School of Business, University of Chicago, Chicago, IL).
Nelson, Daniel, 1992, Filtering and forecasting with misspecified ARCH models I: Getting the right
    variance with the wrong model, Journal of Econometrics, forthcoming.
Nelson, Daniel and Dean Foster, 1991a, Estimating conditional variances with misspecified ARCH
    models: Asymptotic theory, Working paper (University of Chicago, Chicago, IL).

Nelson, Daniel and Dean Foster, 1991b, Filtering and forecasting with misspecified ARCH models II: Making the right forecast with the wrong model, Working paper (University of Chicago, Chicago, IL).

Schwert, William and Paul Seguin, 1990, Heteroskedasticity in stock returns, Journal of Finance 45, 1129–1155.

Sercu, Piet, 1980, A generalization of the international asset pricing model, Revue de l'Association Francaise de Finance 1, 91–135.

Solnik, Bruno, 1974, Equilibrium in international asset markets under uncertainty, Journal of Economic Theory 8, 500–524.

Stoll, Hans and Robert Whaley, 1990, The dynamics of stock index and stock index futures returns, Journal of Financial and Quantitative Analysis 25, 441–468.

Stulz, René M., 1981, A model of international asset pricing, Journal of Financial Economics 9, 383–406.

Stulz, René M., 1983, Pricing capital assets in an international setting: An introduction, Journal of International Business Studies, Winter, 55–73.

Wheatley, Simon, 1988, Some tests of international equity integration, Journal of Financial Economics 21, 177–212.

[14]

The Risk and Predictability of International Equity Returns

Wayne E. Ferson
University of Washington

Campbell R. Harvey
Duke University

We investigate predictability in national equity market returns, and its relation to global economic risks. We show how to consistently estimate the fraction of the predictable variation that is captured by an asset pricing model for the expected returns. We use a model in which conditional betas of the national equity markets depend on local information variables, while global risk premia depend on global variables. We examine single- and multiple-beta models, using monthly data for 1970 to 1989. The models capture much of the predictability for many countries. Most of this is related to time variation in the global risk premia.

We investigate the sources of risk and predictability of international equity market returns. We examine several global economic risk factors, including a world market portfolio, exchange rate fluctuations, mea-

Part of this research was conducted while the authors were at the University of Chicago, Graduate School of Business. We thank Warren Bailey, Eugene Fama, Stephen Foerster, Kenneth French, Allan Kleidon, Bruce Lehmann (a referee), Johnny Liew, John D. Martin, Lars Nielson, Bruno Solnik, an anonymous referee, the editor Richard Green, and participants in workshops at the Universities of California at Berkeley, Chicago, Florida, Iowa, Manitoba, Stanford, Texas at Austin, Texas at Dallas, Tel Aviv, Queens, Washington, at the August, 1991 National Bureau of Economic Research Summer Institute's International Studies/Macroeconomics week, the 1992 Utah Winter Finance Conference, the 1992 Western Finance Association, the 1992 French Finance Association and the September 1992 Berkeley Program in Finance for helpful discussions. Ferson acknowledges financial support from the Pigott–Paccar professorship at the University of Washington. Address correspondence to Wayne E. Ferson, Department of Finance and Business Economics, DJ-10, University of Washington, Seattle, WA 98195.

The Review of Financial Studies 1993 Volume 6, number 3, pp. 527–566
© 1993 The Review of Financial Studies 0893-9454/93/$1.50

The Review of Financial Studies / v 6 n 3 1993

sures of global inflation, world interest rates, international default risk, and world industrial production. We formulate an empirical beta pricing model, where country-specific conditional betas measure sensitivity to the global risk factors. Both the betas and the expected risk premia can vary over time.

Most tests of conditional asset pricing models ask the models to explain 100 percent of the predictability of the asset returns. Since a model can be useful even if it does not account for all of the variance, we estimate directly the fraction of the predictability that is explained by the model and the fraction that is left unexplained. We develop an approach for consistently estimating such fractions, using the generalized method of moments.

We study the predictability in 18 national equity market returns, using regressions on predetermined variables. Such regressions have been examined before, but our focus is unique. We concentrate on the marginal impact of local market variables, given a common set of instruments representing the state of the global economy. The local information is often important, and our regressions suggest that its effect on country returns is related to the country-specific betas.

Estimating the beta pricing models, we find that they can capture substantial fractions of the predictability for many of the countries. Single-beta models, using the world market index, are compared with multiple-beta models, which better explain the predictability in returns. Movements in the betas, while statistically significant, contribute only a small fraction to the predicted variation in expected returns. The global risk premia appear to be the dominant source of the predictability.

The paper is organized as follows. Section 1 reviews the models. Section 2 describes our empirical methodology, and Section 3 introduces the data. The empirical results are presented in Section 4, and Section 5 offers some concluding remarks.

1. The Models

The usual objective of empirical work on international asset pricing models is to explain differences in average returns. Average returns are estimates of unconditional expected returns, formed using no information about the current state of the economy. However, asset pricing models may also be interpreted as statements about expected returns *conditional* on currently available information. We focus on the ability of beta pricing models to capture the predictability of international equity market returns through conditional expected risk premia and conditional betas.

Beta pricing models to describe expected returns across countries have been developed by a number of authors, who show that the models require strong assumptions. We assume that the national equity markets are perfectly integrated in a global economy, with no barriers to extranational equity investments, no transactions or information costs, and no taxes. Such extreme assumptions are unlikely to provide a good approximation to the actual complexity of international invest-ments. Our approach is to see how far one can go in capturing equity market predictability by using such a simple framework. The results are encouraging, and we expect that further refinements of the models should produce even better explanatory power.

If we assume rational expectations, actual returns differ from their conditional expected values in the model by an error term that is orthogonal to the conditioning information. The conditioning infor-mation, Ω_{t-1}, is assumed to be public knowledge at time $t - 1$. Pre-dictability of returns is attributed to the correlation between expected returns and the current information. Following previous studies, the information, Ω_{t-1}, is persistent over time, and the expected returns inherit this persistence. We model expected returns as functions of betas and risk premia. Therefore, predictability should arise because betas or risk premia are correlated with the information variables. We assume that conditional expected returns can be written as

$$E(R_{it} \mid \Omega_{t-1}) = \lambda_0(\Omega_{t-1}) + \sum_{j=1}^{K} b_{ij}(\Omega_{t-1})\lambda_j(\Omega_{t-1}), \qquad (1)$$

where the $b_{ij}(\Omega_{t-1})$ are the conditional regression betas of the returns, R_{it}, measured in a common currency, on K global risk factors, $j = 1,...,K$. The expected risk premia, $\lambda_j(\Omega_{t-1})$, $j = 1,...,K$, are the expected excess returns on *mimicking portfolios* for the risk factors, similar to the static models of Huberman, Kandel, and Stambaugh (1987) and Lehmann and Modest (1988).[1] The intercept $\lambda_0(\Omega_{t-1})$ is the expected return of portfolios with all of their betas equal to zero. If there is a risk-free asset available at time $t - 1$, then its rate of return equals $\lambda_0(\Omega_{t-1})$. Equation (1) implies an expression for the expected *excess* returns:

$$E(r_{it} \mid \Omega_{t-1}) = \sum_{j=1}^{K} \beta_{ij}(\Omega_{t-1})\lambda_j(\Omega_{t-1}), \qquad (2)$$

where $\beta_{ij}(\Omega_{t-1}) = b_{ij}(\Omega_{t-1}) - b_{fj}(\Omega_{t-1})$ are the conditional betas of the excess returns and $b_{fj}(\Omega_{t-1})$, $j = 1,...,K$, are the conditional betas of a Treasury bill.

---

[1] Mimicking portfolios are defined as portfolios that may be substituted for the factors in a factor model regression, to measure the betas, and whose expected excess returns are the risk premiums.

The Review of Financial Studies / v 6 n 3 1993

1.1 Choosing the factors

The mean-variance mathematics [e.g., Roll (1977)] implies that some portfolio can always serve as a single factor, such that Equations (1) and (2) are satisfied. Therefore, the choice of factors determines the empirical content of the models. Although we do not attempt to test specific international asset pricing theories, our choice of factors follows previous theoretical and empirical work on international asset pricing. We study both single- and multiple-factor models. The single-factor model is similar to the capital asset pricing model (CAPM) of Sharpe (1964) and Lintner (1965). Stulz (1981b, 1984) and Adler and Dumas (1983) provide conditions under which a single-beta CAPM based on the world market portfolio holds globally. They assume no exchange risk and a constant investment opportunity set, in addition to the general assumptions we have described. Our investigation of the CAPM should therefore be viewed as extending static model restrictions to a conditional setting, similar to Harvey (1991).

When purchasing power parity does not hold, then consumers face exchange risk for investing internationally. Solnik (1974) showed that exchange risks should be "priced" even in a world otherwise similar to that of the static CAPM. Adler and Dumas [1983, Equation (14)] present a model in which a combination of the world market and measures of exchange risk is mean-variance efficient. The exchange risk can be broken down into a separate factor for each currency, as in Dumas and Solnik (1992), or approximated by a single variable. We study a two-beta model in the spirit of the latter approach, using the world market portfolio and an aggregate of exchange risks as the two factors.

International equilibrium and arbitrage pricing (APT) models with several risk factors are described by Stulz (1981a), Hodrick (1981), Ross and Walsh (1983), and Bansal, Hsieh, and Viswanathan (1992), among others. The central intuition of such models is that only the pervasive sources of common variation should be priced. Korajczyk and Viallet (1989) and Heston, Rouwenhorst, and Wessels (1991) find evidence for several common sources of variation in U.S. and European stocks, which suggests that a number of worldwide risk factors may be important. We therefore study models with several global risk factors.

1.2 Modeling conditioning information

We study the *predictable variation,* which we define as the unconditional variance of the conditional expected excess returns. We measure to what extent various specifications of Equation (2) can capture the predictable variation, using time-varying country-specific conditional betas and global risk premia. Previous studies find that the conditional second moments of national equity market returns move over time in association with lagged variables [e.g., King, Sentana, and Wadhwani (1990), Harvey (1991)]. Other studies find evidence of time-varying betas for international asset returns [e.g., Giovannini and Jorion (1987, 1989), Mark (1985)]. We therefore allow for time variation in both the expected risk premia and the conditional betas.

Let $\Omega_{t-1} = \{Z_{t-1}, Z^i_{t-1}, i = 1,...,n\}$, where Z_{t-1} represents our global information variables and Z^i_{t-1}, our local information variables for country i. We assume globally integrated capital markets, which implies that the risk premia should not be country-specific. We therefore restrict the risk premia in (2) to depend only on the global variables, Z_{t-1}. Exploratory regressions, described here, suggest that the local market information variables are related to country-specific betas. In the interest of parsimony, therefore, we assume that the betas are functions only of the local market information and model the predictable variance, using Equation (2), as

$$\text{Var}\{E(r_{it} \mid \Omega_{t-1})\} = \text{Var}\left\{\sum_{j=1}^{K} \beta_{ij}(Z^i_{t-1})\lambda_j(Z_{t-1})\right\}. \qquad (3)$$

Some informal intuition for the impact of the restrictions in (3) for country i can be obtained by assuming that $E(r_{it} \mid \Omega_{t-1})$ is a function $f(Z^i_{t-1}, Z_{t-1})$. Dropping the subscripts, consider an example where there is a single factor ($K = 1$), where β, λ, Z^i, and Z are scalars and where Z^i is uncorrelated with Z. Writing $f(Z^i, Z) = \beta(Z^i, Z)\lambda(Z^i, Z)$ and taking a first-order Taylor series about the means, we have

$$\text{Var}(f) \approx \left[\lambda(\cdot)\frac{\partial\beta}{\partial Z^i} + \beta(\cdot)\frac{\partial\lambda}{\partial Z^i}\right]^2 \text{Var}(Z^i)$$

$$+ \left[\lambda(\cdot)\frac{\partial\beta}{\partial Z} + \beta(\cdot)\frac{\partial\lambda}{\partial Z}\right]^2 \text{Var}(Z), \qquad (4)$$

where $\lambda(\cdot)$ and $\beta(\cdot)$ are evaluated at the means. The first term captures the contribution of the local information to the predictable variance of country i's return, and the second term captures the contribution of the global information. Market integration can be interpreted as implying that $\partial\lambda/\partial Z^i = 0$ in the first term. The assumption that the betas depend only on the local market information implies that $\partial\beta/\partial Z = 0$ in the second term. By setting $\partial\beta/\partial Z = 0$, we are ignoring what should be the smaller of the coefficients that scale the variance in the second term of (4). This occurs because the square of an average risk premium is a small number compared with the square of an average beta. The term that we retain should capture the dominant effect of the global information variables on the predictable variation.

The Review of Financial Studies / v 6 n 3 1993

2. Methodology

To estimate the fraction of the predictable variation that a beta pricing model captures, we use a regression of the excess country return, r_{it}, on the information variables as a base case. Returns are measured in a common currency, which we choose to be the U.S. dollar. (Later, we investigate the sensitivity of the results to the currency of denomination.) With a linear regression model for the conditional expected return given Z_{t-1}, $E(r_{it} \mid Z_{t-1}) = Z'_{t-1}\delta_i$, where δ_i is the coefficient vector. The predictable variance of the return, using Z_{t-1}, is $\mathrm{Var}[E(r_{it} \mid Z_{t-1})] = \mathrm{Var}[Z'_{t-1}\delta_i].$[2]

The predictable variation captured by the model depends on the conditional betas and the risk premia. We use a linear regression to model the expected risk premia, following much of the literature on conditional asset pricing. That is, we assume that $\lambda(Z_{t-1}) = E(F_t \mid Z_{t-1}) = \gamma' Z_{t-1}$, where γ is an $L \times K$ matrix of coefficients and the F_t are mimicking portfolio excess returns for K risk factors. We approximate the conditional betas as linear functions of the local information variables: $\beta_{ij}(Z^i_{t-1}) = \kappa'_i Z^i_{t-1}$, where κ_i is an $L \times K$ matrix of coefficients that describe the conditional betas for country i as a linear function of the lagged, local market variables.[3] With these assumptions, the predictable variance of the return captured by the beta pricing model is $\mathrm{Var}[\Sigma_j E(F_{jt} \mid Z_{t-1})\beta_{ij}(Z^i_{t-1})] = \mathrm{Var}[Z'_{t-1}\gamma\kappa'_i Z^i_{t-1}]$. We express this as a proportion, defining the following variance ratio:

$$VR1_i = \frac{\mathrm{Var}\left[E\left(\sum_{j=1}^{K} F_{jt} \mid Z_{t-1}\right)\beta_{ij}(Z^i_{t-1})\right]}{\mathrm{Var}[E(r_{it} \mid Z_{t-1})]}$$

$$= \frac{\mathrm{Var}[Z'_{t-1}\gamma\kappa'_i Z^i_{t-1}]}{\mathrm{Var}[Z'_{t-1}\delta_i]}. \tag{5}$$

The variance ratio VR1 measures the fraction of the predictable variance in the return attributed to the model.

We estimate the model by first defining the following error terms for each country i:

$$u1_{it} = (r_{it} - Z'_{t-1}\delta_i), \tag{6a}$$

---

[2] We also report results where the conditional variance of the expected return is formed by regressing the country return on both the global and the local information variables.

[3] Linear approximations for betas are used by Campbell (1987) and Shanken (1990), among others. A problem common to all such approaches, including ours, is that the information set used in the empirical work is implicitly assumed to represent all publicly available information. Our "unrestricted" regression for the predictable variation does not nest the expected return predicted by the model, as would normally be the situation for hypothesis tests. The large number of product terms would make such an approach unwieldy here.

$$u2_{it} = (F'_t - Z'_{t-1}\gamma)',$$ (6b)

$$u3_{it} = [(u2_{it}u2'_{it})(\kappa'_i Z^i_{t-1}) - (F_t u1'_{it})],$$ (6c)

$$u4_{it} = (Z'_{t-1}\delta_i - \theta_i),$$ (6d)

$$u5_{it} = (Z'_{t-1}\gamma)(\kappa'_i Z^i_{t-1}) - \theta_i + \alpha_i,$$ (6e)

$$u6_{it} = (u4^2_{it})VR1_i - u5^2_{it}.$$ (6f)

The parameters are $\{\theta_i, \alpha_i, VR1_i, \gamma, \delta_i, \kappa_i\}$, where the first three parameters are scalars. The parameter α_i is the difference between the unconditional mean return and the unconditional mean of the model fitted return. It therefore measures an "average pricing error," analogous to the traditional α measure of performance. If the model is well specified, α_i should be zero.

The model implies the orthogonality conditions[4]

$$E(u1_{it}Z_{t-1}, u2_{it}Z'_{t-1}, u3_{it}Z''_{t-1}, u4_{it}, u5_{it}, u6_{it}) = 0.$$

The number of orthogonality conditions and the number of parameters in the system are $2LK + L + 3$, and the system is exactly identified. The model is estimated for each country by using Hansen's (1982) generalized method of moments (GMM).[5]

We also modify system (6) to obtain a complementary variance ratio:[6]

$$VR2_i = \frac{Var\left[E(r_{it} \mid Z_{t-1}) - \sum_{j=1}^{K} \beta_{ij}(Z^i_{t-1})E(F_{jt} \mid Z_{t-1})\right]}{Var[E(r_{it} \mid Z_{t-1})]}$$

$$= \frac{Var[Z'_{t-1}\delta_i - Z'_{t-1}\gamma\kappa'_i Z^i_{t-1}]}{Var[Z'_{t-1}\delta_i]}.$$ (7)

The ratio VR2 measures the predictable variation in the return that is not captured by the model.

The difference between the returns and the model expected returns should have the property that their expected values, given *all* of the

---

[4] As a check, we reestimated the model for a number of cases, forcing the error term in the conditional beta equation (6c) to be orthogonal to the global instruments, Z_{t-1}, instead of the local instruments. The results were broadly similar.

[5] The system is estimated separately for each country in order to keep the size of the problem tractable. As the system is exactly identified, the point estimates of the parameters are the same as they would be if the same system was estimated jointly across the countries. We use $L = 7$ global information variables, so the number of moment conditions in a model with $K = 5$ factors is 80. We also have seven local market information variables for each country, and 239 monthly return observations. We are unable to estimate system (6) using all of the variables, as the number of orthogonality conditions would exceed the number of observations.

[6] To estimate $VR2_n$, we replace the model-fitted part of the return $Z'_{t-1}\gamma\kappa'_i Z^i_{t-1}$ in (6e) with $Z'_{t-1}\delta_i - Z'_{t-1}\gamma\kappa'_i Z^i_{t-1}$.

The Review of Financial Studies / v 6 n 3 1993

conditioning information, Ω_{t-1}, are zero. We have imposed many restrictions on the model, requiring the local information variables to enter only through the betas and the world information to enter only through the risk premia. Although we are forced to estimate the models by using subsets of the information, we conduct diagnostics on the model "pricing errors," which are

$$\epsilon_{it} = r_{it} - Z'_{t-1}\gamma\kappa'_i Z^i_{t-1}. \tag{8}$$

The pricing errors are the sum of the unexpected part of the returns and any specification error in the model for the expected returns. If the model is well specified, we should find that $E(\epsilon_{it} \mid Z^i_{t-1}) = E(\epsilon_{it} \mid Z_{t-1}) = 0$; that is, the pricing errors should be unpredictable. (The unconditional mean of the pricing error is α_i, which should also equal zero.)

As a check on the sensitivity of our results, we estimate variance ratios by the cross-sectional regression (CSR) methods of Fama and MacBeth (1973), as employed by Ferson and Harvey (1991) in a domestic context. This approach, which we review in the Appendix, is a multistep procedure that allows for time-varying covariances, variances, betas, and expected returns.

3. The Data

3.1 Country returns
We study equity returns for 18 national markets as provided by Morgan Stanley Capital International (MSCI). Total monthly returns are used for 1970 to 1989. The U.S. dollar returns are measured in excess of the U.S. Treasury bill that is the closest to 30 days to maturity, as provided by the Center for Research in Security Prices (CRSP) at the University of Chicago. To convert from local currency values to U.S. dollar values, we use the closing European interbank currency rates from MSCI on the last trading day of the month.

3.2 Global economic risk variables
We construct a set of variables to represent global economic risks. Our approach is to choose variables a priori and to investigate their importance with simple, factor model regressions. Then we study the pricing of the most important risks. Summary statistics for the variables are presented in Table 1; details about the data sources and definitions are provided in the Appendix.

WDRET is the U.S. dollar return of the MSCI world equity market in excess of a short-term interest rate. Asset pricing models usually include a role for a "market portfolio" as a measure of risk. Harvey

(1991) studies the risk premium associated with conditional covariances of returns with the world stock return index and concludes that it partially explains the differential performance of the U.S. and Japanese stock markets. The world equity market index is a value-weighted combination of the country returns.[7]

dG10FX is the log first difference in the trade-weighted U.S. dollar prices of the currencies of 10 industrialized countries. The G-10 countries are defined as the G-7 (not including the United States), plus the Netherlands, Belgium, Sweden, and Switzerland. The G-7 countries are Canada, France, Germany, Italy, Japan, the United Kingdom, and the United States. This series is from the International Monetary Fund (IMF), as reported by Citibase. A positive change (dG10FX > 0) indicates a depreciation of the dollar. In Adler and Dumas (1983, Equation 14), the theoretical exchange risk factor depends on exchange rates, consumer price index changes, and risk tolerance in each country. This factor is difficult to replicate empirically, so Dumas and Solnik (1992) break it down into separate variables for each country. We use a single aggregate measure as a parsimonious alternative to the approach of Dumas and Solnik (1992). Previous studies examine the pricing of exchange risks in national equity markets. They find little evidence that exchange risks are priced on average, but there is some evidence for time-varying currency risk premia.[8] A unique feature of our study is to use a global measure of exchange risk in a multicountry asset pricing model.

G7UI is the unexpected component of a monthly global inflation measure. The G-7 inflation rate is a weighted average of the percentage changes in the consumer price indices (CPI) in the G-7 countries, using the relative shares of the total real, gross domestic product (GDP) as the weights. An inflation state variable could arise in a multibeta model if inflation has real effects, in the general sense that global inflation is correlated with marginal utility. For example, higher inflation may signal higher levels of economic uncertainty, which make consumers worse off. If national equity market returns differ in their exposure to changes in the global inflation outlook, there may be an inflation risk premium in global equity markets.[9]

---

[7] MSCI attempts to avoid the double counting of firms whose equity is traded on the stock markets of more than one country. There are, however, other problems with the index. For example, French and Poterba (1991) show that the MSCI world index gives too much weight to Japan because the amount of cross-corporate ownership of shares in Japan has been unusually high. Alternative indices, such as the FT-Actuaries world index, suffer from the same problem. Harvey (1991) reports that in March of 1989 Japan accounted for 43 percent of the MSCI world index and 41 percent of the FT-Actuaries index. We choose the MSCI data over the FT-Actuaries data because the latter are only available from 1981.

[8] See Hamao (1988), Bodurtha, Cho, and Senbet (1989), Brown and Otsuki (1990a,b), and Dumas and Solnik (1992).

[9] If higher inflation makes consumers worse off and therefore is associated with higher real marginal utility, we would expect a negative inflation premium.

The Review of Financial Studies / v 6 n 3 1993

Table 1
Summary statistics for the world risk factors and instrumental variables: 1970:2–1989:12
(239 observations)

Variable	Symbol	Mean	Std. dev.	ρ_1	ρ_2	ρ_3	ρ_4	ρ_{12}	ρ_{24}
			World risk factors						
World excess return	wdret	0.545	4.189	.15	−.03	.05	.03	.09	.00
Change in Eurodollar–Treasury yield	dted	−0.046	3.988	−.08	−.09	−.07	−.13	.02	.09
Log change in G-10 foreign exchange rate	dG10fx	0.104	2.099	.31	.06	.09	.08	.06	−.07
Unexpected G-7 inflation	dG7ui	−0.005	0.204	.00	.04	−.02	−.09	.01	.08
Change in long-term G-7 expected inflation	dG7elt	−0.039	1.275	−.34	−.12	.09	−.16	−.08	.01
Change in price of oil	doil	0.062	0.861	.56	.22	.08	.03	−.02	−.02
Change in G-7 industrial production	dG7ip	0.215	0.817	.11	.27	.24	.15	−.08	−.17
G-7 real interest rate	G7rtb	0.132	0.316	.67	.52	.53	.52	.67	.55
			World instrumental variables						
Lagged world excess return	wr	0.523	4.211	.14	−.02	.07	.04	.08	−.00
Lagged world dividend yield	wrddiv	0.320	0.080	.98	.96	.95	.93	.76	.57
Lagged Eurodollar–Treasury yield spread	ted	0.121	0.084	.74	.57	.40	.44	.26	−.01
Lagged slope of U.S. term structure	term	0.111	0.118	.87	.76	.70	.64	.28	−.08
30-day U.S. Treasury bill rate	tb1	0.597	0.224	.93	.87	.82	.78	.59	.28

| | | | Correlations of the world risk factors | | | | |
Variable	wdret	dted	dG10fx	G7ui	dG7elt	doil	dG7ip	G7rtb
wdret	1.000							
dted	−0.154	1.000						
dG10fx	0.314	0.010	1.000					
G7ui	−0.005	0.166	−0.015	1.000				
dG7elt	−0.253	0.238	−0.110	0.005	1.000			
doil	−0.066	−0.107	−0.143	0.207	−0.098	1.000		
dG7ip	−0.053	0.128	−0.075	0.128	0.053	−0.055	1.000	
G7rtb	0.101	−0.058	−0.059	−0.564	−0.007	−0.289	−0.031	1.000

| | | | Correlations of the world instruments | | |
Variable	wr	jan	divwrd	ted	term	tb1
wr	1.000					
jan	0.091	1.000				
divwrd	−0.156	0.016	1.000			
ted	−0.347	0.078	0.350	1.000		
term	0.138	−0.006	−0.271	−0.414	1.000	
tb1	−0.230	−0.059	0.518	0.390	−0.530	1.000

World risk factors

The world excess return is the arithmetic return on the Morgan Stanley Capital International world equity index (including dividends) minus the Ibbotson Associates one-month bill rate. The change in the Eurodollar–Treasury yield spread is the first difference of the spread between the 90-day Eurodollar yield and the 90-day Treasury-bill yield (from the Federal Reserve Bulletin). The log change in the G-10 foreign exchange rate is based on the trade-weighted dollar per foreign exchange

dG7ELT is the monthly change in a measure of long-term inflationary expectations. Chen, Roll, and Ross (1986) include a measure of unexpected inflation and a measure of changes in expected inflation in their study for the United States. dG7ELT is formed by regressing a 48-month moving average of the G-7 inflation rate on our predetermined global information variables and taking the first difference of the fitted values.

dTED is the change in the spread between the 90-day Eurodollar deposit rate and the 90-day U.S. Treasury-bill yield. The "TED spread" is a measure of the premium on Eurodollar deposit rates in London, relative to the U.S. Treasury. Fluctuations in the spread may capture fluctuations in global credit risks.

G7RTB is a weighted average of short-term interest rates in the G-7 countries, using the shares of G-7 GDP as the weights, minus the G-7 inflation rate. Real interest rates are often used in economic models to capture the state of investment opportunities. For example, Merton (1973) and Cox, Ingersoll, and Ross (1985) develop models in which interest rates are state variables. Chen, Roll, and Ross (1986) and Ferson and Harvey (1991) include real interest rate risk in empirical models for the U.S. market.[10]

dOIL is the change in the monthly average U.S. dollar price per barrel of crude oil. Chen, Roll, and Ross (1986) propose oil prices as a measure of economic risk in the U.S. market, and Hamao (1988)

---

[10] Although the correlation between G7RTB and G7UI is relatively high (at −.56), it is not perfect because the G-7 nominal interest rates are not part of the conditioning information used to form G7UI and because G7RTB is not prewhitened.

←

rate of 10 industrialized countries (G-7 plus the Netherlands, Belgium, Sweden, and Switzerland), from the International Monetary Fund. The unexpected inflation for the G-7 countries is derived from a time-series model applied to an aggregate G-7 inflation rate where the (varying) weights in the aggregate are determined by country weights in total G-7 gross domestic product. The change in long term G-7 expected inflation is found by regressing a 48-month moving average of the G-7 inflation rate on the lagged instrumental variables and taking the first difference of the fitted values. The change in the price of oil is the log change in the average U.S. dollar price per barrel at the wellhead from 1974 to 1989 and the posted West Texas Intermediate price from 1969 to 1973. The change in G-7 industrial production is calculated by weighting local industrial production index levels by the following weights: Canada, .04314; France, .09833; Germany, .05794; Italy, .13093; Japan, .07485; U.K., .11137; U.S., .48343, which are the weights in G-7 gross domestic product in the third quarter of 1969. The growth rate is the logarithmic difference in the aggregate industrial production index. The G-7 real interest rate is calculated by aggregating individual countries' short-term interest rates minus inflation rates using (varying) weights based on quarterly shares in G-7 gross domestic product.

World instrumental variables

The instrumental variables are the lagged return of the Morgan Stanley Capital International world index in excess of the CRSP 30-day bill, a dummy variable for the month of January, the dividend yield (based on the past 12 months' dividends) on the Morgan Stanley Capital International world equity index, the difference between the 90-day Eurodollar rate and the CRSP three-month Treasury-bill yield, the difference between the U.S. 10-year Treasury-bond yield and the CRSP three-month bill yield, and the CRSP 30-day Treasury-bill yield.

The Review of Financial Studies / v 6 n 3 1993

and Brown and Otsuki (1990b) study oil prices in the Japanese equity market.[11]

dG7IP is a weighted average of industrial production growth rates in the G-7 countries, where a measure of relative production shares is used as the weights. Chen, Roll, and Ross (1986) and Shanken and Weinstein (1990) examine the average pricing of U.S. industrial production in the U.S. market. Hamao (1988) examines domestic industrial production risk in the Japanese equity market, and Bodurtha, Cho, and Senbet (1989) estimate the average risk premia for domestic industrial production risk in several countries. No previous study has examined the pricing of global industrial output risks in a conditional asset pricing model.

Our application of beta pricing models requires mimicking portfolios for the risk factors. When a factor is an excess return, the best way to estimate a mimicking portfolio is to use the excess return of the asset directly [Shanken (1992)]. Among our global risk factors, only WDRET is an excess return. We estimate mimicking portfolios for the other variables. One way to estimate mimicking portfolios is to use a large cross section of asset returns [Connor and Korajczyk (1986), Lehmann and Modest (1988), Korajczyk and Viallet (1989)], an approach not available to us. We estimate mimicking portfolios by two common methods, which we describe, and compare them to check the sensitivity of the results.

3.3 The predetermined instruments

We include a list of predetermined instrumental variables similar to previous studies of predictability in country returns. The global information variables, Z_{t-1}, are (1) the yield of a one-month U.S. Treasury bill, (2) the dividend yield of the MSCI world stock market index, (3) a spread between the yields to maturity of 10-year U.S. Treasury bonds and 90-day U.S. Treasury bills, (4) the lagged value of the Eurodollar–U.S. Treasury (TED) spread, (5) the lagged return on the MSCI world market index, and (6) a dummy variable for the month of January. These variables represent readily available, global information that may influence expectations about future equity returns.

For our country-specific instruments, Z_{t-1}^i, we replace the U.S. Treasury bill with a short-term interest rate from the specific country. The world dividend yield is replaced with the dividend yield for the national stock market. The term spread is replaced with a yield spread

---

[11] We used a spliced series of the posted West Texas intermediate crude and the average U.S. wellhead price, as described in the Appendix. These are not the best indicators of market prices, but they are the best available to us for this period. Futures markets for crude oil did not develop until 1983 (heating oil futures began trading in 1978). Chen, Roll, and Ross (1986) used the energy component of the Producer Price Index. Given the prevalence of long-term oil price contracts over much of the sample, this measure is not likely to better reflect current oil market conditions.

of domestic long-term over short-term, low-risk bonds. The lagged world index return is replaced with the lagged return of the national stock market index. These variables represent information specific to the domestic markets, to the extent that the global aggregates are not sufficient for the local market information. Of course, the distinction between national market information and global information is artificial, because the information sets of investors overlap in more complicated ways. We choose this design on the basis of data availability, parsimony, and empirical tractability. Our data sources and definitions are provided in the Appendix.[12] Table 1 presents monthly summary statistics of the world information variables.

Since the predetermined variables follow previous empirical work, there is a natural concern about predictability uncovered through collective "data snooping" by a series of researchers. Solnik (1993) uses a set of country-specific instruments similar to a subset of ours and argues that step-ahead tests provide evidence that the predictive ability of the instruments is economically significant. Such results increase our confidence that the predictability is an economic phenomenon.[13]

4. Empirical Results

4.1 Preliminary regressions

Table 2 summarizes factor models, where each national equity market return is regressed over time on the eight global risk factors. We use 60-month rolling regressions as a simple way to approximate a factor model with time-varying betas.[14] The right-hand column of Table 2 presents the average of the adjusted R^2's of the rolling regressions for each country. By this measure the global risk factors explain, ex post, 14 to 80 percent of the variance over the 1975–1989 period. In separate regressions, we found that the world market portfolio is by

---

[12] We studied one other variable, a lagged measure of volatility for the S&P 500 stock market index, constructed from daily returns in the fashion of French, Schwert, and Stambaugh (1987). This variable was also studied by Cutler, Poterba, and Summers (1990). We found that the lagged volatility had no marginal explanatory power for our sample of monthly returns.

[13] The direction of any bias due to data snooping is not clear. On the one hand, the ability of beta pricing models to explain the predictability has not been a criterion for the choice of the lagged information variables. Spurious predictability of the returns, as would be implied by data snooping, should therefore be difficult to "explain" using the models. On the other hand, we choose the global risk variables following previous studies. Most of the previous studies used the factors in unconditional models and did not focus on predictability. Data snooping biases in the risk factors should therefore not be strongly correlated with those in the predetermined variables. However, there must be some correlation between the returns and the factors, which implies that any data-snooping bias may not be independent across the two.

[14] See Braun, Nelson, and Sunier (1991) for evidence that such betas are similar to EGARCH models of conditional betas.

The Review of Financial Studies / v 6 n 3 1993

Table 2
The proportion of times that the right-tail probability value was less than 10% for the statistic testing whether the beta coefficients are equal to zero or equal across all countries, based on rolling time series regressions on eight world risk factors. The sample is 1975: 2–1989:12 (179 observations)

Country, i	wdret	dted	dG10fx	G7ui	dG7elt	doil	dG7ip	G7rtb	$\bar{R}^2$
Australia	0.972	0.358	0.229	0.140	0.553	0.112	0.061	0.173	0.406
Austria	0.475	0.279	0.838	0.073	0.162	0.078	0.000	0.151	0.294
Belgium	1.000	0.128	0.777	0.011	0.168	0.050	0.028	0.145	0.444
Canada	1.000	0.061	0.145	0.285	0.553	0.307	0.000	0.196	0.566
Denmark	1.000	0.011	0.274	0.073	0.369	0.017	0.000	0.212	0.233
France	1.000	0.229	0.514	0.184	0.173	0.017	0.341	0.078	0.408
Germany	0.989	0.380	0.804	0.034	0.000	0.291	0.006	0.106	0.358
Hong Kong	0.899	0.291	0.162	0.000	0.156	0.341	0.257	0.017	0.190
Italy	0.894	0.469	0.212	0.112	0.330	0.274	0.056	0.106	0.241
Japan	1.000	0.095	0.503	0.207	0.318	0.201	0.251	0.173	0.430
Netherlands	1.000	0.140	0.570	0.017	0.045	0.101	0.039	0.263	0.555
Norway	0.972	0.034	0.291	0.251	0.430	0.453	0.240	0.179	0.313
Singapore/Malaysia	0.961	0.050	0.391	0.101	0.240	0.469	0.006	0.162	0.324
Spain	0.760	0.486	0.285	0.106	0.307	0.475	0.000	0.084	0.138
Sweden	0.944	0.006	0.458	0.112	0.212	0.073	0.218	0.263	0.249
Switzerland	1.000	0.084	0.626	0.017	0.391	0.173	0.011	0.436	0.530
United Kingdom	1.000	0.039	0.419	0.078	0.106	0.134	0.140	0.156	0.444
United States	1.000	0.034	0.972	0.196	0.324	0.402	0.168	0.050	0.790
$\beta_{ij} = 0$ for $i = 1,...,18$	1.000	0.425	0.978	0.123	0.939	0.670	0.095	0.425	
$\beta_{ij} = \beta_i$ for $i = 1,...,18$	0.832	0.374	0.983	0.112	0.816	0.665	0.061	0.402	

Proportions are based on heteroskedasticity consistent test statistics. The standard error of the fraction rejected (adjusted for overlapping observations) is .143. The R^2's are average time-series R^2's adjusted for degrees of freedom. The values in rows 1–18 represent the proportion of times that the probability value for the statistic, testing whether the beta coefficient is zero, was less than 10 percent. The values in rows 19 and 20 represent the proportion of times that the probability value was less than 10 percent for the tests that the beta associated with each source of risk is zero across 18 country portfolios or equal across 18 country portfolios, respectively. The world excess return, wdret, is the arithmetic return on the Morgan Stanley Capital International world equity index (including dividends) minus the Ibbotson Associates one-month bill rate. The change in the Eurodollar–Treasury yield spread, dted, is the first difference of the spread between the 90-day Eurodollar yield and the 90-day Treasury-bill yield (from the Federal Reserve Bulletin). The log change in the G-10 foreign exchange rate, dG10fx, is based on the trade-weighted dollar per foreign exchange rate of 10 industrialized countries (G-7 plus the Netherlands, Belgium, Sweden, and Switzerland). The unexpected inflation for the G-7 countries, G7ui, is derived from a time-series model applied to an aggregate G-7 inflation rate where the (varying) weights in the aggregate are determined by country weights in total G-7 gross domestic product. The change in long-term expected G-7 inflation, dG7elt, is a result of projecting the four-year moving average of G-7 inflation on the set of lagged instrumental variables. The change in the price of oil, doil, is the log change in the average U.S. dollar price per barrel at the wellhead from 1974 to 1989 and the posted West Texas Intermediate price from 1969 to 1973. dG7ip is the change in G-7 industrial production. The G-7 real interest rate, G7rtb, is calculated by aggregating individual countries' short-term interest rates minus inflation rates using (varying) weights based on quarterly shares in G-7 gross domestic product.

far the most important factor in this sense. It alone explains 5 to 71 percent of the ex post variance, depending on the country.

We use the regressions in Table 2 to delete a subset of our initial risk factors from the subsequent analysis. If there is a variable whose betas are not different across the countries or different from zero, then that variable will not be priced. The bottom row of Table 2 presents tests of the hypothesis that the betas for each global risk variable are zero in all of the countries and of the hypothesis that they are equal across the countries. The first number is the fraction of the 60-month regressions in which a Wald test rejects the hypothesis that the betas are equal to zero for all countries, using a 10 percent significance level. The second number is the fraction of the 60-month regressions in which the test rejects the hypothesis that the betas are jointly equal across the countries but not necessarily equal to zero. If the null hypotheses are true, then we expect to reject in 10 percent of the cases. We calculate an approximate standard error for the fraction rejected, given 179 trials, as equal to 0.143.[15] To include a risk variable in our model, we require that the fraction rejected in Table 2 be at least two standard errors above the expected fraction of 0.10. This leads us to drop the variables G7UI, G7IP, and dTED.

Table 3 summarizes regressions that use the lagged world information variables to predict the excess country returns. The apparent predictable variation measured by the adjusted R^2's ranges across the countries, from virtually zero to over 10 percent. Table 4 shows the marginal explanatory power of additional lagged variables. The first three columns report R^2's for regressions of the returns on the global information variables, augmented with either the local versions of the information variables or with the lagged values of the rolling regression betas from Table 2.[16] The fourth column of the table presents F-tests for the incremental explanatory power of the local information variables, given the global variables. They are significant at the 5 percent level for 7 of the 18 countries, which provides some evidence that local information is important.[17] A joint heteroskedasticity-consistent Wald test for all 18 countries produces a test statistic of 180.1. The right-tail p value from the χ^2 distribution is less than .001.

The beta pricing model assumes that expected returns are determined by conditional betas, which are country specific, and by expected risk premia, which are global measures. If conditional betas

---

[15] Each joint test based on one rolling regression, using a test of size α, is viewed as generating a binomial trial. If these trials were independent, then the variance of the fraction rejected in n trials is approximately given by $\alpha(1 - \alpha)/n$. But the rolling regressions are not independent, because of the overlapping data. The variance of the fraction rejected, p, is adjusted for the overlap as follows. Assuming that the underlying data are independent across the months, then the autocovariance of the p_i's that is induced by overlapping data is $\mathrm{Cov}(p_i, p_{i-j}) = [(60 - j)/60]\mathrm{Var}(p_i)$ if j < 60, and zero otherwise. We construct the covariance matrix of the vector of the p_i's and find the standard error of p for 179 trials, using the 60-month regression approach and $\alpha = .10$, to be .143.

[16] The rolling regression betas for time $t - 1$ are not strictly predetermined to the extent that publication lags and data revisions imply that the economic series were not actually available to market participants at time $t - 1$. We therefore estimated these regressions with betas lagged back two months. Also, for the first 60 months of the sample, the betas are constant.

[17] This is so in spite of the fact that in some of the more regulated economies (e.g., Sweden) the interest rates used as instruments are not competitively determined market rates.

The Review of Financial Studies / v 6 n 3 1993

542

Table 3
Regression of asset returns on world instrumental variables. The sample is 1970:2–1989:12 (239 observations)

Country	intercept	wr_{t-1}	jan.	Instrument $divwrd_{t-1}$	ted_{t-1}	$term_{t-1}$	$tb1_t$	$\bar{R}^2$
Australia	0.040 (0.025)	0.190 (0.142)	0.027 (0.020)	12.985 (8.826)	−18.619 (7.642)	−11.911 (5.642)	−7.482 (3.566)	0.068
Austria	0.066 (0.021)	0.069 (0.084)	−0.033 (0.011)	−9.252 (5.454)	−9.797 (4.055)	−3.182 (4.171)	−1.850 (1.974)	0.074
Belgium	0.039 (0.019)	−0.042 (0.090)	0.022 (0.012)	1.669 (5.416)	−9.274 (5.181)	0.785 (3.596)	−4.481 (2.278)	0.042
Canada	0.030 (0.020)	0.077 (0.086)	0.019 (0.016)	11.999 (5.615)	−9.768 (5.898)	−10.176 (4.143)	−7.226 (2.443)	0.064
Denmark	0.039 (0.020)	−0.196 (0.087)	0.020 (0.015)	−3.129 (5.213)	−9.065 (4.615)	1.605 (3.387)	−2.041 (2.047)	0.032
France	0.027 (0.023)	−0.001 (0.099)	0.021 (0.019)	9.103 (7.402)	−16.422 (7.146)	−3.642 (4.829)	−4.442 (3.061)	0.026
Germany	0.023 (0.023)	0.073 (0.112)	−0.005 (0.015)	5.338 (5.754)	−9.273 (5.629)	−1.842 (4.057)	−3.473 (2.224)	0.013
Hong Kong	0.069 (0.046)	0.127 (0.164)	0.074 (0.026)	9.510 (11.681)	−31.837 (10.542)	−10.652 (7.544)	−6.656 (4.587)	0.057
Italy	0.009 (0.026)	0.124 (0.112)	0.030 (0.018)	0.889 (6.864)	−12.733 (6.281)	−1.112 (4.469)	0.726 (2.967)	0.011
Japan	0.038 (0.022)	0.206 (0.110)	0.008 (0.012)	0.874 (5.926)	−7.769 (5.968)	1.399 (3.876)	−3.582 (2.309)	0.063
Netherlands	0.021 (0.019)	−0.030 (0.091)	0.031 (0.014)	10.720 (5.186)	−16.574 (5.242)	−2.796 (3.742)	−4.373 (2.318)	0.076

International Equity Returns

Table 3
Continued

Country	intercept	wr_{t-1}	jan_t	Instrument $divwrd_{t-1}$	ted_{t-1}	$term_{t-1}$	$tb1_t$	$\bar{R}^2$
Norway	0.070 (0.027)	−0.041 (0.154)	0.048 (0.018)	−5.766 (7.863)	−13.773 (8.189)	−11.186 (5.493)	−2.801 (3.350)	0.032
Singapore/Malaysia	0.072 (0.030)	0.051 (0.152)	0.081 (0.027)	11.648 (9.406)	−14.650 (8.083)	−17.227 (5.409)	−11.381 (3.520)	0.105
Spain	0.048 (0.019)	0.117 (0.099)	0.019 (0.016)	−17.163 (6.496)	−1.116 (5.583)	−0.172 (3.718)	1.586 (2.313)	0.030
Sweden	0.018 (0.020)	0.154 (0.114)	0.025 (0.015)	−0.861 (5.857)	−3.416 (5.782)	−2.423 (4.144)	−0.318 (2.524)	0.005
Switzerland	0.025 (0.019)	−0.073 (0.097)	0.012 (0.016)	9.226 (5.699)	−12.698 (5.487)	−2.580 (3.735)	−5.306 (2.262)	0.039
United Kingdom	0.009 (0.022)	−0.023 (0.142)	0.050 (0.029)	20.683 (8.430)	−19.979 (7.038)	−5.257 (5.153)	−6.881 (3.297)	0.074
United States	0.006 (0.015)	−0.041 (0.086)	0.024 (0.013)	11.497 (5.231)	−11.277 (4.601)	−2.537 (3.309)	−4.134 (1.948)	0.061
World	0.017 (0.014)	0.033 (0.065)	0.022 (0.011)	9.140 (4.265)	−12.056 (3.869)	−2.877 (2.848)	−4.175 (1.682)	0.095

R^2's are adjusted for degrees of freedom. Standard errors in parentheses are heteroskedasticity consistent. The instrumental variables are the following: a constant, a dummy variable for the month of January, the lagged excess return of the Morgan Stanley Capital International world index minus the CRSP 30-day bill, the dividend yield (over the past 12 months) on the Morgan Stanley Capital International world equity index, the difference between the 90-day Eurodollar rate and the CRSP three-month Treasury-bill yield, the difference between the U.S. 10-year Treasury-bond yield and the CRSP three-month bill yield, and the CRSP 30-day Treasury-bill yield.

The Review of Financial Studies / v 6 n 3 1993

Table 4
The incremental explanatory power of local information variables in predicting 18 countries' equity returns. The sample is 1970:2–1989:12 (239 observations)

Country	R^2 world	R^2 world + local	R^2 world + 5 betas	World + local F-test: exclude local p value	World + local + 1 beta F-test: exclude local p value	World + local + 5 betas F-test: exclude local p value
Australia	0.091	0.133	0.143	2.642 0.035	1.915 0.109	1.861 0.118
Austria	0.097	0.118	0.139	1.368 0.246	1.854 0.119	1.885 0.114
Belgium	0.067	0.089	0.142	1.385 0.240	0.552 0.698	1.398 0.236
Canada	0.087	0.128	0.182	2.563 0.039	2.566 0.039	1.798 0.130
Denmark	0.056	0.079	0.090	1.402 0.234	1.550 0.189	1.403 0.234
France	0.051	0.056	0.104	0.320 0.864	0.579 0.678	1.286 0.276
Germany	0.037	0.041	0.067	0.200 0.938	0.734 0.569	0.320 0.864
Hong Kong	0.081	0.081	0.103	0.013 0.987	0.027 0.974	0.475 0.623
Italy	0.036	0.061	0.085	1.504 0.202	1.413 0.230	0.991 0.413
Japan	0.086	0.092	0.112	0.349 0.844	0.427 0.789	1.001 0.408
Netherlands	0.099	0.133	0.172	2.202 0.070	1.639 0.165	2.979 0.020
Norway	0.056	0.102	0.101	2.822 0.026	2.860 0.024	1.935 0.105
Singapore/Malaysia	0.128	0.182	0.147	3.626 0.007	3.601 0.007	5.021 0.001
Spain	0.055	0.085	0.086	1.880 0.115	1.804 0.129	2.775 0.028
Sweden	0.030	0.068	0.056	2.269 0.063	2.780 0.028	3.502 0.008
Switzerland	0.063	0.103	0.103	2.445 0.047	2.048 0.089	2.116 0.080
United Kingdom	0.097	0.202	0.152	6.702 0.000	4.153 0.003	4.504 0.002
United States	0.084	0.148	0.202	4.061 0.003	2.078 0.084	0.576 0.680

The "world" regressions are time-series regressions of each country's excess return on the set of lagged world instruments. The "world" instrumental variables are the following: a constant, a dummy variable for the month of January, the lagged Morgan Stanley Capital International world return minus the CRSP 30-day bill, the dividend yield on the Morgan Stanley Capital International world equity index, the difference between the 90-day Eurodollar rate and the CRSP three-month bill yield, the difference between the U.S. 10-year Treasury-bond yield and the CRSP three-month bill yield, and the CRSP 30-day Treasury-bill yield.

The "world + local" regressions include the additional instrumental variables, which are the lagged excess return of the local equity market, the dividend yield for the local equity market, the difference between the long-term and short-term interest rates in the country and the local short-term interest rate.

The "world + local + 1 beta" regressions use the same regressors as the "world + local" are approximately constant, then predictable variation should be captured by global variables. If time variation in the betas is important, then local information may enter through the betas. Table 4 shows that the lagged betas deliver an increase in the explanatory power of the regressions. Their incremental forecast power is comparable to the local versions of the information variables. This suggests that the betas may capture information about the future returns, similar to the local variables.

In the fifth and sixth columns of Table 4 the incremental explanatory power of the local information variables is illustrated, in regressions which include both the lagged betas and the global variables. In the fifth column the lagged beta for each country with respect to the world market index is used. The sixth column introduces betas for all five of the global risk factors. An F-test examines the marginal explanatory power of the local variables. Their marginal impact is reduced, although not completely eliminated, when the lagged betas are included. Overall, the regressions provide some support for our specification of the empirical asset pricing model, in which we assume that local information variables enter through the betas. Of course, the regressions are only suggestive of how such a model will actually perform.

4.2 Explaining predictability using global economic risk factors

Table 5 addresses the extent to which the models can explain predictable variation in the country returns. The table reports for each country the average pricing error, α_i, its standard error, the variance ratios and their standard errors, and some analysis of the predictability that remains in the model pricing errors.

Panel A of Table 5 summarizes the single-factor model, in which the world market portfolio is the factor. The average pricing error is smaller than the average excess return for all countries and is more than two standard errors from zero in only three cases. However, the standard errors are large. Regressing the pricing errors over time on the lagged global information variables, the adjusted R^2's are negative for 10 of the 18 countries. Regressing the pricing errors on the local

---

←

regressions, in addition to the beta coefficient from a regression of the asset return on the excess world market return from $t - 62$ to $t - 2$.

The "world + local + 5 betas" regressions use the same regressors as the "world + local" regressions, in addition to the beta coefficients from a regression of the asset return on five world risk factors from $t - 62$ to $t - 2$. The risk factors are the excess world market return, the log change in a U.S. dollar versus G-10 currency index, the change in long-term expected G-7 inflation, the log change in the price of oil and the G-7 real interest rate.

The Review of Financial Studies / v 6 n 3 1993

Table 5
A decomposition of the predictable variation in international equity returns

Country	Average return	Average pricing error α_i	VR1	VR2	χ^2 constant betas	$\bar{R}^2$ pricing errors on Z	$\bar{R}^2$ pricing errors on Z'
A: 1-factor model[1]							
Australia	0.468	0.251 (0.477)	0.523 (0.240)	0.267 (0.134)	5.959 [0.428]	−0.004	0.003
Austria	0.756	0.633 (0.361)	0.091 (0.068)	0.809 (0.164)	2.703 [0.845]	0.055	0.070
Belgium	0.897	0.646 (0.316)	0.644 (0.387)	0.310 (0.179)	12.287 [0.056]	−0.007	−0.020
Canada	0.451	0.157 (0.284)	1.169 (0.496)	0.402 (0.236)	17.096 [0.009]	0.003	0.000
Denmark	0.816	0.473 (0.330)	0.494 (0.321)	0.708 (0.337)	1.790 [0.938]	0.015	−0.009
France	0.729	0.233 (0.379)	0.925 (0.520)	0.079 (0.124)	3.798 [0.704]	−0.023	−0.020
Germany	0.651	0.300 (0.325)	0.841 (0.529)	0.151 (0.182)	2.930 [0.818]	−0.021	−0.020
Hong Kong	1.630	1.397 (0.820)	0.274 (0.170)	0.334 (0.149)	7.143 [0.308]	0.001	0.004
Italy	0.296	−0.053 (0.472)	0.790 (0.545)	0.906 (0.642)	18.022 [0.006]	−0.000	0.023
Japan	1.313	0.784 (0.306)	0.510 (0.224)	0.386 (0.204)	16.769 [0.010]	0.006	−0.011
Netherlands	0.830	0.444 (0.257)	0.696 (0.242)	0.097 (0.074)	6.709 [0.349]	−0.018	0.011
Norway	0.932	0.889 (0.493)	0.726 (0.434)	0.647 (0.344)	16.299 [0.012]	0.004	0.006
Singapore/Malaysia	1.114	0.646 (0.519)	0.407 (0.192)	0.389 (0.166)	18.910 [0.004]	0.019	0.032
Spain	0.361	0.105 (0.390)	0.464 (0.359)	1.118 (0.443)	21.545 [0.001]	0.029	−0.004
Sweden	0.964	0.810 (0.384)	1.169 (1.070)	0.970 (0.831)	8.733 [0.189]	−0.001	0.007
Switzerland	0.548	0.224 (0.286)	1.025 (0.499)	0.212 (0.177)	6.373 [0.383]	−0.016	−0.013
United Kingdom	0.761	0.060 (0.403)	0.708 (0.311)	0.252 (0.147)	13.573 [0.035]	−0.012	0.066
United States	0.380	−0.052 (0.183)	1.218 (0.403)	0.179 (0.133)	20.141 [0.003]	−0.016	0.005
Average		0.442	0.704	0.456			
B: 2-factor model with BGL mimicking portfolio[2]							
Australia	0.468	−0.008 (0.482)	0.602 (0.263)	0.402 (0.175)	24.250 [0.019]	0.001	0.011
Austria	0.756	−0.110 (0.250)	0.465 (0.181)	0.394 (0.143)	19.094 [0.086]	0.012	0.014
Belgium	0.897	0.293 (0.250)	1.074 (0.428)	0.227 (0.179)	20.974 [0.051]	−0.013	−0.013

[1] The excess world market return is the single factor.
[2] In this two-factor model, the second factor is the change in the log of the U.S. versus G-10 countries exchange rate index. A mimicking portfolio is formed for the exchange rate index using the technique of Breeden, Gibbons, and Litzenberger (1989).

International Equity Returns

Table 5
Continued

Country	Average return	Average pricing error α_i	VR1	VR2	χ^2 constant betas	$\bar{R}^2$ pricing errors on Z	$\bar{R}^2$ pricing errors on Z'
Canada	0.451	0.247 (0.268)	1.174 (0.445)	0.361 (0.189)	23.581 [0.023]	−0.003	−0.003
Denmark	0.816	0.046 (0.284)	0.868 (0.476)	0.504 (0.300)	10.672 [0.557]	0.002	−0.013
France	0.729	−0.185 (0.351)	1.266 (0.619)	0.290 (0.275)	10.382 [0.582]	−0.014	−0.013
Germany	0.651	0.019 (0.291)	1.250 (0.640)	0.237 (0.257)	16.373 [0.175]	−0.020	−0.017
Hong Kong	1.630	0.647 (0.789)	0.428 (0.235)	0.419 (0.195)	13.050 . [0.365]	0.002	0.006
Italy	0.296	−0.492 (0.444)	1.228 (0.775)	1.086 (0.827)	21.511 [0.043]	0.001	0.024
Japan	1.313	0.438 (0.255)	0.751 (0.235)	0.277 (0.157)	41.392 [0.000]	−0.009	−0.022
Netherlands	0.830	0.284 (0.251)	0.793 (0.268)	0.148 (0.103)	17.597 [0.128]	−0.012	0.018
Norway	0.932	0.779 (0.490)	0.856 (0.500)	0.727 (0.381)	24.087 [0.020]	0.005	0.005
Singapore/Malaysia	1.114	0.663 (0.542)	0.418 (0.190)	0.395 (0.173)	26.163 [0.010]	0.019	0.030
Spain	0.361	−0.310 (0.376)	0.704 (0.471)	0.763 (0.381)	29.886 [0.003]	0.009	−0.008
Sweden	0.964	0.636 (0.389)	1.453 (1.275)	1.173 (1.020)	12.164 [0.433]	0.003	0.014
Switzerland	0.548	−0.091 (0.244)	1.357 (0.520)	0.405 (0.247)	21.769 [0.040]	−0.003	0.007
United Kingdom	0.761	−0.144 (0.417)	0.768 (0.332)	0.367 (0.264)	17.122 [0.145]	−0.006	0.069
United States	0.380	0.116 (0.151)	1.252 (0.260)	0.151 (0.084)	23.457 [0.024]	−0.017	0.001
Average		0.157	0.928	0.463			
		C: 2-factor model with FM mimicking portfolio[3]					
Australia	0.468	0.410 (0.469)	0.539 (0.247)	0.308 (0.143)	19.954 [0.068]	−0.002	0.006
Austria	0.756	0.455 (0.337)	0.135 (0.082)	0.784 (0.190)	29.191 [0.004]	0.049	0.060
Belgium	0.897	0.450 (0.300)	0.672 (0.387)	0.337 (0.202)	20.959 [0.051]	−0.005	−0.020
Canada	0.451	0.351 (0.275)	1.186 (0.536)	0.510 (0.296)	49.514 [0.000]	0.008	0.004
Denmark	0.816	0.421 (0.326)	0.544 (0.340)	0.712 (0.357)	5.514 [0.939]	0.015	−0.007
France	0.729	0.144 (0.382)	0.923 (0.549)	0.156 (0.209)	12.567 [0.401]	−0.021	−0.017
Germany	0.651	−0.061 (0.315)	1.258 (0.760)	0.449 (0.410)	37.869 [0.000]	−0.016	−0.015
Hong Kong	1.630	1.042 (0.548)	0.748 (0.298)	0.224 (0.129)	38.665 [0.000]	−0.010	−0.008

[3] In this two-factor model, the mimicking portfolio for the exchange rate index is formed using the method of Fama and MacBeth (1973).

The Review of Financial Studies / v 6 n 3 1993

Table 5
Continued

Country	Average return	Average pricing error α_i	VR1	VR2	χ^2 constant betas	$\bar{R}^2$ pricing errors on Z	$\bar{R}^2$ pricing errors on Z'
Italy	0.296	−0.227 (0.479)	0.921 (0.636)	0.954 (0.688)	38.695 [0.000]	0.001	0.022
Japan	1.313	0.816 (0.300)	0.645 (0.261)	0.381 (0.223)	48.863 [0.000]	0.005	−0.014
Netherlands	0.830	0.339 (0.248)	0.746 (0.236)	0.061 (0.058)	30.669 [0.002]	−0.020	0.013
Norway	0.932	0.748 (0.497)	0.724 (0.433)	0.588 (0.332)	24.670 [0.016]	0.000	0.003
Singapore/Malaysia	1.114	0.922 (0.497)	0.457 (0.318)	0.593 (0.225)	78.739 [0.000]	0.045	0.059
Spain	0.361	0.105 (0.388)	0.427 (0.321)	1.101 (0.422)	22.996 [0.028]	0.027	−0.007
Sweden	0.964	0.814 (0.388)	1.308 (1.160)	0.994 (0.833)	12.792 [0.384]	−0.002	0.006
Switzerland	0.548	0.029 (0.292)	1.266 (0.578)	0.269 (0.253)	28.797 [0.004]	−0.011	−0.010
United Kingdom	0.761	0.148 (0.421)	0.753 (0.358)	0.432 (0.259)	75.157 [0.000]	0.006	0.089
United States	0.380	0.028 (0.195)	1.305 (0.447)	0.258 (0.178)	34.513 [0.001]	−0.013	0.008
Average		0.382	0.809	0.506			
		D: 5-factor model with BGL mimicking portfolios[a]					
Australia	0.468	0.115 (0.442)	0.951 (0.406)	0.458 (0.300)	52.191 [0.007]	−0.009	0.009
Austria	0.756	−0.114 (0.212)	0.610 (0.184)	0.292 (0.123)	68.107 [0.000]	−0.005	0.002
Belgium	0.897	0.418 (0.258)	1.172 (0.481)	0.352 (0.248)	48.992 [0.016]	−0.015	−0.010
Canada	0.451	0.130 (0.296)	1.489 (0.476)	0.388 (0.207)	48.977 [0.016]	−0.005	−0.001
Denmark	0.816	−0.032 (0.274)	1.198 (0.572)	0.667 (0.419)	66.355 [0.000]	0.010	−0.012
France	0.729	0.122 (0.356)	1.405 (0.715)	0.505 (0.354)	72.931 [0.000]	−0.009	−0.007
Germany	0.651	−0.013 (0.283)	1.432 (0.708)	0.224 (0.222)	79.956 [0.000]	−0.023	−0.017
Hong Kong	1.630	0.560 (0.796)	0.701 (0.378)	0.650 (0.318)	63.312 [0.000]	0.003	0.003
Italy	0.296	−0.234 (0.392)	1.122 (0.687)	1.262 (0.992)	72.547 [0.000]	0.012	0.023
Japan	1.313	0.390 (0.244)	0.744 (0.257)	0.360 (0.196)	77.714 [0.000]	−0.006	−0.020
Netherlands	0.830	0.195 (0.250)	0.975 (0.359)	0.204 (0.148)	29.562 [0.488]	−0.012	0.013

[a] The risk factors are the excess world market return, the log change in a U.S. dollar versus G-10 currency index, the change in long-term expected G-7 inflation minus the Treasury-bill return, the change in the price of oil minus the Treasury-bill return and the G-7 real interest rate. Mimicking portfolios for the last four factors are formed with the technique of Breeden, Gibbons, and Litzenberger (1989).

International Equity Returns

Table 5
Continued

Country	Average return	Average pricing error α_i	VR1	VR2	χ^2 constant betas	$\bar{R}^2$ pricing errors on Z	$\bar{R}^2$ pricing errors on Z^i
Norway	0.932	0.830 (0.426)	1.736 (0.802)	0.718 (0.503)	92.306 [0.000]	−0.009	0.007
Singapore/Malaysia	1.114	0.115 (0.488)	0.718 (0.279)	0.409 (0.218)	70.742 [0.000]	0.006	0.023
Spain	0.361	0.013 (0.321)	1.149 (0.674)	0.545 (0.367)	50.345 [0.011]	−0.006	−0.010
Sweden	0.964	0.703 (0.387)	1.276 (1.094)	1.141 (0.976)	50.396 [0.011]	−0.003	0.004
Switzerland	0.548	−0.095 (0.226)	1.619 (0.515)	0.347 (0.282)	56.521 [0.002]	−0.012	0.009
United Kingdom	0.761	0.036 (0.413)	1.349 (0.941)	0.955 (0.944)	55.936 [0.003]	0.004	0.045
United States	0.380	0.124 (0.168)	1.507 (0.349)	0.273 (0.187)	100.423 [0.000]	−0.015	0.006
Average		0.181	1.175	0.542			
E: 5-factor model with FM mimicking portfolios[s]							
Australia	0.468	−0.441 (0.554)	1.837 (1.640)	1.427 (1.515)	153.978 [0.000]	0.028	0.012
Austria	0.756	0.168 (0.263)	0.301 (0.155)	0.651 (0.203)	69.248 0.001	0.028	0.029
Belgium	0.897	0.382 (0.296)	0.674 (0.369)	0.457 (0.294)	101.254 [0.000]	−0.001	−0.009
Canada	0.451	0.491 (0.333)	2.103 (0.849)	0.878 (0.467)	134.101 [0.000]	0.018	0.024
Denmark	0.816	0.559 (0.359)	0.471 (0.303)	0.770 (0.386)	102.177 [0.000]	0.009	−0.008
France	0.729	0.150 (0.419)	0.958 (0.577)	0.702 (0.434)	110.318 [0.000]	−0.014	−0.014
Germany	0.651	−0.108 (0.309)	1.458 (0.810)	0.578 (0.510)	87.854 [0.000]	−0.019	−0.015
Hong Kong	1.630	0.336 (0.534)	1.629 (0.779)	0.510 (0.453)	129.590 [0.000]	−0.020	−0.018
Italy	0.296	−0.122 (0.419)	1.957 (1.375)	2.059 (1.407)	152.785 [0.000]	−0.009	−0.001
Japan	1.313	1.136 (0.311)	1.038 (0.467)	0.640 (0.401)	177.925 [0.000]	−0.004	−0.012
Netherlands	0.830	0.308 (0.268)	0.799 (0.330)	0.171 (0.108)	102.242 [0.000]	−0.017	0.009
Norway	0.932	0.610 (0.551)	2.185 (1.289)	1.357 (0.972)	166.421 [0.000]	−0.007	0.006
Singapore/Malaysia	1.114	0.244 (0.595)	0.873 (0.403)	0.693 (0.377)	101.276 [0.000]	0.017	0.022
Spain	0.361	0.367 (0.352)	0.874 (0.584)	0.824 (0.480)	97.672 [0.000]	0.001	−0.016
Sweden	0.964	0.684 (0.427)	1.252 (1.101)	1.374 (1.117)	81.206 [0.000]	−0.004	−0.008
Switzerland	0.548	0.163 (0.328)	1.142 (0.552)	0.444 (0.339)	76.119 [0.000]	−0.012	−0.012

[s] In this model, Fama and MacBeth (1973) mimicking portfolios are used.

The Review of Financial Studies / v 6 n 3 1993

Table 5
Continued

Country	Average return	Average pricing error α_i	VR1	VR2	χ^2 constant betas	$\bar{R}^2$ pricing errors on Z	$\bar{R}^2$ pricing errors on Z'
United Kingdom	0.761	−0.177 (0.391)	1.856 (2.089)	1.311 (1.916)	104.485 [0.000]	−0.014	0.014
United States	0.380	−0.022 (0.258)	1.510 (0.641)	0.415 (0.338)	101.549 [0.000]	−0.016	0.010
Average		0.262	1.293	0.848			

The following system is estimated for each asset i:

Disturbance	Orthogonal to
$u1_{it} = (r_{it} - \mathbf{Z}'_{t-1}\delta_i)$	$\mathbf{Z}_{t-1}$
$u2_t = (\mathbf{F}_t - \mathbf{Z}'_{t-1}\gamma)'$	$\mathbf{Z}_{t-1}$
$u3_{it} = [(u2_t u2'_t)(\kappa'_i\mathbf{Z}'_{t-1}) - (F_t u1'_{it})]$	$\mathbf{Z}_{t-1}$
$u4_{it} = (\mathbf{Z}'_{t-1}\delta_i - \theta_i)$	1
$u5_{it} = (\mathbf{Z}'_{t-1}\gamma)(\kappa'_i\mathbf{Z}'_{t-1}) - \theta_i + \alpha_i$	1
$u6_{it} = (u4^2_{it})\text{VR1}_i - u5^2_{it}$	1

where r_i represents the return on asset i, $\mathbf{Z}$ is the common world predetermined information, $\mathbf{Z}'$ is the local information, δ are coefficients from a linear projection of the asset returns on the information, $\kappa'_i\mathbf{Z}'$ are the fitted conditional betas, $\mathbf{F}$ are the factor returns, γ are the coefficients from a linear projection of the factor returns on the information, θ_i is the mean asset return, α_i is the difference between the mean asset return and the model-fitted mean asset return, and VR1 is the ratio of the variance of the asset pricing model's fitted values to the variance of the statistical model's fitted values. In a separate estimation, the last two equations are replaced with

$u5_{it} = (\mathbf{Z}'_{t-1}\delta_i - \mathbf{Z}'_{t-1}\gamma\kappa'_i\mathbf{Z}'_{t-1}) - \theta_{2i}$	1
$u6_{it} = (u4^2_{it})\text{VR2}_i - u5^2_{it}$	1

where VR2 is the ratio of the variance of the model's unexplained expected returns to the variance of the statistical model's fitted values. χ^2 is the Wald test for the hypothesis that the conditional betas are constant over time (κ_i's zero except for the intercept). The $\bar{R}^2$ are for regressions of the model pricing errors, defined as $\epsilon_{it} = r_{it} - \mathbf{Z}'_{t-1}\gamma\kappa'_i\mathbf{Z}'_{t-1}$ on the lagged instruments. The sample is 1970:2–1989:12 (239 observations).

versions of the information variables, 7 of the 18 adjusted R^2's are negative. The largest of the 36 adjusted R^2's for the pricing errors are 7 percent (Austria) and 6.6 percent (United Kingdom). The variance ratios VR1 are larger than the VR2's in 13 of the 18 countries, which suggests that the model captures more of the predictability than it leaves in the residuals. The average VR1 is 0.704, and the average VR2 is 0.456. However, the large standard errors preclude precise inferences.[18]

Panels B and C of Table 5 show results for two-factor models, in which the exchange risk variable is a second factor. Since the exchange risk variable is not an excess return, we construct a mimicking port-

---

[18] Joint tests would be preferred in order to account for correlation across the countries. However, with 80 orthogonality conditions per country in the five-factor model and only 236 time-series observations, we are unable to provide joint tests. We leave it to the reader to make these judgments informally.

folio.[19] Mimicking portfolios for the factors are constructed in two ways. The first is a variation of the approach in Breeden, Gibbons, and Litzenberger (BGL, 1989). BGL construct a maximum correlation portfolio by regressing the factor over time on the test assets. The slope coefficients are proportional to the portfolio weights. Our modification of the BGL approach is to include the world information variables in the regressions, thereby approximating a maximum conditional correlation portfolio. The results using this portfolio for the exchange risk factor are reported in panel B.

The BGL approach assumes that the mimicking portfolio weights are fixed parameters over the sample, which is a potential weakness. An alternative method uses cross-sectional regressions of the country returns each month on the lagged, rolling regression betas for dG10FX, which is similar to Fama and MacBeth (1973). The cross-sectional regression coefficients are the excess returns on a mimicking portfolio and are used in panel C. This approach allows the mimicking portfolio weights to vary month by month. The details of the approach are described in the Appendix.[20]

The results for the two-factor model show modest improvement over the single-factor model. The average pricing error α_i is reduced, relative to the single-factor model for 11 of the countries. The estimates of the α_i are more than two standard errors from zero in only 3 of 36 cases. The adjusted R^2's from regressing the pricing errors on the lagged variables present a similar pattern to the one-factor model. Twelve to 17 of the 18 VR1's are larger than the VR2's.

Panels D and E of Table 5 summarize the five-factor models. The world excess return WDRET is used directly as a factor, while mimicking portfolios are used for the variables G7RTB, dOIL, dG7ELT, and dG10FX. In panel D the modified BGL mimicking portfolios are used, and in panel E the Fama–MacBeth portfolios are used. The statistics point to a fairly dramatic improvement in the fit of the model relative to the single-factor models. Only 1 of the 36 average pricing errors, α_i, is more than two standard errors from zero. Thirty-one of the 36 VR1's are larger than the corresponding VR2's, and only 3 of 36 VR2's are more than two standard errors greater than zero. The regressions of the model residuals on the lagged world and on the

---

[19] The variable dG10FX approximates an excess return when the trade weights are known and a trade-weighted combination of foreign currency deposit rates is close to the U.S. bill rate. We therefore estimated a two-factor model in which we used dG10FX directly instead of a mimicking portfolio. The results were broadly similar.

[20] Both the BGL and the cross-sectional regression approach have the disadvantage that the estimation of system (6) does not account for the fact that mimicking portfolios were formed in a previous step. See Wheatley (1989) for an analysis of this problem. We experimented with GMM systems in which mimicking portfolio weights were estimated simultaneously with the other model parameters, but we found the systems empirically intractable.

551

The Review of Financial Studies / v 6 n 3 1993

lagged local market variables show little evidence of remaining predictability. These results show that the five-factor models can capture
much of the predictable variation in most of the country returns. There
are a few countries, however, where the models have difficulties.
Austria and Italy are two cases where there is apparent predictability
that the models do not capture well.[21]

Finally, Table 5 shows a Wald test of the hypothesis that the conditional betas may be regarded as constant over time, where the
alternative is the linear model.[22] The test rejects constant betas in the
one-factor model at the 5 percent level, for 8 of the 18 countries. For
the two-beta models, the tests reject in 9 to 13 countries. In the five-
beta models, constant betas are rejected in all but 1 of the 36 cases.
Therefore, time variation in conditional betas appears to be statistically significant in our model.[23]

4.3 The importance of changing betas
Although statistical tests reject the hypothesis that the conditional
betas are constant, this does not provide a measure of how important
movements in the betas are for explaining return predictability. We
investigate this question by estimating the following decomposition:

$$\text{Var}\{E(\beta'\lambda\,|\,Z)\} = E(\beta)'\text{Var}\{E(\lambda\,|\,Z)\}E(\beta)$$
$$+ E(\lambda)'\text{Var}\{\beta(Z)\}E(\lambda) + \phi. \qquad (9)$$

The left-hand side of (9) is the predictable variation that is captured
by the model. The first term on the right-hand side is the part attributed to movements in expected risk premia. The second term is the
part attributed to time variation in the betas. The term ϕ represents
interaction effects that arise because the expected risk premia and
betas may be correlated through time. Ferson and Harvey (1991) used
a similar decomposition in domestic data, which they estimated with
a multistep regression procedure.

We employ the GMM to consistently estimate the decomposition
(9). We start with the first three equations of system (6). Two additional equations are added to the system to identify parameters for
the unconditional means of the betas and of the risk premia. A third
equation identifies the unconditional means of the products of the

---

[21] We estimated versions of the models in which the variance ratios used projections of returns on
both the global and the local information variables in the denominator. Not surprisingly, these
larger models produced less precise results. There was evidence that a five-factor model performs
better than a one- or two-factor model, but the overall performance of the models was worse.

[22] The statistic is a quadratic form in the coefficients that model the betas as functions of the lagged
Z'_{t-1}, where the matrix is the inverse of a heteroskedasticity-consistent estimate of their covariance
matrix. The statistic is asymptotically a χ^2 variable under the null hypothesis.

[23] One should be cautious about interpreting the Wald tests, because the number of restrictions is
large relative to the sample size. The tests are also likely to be correlated across the countries.

betas and risk premia. The variances are constructed as the means of the products minus the products of the means. A fourth equation defines a parameter equal to the ratio of the first term on the right-hand side of (9) to the left-hand side of (9). This is the fraction of the model predicted variance of return that is attributed to variation in expected risk premia. A complementary ratio, calculated in a separate estimation, measures the fraction that is attributed to variation in betas. The notes to Table 6 display the equations in detail.

Table 6 shows that there is only a small direct contribution of time-varying betas to the model variation in expected country returns. Most of the predictable variation that is captured by our model is attributed to movements in the global risk premia.[24] There are, however, sizable interaction effects. The sum of the direct beta and risk premia effects is less than 1.0 for most of the countries. This implies that the betas and the expected risk premia are positively related for those countries, which has an interesting interpretation. If the expected risk premia are countercyclical in the aggregate, the estimates suggest that the sensitivity to the global risk factors are higher for most of the countries in a weak global economy.[25] Apparent exceptions are Japan and Germany, where the point estimates suggest that the betas are lower in a weak global economy.

4.4 Diagnostics

Table 7 shows some regressions to further check the specification of the models. In the first two panels, the pricing errors for each country are regressed on dummy variables, indicating one of three currency market regimes. They are the 1970:2–1973:2 period of fixed exchange rates, the "dirty float" period from 1973:3 to 1980:12, and the subsequent period of more flexible exchange rates. Of course, the use of three fixed regimes for each country is a dramatic simplification, but it could still be informative to see if the average pricing errors are significantly different in these three regimes. The first panel shows results for the one-factor model, in which the coefficient on a dummy variable exceeds two standard errors for five of the countries. The second panel summarizes the five-factor model, using the BGL mimicking portfolios. There are only two cases of coefficients that are more than two standard errors from zero, and none exceed 2.5 standard errors. There is little evidence of misspecification associated with the currency regimes.

---

24 Ferson and Harvey (1991) find similar results for portfolios of U.S. stocks. To assess the importance of the functional form of the betas for this result, we estimated single-factor models in which the squares of the local information variables are included in the beta equations. The results are similar to the first panel of Table 6.

25 See Harvey, Solnik, and Zhou (1992) for evidence that the expected risk premium on the world market index, which we use in the one-factor model, is countercyclical.

The Review of Financial Studies / v 6 n 3 1993

Table 6
The role of changing risk and changing risk premia in the predictable variation in international equity returns.

Country	Proportion of variance due to changing risk premia (Γ_1)	Proportion of variance due to changing betas (Γ_2)
	A: 1-factor model[1]	
Australia	0.610 (0.229)	0.010 (0.016)
Austria	0.957 (0.343)	0.023 (0.045)
Belgium	0.909 (0.224)	0.010 (0.012)
Canada	0.552 (0.129)	0.011 (0.013)
Denmark	0.931 (0.270)	0.004 (0.009)
France	0.862 (0.227)	0.005 (0.006)
Germany	1.154 (0.183)	0.005 (0.009)
Hong Kong	0.610 (0.263)	0.011 (0.015)
Italy	0.701 (0.208)	0.040 (0.048)
Japan	1.240 (0.193)	0.018 (0.022)
Netherlands	0.801 (0.154)	0.004 (0.007)
Norway	0.524 (0.227)	0.024 (0.030)
Singapore/Malaysia	0.441 (0.183)	0.027 (0.033)
Spain	0.881 (0.352)	0.043 (0.055)
Sweden	0.812 (0.290)	0.016 (0.022)
Switzerland	0.735 (0.193)	0.006 (0.008)
United Kingdom	0.603 (0.209)	0.019 (0.025)
United States	0.762 (0.148)	0.007 (0.007)
Average	0.783	0.016
	B: 5-factor model[2]	
Australia	0.495 (0.199)	0.032 (0.035)
Austria	0.731 (0.209)	0.020 (0.022)
Belgium	0.544 (0.138)	0.013 (0.013)

[1] The excess world market return is the single factor.

[2] The risk factors are the excess world market return, the log change in a U.S. dollar versus G-10 currency index, the change in long-term expected G-7 inflation minus the Treasury-bill return, the change in the price of oil minus the Treasury-bill return and the G-7 real interest rate. Mimicking portfolios for the last four factors are formed with the technique of Breeden, Gibbons, and Litzenberger (1989).

International Equity Returns

Table 6
Continued

Country	Proportion of variance due to changing risk premia (Γ_1)	Proportion of variance due to changing betas (Γ_2)
Canada	0.606 (0.155)	0.005 (0.008)
Denmark	0.910 (0.232)	0.011 (0.017)
France	0.663 (0.210)	0.021 (0.021)
Germany	1.036 (0.183)	0.012 (0.021)
Hong Kong	0.333 (0.175)	0.068 (0.066)
Italy	0.669 (0.236)	0.042 (0.046)
Japan	1.107 (0.280)	0.038 (0.033)
Netherlands	0.738 (0.207)	0.010 (0.035)
Norway	0.448 (0.168)	0.034 (0.035)
Singapore/Malaysia	0.558 (0.223)	0.040 (0.041)
Spain	0.516 (0.210)	0.023 (0.057)
Sweden	0.537 (0.222)	0.042 (0.057)
Switzerland	0.660 (0.205)	0.007 (0.009)
United Kingdom	0.277 (0.302)	0.040 (0.036)
United States	0.674 (0.169)	0.008 (0.011)
Average	0.639	0.026

The following system is estimated for each asset i:

Disturbance	Orthogonal to
$u1_{it} = (r_{it} - Z'_{t-1}\delta_i)$	Z_{t1}
$u2_t = (F'_t - Z'_{t-1}\gamma)'$	Z_{t-1}
$u3_{it} = [(u2_t u2'_t)(\kappa'_i Z'_{t-1}) - (F_t u1'_{it})]$	Z'_{t-1}
$u4_{it} = (Z'_{t-1}\gamma)(\kappa'_i Z'_{t-1}) - \mu_{1t}$	1
$u5_{it} = (\kappa'_i Z'_{t-1}) - \mu_{2t}$	1
$u6_t = (\gamma Z_{t-1}) - \mu_3$	1
$u7_{it} = (u4^2_{it})\Gamma_{1i} - [\mu'_{1i}(u6_t u6'_t)\mu_{1t}]$	1

where r_i represents the return on asset i, Z is the common world predetermined information, Z' is the local information, F are the factor returns, δ are coefficients from a linear projection of the asset returns on the information, γ are coefficients from a linear projection of the factor returns on the information, $\kappa'_i Z'_{t-1}$ are the fitted conditional betas, μ_1 is the mean fitted value from the model, μ_2 are the mean conditional betas, μ_3 are the mean conditional risk premiums, Γ_1 is the ratio of the predictable variance due to the risk premiums to the variance of the model-fitted returns. In a separate estimation, the last equation is replaced with

$$u7_{it} = (u4^2_{it})\Gamma_{2i} - [\mu'_1(u5_{it}u5'_{it})\mu_{2t}] \qquad\qquad 1$$

where Γ_2 is the ratio of the predictable variance due to changing conditional betas to the variance of the model-fitted returns. The sample is 1970:2–1989:12 (239 observations).

555

The Review of Financial Studies / v 6 n 3 1993

Table 7   Continued
The performance of the asset pricing models during different exchange regimes and under different capital controls.

Country	Intercept	Fixed Exchange Rates 1970:2–1973:2	Dirty Float Exchange Rates 1973:3–1980:12	$\bar{R}^2$
A: 1-factor model pricing errors[1]				
Australia	0.621 (0.797)	−1.297 (1.297)	−0.434 (1.130)	−0.005
Austria	1.030 (0.693)	0.396 (0.920)	−1.177 (0.803)	0.004
Belgium	1.427 (0.620)	−0.229 (0.857)	−1.919 (0.844)	0.016
Canada	0.250 (0.547)	0.292 (0.887)	−0.357 (0.815)	−0.007
Denmark	0.975 (0.578)	0.992 (1.073)	−1.682 (0.758)	0.024
France	0.853 (0.683)	−1.002 (1.042)	−1.192 (1.055)	−0.002
Germany	0.947 (0.640)	−0.877 (1.028)	−1.314 (0.853)	0.002
Hong Kong	0.775 (1.009)	6.215 (2.902)	−0.873 (1.564)	0.031
Italy	0.903 (0.729)	−1.773 (1.047)	−1.752 (1.141)	0.005
Japan	1.423 (0.606)	1.080 (1.060)	−2.071 (0.812)	0.034
Netherlands	1.026 (0.523)	−0.791 (0.893)	−1.181 (0.752)	0.003
Norway	0.933 (0.737)	0.631 (1.257)	−0.364 (1.185)	−0.007
Singapore/Malaysia	0.271 (0.757)	3.128 (1.672)	−0.278 (1.232)	0.010
Spain	1.189 (0.659)	−0.168 (0.912)	−2.721 (0.922)	0.034
Sweden	1.800 (0.657)	−1.246 (1.045)	−2.048 (0.874)	0.015
Switzerland	0.593 (0.537)	−0.139 (0.904)	−0.893 (0.802)	−0.003
United Kingdom	0.642 (0.604)	−0.449 (1.047)	−1.315 (1.088)	−0.001
United States	0.465 (0.427)	−0.539 (0.721)	−1.114 (0.638)	0.005
B: 5-factor model (with BGL mimicking portfolios) pricing errors[2]				
Australia	0.479 (0.790)	−1.466 (1.299)	−0.352 (1.106)	−0.004
Austria	−0.034 (0.648)	0.498 (0.870)	−0.405 (0.763)	−0.005
Belgium	0.870 (0.612)	−0.036 (0.841)	−1.149 (0.844)	0.001

[1] The excess world market return is the single factor.
[2] The risk factors are the excess world market return, the log change in a U.S. dollar versus G-10 currency index, the change in long-term expected G-7 inflation minus the Treasury-bill return, the change in the price of oil minus the Treasury-bill return and the G-7 real interest rate. Mimicking portfolios for the last four factors are formed with a technique similar to Breeden, Gibbons, and Litzenberger (1989).

International Equity Returns

Table 7
Continued

Country	Intercept	Fixed Exchange Rates 1970:2–1973:2	Dirty Float Exchange Rates 1973:3–1980:12	$\bar{R}^2$
Canada	0.563 (0.546)	0.005 (0.879)	−1.115 (0.800)	0.001
Denmark	0.333 (0.577)	0.654 (1.028)	−1.197 (0.767)	0.008
France	0.239 (0.672)	−0.801 (1.030)	0.020 (1.071)	−0.007
Germany	0.484 (0.630)	−0.868 (1.022)	−0.931 (0.852)	−0.003
Hong Kong	0.230 (1.011)	4.525 (2.873)	−0.953 (1.568)	0.015
Italy	0.170 (0.731)	−1.568 (1.041)	−0.413 (1.138)	−0.003
Japan	1.024 (0.605)	0.051 (1.053)	−1.648 (0.817)	0.011
Netherlands	0.748 (0.523)	−0.959 (0.887)	−1.038 (0.751)	0.001
Norway	0.596 (0.733)	0.647 (1.249)	0.342 (1.153)	−0.008
Singapore/Malaysia	0.456 (0.757)	1.531 (1.695)	−1.485 (1.199)	0.007
Spain	0.231 (0.650)	0.800 (0.879)	−0.876 (0.919)	0.001
Sweden	1.416 (0.657)	−0.791 (1.043)	−1.516 (0.875)	0.004
Switzerland	0.255 (0.525)	−0.354 (0.900)	−0.759 (0.789)	−0.004
United Kingdom	0.609 (0.620)	−0.483 (1.048)	−1.278 (1.036)	−0.001
United States	0.831 (0.425)	−0.672 (0.718)	−1.549 (0.622)	0.018
	C: 1-factor model pricing errors[1]			
Japan	1.423 (0.606)	0.095 (1.041)	−1.870 (0.824)	0.015
	D: 5-factor model pricing errors[2]			
Japan	1.024 (0.605)	−0.793 (1.025)	−1.368 (0.827)	0.003

The following system is estimated for each asset i:

Disturbance	Orthogonal to
$u1_{it} = (r_{it} - Z'_{t-1}\delta_i)$	Z_{t-1}
$u2_t = (F'_t - Z'_{t-1}\gamma)'$	Z_{t-1}
$u3_{it} = [(u2_t u2'_t)(\kappa'_i Z'_{t-1}) - (F_t u1'_{it})]$	Z'_{t-1}

where r_i represents the return on asset i, Z is the common world predetermined information, Z' is the local information, δ are coefficients from a linear projection of the asset returns on the information, $\kappa'_i Z'_{t-1}$ are the fitted conditional betas, γ are coefficients from a linear projection of factor returns on the information, and F are the factor returns. The pricing errors are $\epsilon_{it} = r_{it} - Z_{t-1}\gamma\kappa'_i Z'_{t-1}$. The pricing errors are regressed on two dummy variables and a constant. The table shows the regression coefficients and their standard errors. The first dummy is set equal to one during 1970:2–1973:2, the period of fixed exchange rates. The second dummy is set equal to one

The Review of Financial Studies / v 6 n 3 1993

Table 7
Continued

during 1973:3–1980:12, the period of active central bank intervention in the foreign currency markets (the so-called dirty float). In the analysis of Japanese capital controls, three regimes are examined. The first dummy variable is set equal to one during 1970:2–1973:12, the period when no foreign corporation could invest in Japanese securities. The second dummy variable is set equal to one during 1974:1–1980:12, a period of severe capital controls. The sample is 1970:2–1989:12 (239 observations).

The currency regime periods are similar to periods of different capital control restrictions in Japan. In the third panel of Table 7 the pricing errors for Japan are regressed on dummy variables, indicating different capital control regimes. The first is the 1970:2–1973:12 period, in which most capital flows were not officially allowed. The second is the 1974:1–1980:12 period, when capital flows were severely restricted.[26] A dummy variable coefficient is significant in the one-factor model but not in the five-factor model. This is additional evidence that systematic errors in a one-factor asset pricing model can be reduced by moving to a five-factor model.

We conducted a number of further experiments to check the sensitivity of our results to the econometric methods. We estimated predictable variance ratios using cross-sectional regression techniques similar to Ferson and Harvey (1991), as described in the Appendix. We found that the results were broadly similar. For example, in only 3 of the 18 countries were the fractions of the predictable variance explained by the five-factor model smaller than the fraction unexplained. The average value of the ratio VR1 across the countries was 0.67 in the one-factor model and 0.93 in the five-factor model. Repeating this analysis while using the first and second halves of the sample provided no strong evidence that the models perform better in the second half. The VR1's in the one-factor model were slightly higher in the first half of the sample.[27]

We also examined the time series of the adjusted R^2's from the rolling regressions of the country returns on the global risk variables, and we saw no tendency for them to increase over the sample period. The correlation between the ratios VR1 from the five-factor model

---

[26] Capital controls in Japan were actually relaxed in a series of steps, which raises the possibility that a more detailed analysis could detect their effects [see, for example, Bonser-Neal et al. (1990)].

[27] We repeated this analysis, using the local instrument set to capture the predictable variation in the returns, and the overall impressions were similar. In the one-factor (five-factor) model the ratio VR2 was larger than the ratio VR1 for 11 (15) of the countries, and the average of the VR2's was greater than the VR1's. We also repeated the analysis, using the world instrument set augmented by the lagged betas, and the results were similar. We checked the sensitivity to using an alternative beta estimation technique. We estimated the betas as the slope coefficients in rolling regressions that included both the risk factors and the lagged instruments Z_{t-1} on the right-hand side. When we used these rolling betas conditioned on Z_{t-1}, we found a slight decline in the average of the VR1's in the single-beta model. With five factors, however, the variance ratios were slightly more favorable to the models.

and the average adjusted R^2's is 0.7. On average, a country for which the factor model regressions have higher explanatory power is a country for which the beta pricing model explains more of the predictability in returns. When we examined the relation between the VR1's and the R^2's of the predictive regressions, we found virtually no relation.

To assess the sensitivity of the results to the currency of denomination, we reestimated system (6) for a number of the cases, using returns denominated in local currency units, in excess of a local short-term interest rate, as described in the Appendix. The overall results for those cases are not dramatically different.

5. Concluding Remarks

Using global risk factors to model returns across countries implies some strong assumptions. Such a model ignores, for example, the costs of extranational investment and information problems. Our model assumes that expected returns are determined by country-specific betas and global risk premia. We allowed the betas to vary over time with local market information variables. Assuming market integration, we forced the risk premia to depend only on global information variables. Despite these restrictions, our evidence suggests that the models can capture much of the predictable variation in a sample of returns for 18 countries. Models that incorporate additional considerations should produce even better explanatory power.

We showed how to estimate the predictable variance of returns that is explained by an asset pricing model jointly with the other parameters of the model. This approach avoids many of the econometric problems of multistep procedures and is flexible enough to address other research questions. We used the approach to estimate the contributions of time-varying betas and time-varying risk premia to the predictability in returns. We found that the largest component is the time-varying risk premia.

Appendix

This appendix describes the cross-sectional regression methods and records our data sources and definitions.

Cross-sectional regression methods
The cross-sectional regression (CSR) methods of Fama and MacBeth (1973) have typically been used to investigate the average pricing of economic risks. Ferson and Harvey (1991) use a multistep CSR methodology to estimate conditional asset pricing models. In the first step,

The Review of Financial Studies / v 6 n 3 1993

instruments for the conditional betas in month t are obtained by regressing the excess country returns on the risk factors and using the time series for months $t - 60$ to $t - 1$. The second step is a cross-sectional regression for each month t of the asset returns on the predetermined betas:

$$r_{it} = \gamma_{0t} + \sum_{j=1}^{K} \gamma_{jt}\beta_{ij,t-1} + \epsilon_{it}, \qquad i = 1,...,N, \qquad \text{(A1)}$$

where the $\beta_{ij,t-1}$ are the betas of the excess returns for month t. The slope coefficient, γ_{jt}, $j = 1,...,K$, is a portfolio excess return. The portfolio has maximum conditional correlation with the factor, as measured by the betas and the cross-sectional regression residuals.[28] The cross-sectional regression provides a decomposition of each excess return for each month. The first component, $\sum_{j=1}^{K} \gamma_{jt}\beta_{ij,t-1}$, represents the part of the return that is related to the cross-sectional structure of risk, as measured by the betas. The predictability of returns should be due to this component. The remaining component of return is the sum of the residual for the asset and the intercept for month t, $\epsilon_{it} + \gamma_{0t}$. This is the part of the return that is uncorrelated with the measures of risk. The part of the return that is unrelated to risk should be unpredictable.

We regress each excess return on the lagged instruments and calculate the time-series variance of the fitted values. The objective is to see how much of this predictable variance is "explained" by the model. The part captured by the model is the variance of the projection of the model fitted values [$\sum_{j=1}^{K} \gamma_{jt}\beta_{ij,t-1}$, from Equation (A1)] on the instruments. We calculate a ratio, VR1 for each i, dividing this variance by the variance of the fitted values of the excess return. The predictable component of a return that is not captured by the model is measured as the variance of the projection of $u_t = \gamma_{0t} + \epsilon_{it}$ on the lagged variables. This is summarized, using Z_{t-1} as the lagged variable in the following variance ratios:

$$\text{VR1} = \frac{\text{Var}\left\{ P\left(\sum_{j=1}^{K} \gamma_{jt}\beta_{ij,t-1} \mid Z_{t-1} \right) \right\}}{\text{Var}\{P(r_t \mid Z_{t-1})\}},$$

$$\text{VR2} = \frac{\text{Var}\{P(\epsilon_{it} + \gamma_{0t} \mid Z_{t-1})\}}{\text{Var}\{P(r_t \mid Z_{t-1})\}}, \qquad \text{(A2)}$$

---

[28] The correlation for a given factor is maximized among all portfolios with zero betas on the other factors, if the betas are the true conditional betas and a GLS cross-sectional regression is used. We report results using the simpler OLS cross-sectional regressions.

where $P(\cdot \mid Z_{t-1})$ stands for the linear projection onto Z_{t-1} and Var$\{\cdot\}$ is the variance.

The CSR approach presents certain econometric problems. One problem is measurement errors in the betas, which can bias the second step, cross-sectional regressions. Shanken (1992) provides a review and analysis of the large-sample issues, assuming that the betas are constant parameters. Amsler and Schmidt (1985) provide evidence on the small-sample properties of the time-series averages of cross-sectional regression estimators. Little is known, however, about the finite-sample properties of CSR approaches for conditional asset pricing.

Connor and Uhlaner (1989) show that an iterated version of the CSR methodology can deliver consistent estimates of the risk premia under certain assumptions.[29] We use a two-stage version of the Fama–MacBeth regressions. Specifically, we use the estimated risk premia from the first-stage, cross-sectional regressions in a second stage as proxies for the risk factors. We calculate a new set of rolling regression betas for the country returns on these factors, and we use these second-round betas in a second stage of cross-sectional regressions to estimate a new set of risk premia. Our results are based on these second-round cross-sectional regressions.[30]

The world risk factors

WDRET is the arithmetic return on the Morgan Stanley Capital International world equity index, including dividends, minus the Ibbotson Associates one-month U.S. Treasury bill rate. dTED is the difference between the 90-day Eurodollar yield (Citibase FYUR3M) and the 90-day Treasury-bill yield (Citibase FYGM3 secondary market, converted from discount to true yield to maturity). dG10FX is the difference in the trade-weighted dollar prices of foreign exchange for 10 industrialized countries (Citibase FXG10).

G7UI is derived from a time-series model applied to an aggregate G-7 inflation rate. The G-7 inflation rate is constructed by weighting the individual countries' inflation rates (Citibase: PC6CA, PC6FR, PC6IT, PC6JA, PC6UK, PC6WG, and ZUNEW) by their shares in the previous quarter's real U.S. dollar G-7 gross domestic product. These weights change through time. The time-series model is ARIMA(0, 1, 2)(0, 1, 2) and the parameters estimates are

---

[29] They assume there is a factor structure with constant loadings.

[30] Connor and Uhlaner (1989) show that iterated Fama–MacBeth estimates suffer from the same rotational indeterminacy as does factor analysis. Therefore, a cost of our approach is that we are unable to isolate the pricing effects of specific factors in a multiple-beta model.

The Review of Financial Studies / v 6 n 3 1993

	Parameter	Std. Error	T-ratio
Intercept	0.00000	0.000057	0.10
MA1,1	0.432613	0.061754	7.01
MA1,2	0.271394	0.061544	4.41
MA2,1	−0.305806	0.065162	−4.69
MA2,2	−0.180382	0.065377	−2.76

The parameters are estimated with 250 monthly observations. The χ^2 test for significance of the first six residual autocorrelations has a p value of .111, and the corresponding statistic for the first 12 autocorrelations has a p value of .275.

dG7ELT is the result of projecting the four-year moving average of G-7 inflation on the lagged global information variables specified below. dOIL is the natural log of the average U.S. dollar price of per barrel at the wellhead from 1974 to 1989 and the posted West Texas Intermediate price from 1969 to 1973. Since the West Texas price is consistently higher than the average wellhead price, the 1969–1973 data is grossed down by 65 percent. This represents the average premium of West Texas over the average wellhead during 1974–1976. dG7IP is calculated by weighting local industrial production indices by the following (fixed) factors: Canada .04314, France .09833, Germany .05794, Italy .13093, Japan .07485, U.K. .11137, U.S. .48343, which are the weights in G-7 gross domestic product in the third quarter of 1969. The logarithmic difference in this aggregate index is the growth in G-7 industrial production. G7RTB is calculated by aggregating individual countries' short-term interest rates. The following interest rates are used (Citibase FYCA3M–Canada 90-day Treasury bill, FYFR3M–France 90-day bill, FYGE3M–Germany 90-day bill, FYIT6M–Italy 180-day bill, FYCMJP–Japan commercial paper 1969–1976 and FYJP3M–Japan Gensaki rate 1977–1989, FYUK3M–United Kingdom 90-day bill, FYUS3M–United States 90-day bill). The aggregated G-7 interest rate is calculated by using the countries' previous quarter's shares in G-7 gross domestic product. The real G-7 interest rate is calculated by subtracting the G-7 inflation rate.

The global information variables
The Eurodollar–Treasury yield spread is the difference between the 90-day Eurodollar rate (Citibase FYUR3M) and the CRSP–Fama 90-day bill yield. The slope of the term structure is the difference between the U.S. 10-year Treasury-bond yield (Citibase FYGT10) and the CRSP Fama 90-day-bill yield. The U.S. Treasury-bill yield is the 30-day yield from the CRSP–Fama files. This variable is not lagged, because the nominal one-month yield is known at the end of the previous month.

International Equity Returns

The country-specific information variables

The lagged country returns are 18 Morgan Stanley Capital International equity indices. These returns are in excess of the CRSP–Fama 30-day bill. The lagged value of the dividend yields for 18 MSCI equity indices are used in place of the MSCI world dividend yield. The numerator is a 12-month moving sum of the dividends, and the denominator is the current index level. The short-term interest rates for the various countries are listed together with their series codes from IFS or Citibase. These are as follows: Australia, 13-week bill (IFS 61C); Austria, money market rate (IFS 60B); Belgium, 3-month bill (Citibase FYBE3M); Canada, 3-month bill (IFS 60C); Denmark, discount rate 1969–1971 (IFS 60A); call money rate 1972–1989 (IFS 60B); France, 3-month interbank (Citibase FYFR3M); Germany, Frankfurt 90-day rate (Citibase FYWG3M); Hong Kong, no data, U.S. 3-month bill used; Italy, 6-month bill (Citibase FYIT6M); Japan, call money rate 1969–1976 (Citibase FYCMJP); Gensaki rate, 1977–1989 (Citibase FYJP3M); Netherlands, call money rate 1969–1978:11 (IFS 60B), 3-month bill 1979:12–1989; Norway, prime rate 1969–1971:1, call money rate 1971:12–1989 (IFS60B); Singapore/Malaysia, no data, U.S. bill; Spain, prime rate 1969–1973:12, call money rate 1974–1976 (IFS 60B), 3-month bill 1977–1989 (IFS 60C); Sweden, 3-month bill (IFS 60C); Switzerland, 3-month deposit rate (Citibase FYSW3M); United Kingdom, 3-month bill (Citibase FYUK3M); United States, 3-month bill (Citibase FYUS3M).

TERM = the lagged term premium: The difference between long-term interest rates and the above short-term rates: Australia, 15-year Treasury bond (IFS 61C); Austria, government bond (IFS 61); Belgium, government bond (Citibase FYBEGB); Canada, government bond (IFS 61); Denmark, government bond (IFS 61); France, government bond (Citibase FYFRGB); Germany, government bond (Citibase FYWGGB); Hong Kong, no data, U.S. Treasury bond; Italy, government bond (Citibase FYITGB); Japan, government bond (Citibase FYJPGB); Netherlands, government bond (IFS 61); Norway, government bond (IFS 61); Singapore/Malaysia, no data, U.S. Treasury bond; Spain, government bond (IFS 61); Sweden, government bond (Citibase FYSDGB); Switzerland, government bond (Citibase FYSWGB); United Kingdom, government bond (Citibase FYUKGB), United States, government bond (Citibase FYUSGB).

References

Adler, Michael, and Bernard Dumas, 1983, "International Portfolio Selection and Corporation Finance: A Synthesis," *Journal of Finance*, 38, 925–984.

Amsler, Christine, and P. Schmidt, 1985, "A Monte Carlo Investigation of the Accuracy of Multivariate CAPM Tests," *Journal of Financial Economics*, 14, 359–375.

563

The Review of Financial Studies / v 6 n 3 1993

Bansal, Ravi, David Hsieh, and S. Viswanathan, 1992, "A New Approach to International Arbitrage Pricing Theory," working paper, Duke University.

Bodurtha, James N., D. Chinhyung Cho, and Lemma W. Senbet, 1989, "Economic Forces and the Stock Market: An International Perspective," *Global Finance Journal,* 1, 21–46.

Bonser-Neal, Catherine, Greggory Brauer, Robert Neal, and Simon Wheatley, 1990, "International Investment Restrictions and Closed-end Country Fund Prices," *Journal of Finance,* 45, 523–548.

Braun, Phillip, Dan Nelson, and Alan Sunier, 1991, "Good News, Bad News, Volatility and Betas," working paper, University of Chicago.

Breeden, Douglas T., Michael R. Gibbons, and Robert H. Litzenberger, 1989, "Empirical Tests of the Consumption-Oriented CAPM," *Journal of Finance,* 44, 231–262.

Brown, Stephen J., and Toshiyuki Otsuki, 1990a, "Macroeconomic Factors and the Japanese Equity Markets: The CAPMD Project," in Edwin J. Elton and Martin J. Gruber (eds.), *Japanese Capital Markets,* Harper and Row, New York, pp. 175–192.

Brown, Stephen J., and Toshiyuki Otsuki, 1990b, "A Global Asset Pricing Model," working paper, New York University.

Campbell, John Y., 1987, "Stock Returns and the Term Structure," *Journal of Financial Economics,* 18, 373–400.

Chen, Nai-fu., Richard R. Roll, and Stephen A. Ross, 1986, "Economic Forces and the Stock Market," *Journal of Business,* 59, 383–403.

Cho, David, C. Eun, and Lemma Senbet, 1986, "International Arbitrage Pricing Theory: An Empirical Investigation," *Journal of Finance,* 41, 313–329.

Connor, Gregory, and Robert Korajczyk, 1986, "Performance Measurement with the Arbitrage Pricing Theory: A New Framework for Analysis," *Journal of Financial Economics,* 15, 373–394.

Connor, Gregory, and Robert Uhlaner, 1989, "A Synthesis of Two Approaches to Factor Estimation," working paper, University of California at Berkeley.

Cox, John C., Jonathan E. Ingersoll, Jr., and Stephen A. Ross, 1985, "A Theory of the Term Structure of Interest Rates," *Econometrica,* 53, 385–407.

Cutler, David M., J. Poterba, and L. Summers, 1990, "International Evidence on the Predictability of Stock Returns," working paper, Massachusetts Institute of Technology.

Dumas, Bernard, and Bruno Solnik, 1992, "The World Price of Exchange Rate Risk," working paper, Wharton School and HEC.

Fama, Eugene F., and James D. MacBeth, 1973, "Risk, Return and Equilibrium: Empirical Tests," *Journal of Political Economy,* 81, 607–636.

Ferson, Wayne E., and Campbell R. Harvey, 1991, "The Variation of Economic Risk Premiums," *Journal of Political Economy,* 99, 385–415.

French, Kenneth R., G. William Schwert, and Robert F. Stambaugh, 1987, "Expected Stock Returns and Volatility," *Journal of Financial Economics,* 19, 3–29.

French, Kenneth R., and James Poterba, 1991, "Were Japanese Stock Prices Too High?," *Journal of Financial Economics,* 29, 337–364.

Giovannini, Alberto, and Phillipe Jorion, 1987, "Interest Rates and Risk Premia in the Stock Market and in the Foreign Exchange Market," *Journal of International Money and Finance,* 6, 107–123.

Giovannini, Alberto, and Phillipe Jorion, 1989, "Time Variation of Risk and Return in the Foreign Exchange and Stock Markets," *Journal of Finance,* 44, 307–325.

Hamao, Yasushi, 1988, "An Empirical Examination of Arbitrage Pricing Theory: Using Japanese Data," *Japan and the World Economy,* 1, 45–61.

Hansen, Lars P., 1982, "Large Sample Properties of the Generalized Method of Moments Estimators," *Econometrica*, 50, 1029–1054.

Harvey, Campbell R., 1991, "The World Price of Covariance Risk," *Journal of Finance*, 46, 111–157.

Harvey, Campbell R., Bruno Solnik, and Guofu Zhou, 1992, "What Determines Expected Asset Returns?," working paper, Duke University.

Heston, Steven, Geert Rouwenhorst, and Roberto E. Wessels, 1991, "The Structure of International Stock Returns," working paper, Yale School of Organization and Management.

Hodrick, Robert J., 1981, "Intertemporal Asset Pricing with Time-varying Risk Premia," *Journal of International Economics*, 11, 573–587.

Huberman, Gur, Shmuel A. Kandel, and Robert F. Stambaugh, 1987, "Mimicking Portfolios and Exact Arbitrage Pricing," *Journal of Finance*, 42, 1–10.

Jorion, Phillipe, 1991, "The Pricing of Exchange Risk in the Stock Market," *Journal of Financial and Quantitative Analysis*, 26, 363–376.

King, Mervyn, Enrique Sentana, and Sushil Wadhwani, 1990, "A Heteroskedastic Factor Model of Asset Returns and Risk Premia with Time-varying Volatility: An Application to Sixteen World Stock Markets," working paper, London School of Economics.

Korajczyk, Robert A., and Claude J. Viallet, 1991, "Equity Risk Premia and the Pricing of Foreign Exchange Risk," forthcoming in *Journal of International Economics.*

Korajczyk, Robert A., and Claude J. Viallet, 1989, "An Empirical Investigation of International Asset Pricing," *Review of Financial Studies*, 2, 553–586.

Lehmann, Bruce N., and David M. Modest, 1988, "The Empirical Foundations of the Arbitrage Pricing Theory," *Journal of Financial Economics*, 21, 213–254.

Lintner, John, 1965, "The Valuation of Assets and the Selection of Risky Investments in Stock Portfolios and Capital Budgets," *Review of Economics and Statistics*, 47, 13–37.

Lo, Andrew W., and A. Craig MacKinlay, 1990, "Data Snooping Biases in Tests of Financial Asset Pricing Models," *Review of Financial Studies*, 3, 431–468.

Mark, Nelson C., 1985, "On Time-Varying Risk Premia in the Foreign Exchange Market: An Econometric Analysis," *Journal of Monetary Economics*, 16, 3–18.

Merton, Robert C., 1973, "An Intertemporal Capital Asset Pricing Model," *Econometrica*, 41, 867–887.

Roll, Richard R., 1977, "A Critique of the Asset Pricing Theory's Tests. I: On Past and Potential Testability of the Theory," *Journal of Financial Economics*, 4, 349–357.

Ross, Stephen A., and Michael Walsh, 1983, "A Simple Approach to the Pricing of Risky Assets with Uncertain Exchange Rates," in R. Hawkins, R. Levich, and C. Wihlborg (eds.), *The Internationalization of Financial Markets and National Economic Policy*, JAI Press, Greenwich, CT.

Shanken, Jay, 1990, "Intertemporal Asset Pricing: An Empirical Investigation," *Journal of Econometrics*, 45, 99–120.

Shanken, Jay, 1992, "On the Estimation of Beta Pricing Models," *Review of Financial Studies*, 5, 1–34.

Shanken, Jay, and Mark I. Weinstein, 1990, "Macroeconomic Variables and Asset Pricing: Estimation and Tests," working paper, University of Rochester.

Sharpe, William F., 1964, "Capital Asset Prices: A Theory of Market Equilibrium under Conditions of Risk," *Journal of Finance*, 19, 425–442.

The Review of Financial Studies / v 6 n 3 1993

Solnik, Bruno, 1974, "An Equilibrium Model of the International Capital Market," *Journal of Economic Theory*, 8, 500–524.

Solnik, Bruno, 1993, "The Performance of International Asset Allocation Strategies Using Conditioning Information," *Journal of Empirical Finance*, 1, 33–55.

Stulz, René M., 1981a, "A Model of International Asset Pricing," *Journal of Financial Economics*, 9, 383–406.

Stulz, René M., 1981b, "On the Effects of Barriers to International Investment," *Journal of Finance*, 36, 923–934.

Stulz, René M., 1984, "Pricing Capital Assets in an International Setting: An Introduction," *Journal of International Business Studies*, 15, 55–74.

Wheatley, Simon, 1989, "Testing Asset Pricing Models with Infrequently Measured Factors," working paper, University of Washington.

[15]

THE JOURNAL OF FINANCE • VOL. LII, NO. 5 • DECEMBER 1997

International Asset Pricing and Portfolio Diversification with Time-Varying Risk

GIORGIO DE SANTIS and BRUNO GERARD*

ABSTRACT

We test the conditional capital asset pricing model (CAPM) for the world's eight largest equity markets using a parsimonious generalized autoregressive conditional heteroskedasticity (GARCH) parameterization. Our methodology can be applied simultaneously to many assets and, at the same time, accommodate general dynamics of the conditional moments. The evidence supports most of the pricing restrictions of the model, but some of the variation in risk-adjusted excess returns remains predictable during periods of high interest rates. Our estimates indicate that, although severe market declines are contagious, the expected gains from international diversification for a U.S. investor average 2.11 percent per year and have not significantly declined over the last two decades.

IN THIS ARTICLE, WE TEST a conditional version of the capital asset pricing model (CAPM) in an international setting, and analyze its implications for international portfolio diversification. First, we investigate both the cross-sectional and time-series restrictions of the model using data from the eight largest equity markets in the world. Then, we take the perspective of a U.S. investor and use the estimated model to examine how the ex ante benefits of international diversification have changed over the last two and one-half decades in response to changing conditions in international security markets. In particular, we focus our attention on two issues. First, we analyze the effects of the increasing level of integration among financial markets on the expected gains from international diversification. Second, we study whether, over short horizons, an internationally diversified portfolio provides a good hedge against large declines in the U.S. market.

The evidence shows that the world price of covariance risk is equal across countries and changes over time in a predictable way, whereas the price of

* Marshall School of Business, University of Southern California. An earlier version of this article was circulated under the title "Time-varying risk and international portfolio diversification with contagious bear markets." We thank the editor, René Stulz, an anonymous referee, Geert Bekaert, Fischer Black, Tim Bollerslev, Peter Bossaerts, Andrea Buraschi, John Cochrane, Campbell Harvey, Selo Imrohoroglu, Philippe Jorion, John Matsusaka, Hans Mikkelsen, Franz Palm, Aris Protopadakis, Allan Timmermann, and Arnold Zellner, as well as seminar participants at the University of Southern California, the Federal Reserve Bank of Minneapolis, UC Santa Barbara, UCLA, UC San Diego, HEC Lausanne, Free University of Brussels, University of Michigan, University of Washington, CEPR-LIFE Workshop on International Finance in Maastricht, WFA meetings in Aspen, CEPR Summer Symposium in Gerzensee and EFA meetings in Milan for many valuable comments. Gérard acknowledges research support from the ZFRIF fund at USC.

country-specific risk is not different from zero. This is consistent with the CAPM and supports the hypothesis of international market integration. However, we find that when the price of market risk is restricted to be positive, as the theory implies, some of the variation in residual returns remains predictable. Interestingly, the predictability disappears when we relax the nonnegativity restriction on the price of risk. This might be due to the inability of the model to accommodate negative risk premia during periods of high short-term interest rates. We conclude that although the conditional version of the traditional CAPM provides useful information on the dynamics of market premia, a more adequate model of international asset pricing should probably include additional factors. Along these lines, recent work by Dumas and Solnik (1995) and De Santis and Gérard (1997) suggests that, in international markets, currency risk is priced in addition to market risk.

Our results have interesting implications for investors who want to diversify their portfolios internationally. We find that severe U.S. market declines are contagious at the international level, and often imply a significant reduction in the gains from holding an internationally diversified portfolio. Our estimates indicate that, on average, the expected gains from international diversification are equal to 2.11 percent on an annual basis and have not been significantly affected by the increasing level of integration of international markets.

To implement the tests, we extend the multivariate generalized autoregressive conditional heteroskedasticity (GARCH) parameterization recently proposed by Ding and Engle (1994) to accommodate GARCH-in-Mean effects, which are essential to most asset pricing models. Since this specification is considerably more parsimonious than those used in previous studies, we can test the pricing restrictions of the model and analyze international comovements for a relatively large number of markets. This is an important methodological contribution of our article. Finally, we develop an alternative to the test of the conditional CAPM proposed by Bollerslev, Engle, and Wooldridge (1988). Our specification can be used to test the cross-sectional restrictions of the model on any subset of the assets, even when observations of asset supplies at each point in time are unavailable to the econometrician. Implementation of the test only requires returns on a market-wide index. This specification can easily be extended to accommodate multiple risk factors.

The rest of the article is organized as follows. Section I presents the asset pricing model and the methodology used to test it. Section II describes the data. Section III contains the estimation and test results. Section IV discusses the implications of our findings for international portfolio diversification. Section V concludes the article.

I. Model and Empirical Methods

A. *A Model of International Asset Pricing*

One of the most widely used models in finance is the CAPM originally derived by Sharpe (1964) and Lintner (1965). In a two-period framework, the model predicts that the expected return on any traded asset, in excess of a risk-free return, is proportional to the systematic risk of the asset, as measured by its covariance with a market-wide portfolio return.

Merton (1973) shows that, in an intertemporal model, economic agents need to hedge against changes in the investment opportunity set. This implies that the expected return on any asset is a function of the covariances between its return and the return on a number of hedging portfolios. A simple specification where the market portfolio is the only pricing factor can be obtained by introducing additional assumptions, for example, by assuming that investors have logarithmic preferences.

We use the conditional CAPM with one factor as our benchmark model and then test alternative specifications. Formally, the asset pricing equations can be written

$$E(R_{it}|\Im_{t-1}) - R_{ft} = \delta_{t-1}\text{cov}(R_{it}, R_{mt}|\Im_{t-1}) \quad \forall i \tag{1}$$

where R_{it} is the return on asset i between time $t-1$ and t; R_{ft} is the return on a (conditionally) risk-free asset; R_{mt} is the return on the market portfolio and $\Im_{t-1}$ is the set of market-wide information available at the end of time $t-1$. Equation (1) implies that δ_{t-1} can be interpreted as the price of covariance risk. Because the same equation has to hold for the market portfolio, δ_{t-1} is also referred to as the price of market risk.

The same model is often used in an international framework (see, among others, Giovannini and Jorion (1989), Harvey (1991) and Chan, Karolyi, and Stulz (1992)). In most applications, all returns in equation (1) are measured in a common currency, usually the U.S. dollar. This approach assumes that investors do not cover their exposure to exchange rate risk or, equivalently, that the price of exchange risk is equal to zero.[1]

B. Empirical Methods

Equation (1) appears to be the natural relation to use in empirical tests of the CAPM because it takes into account investors' use of newly acquired information in making portfolio decisions. The model requires equation (1) to hold for every asset, including the market portfolio. Therefore, in an economy with N risky assets, the following system of pricing restrictions has to be satisfied, at each point in time

$$E(R_{1t}|\Im_{t-1}) - R_{ft} = \delta_{t-1}\text{cov}(R_{1t}, R_{mt}|\Im_{t-1})$$

$$\vdots \qquad\qquad\qquad \vdots$$

$$E(R_{N-1t}|\Im_{t-1}) - R_{ft} = \delta_{t-1}\text{cov}(R_{N-1t}, R_{mt}|\Im_{t-1}) \tag{2}$$

$$E(R_{mt}|\Im_{t-1}) - R_{ft} = \delta_{t-1}\text{var}(R_{mt}|\Im_{t-1}).$$

---

[1] A more general framework with optimal hedging is discussed in Solnik (1974), Sercu (1980), Stulz (1981, 1995), and Adler and Dumas (1983).

The system includes only $(N - 1)$ risky securities plus the market portfolio to avoid redundancies. If all the risky assets were included in the system, the last equation would just be a linear combination of the first N equations in each period. In empirical work, any subset of the assets can be used if N is too large. However, the cost of reducing the size of the system is that information on cross-correlations is lost and tests of the asset pricing restrictions imposed by the model have less power.

Formally, let R_t denote the $(N \times 1)$ vector which includes $(N - 1)$ risky assets and the market portfolio. Then, the following system of equations can be used as a benchmark model to test the conditional CAPM:

$$R_t - R_{ft}\iota = \delta_{t-1}h_{Nt} + \epsilon_t \qquad \epsilon_t|\mathfrak{I}_{t-1} \sim N(0, H_t) \qquad (3)$$

where ι is an N-dimensional vector of ones, H_t is the $(N \times N)$ conditional covariance matrix of asset returns, h_{Nt} is the Nth column of H_t and contains the conditional covariance of each asset with the market.

Equation (3) follows directly from the conditional CAPM. However, the model does not impose any restrictions on the dynamics of the conditional second moments. GARCH processes can be used to fill this gap and obtain a testable version of the model.

A popular GARCH $(1, 1)$ parameterization for H_t is

$$H_t = C'C + A'\epsilon_{t-1}\epsilon'_{t-1}A + B'H_{t-1}B \qquad (4)$$

where C is an $(N \times N)$ symmetric matrix and A and B are $(N \times N)$ matrices of constant coefficients.[2]

The specification in equation (4) is very appealing, given the success of univariate GARCH processes in fitting financial time series. It is also very difficult to estimate due to the large number of unknown parameters. For this reason, most studies that use multivariate GARCH processes limit the analysis to a small number of assets and/or impose several restrictions on the process generating H_t. Often, either the correlations are restricted to be constant (Bollerslev (1990) and Ng (1991)) or both A and B are restricted to be diagonal matrices (see, for example, Bollerslev, Engle, and Wooldridge (1988)). The latter restriction implies that the variances in H_t depend only on past squared residuals and an autoregressive component, while the covariances depend upon past cross-products of residuals and an autoregressive component. We choose the diagonal representation because the constant correlation model appears to be too restrictive for the issues we want to address. In particular, some authors (see, for example, Longin and Solnik (1995) and Karolyi and Stulz (1996)) have suggested that correlations among asset returns change with market conditions, and this feature cannot be accommodated by a constant correlation model. One could argue that the diagonal parameterization is also quite restrictive in light of the cross-market dependences in conditional volatility documented in recent studies (see, for example,

---

[2] See Engle and Kroner (1995) for a detailed discussion of this parameterization.

Hamao, Masulis, and Ng (1990) and Chan, Karolyi, and Stulz (1992)). However, most of those studies use high frequency data. Because we use returns measured at monthly frequencies, we believe that the spillover in volatility may not be very strong. In the data section we provide some evidence in support of this conjecture.

In this case, equation (4) can be written in a simpler form

$$H_t = C'C + aa' * \epsilon_{t-1}\epsilon'_{t-1} + bb' * H_{t-1} \tag{5}$$

where a and b are $(N \times 1)$ vectors which include the diagonal elements of A and B respectively, and $*$ denotes the Hadamard matrix product (element by element).

Unfortunately, if the researcher is interested in analyzing a relatively large number of assets, even the diagonal model is still difficult to estimate, unless more restrictions are imposed on the process driving H_t. To further reduce the number of parameters, we adopt a specification recently proposed by Ding and Engle (1994) which assumes the process to be covariance stationary. The next subsection describes the details of this parameterization.

C. Parsimonious Multivariate GARCH-in-Mean Parameterization

Consider the following system of equations, in which the conditional expectation of the vector of returns R_t is not explicitly parameterized

$$R_t = E_{t-1}(R_t) + \epsilon_t \qquad \epsilon_t|\Im_{t-1} \sim N(0, H_t)$$

and the dynamics for H_t are as described in equation (5). If the ϵ_t process is covariance stationary, its unconditional variance-covariance matrix is equal to

$$H_0 = C'C *(\iota\iota' - aa' - bb')^{-1}.$$

Ding and Engle suggest to replace $C'C$ in equation (5) with $H_0 * (\iota\iota' - aa' - bb')$ during estimation. If a consistent estimator of H_0 is available, optimization needs to be performed only with respect to the parameters in a and b, but not with respect to the parameters in $C'C$. In a diagonal system with N assets, this implies that the number of unknown parameters in the conditional variance equation is reduced from $2N + N(N + 1)/2$ to $2N$.[3]

The essential ingredient to implement this methodology is H_0. If there is no GARCH-in-Mean component in the model, estimation can be performed in two stages. First, a series of estimated residuals is obtained from a model without a GARCH correction for the second moments. Then, the residuals from the first stage are used to estimate the multivariate GARCH process.

In most asset pricing applications, however, the pricing restrictions postulate a relation between conditional expected returns and conditional second moments. In this case, the information matrix of the parameters is no longer

---

[3] In our implementation, with nine assets, the total number of parameters to estimate for the GARCH process is reduced from 63 to 18 by adopting the Ding and Engle specification.

block-diagonal, because of the GARCH-in-Mean feature of the model, and the two-stage estimation procedure suggested by Ding and Engle must be modified.

If investors have rational expectations, the error term that measures the difference between actual returns and their conditional expectations must be orthogonal to the conditioning information. Therefore, the following relation exists between the unconditional covariance matrix of the returns and the unconditional covariance matrix of the residuals

$$\text{cov}(R_t) = \text{cov}[E_{t-1}(R_t)] + H_0.$$

Obviously, H_0 is not directly observable. However, an iterative procedure can be implemented as follows. In the first iteration H_0 is set equal to the sample covariance matrix of the returns. Thereafter it is updated using the covariance matrix of the estimated residuals at the end of each iteration.[4]

In either case, equation (5) is replaced by

$$H_t = H_0 * (\iota\iota' - aa' - bb') + aa' * \epsilon_{t-1}\epsilon_{t-1}' + bb' * H_{t-1}. \qquad (6)$$

The advantages of this multivariate GARCH-in-Mean parameterization are obvious to researchers in asset pricing. First, the reduction in the number of parameters to estimate makes the model applicable to relatively large cross-sections of assets, while preserving flexibility in the dynamics of the conditional second moments. Second, it restricts the unconditional second moments implied by the estimated model to closely match the corresponding sample moments.

Inevitably, parsimony comes at a cost. If the assumption of covariance stationarity does not hold over the sampling period, the inferences are incorrect. Further, some generalizations of standard GARCH processes, like the asymmetric response of conditional second moments to past innovations, can be hard to implement.[5]

An alternative approach to study large systems of assets is the Factor-GARCH model of Engle, Ng, and Rothschild (1990) and King, Sentana and Wadhwani (1994). In this case, the dynamics of the conditional covariance matrix are driven by a limited number of factors that follow GARCH processes. Such a parameterization is a parsimonious alternative to the one proposed here. However, also in this case, parsimony can only be obtained by sacrificing the flexibility of the process. For example, if only one factor is used to model the entire covariance matrix, and the parameters of the model are assumed to be constant, then the chances to detect changes in covariances and differences in volatility across markets are limited (see De Santis (1993)).

---

[4] The procedure is similar to iterated GMM estimation and is likely to improve the small sample properties of the estimators, even when the two-stage procedure delivers consistent results (see Ferson (1995)).

[5] If the asymmetric response is modeled using information variables not observed at time zero, this parameterization requires the use of truncated multivariate distributions.

We use equations (3) and (6) as our benchmark model. Under the assumption of conditional normality, the log-likelihood function can be written as follows:

$$\ln L(\theta) = -\frac{TN}{2} \ln 2\pi - \frac{1}{2} \sum_{t=1}^{T} \ln|H_t(\theta)| - \frac{1}{2} \sum_{t=1}^{T} \epsilon_t(\theta)' H_t(\theta)^{-1} \epsilon_t(\theta) \quad (7)$$

where θ is the vector of unknown parameters in the model. Since the normality assumption is often violated in financial time series, we estimate the model and compute all our tests using the quasi-maximum likelihood (QML) approach proposed by Bollerslev and Wooldridge (1992). Under standard regularity conditions, the QML estimator is consistent and asymptotically normal and statistical inferences can be carried out by computing robust LM or Wald statistics. Optimization is performed using the BHHH (Berndt, Hall, Hall, and Hausman (1974)) algorithm.

D. Related Work

Multivariate GARCH models have been used widely to test the pricing restrictions of the conditional CAPM. An incomplete list includes Bollerslev, Engle, and Wooldridge (1988), Giovannini and Jorion (1989), Ng (1991), and Chan, Karolyi, and Stulz (1992). The parameterization used in these studies can be formalized as follows[6]

$$R_t - R_{ft}\iota = \delta H_t \omega_{t-1} + \epsilon_t \qquad \epsilon_t|\Im_{t-1} \sim N(0, H_t) \quad (8)$$

where ι and H_t are defined earlier, and ω_{t-1} is an $(N \times 1)$ vector of market weights for the risky assets, measured at the end of time $t - 1$.

As discussed earlier, the parsimonious GARCH parameterization that we propose allows us to test the restrictions of the model simultaneously on a large number of assets while preserving the flexibility of the most general GARCH processes. In addition, our specification of the mean equation (equation (3)) differs from equation (8) in that we replace the last element of vector R_t with the return on the market portfolio. This simple variation has two advantages.

First, once the dynamics of H_t are specified, the model in equation (8) can be estimated and tested as long as the market weights are observed by the econometrician at each time t. Often, when market capitalizations are not available, the net supply ω_t of each asset is estimated from multiple sources, thus introducing measurement errors. The parameterization that we propose

---

[6] This notation does not necessarily reflect all the features of each of the studies cited above. However, it provides a good framework to characterize the common aspects among them.

requires a market index, but not the individual asset weights, to be available to the econometrician at each t.[7]

Second, in our approach, equation (3) can be extended to the case where asset returns depend on multiple risk factors, by augmenting R_t with the returns on factor portfolios and adding the risk premium for each factor to the right-hand side of the equation.[8]

A different approach to testing the conditional version of the international CAPM is proposed by Harvey (1991) who combines the hypothesis of conditional mean-variance efficiency of the world portfolio with the auxiliary assumption that investors use a linear filter to predict asset returns. His test is based on Hansen's (1982) generalized method of moments (GMM) and can be implemented without prespecifying the dynamics of the conditional second moments.

Our approach differs from that of Harvey in two respects. First, in our auxiliary assumption, we parameterize the dynamics of the conditional second moments instead of the first moments. Because a large body of research in finance shows that models that predict second moments have been more successful than models that predict first moments, our approach is likely to have more power.[9] Moreover, using Harvey's method, many variables of interest that are functions of conditional second moments cannot be recovered. Obviously, these variables could be estimated by imposing additional moment restrictions. Unfortunately, it is well known that the properties of GMM-based tests deteriorate quickly as the dimension of the system increases.[10]

Second, we use maximum likelihood to test the model. As long as the model is correctly specified, our approach is more efficient. Of course, the method may yield incorrect inferences if the assumptions underlying the likelihood function are violated. However, this problem can be alleviated by using QML estimates for the standard errors, which are robust to violations of the normality assumption.

In a recent article, Dumas and Solnik (1995) use an instrumental variable approach similar to Harvey's to test whether currency risk is priced in international financial markets, when investors use optimal hedging strategies. In their study, they parameterize only the dynamics of the intertemporal marginal rate of substitution, while leaving conditional first and second moments

---

[7] In a recent study, Bekaert and Harvey (1995) use a similar approach. However, due to the complex parameterization of their model, their implementation is limited to the world index and one country at a time.

[8] With multiple factors equation (3) would become:

$$R_t - R_{ft}\iota = \delta_{1,t-1}h_{(N-K+1)t} + \delta_{2,t-1}h_{(N-K+2)t} + \cdots + \delta_{K,t-1}h_{Nt} + \epsilon_t, \quad \epsilon_t|\mathfrak{I}_{t-1} \sim N(0, H_t)$$

where R_t denotes the $(N \times 1)$ vector of returns which includes $(N - K)$ risky assets and the K factor mimicking portfolios, $h_{N-K+k,t}$ is the $(N - K + k)$th column of H_t and contains the conditional covariances of each asset with factor mimicking portfolio k.

[9] See Engel, Frankel, Froot, and Rodrigues (1995) for a discussion of this issue.

[10] See, for example, Ferson (1995). For this reason, in most cases Harvey (1991) tests the pricing restrictions for one country at a time against the world portfolio.

unspecified. Also in this case, the methodology is very general and parsimonious; however, the lack of parameterization of the conditional second moments limits the number of questions that can be addressed. For example, as the authors point out, they cannot compare the dimension of the exchange risk premia relative to the reward for market risk. Our methodology can be extended to test their model and answer some of the questions that cannot be addressed by their method. However, since this extension raises nontrivial issues that go beyond the scope of this study, we leave it to future work.[11]

II. Data

We use monthly dollar-denominated returns on stock indices for the G7 countries (Canada, France, Germany, Italy, Japan, United Kingdom, and U.S.A.) and Switzerland, the largest European market not included in the G7. To approximate the market portfolio, we use a value-weighted world index. All the data are from Morgan Stanley Capital International (MSCI) and cover the period from January 1970 through December 1994.[12]

Table I contains summary statistics for the U.S. dollar returns on the eight national indices and on the value-weighted world index. All values are computed in excess of the return on the U.S. T-Bill closest to 30 days to maturity, as reported in the CRSP risk-free files. Panel A in the table contains means, standard deviations, skewness, kurtosis, Bera-Jarque (1982) statistics, and the sample correlation matrix. The index of kurtosis shows that the unconditional distribution of excess returns has heavier tails than the normal for all the countries in our sample. The Bera-Jarque statistic also indicates that the hypothesis of normality is rejected in all instances.

Most correlations in the table are below 0.5 and the average, excluding the world index, is equal to 0.435. These numbers tend to be lower than the correlations between portfolios of U.S. assets. For example, Elton and Gruber (1992) document that, during the period 1980–1988, the correlation between a value-weighted index of the largest 1000 stocks traded in the U.S. and a value-weighted index of the next 2000 largest stocks is equal to 0.92.

Panel B reports autocorrelations for the excess returns and excess returns squared. The lack of statistically significant autocorrelations in the return series reveals that we do not need to include an AR correction in the mean equations. On the other hand, autocorrelation is detected, at short lags, in the squared returns, suggesting that a GARCH parameterization for the second moments might be appropriate.

Finally, the table contains the cross-correlations of squared returns, at different leads and lags, between the world and the other countries. With few exceptions, only the contemporaneous correlations are statistically significant. The same holds for cross-correlations between other pairs of countries. Of the

---

[11] See De Santis and Gérard (1997).

[12] The MSCI data set has been widely used in previous work. The MSCI methodological notes provide a detailed description of the data.

The Journal of Finance

Table I

Summary Statistics of Excess Returns

Monthly dollar-denominated returns on the equity indices of eight countries, and the value-weighted world index are from MSCI (Morgan Stanley Capital International). Excess returns are obtained by subtracting the return on the United States T-Bill that is closest to 30 days to maturity. R_{it}^e denotes excess returns in percent per month. The sample covers the period January 1970 through December 1994 (300 observations). B–J is the Bera–Jarque test for normality; Q is the Ljung–Box statistic of order 12.

Panel A: Summary Statistics									
	Canada	Japan	France	Germany	Italy	Switzerland	United Kingdom	United States	World
Weights									
Jan 70	0.035	0.039	0.023	0.028	0.014	0.011	0.090	0.691	1.00
Dec 82	0.038	0.182	0.013	0.034	0.009	0.018	0.079	0.555	1.00
Dec 94	0.021	0.289	0.033	0.041	0.012	0.030	0.101	0.361	1.00
Mean	0.33	1.00	0.64	0.57	0.23	0.63	0.72	0.38	0.45
Std. Dv.	5.50	6.70	6.97	6.06	7.76	5.60	7.46	4.48	4.22
Skewness	−0.34*	0.18	0.00	−0.09	0.31*	0.01	1.31**	−0.20	−0.35*
Kurtosis[a]	2.07**	0.77**	1.40**	0.88**	0.87**	1.72**	9.90**	2.44**	1.57**
B–J	56.46**	8.37*	22.95**	9.28*	13.47**	23.68**	1264.67**	72.95**	35.23**
Q_{12}	11.90	16.71	12.40	18.93	21.64*	6.73	14.50	9.29	12.86

Unconditional Correlations of R_{it}^e									
	Canada	Japan	France	Germany	Italy	Switzerland	United Kingdom	United States	World
Canada	1	0.273	0.423	0.293	0.288	0.464	0.513	0.701	0.702
Japan		1	0.396	0.387	0.381	0.441	0.364	0.269	0.687
France			1	0.599	0.431	0.610	0.540	0.437	0.620
Germany				1	0.379	0.701	0.426	0.348	0.556
Italy					1	0.373	0.337	0.215	0.427
Switzerland						1	0.571	0.504	0.687
United Kingdom							1	0.508	0.684
United States								1	0.828

144 nonsimultaneous correlations (of order −2, −1, 1, 2) between all pairs of indices, only eight are statistically significant, which can be imputed to chance. This evidence suggests that, at least in our sample, cross-market dependences in volatility are not strong and, therefore, the diagonal GARCH parameterization that we adopt is not too restrictive.

Table II contains summary statistics for the conditioning variables. We select a set of instruments that have been widely used in the international asset pricing literature (see, among others, Bekaert and Hodrick (1992), Ferson and Harvey (1993), and Bekaert and Harvey (1995)). In particular, in addition to a January dummy, our instruments include the lagged dividend-price ratio for the world index in excess of the risk-free rate; the month-to-month change in the U.S. term premium, measured by the yield on the ten-year U.S. Treasury note in excess of the one-month T-Bill rate; the U.S.

Table I—*Continued*

Panel B: Autocorrelations and Cross-Correlations

Autocorrelations of R_{it}^e

Lag	Canada	Japan	France	Germany	Italy	Switzerland	United Kingdom	United States	World
1	0.002	0.088	0.080	0.008	0.099	0.062	0.091	0.015	0.095
2	−0.086	−0.008	−0.008	−0.019	−0.038	−0.053	−0.099	−0.032	−0.042
3	0.065	0.086	0.128*	0.089	0.100	0.060	0.062	0.007	0.045
4	−0.036	0.044	0.032	0.073	0.072	0.005	0.014	−0.008	0.004
5	0.094	0.021	0.014	−0.109	0.009	0.027	−0.130*	0.098	0.092
6	0.044	−0.021	0.005	0.011	0.136*	−0.049	−0.043	−0.096	−0.083

Autocorrelations of $(R_{it}^e)^2$

Lag	Canada	Japan	France	Germany	Italy	Switzerland	United Kingdom	United States	World
1	0.070	0.125*	0.061	0.176**	0.188**	0.084	0.167*	0.117*	0.066
2	0.228**	0.061	−0.002	−0.033	−0.010	−0.108	0.087	0.050	0.010
3	0.016	−0.000	0.046	0.076	0.022	0.031	0.052	0.129*	0.035
4	0.079	0.024	0.167*	0.058	0.023	0.036	0.029	0.035	0.047
5	0.043	0.053	0.018	0.060	0.088	0.041	0.112	0.002	0.094
6	−0.006	0.053	0.035	0.038	0.035	−0.001	−0.002	0.028	0.033

Cross-correlations of $(R_{it}^e)^2$—World and Country j

Lag	Canada	Japan	France	Germany	Italy	Switzerland	United Kingdom	United States
−6	−0.010	−0.084	−0.051	0.025	0.007	−0.013	−0.032	−0.074
−5	0.047	0.069	0.069	0.049	0.078	0.079	−0.093	0.108
−4	−0.035	0.046	−0.007	−0.051	0.025	−0.060	−0.014	−0.001
−3	0.035	0.071	0.116*	0.042	0.066	0.058	0.093	0.011
−2	−0.075	−0.003	−0.030	−0.043	0.048	−0.070	−0.049	−0.048
−1	0.120*	0.143*	0.036	0.061	0.076	0.032	0.054	0.035
0	0.702**	0.687**	0.620**	0.556**	0.427**	0.687**	0.684**	0.828**
1	0.019	0.073	0.083	0.011	0.138*	0.099	0.065	0.099
2	−0.038	−0.015	−0.011	0.006	−0.045	−0.054	−0.040	−0.009
3	0.044	−0.003	0.070	0.016	0.057	0.024	0.030	0.055
4	0.005	0.007	0.043	0.009	0.041	0.014	0.003	−0.031
5	0.007	0.038	0.034	0.075	0.001	0.085	0.053	0.086
6	−0.061	−0.033	−0.081	−0.031	−0.074	−0.085	−0.068	−0.083

Number of significant cross-correlations of order $(-2, -1, 1, 2)$: 8 out of 144.

[a] Equal to zero for the normal distribution.
* and ** denote statistical significance at the 5 percent and 1 percent levels, respectively.

default premium, measured by the yield difference between Moody's BAA and AAA rated bonds; and the month-to-month change in the U.S. interest rate. The table shows that the instruments carry nonredundant information, since their correlations are quite low.

The Journal of Finance

Table II

Summary Statistics of Information Variables

The information set includes the world dividend yield in excess of the return on the United States (U.S.) T-Bill with maturity closest to 30 days (XDPR), the change in U.S. term premium (ΔUSTP), the U.S. default premium (USDP), and the change in the 30-day U.S. T-Bill return (ΔUSRF). The world dividend yield is the dollar-denominated dividend yield on the MSCI world index. The U.S. term premium is equal to the yield on 10-year U.S. T-Notes in excess of the yield of the 3-month U.S. T-Bill. The U.S. default premium is the yield on Moody's BAA rated bonds in excess of the yield on Moody's AAA rated bonds. The sample covers the period January 1970 through December 1994 (300 observations).

	Mean	Std. Dev.	Min.	Max.	Correlations		
					ΔUSTP	USDP	ΔUSRF
XDPR	−0.249	0.189	−0.930	0.029	−0.018	−0.356	0.162
ΔUSTP	0.010	0.476	−2.190	3.330	1	0.135	−0.427
USDP	1.198	0.440	0.580	2.690		1	−0.148
ΔUSRF	−0.001	0.074	−0.467	0.276			1

	Autocorrelations						
Lag	1	2	3	4	5	6	12
XDPR	0.922	0.854	0.792	0.744	0.715	0.694	0.501
ΔUSTP	0.227	−0.150	−0.039	−0.077	−0.087	−0.138	−0.155
USDP	0.952	0.889	0.842	0.806	0.769	0.714	0.479
ΔUSRF	−0.063	−0.051	−0.110	−0.093	−0.032	0.026	0.058

III. Empirical Evidence

As discussed in Section I, the traditional CAPM, applied to international financial markets, postulates that the conditional expected return on any asset is linearly related to the conditional covariance between that asset and the return on a world-wide portfolio. The model, which we refer to as the benchmark model, can be rewritten as follows for convenience

$$R_{it} - R_{ft} = \delta_{t-1}\text{cov}(R_{it}, R_{mt}|\mathfrak{T}_{t-1}) + \epsilon_{it} \qquad \forall i. \qquad (9)$$

If international markets are fully integrated and world market risk is the only relevant factor, the price of covariance-risk δ_{t-1} should be positive and equal across all markets.

We compare the performance of the benchmark model to two alternative specifications which can provide useful insights, should the standard CAPM fail to hold. The first alternative allows for some level of market segmentation. In particular, we introduce two changes. First, we assume that country-specific risk, as measured by the conditional variance, is priced in each market in addition to world-wide risk. Second, we introduce a constant in each pricing equation to accommodate other forms of segmentation, like differences in tax treatment or other institutional arrangements that cannot be captured by the benchmark model. Formally, the first alternative to equation (9), which we refer to as the partial segmentation model, is specified as follows:

$$R_{it} - R_{ft} = \alpha_i + \delta_{t-1}\text{cov}(R_{it}, R_{mt}|\mathfrak{I}_{t-1}) + \gamma_i\text{var}(R_{it}|\mathfrak{I}_{t-1}) + \epsilon_{it} \qquad \forall i. \qquad (10)$$

Under the null hypothesis of full market integration both α_i and γ_i must be equal to zero for all markets.

The second alternative examines whether the variation in conditional expected returns is fully explained by world market risk. Let z_{t-1} be a $(k \times 1)$ vector of variables included in $\mathfrak{I}_{t-1}$. We estimate the following system of equations:

$$R_{it} - R_{ft} = \alpha_i + \lambda'z_{t-1} + \delta_{t-1}\text{cov}(R_{it}, R_{mt}|\mathfrak{I}_{t-1}) + \epsilon_{it} \qquad \forall i. \qquad (11)$$

If the traditional CAPM is misspecified, some of the variables in z_{t-1} could have statistical power in explaining the dynamics of the expected returns.

A. The Conditional CAPM with Constant Price of Risk

We start our investigation by introducing the additional assumption that the price of market risk δ_{t-1} is constant. This implies that, although both the conditional risk-free rate and the conditional mean-standard deviation frontier can change in each period, the slope of the capital market line is fixed. This restriction has been imposed in many studies of the conditional CAPM (e.g., Giovannini and Jorion (1989) and Chan, Karolyi, and Stulz (1992)) and, in this sense, it represents an interesting starting point.

Panel A in Table III contains QML estimates of the parameters for the benchmark model. The point estimate for the price of market risk is equal to 2.37,[13] which is reasonable both in size and sign. However, the 1.61 value for the robust standard error is relatively large and implies that the coefficient is statistically significant only at the 15 percent level.

Next, consider the estimated parameters for the GARCH process. With the exception of Germany, all the elements in the vectors a and b are statistically significant at any conventional level. In addition, the estimates satisfy the stationarity conditions for all the variance and covariance processes.[14] As it is typical in most studies that use GARCH models, all processes display high persistence and the estimates of the b_i coefficients (which link second moments to their lagged value) are considerably larger than the corresponding estimates of the a_is (which link second moments to their past innovations).

Panel B includes a variety of diagnostic statistics to evaluate this specification of the model. The average pricing errors are a relatively small fraction of the corresponding average excess returns. However, for each index, the fraction of total variation in the excess returns explained by the model, which we

---

[13] The number reported in the table is 0.0237 because the estimation uses percentage returns.
[14] Theorem 1 in Bollerslev (1986) implies that for each process in H_t to be covariance stationary, the condition $a_i a_j + b_i b_j < 1 \ \forall i, j$ has to be satisfied.

1894   *The Journal of Finance*

Table III

Quasi-Maximum Likelihood (QML) Estimates of the Conditional International CAPM with Constant Price of Risk

Estimates are based on monthly dollar-denominated returns from January 1970 through December 1994. Data for the country equity indices and the world portfolio are from MSCI (Morgan Stanley Capital International). The risk-free rate is the return on the U.S. T-Bill with maturity closest to 30 days from Center for Research in Security Prices (CRSP). Each mean equation relates the country index excess return R_{it}^e to its world covariance risk cov(R_{it}; $R_{mt}|\Im_{t-1}$):

$$R_{it}^e = \delta \ \text{cov}(R_{it}; R_{mt}\Im_{t-1}) + \epsilon_{it}$$

where δ denotes the price of world covariance risk and $\epsilon_t|\Im_{t-1} \sim N(0, H_t)$. The conditional covariance matrix H_t is parameterized as follows:

$$H_t = H_0 * (\iota\iota' - aa' - bb') + aa' * \epsilon_{t-1}\epsilon'_{t-1} + bb' * H_{t-1}$$

where $*$ denotes the Hadamard matrix product, a and b are 9×1 vectors of constants and ι is an 9×1 unit vector. QML standard errors are reported in parentheses.

RMSE denotes Root Mean Squared Error. Pseudo R^2s are computed for each index as the ratio between the sum of squared fitted values of the risk premia and the sum of squared excess returns. Since the model restricts the price of risk to be constant across indices, individual pseudo R^2 are not guaranteed to be positive. B–J is the Bera–Jarque test statistic for normality. Q is the *p*-value of Ljung–Box test statistic of order 12 for standardized residuals (z) and standardized residuals squared (z^2). EN–S– and EN–S+ are Engle–Ng Lagrange multiplier tests for positive and negative size-bias in standardized residuals squared.

Panel A: Parameter Estimates

Price of Covariance Risk

δ (const)	0.0237
	(0.0161)

GARCH Process

	Canada	Japan	France	Germany	Italy	Switzerland	United Kingdom	United States	World
a_i	0.172	0.188	0.240	0.292	0.158	0.176	0.250	0.227	0.206
	(0.036)	(0.025)	(0.064)	(0.073)	(0.065)	(0.075)	(0.038)	(0.032)	(0.031)
b_i	0.962	0.966	0.872	0.703	0.895	0.922	0.947	0.961	0.965
	(0.016)	(0.009)	(0.044)	(0.501)	(0.066)	(0.027)	(0.019)	(0.012)	(0.010)

Panel B: Summary Statistics and Diagnostics for the Residuals

	Canada	Japan	France	Germany	Italy	Switzerland	United Kingdom	United States	World
Avg. Exc. Return	0.33%	1.00	0.64	0.57	0.23	0.63	0.72	0.38	0.45
Avg. pred. Error	−0.06%	0.54	0.20	0.23	−0.10	0.24	0.20	0.01	0.02
RMSE	5.50	6.70	6.61	6.06	7.76	5.61	7.45	4.46	4.22
Pseudo R^2	0.15%	−0.24	0.17	0.07	0.08	0.04	0.43	0.54	0.33
Kurtosis[a]	1.74**	0.64*	1.42**	0.70*	0.91**	1.28**	4.80**	2.05**	1.76**
B–J	41.72**	6.29*	23.57**	6.53*	13.72**	19.24**	290.91**	55.82**	48.99**
$Q_{12}(z)$	0.62	0.08	0.37	0.11	0.05	0.89	0.73	0.75	0.29
$Q_{12}(z^2)$	0.40	0.65	0.56	0.45	0.73	0.40	0.92	0.51	0.81
EN–S–	−0.38	−0.85	−1.32	−1.03	−0.52	−1.43	0.29	−0.85	−0.69
EN–S+	1.00	0.73	−0.58	1.13	1.98*	−0.37	−0.80	−0.58	−1.43
Likelihood function					−7508.60				

[a] Equal to zero for the normal distribution.
* and ** denote statistical significance at the 5 percent and 1 percent levels, respectively.

refer to as pseudo-R^2, is rather low and reaches its highest value of 0.54 percent for the U.S. market.[15] For most countries, the index of kurtosis for the standardized residuals is lower than the corresponding index for the excess returns. The same is true for the Bera-Jarque test statistic. Still, the hypothesis of normality is rejected in most cases. This suggests that, although the GARCH parameterization can accommodate some of the kurtosis in the data, the use of a fat-tailed conditional distribution might improve the performance of the model. This evidence against normality warrants the use of QML inferential procedures in our analysis.

We also construct the estimated standardized residuals ($\epsilon_t h_t^{-1/2}$) and the estimated standardized residuals squared ($\epsilon_t^2 h_t^{-1}$) and compute the Ljung-Box portmanteau statistic for each series to test the hypothesis of absence of autocorrelation up to order 12. The tests show that the null hypothesis is never rejected and that the GARCH (1, 1) parameterization that we adopt is satisfactory.[16]

Finally, we report test statistics for the presence of asymmetric responses to past innovations in the conditional covariance matrix. This phenomenon has been widely studied using univariate GARCH processes. For example, Engle and Ng (1993) find that bad news has a larger effect on volatility than good news. For this reason, we compute the test statistic for signed size-bias in the residuals that they propose. The test rejects the null hypothesis of no positive size-bias only for Italy. This result is not necessarily surprising, because most previous studies on this issue use higher frequency data. It is possible that volatility asymmetries are present in international markets, but they cannot be detected in monthly data.

Since our parameterization for the conditional covariance process has not yet been used in empirical applications, we also compare the estimation results of this specification to those from the Engle and Kroner (1995) diagonal specification. The latter model is widely used, but less parsimonious, because the intercepts of the conditional covariance process must be estimated. For this reason, we have to limit the comparison to a system of four countries plus the world portfolio.[17] The results show that the dynamics of the conditional second moments are essentially unaffected by the parameterization. Interestingly, the main difference between the two approaches is that the unconditional second moments implied by the Engle and Kroner parameterization are often much larger (sometimes more than double) than those implied by our parameterization or, more importantly, than the corresponding sample moments. Although this result may be sample specific, it suggests that an appealing feature of our parameterization is its ability to capture the dynamics of the conditional

---

[15] Since the model requires the coefficient δ to be equal across all markets, the pseudo-R^2 statistics are not guaranteed to be all nonnegative.

[16] We also find that this specification is selected by the Schwartz information criterion over a set of alternative specifications that go from a constant covariance matrix to a GARCH (2, 2) process.

[17] We include the four largest markets in the MSCI data set: United States, United Kingdom, Japan, and Germany. The results from this experiment are available upon request.

1896   *The Journal of Finance*

Table IV
Specification Tests of the Conditional International CAPM with Constant Price of Risk

This table reports robust Wald test statistics for two alternative specifications of the conditional international capital asset pricing model (CAPM). The first model (equation A) includes country specific risk and country specific intercepts in addition to market risk. The second model (equation B) includes asset specific intercepts and the instruments in z_{t-1} as independent conditioning variables, in addition to market risk. The instruments include a constant, a January dummy (JAN), the world index dividend yield in excess of the return on the 30-day U.S. T-Bill (XDPR), the change in the U.S. term premium (ΔUSTP), the U.S. default premium (USDP) and the change in the 30-day U.S. T-Bill return (ΔUSRF). Estimation is based on monthly dollar-denominated returns from January 1970 through December 1994. Data for the country equity indices and the world portfolio are from MSCI (Morgan Stanley Capital International). The risk-free rate is the return on the U.S. T-Bill with maturity closest to 30 days from the Center for Research in Security Prices (CRSP).

Eq. A

$$R_{it}^e = \alpha_i + \delta_i \mathrm{cov}(R_{it}; R_{mt}|\Im_{t-1}) + \gamma_i \mathrm{var}(R_{it}|\Im_{t-1}) + \epsilon_{it}$$

Eq. B

$$R_{it}^e = \alpha_i + \lambda' z_{t-1} + \delta \, \mathrm{cov}(R_{it}; R_{mt}|\Im_{t-1}) + \epsilon_{it}$$

where δ denotes the price of world covariance risk and $\epsilon_t|\Im_{t-1} \sim N(0, H_t)$. The conditional covariance matrix H_t is parameterized as follows:

$$H_t = H_0 * (\iota\iota' - aa' - bb') + aa' * \epsilon_{t-1}\epsilon'_{t-1} + bb' * H_{t-1}$$

where $*$ denotes the Hadamard matrix product, a and b are 9×1 vectors of constants and ι is an 9×1 unit vector.

Null Hypothesis	χ^2	df	p-level
Equation A			
Is the price of risk equal across countries?			
H_0: $\delta_i = \delta$, $\forall i$	4.767	8	0.782
Are country-specific intercepts jointly equal to zero?			
H_0: $\alpha_i = 0$, $\forall i$	6.534	9	0.685
Is the price of country-specific risk equal to zero?			
H_0: $\gamma_i = 0$, $\forall i$	4.231	8	0.765
Equation B			
Are the information variables z_{t-1} orthogonal to the risk-adjusted excess returns?			
H_0: $\lambda_k = 0$, $\forall k$	22.125	5	0.001

second moments, as well as other standard GARCH processes, while matching closely the sample second moments of the data.

Table IV contains the results of tests that compare the benchmark CAPM to alternative specifications. First, we estimate the partial market segmentation model specified in equation (10). In this model the risk premium for each country depends not only on the covariance with the world portfolio, but also on two country-specific factors: a constant and the conditional variance. The robust Wald tests support the conditional CAPM. Only one of the constant factors is individually significant at the 10 percent level and the p-value for the joint hypothesis that all the α_is are zero is equal to 0.69. None of the prices of country risk (γ_i) is individually significant either, and the p-value for the joint hypothesis that country risk is not priced in any market is equal to 0.77. We also consider an alternative form of market segmentation in which the price of covariance risk δ differs across countries. The null hypothesis of a common price cannot be rejected at any statistically reasonable level.

Second, we test the hypothesis that some of the variation in the excess returns can be explained by a number of information variables, even after accounting for the variation in the market risk premium of each asset. Formally, we test the hypothesis that the λ coefficients in equation (11) are jointly equal to zero. The robust Wald test statistic reported in the table shows that this hypothesis is strongly rejected by the data.

In summary, a number of diagnostic tests support the pricing restrictions of the traditional CAPM when applied to international financial markets. Expected returns are positively related to market risk and the price of covariance risk is equal across markets. In addition, neither idiosyncratic risk nor a country-specific constant factor add any explanatory power to the model. Nevertheless, two main issues emerge from the results discussed so far. First, although the estimates reveal a positive relation between excess returns and covariance risk, the link is statistically weak. Second, the model explains only a small amount of variation in the excess return series and some of the variation is still predictable after accounting for market risk. These results may be due, at least in part, to the auxiliary assumption on the constancy of the price of risk. If excess returns are considerably more variable than their conditional covariance with the market, a model with a constant price of risk may not have enough power to fully explain the dynamics of the risk premia. We analyze this issue in the next subsection by allowing δ to vary through time.

B. The Conditional CAPM with Time-Varying Price of Risk

Since the conditional CAPM is only a partial equilibrium model, the theory does not help identify the state variables that affect the price of market risk. Inevitably, any parameterization of the dynamics of δ_{t-1} can be criticized for being ad hoc. For example, many studies assume that the price of risk is linearly related to a given set of instruments, because this is an easy specification to estimate and test.[18] One limitation of this approach is that, in the absence of additional restrictions, a linear price of market risk can become negative, which is inconsistent with the theory. Merton (1980) points out that the nonnegativity restriction should be incorporated into the specification of the model to avoid biases in the estimation of the market premium. For this

---

[18] For example, Ferson (1989) and Ferson, Foerster, and Keim (1993) use the linearity assumption to test latent variable models.

The Journal of Finance

reason, we assume that the price of market risk can be approximated by an exponential function of the instruments[19]

$$\delta_{t-1} = \exp(\kappa' z_{t-1}).$$

The instrument set z_{t-1} is described in the data section. To accommodate the January effect, we assume that the price of risk in the month of January is equal to $\delta_{t-1} = \kappa_J + \exp(\kappa' z_{t-1})$.

Panel A in Table V contains QML estimates of the parameters for the benchmark model with time-varying δ. The average price of market risk is equal to 3.96 and given a Newey-West consistent standard error of 0.38, is highly significant. The robust Wald test statistic for the hypothesis that the price of risk is constant (Panel B in the table) is equal to 22.59 and, therefore, the null hypothesis is strongly rejected at any conventional level. Individual test statistics reveal that the dynamics of δ are mostly driven by the excess dividend-yield, the change in the short-term interest rate and, in part, by the January dummy variable.[20]

These findings are very interesting, especially when compared to the earlier discussion of the conditional CAPM with constant price of risk. Obviously, the lack of statistical significance in the relation between expected returns and conditional market risk documented in Table III is due to the insufficient variation in the conditional covariances relative to the excess returns. The improved performance of the model is confirmed by the diagnostic statistics reported in Panel C. For example, the average value of the pseudo-R^2s increases from 0.16 percent in the case of constant price of risk to 2.52 percent when δ is time-varying. Most of the indices of kurtosis and the Bera-Jarque statistics are also improved relative to the model with constant δ. The standardized residuals, however, are still fat-tailed.

Figure 1 contains a plot of the estimated price of covariance risk.[21] Part of the volatility in the point estimates is inevitably due to estimation error. Since we believe that the most interesting component of our estimates is the trend in the series, we also include a plot of the price in which the high frequency components are filtered-out using the Hodrick and Prescott (HP) methodology (see Hodrick and Prescott (1996)). The filtered price reaches its highest values in the Seventies, becomes much lower during the Eighties and finally increases again in the early Nineties. The average value of δ_{t-1} between January 1980 and December 1994 is equal to 3.31 and significantly lower than its average value of 4.94 in the first part of the sample.[22]

---

[19] Bekaert and Harvey (1995) and De Santis and Gérard (1997) use a similar parameterization.

[20] We also investigate an alternative specification of the model in which the instruments include an aggregate measure of currency risk computed as the difference between the dollar and local currency returns on the world index. The coefficient of this variable is not statistically significant and none of the results are affected.

[21] To preserve readability, the plot does not include the January component of δ_t.

[22] Our choice to split the sample in 1980 is not completely arbitrary. In 1980 Japan, the country with the largest financial markets after the United States, enacted the Foreign Exchange and Foreign Control Law which lifted many restriction to international investments. Since then many other countries have liberalized their financial markets.

International Asset Pricing and Portfolio Diversification   1899

Another feature of the estimated price of risk is the presence of a pronounced January effect. The average estimated premia, excluding the January component, vary from a minimum of 0.45 percent per month (Germany) to a maximum of 0.72 percent (U.K.). They increase by an average of 1.47 percent in the month of January. This indicates that approximately 25 percent of the annual premium is earned during the first month of the year. Although our approach treats the January effect as a seasonal in the price of risk, rather than as a factor which affects risk premia linearly, our results confirm the findings of Gultekin and Gultekin (1983) and extend them to the Eighties and the first half of the Nineties.

Panel A in Table V shows that the structure of the conditional second moments is essentially unchanged when the price of market risk is allowed to vary. Panel C also includes some diagnostic tests on the squared standardized residuals to evaluate the specification of the conditional second moments. As before, the Ljung-Box statistics reveal that no significant autocorrelation is left in the series obtained from the GARCH (1, 1) parameterization and the Engle-Ng LM tests for signed size-bias suggest that, at least in our sample, there is no evidence of asymmetry in the response of conditional second moments to past innovations. Finally, we compute an extension of the LM test proposed by Engle and Ng (1993) to determine whether the instruments in z_{t-1} are orthogonal to the conditional variances.[23] In seven of nine cases we fail to reject the hypothesis that the instruments cannot predict conditional volatilities. The only exceptions are Canada and the world portfolio. Although this result opens the possibility for further studies on the specification of the GARCH process, we do not believe that the evidence is strong enough, in our context, to require a specification that would be much harder to estimate.

Having established a number of satisfactory features of the conditional CAPM with time-varying price of risk, we proceed to evaluate the two alternative specifications discussed at the beginning of this section. The results for these tests are contained in Table VI. First, we consider the model with partial market segmentation. In light of the previous testing results it is not surprising that neither the constants, nor the country specific volatilities are priced. In fact, the relaxation of the constancy hypothesis on δ_{t-1} should have no bearing on these results.

The second alternative specification is potentially more interesting. Since the model with time-varying price of risk explains a larger fraction of the variation in excess returns, this may eliminate the instruments' ability to predict excess returns, after accounting for market risk. The robust Wald test, however, shows that this is not the case and the null hypothesis that all the λs in equation (11) are equal to zero is strongly rejected again.

Given the persistence of this result, we believe it is worth exploring an additional hypothesis. The predictability may be driven by the nonnegativity restriction that we impose on the market risk premium. For example, Bou-

---

[23] For each country index, we run a regression of the squared standardized residuals on the variables included in z_{t-1}. Under the null hypothesis that the instruments have no predictive power, the regression R^2 multiplied by the number of observations is distributed as a chi-square variable with five degrees of freedom.

Table V

Quasi-Maximum Likelihood (QML) Estimates of the Conditional International CAPM with Time-Varying Price of Risk

Estimates are based on monthly dollar-denominated returns from January 1970 through December 1994. Data for the country equity indices and the world portfolio are from MSCI (Morgan Stanley Capital International). The risk-free rate is the return on the U.S. T-Bill with maturity closest to 30 days from Center for Research in Security Prices (CRSP). All returns are in percent per month. Each mean equation relates the country index excess return R_{it}^e to its world covariance risk $\text{cov}(R_{it}; R_{mt}|\mathfrak{I}_{t-1})$. The price of risk is function of a set of instruments, z_{t-1}, included in the investors' information set. The instruments include a constant, a January dummy (JAN), the world index dividend yield in excess of the return on the 30-day U.S. T-Bill (XDPR), the change in the U.S. term premium (ΔUSTP), the U.S. default premium (USDP) and the change in the 30-day U.S. T-Bill return (ΔUSRF).

$$R_{it}^e = \delta \text{cov}_{t-1}(R_{it}; R_{mt}|\mathfrak{I}_{t-1}) + \epsilon_{it}$$

where $\delta_{t-1} = \exp(\kappa' z_{t-1})$ denotes the price of world covariance risk and $\epsilon_t|\mathfrak{I}_{t-1} \sim N(0, H_t)$. The conditional covariance matrix H_t is parameterized as follows:

$$H_t = H_0 * (\iota\iota' - aa' - bb') + aa' * \epsilon_{t-1}\epsilon'_{t-1} + bb' * H_{t-1}$$

where $*$ denotes the Hadamard matrix product, a and b are 9×1 vectors of constants and ι is an 9×1 unit vector. QML standard errors are reported in parentheses.

RMSE denotes Root Mean Squared Error. Pseudo R^2s are computed for each index as the ratio between the sum of squared fitted values of the risk premia and the sum of squared excess returns. Since the model restricts the price of risk to be constant across indices, individual pseudo R^2s are not guaranteed to be positive. B–J is the Bera–Jarque test statistic for normality. Q is the p-value of Ljung–Box test statistic of order 12 for standardized residuals (z) and standardized residuals squared (z^2). EN–S– and EN–S+ are Engle–Ng Lagrange multiplier tests for positive and negative size-bias in standardized residuals squared. EN-z denotes the Engle-Ng Lagrange multiplier test of the predictability of standardized residuals squared with the z variables.

Panel A: Parameter Estimates

Price of Covariance Risk

κ_0 (const)	κ_1 (JAN)	κ_2 (XDPR)	κ_3 (ΔUSTP)	κ_4 (USDP)	κ_5 (ΔUSRF)
-2.942	0.089	6.783	-0.652	0.414	-13.683
(2.570)	(0.054)	(2.483)	(2.263)	(2.288)	(5.517)

GARCH Process

	Canada	Japan	France	Germany	Italy	Switzerland	United Kingdom	United States	World
a_i	0.171	0.189	0.251	0.293	0.163	0.169	0.244	0.229	0.206
	(0.038)	(0.025)	(0.066)	(0.060)	(0.065)	(0.072)	(0.040)	(0.031)	(0.030)
b_i	0.961	0.966	0.868	0.671	0.888	0.921	0.950	0.960	0.965
	(0.018)	(0.009)	(0.044)	(0.438)	(0.070)	(0.033)	(0.018)	(0.012)	(0.010)

ctd. overleaf

Table V—*Continued*

Panel B: Specification Test				
Null Hypothesis	χ^2	df	*p*-level
Is the price of market risk constant?			
H_0: $\kappa_k = 0$, $\forall k > 1$	22.587	5	0.000

Panel C: Summary Statistics and Diagnostics for the Residuals

	Canada	Japan	France	Germany	Italy	Switzerland	United Kingdom	United States	World
Avg. exc. return	0.33%	1.00	0.64	0.57	0.23	0.63	0.72	0.38	0.45
Premia: exc. Jan.	0.51%	0.61	0.58	0.45	0.46	0.52	0.72	0.51	0.57
January	1.38%	1.66	1.59	1.27	1.26	1.41	1.80	1.33	1.53
Avg. pred. error	−0.29%	0.25	−0.08	0.01	−0.33	−0.00	−0.15	−0.23	−0.25
RMSE	5.40	6.66	6.93	6.06	7.77	5.56	7.32	4.33	4.10
Pseudo R^2 [a]	3.80%	1.06	1.03	0.01	−0.31	1.44	3.80	6.27	5.55
Kurtosis[a]	1.58**	0.58*	1.21**	0.60*	0.95**	1.03**	3.91**	1.83**	1.55**
B–J	35.91**	6.86*	17.20**	4.55	15.45**	12.43**	195.62**	45.64**	37.71**
$Q_{12}(z)$	0.52	0.22	0.50	0.10	0.02	0.93	0.73	0.68	0.28
$Q_{12}(z^2)$	0.67	0.60	0.52	0.25	0.76	0.38	0.78	0.71	0.89
EN–S−	−0.21	−0.95	−1.42	−0.72	−0.39	−1.26	0.38	−0.36	−0.02
EN–S+	1.41	0.37	−0.96	1.36	1.93	0.01	−0.67	−0.39	−1.07
EN–z	18.67**	2.11	5.83	4.08	6.27	10.40	8.01	7.01	16.34**
Likelihood function:					−7499.94				

[a] Equal to zero for the normal distribution.
* and ** denote statistical significance at the 5 percent and 1 percent levels, respectively.

doukh, Richardson, and Smith (1993) find that, for the U.S. market, negative risk premia are associated with periods of high expected inflation and downward sloping term structures. It is plausible that international financial markets display similar features, which obviously cannot be captured by the CAPM alone. To test this hypothesis we estimate the model in equation (11) assuming, this time, that the price of market risk is linear in the instruments, then we repeat the predictability test on the risk-adjusted returns. Figure 2 contains a plot of the estimated price of market risk with and without the nonnegativity restriction imposed. Although the two series have a correlation of 0.65, the difference is quite dramatic in some periods. Specifically, between the end of the Seventies and the early Eighties the unrestricted price of market risk is consistently negative. During those years, interest rates and inflation were unusually high and the slope of the yield curve was often negative. This shows that the findings of Boudoukh, Richardson, and Smith (1993) hold also in an international setting. Interestingly, when we allow risk premia to become negative, the joint test that all the λs in equation (11) are equal to zero has a *p*-value of 0.68, which implies that the predictability documented earlier is indeed driven by the inability of the CAPM to accommodate negative expected returns.

To summarize, we find that expected excess returns are positively related to their conditional covariance with a world-wide portfolio whereas country specific risk is not priced. Explicitly modeling the time-variation of the price of

The Journal of Finance

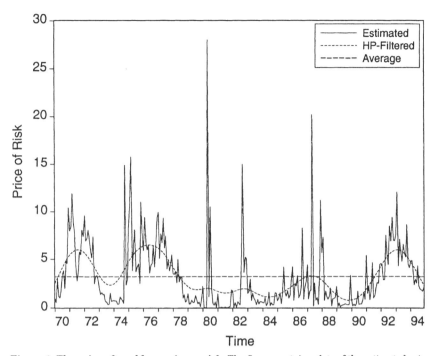

Figure 1. The price of world covariance risk. The figure contains plots of the estimated price of covariance risk, the corresponding HP-filtered series and a horizontal line that corresponds to the average price of risk. The estimates are obtained from the conditional version of the international CAPM. The plotted series do not include the January component.

market risk improves the ability to explain the dynamics of the risk premia. However expected excess returns remain predictable after accounting for world market risk. This is the most concerning result for advocates of the traditional CAPM as a model of international asset pricing: a one-factor model which imposes a nonnegativity constraint on the market risk premium cannot fully explain the dynamics of international expected returns.[24] If the premium for market risk has to be positive, an alternative model is needed to accommodate negative equity premia for some periods of time. For example, the recent findings of Dumas and Solnik (1995) and De Santis and Gérard (1997) indicate that currency risk is likely to be an important omitted factor for international assets. Or it is possible that national equity indices contain characteristics which are not accounted for by market risk.[25] Alternatively, a nonlinear pricing model like the one suggested by Bansal, Hsieh, and

[24] To verify the robustness of our results, we replicate all our tests using local currency returns in excess of the local risk free rate. This model assumes that investors use a unitary hedge ratio to offset their exposure to exchange rate risk (see, e.g., Chan, Karolyi, and Stulz (1992)). The evidence is essentially unaffected. All the results are available upon request.

International Asset Pricing and Portfolio Diversification   1903

Table VI

Specification Tests of the Conditional International CAPM with Time-Varying Price of Risk

This table reports robust Wald test statistics for two alternative specifications of the conditional international capital asset pricing model (CAPM). The first model (equation A) includes country specific risk and country specific intercepts in addition to market risk. The second model (equation B) includes asset specific intercepts and the instruments in z_{t-1} as independent conditioning variables, in addition to market risk. The instruments include a constant, a January dummy (JAN), the world index dividend yield in excess of the return on the 30-day U.S. T-Bill (XDPR), the change in the U.S. term premium (ΔUSTP), the U.S. default premium (USDP) and the change in the 30-day U.S. T-Bill return (ΔUSRF). Estimation is based on monthly dollar-denominated returns from January 1970 through December 1994. Data for the country equity indices and the world portfolio are from MSCI (Morgan Stanley Capital International). The risk-free rate is the return on the U.S. T-Bill with maturity closest to 30 days from the Center for Research in Security Prices (CRSP).

Eq. A $R_{it}^e = \alpha_i + \delta \, \text{cov}(R_{it}; R_{mt}|\mathfrak{I}_{t-1}) + \gamma_i \text{var}(R_{it}|\mathfrak{I}_{t-1}) + \epsilon_{it}$

Eq. B $R_{it}^e = \alpha_i + \lambda' z_{t-1} + \delta_{t-1} \text{cov}(R_{it}; R_{mt}|\mathfrak{I}_{t-1}) + \epsilon_{it}$

where $\delta_{t-1} = \exp(\kappa' z_{t-1})$ denotes the price of world covariance risk and $\epsilon_t|\mathfrak{I}_{t-1} \sim N(0, H_t)$. The conditional covariance matrix H_t is parameterized as follows

$$H_t = H_0 * (\iota\iota' - aa' - bb') + aa' * \epsilon_{t-1}\epsilon_{t-1}' + bb' * H_{t-1}$$

where $*$ denotes the Hadamard matrix product, a and b are 9×1 vectors of constants and ι is an 9×1 unit vector.

Null Hypothesis	χ^2	df	p-level
Equation A			
Are country specific intercepts jointly equal to zero?			
H_0: $\alpha_i = 0$, $\forall i$	7.566	9	0.578
Is the price of country specific risk equal to zero?			
H_0: $\gamma_i = 0$, $\forall i$	4.182	8	0.840
Equation B			
Are the information variables z_{t-1} orthogonal to the risk-adjusted excess returns?			
H_0: $\lambda_k = 0$, $\forall k$	25.096	5	0.000

Viswanathan (1993) may be needed to explain the cross-section of returns that we analyze.

IV. Should U.S. Investors Diversify Internationally?

The evidence discussed so far suggests that world risk is priced in international financial markets and that a number of restrictions of the traditional CAPM hold when the model is applied to an international setting. However,

---

[25] The possibility that the dynamics of expected returns can be explained by asset characteristics rather than risk has recently been suggested by Daniel and Titman (1997).

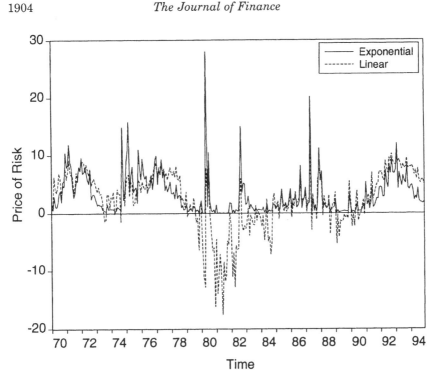

Figure 2. Restricted versus unrestricted price of world covariance risk. The figure contains plots of the estimated price of covariance risk with and without the nonnegativity restriction. The restricted value is obtained by assuming that the price is an exponential function of the instruments whereas the unrestricted value is obtained assuming linearity. The plotted series do not include the January component.

our results also indicate that a model with multiple sources of risk would probably perform better than a single factor model. This implies that the standard approach to portfolio choice proposed by Markowitz (1952) may not be completely adequate when evaluating the benefits of international diversification. Nevertheless, since it is common practice to use this framework also in international finance, in this section we discuss the implications of our findings for mean-variance analysis.[26]

International diversification is often regarded as the best way to improve portfolio performance. In fact, as long as financial markets are affected by country specific factors, correlations between asset returns from different countries are likely to be lower than correlations within the same country. Based on this reasoning, researchers and investment advisors alike have strongly promoted the idea of global diversification. Recently, however, a more

---

[26] Implicitly we make the assumption that all the markets in our study were financially integrated throughout the sample. Bekaert and Harvey (1995) analyze whether the degree of financial integration varies through time.

cautious attitude has been fostered by two arguments. First, international financial markets have become increasingly more integrated, due to the lifting of many restrictions to international investment during the Eighties. If the legal barriers were binding, cross-country correlations may have increased in recent years, thus reducing the benefits of diversification.[27] Second, recent studies suggest that global diversification may not be as good a safety net against bear markets in the United States as most people think. For example, Odier and Solnik (1993) and Lin, Engle, and Ito (1994) suggest that bear markets are contagious at the international level; when the U.S. market tumbles, cross-country correlations increase. In this sense, the benefits of holding an international portfolio may be reduced even further when investors need them the most.

To investigate those two issues, we first construct a measure of the expected gains from international diversification, then focus on its trend and cycle components. In particular, since the process of liberalization has taken place over several years, its effects on asset prices are better identified with the trend in the data. On the other hand, the behavior of international returns during U.S. bear and bull markets is mostly a short-term phenomenon and, therefore, should be reflected by the high frequency component in the data.

In practice, although correlations are the typical measure that analysts refer to, the model that we estimate suggests that the expected benefits of international diversification are driven by the interaction between conditional second moments and the time-varying price of market risk. Consider a U.S. investor who wants to evaluate the potential benefits of adding foreign assets to a portfolio which is fully invested in domestic stocks. The model predicts that the expected excess return on the U.S. portfolio should be equal to $\delta_{t-1}\mathrm{cov}(R_{USt}, R_{mt}|\Im_{t-1})$. Obviously if the investor is not diversified, his risk exposure will be equal to the conditional volatility of the U.S. market. For the same level of volatility, the world portfolio of stocks, combined with the risk-free asset, has an expected excess return equal to $\delta_{t-1}\mathrm{var}(R_{USt}|\Im_{t-1})$. Therefore, the expected gains of international diversification, for a level of risk equal to the volatility of the U.S. market, can be measured as

$$E(R_{dt} - R_{USt}|\Im_{t-1}) = \delta_{t-1}[\mathrm{var}(R_{USt}|\Im_{t-1}) - \mathrm{cov}(R_{USt}, R_{mt}|\Im_{t-1})] \qquad (12)$$

where R_{dt} is the return on an internationally diversified portfolio which includes R_m and R_f and has the same volatility as the U.S. portfolio. The term in brackets in equation (12) can be interpreted as a measure of the (time-varying) nonsystematic risk of the U.S. market, for which investors are not compensated. We discuss the benefits of international diversification by considering the dynamics of both the conditional second moments and the price of world risk.

---

[27] This argument is often found in the business press. However, an economic model that clearly predicts this result is not yet available. For example, in personal conversations with us, Fischer Black argued that the opposite effect could be expected.

1906   *The Journal of Finance*

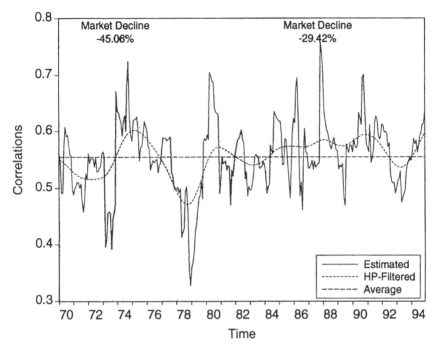

Figure 3. Portfolio correlation with the U.S. market. The figure contains plots of the correlation between the returns on the U.S. index and those of an equally-weighted portfolio which includes the remaining countries. The HP-filtered series and the average value of the correlation are also included. The shaded regions indicate periods of decline in the U.S. market, as identified by Forbes magazine. The two most severe declines in the sample (1973:01–1974:09 and 1987:09–1987:11) are explicitly labeled.

A. The Effects of Liberalization

First, consider the effect of market liberalization on the correlation of returns. Figure 3 contains plots of the time-varying correlations between the U.S. market and an equally weighted portfolio of the foreign assets. The estimated series reveals some interesting regularities. The twenty lowest correlations, with values ranging from 0.33 to 0.46, are all concentrated in the first part of the sample, prior to 1980. On the other hand, sixteen of the twenty largest correlations, with values between 0.68 and 0.76, correspond to the last fourteen years in the data.[28] These results suggest that the tendency of international markets to react simultaneously to innovations has increased with liberalization.

However, concluding that the reduction of legal barriers to international investments has significantly increased correlations would be premature. In

---

[28] All four remaining large correlations are associated with the bear market of 1973–1974.

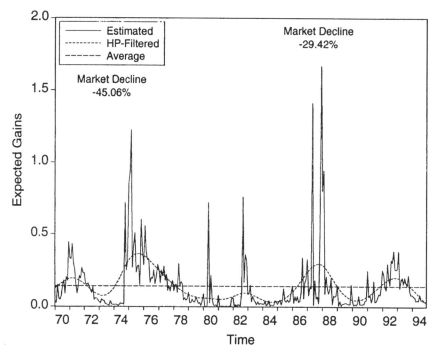

Figure 4. Expected gains from international diversification. The expected gains are measured as the increase in expected returns at the level of the U.S. market conditional volatility. The figure contains plots of the estimated gains, the HP-filtered series, and the average expected gains over the whole sample. The plotted series do not include the January component.

fact, the filtered series in the plot reveals that even recent values are well below the correlations that one would expect for U.S. portfolios. In this sense, the changes in correlations that we document can only be responsible for small changes in the expected gains from diversification.

Figure 4 contains plots of the expected gains from diversification, measured according to equation (12). Here, we focus on the low frequency component of the series to assess whether and how the expected benefits of diversification have been affected by market liberalization. Over the entire sample, the average premium for diversification is equal to 2.11 percent on an annual basis. The Newey-West consistent standard error for this estimate is equal to 0.284, which implies that the average expected gains are statistically significant. Our estimates indicate that the market risk premium for the U.S. index, including the January component, averages 7.45 percent per year. Therefore, for the same level of risk, the premium for an internationally diversified portfolio would be 28 percent higher. Interestingly, prior to 1980, the average gain is equal to 2.51 percent, whereas it is only equal to 1.84 percent for the last fourteen years. However the difference between the two means is not statistically significant. The plot of the filtered series reveals that for most of the Eighties the expected gains were lower than the average for the entire sample. In the early Nineties, however, the data again show relatively large expected benefits. Overall, although liberalization may have reduced the potential gains of diversifying internationally, the trend is rather weak, and the benefits remain economically significant.

B. U.S. Bear Markets and Portfolio Diversification

Next, we discuss whether bear markets are contagious across countries and how this may affect portfolio decisions. In Figures 3 and 4, we identify seven bear markets and seven bull markets for the United States, as defined by Forbes magazine.[29] The different periods are identified using the S&P 500 index as a benchmark. Some of the evidence seems to validate the claim that bear markets are contagious. In particular, we find that three of the largest correlations are associated with the most severe market declines in our sample. For example, between January 1973 and September 1974 the U.S. market dropped 45.06 percent. The estimated correlation at the end of that period is equal to 0.72, which is significantly larger than the sample average of 0.56. Similarly, after the 29.42 percent decline between September and November 1987, the correlation increases to 0.76. Finally, the model predicts another significant increase in correlation at the end of the market decline in the last part of 1990. In general, however, the plot shows that increases in international correlations are only obvious for large declines in the U.S. market and are often not very persistent.

When poor performance is spread across markets, investors have only limited opportunities to shield their portfolios. For example, our data show that the average benefits from international diversification are equal to only 0.08 percent per month during the seven bear markets in the sample, as opposed to 0.21 percent in the remaining periods. However, this result is not sufficient to discard the theory of international portfolio diversification. First, as long as diversification generates positive gains on average and investors are not able to predict bear and bull markets, it is still optimal to hold internationally diversified portfolios. Second, although the financial press often focuses on correlations, our measure in equation (12) suggests that a more appropriate assessment of the time-varying gains from diversification should be based on the dynamics of both nonsystematic risk and the price of market risk. For this reason, in Figure 5 we plot the difference between the conditional volatility of the U.S. market and the conditional covariance between the U.S. market and the World portfolio. It is interesting how, at the end of the 1974 and 1987 bear markets, the estimated difference increases rather dramatically. This implies that, after severe market declines, country specific volatility in the U.S. in-

---

[29] See recent issues of Forbes on mutual fund performance. The seven bear markets cover the following periods: January 1, 1970 to June 30, 1970; January 1, 1973 to September 30, 1974; January 1, 1977 to February 28, 1978; December 1, 1980 to July 31, 1982; July 1, 1983 to July 31, 1984; September 1, 1987 to November 30, 1987; June 1, 1990 to October 31, 1990.

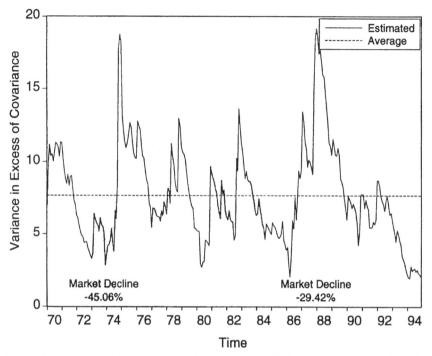

Figure 5. Variance risk in excess of world covariance risk for the U.S. stock market. The plot describes the dynamics of the estimated conditional volatility for the U.S. market, in excess of the conditional covariance between the U.S. market and the World portfolio. The shaded regions indicate periods of decline in the U.S. market, as identified by Forbes magazine. The two most severe declines in the sample (1973:01–1974:09 and 1987:09–1987:11) are explicitly labeled.

creases more than systematic risk. When combined with the estimated price of world risk plotted in Figure 1, this leads to the pattern in expected gains documented in Figure 4. Although the gains are often very low during declines of the U.S. market, they increase considerably when the market starts to recover. Given their inability to predict turns in market conditions, investors are better off holding internationally diversified portfolios even during periods of poor market performance.

V. Conclusions

In this article, we test the pricing restrictions of the conditional CAPM simultaneously for the world's eight largest equity markets. Since our approach fully specifies the dynamics of the conditional moments, we can also investigate how, from the perspective of a U.S. investor, the expected gains from international diversification respond to changing market conditions. In particular, we examine whether the expected benefits have been affected by the increasing integration of international financial markets and whether an internationally diversified portfolio provides a good hedge against large declines in the U.S. market.

Methodologically, we extend the multivariate GARCH process of Ding and Engle (1994) to accommodate GARCH-in-Mean effects and propose an alternative to the test of the CAPM of Bollerslev, Engle, and Wooldridge (1988). Our approach has several advantages. We can estimate the model and analyze international comovements for a large number of assets simultaneously without losing the flexibility of standard GARCH processes. The tests can be implemented on any subset of assets even when asset supplies are unobservable, as long as returns on a market-wide index are available. Finally, our specification can easily be extended to accommodate multiple risk factors.

The evidence supports most of the pricing restrictions of the conditional CAPM. Market risk, measured by the conditional covariance between the return on each asset and a world-index, is equally priced across countries. On the other hand, the price of country-specific risk, measured by the conditional variance of each country index, is not different from zero. Allowing for time-variation in the price of market risk significantly improves the performance of the model. However, when the price of market risk is restricted to be positive, as the theory implies, some of the variation in residual returns remains predictable. Interestingly, the predictability disappears when we relax the nonnegativity restriction. This result may be driven by the inability of the CAPM to accommodate negative risk premia during periods of high short-term interest rates. Even though the conditional version of the traditional CAPM provides useful information on the dynamics of market premia, a more adequate model of international asset pricing should probably include additional factors. Along these lines, recent work by Dumas and Solnik (1995) and De Santis and Gérard (1997) suggests that currency risk is priced in addition to market risk.

Our results have interesting implications for investors who want to diversify their portfolios internationally. We find that severe U.S. market declines are contagious at the international level, and often imply a significant reduction in the expected gains from international diversification. However, our estimates indicate that the ex ante gains for a U.S. investor average 2.11 percent a year and have not significantly declined over the last two and one-half decades. Hence, while holding an internationally diversified portfolio provides little protection against severe U.S. market declines, the long-term gains from international diversification remain economically attractive.

REFERENCES

Adler, Michael, and Bernard Dumas, 1983, International portfolio choice and corporation finance: A synthesis, *Journal of Finance* 38, 925–984.

Bansal, Ravi, David A. Hsieh, and S. Viswanathan, 1993, A new approach to international arbitrage pricing, *Journal of Finance* 48, 1719–1747.

Bekaert, Geert, and Robert Hodrick, 1992, Characterizing predictable components in excess returns on equity and foreign exchange markets, *Journal of Finance* 47, 467–510.

International Asset Pricing and Portfolio Diversification   1911

Bekaert, Geert, and Campbell R. Harvey, 1995, Time-varying world market integration, *Journal of Finance* 50, 403–444.

Bera, Anil K., and Carlos M. Jarque, 1982, Model specification tests: A simultaneous approach, *Journal of Econometrics* 20, 59–82.

Berndt, E. K., B. H. Hall, Robert E. Hall, and Jerry A. Hausman, 1974, Estimation and inference in nonlinear structural models, *Annals of Economic and Social Measurement* 3, 653–665.

Bollerslev, Tim, 1986, Generalized autoregressive conditional heteroskedasticity, *Journal of Econometrics* 31, 307–328.

Bollerslev, Tim, 1990, Modelling the coherence in short-run nominal exchange rates: A multivariate generalized ARCH model, *Review of Economics and Statistics* 72, 498–505.

Bollerslev, Tim, and Jeffrey M. Wooldridge, 1992, Quasi-maximum likelihood estimation and inference in dynamic models with time-varying covariances, *Econometric Reviews* 11, 143–172.

Bollerslev, Tim, Robert F. Engle, and Jeffrey M. Wooldridge, 1988, A capital asset pricing model with time-varying covariances, *Journal of Political Economy* 96, 116–131.

Boudoukh, Jacob, Matthew Richardson, and Tom Smith, 1993, Is the ex ante risk premium always positive? A new approach to testing conditional asset pricing models, *Journal of Financial Economics* 34, 387–408.

Chan, K. C., G. Andrew Karolyi, and René M. Stulz, 1992, Global financial markets and the risk premium on U.S. equity, *Journal of Financial Economics* 32, 137–168.

Daniel, Kent, and Sheridan Titman, 1997, Evidence on the characteristics of cross sectional variation in stock returns, *Journal of Finance* 52, 1–34.

De Santis, Giorgio, 1993, Globalization of equity markets: A test using time-varying conditional moments, Working paper, University of Southern California.

De Santis, Giorgio, and Bruno Gérard, 1997, How big is the premium for currency risk?, *Journal of Financial Economics*, forthcoming.

Ding, Zhuanxin, and Robert F. Engle, 1994, Large scale conditional covariance matrix modeling, estimation and testing, Working paper, University of California at San Diego.

Dumas, Bernard, and Bruno Solnik, 1995, The world price of foreign exchange risk, *Journal of Finance* 50, 445–479.

Elton, Edwin J., and Martin J. Gruber, 1992, International diversification, in Sumner N. Levine, Ed.: *Global Investing* (Harper Business, New York, NY).

Engel, Charles, Jeffrey A. Frankel, Kenneth A. Froot, and Anthony P. Rodrigues, 1995, Tests of conditional mean-variance efficiency of the U.S. stock market, *Journal of Empirical Finance* 2, 3–18.

Engle, Robert F., and Kenneth F. Kroner, 1995, Multivariate simultaneous generalized ARCH, *Econometric Theory* 11, 122–150.

Engle, Robert F., and Victor K. Ng, 1993, Measuring and testing the impact of news on volatility, *Journal of Finance* 48, 1749–1778.

Engle, Robert F., Victor K. Ng, and Michael Rothschild, 1990, Asset pricing with a factor ARCH covariance structure: Empirical estimates for Treasury bills, *Journal of Econometrics* 45, 213–238.

Ferson, Wayne E., 1989, Changes in expected security returns, risk and the level of interest rates, *Journal of Finance* 44, 1191–1218.

Ferson, Wayne E., 1995, Theory and testing of asset pricing models, in R. A. Jarrow, V. Maksimovic, and W. T. Ziemba, Eds.: *Finance*, Handbooks in Operations Research and Management Science, Vol. 9 (North Holland, Amsterdam).

Ferson, Wayne E., and Campbell R. Harvey, 1993, The risk and predictability of international equity returns, *Review of Financial Studies* 6, 527–566.

Ferson, Wayne E., Stephen R. Foerster, and Donald B. Keim, 1993, General tests of latent variable models and mean-variance spanning, *Journal of Finance* 48, 131–156.

Giovannini, Alberto, and Philippe Jorion, 1989, The time variation of risk and return in the foreign exchange and stock markets, *Journal of Finance* 44, 307–325.

Gultekin, Mustafa, and N. Bulent Gultekin, 1983, Stock market seasonality: International evidence, *Journal of Financial Economics* 12, 469–481.

The Journal of Finance

Hamao, Yasushi, Ronald W. Masulis, and Victor Ng, 1990, Correlations in price changes and volatility across international stock markets, *Review of Financial Studies* 3, 281–308.

Hansen, Lars Peter, 1982, Large sample properties of generalized methods of moments estimators, *Econometrica* 50, 1029–1054.

Harvey, Campbell R., 1991, The world price of covariance risk, *Journal of Finance* 46, 111–158.

Hodrick, Robert J., and Edward Prescott, 1996, Post-war business cycles: A descriptive empirical investigation, in Mark Watson, Ed.: Federal Reserve Bank of Chicago.

Karolyi, G. Andrew, and René M. Stulz, 1996, Why do markets move together? An investigation of U.S.–Japan stock return comovements, *Journal of Finance* 51, 951–986.

King, Mervyn, Enrique Sentana, and Sushil Wadhwani, 1994, Volatility and links between national stock markets, *Econometrica* 62, 901–933.

Lin, Weng-Ling, Robert F. Engle, and Takatoshi Ito, 1994, Do bulls and bears move across borders? International transmission of stock returns and volatility, *Review of Financial Studies* 7, 507–538.

Lintner, John, 1965, The valuation of risk assets and the selection of risky investments in stock portfolios and capital budgets, *Review of Economics and Statistics* 47, 13–37.

Longin, Francois, and Bruno Solnik, 1995, Is the correlation in international equity returns constant: 1970–1990?, *Journal of International Money and Finance* 14, 3–26.

Markowitz, Harry, 1952, Portfolio selection, *Journal of Finance* 7, 77–91.

Merton, Robert C., 1973, An intertemporal capital asset pricing model, *Econometrica* 41, 867–888.

Merton, Robert C., 1980, On estimating the expected return on the market: An explanatory investigation, *Journal of Financial Economics* 8, 323–361.

Ng, Lilian, 1991, Tests of the CAPM with time-varying covariances: A multivariate GARCH approach, *Journal of Finance* 46, 1507–1521.

Odier, Patrick, and Bruno Solnik, 1993, Lessons for international asset allocation, *Financial Analyst Journal* 49, 63–77.

Sercu, Piet, 1980, A generalization of the international asset pricing model, *Revue de l'Association Française de Finance* 1, 91–135.

Sharpe, William, 1964, Capital asset prices: A theory of market equilibrium under conditions of risk, *Journal of Finance* 19, 425–442.

Solnik, Bruno, 1974, An equilibrium model of the international capital market, *Journal of Economic Theory* 8, 500–524.

Stulz, René M., 1981, A model of international asset pricing, *Journal of Financial Economics* 9, 383–406.

Stulz, René M., 1995, International portfolio choice and asset pricing: An integrative survey, in V. Maksimovic and W. Ziemba, Eds.: *The Handbook of Modern Finance* (North Holland, Amsterdam).

Name Index

The International Library of Critical Writings in Financial Economics

A History of
NEW ZEALAND

John Lockyer
in association with the Alexander Turnbull Library

REED

CONTENTS

9

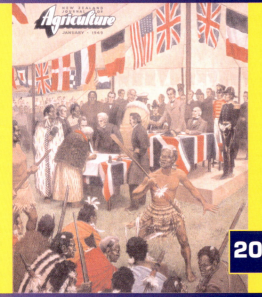

20

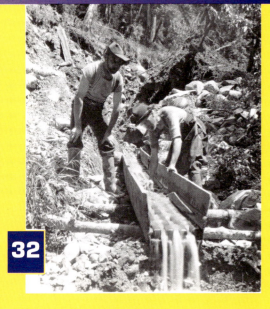

32

46

55

71

79

CHAPTER 1

A land apart

The earth's crust is made up of enormous pieces of rock called plates. Strong forces inside the earth shift, twist, crack and crumble these plates. New Zealand is on the edge of the Pacific Plate.

Two islands

By five million years ago, both the North Island and the South Island could be seen above water. The Indo-Australian and Pacific plates moving against each other formed the volcanoes Ruapehu, Tongariro and Ngauruhoe.

The Southern Alps

These mountains were formed where the Indo-Australian and Pacific plates overlap. The thick crusts of the two plates pushed upwards, forming the mountain ranges that run down through the middle of the South Island.

Volcanoes

New Zealand has lots of volcanic activity because it is on the edge of two plates. The Taupo eruptions 30,000 and 1800 years ago were among the biggest in the world. The last Taupo eruption caused changes to the climate of countries as far away as China.

Glaciers

New Zealand landscapes have been shaped by a cool climate. The South Island's fiords, steep valleys, small rounded hills and wide shallow rivers have been formed by glaciers. Twelve thousand years ago almost all of the South Island high country was covered in glaciers.

Moa.

Te Matua Ngahere Kauri, Waipoua Forest.

Warmer temperatures have reduced this to only a few glaciers today.

Gondwanaland

New Zealand was once part of a huge continent. The continent was called Gondwanaland and it was near the South Pole.

About 200 million years ago, Gondwanaland split into South America, Africa, India, Australia, Antarctica and New Zealand. Over time these new lands slowly drifted apart. This is called 'continental drift'.

Ancient animals and trees

As the continents drifted, birds and windblown seeds could still cross the narrow seas but slowly the area of water between the countries became too great.

The Tasman Sea reached its full width 60 million years ago. This wide area of water protected many New Zealand species from diseases and enemies.

The tuatara, weta and native frog have survived from ancient times and the kauri, kahikatea and rimu trees developed from the Gondwanaland forests. Most of the plants in early New Zealand were not found growing anywhere else.

Mammals and birds

Bats were the first land mammals in New Zealand. Like birds, they probably flew there or were blown in by storms.

The trees were full of fantails, tui and stitchbirds, and moa, takahe and kiwi found their food on the forest floor. With no mammals or other enemies, birds thrived in early New Zealand.

Tuatara.

DID YOU KNOW?

New Zealand is 1600 kilometres from Australia and 2300 kilometres from Antarctica.

The Pacific Plate is sliding past North America by 6 centimetres a year.

Many earthquakes and volcanoes occur in countries on the edge of plates.

Tane Mahuta, New Zealand's largest tree, is one of the oldest living things on earth. It is around 2000 years old.

Haast's eagle was the world's largest and strongest eagle. It lived in the South Island forests. It had a wingspan of three metres and could fly as fast as 80 kilometres per hour. Perching on high branches, it dived on its prey, feeding on moa, takahe, pigeons and other large birds. Haast's eagle is now extinct.

New Zealand's oldest known rocks are about 680 million years old.

Thirty million years ago most of present-day New Zealand was under water.

Warmer world temperatures caused sea levels to rise. By 12,000 years ago water separated the North Island and the South Island.

The last major eruption in the Auckland area was Rangitoto, 600 years ago. The Tarawera eruption in 1886 lasted just five hours.

CHAPTER 2

The Maori

Because New Zealand is a long way from anywhere, it was one of the last countries in the world to be settled.

Polynesians were the first people to live in New Zealand. They came by canoe from East Polynesia over a thousand years ago. The ocean-going canoes used by early Maori were 15–25 metres long with a single hull and outrigger or double hulls. They were made of planks lashed together and had woven sails.

A new land

Trained navigators steered a course by the stars at night and the direction of the sea swells by day. They searched for signs such as birds feeding at sea that told them land was near.

Although many canoes set out from East Polynesia, it is possible only one managed to cross the empty, stormy seas to reach Aotearoa.

When the Europeans arrived a thousand years later, the Maori population was about 100,000. This number could easily have come from one canoe-load.

The arrival of the canoes

Legends say that Maori came to New Zealand in a fleet of canoes. Each area in New Zealand was settled by people from different canoes, but usually only one canoe was remembered as belonging to that place.

However, while it is true that the Maori arrived by canoe, the idea of a 'fleet' is a legend only.

Canoe names:
Kurahaupo, Mamari — Northland and Auckland
Tainui — Waikato
Te Arawa — Rotorua
Mataatua — Bay of Plenty
Takitimu, Horouta — North Island East Cape and east coast
Aotea, Tokomaru — North Island west coast
Te Waka-o-Aoraki — South Island

Food and animals

The Maori brought the rat, dog, kumara, taro, gourd and yam with them. Once on land, they found plenty of food.

They hunted for birds, fish and seals. Giant flightless moa, heavier than 200 kilograms, were easy prey.

Size

The Maori were bigger than the Europeans of that time. Two hundred years ago, the average height of European men was 160 centimetres while the average height of Maori men was 175 centimetres.

Life

The people worked hard. They cleared and cultivated the land with primitive tools. They carved, carried, paddled and sailed canoes.

They had few medicines but they also had few diseases. Like most ancient people they lived only about thirty years. Very few lived into their forties or later.

Maui

There are many legends about the mythical, magical Maui. Many stories say he was a mischievous boy who liked to play tricks on others. Once he turned himself into a pigeon and threw berries at his parents.

He and his brothers also snared Ra, the sun, who they beat until he promised to move more slowly across the sky.

Te Ika-a-Maui

This legend tells how Maui went fishing with his brothers into unknown waters.

Using his grandmother's jawbone for a hook and blood from his own nose for bait, Maui fished up the North Island of New Zealand. This is called Te Ika-a-Maui (The Fish of Maui). The South Island was his canoe and Stewart Island its anchor stone.

Changes

New Zealand was much colder than Polynesia and so the Maori had to make many changes to how they lived.

They made warmer clothing and houses, and kumara had to be lifted and stored in earth pits over the winter.

They made tapa cloth from the paper mulberry plant and plaited cloth from flax to make rain capes and skirts.

Villages

The houses were small and sometimes smoky from fires. They were grouped in villages and often close to a pa.

Food was stored at the pa so if the village was attacked the people knew they would be safe on the fortified hilltop.

THE MAORI

DID YOU KNOW?

Aotearoa probably means Land of the Long Daylight because the Polynesians would have found the long twilight in New Zealand unusual. Places close to the equator have no twilight.

Computers have predicted that the voyage from East Polynesia to New Zealand took about a month.

The Polynesians came from a place they called Hawaiki, in eastern Polynesia. This place could have been the Cook Islands, Tahiti or the Marquesas Islands. No one knows for sure.

Legends say Kupe discovered Te Ika-a-Maui. He arrived in Aotearoa chasing a giant octopus.

Early Maori believed sickness was caused by makutu (witchcraft) or from doing tapu (forbidden) things

Maori were great seafarers and river travellers.

Drowning was always a risk, and was probably the cause of most accidental deaths for Maori.

A painting showing Maori life before the arrival of the European.

Warfare

Warfare was a major part of early Maori life and tribes often fought each other. Danger was a daily hazard.

They often fought for utu (revenge) or payment.

Sometimes the Maori were cannibals.

Communication

But life was not always violent. Many tribes were friendly and entertained and traded gifts with each other. Muttonbirds, greenstone (pounamu) and obsidian were highly prized. The greenstone and obsidian were used to make ornaments, knives and other sharp tools.

The tribe

Maori families (whanau) lived closely together. The extended family (hapu) — cousins and other relations — lived nearby too. People who belonged to the same village or villages were called iwi.

The Maori did not think of themselves as one people. They belonged to their tribes.

Chiefs

The tribes were ruled by chiefs (rangatira). Most chiefs were men and some were very well known.

Te Rauparaha was a great warrior.

Te Wherowhero, a Waikato chief, was the first Maori king. He called himself Potatau.

Topeora was a famous woman chief. She was a poet

and a sister of Te Rauparaha and was one of the few women who signed the Treaty of Waitangi.

A chief has importance and power (mana) and he or she was sacred (tapu).

Tapu

Tapu is central to Maori life. The kumara gardens were tapu. The birth of a child was tapu too. Anyone who didn't respect tapu would be punished by the gods.

The Maori believed in many gods — Tane, the god of the forests; Tangaroa, the god of the sea; Tu-Matauenga, the god of war.

Not all Maori gods were friendly.

Children

Maori children worked hard gathering seafood, snaring birds and helping in the gardens. They often had lessons about their ancestors from their elders (kaumatua).

When they weren't working, the children played with darts, knucklebones, stilts, spinning tops, puppets and kites.

The older boys liked stick games and wrestling while the girls wove cloaks and preserved food.

DID YOU KNOW?

On Coromandel Peninsula there is a beach called Kikowhakarere. This means 'the flesh thrown away or left behind'. It is said that the beach is named to remember a cannibal feast that was suddenly interrupted by an enemy attack.

Most Maori knowledge was passed on by speech.

Knowledge of the ancestors (whaka-papa) was learned by heart.

Te Wherowhero.

Display of Maori weaponry.

CHAPTER 3

Early explorers

In 1642 a Dutchman, Abel Tasman, set out from a Dutch trading post in Java, Indonesia hoping to find another large continent east of Australia.

He had two ships — the *Heemskerck*, which was armed for fighting, and the *Zeehaen*, which carried goods to trade.

The *Heemskerck* was a sailing warship. It carried long-range cannons that were usually made of bronze, and iron short-range guns.

The *Zeehaen* carried the following goods for trade:
10 Golconda blankets
500 Chinese small mirrors
90 kilograms of ironmongery
quantities of cloves, mace,
 nutmegs and pewter
50 Chinese gold wire
10 packets Chinese gold wire
25 pieces of assorted iron pots
3 pearls and a large brass basin

Land ahoy

Five months after leaving Java, Tasman sighted the west coast of the South Island.

He sailed north and anchored in Tasman Bay at the top of the South Island. Warriors from Ngati Tumata Kokiri tribe attacked his landing boat. The boat was rammed by canoes and the warriors struck the Dutchmen with short, thick pieces of wood (mere). Three sailors were killed and one died later of his wounds. Tasman quickly weighed anchor and sailed off.

He named the bay Murderers' Bay.

Another landing

Tasman continued to sail up the west coast of the North Island. He named the northern cape after the wife of his Governor-General, Maria van Diemen.

Tasman hoped not all the 'natives' were unfriendly but when he tried to land on

Abel Tasman.

Three Kings Islands he was driven away by Maori again.

Novo Zeelandia

Tasman called the land he'd found Staten Landt. But after a few years it became known in Europe as Novo Zeelandia

CAPTAIN COOK.

(New Zeeland). Zeeland is a coastal area in the Netherlands.

James Cook

James Cook was born on 28 October 1728 in England. When he was 19 he worked as a seaman on a coal freighter. When he was 27 he joined the Royal Navy.

He was an excellent navigator and chart-maker.

New land

Captain Cook was sent to the South Pacific to learn more about the land discovered by Abel Tasman. He wanted to know if it was the great southern continent that people talked about.

Captain James Cook.

DID YOU KNOW?

Murderers' Bay is now called Golden Bay.

Before sailing to New Zealand Captain Cook was in Tahiti on a scientific exploration. He was observing Venus moving across the face of the sun. This information would help scientists work out how far the earth was from the sun.

French explorer Jean-Francois Marie de Surville also sailed to New Zealand in 1769. Many of his men were ill with scurvy. He anchored in Doubtless Bay in the Bay of Islands. This ship was attacked by local Maori so de Surville took to sea again, leaving New Zealand.

French explorer Marion du Fresne and fifteen of his crew were killed and eaten by Maori in the Bay of Islands in 1772.

The rest of his crew took revenge, burning villages and killing nearly 300 Maori.

A few Polynesians returned to Europe with the explorers. Omai, a Tahitian, was introduced to many important Europeans. He was admired and was given lots of presents to take home.

Captain James Cook.
1768 – 1771.
Scale, 1 inch = 12 feet.

HMS Endeavour.

Plate XXIV.

S. Parkinson del.   J. Newton sculp.

View of an Arched Rock, on the Coast of New Zealand; with an Hippa, or Place of Retreat, on the Top of it.

View of an arched rock on the coast of New Zealand, by Sydney Parkinson.

Young Nick

At 2 p.m. on 6 October 1769, Nicholas Young, a boy on the masthead of Cook's ship *Endeavour*, shouted, 'Land!' He was the first European to see the North Island's east coast. The land he sighted was named after him — Young Nick's Head. A bottle of rum was his reward for seeing it first.

Landing trouble

Cook anchored the *Endeavour* in a bay near the site of modern Gisborne. When he tried to meet with local Maori, his men were attacked. In the fight, many Maori were killed.

Cook left and named the area Poverty Bay.

More trouble

Further down the coast, Cook met more Maori. When he tried to barter some cloth for dried fish, they grabbed a boy off the ship and dragged him into a canoe. Cook's men fired on the canoe and the boy escaped over the side and swam back to the *Endeavour*.

Cook named the area Cape Kidnappers.

Friends at last

Cook did make friends with many tribes along the east coast.

He spent eleven days at Mercury Bay, off Whitianga.

Years later, a famous chief, Te Horeta Taniwha, said when he had been a boy his people had called the Europeans goblins with eyes in the backs of their heads when they saw them rowing ashore.

Captain Cook gave Te Horeta a nail as a present. It was the first time Maori in this area had seen metal.

Te Horeta treasured the nail, fitting it to his spear tip and also using it to make holes in the side-boards of canoes.

Guns

Cook's men had guns. The Maori called the guns walking-sticks.

When the Europeans pointed them at the trees, thunder and lightning was heard and birds fell to the ground. The Maori children were terrified and fled into the bush.

Around New Zealand

Captain Cook sailed round North Cape, then down the west coast of the North Island and anchored in Queen Charlotte Sound. He spent three weeks there collecting fresh food and repairing the ship.

Afterwards he sailed through Cook Strait and up to Cape Turnagain. Then he turned southwards to circumnavigate the South Island.

He made good maps of the main islands and kept full records of his meetings with the Maori tribes.

Banks and Parkinson

Not everyone on the *Endeavour* was a sailor.

Joseph Banks was a botanist who was on the voyage to collect and catalogue any new plants, birds and insects they found.

Artist Sydney Parkinson sketched scenes from the new land.

Return trips

James Cook returned to New Zealand in 1773 and 1777.

On all his trips he introduced new crops and animals like potatoes and pigs.

He also found and fixed many mistakes on the maps that he'd made on earlier voyages.

Blunders

The Europeans and Maori were keen to trade but because they didn't understand each other, there were lots of misunderstandings and fights.

Both sides were bloodthirsty.

News of New Zealand

James Cook's journals were read throughout Europe. He described the land as full of promise — a place where new settlers could build a comfortable life. He said the Maori people were strong, active, brave, artistic and war-like. New Zealand was suddenly big news in Europe.

A botanical plate of a kowhai plant, drawn by Sydney Parkinson.

CHAPTER 4

Early settlers

After 1790, men from Sydney, Hobart, North America and Britain landed on the southern coast of the South Island to collect sealskins.

The hunters stayed for months and collected as many as 14,000 skins in a season.

These skins were sold to China, America and England to be made into hats.

By 1810 fashions had changed and seal numbers had dwindled, so the sealers stopped coming.

Deep-sea whalers

Whalers stopped by New Zealand too. They were after cachalot (sperm whales).

They visited New Zealand for fresh food, water and replacement crews.

Many Maori travelled the world working on the whaling ships.

Bay whaling

After 1820, more whalers worked from the shore.

The whalers went to sea in small, strong boats. They were after the black or right whale.

They set up stations mainly in the South Island. These stations were small villages and some villages had more than a hundred families.

Killing season

From May to October, female whales came inshore to give birth to calves. The whalers killed the calves and then the mothers after they refused to leave their dead babies.

The rest of the year, most of the whalers ran small farms.

Eventually too many whales were killed and they disappeared from the coast.

In the 1850s people started using vegetable oil more than whale oil, forcing the whaling stations to shut down.

Flax workers with bales of flax.

Flax

From 1815, ships came often to New Zealand to collect a cargo of flax.

New Zealand flax was good quality and fetched high prices. It was used to make ropes and cords.

The fibre was prepared by Maori women, who scraped away the fleshy part with a sharp mussel shell. This process took a long time and it was hard to keep up with orders. The business died out after 1831, when traders found superior flax in the Philippines.

Timber

The British navy wanted long, straight kauri and kahikatea timber for hulls, masts and booms on their sailing ships.

Sawmills were built at Thames and the Hokianga harbour. These places were close to the sea and

View of a building where logs were cut.

The oil from cachalot (sperm whales) was used in Europe for lighting. Ambergris, a waxy material from the intestines of sperm whales, was used for perfumes.

Whales were hunted for their bones too. Whalebone was used for women's corsets and umbrella ribs.

Many traders exchanged guns for flax collected by Maori. One ton of fibre was worth two muskets.

Pakeha-Maori were European traders who had married Maori women and settled with the tribe.

In 1806 James Caddell came to New Zealand with some sealers. He was thirteen years old. His party was attacked by Maori and all were killed (and later eaten) except for James. He got away and ran up to a chief called Tako and grabbed his cloak. The chief was tapu at the time, which meant no one could touch James without risking punishment.

James was allowed to live. He grew up with the tribe and married Tako's daughter.

He later became a chief himself and tattooed his face.

The only equipment needed in a whaling station apart from a boat were tray pots in which to boil the blubber, windlasses, knives and barrels.

rivers so that when the trees were felled they were floated down the rivers to the sawmills.

At the sawmills, the timber was cut and loaded on to ships for export.

Bartering

All the traders needed food and water.

Maori bartered with the strangers they called Pakeha. Potatoes and pigs were popular items of trade.

The traders also wanted mats, carvings and especially shrunken human heads.

In return, Maori wanted nails, axes, muskets and blankets.

Muskets

Maori warriors wanted guns because a tribe with muskets had a great advantage.

Hongi Hika, a Ngapuhi chief, was one of the first warriors to fight with guns.

The other tribes soon realised they would not survive without muskets.

Twenty-five bags of potatoes bought one musket.

Hongi Hika

In 1820, Hongi Hika went to England with the missionary Thomas Kendall. There he helped scholars compile a Maori dictionary.

The English people admired Hongi Hika and gave him many gifts. King George IV presented him with a suit of chain mail.

Before he returned to New Zealand, Hongi Hika sold all his gifts except for the suit of mail and bought 300 muskets.

Back home, he attacked and slaughtered his old enemies in the Thames–Waikato area.

European settlements

One of the first Pakeha towns was Kororareka (now Russell) in the Bay of Islands.

Kororareka ('sweet penguin') was a supply post for traders. As many as 30 ships anchored at any one time in the bay to trade. Maori farmers supplied the traders with water, pigs, potatoes, barley, maize, oats and wheat.

The Hokianga was the second largest Pakeha settlement. Ships sailed up the harbour to Horeke, where there was a shipyard and sawmill.

The Reverend Samuel Marsden.

The missionaries

In 1814 Samuel Marsden, a schoolmaster, carpenter and ropemaker, arrived to set up the first mission in the Bay of Islands.

The Anglican Church wanted to teach Christianity to the Maori people but few were interested. The Roman Catholic Bishop Pompallier and other missionaries experienced the same problems.

Russell today.

The power of God's Word, artist unknown (1956).

The Bible

After 1825, when the mission moved to Kerikeri then Waimate, and other missionaries like Henry Williams and William Colenso arrived, some Maori started to listen.

The missionaries had real success when the Bible and prayer books were translated into Maori.

Maori were keen to read and write their own language.

Changes

Many Maori turned to Christianity when they found their own gods couldn't protect them from the terrible Pakeha diseases that had arrived with the early Europeans.

They were expected to make changes in their way of life. The missionaries made Sunday a day of rest. They also tried to stop cannibalism and the chiefs from having more than one wife.

More changes

Guns meant that many more Maori were killed in tribal wars but sickness was the biggest killer. Maori had no protection from colds, influenza and measles. These European diseases wiped out thousands.

Europeans also brought iron and metals, which Maori hadn't seen before, as well as, books, clocks, compasses and money.

The Europeans had changed Maori life for ever.

CHAPTER 5

The British and the Treaty

ON THIS SPOT ON THE SIXTH DAY OF FEBRUARY 1840 WAS SIGNED THE TREATY OF WAITANGI UNDER WHICH NEW ZEALAND BECAME PART OF THE BRITISH EMPIRE

Mild weather, good farming and friendly Maori brought many new settlers. Most came from New South Wales where land prices were high and wool prices were low.

James Busby

In 1833 James Busby was appointed British Resident for New Zealand. The resident's job was like an ambassador's. He sent reports to England about happenings in New Zealand.

At Waitangi, he and some Maori chiefs chose the first national flag. It had a red St George's Cross on a white background and four eight-pointed stars.

Busby had no soldiers so he couldn't keep order. Even when his own house was raided, he could do nothing.

His only help came from the British navy when one of its ships visited New Zealand.

The French

The French navy also visited often. They called on Bishop Pompallier, the French leader of the Catholic mission.

Busby thought the French were becoming too interested in New Zealand.

Then in 1837 Frenchman Baron Charles de Thierry announced himself as the sovereign chief of New Zealand.

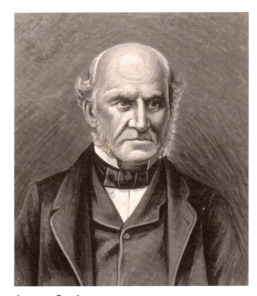

James Busby.

He said he had bought 40,000 acres (16,187 hectares) of land in Hokianga.

Independence

Even though the French government didn't support de Thierry, Busby quickly gathered 34 northern chiefs at Waitangi. Together they announced New Zealand to be independent. They also asked the British government for protection.

Edward Wakefield.

Edward Gibbon Wakefield

Wakefield wanted to make money by settling people in New Zealand. He hoped to buy Maori land cheaply and then sell it at a higher price to the wealthy. The profits would pay for the fares of workers. In return for the fare, the workers would labour on the land for a few years.

As on English farms, the owners would be gentlemen while the workers did the hard labour.

Edward Wakefield came up with his scheme to colonise New Zealand while he was in prison. He spent three years in Newgate jail for running away with and marrying Ellen Turner, a wealthy manufacturer's school-aged daughter.

The New Zealand Company

In 1838 Wakefield formed the New Zealand Company. The company offered land for sale in New Zealand even before Wakefield had bought it.

After hearing rumours that the British were about to make New Zealand part of the empire, Wakefield quickly sent the ship *Tory* to New Zealand with surveyors and land buyers.

Arthur Wakefield, Edward Wakefield's brother, was captain of the *Tory*.

William Hobson

Meanwhile the British government sent William Hobson, a naval captain, to New Zealand with instructions to persuade the Maori chiefs to accept Queen Victoria's rule and be governed by Britain.

Hobson arrived in the Bay of Islands on 29 January 1840.

The Treaty of Waitangi

Hobson met with Maori chiefs at Waitangi on 5 February 1840. He showed them a

William Hobson.

document he and his staff had made up. The document was called the Treaty of Waitangi.

The chiefs were asked to give up to the Queen the right to buy their land. In return, Maori would keep possession of their land and property and they would get full rights and privileges as British subjects.

The gathering

Ships anchored in the bay and boats with settlers and residents landed on the shore. On the lawn was a large tent decorated with the flags of their nations.

The Maori chiefs looked splendid in black and white striped dogskin mats and new woollen cloaks of crimson, blue, brown and plaid.

Here and there, taiaha (long clubs), decorated with white dog hair and crimson and red

NEW ZEALAND JOURNAL OF **Agriculture**

JANUARY · 1949

The signing of the Treaty.

James Busby called out their names one by one. Hone Heke was the first Maori to sign.

The chiefs' version of the Treaty was in Maori. Henry Williams' translation used words that were invented to describe ideas not part of Maori culture.

Kawanatanga

In the Treaty, Williams used the word 'kawanatanga' to describe the idea of rule or sovereignty, but kawanatanga means governorship only. A better word would have been 'mana' (power).

Had the chiefs understood what they were giving away, they might not have signed.

It has been said that Williams didn't want to translate too many land details in the Treaty because he wanted

Henry Williams.

feathers, had been thrust into the ground.

A day of speeches

Henry Williams translated the Treaty for the chiefs. Some of the chiefs were against the Treaty. They didn't trust this new government. They thought Maori would become slaves. They wanted to go back to the time before blankets, bread, muskets and disease.

Other chiefs disagreed. They said the white man was here to stay, so they needed to protect their customs and land.

Signing the Treaty

The next day the chiefs signed the Treaty, even those who were against it.

to protect the 11,000 acres (4452 hectares) he had bought.

Confusion

The Maori at Waitangi signed the Maori version. Later, some Waikato chiefs signed the English version.

The two documents are different. One clause in the English version promises Maori 'full exclusive and undisturbed possession of their lands and estates, forests and fisheries'. The Maori version promises the tribes 'the entire chieftainship of their lands, their villages and all their property'.

Many Maori also believed they had not given the Queen the sole right to buy their land.

The proclamation

While the Treaty was taken round the country to collect chiefs' signatures, the New Zealand Company settlers had formed a government at Port Nicholson (Wellington) and were making their own laws.

To stop this, Hobson issued a proclamation on 21 May 1840. New Zealand was now governed by Britain.

DID YOU KNOW?

In 1830 about 330 Europeans lived in New Zealand. By 1840 there were about 2000 Europeans.

Maori called James Busby 'Man-o-war without guns'.

At Waitangi, Bishop Pompallier had a massive gold chain and crucifix draped over a purple gown. The Maori said, 'Ko ia ano te tino rangatira!' ('He indeed is the chief gentleman!')

Tareha, a chief of Ngati Rehia (Ngapuhi), did not want the Treaty. He deliberately dressed in old floor-matting and carried a bunch of dried fern-root. He shouted angrily at Hobson, 'Go back, return; make haste away See this is my food, the food of my ancestors.' To think of tempting men — us Natives — with baits of clothing and food!'

Tamati Waka Nene, a Ngapuhi chief, liked the Treaty. He wanted the British to preserve Maori customs, to protect their land ownership and to save them from slavery. He shouted to Hobson, 'Stay thou, our friend, our father, our Governor!'

For the signing of the Treaty, Hobson had learnt a few Maori words: 'He iwi tahi tatou' ('We are one people')

CHAPTER 6

Early Governors and the Maori

Hone Heke's pa at Ohaeawai.

Governor Fitzroy William Hobson died in 1842. He was replaced by naval officer Robert FitzRoy.

Trouble was waiting for FitzRoy in New Zealand. The New Zealand Company had sold land to many new settlers in Wellington and Nelson but Maori said the land was still theirs.

Wairau

In 1843, settlers started surveying land at Wairau, Nelson, but the great chiefs Te Rauparaha and Te Rangihaeata said they wanted the sale investigated.

The surveyors carried on so the Maori burned their huts. The Company sent 35 armed men to arrest Te Rauparaha but he wouldn't surrender. A settler killed Te Rangihaeata's wife and the Maori then killed 22 Europeans.

Governor FitzRoy believed the settlers were wrong so he did nothing. But there were more problems at the Bay of Islands

Hone Heke

Hone Heke was the nephew of the great Hongi Hika. He no longer believed in the Treaty and said he had been tricked. He thought the Pakeha were after all the land.

A British flag flew at Waitangi. In protest, Heke and his followers cut down the flagstaff.

Three times the flagstaff was put back up and three times the Maori cut it down.

Hone Heke (centre) with his wife, Harriet (left), and uncle, Kawiti (right).

Kororareka

A soldier guarded the fourth flagstaff so Heke attacked the troops at Kororareka. Twelve Maori and fifteen soldiers and sailors were killed. The town was left a smoking ruin. FitzRoy sent for more British troops from Sydney.

Lake Omapere

Four hundred troops attacked Heke at his Lake Omapere pa.

Hone Heke had about 300 men and his ally, Kawiti, had another 150.

It was a Maori victory, although fourteen European and fourteen Maori were killed.

Ohaeawai

Even more troops arrived from Sydney and FitzRoy sent them all to Ohaeawai, where Heke and Kawiti had strengthened another pa. This pa was surrounded by three wooden walls and inside there were many pits and trenches.

Without cover, the British charged straight at Maori muskets. Over a hundred British

Tamati Waka Nene.

By 1846 he and the friendly Tamati Waka Nene of Ngapuhi had 1500 men between them. They attacked Kawiti's pa at Ruapekapeka ('bat's nest').

When Kawiti and Hone Heke escaped, Governor Grey decided to make peace with them after Hone Heke said he would stop fighting if Grey did not confiscate his land. Governor Grey agreed to this and gave him a pardon.

More trouble

Throughout the country more land disputes were happening.

In the Hutt Valley, near Wellington, Te Rangihaeata ordered warriors to attack an army stockade that was built on Maori land. Six soldiers were killed.

The capture of Te Rauparaha

Grey believed Te Rauparaha was organising many of the attacks on settlers in the Wellington area.

He sent most of his troops and ships south.

One day, he sailed past Te Rauparaha's pa (near modern Plimmerton). He hoped Te Rauparaha would think the ships were going to Wellington. Once he was out of sight, Grey turned back, waited until dawn then raided Te Rauparaha's pa and captured him.

were killed or wounded and only ten Maori.

The British were beaten again.

The sack

Governor FitzRoy had failed.

When he was ordered back to England many settlers were glad. They hated him for not punishing Te Rauparaha over the land dispute at Wairau.

Governor Grey

Captain George Grey, an army man, became New Zealand's most famous governor. Much later, he became a politician and premier (prime minister).

In 1845, when he was 33 years old, he was sent to New Zealand with many troops.

In jail

Grey locked Te Rauparaha in jail. He laid no charges and there was no trial.

With the famous chief out of the way and the capture of Te Rangihaeata's pa by troops and friendly Maori, the fighting stopped.

Grey and the Maori

Grey learned to speak Maori.

He got on well with the Maori chiefs and encouraged them to write down their stories and legends. Grey published these in Maori and English.

He gave money to mission schools where Maori children learned reading, writing and arithmetic. He also built four hospitals for Maori and lent money to tribes for farming equipment and coastal ships. The ships were used to transport their trading goods like flour.

He made sure the land deals were fair to all.

1854

By this time Grey had left New Zealand to become Governor of Cape Province in South Africa, but not before he helped write the 1852 Constitution.

DID YOU KNOW?

Eliza Grey
While her husband was enjoying the excitement of war, Eliza Grey was bored and unhappy. She wrote to a friend Maggie Watts: 'I really ought to be accustomed to live alone by this time. I am so constantly left now — and I am growing graver and gloomier than ever I fear. The country, place and (up to now) the people are very distasteful to me — there is scarcely a lady here — and were it not for the large military and naval force stationed here, there would be scarcely a gentleman.'

The 1852 Constitution set up a democratic system of government. Most white men could vote but no women. There were elected assemblies in each province and a General Assembly that first met in Auckland in 1854.

The military built blockades or forts like those built in the USA for defence against the Indians. But even these formidable buildings couldn't stop the attacking Maori.

The Constitution is the system of laws under which New Zealand exists.

Sir George Grey and Te Riwai Ropiha.

CHAPTER 7

A new life

Fagan, James. The emigrants' farewell.

The emigrants who came to New Zealand wanted a better life. Most hoped to buy their own land but they had to be skilled, trustworthy, healthy and to want to work hard.

They had to prove they were of good character. Many got letters from their church leaders to say this.

Shipboard life

The voyage to New Zealand often took longer than four months.

On board ship the passengers either had their own cabin (if they paid extra) or stayed in large dormitories in the hold.

Most of the new immigrants were in the hold. There were no portholes and it was

FREE AND ASSISTED EMIGRATION TO NEW ZEALAND.

FREE AND ASSISED PASSAGES
ARE granted by the GOVERNMENT of NEW ZEALAND as under:—
to Married Agricultural Labourers, Navvies, Ploughmen, Shepherds, and a few Country Mechanics, on their giving a Promissory Note for £10, payable in the Colony by instalments; or by paying £5 in cash.
FREE PASSAGES ARE GIVEN TO SINGLE FEMALE DOMESTIC SERVANTS.
Daughters and sons of twelve years of age and upwards, and going out with their Parents, are taken, the former FREE OF CHARGE, and the latter on payment of £4 in cash, or on giving a Promissory Note for £6.
SINGLE MEN are taken on payment (before Sailing) of the sum of £8; or on payment of £4 in cash, and giving a Promissory Note for £8.
For Terms and Conditions apply personally, or by letter, to the Agent General for New Zealand, 7, Westminster Chambers, London, S.W.
London, October 18th, 1873.
Galway—James J. Fynn, Victoria Place.

Montage of sketches showing life on board an emigrant ship.

too dark to read or work.

A family of six was squashed into a cubicle 1.8 metres by 2.4 metres.

Disease spread quickly in the cramped quarters.

Equipment

Emigrants were given a mattress, pillow and cooking pots.

They had to provide cutlery and drinking mugs.

They could keep a month's supply of clothing with them, while the rest of their gear was stowed deeper in the hold.

Settling in

In 1840 one thousand new settlers landed on Petone Beach, Wellington. All they could see was thick bush and swamps. Their gear was heaped in piles on the sand.

Until they could buy land, most settlers lived in tents or under tarpaulins.

The first houses were raupo (flax) huts measuring 3.6 metres by 4.2 metres, built of upright and cross poles and plastered with clay.

Riches

By 1846 there were 9000 new settlers scattered between Auckland, Wellington and then later Christchurch and Dunedin.

New Zealand was a rich land.

Fish, wild pigs and birds were easily hunted.

The raupo huts were replaced with wooden and stone houses.

By the 1860s grand houses were being built, especially in the South Island where farming was excellent.

Huts in the 1860s.

Group outside a timber camp hut.

Daily life

Shoes were expensive so children played barefoot.

Washing clothes was difficult but everyone dressed neatly.

On Sunday people wore their best clothes and went to church services.

Many children didn't go to school regularly. They worked on the farms.

Families were large but many children died young from diphtheria, whooping cough, typhoid fever and diarrhoea.

Women

Men found breaking in the land was too difficult without a wife to help.

Most women in early New Zealand were married. Nearly all of them worked in the home — cooking, washing and looking after the children. They earned cash from dairy goods like homemade butter.

They often schooled their children and with no hospitals they looked after the sick.

They also made sure the men didn't drink too much and minded their manners in company.

Sketch of a kitchen in an emigrant's hut.

DID YOU KNOW?

David Home was a new emigrant. His fare was paid by the Manukau and Waitemata Company in 1840.

In return, he had to work as a farm ploughman for twelve months for lodgings and five shillings (50 cents) a day.

Harriet Bracken, aged twelve, was paid two shillings (20 cents) a week for doing housework for a neighbour.

Out of this she paid for her own shoes and schooling.

In 1842, on one voyage to New Zealand, 65 children aboard the ship *Lloyds* died from diseases.

When settlers arrived in New Zealand they quickly learned how to make tea from the manuka tree (tea tree), how to shoot a fat wood pigeon, and how to smoke fish.

They also learned to beware of the poisonous tutu berries.

The Maori were keen to trade food for European clothes.

Working men wore coloured check shirts made of flannel or cotton. Women wore skirts that hid their ankles with lots of petticoats.

Two young men were about to take over a sheep station in Canterbury. Charlotte Godley, their mother, thought they would become semi-barbarous in the wilds without a woman's company, so she begged them to have a 'pretend figure of a lady carefully draped, set up in their usual sitting room and always behave before it as if it were their mother'.

Wool, timber and gold!

Sheep for transportation at Waipiro Bay beach.

In 1848, after the Free Church of Scotland settled immigrants in Otago and the Church of England did the same in Canterbury, there were suddenly more workers than work. A few adventurous people bought stock from Australia to farm.

Sheep farming

In Wellington, in 1844, Charles Clifford landed one of the first flocks of sheep. They were driven up to the Wairarapa Plains for grazing.

The rich grasslands gave good feed and farmers made lots of money selling wool.

Sheep farming quickly became popular, especially in the South Island.

Sheep country

The land grazed by sheep was not usable for much else.

For a small fee, farmers in the South Island could lease a 10,000-acre (4047-hectare) run from the government. The hardy Australian merino was the best sheep for these high country runs.

There were no fences on the runs. Shepherds lived in huts on the boundaries to watch for strays.

Sketches of a sheep station during the wool season.

Cutting down a kauri tree.

A large nugget of kauri gum.

Felling the forest

To earn a living, other settlers sold timber. They cleared the native forests for farming.

The North Island forests were rimu and kauri. The timber was used for houses, shops, halls and churches. Some kauri was exported to Britain for ship-building.

Gum was also collected from kauri trees and used to make paint, glue and varnish.

Gold

The Otago council offered a £500 ($1000) reward for the discovery of gold.

Australian Gabriel Read heard of a find in the Tuapeka area. He took a tent, a blanket, a spade, a tin dish, a butcher's knife and a week's food into a Tuapeka gully. After ten hours, using the knife and dish, he panned seven ounces (198 grams) of gold.

Gold fever

When they heard the news, other diggers with picks and shovels invaded what became known as Gabriel's Gully.

Within months, the number grew to 11,000. Almost all were men. They lived in tents.

In 1862 gold was discovered round the Clutha River.

Later finds were made on the Arrow River, Shotover River and at Naseby.

Miners' equipment

The miners carried their gear — clothes, pick, shovel and tin pan — in a 'swag' (rolled-up blanket). They wore nugget boots, moleskin trousers, flannel shirts and floppy hats.

They ate mutton and damper (a mixture of flour and water), and drank strong tea, boiled in a billy. They also hunted for birds and pigs.

On their way north, at Mukamukaiti, the drovers stood in the sea to pass Charles Clifford's flock of sheep from hand to hand round the rocks.

In 1843 there were only a few hundred sheep scattered round the missionary settlements. Ten years later there were over half a million sheep and after twenty years the number had grown to three million. Selling wool was big business.

In 1849 a ten-month-old lamb was worth three guineas ($6.30). A breeding ram was worth twenty guineas ($42).

The massive kauri and rimu trees were felled with saws and axes. The saws were up to 3.5 metres long.

Bushmen also used steel wedges, and a wooden hammer, to keep the cut open.

To stop their saws sticking with kauri gum, bushmen rubbed them with madoo.

Madoo is a mixture of kerosene and salt-free fat.

When gold fever hit New Zealand, prospectors came from Australia, sailors jumped ship and soldiers deserted the army.

Men at Burkett's claim, Collingwood.

Sluicing for gold.

Gold mining was hard, dangerous work. Blizzards, floods and landslides killed many miners.

Chinese miners

Between 1874 and 1881 there were about 5000 Chinese working the New Zealand minefields. Half of these were in Otago.

These miners wore their hair in pigtails, wore bamboo hats and carried their gear in baskets hung on the end of bamboo poles.

The other miners were suspicious of them and let them work only in worthless claims. The Chinese were hard workers and found plenty of gold in the abandoned diggings. They were also clever miners who helped improve gold-dredging systems. Many returned to

their families in China after they had saved about £100 ($200).

Life on the goldfields

Thick mud, narrow tracks and crumbling cliffs made the roads to the goldfields dangerous.

Chinese goldminers.

Women were in great demand in the tent towns. Any single woman who came to the fields was usually married within a week.

The towns often got their water from the same place that rubbish was thrown, so

typhoid was a common disease.

Because rats infested the fields, a cat was a treasure.

For entertainment, the men went to the 'pub' and gambled. They bet on rat fights.

Dunedin

The people who made the most money were the traders who travelled to the goldfields.

They charged high prices for their equipment: picks 16s ($1.60), newspaper 2s 6d (25 cents) a copy, candles 1s (10 cents), butter 3s 6d per pound (35 cents per 454 grams), tobacco 6s per pound (60 cents per 454 grams), eggs 21s ($2.10) per dozen.

Most of the supplies came from Dunedin. In the 1860s it was New Zealand's largest town.

End of the boom

After 1863, gold in the Otago fields ran out.

Miners moved up the west coast to Hokitika but the thick bush, heavy rain, sandflies and mosquitoes made mining even tougher.

In 1867 gold was found deep in the Coromandel coast. Ordinary miners couldn't afford the expensive machinery needed to work the quartz reefs.

Gold mining continued in Otago, Reefton and Waihi but the gold rush was over.

An early gumdigger.

DID YOU KNOW?

When miners arrived at a field they had to stake out a claim by banging pegs in at each corner. Then the claim had to be registered with officials. There were many arguments and fights over the claims.

Firewood was scarce on the goldfields. Some miners had to walk 20 kilometres to get enough wood to boil the billy.

Often on winter mornings, the miners' boots were frozen solid.

Sometimes hungry miners stole sheep from the large unguarded flocks.

At the goldfields, one single woman boasted she'd had fifty offers of marriage in one week.

Dan Ellison and Hakaria Haeroa were panning for gold in the Shotover River.

While crossing the river, Dan's dog was swept downstream. It scrambled ashore on a rocky point. When Dan swam to rescue it, he found the cracks on the point filled with gold.

He and Hakaria collected 300 ounces (8.5 kilograms) before nightfall, worth more than £1,200 ($2,400).

The miners worked six days a week. On Sundays they washed their clothes, darned their socks and sat around smoking pipes or went hunting.

CHAPTER 9

Conflicts begin, 1860-72

As more settlers came to New Zealand they wanted to get land faster than the Maori would sell it.

For Maori the land was their country; they loved it. For settlers, the land meant new farms to make money.

As the Pakeha population increased, more Maori decided not to sell their land. This caused trouble for everyone.

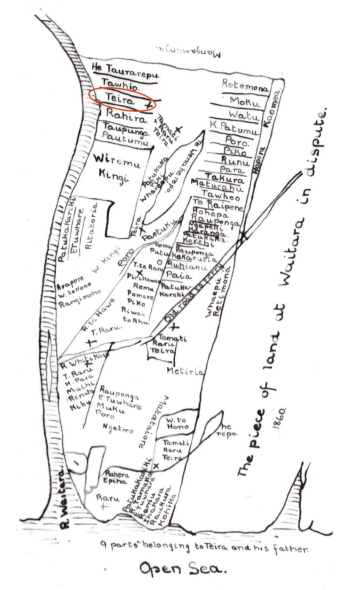

Maori land claims, Waitara, 1861.

The Maori king movement

The settlers had had their own government since 1856 but there were no Maori politicians and almost no Maori had a vote.

At a large meeting in 1858, Wiremu Tamihana (William Thompson), chief of Ngatihaua tribe, united other tribes from Waikato, Taupo, East Coast and Taranaki. They elected a famous old chief, Te Wherowhero, as the first Maori king. He took the name Potatau and soon had his own courts, a flag, troops and constables.

All the tribes agreed not to sell their land.

The Waitara dispute

In 1859 a Maori named Teira (Taylor) tried to sell land at the Waitara River, near New Plymouth. The powerful chief Wiremu Kingi (William King) said the land wasn't Teira's to sell.

The government decided Teira and his family owned at least some of the land so they bought it. They told Wiremu Kingi to stop interfering. This made Kingi very angry.

Land customs

The new governor, Colonel Gore Browne, and the government didn't understand Maori land customs.

Most Maori land is owned by the tribe, not individuals. Almost everyone in the tribe had to agree before any land could be sold.

The battle

Wiremu Kingi got his people to pull up the survey pegs at Waitara. He sent warriors to burn settlers' farmhouses.

He built a new pa on the land.

Maori from south Taranaki, Waikato and Ngati Maniapoto tribes joined the fight.

There were 3000 European troops fighting 1500 Maori. Maori were outnumbered. They lost Waitara but in revenge captured some British land close to New Plymouth.

In 1861, with the help of Wiremu Tamihana, a truce was made but the fighting was not over.

Meeting between Maori and British authorities at Waitara, 1878.

Governor Gore Browne.

Governor Grey returns

Governor Gore Browne wanted more Maori land for new settlers. He decided to invade the Waikato to defeat the Maori king but the British government did not agree.

Gore Browne was sacked and Governor Grey returned.

The 'King' Maori did not trust Grey. When he sent troops to Taranaki to take back land captured by hostile Maori, war broke out.

War in the Waikato

General Duncan Cameron and his troops defeated the Maori in Taranaki. General Duncan then led his troops to the Waikato.

By 1864 there were 12,000 European troops plus 1000 'friendly' Maori fighting 4000 'King' Maori.

Part-time warriors

To stop the advancing British army, Maori built big pa in their way. They defended these fortresses easily but they were always short of men.

Maori warriors often had to leave battle to visit home to check on their families, get more supplies and help grow food.

Rewi Maniapoto.

Sir Duncan Alexander Cameron and his troops.

Orakau

Rewi Maniapoto built a pa in a peach grove at Orakau.

He and 300 Maori from several tribes were attacked by 2000 British troops. They held off cannon fire and bayonet charges, but after three days they had only raw potatoes to eat and wooden bullets to fire.

General Cameron asked them to surrender. Rewi replied, 'Ka whawhai tonu ake! Ake! Ake!' ('We will fight on for ever, for ever, for ever!')

Then suddenly they walked out of the pa. Maniapoto and about 150 others escaped into the swamps but many others, including women and children, were killed.

The battle of Gate Pa

General Cameron marched on to Tauranga to capture Gate Pa, the pa of Ngai te Rangi. Here 1650 British attacked 250 Maori.

After bombing the pa with 50-kilogram shells, they charged forward with bayonets.

The Maori had survived by sheltering in trenches and pits. They wounded and killed 112 British troops.

The British lost the battle, but they had already confiscated lots of land in the Waikato, Taranaki and Tauranga areas. This confiscation was against the Treaty of Waitangi and caused the fighting to go on for another eight years.

The Hau-Hau

The Hau-hau was a religious group. During battle they shouted, 'Pai marire hau-hau!' They believed this would save them from Pakeha bullets but it didn't.

The Pai Marire (Good and Peaceful) religion was started by Te Ua from Taranaki. One of his chiefs, Titokowaru, was a fearsome warrior. He recaptured most of the land between Mount Egmont/ Taranaki and Wanganui. He frightened the settlers by reviving cannibalism.

Te Kooti

Te Kooti was a British 'friendly' fighting on the East Coast.

The British accused him of helping the Hau-hau. He denied this, but wasn't believed.

Te Kooti was banished to the Chatham Islands without a trial. There, he studied the Bible and started a new religion, Ringatu (the Upraised Hand).

In 1868, he and his friends stole a schooner. They sailed back to New Zealand where they attacked and killed many settlers and 'friendly' Maori round the East Coast.

Parihaka

Te Whiti was a Maori prophet. He believed in peaceful protest.

He was against drinking alcohol and held large prayer meetings at Parihaka, his Taranaki village.

When Pakeha tried to settle on his tribe's confiscated land, his people pulled up survey pegs and ploughed up farms.

When the government sent 1600 troops to take over Parihaka, they were met by hundreds of dancing, singing children.

Te Whiti was arrested and locked up for a year.

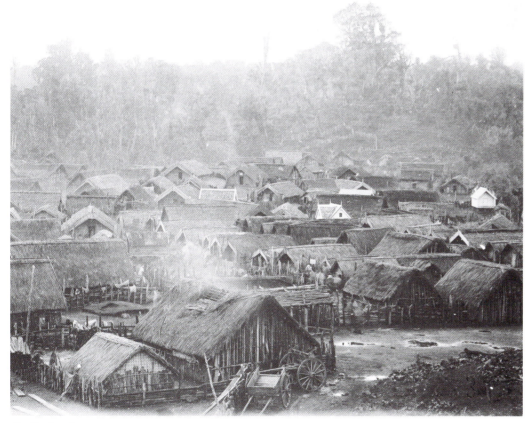

Parihaka Pa.

DID YOU KNOW?

The Arawa tribe from Rotorua were British 'friendlies'. They defeated the Maori king's supporters on the East Coast.

During the New Zealand wars about one thousand men were killed on each side.

Titokowaru was never defeated in a battle.

In 1869 his followers mysteriously left him and he could fight no longer.

The Maori king and his tribes stopped settlers from entering the 'King Country' until around 1880. After that it became too difficult to defend the large area and they began to sell land again.

When Te Whiti returned to Parihaka he built a model village with piped water and electricity. This was an effort to lead his people to successful life in the Pakeha world.

CHAPTER 10

The late nineteenth century

By the end of the 1860s the fighting was almost over and the gold was running out.

Although the South Island was rich from farming, the North Island had suffered badly from the wars.

The future looked gloomy. Many people left for Australia or to seek their fortunes in California.

Sir Julius Vogel

Julius Vogel was a gold assayer in the Australian goldfields. An assayer tests rock ore to find out how much gold it has.

He came to Otago to work as a newspaper reporter.

He had ideas about how to improve life in New Zealand. He was elected to Parliament in 1863 and in 1869 he became Colonial Treasurer (Minister of Finance).

Borrowing for growth

In 1870 Vogel announced his plan. Over ten years the government would borrow £6 million ($12 million) to build roads, railways and ports. The roads and railways would connect the scattered towns. This would open up the country and, hopefully,

attract thousands of new settlers.

The new immigrants

Before 1870 most immigrants were men — whalers, sealers, sailors, soldiers and miners.

In the 1870s over 100,000 people came to New Zealand and most of them were families. These people built the roads and railways and cleared the thick North Island forests.

The forests

The forests were made up of huge rimu and totara trees. These trees stood in the way of roads and farms.

First the trees were killed by fire, then cut down with axes and handsaws.

Some of the timber was used for building but most of it was burnt or left to rot.

The Scandinavians

The families that cleared the forests came from Scandinavia. They were young, poor, knew little English and had never seen such thick bush.

Each family was given 40 acres (16 hectares) of

Advertising for domestic servants in New Zealand.

Sir Julius Vogel.

Road construction.

land. Before they could start work on their own land, they had to clear the bush for roads and railways.

A home in the bush

The first homes were made out of timber slabs or ponga logs. They had two rooms — a bedroom and a kitchen. There were no windows; the floor was stamped-down earth.

While the men cut the trees the women and children gathered food — eels, pigeons, wild honey and weka eggs.

There were no schools.

A new farm

As the land was cleared, small farms replaced the bush huts and roads replaced the bush tracks.

Farmers planted wheat and

children went to school.

By the 1900s travelling salesmen — dentists, tailors, watchmakers, piano tuners and photographers — were visiting most farms.

Pioneer children

In 1881, 42 per cent of the people were younger than fifteen.

New Zealand was a healthy place to bring up children. Unlike most of Europe, there was plenty of meat, cheese, bread and milk.

Schools were built in towns and in the country.

In Maori communities parents gave the land for the school and helped pay for the teacher. The teaching was in English and the teacher was usually Pakeha.

By 1879 there were 57 of these schools set up.

DID YOU KNOW?

In 1861 Julius Vogel helped start New Zealand's first newspaper, the *Otago Daily Times.*

Before 1870 most people travelled round New Zealand by horseback or coastal ship.
There was no road from Auckland to Wellington.

In 1874 there were only 417 kilometres of railway tracks in the country.

Trees in the forests were hundreds of years old. Many rimu and totara were 25 metres high and two metres thick.

Scandinavian families were paid five shillings (50 cents) a day for clearing land for roads and railways. The cost of the fare from Europe was taken out of this pay.

After cutting down the trees and undergrowth and leaving it to dry for three or four months, the men then lit fires.
The ash was used as fertiliser.

In 1888 a burn-off fire got out of control and destroyed 30 homes.

Many children ground their family's wheat grain. It took two hours every day to make enough flour for a family's bread.

This wide range of toys from the 1950s was unavailable to the Victorian child.

Work, work, work

During the nineteenth century most children worked. Girls often worked as home helpers when they were about eleven or twelve. Many boys at the same age worked on farms or in factories.

Toys and games

In their free time, pioneer children played with toys — spinning tops, hoops, dolls, prams and doll houses. They also played tennis, rounders, tag, hopscotch and marbles.

Bicycles

In 1888 pneumatic tyres and a diamond frame made the bicycle very popular. It was safe, cheap, comfortable and fast. A rider could easily cover 80–120 kilometres a day.

The piano

Many girls learned to play the piano. Many rode horses or bicycles to get to their lessons.

In 1901 there were 1400 music teachers and about 43,000 pianos. The population at the time was less than 800,000.

The Tarawera eruption

On 10 June 1886 Mount Tarawera, near Rotorua, erupted. The blast was heard in Christchurch. It rattled windows in Blenheim and Nelson. In Auckland it sounded like battle gunfire.

A continuous roar could be heard closer to the volcano.

Te Wairoa was the closest village to Tarawera; 65 of the 70 homes were destroyed.

Eleven people from Te Wairoa were killed.

Nearby villages — Tokiniho, Moura, Rotomahana, Waingongoro and Totariki — were swept away altogether.

Over 100 Maori and seven Pakeha died.

The land was covered in ash and the famous Pink and White

Bicycles became a popular form of transport.

Mount Tarawera in eruption, 10 June 1886.

Terraces were completely destroyed.

On 1 June, a week before the Tarawera eruption, a group of Maori and tourists were out on the lake. They saw a large waka (canoe) travelling very fast towards Mount Tarawera.

The paddlers were silent and ignored the calls of the Maori and tourists. Up to that day no such canoe had existed on the lake. Later, people said it was a 'ghost canoe', warning of the coming disaster.

Te Wairoa pa, after the eruption of Mount Tarawera.

CHAPTER 11

Many settlements become one

Clothing industry c. 1900.

The Dunedin.

Life was hard in the 1880s. Overseas prices for wool were low. With low prices for exports it was hard to pay for imports.

In towns there weren't enough jobs for everyone.

Many men were out of work. Their families lived in rough homes and had little to eat.

The government did not give money to the unemployed.

Bad working conditions

Factory jobs were terrible. People worked long hours. The buildings were overcrowded and poorly lit, and machinery had no safety guards. Many young children worked in these places because their parents needed the money.

Progress

In 1882 the first cargo of frozen meat left for Britain aboard the *Dunedin*. The *Dunedin* had an iron hull and was fitted with machinery for freezing.

The meat arrived in good condition and fetched one shilling and six pence (15 cents) a kilogram — a good price.

During this time more railways were built. Telegraph and telephone networks were set up. But times were still hard.

The Liberal Party, led by John Ballance, won the 1890 election. They promised to help all citizens have a better life.

The Liberal government

The new government bought large blocks of land like the Cheviot Estate in North Canterbury. Its 34,000 acres (13,759 hectares) were cut into small farms; 650 new settlers moved in and a small town was built.

Frozen meat and dairy products were selling well in Britain so the government had money to build a school in every district. Many districts had halls and libraries too.

New laws were made to help workers in factories.

The Arbitration Court

To stop strikes, the government set up a system for deciding wages and working conditions. The system let workers and employers sort out their arguments in a committee.

If this failed then the problem was taken to the Arbitration Court, where a judge made a decision that both sides had to accept.

This did not always work and by 1908 workers were striking.

A better deal for women

At this time, only men could vote. They owned everything, even a wife's wages.

After 1884 women were able to keep their wages and property.

By 1900 fewer women wanted to work as home help. Many became teachers, journalists and factory workers. Some were trying to get into law and medicine.

They wanted to vote and stand for Parliament. They also wanted better education for girls.

The temperance movement

Alcohol was a big problem. In the 1880s the drinks were stronger, cheaper and anyone could buy them.

In 1885 some women formed a group to stop the sale of alcohol. They called themselves the Women's Christian Temperance Union. They stopped alcohol being sold to children.

If they got the vote, women hoped they could stop the sale of all alcohol.

Kate Sheppard

A Christchurch Temperance leader, Kate Sheppard, organised petitions to allow women to vote.

In 1893 a petition was signed by 30,000 women. By this time most politicians wanted women

DID YOU KNOW?

In factories boys and girls were paid 75 cents or less a week. Some were paid nothing for the first year because they were being 'trained'. Outworkers who finished shirts and trousers at home got worse pay. Women often worked until 11.00 p.m. and earned just 4 cents a day.

In the 1890s new factory laws said no boy or girl under fourteen could work in a factory. Boys under sixteen and all women and girls could not work more than 48 hours a week. Hours of work were between 7.45 a.m. and 6.00 p.m.

The *Dunedin* voyage took 98 days. The captain feared the masts would catch alight because cinders from the boilers kept burning holes in the sails.

In 1912 there was a long and bitter miners' strike in Waihi.

In 1897, in Dunedin, Ethel Benjamin became the first woman lawyer to graduate and practise in New Zealand.

The first woman member of Parliament (MP) was Elizabeth McCombs. She was elected in 1933.

A temperance poster.

Kate Sheppard.

Classes in the early 1900s.

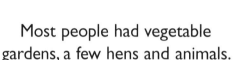
An early house.

to have the vote too.

In 1893 New Zealand was the first country to give women the vote.

By 1919 women were also able to stand for Parliament.

Schools in the 1890s
In the 1890s, most children could attend school. To get there, many of them rode horses or walked.

Written work was done on slates with a special pencil. Lessons were learned by chanting after the teacher.

Town schools had large classes — 90 to 100 pupils. Teachers were strict and used the strap or cane often.

Home life
By the 1890s a few homes had a wood-burning kitchen stove.

Clothes were washed by boiling them in a copper in a shed.

Most people had vegetable gardens, a few hens and animals.

House walls were often papered with old newspapers.

The toilet was a small shed outside built over a 'longdrop'.

Town sewage was pumped into the harbour or collected by the 'night cart' and dumped.

'King Dick' Seddon
In the 1890s the prime minister was Richard John Seddon. He was very popular and known as 'King Dick'.

In 1898, he introduced an old-age pension.

He set up state fire insurance and built maternity hospitals in the four main centres.

He was against Asian immigration, though, and stopped Chinese and Indian settlers from getting the pension.

The turn of the century
Telegraph, telephone and rail-

Richard John Seddon.

way networks joined most of the settled areas.

In 1901, postage was introduced. Letters could be sent round the country and overseas for one penny (one cent).

In 1908, after 40 years' work, the North Island Main Trunk Railway was finished.

In 1892 the New Zealand Rugby Football Union was set up.

Railways construction.

The government worked on land affairs, welfare, education and health.

Mount Cook was climbed in 1894.

By 1910 people thought of themselves as part of New Zealand rather than a province like Otago or Wellington. The country was no longer a pioneer land.

The early postal service.

DID YOU KNOW?

Boys liked to smash the telephone cups on the new telephone poles using catapults.

In a raid on a small Feilding school in 1884, the policeman confiscated 30 catapults.

The Boys' and Girls' Brigade and the Scouts and Girl Guides were founded in the 1890s.

Saturday was shopping day. All shops stayed open until 10 p.m. Wednesday was a half holiday.

Food was cheap. A loaf of bread was 3d (3 cents). A pound of butter (454 grams) was one shilling (10 cents). A good meal could be bought for 1 shilling and 6 pence (15 cents).

St John Ambulance and the Foundation for the Blind were set up in 1890.

In 1898, the old people's pension was almost six shillings and 11 pence (70 cents) per week.

If people grew a few vegetables and kept some chickens this was just enough to survive on.

The maternity hospitals were all called St Helen's after Seddon's birthplace in Lancashire, England.

In 1902, thirteen million letters were posted.

CHAPTER 12

A farming country

Between 1900 and 1920 the most common type of business was the family farm of 40 acres (16 hectares).

Dairy farms

With refrigeration, New Zealand meat and butter could be sold round the world.

By 1911 there were more than 15,000 dairy farms. The cows were milked by hand twice a day.

Other animals

Every farmer had a team of horses for ploughing, hauling and carrying. The farmer worked six days a week.

Each day started at 5.30 a.m. with the horses' first feed and finished at 10 p.m. when the horses returned to the stable.

Most farms had cats and dogs too. The dogs were used for herding and hunting and the cats were rat catchers.

Busy families

Men and boys looked after the fields, animals and crops.

Sheep were dipped in the district sheep-dip. They were shorn with hand shears, then the wool was baled and carted to the railway station.

Women and older children tended the vegetable garden and orchard. Fruit was pre-served or made into jam.

Younger children collected firewood, looked for fresh hens' eggs and fed the pigs. Pigs were killed for bacon.

Pocket money

Children killed rabbits for their skins that they sold.

In the South Island they went bird-nesting. Birds were pests. They ate farmers' seeds and grain. Local councils paid two cents a dozen for birds' eggs or birds' heads.

William Massey.

The move north

Pakeha families moved on to good dairy-farming land in Taranaki, Bay of Plenty and the Waikato.

The land was taken or bought from the Maori after the wars. Farmers in Wairarapa started farming fat lamb.

The Pakeha population of the North Island passed that of the South Island in 1901.

New political party

The Liberal Party had been in government for 20 years.

By 1911 farmers were beginning to follow the Reform Party. The leader of the party was 'Farmer' Bill Massey. Because he was a farmer, he understood what they wanted.

The 1911 election was a tie. The Liberals formed a government but they were in a muddle.

Then in July 1912 they lost a confidence vote and Bill Massey became prime minister.

A farmers' government

'Farmer' Bill thought the farmers were the 'backbone of the country'. His government gave them lots of help to export goods to Britain; but the towns were growing larger and the townspeople said this was unfair.

Rents, food and clothing were getting dearer but wages stayed the same. Once again there weren't enough jobs for everyone. Some people wanted to strike against their bosses.

Disease

In the towns, some rich families had indoor plumbing but most people still had an outside toilet and bathed once a week in an outside tub.

Many people threw their rubbish into the street or the backyard, so disease spread quickly.

In 1900 the Department of Health was set up to improve sanitation, water supply and sewerage.

The 'Red Feds'

Work on the waterfront, railways and in the mines was dangerous and wages were low. The workers wanted to strike for better conditions.

In 1909 the West Coast and Waihi miners formed the Federation of Labour. Their

DID YOU KNOW?

A team of horses usually drank 20 buckets of water at each watering.

Boys liked to hunt rabbits with ferrets. If a ferret killed a rabbit underground it often stayed there to sleep off its meal and the owner had to dig it out.

In 1880 Dunedin was the most important city in the country. In 1911 Auckland was the largest, with a population of 102,676.
Although farming was our most important business (and probably still is), in 1911 more people were living in towns than on the land.

'Farmer' Bill Massey was pitching hay on his farm in Mangere when a telegram was passed to him on a pitchfork. It was an invitation to stand in the by-election for the west Auckland seat of Waitemata.
He won the seat, then in 1896 moved to Franklin. He held this seat until his death in 1925.

The main difference between the 'Red Feds' and other unions was that they used the strike as a weapon against their employers.

The strikes of 1913.

Some of the 'specials' taken on to break the strikes of 1913.

nickname was the 'Red Feds'. Red is the colour connected with communists and socialists. The flags of communist countries are often red.

In 1912 and 1913 the engineers at the Waihi mine tried to break away from the old union to join the mine owners' new union. There were fights between the two unions. The government gave police protection to the new union members. More than 60 old union members were put in prison. A policeman was shot and an engine driver was killed during one clash.

Massey's Cossacks

In 1913, when the 'Red Feds' organised other strikes, the government took on extra police. They were called 'specials'. They had horses and carried long batons. People called them 'Massey's Cossacks'.

The waterfront strike

On 8 November 1913 over a thousand 'specials' fought against the Auckland wharfies to try and break their strike. The 'specials' won the battle.

Workers in Dunedin, Wellington and Lyttelton were on strike too. The 'Red Feds' wanted the whole country to strike in support of the wharfies but people knew they

'Specials' in Waterloo Quay, Wellington.

wouldn't win a strike against both the bosses and the government.

By January 1914 everyone was back at work.

A change of heart

Most people didn't agree with the 1913 strike but they didn't like the government's actions either.

Voters turned away from

Massey's Reform Party government. They didn't vote for the 'Red Feds' either. They gave their votes to the Liberal Party instead.

In the 1914 election Massey's party won by two seats, so the Reform Party and the Liberal Party formed a coalition government.

The Plunket Society

In 1907 Dr Frederick Truby King and his wife formed the Plunket Society. The Society improved the health of women and children.

At this time, 51 out of every 1000 babies died in their first year, mostly from disastrous sicknesses caused by bad feeding and unclean habits.

Plunket nurses and district nurses visited mothers to make sure babies were kept clean and well fed.

The Health Department made regular health checks on children at school after 1912.

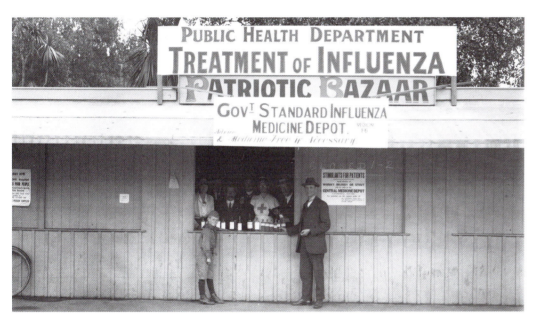

The influenza depot, Christchurch, set up to cope with the influenza epidemic.

Staff outside the South Durham Street District Nursing Office.

Dr Frederick Truby King.

CHAPTER 13

The Maori rebuild

Maori housing in the early 1900s.

In the early 1900s the best Maori land had been taken by Pakeha or sold to them.

Very few Maori lived in towns. They lived in villages, but without land it was hard to earn money.

Some Maori worked for Pakeha farmers. Others dug for kauri gum or gathered flax.

They still grew or caught most of their food.

Apirana Ngata.

Living conditions

Maori villages were small, with usually less than 50 people. The homes were built of nikau, ponga, raupo, bark and earth. They had no toilets and the cooking area was outside. Water for washing and drinking was collected from streams.

The poor housing and Pakeha diseases like measles, whooping cough and flu killed many Maori.

The Young Maori Party

In 1905 Apirana Ngata, a lawyer, of Ngati Porou, joined Parliament as the MP for Eastern Maori.

Peter Buck (Te Rangi Hiroa) from Taranaki was a doctor and a Native Health Officer from 1905 to 1909. He became the MP for Northern Maori in 1909.

Maui Pomare was a doctor also. He was a Native Health Officer from 1901 to 1911 when he became MP for Western Maori.

These men belonged to the Young Maori Party. All of them went to Te Aute College in Hawkes Bay. They were determined to use their education to help their people.

Maui Pomare.

Two worlds

The Young Maori Party believed Maori had to take on some of the Pakeha ways of life. Ngata, Pomare and Buck had done it successfully but it was impossible for most Maori in the 1890s. Much of their land had been taken or sold. The government gave loans to Pakeha farmers but not to Maori. More schools and hospitals were built for Pakeha. Maori had no money to pay for books or health care.

Maori leadership

After the wars and the 'land grabbing', Maori would not listen to outsiders. They trusted only leaders who belonged to their tribe. Some of these leaders founded their own religions. People seemed to feel better knowing God and the wairua (spirits of their ancestors) were helping them.

Ringatu

This religion was started by Te Kooti Rikirangi.

Like the Jews of the Old Testament, Te Kooti said, Maori had lost their land and were treated unfairly by men in power. But God would save them like he had saved the Jews. Te Kooti taught his people to beware of Pakeha.

Rua Kenana.

Rua Kenana

Before Te Kooti died he said, 'In twice seven years a man shall arise in the mountains to succeed me. He shall be the new prophet of the people.'

Rua Kenana said he was that man.

Like Te Kooti, Rua compared the Jews to his Tuhoe people. His followers called themselves Nga Iharaira (the Israelites). His settlement at Maungapohatu in the Urewera hills was called New Jerusalem.

The wooden circular temple at Maungapohatu.

DID YOU KNOW?

Favourite foods of the Maori were berries — taraire, tawa, karaka and miro — cooked in the hangi. Pigeons, tui and parrots cooked in their own fat were delicious, along with wild pigs and fish.

A special food was the kiore (grey rat).

When Tawhiao, the Maori king, died in 1894 his tangi lasted more than a month and 4000 people followed his body to Taupiri mountain where he was buried.

The first Maori to get a university degree — a BA at Canterbury in 1893 — was Apirana Ngata. He also gained a law degree from Auckland University in 1896.

In 1927 Peter Buck left New Zealand to become director of the Bishop Museum in Hawaii. Later, he became a professor at Yale University in the United States.

Maui Pomare was a minister in the Reform Government from 1912 to 1928. For three of those years he was Minister of Health.

In 1906 only four doctors in the Waikato area would take Maori patients.

New Jerusalem

Rua had more than a thousand followers at Maungapohatu. It was so far out in the bush, few Pakeha went there.

Terrible stories were made up about Rua that scared many Pakeha. Then when Rua told his followers not to join the First World War because the time for fighting had passed, Pakeha started saying he was on Germany's side. So in March 1916 the government sent 70 police to break up his stronghold.

Rough justice

Rua and his two eldest sons, Whatu and Toko, met the police. There was no fight but when the police tried to grab Rua, a gun went off — no one knows whose. Toko ran for his gun and wounded four policemen before he was shot and killed.

When the shooting stopped, Rua, Whatu and four others were arrested. Rua was charged with sedition (treason) but was only found guilty of another offence — unwilling to be arrested at Te Waiiti on 12 February.

He was given a very harsh sentence — twelve months' hard labour and eighteen months' imprisonment.

Big costs

To pay for the trial, Rua's people had to sell much of their land. They were given no help from the government.

In 1918, when Rua returned to Maungapohatu, most people had left the settlement. A few stayed with him until his death on 20 February 1937.

The Ratana religion

Tahupotiki Wiremu Ratana was also a religious leader.

He was a farmer who lived near Wanganui. On 8 November 1918 he had a vision. A voice told him to 'unite the Maori people'.

As news of Ratana's vision spread, people came to his farm. On Christmas Day, 1920 three thousand people listened to him speak.

Ratana also travelled up and down the country gathering followers from different tribes.

In 1925 he formed the Ratana Church.

Ratana also wanted a strong voice for Maori in Parliament. He supported the Labour Party and in 1928 four of his followers stood for Parliament.

Ratana died on 18 September 1939 but his message lived on: his people could survive in a Pakeha world.

Princess Te Puea

Princess Te Puea Herangi of Waikato was a different type of leader.

Her mother was the eldest child of King Tawhiao. When her mother died in 1898 Te Puea became a leader of her mother's

Princess Te Puea Herangi.

people. She was fifteen years old.

The Waikato tribes were still angry about the wars and their loss of land. They would have nothing to do with the Pakeha, especially doctors and schools where Maori children had to speak English.

Epidemics

In 1913 there was a smallpox epidemic. The tribes had no money for doctors or nurses. Many Maori people died in the Waikato.

Then in 1918 there was a Spanish flu epidemic.

Only three out of 200 people in Te Puea's village did not get sick.

Again there was no help from the government.

Turangawaewae

Te Puea's village was near Meremere on low ground that flooded in winter. After the epidemics Te Puea decided to move the village back to where the first king's house had been at Ngaruawahia. She wanted to build a new home, where her people could have healthier lives. It was called Turangawaewae (a place to stand).

Self-help

Turangawaewae is a magnificent marae. It showed the Waikato tribes and the rest of New Zealand that Maori could help themselves.

It also showed that some Pakeha things were useful. Turangawaewae had a sewerage system and a clean water supply. Te Puea taught her people to remember Maori culture and values — songs, stories, dances and tribal histories. She encouraged carving and canoe building. But best of all, she convinced her people to send their children to school and to take them to a doctor when they were sick.

Better times

In the 1920s and 1930s governments began to help Maori. Money was spent on housing. More children went on to high school.

Eight Maori district high schools were set up in the 1940s.

Money was lent to Maori farmers for land development. Some of the land taken unfairly during the wars was returned.

Moving to the cities

In 1890, 95 per cent of Maori lived outside towns. By 1990 most Maori lived in towns and cities. In 1984 there were 69,000 Maori in Auckland. New city marae were built.

The Maori Women's Welfare League was set up in 1951. In 1962 the New Zealand Maori Council was established. These organisations were formed to help all Maori.

Balancing the past

In 1975 Whina Cooper formed Te Roopu o te Matakite (The People with a Vision). She led a march from the Far North to Wellington to protest against the taking of Maori land.

Kohanga reo (language nests) for preschoolers were set up to save the Maori language.

In 1975 the Waitangi Tribunal was formed to look into and settle Maori claims on land, fishing rights, language and customs.

New Maori parties

In 1979 Matiu Rata, Ranginui Walker, Pat Hohepa and others formed Mana Motuhake (The Separate Mana of the People).

In the first MMP election in 1996, the New Zealand First Party represented many Maori.

DID YOU KNOW?

Taumau (arranged marriages) were common. Taumau was sometimes used when a leader needed a helper.

When Princess Te Puea of Waikato was 38 years old, her family chose a much younger man to marry her so he could be her helper. He was called Tumokai — the worker.

As late as 1981, 6114 Maori, mostly in the Bay of Plenty and the East Cape, followed the Ringatu religion.

Rua Kenana's trial in Auckland lasted 47 days. This was the longest trial in New Zealand until 1977.

After Kenana's trial, eight jury members signed a petition protesting at Rua's harsh sentence.

The first Ratana MP was Eruera Tirikatene, who won Southern Maori in a by-election in 1932.

In 1769, when Captain Cook was in New Zealand, the Maori population was estimated to be around 100,000. By 1896 the number had dropped to 42,113. In 1901 there were 45,500 Maori and the population had started to rise again. In 1936 there were 82,000 Maori. By 1951 there were 115,676.

In 1991 there were 434,847 (12.9 per cent of the population).

CHAPTER 14

The growth of a nation

Soldiers in the South African war.

In the 1800s New Zealand and the six Australian colonies (such as New South Wales and Victoria) were known as Australasia. In the 1890s when many Australians wanted to make the seven colonies a new nation, most New Zealanders said no. They thought New Zealand should be a nation on its own.

In 1901, when the Australian Commonwealth was formed, New Zealand was not part of it.

The Boer War

From 1899 to 1902 the British Army, helped by the Australians, Canadians and New Zealanders, fought two small Boer countries in South Africa.

Many of the Boers were part-time fighters — they fought for a while then went home to their farms. The British followed them, burnt their houses and put the women and children in 'concentration' camps where thousands died of diseases.

Bold, brave soldiers

The New Zealanders were used to sleeping out and roughing it. They were called 'Maorilanders' or 'Rough Riders'. They made excellent scouts and patrollers. They proved they were as bold and brave as the best British soldiers.

A sense of pride

By the 1900s most New Zealanders felt proud about their country. Many said it was the most beautiful country in the world.

They were also proud of their sporting glory. Horses were winning important races in Australia.

Anthony Wilding won the men's singles at Wimbledon every year from 1910 to 1913. He also won the Davis Cup several times for Australasia with his Australian partner Norman Brookes. Wilding was later killed during the First World War.

Rugby greats

In 1905 during a tour of Great Britain the All Blacks beat England, Scotland and Ireland, losing only one game to Wales, out of a total of 32 played. And it's been said that in the game against Wales the All Blacks scored a try that had been disallowed! Altogether they scored 830 points against 39. The New Zealanders were now considered to be among the best rugby players in the world.

Women

New Zealand women were proud that they had helped New Zealand to be the first country in the world to give women the vote.

Organisations like the National Council of Women encouraged governments to improve education for everyone, especially girls.

Schools

A School Reader was published in 1899. It taught children to be proud of their country's life, literature and history.

In 1901 an ensign flown by New Zealand ships (a Union Jack with four stars) became the

Early classes being taught in the open air.

DID YOU KNOW?

In 1886 out of a total New Zealand population of 578,500 people, some 300,000 were born in New Zealand. Only 43,500 of these were aged twenty or more. 215,000 were under fifteen and 256,000 were under twenty-one.

In 1882 New Zealanders sent 1,500,000 telegrams.

By 1896 there were 5000 telephones and by 1904 there were 12,000.

New Zealand was the first colony to send troops — mounted infantry — to the Boer War.

Some seventy New Zealanders led by Captain Madocks charged a group of a hundred Boers on a hill, who had attacked some soldiers from Yorkshire. They drove the Boers back but two New Zealanders were killed. The hill was named 'New Zealand Hill'.

In 1883 the racehorse Martini-Henry won both the Victorian Derby and the Melbourne Cup in record time.

New Zealand was one of the first countries in the world to give the elderly old-age pensions.

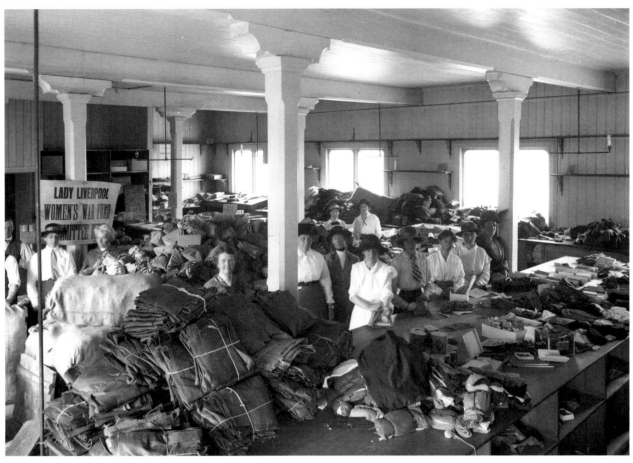
Women working during the First World War.

New Zealand flag. It was issued to every school and was often saluted during ceremonies.

'God of nations! At thy feet; In the bonds of love we meet' was written by Thomas Bracken in 1875. It was set to music by John J. Woods, an Otago teacher, and was sung in many schools. In 1940 it became the national hymn.

The First World War

Many New Zealanders fought in the First World War from 1914 to 1918. On 25 April 1915 Australian and New Zealand troops (Anzacs) landed at Anzac Cove, Gallipoli. They were fighting the Turks who were hidden in the rugged hills above the beach. Many mistakes were made and the Anzacs and the British could not conquer the Turks. A large number of British, Anzac and Turkish troops were killed.

Chunuk Bair

In 1915 Colonel W.G. Malone and his Wellington Battalion captured the high hill, Chunuk Bair. This gave them a chance to attack the Turks but there were too many of them. They were slaughtered by Turkish rifles and machine-gun fire. Malone and some of his men were killed by shells fired by a British warship. The Turks retook the hill and drove the Anzacs back to the beach.

In December 1915 all the troops were evacuated from Gallipoli.

In many ways the war in Gallipoli helped New Zealanders start to think of themselves as a separate country from Britain. Ormond Burton of the New Zealand Field Ambulance summed up the feelings of the time: 'The way men died on Chunuk is shaping the deeds yet to be done by generations still unborn.' When the August fighting died down there was no longer any question that the New Zealanders had commenced to realise themselves as a nation'.

Heroes

Although they lost the battle, the Anzacs were heroes. Their fighting skills and bravery were reported round the world. They proved they were as good as the best soldiers in the world.

More fighting

The New Zealand Army went on to fight against the Germans in France and Belgium. Before the war was over nearly 50,000 New Zealanders, over half of those who went to war, were killed or wounded.

Wounded troops.

Dressing station at Gallipoli, 1915.

DID YOU KNOW?

In 1878 there were 231,000 men and only 183,000 women.

By 1900 all children spoke with a 'colonial twang'. Some of it came from Australia and some they made up themselves. They called a dog a 'guri', which is from the Maori word 'kuri'.

At Gallipoli the Anzacs' aim was to help the Royal Navy break through the narrow Dardanelles straits to threaten Constantinople, the capital of Turkey. Turkey was an ally of Germany.

At Gallipoli between 6 and 9 August, 1800 New Zealanders — Pakeha and Maori — out of 4500 men fighting had been killed or wounded.

Altogether 2700 New Zealanders died at Gallipoli and 4700 were wounded.

Anzac Day, 25 April, is the day New Zealanders and Australians remember those who died or were wounded in war.

CHAPTER 15

Between the wars

Three teams of horses hauling ploughs, probably in the Christchurch region.

The First World War ended on 11 November 1918.
Up and down the country memorials were set up to remember those who fought and died.
Those who survived just wanted to go back to life as it had been before.

One big farm

After the war, farmers' exports — wool, frozen meat (mostly lamb), butter and cheese — earned the country good prices. There were a few farms for cattle, cereals and timber but almost no orchards, vineyards or market gardens.

Many soldiers were given help so they could buy land to start more farms but much of the land was expensive.

Then export prices suddenly dropped and many families couldn't pay their loans so were forced off their farms.

Scientific farming

New Zealand was one of the first countries to use science to improve farming. Farms were top-dressed with fertiliser to keep the land in grass all year. Experiments with animals showed Jersey cows gave milk with more butterfat.

When the milking machine was invented, farmers increased their herds and milked more cows faster.

Milking and shearing were made easier when electricity reached the farms.

The inside of a typical general store.

A transport revolution

In the 1920s motor cars became popular. Most had electric lights, an automatic starter and a vacuum pump system to feed petrol into the engine. But tyres were poor quality so two spares were always carried.

There were no petrol stations. Petrol came in four-gallon (18-litre) tins and was bought from the grocer for one dollar.

In winter chains were put on the wheels to help the car over muddy clay roads. A 50-kilometre drive could take four hours.

Forty kilometres an hour was a good speed. Many cars went 70 kilometres per hour but not for long because the radiator would boil.

Towns grow suburbs

In 1926 the population of New Zealand was nearly one and half million. Sixty per cent of people lived in towns.

Towns and cities were spreading out. Suburbs grew along main roads and railways. Trams and buses took people from home to work. Even though shops were built where the trams and buses stopped,

Living room.

butchers, grocers and bakers still called at homes.

The coal house was filled up every few weeks and the ice man called once a week. He brought a block of ice for the ice box which lasted exactly one week.

The 'flicks'
In 1896 the first moving pictures, 'kinematographs', were seen in New Zealand. They had no story, just moving pictures.

After 1900 the films started to tell stories but there was no colour or sound and they flickered. The film was flammable and often caught fire.

By the 1920s movies were very popular. Auckland had 25 picture theatres. Saturday afternoon sessions showed cartoons and serials like *Buffalo Bill, Tarzan* and *Flash Gordon*.

On 8 March 1929, at the Paramount Theatre in Wellington, the first 'talkie' was shown. Queues stretched along Courtenay Place and Cambridge Terrace.

Tasman crossing
In 1928 Charles Kingsford Smith flew the Tasman in his plane, the *Southern Cross*. It took him fourteen hours and twenty-five minutes. Thirty thousand people went to Wigram airfield to watch him land.

Trouble again
Prices for New Zealand goods overseas were low.

Bill Massey, Prime Minister from 1912 to 1925, and Gordon Coates, Prime Minister from 1925 to 1928, borrowed money from overseas to help the economy.

Most of the money went to farmers to make more butter, meat and wool. For many

Crowds turned up to greet Charles Kingsford Smith when he landed at Wigram airfield.

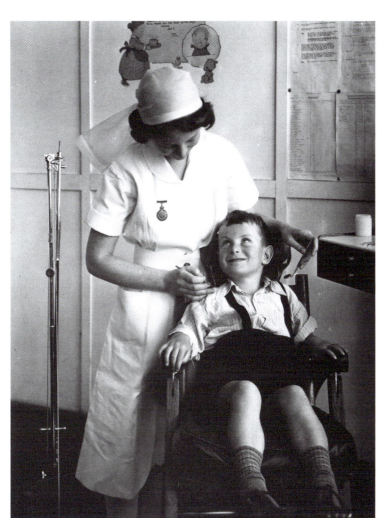

The Wellington Dental Clinic in Willis Street.

families, especially those in the towns, it was hard times. Food prices kept going up. Rents and housing were expensive. Many people had no work.

With little money for essentials, children's health suffered. School medical checks showed that most children had bad teeth, and eye, ear and skin diseases.

The government helps

Health camps were started in 1919 to look after unhealthy children. At the same time the School Dental Service began to train dental nurses.

In 1926 the government paid poor families with an income less than £4 ($8) two shillings (20 cents) a week for every child after the first two. The allowance was not paid to 'foreigners', or 'bad' or unmarried parents. By 1930, 3868 families got the allowance.

Another loan

In the 1928 election Sir Joseph Ward promised to borrow another £70 million ($140 million) to improve everyone's lives. His party won the election but he was not able to keep his promise.

61

CHAPTER 16

Depression and the welfare state

Crowds awaiting the result of the 1931 elections.

In the early 1930s business around the world was bad. Prices for New Zealand goods overseas dropped even lower. Sir Joseph Ward could not borrow his millions. He died in 1930 leaving a government with no money and no ideas.

Work programmes

In 1929 there were 6000 people out of work.

A year later it was 11,000. The government got local councils and private businesses to organise jobs for these people and helped to pay them.

Scheme 5

This was a huge programme to keep men and boys in work. Councils got them to garden and kill weeds along the roadsides. They made new roads and drains. They planted thousands of hectares of pine trees. They built tourist roads like

Auckland's Scenic Drive and the road to Milford Sound through the Homer Tunnel.

Building school playgrounds was a Scheme 5 project.

The councils wanted to keep the workers busy for as long as possible so they gave them shovels and wheelbarrows instead of diggers and bulldozers.

Scheme 5 wages
The pay was poor. Single men were paid fifteen shillings ($1.50) a week. Married men were paid more.

The highest pay of £2 ($4) a week was for a married man with three or more children.

Food riots
On 9 January 1932 a crowd of unemployed people, many of them women, shouting, 'We want food!', smashed the windows of Wardell's grocery shop in Dunedin.

In April the government cut wages for all its employees. On 14 April, after a protest meeting in the Auckland Town Hall, the crowd ran down Queen Street, smashing shop windows. The next night shop windows were broken in Karangahape Road. A force of 2000 police, army, navy and volunteers was brought in to keep the peace.

Hope
The government spent little and hoped prices for exports would improve, which they did by 1935.

Unemployment dropped to 50,000 but life was still hard, especially for the unskilled, young people, women and Maori.

Life in the Depression
In 1935 there were still thousands of families on Scheme 5.

Many lived in shacks. They used anything they could find for clothing. Hessian sacks were used for boys' pants. Towels and aprons were made out of flour sacks. Woollen jerseys with holes were unpicked and reknitted. Pieces of cardboard were put inside shoes when the soles wore out.

Michael Joseph Savage.

Micky Savage
In 1933 Michael Joseph Savage became the leader of the Labour Party. The people called him 'Micky'.

He went up and down the country, talking to them about jobs, houses, schools and hospitals. People were tired of hardship and wanted a change. They trusted Micky. The Labour Party won the 1935 election easily.

The Labour government
Savage's government improved

DID YOU KNOW?

The worst unemployment was in 1932 and 1933.

In 1933 there were 81,000 out of work. This did not include thousands of women and teenage boys and girls who worked on farms or in homes for board and a few shillings a week.

In 1935, when one woman's grandfather died she took all his underwear and made them into woollen singlets for her children.

Micky Savage started all his important sentences with 'Now then...'.

Before 1935, families who could not afford houses rented them. Poorer families rented rooms. In bad times people lived in sheds and crowded into shared houses.

The new state houses were on large sections so families could grow their own vegetables.

In the late 1930s life got easier. Carpets covered floors in houses. Radios, refrigerators, electric stoves, water heaters and washing machines were bought.

Passenger aeroplanes linked the major cities in 1939.

A regular flying boat service between Auckland and Sydney started in 1940.

Some of the first state houses.

the lives of ordinary New Zealanders. In 1936 a new Department of Housing was set up. Minister of Finance Walter Nash gave £5 million ($10 million) for housing. The first 52 state houses were built in Miramar, Wellington. Between 1937 and 1949 the government built an average of 2475 houses every year. It also lent money to people to build their own houses.

This project gave jobs to the men who built them and to the people who made the fittings that went into them.

More work
The government also started bigger work projects.

Hydro-electric dams were built to generate electricity. There were more cars so better roads were made. Flying became a way of transport so aerodromes were built too.

Welfare
Old-age pensions were improved.

All children, if they chose to, could go on to secondary school.

The working week was set at 40 hours.

Wages were fixed so families could live without hardship.

Social security
On 2 April 1938 Micky Savage announced his social security scheme. He promised better pensions for widows, the disabled, and old people.

People at 60, who needed it, would get £1 10s ($3) a week. And at 65 everyone would get a living pension. He also said there would be no charge for medicines, medical care, public hospital treatment, or maternity care.

In 1938 the Labour Party won the election again, easily.

Primary schools
In the 1880s primary schools went from primer one to standard six (now year eight). Each class finished with an exam. No one could go on to the next class without passing the exam.

Clever children could pass more than one exam in a year.

Those who passed the six standard exams were given a 'Certificate of Proficiency'. Some children stayed on until they got their 'Proficiency' but most left school before this.

At this time only 3 per cent of children stayed past standard four.

Secondary schools

In 1900 there were only 25 secondary schools, and they weren't free. Fees were about £10 ($20) a year. Most schools taught only Latin, foreign languages (usually French) and mathematics. Some larger schools also taught science.

In 1902 cooking for girls and woodwork for boys were offered in some schools.

Better education

In 1936 education was free until a student turned fourteen.

In 1944 the leaving age was raised to fifteen.

By the end of the 1940s, 97 per cent of children went to secondary school. More schools had to be built. Government money was given for libraries, art materials, and music and science equipment.

A better life

By the end of the 1930s New Zealand had changed. New homes, more jobs, higher pay, pensions, free health care and improved education had made it a better place.

Higher prices for New Zealand goods overseas meant the government could look after almost all of the people.

Engineering classes at Hutt Valley Memorial Technical College, Petone.

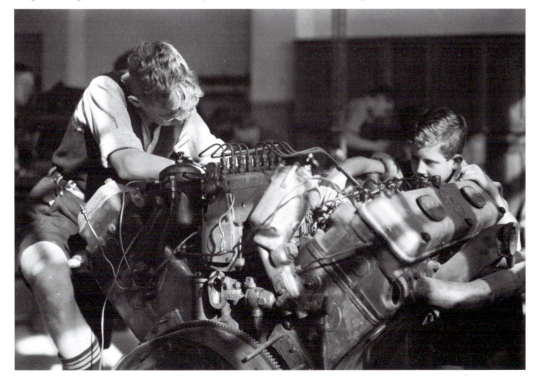

DID YOU KNOW?

Scheme 5 finished in 1939.

In the 1930s there were less than a thousand doctors in New Zealand.

In 1938 most doctors charged 10s 6d ($1.05) a visit.
In 1941 the government paid doctors 7s 6d (75 cents) and the doctors charged their patients the rest.

The health care system set up in 1939 gave New Zealanders an almost free system for over 20 years.

In 1900 the 25 secondary schools taught 2800 students (1800 boys and 1000 girls).
The biggest was Auckland Grammar School with 344 pupils (both boys and girls).

In 1920 only 13 per cent of students went to secondary school. Most of those stayed less than a year.

In 1944 the School Certificate examination was offered to students who didn't want to go to university but needed a qualification.

CHAPTER 17

Further war

New Zealand troops leaving to fight in the Second World War.

New Zealand troops at Cassino, Italy in the Second World War.

In the years 1914–18 Great Britain, France, Russia, the United States and their allies including New Zealand won the First World War against Germany and its allies.

Wars

In the years 1939–45 Great Britain, France, the United States and the Soviet Union and their allies including New Zealand won the Second World War against Nazi Germany, Italy and their allies.

New Zealand at war

In the Second World War New Zealand troops fought bravely in the deserts of North Africa against the Germans and the Italians. They also fought unsuccessfully to save Greece and Crete from the Germans.

Cassino

After helping to win the battle in North Africa, the New Zealanders joined the battle for Italy.

The Germans had a stronghold in a famous abbey on top of a hill in Cassino. The British, Indians and New Zealanders attacked the monastery, ruining it with bombs, but the Germans held on. For two months both sides fought bravely. In the end the Allies pulled out their forces and moved on.

Maori at war

More than 17,000 Maori fought in the Second World War. Many fought for the famous Maori Battalion.

Te Moananui-a-Kiwa Ngarimu was awarded the Victoria Cross, the highest award for bravery.

Japan

On 7 December 1941 Japan joined the war on Germany's side. They bombed the American naval base at Pearl Harbour. They also conquered Malaysia, French Indo-China and the Dutch East Indies.

For the first time New Zealand was threatened by attack. The Japanese invaded New Guinea and bombed Darwin in Australia. They also sent some mini submarines to attack ships in the Sydney Harbour.

Thousands of American marines and sailors were sent

End-of-war celebrations.

to protect New Zealand but there was no attack.

The end

In 1945 the Russian, American and British armies reconquered Europe. The Germans and Italians were beaten. The Japanese surrendered after the Americans dropped the first atom bomb on Hiroshima and then Nagasaki, killing thousands of people.

New Zealanders fought all over the world in the air force, navy and army. Once again they showed they were brave and bold.

Women at home

Everyone helped during the war. With most of the men away

Making munitions during the Second World War.

New Zealand troops in Malaya, 1955.

fighting, many 'land girls' worked as farmhands. Other women helped by sewing and knitting clothing for the men and baking fruit cakes for food parcels to send overseas.

Children at home

To help raise money, children collected ergot, a sticky fungus growing on grass. This was used to make an ointment that helped stop bleeding. Other children collected and sold scrap metal, bottles and paper.

At school they practised air-raid drills — what to do if they were bombed.

Hard times again

Many things couldn't be bought in the shops because they couldn't be imported. Petrol, meat and other foods were rationed. People took ration coupons to the butcher, grocer and petrol stations to get their share.

Cold War

A war of words and threats broke out between Russia and the United States. The Russians had a communist government and the US had a democratic government. The Americans thought the Russian communists wanted to rule the world while the Russians feared an attack by American atom bombs. In 1949 Chinese Communists took over their own country.

Anzus

In 1951 Australia and New Zealand signed a treaty of friendship with the US. If attacked, they agreed to help each other.

More hot wars

In the early 1950s New Zealand armed forces helped fight the Communist North Koreans when they invaded South Korea.

In the mid-1960s New Zealand forces were sent to help the Americans fight the North Vietnam Communists.

Protests

Many people thought these smaller wars might turn into another 'great' war. They also thought countries should be allowed to decide their own governments.

Thousands of citizens, especially young people, protested against the Vietnam War. Finally in 1972–73, the Americans and their allies pulled out of Vietnam. They had lost the war.

Nuclear tests

Countries like France and Great Britain often tested nuclear weapons in the South Pacific Ocean.

In 1973, when the French were testing bombs at Mururoa, Prime Minister Norman Kirk sent two navy ships, *Otago* and *Canterbury*, to steam close by. This was reported round the world.

People were frightened of nuclear explosions. In 1987 the New Zealand Labour government passed a law that banned nuclear-armed or nuclear-powered war-ships in our coastal waters.

FURTHER WAR

DID YOU KNOW?

During the war many women and old men helped with fundraising for the war effort. Women knitted and sewed clothing for the servicemen. Fruit cakes were baked. Food parcels were packed and sent overseas.

Children helped at 'bring and buy' stalls to raise money.

In public parks and schools trenches were often dug and covered to be used as air raid shelters.

The newspaper was full of the Second World War. One day a little girl in Auckland went home from school and her mother said, 'The war is over'. The little girl asked, 'Won't there be any more newspapers now?'

New Zealanders asked why, if nuclear bombs were safe as the French said, they did not test them near Paris.

Protesting against the war in Vietnam.

CHAPTER 18

Changing fortunes

Peter Fraser.

Keith Holyoake.

After Micky Savage died in 1940, Peter Fraser became the prime minister. He was clever and a hard worker but he didn't have Savage's personality and people didn't like him as much.

The first National government

There were still food shortages after the war. The people blamed the government and in the 1949 election Labour lost to the National Party. Sidney Holland, a Canterbury businessman, was the National Party leader. He promised to 'make the pound go further'.

A rich land

From the end of 1940s to the late 1960s New Zealand was one of the richest countries in the world. Everyone paid high prices for our meat, wool and butter. In 1951, during the Korean War, wool reached 240d a pound (the equivalent of 600 cents a kilo).

Good times

During the depression of the 1930s people couldn't afford to buy what they wanted. Then during the war everything was in short supply.

In the 1950s life was much easier. People had more money. There were pensions. Farms and stock numbers were larger. People could get telephones, motor vehicles, houses, electric toasters, vacuum cleaners, washing machines, radios, overseas trips and university scholarships.

Ups and downs

The good years continued with Prime Minister Keith Holyoake. But in 1967–68 overseas prices for our goods dropped again.

From 1970 through to the 1980s prices for almost everything in the shops went up.

From 1974 onwards our exports did not earn enough to pay for our imports. Governments began borrowing money again to keep up the standard of living.

Old jobs

Machinery changed the way New Zealanders lived and worked. Farmers replaced their horses with tractors. Thousands of female telephone operators were replaced by automatic telephone exchanges.

Thousands of milliners and machinists lost their jobs in the 1950s when hats went out of style.

New jobs

Steel-making factories were started. A glassworks was set up in Whangarei. Large hydro-electric projects made power for the nation. An aluminium smelter was built at Bluff. Mills produced pulp, paper and particle board from the huge pine forests planted in the 1920s and 1930s.

Hydroelectric power station.

Women's work

In 1936 less than 4 per cent of married women worked.

In 1981 35 per cent worked.

When women did the same job as men they were paid less. Men argued they had families to feed and women did not. This was unfair and 'equal pay for equal work' came about in the 1960s.

Maori

In 1936 there were only 1700 Maori living in Auckland.

By 1945, 20 per cent of Maori lived in towns and by 1976, 76 per cent lived in towns or cities.

Immigrants

By 1991 there were 123,000 Pacific Islanders living in New Zealand. They came from

Polynesian churchgoers.

DID YOU KNOW?

From the late 1940s to the mid-1960s only the Americans, Canadians and Swedish were said to be wealthier than New Zealanders.

During the Korean War, wool was so valuable farmers paid children to collect tufts of wool from their barb-wire fences.

In 1937 there were only 250,000 radios in the whole country. By 1981, 67 per cent of houses had colour television and 34 per cent had black and white television.

By 1995, New Zealanders, on average, watched two hours and forty-two minutes of television a day.

In 1967 dollars and cents replaced pounds, shillings and pence. The new dollar was worth ten shillings.

By 1937 there were 211,000 cars, trucks, taxis and motorcycles in the country. By 1981 there were 1,700,000 motor vehicles owned by a population of 3 million. By 1996 there were 2,487,722 vehicles while the population was only 3.5 million.

Western Samoa, Tonga, the Cook Islands, Niue and other islands. In the past most Pakeha in towns and cities had not met many Maori or Asian people. Now, Maori, Cook Islanders, Tongans, Chinese and Cambodians had to get to know each other and 'get on'.

New problems

Since about 1972, New Zealand, like many other countries, has had difficult times. In 1973 the price of oil went up four times in a few months. Exports did not pay enough for the oil and petrol. People lost their jobs again.

Many New Zealanders left to find new jobs in Australia.

Sir Robert Muldoon

Muldoon was prime minister from 1975 to 1984.

Like other prime ministers

Sir Robert Muldoon.

before him he also borrowed money from overseas to try to fix the nation's problems ($10 billion was borrowed to pay for huge power projects called Think Big). This didn't help. Prices in shops increased again.

By 1982 inflation was 20 per cent.

In 1984 Muldoon lost the election to David Lange.

David Lange

Lange was the leader of the Labour Party and Sir Roger Douglas was the minister of finance. They made huge changes to the economy.

Saturday shopping was extended and Sunday shopping was allowed. They sold off government businesses like the railways, forests, airlines and telephone systems. Many government workers lost their jobs.

National again

In 1991, after Labour lost the election, the new National government's minister of finance, Ruth Richardson, and Bill Birch, the minister of labour, made more changes. People no longer had to belong to a union and cuts were made to the welfare system. But slowly the country's debt fell and the number of jobs rose.

MMP

The changes made many people unhappy. Some thought that politicians couldn't be trusted.

They wanted to change the way MPs were elected. In 1993, after two referendums, it was shown that more than 55 per cent of people wanted the 1996 election to be under the MMP (Mixed Member Proportional) electoral system.

The 1996 vote

With MMP each voter had two votes — one to choose the party and one for the electorate member. After the 1996 election there was no clear winner so a coalition government was made from the National Party, with Jim Bolger as prime minister, and the New Zealand First Party, with Winston Peters as deputy prime minister and treasurer.

John Walker.

Famous modern New Zealanders

Yvette Williams, Peter Snell, John Walker and Danyon Loader were a few sportspeople who gained international honours.

New Zealanders are also proud of their famous writers like poet James K. Baxter and novelists Janet Frame, Sylvia Ashton-Warner, Maurice Gee and Witi Ihimaera. Short-story writers Katherine Mansfield and Frank Sargeson, and children's writer Margaret Mahy are also known throughout the world. Painters like Frances Hodgkins and Colin McCahon also helped New Zealanders feel proud.

Witi Ihimaera.

CHANGING FORTUNES

DID YOU KNOW?

In 1968 unemployment reached 7000.

In 1901 the workforce was divided into the following broad areas:

Agriculture	74.5%
Industries	13.1%
Services	11%
Other	1.4%

In 1981 the total workforce was 1,325,000 people.

Farming, forestry, etc. (Agriculture)	11.2%
Factories, mills, etc. (Industries)	23.2%
Drivers, shop assistants, bank clerks, etc. (Services)	62%
Other	3.6%

Maori and Pacific Islanders make up 13.5 per cent of the population.

There are more Polynesians in Auckland than in any other Pacific town.

In 1956 New Zealand had the highest income per person in the world. In 1980s it had slipped to seventeenth.

In 1985 government workers were cut from 88,000 to 34,500.

The 1996 MMP election put more women and Maori into government and the first Asian was elected into Parliament.

CHAPTER 19

The changing world of children

Children in the 1800s did not have much free time. They were too busy working to help the family.

When they did play they liked to explore, fish, look for birds' nests, and sail homemade rafts and boats. They also played hide and seek just as children do today.

Chasing games like 'Cowboys and Indians', 'Pakehas and Maori', or 'Boers and British' were played in the bush. 'Oranges and Lemons', 'Farmer in the Dell', 'Postman's Knock,' 'Musical Chairs' and 'Pass the Parcel' were singing games played by all ages.

Sunday School
Most Victorian children went to Sunday School.

They played indoor games, dressing up, charades, word games and sang hymns. They all looked forward to picnic days, where they had sandwiches, cake and lemonade.

School games
After 1877, when children had to go to school, playgrounds were split into boys' and girls' areas.

The girls had less space and played quieter games like cat's cradle, knucklebones, skipping and swinging.

Boys liked piggy-back fighting and bullrush.

Pressed flowers, stamps, birds' eggs and cigarette cards were collected and swapped. Instead of cricket children played rounders. The bat was the heavy stem of a flax plant and the ball was a pair of rolled-up socks.

Footballs were sacks sewn up with rags.

The early 1900s
After 1900 children played more organised games. Girls played softball, basketball and netball. Boys played rugby and cricket.

Piggy-back fighting in 1906.

By the 1920s sports gear like balls could be bought in shops. Dolls and dolls' houses were popular as were teddy bears and golliwogs.

Both boys and girls liked spinning tops, kites, stilts, hobby-horses and knucklebones. Hopscotch, 'Tiggy', and 'Hidey-go-seek' were year-round games.

Marbles

A bag of marbles was a prized possession.

The target marbles were called 'dakers', 'dubs', 'dukes', 'glassies' or 'changers'. The thrown marble was a 'taw' or a 'shooter'.

The latest craze

Railways, roads, telephones, radios, televisions, movies and magazines made the world seem smaller. Fashions from overseas were now seen in New Zealand. The first chocolate-covered ice creams — 'Eskimo pies' — appeared in the 1930s.

Playing marbles.

75

An early radio programme.

During the Second World War, American soldiers often had bubblegum, double-decker sandwiches and hamburgers.

In the 1950s kewpie and walkie-talkie dolls, Meccano and Monopoly sets were the craze.

Teenagers
In the 1950s some teenagers and older children formed their own groups. They had special names like 'milk-bar cowboys', 'bodgies', 'widgies' and 'punks'.

Each group was known by its clothing and hairstyle.

Music
Early on, most music was played in homes, halls or park bandstands. Technology changed this. Gramophones were sold in the 1890s. In the 1930s, when almost all families had radios, popular songs from round the world were heard in New Zealand living rooms.

Pop stars
From the 1950s and 1960s teenagers tuned into their own music on portable record players and transistor radios. Bill Haley and his Comets and Elvis Presley's rock-and-roll songs were the hits. In 1964 when the Beatles visited, crowds of fans mobbed them wherever they went. New Zealand was also visited by many famous dancers, actors and musicians like Anna Pavlova, Laurence Olivier, Vivien Leigh and Dame Nellie Melba.

Public entertainment
In the 1800s any public event was a good time for Pakeha and Maori to sing a few songs, listen to the band and make speeches. The prime minister or governor-general coming to town usually meant a holiday from school and a parade.

Exhibitions

These celebrated culture and history as well as new ideas.

From 1862 to 1897 New Zealand sent exhibitions overseas. These included Maori cloaks and carvings, gold, flax and wood samples.

Exhibitions were also held in New Zealand. The most popular was the Christchurch Exhibition of 1906–07. It had a Maori pa, Fijian firewalkers, a brass band competition and a sideshow alley that had a water chute eighteen metres high.

Home entertainment

With radios people started staying at home for a lot of their entertainment. People tuned in every day for their favourite programmes with people like 'Uncle Tom', 'Aunt Daisy' and 'Uncle Scrim'.

Selwyn Toogood's famous programme *It's in the Bag* started on radio in the 1950s.

Television came to New Zealand in the 1960s. By 1968, 75 per cent of homes had a television set.

Now, FM radio, video, DVD, Walkmans and personal computers give people more choice about how and when they get their entertainment.

DID YOU KNOW?

More than two million people went to the Christchurch Exhibition in 1906–07.

The grandest exhibition in Wellington was the New Zealand Centennial in 1939. It had huge models of the Waitomo Caves and the Main Trunk railway line with trains and Cook Strait ferries.

A wool arch at one of the entrances to the New South Wales Court at the New Zealand International Exhibition, Christchurch.

CHAPTER 20

New Zealand today

Maori culture group.

From left: Sian Elias, Chief Justice; Jenny Shipley, then leader of the Opposition; Dame Silvia Cartwright, Governor-General; and Helen Clark, Prime Minister.

Maori

Since the Second World War Maori have moved from the country to the city for jobs and entertainment. Separated from their land, families and marae, many felt lost.

Today many have regained their culture by learning Maori language and customs at school and on new city marae. Preschoolers are learning Maori at kohanga reo (language nests).

There are more Maori in parliament than ever before.

Waitangi Tribunal

This was established to settle the many disputes between Maori tribes and the government. Compensation (payout) was paid to many Maori tribes to help right past wrongs like the land confiscation that had taken place during the1800s.

In 1992 the government agreed to pay compensation to Maori tribes to settle a 150-year-old argument over fishing rights.

Women

The role of women has changed greatly too. Today many married women have returned to work. Children are placed in childcare centres, or partners help look after them. Women have the same job opportunities as men and many are working in important positions.

Jenny Shipley has been prime minister and Helen Clark is the current prime minister.

Dame Cath Tizard has been governor-general. The governor-general today is Dame Sylvia Cartwright and the Chief Justice is also a woman — Dame Sian Elias.

The environment

In the past forests were destroyed for farms. Now, many native trees are protected. Special areas round the country like Fiordland have been set up as national or regional parks.

Native species like the kiwi

Kiwi.

Children benefit from learning other countries' customs.

and tuatara are protected.

There are laws to stop people catching too many fish.

Many towns and cities have recycling programmes.

Immigrants

Throughout the years immigrants have continued to come to New Zealand. Scandinavian, Dutch, Chinese and Indian have all settled here.

In the 1960s, Pacific Islanders became the largest immigrant group.

New Zealand is a truly Pacific nation. Pacific Islanders make up 13 per cent of Auckland's population while Maori make up 10 per cent.

In the 1970s the Asian population started to increase with war refugees from Vietnam, Cambodia and Laos.

People from Taiwan, Hong Kong and Korea with skills and money came to New Zealand in the late 1980s and early 1990s.

Every year New Zealand takes refugees from all over the world who want the opportunity to settle in a new country.

Unions

In 1993 the government broke down the large national unions into much smaller plant-centred ones. Workers could choose which union they wanted to join.

Changes for everyone

In the mid-1980s the government made many changes.

Farmers lost income support. GST (goods and services tax), tax on everything bought and sold, was introduced.

There was a downturn in farming and a boom in the cities.

The boom ended with the stockmarket crash in October 1987.

Amongst all the changes were many job losses, especially in manufacturing.

Native bush.

New Zealand troops in East Timor.

East Timor

Since 1859 East Timor had been ruled by Portugal. After the Second World War, some East Timorese wanted their country to be independent while others said it should be part of Indonesia. In 1974 war broke out between the two groups. Indonesian troops helped defeat the independents and in 1976 Indonesia declared East Timor to be the twenty-seventh Indonesian province.

In 1999, after Indonesian President Suharto lost power, the people of East Timor got the chance to vote on how their country should be run. Seventy-five per cent of voters decided East Timor should be independent. Military groups who wanted to stay under Indonesian rule went on a rampage across East Timor killing thousands of independence supporters and driving tens of thousands of others into West Timor.

In February 2000, the United Nations set up the United Nations Transitional Administration in East Timor (UNTAET).

UNTAET is a peace-keeping force made up of military and civilian people from around the world. Its job is to keep law and order while the independent government is formed.

New Zealand forces — a battalion and four helicopters with crew — are part of UNTAET.

Liquor laws

Before 1999, eighteen-year-olds (legally adults) couldn't buy alcohol from hotels and liquor stores but they could be served alcohol with food in licensed restaurants and nightclubs.

Overseas tourists also found it odd that they couldn't buy alcohol on a Sunday unless they were having a meal at a licensed restaurant.

To make the liquor laws fairer for everyone, on 1 December 1999 the minimum legal age to buy alcohol was dropped from 20 to 18.

Hotels and liquor stores were able to trade on Sundays and supermarkets could sell beer as well as wine.

What next?

The effects of the changes that recent governments have made to the health, education, housing and welfare systems won't be known for many years. Many people hope that the gap between what is expected to happen and what really happens won't be too great. Only time will tell.

INDEX

Photographs

page 4 above Holger Leue
below Alexander Turnbull Library *ref PUBL 0044 42*
page 5 above Holger Leue
below Holger Leue
page 6 Reed Publishing (NZ) Ltd
page 8 Reed Publishing (NZ) Ltd
page 9 left Reed Publishing (NZ) Ltd
right Alexander Turnbull Library *ref C 25663 1/2*
page 10 top Reed Publishing (NZ) Ltd
bottom Reed Publishing (NZ) Ltd
page 11 top Alexander Turnbull Library *ref A 217 010*
bottom Alexander Turnbull Library *ref B 011 022*
page 12 Alexander Turnbull Library *ref PUBL 0037 24*
page 13 Alexander Turnbull Library *ref B 026 050*
page 14 Alexander Turnbull Library *ref PUBL 0017 02*
page 15 top Alexander Turnbull Library *ref F 62685 1/2*
bottom Alexander Turnbull Library *ref G 12579 1/1*
page 16 top Alexander Turnbull Library *ref G 620*
bottom Holger Leue
page 17 Alexander Turnbull Library *ref PUBL 0151 2 013*
page 18 Alexander Turnbull Library *ref A 044 008*
page 19 left Alexander Turnbull Library *ref PUBL 0128 001*
right Alexander Turnbull Library *ref G 826 1*
page 20 top Alexander Turnbull Library *ref A 242 002*
bottom Alexander Turnbull Library *ref F 11119 1/2*
page 21 Reed Publishing (NZ) Ltd
page 22 Alexander Turnbull Library *ref A 079 005*
page 23 Alexander Turnbull Library *ref C 012 019*
page 24 Alexander Turnbull Library *ref 1/1 017878*
page 25 Alexander Turnbull Library *ref F 5088 1/2*
page 26 top Alexander Turnbull Library *ref C 015 001*
bottom Reed Publishing (NZ) Ltd
page 27 Alexander Turnbull Library Making New Zealand Collection *ref F 661 1/4 MNZ*
page 28 top Alexander Turnbull Library *ref F 4135 1/2*
bottom Alexander Turnbull Library Northwood Collection *ref PA1 o 395 05*
page 29 Alexander Turnbull Library William Bambridge Diary 1843-1845 *ref MS 0130 280*
page 30 top Alexander Turnbull Library FA Hargreaves Collection *ref G 23296 1/1*
bottom Alexander Turnbull Library *ref PUBL 0110 1883 001*
page 31 left Alexander Turnbull Library *ref G 19068 1/4*
right Alexander Turnbull Library Northwood Collection *ref F 51968 1/2*
page 32 top left Alexander Turnbull Library *ref G 548 10x8*
top right Alexander Turnbull Library *ref F 15790 1/2*

bottom Alexander Turnbull Library McNeur Collection *ref F 19165 1/2*
page 33 Reed Publishing (NZ) Ltd
page 34 Alexander Turnbull Library *ref G 51619 1/2*
page 35 top Alexander Turnbull Library *ref A 018 003*
bottom Alexander Turnbull Library *ref F 71666 1/2*
page 36 left Alexander Turnbull Library *ref F 21458 1/2*
right Alexander Turnbull Library *ref F 29252 1/2*
page 37 Alexander Turnbull Library *ref G 1071 10x8*
page 38 top Alexander Turnbull Library *ref C 19563 1/2*
bottom Alexander Turnbull Library *ref F 53949 1/2*
page 39 Alexander Turnbull Library *ref F 75789 1/2*
page 40 top Alexander Turnbull Library Kwok Collection *ref F 171531 1/2*
bottom Alexander Turnbull Library *ref F 76263 1/2*
page 41 top Alexander Turnbull Library *ref F 80869 1/2*
bottom Alexander Turnbull Library Burton Bros Collection *ref F 2925 1/4*
page 42 left Alexander Turnbull Library Making New Zealand Collection *ref F 702 1/4 MNZ*
right Alexander Turnbull Library DA De Maus Collection *ref G 2024 1/4*
page 43 left Alexander Turnbull Library *ref F 53670 1/2*
right Alexander Turnbull Library *ref C 16138 1/2*
page 44 top left Alexander Turnbull Library Northwood Collection *ref F 29087 1/2*
top right Alexander Turnbull Library *ref G 66719 1/2*
bottom Alexander Turnbull Library SP Andrew Collection *ref G 14825 1/1*
page 45 top Alexander Turnbull Library *ref F 151341 1/2*
bottom Alexander Turnbull Library Northwood Collection *ref F 30466 1/2*
page 46 Reed Publishing (NZ) Ltd
page 47 Alexander Turnbull Library General Assembly Library Collection *ref F 88 35mm A*
page 48 top left Reed Publishing (NZ) Ltd
top right Alexander Turnbull Library *ref F 29096 1/2*
bottom Alexander Turnbull Library *ref 6171 1/2*
page 49 top Alexander Turnbull Library The Press (Christchurch) Collection *ref G 8542 1/1*
bottom left Alexander Turnbull Library Steffano Webb Collection *ref G 5293 1/1*
bottom right Reed Publishing (NZ) Ltd
page 50 top Alexander Turnbull Library FG Radcliffe Collection *ref F 51741 1/2*
middle Alexander Turnbull Library *ref F 181 35mm F*

bottom Alexander Turnbull Library *ref F 32139 1/2*
page 51 top Alexander Turnbull Library *ref F 42965 1/2*
bottom Alexander Turnbull Library *ref 2915 1/2*
page 52 Alexander Turnbull Library *ref F 45546 1/2*
page 54 Alexander Turnbull Library Rausch Collection *ref F 25283 1/2*
page 55 Alexander Turnbull Library *ref F 68959 1/2*
page 56 Alexander Turnbull Library The Press (Christchurch) Collection *ref G 8352 1/1*
page 57 top Alexander Turnbull Library *ref no negative number*
bottom Alexander Turnbull Library C Athol Williams Collection *ref F 61561 1/2*
page 58 Alexander Turnbull Library Photographer: William George Weigel 1890-1980 *ref F 92046 1/2*
page 59 top Alexander Turnbull Library *ref G 37512 1/2*
bottom Reed Publishing (NZ) Ltd
page 60 Alexander Turnbull Library *ref F 30845 1/2*
page 61 Alexander Turnbull Library *ref F 105158 1/2*
page 62 Reed Publishing (NZ) Ltd
page 63 Alexander Turnbull Library *ref F 53946 1/2*
page 64 Reed Publishing (NZ) Ltd
page 65 Alexander Turnbull Library *ref F 76227 1/2*
page 66 top left Reed Publishing (NZ) Ltd
top right Alexander Turnbull Library War History Collection *ref DA 05307*
page 67 top Reed Publishing (NZ) Ltd
bottom Reed Publishing (NZ) Ltd
page 68 Alexander Turnbull Library War History Collection *ref F 51936 1/2*
page 69 Reed Publishing (NZ) Ltd
page 70 left Reed Publishing (NZ) Ltd
right Reed Publishing (NZ) Ltd
page 71 top Holger Leue
bottom Holger Leue
page 72 left Reed Publishing (NZ) Ltd
page 73 Reed Publishing (NZ) Ltd
page 74 left Alexander Turnbull Library Tesla Collection *ref G 16844 1/1*
right Alexander Turnbull Library William Berry Collection *ref G 38089 1/2*
page 75 top Alexander Turnbull Library R McIndoe Collection *ref G 23867 1/2*
bottom Alexander Turnbull Library Thresh Collection *ref G 10529 1/1*
page 76 Alexander Turnbull Library Earle Andrew Collection *ref G 18312 1/1*
page 77 Alexander Turnbull Library The Press (Christchurch) Collection *ref G 17775 1/1*
page 78 top left Holger Leue
top right Reed Publishing (NZ) Ltd
page 79 top left Holger Leue
top right Holger Leue
bottom left Holger Leue
page 80 New Zealand Defence Force
page 81 Greenwood Photography

REED PUBLISHING (NZ) LTD
TE KARUHI TĀ TĀPUI O REED (AOTEAROA)

Established in 1907, Reed is New Zealand's largest
book publisher, with over 600 titles in print.
www.reed.co.nz

Published by Reed Books, a division of Reed Publishing (NZ) Ltd,
39 Rawene Rd, Birkenhead, Auckland.
Associated companies, branches and representatives throughout the world.

ISBN-13: 978 1 86948 719 5
ISBN-10: 1 86948 719 2

First published 2002
Reprinted 2003, 2004, 2005 (twice)

Printed in New Zealand